Stanley Gibbo

Stamp Catalogue

Southern Africa

2nd edition 2007

Stanley Gibbons Ltd
London and Ringwood

By Appointment to Her Majesty The Queen
Stanley Gibbons Ltd, London
Philatelists

Published by Stanley Gibbons Ltd
Editorial, Publications Sales Offices
and Distribution Centre:
Parkside, Christchurch Road, Ringwood,
Hants BH24 3SH

ISBN13: 978-0-85259-654-8
ISBN: 0-85259-654-5

Item No. 2978 (07)

Printed in Great Britian by the Friary Press,
Dorchester

General Philatelic Information and Guidelines to the Scope of Stanley Gibbons Commonwealth Catalogues

The notes which follow seek to reflect current practice in compiling the Stanley Gibbons Commonwealth Catalogues.

It scarcely needs emphasising that the Stanley Gibbons Stamp Catalogue has a very long history and that the vast quantity of information it contains has been carefully built up by successive generations through the work of countless individuals. Philately is never static and the Catalogue has evolved and developed over the years. These notes relate to the current criteria upon which a stamp may be listed or priced. It should be recognised that these criteria have developed over time and may have differed somewhat in the early years of this catalogue. These notes are not intended to suggest that we plan to make wholesale changes to the listing of classic issues in order to bring them into line with today's listing policy, they are designed to inform catalogue users as to the policies currently in operation.

PRICES

The prices quoted in this Catalogue are the estimated selling prices of Stanley Gibbons Ltd at the time of publication. They are, unless it is specifically stated otherwise, for examples in fine condition for the issue concerned. Superb examples are worth more; those of a lower quality considerably less.

All prices are subject to change without prior notice and Stanley Gibbons Ltd may from time to time offer stamps below catalogue price. Individual low value stamps sold at 399 Strand are liable to an additional handling charge. Purchasers of new issues are asked to note the prices charged for them contain an element for the service rendered and so may exceed the prices shown when the stamps are subsequently catalogued. Postage and handling charges are extra.

No guarantee is given to supply all stamps priced, since it is not possible to keep every catalogued item in stock. Commemorative issues may, at times, only be available in complete sets and not as individual values.

Quotation of prices. The prices in the left-hand column are for unused stamps and those in the right-hand column are for used.

A dagger (†) denotes that the item listed does not exist in that condition and a blank, or dash, that it exists, or may exist, but we are unable to quote a price.

Prices are expressed in pounds and pence sterling. One pound comprises 100 pence (£1 = 100p).

The method of notation is as follows: pence in numerals (e.g. 10 denotes ten pence); pounds and pence, up to £100, in numerals (e.g. 4.25 denotes four pounds and twenty-five pence); prices above £100 are expressed in whole pounds with the '£' sign shown.

Unused stamps. Great Britain and Commonwealth: the prices for unused stamps of Queen Victoria to King George V are for lightly hinged examples. Unused prices for King Edward VIII, King George VI and Queen Elizabeth issues are for unmounted mint.

Some stamps from the King George VI period are often difficult to find in unmounted mint condition. In such instances we would expect that collectors would need to pay a high proportion of the price quoted to obtain mounted mint examples. Generally speaking lightly mounted mint stamps from this reign, issued before 1945, are in considerable demand.

Used stamps. The used prices are normally for stamps postally used but may be for stamps cancelled-to-order where this practice exists.

A pen-cancellation on early issues can sometimes correctly denote postal use. Instances are individually noted in the Catalogue in explanation of the used price given.

Prices quoted for bisects on cover or large piece are for those dated during the period officially authorised.

Stamps not sold unused to the public (e.g. some official stamps) are priced used only.

The use of 'unified' designs, that is stamps inscribed for both postal and fiscal purposes, results in a number of stamps of very high face value. In some instances these may not have been primarily intended for postal purposes, but if they are so inscribed we include them. We only price such items used, however, where there is evidence of normal postal usage.

Cover prices. To assist collectors, cover prices are quoted for issues up to 1945 at the beginning of each country.

The system gives a general guide in the form of a factor by which the corresponding used price of the basic loose stamp should be multiplied when found in fine average condition on cover.

Care is needed in applying the factors and they relate to a cover which bears a single of the denomination listed; if more than one denomination is present the most highly priced attracts the multiplier and the remainder are priced at the simple figure for used singles in arriving at a total.

The cover should be of non-philatelic origin; bearing the correct postal rate for the period and distance involved and cancelled with the markings normal to the offices concerned. Purely philatelic items have a cover value only slightly greater than the catalogue value for the corresponding used stamps. This applies generally to those high-value stamps used philatelically rather than in the normal course of commerce. Low-value stamps, e.g. ¼d. and ½d., are desirable when used as a single rate on cover and merit an increase in 'multiplier' value.

First day covers in the period up to 1945 are not within the scope of the system and the multiplier should not be used. As a special category of philatelic usage, with wide variations in valuation according to scarcity, they require separate treatment.

Oversized covers, difficult to accommodate on an album page, should be reckoned as worth little more than the corresponding value of the used stamps. The condition of a cover also affects its value. Except for 'wreck covers', serious damage or soiling reduce the value where the postal markings and stamps are ordinary ones. Conversely, visual appeal adds to the value and this can include freshness of appearance, important addresses, old-fashioned but legible hand-writing, historic town-names, etc.

The multipliers are a base on which further value would be added to take account of the cover's postal historical importance in demonstrating such things as unusual, scarce or emergency cancels, interesting routes, significant postal markings, combination usage, the development of postal rates, and so on.

Minimum price. The minimum catalogue price quoted is 10p. For individual stamps prices between 10p. and 95p. are provided as a guide for catalogue users. The lowest price charged for individual stamps or sets purchased from Stanley Gibbons Ltd is £1

Set prices. Set prices are generally for one of each value, excluding shades and varieties, but including major colour changes. Where there are alternative shades, etc., the cheapest is usually included. The number of stamps in the set is always stated for clarity. The mint prices for sets containing *se-tenant* pieces are based on the prices quoted for such combinations, and not on those for the individual stamps.

Varieties. Where plate or cylinder varieties are priced in a used condition the price quoted is for a fine used example with the cancellation well clear of the listed flaw.

Specimen stamps. The pricing of these items is explained under that heading.

Stamp booklets. Prices are for complete assembled booklets in fine condition with those issued before 1945 showing normal wear and tear. Incomplete booklets and those which have been 'exploded' will, in general, be worth less than the figure quoted.

Repricing. Collectors will be aware that the market factors of supply and demand directly influence the prices quoted in this Catalogue. Whatever the scarcity of a particular stamp, if there is no one in the market who wishes to buy it cannot be expected to achieve a high price. Conversely, the same item actively sought by numerous potential buyers may cause the price to rise.

All the prices in this Catalogue are examined during the preparation of each new edition by the expert staff of Stanley Gibbons and repriced as necessary. They take many factors into account, including supply and demand, and are in close touch with the international stamp market and the auction world.

Commonwealth cover prices and advice on postal history material originally provided by Edward B Proud.

GUARANTEE

All stamps are guaranteed originals in the following terms:

If not as described, and returned by the purchaser, we undertake to refund the price paid to us in the original transaction. If any stamp is certified as genuine by the Expert Committee of the Royal Philatelic Society, London, or by BPA Expertising Ltd, the purchaser shall not be entitled to make any claim against us for any error, omission or mistake in such certificate.

Consumers' statutory rights are not affected by the above guarantee.

The recognised Expert Committees in this country are those of the Royal Philatelic Society, 41 Devonshire Place, London W1G, 6JY, and BPA Expertising Ltd, PO Box 137, Leatherhead, Surrey KT22 0RG. They do not undertake valuations under any circumstances and fees are payable for their services.

CONDITION GUIDE

To assist collectors in assessing the true value of items they are considering buying or in reviewing stamps already in their collections, we now offer a more detailed guide to the condition of stamps on which this catalogue's prices are based.

For a stamp to be described as 'Fine', it should be sound in all respects, without creases, bends, wrinkles, pin holes, thins or tears. If perforated, all perforation 'teeth' should be intact, it should not suffer from fading, rubbing or toning and it should be of clean, fresh appearance.

Margins on imperforate stamps: These should be even on all sides and should be at least as wide as half the distance between that stamp and the next. To have one or more margins of less than this width, would normally preclude a stamp from being described as 'Fine'. It should be remembered that some early stamps were positioned very close together on the printing plate and in such cases 'Fine' margins would necessarily be narrow. On the other hand, some plates were laid down to give a substantial gap between individual stamps and in such cases margins would be expected to be much wider.

An 'average' four-margin example would have a narrower margin on one or more sides and should be priced accordingly, while a stamp with wider, yet even, margins than 'Fine' would merit the description 'Very Fine' or 'Superb' and, if available, would command a price in excess of that quoted in the catalogue.

Gum: Since the prices for stamps of King Edward VIII, King George VI and Queen Elizabeth are for 'unmounted' or 'never hinged' mint, it should be anticipated that even stamps from these reigns which have been very lightly mounted should be available at a discount from catalogue price, the more obvious the hinge marks, the greater the discount.

Catalogue prices for stamps issued prior to King Edward VIII's reign are for mounted mint, so unmounted examples would be worth a premium, Hinge marks on 20th century stamps should not be too obtrusive, and should be at least in the lightly mounted category. For 19th century stamps more obvious hinging would be acceptable, but stamps should still carry a large part of their original gum—'Large part o.g.'—in order to be described as 'Fine'.

Centring: Ideally, the stamp's image should appear in the exact centre of the perforated area, giving equal margins on all sides. 'Fine' centring would be close to this ideal with any deviation having an effect on the value of the stamp. As in the case of the margins on imperforate stamps, it should be borne in mind that the space between some early stamps was very narrow, so it was very difficult to achieve accurate perforation, especially when the technology was in its infancy. Thus, poor centring would have a less damaging effect on the value of a 19th century stamp than on a 20th century example, but the premium put on a perfectly centred specimen would be greater.

Cancellations: Early cancellation devices were designed to 'obliterate' the stamp in order to prevent it being reused and this is still an important objective for today's postal administrations. Stamp collectors, on the other hand, prefer postmarks to be lightly applied, clear, and to leave as much as possible of the design visible. Dated, circular cancellations have long been 'the postmark of choice', but the definition of a 'Fine' cancellation will depend upon the types of cancellation in use at the time a stamp was current—it is clearly illogical to seek a circular datestamp on a Penny Black.

'Fine', by definition, will be superior to 'Average', so, in terms of cancellation quality, if one begins by identifying what 'Average' looks like, then one will be half way to identifying 'Fine'. The illustrations will give some guidance on mid-19th century and mid-20th century cancellations of Great Britain, but types of cancellation in general use in each country and in each period will determine the appearance of 'Fine'.

As for the factors discussed above, anything less than 'Fine' will result in a downgrading of the stamp concerned, while a very fine or superb cancellation will be worth a premium.

Combining the factors: To merit the description 'Fine', a stamp should be fine in every respect, but a small deficiency in one area might be made up for in another by a factor meriting an 'Extremely Fine' description.

Some early issues are so seldom found in what would normally be considered to be 'Fine' condition, the catalogue prices are for a slightly lower grade, with 'Fine' examples being worth a premium. In such cases a note to this effect is given in the catalogue, while elsewhere premiums are given for well-centred, lightly cancelled examples.

It should be emphasised that stamps graded at less than fine remain collectable and, in the case of more highly priced stamps will continue to hold a value. Nevertheless, buyers should always bear condition in mind.

MARGINS ON IMPERFORATE STAMPS

Superb | Very fine | Fine | Average | Poor

GUM

Unmounted | Very lightly mounted | Lightly mounted | Mounted/large part original gum (o.g.). | Heavily mounted small part o.g

CENTRING

Superb | Very fine | Fine | Average | Poor

CANCELLATIONS

Superb | Very fine | Fine | Average | Poor

Superb | Very fine

Fine | Average | Poor

THE CATALOGUE IN GENERAL

Contents. The Catalogue is confined to adhesive postage stamps, including miniature sheets. For particular categories the rules are:

(a) Revenue (fiscal) stamps or telegraph stamps are listed only where they have been expressly authorised for postal duty.
(b) Stamps issued only precancelled are included, but normally issued stamps available additionally with precancel have no separate precancel listing unless the face value is changed.
(c) Stamps prepared for use but not issued, hitherto accorded full listing, are nowadays foot-noted with a price (where possible).
(d) Bisects (trisects, etc.) are only listed where such usage was officially authorised.
(e) Stamps issued only on first day covers or in presentation packs and not available separately are not listed but may be priced in a footnote.
(f) New printings are only included in this Catalogue where they show a major philatelic variety, such as a change in shade, watermark or paper. Stamps which exist with or without imprint dates are listed separately; changes in imprint dates are mentioned in footnotes.
(g) Official and unofficial reprints are dealt with by footnote.
(h) Stamps from imperforate printings of modern issues which occur perforated are covered by footnotes, but are listed where widely available for postal use.

Exclusions. The following are excluded:

(a) non-postal revenue or fiscal stamps;
(b) postage stamps used fiscally;
(c) local carriage labels and private local issues;
(d) bogus or phantom stamps;
(e) railway or airline letter fee stamps, bus or road transport company labels;
(f) cut-outs;
(g) all types of non-postal labels and souvenirs;
(h) documentary labels for the postal service, e.g. registration, recorded delivery, air-mail etiquettes, etc.;
(i) privately applied embellishments to official issues and privately commissioned items generally;
(j) stamps for training postal officers.

Full listing. 'Full listing' confers our recognition and implies allotting a catalogue number and (wherever possible) a price quotation.

In judging status for inclusion in the catalogue broad considerations are applied to stamps. They must be issued by a legitimate postal authority, recognised by the government concerned, and must be adhesives valid for proper postal use in the class of service for which they are inscribed. Stamps, with the exception of such categories as postage dues and officials, must be available to the general public, at face value, in reasonable quantities without any artificial restrictions being imposed on their distribution.

For errors and varieties the criterion is legitimate (albeit inadvertent) sale through a postal administration in the normal course of business. Details of provenance are always important; printers' waste and deliberately manufactured material are excluded.

Certificates. In assessing unlisted items due weight is given to Certificates from recognised Expert Committees and, where appropriate, we will usually ask to see them.

Date of issue. Where local issue dates differ from dates of release by agencies, 'date of issue' is the local date. Fortuitous stray usage before the officially intended date is disregarded in listing.

Catalogue numbers. Stamps of each country are catalogued chronologically by date of issue. Subsidiary classes are placed at the end of the country, as separate lists, with a distinguishing letter prefix to the catalogue number, e.g. D for postage due, O for official and E for express delivery stamps.

The catalogue number appears in the extreme left-column. The boldface Type numbers in the next column are merely cross-references to illustrations.

Once published in the Catalogue, numbers are changed as little as possible; really serious renumbering is reserved for the occasions when a complete country or an entire issue is being rewritten. The edition first affected includes cross-reference tables of old and new numbers.

Our catalogue numbers are universally recognised in specifying stamps and as a hallmark of status.

Illustrations. Stamps are illustrated at three-quarters linear size. Stamps not illustrated are the same size and format as the value shown, unless otherwise indicated. Stamps issued only as miniature sheets have the stamp alone illustrated but sheet size is also quoted. Overprints, surcharges, watermarks and postmarks are normally actual size. Illustrations of varieties are often enlarged to show the detail. Stamp booklet covers are illustrated half-size, unless otherwise indicated.

Designers. Designers' names are quoted where known, though space precludes naming every individual concerned in the production of a set. In particular, photographers supplying material are usually named only where they also make an active contribution in the design stage; posed photographs of reigning monarchs are, however, an exception to this rule.

CONTACTING THE CATALOGUE EDITOR

The editor is always interested in hearing from people who have new information which will improve or correct the Catalogue. As a general rule he must see and examine the actual stamps before they can be considered for listing; photographs or photocopies are insufficient evidence.

Submissions should be made in writing to the Catalogue Editor, Stanley Gibbons Publications at the Ringwood office. The cost of return postage for items submitted is appreciated, and this should include the registration fee if required.

Where information is solicited purely for the benefit of the enquirer, the editor cannot undertake to reply if the answer is already contained in these published notes or if return postage is omitted. Written communications are greatly preferred to enquiries by telephone or e-mail and the editor regrets that he or his staff cannot see personal callers without a prior appointment being made. Correspondence may be subject to delay during the production period of each new edition.

The editor welcomes close contact with study circles and is interested, too, in finding reliable local correspondents who will verify and supplement official information in countries where this is deficient.

We regret we do not give opinions as to the genuineness of stamps, nor do we identify stamps or number them by our Catalogue.

TECHNICAL MATTERS

The meanings of the technical terms used in the catalogue will be found in our *Philatelic Terms Illustrated.*

References below to (more specialised) listings are to be taken to indicate, as appropriate, the Stanley Gibbons *Great Britain Specialised Catalogue* in five volumes or the *Great Britain Concise Catalogue*.

1. Printing

Printing errors. Errors in printing are of major interest to the Catalogue. Authenticated items meriting consideration would include: background, centre or frame inverted or omitted; centre or subject transposed; error of colour; error or omission of value; double prints and impressions; printed both sides; and so on. Designs *tête-bêche*, whether intentionally or by accident, are listable. *Se-tenant* arrangements of stamps are recognised in the listings or footnotes. Gutter pairs (a pair of stamps separated by blank margin) are not included in this volume. Colours only partially omitted are not listed. Stamps with embossing omitted are reserved for our more specialised listings.

Printing varieties. Listing is accorded to major changes in the printing base which lead to completely new types. In recess-printing this could be a design re-engraved; in photogravure or photolithography a screen altered in whole or in part. It can also encompass flat-bed and rotary printing if the results are readily distinguishable.

To be considered at all, varieties must be constant.

Early stamps, produced by primitive methods, were prone to numerous imperfections; the lists reflect this, recognising re-entries, retouches, broken frames, misshapen letters, and so on. Printing technology has, however, radically improved over the years, during which time photogravure and lithography have become predominant. Varieties nowadays are more in the nature of flaws and these, being too specialised for this general catalogue, are almost always outside the scope.

In no catalogue, however, do we list such items as: dry prints, kiss prints, doctor-blade flaws, colour shifts or registration flaws (unless they lead to the complete omission of a colour from an individual stamp), lithographic ring flaws, and so on. Neither do we recognise fortuitous happenings like paper creases or confetti flaws.

Overprints (and surcharges). Overprints of different types qualify for separate listing. These include overprints in different colours; overprints from different printing processes such as litho and typo; overprints in totally different typefaces, etc. Major errors in machine-printed overprints are important and listable. They include: overprint inverted or omitted; overprint double (treble, etc.); overprint diagonal; overprint double, one inverted; pairs with one overprint omitted, e.g. from a radical shift to an adjoining stamp; error of colour; error of type fount; letters inverted or omitted, etc. If the overprint is handstamped, few of these would qualify and a distinction is drawn. We continue, however, to list pairs of stamps where one has a handstamped overprint and the other has not.

Varieties occurring in overprints will often take the form of broken letters, slight differences in spacing, rising spaces, etc. Only the most important would be considered for listing or footnote mention.

Sheet positions. If space permits we quote sheet positions of listed varieties and authenticated data is solicited for this purpose.

De La Rue plates. The Catalogue classifies the general plates used by De La Rue for printing British Colonial stamps as follows:

VICTORIAN KEY TYPE

Die I

1. The ball of decoration on the second point of the crown appears as a dark mass of lines.
2. Dark vertical shading separates the front hair from the bun.
3. The vertical line of colour outlining the front of the throat stops at the sixth line of shading on the neck.
4. The white space in the coil of the hair above the curl is roughly the shape of a pin's head.

Die II

1. There are very few lines of colour in the ball and it appears almost white.
2. A white vertical strand of hair appears in place of the dark shading.

3. The line stops at the eighth line of shading.
4. The white space is oblong, with a line of colour partially dividing it at the left end.

Plates numbered 1 and 2 are both Die I. Plates 3 and 4 are Die II.

GEORGIAN KEY TYPE

Die I

A. The second (thick) line below the name of the country is cut slanting, conforming roughly to the shape of the crown on each side.
B. The labels of solid colour bearing the words "POSTAGE" and "& REVENUE" are square at the inner top corners.
C. There is a projecting "bud" on the outer spiral of the ornament in each of the lower corners.

Die II

A. The second line is cut vertically on each side of the crown.
B. The labels curve inwards at the top.
C. There is no "bud" in this position.

Unless otherwise stated in the lists, all stamps with watermark Multiple Crown CA (w **8**) are Die I while those with watermark Multiple Crown Script CA (w **9**) are Die II. The Georgian Die II was introduced in April 1921 and was used for Plates 10 to 22 and 26 to 28. Plates 23 to 25 were made from Die I by mistake.

2. Paper

All stamps listed are deemed to be on (ordinary) paper of the wove type and white in colour; only departures from this are normally mentioned.

Types. Where classification so requires we distinguish such other types of paper as, for example, vertically and horizontally laid; wove and laid bâtonné; card(board); carton; cartridge; glazed; granite; native; pelure; porous; quadrillé; ribbed; rice; and silk thread.

Wove paper Laid paper

Granite paper Quadrillé paper

Burelé band

The various makeshifts for normal paper are listed as appropriate. The varieties of double paper and joined paper are recognised. The security device of a printed burelé band on the back of a stamp, as in early Queensland, qualifies for listing.

Descriptive terms. The fact that a paper is handmade (and thus probably of uneven thickness) is mentioned where necessary. Such descriptive terms as "hard" and "soft"; "smooth" and "rough"; "thick", "medium" and "thin" are applied where there is philatelic merit in classifying papers.

Coloured, very white and toned papers. A coloured paper is one that is coloured right through (front and back of the stamp). In the Catalogue the colour of the paper is given in italics, thus:
black/*rose* = black design on rose paper.

Papers have been made specially white in recent years by, for example, a very heavy coating of chalk. We do not classify shades of whiteness of paper as distinct varieties. There does exist, however, a type of paper from early days called toned. This is off-white, often brownish or buffish, but it cannot be assigned any definite colour. A toning effect brought on by climate, incorrect storage or gum staining is disregarded here, as this was not the state of the paper when issued.

"Ordinary" and "Chalk-surfaced" papers. The availability of many postage stamps for revenue purposes made necessary some safeguard against the illegitimate re-use of stamps with removable cancellations. This was at first secured by using fugitive inks and later by printing on paper surfaced by coatings containing either chalk or china clay, both of which made it difficult to remove any form of obliteration without damaging the stamp design.

This catalogue lists these chalk-surfaced paper varieties from their introduction in 1905. Where no indication is given, the paper is "ordinary".

Our chalk-surfaced paper is specifically one which shows a black mark when touched with a silver wire. The paper used during the Second World War for high values, as in Bermuda, the Leeward Islands, etc., was thinly coated with some kind of surfacing which does not react to silver and is therefore regarded (and listed) as "ordinary". Stamps on chalk-surfaced paper can easily lose this coating through immersion in water.

Another paper introduced during the War as a substitute for chalk-surfaced is rather thick, very white and glossy and shows little or no watermark, nor does it show a black line when touched with silver. In the Bahamas high values this paper might be mistaken for the chalk-surfaced (which is thinner and poorer-looking) but for the silver test.

Some modern coated papers show little or no reaction to the silver test and, therefore, cannot be classed as chalk-surfaced.

Green and yellow papers. Issues of the First World War and immediate postwar period occur on green and yellow papers and these are given separate Catalogue listing. The original coloured papers (coloured throughout) gave way to surface-coloured papers, the stamps having "white backs"; other stamps show one colour on the front and a different one at the back. Because of the numerous variations a grouping of colours is adopted as follows:

Yellow papers

(1) The original *yellow* paper (throughout), usually bright in colour. The gum is often sparse, of harsh consistency and dull-looking. Used 1912–1920.
(2) The *white-backs*. Used 1913–1914.
(3) A bright lemon paper. The colour must have a pronounced greenish tinge, different from the "yellow" in (1). As a rule, the gum on stamps using this lemon paper is plentiful, smooth and shiny, and the watermark shows distinctly. Care is needed with stamps printed in green on yellow paper (1) as it may appear that the paper is this lemon. Used 1914–1916.
(4) An experimental *orange-buff* paper. The colour must have a distinct brownish tinge. It is not to be confused with a muddy yellow (1) nor the misleading appearance (on the surface) of stamps printed in red on yellow paper where an engraved plate has been insufficiently wiped. Used 1918–1921.
(5) An experimental *buff* paper. This lacks the brownish tinge of (4) and the brightness of the yellow shades. The gum is shiny when compared with the matt type used on (4). Used 1919–1920.
(6) A *pale yellow* paper that has a creamy tone to the yellow. Used from 1920 onwards.

Green papers

(7) The original "green" paper, varying considerably through shades of blue-green and yellow-green, the front and back sometimes differing. Used 1912–1916.
(8) The *white backs*. Used 1913–1914.
(9) A paper blue-green on the surface with *pale olive* back. The back must be markedly paler than the front and this and the pronounced olive tinge to the back distinguish it from (7). Used 1916–1920.
(10) Paper with a vivid green surface, commonly called *emerald-green*; it has the olive back of (9). Used 1920.
(11) Paper with *emerald-green* both back and front. Used from 1920 onwards.

3. Perforation and Rouletting

Perforation gauge. The gauge of a perforation is the number of holes in a length of 2 cm. For correct classification the size of the holes (large or small) may need to be distinguished; in a few cases the actual number of holes on each edge of the stamp needs to be quoted.

Measurement. The Gibbons *Instanta* gauge is the standard for measuring perforations. The stamp is viewed against a dark background with the transparent gauge put on top of it. Though the gauge measures to decimal accuracy, perforations read from it are generally quoted in the Catalogue to the nearest half. For example:

Just over perf 12¾ to just under 13¼ = perf 13
Perf 13¼ exactly, rounded up = perf 13½
Just over perf 13¼ to just under 13¾ = perf 13½
Perf 13¾ exactly, rounded up = perf 14

However, where classification depends on it, actual quarter-perforations are quoted.

Notation. Where no perforation is quoted for an issue it is imperforate. Perforations are usually abbreviated (and spoken) as follows, though sometimes they may be spelled out for clarity. This notation for rectangular stamps (the majority) applies to diamond shapes if "top" is read as the edge to the top right.

P 14: perforated alike on all sides (read: "perf 14").
P 14×15: the first figure refers to top and bottom, the second to left and right sides (read: "perf 14 by 15"). This is a compound perforation. For an upright triangular stamp the first figure refers to the two sloping sides and second to the base. In inverted triangulars the base is first and the second figure to the sloping sides.
P 14–15: perforation measuring anything between 14 and 15: the holes are irregularly spaced, thus the gauge may vary along a single line or even along a single edge of the stamp (read: "perf 14 to 15").
P 14 *irregular*: perforated 14 from a worn perforator, giving badly aligned holes irregularly spaced (read: "irregular perf 14").

P *comp(ound)* 14×15: two gauges in use but not necessarily on opposite sides of the stamp. It could be one side in one gauge and three in the other; or two adjacent sides with the same gauge. (Read: "perf compound of 14 and 15".) For three gauges or more, abbreviated as "P 12, 14½, 15 *or compound*" for example.

P 14, 14½: perforated approximately 14¼ (read: "perf 14 or 14½"). It does *not* mean two stamps, one perf 14 and the other perf 14½. This obsolescent notation is gradually being replaced in the Catalogue.

Imperf: imperforate (not perforated)

Imperf×P 14: imperforate at top ad bottom and perf 14 at sides.

P 14×*imperf*: perf 14 at top and bottom and imperforate at sides.

Such headings as "P 13×14 (*vert*) and P 14×13 (*horiz*)" indicate which perforations apply to which stamp format—vertical or horizontal.

Some stamps are additionally perforated so that a label or tab is detachable; others have been perforated for use as two halves. Listings are normally for whole stamps, unless stated otherwise.

Imperf×perf

Other terms. Perforation almost always gives circular holes; where other shapes have been used they are specified, e.g. square holes; lozenge perf. Interrupted perfs are brought about by the omission of pins at regular intervals. Perforations merely simulated by being printed as part of the design are of course ignored. With few exceptions, privately applied perforations are not listed.

In the 19th century perforations are often described as clean cut (clean, sharply incised holes), intermediate or rough (rough holes, imperfectly cut, often the result of blunt pins).

Perforation errors and varieties. Authenticated errors, where a stamp normally perforated is accidentally issued imperforate, are listed provided no traces of perforation (blind holes or indentations) remain. They must be provided as pairs, both stamps wholly imperforate, and are only priced in that form.

Stamps imperforate between stamp and sheet margin are not listed in this catalogue, but such errors on Great Britain stamps will be found in the *Great Britain Specialised Catalogue*.

Pairs described as "imperforate between" have the line of perforations between the two stamps omitted.

Imperf between (horiz pair): a horizontal pair of stamps with perfs all around the edges but none between the stamps.

Imperf between (vert pair): a vertical pair of stamps with perfs all around the edges but none between the stamps.

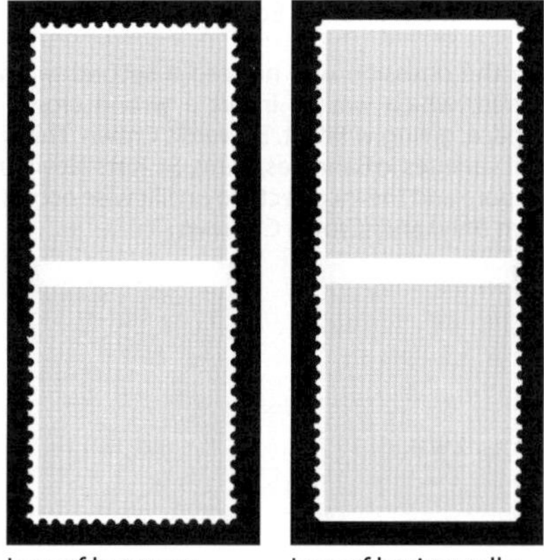

Imperf between (vertical pair) — Imperf horizontally vertical pair)

Where several of the rows have escaped perforation the resulting varieties are listable. Thus:

Imperf vert (horiz pair): a horizontal pair of stamps perforated top and bottom; all three vertical directions are imperf—the two outer edges and between the stamps.

Imperf horiz (vert pair): a vertical pair perforated at left and right edges; all three horizontal directions are imperf—the top, bottom and between the stamps.

Straight edges. Large sheets cut up before issue to post offices can cause stamps with straight edges, i.e. imperf on one side or on two sides at right angles. They are not usually listable in this condition and are worth less than corresponding stamps properly perforated all round. This does not, however, apply to certain stamps, mainly from coils and booklets, where straight edges on various sides are the manufacturing norm affecting every stamp. The listings and notes make clear which sides are correctly imperf.

Malfunction. Varieties of double, misplaced or partial perforation caused by error or machine malfunction are not listable, neither are freaks, such as perforations placed diagonally from paper folds, nor missing holes caused by broken pins.

Types of perforating. Where necessary for classification, perforation types are distinguished. These include:

Line perforation from one line of pins punching single rows of holes at a time.

Comb perforation from pins disposed across the sheet in comb formation, punching out holes at three sides of the stamp a row at a time.

Harrow perforation applied to a whole pane or sheet at one stroke.

Rotary perforation from toothed wheels operating across a sheet, then crosswise.

Sewing machine perforation. The resultant condition, clean-cut or rough, is distinguished where required.

Pin-perforation is the commonly applied term for pin-roulette in which, instead of being punched out, round holes are pricked by sharp-pointed pins and no paper is removed.

Mixed perforation occurs when stamps with defective perforations are re-perforated in a different gauge.

Punctured stamps. Perforation holes can be punched into the face of the stamp. Patterns of small holes, often in the shape of initial letters, are privately applied devices against pilferage. These (perfins) are outside the scope except for Australia, Canada, Cape of Good Hope, Papua and Sudan where they were used as official stamps by the national administration. Identification devices, when officially inspired, are listed or noted; they can be shapes, or letters or words formed from holes, sometimes converting one class of stamp into another.

Rouletting. In rouletting the paper is cut, for ease of separation, but none is removed. The gauge is measured, when needed, as for perforations. Traditional French terms descriptive of the type of cut are often used and types include:

Arc roulette (percé en arc). Cuts are minute, spaced arcs, each roughly a semicircle.

Cross roulette (percé en croix). Cuts are tiny diagonal crosses.

Line roulette (percé en ligne or *en ligne droite)*. Short straight cuts parallel to the frame of the stamp. The commonest basic roulette. Where not further described, "roulette" means this type.

Rouletted in colour or coloured roulette (percé en lignes colorées or *en lignes de coleur)*. Cuts with coloured edges, arising from notched rule inked simultaneously with the printing plate.

Saw-tooth roulette (percé en scie). Cuts applied zigzag fashion to resemble the teeth of a saw.

Serpentine roulette (percé en serpentin). Cuts as sharply wavy lines.

Zigzag roulette (percé en zigzags). Short straight cuts at angles in alternate directions, producing sharp points on separation. US usage favours "serrate(d) roulette" for this type.

Pin-roulette (originally *percé en points* and now *perforés trous d'epingle*) is commonly called pin-perforation in English.

4. Gum

All stamps listed are assumed to have gum of some kind; if they were issued without gum this is stated. Original gum (o.g.) means that which was present on the stamp as issued to the public. Deleterious climates and the presence of certain chemicals can cause gum to crack and, with early stamps, even make the paper deteriorate. Unscrupulous fakers are adept in removing it and regumming the stamp to meet the unreasoning demand often made for "full o.g." in cases where such a thing is virtually impossible.

5. Watermarks

Stamps are on unwatermarked paper except where the heading to the set says otherwise.

Detection. Watermarks are detected for Catalogue description by one of four methods: (1) holding stamps to the light; (2) laying stamps face down on a dark background; (3) adding a few drops of petroleum ether 40/60 to the stamp laid face down in a watermark tray; (4) by use of the Stanley Gibbons Detectamark, or other equipment, which work by revealing the thinning of the paper at the watermark. (Note that petroleum ether is highly inflammable in use and can damage photogravure stamps.)

Listable types. Stamps occurring on both watermarked and unwatermarked papers are different types and both receive full listing.

Single watermarks (devices occurring once on every stamp) can be modified in size and shape as between different issues; the types are noted but not usually separately listed. Fortuitous absence of watermark from a single stamp or its gross displacement would not be listable.

To overcome registration difficulties the device may be repeated at close intervals *(a multiple watermark)*, single stamps thus showing parts of several devices. Similarly, a *large sheet watermark* (or *all-over watermark*) covering numerous stamps can be used. We give informative notes and illustrations for them. The designs may be such that numbers of stamps in the sheet automatically lack watermark: this is not a listable variety. Multiple and all-over watermarks sometimes undergo modifications, but if the various types are difficult to distinguish from single stamps notes are given but not separate listings.

Papermakers' watermarks are noted where known but not listed separately, since most stamps in the sheet will lack them. Sheet watermarks which are nothing more than officially adopted papermakers' watermarks are, however, given normal listing.

Marginal watermarks, falling outside the pane of stamps, are ignored except where misplacement caused the adjoining row to be affected, in which case they may be footnoted.

Watermark errors and varieties. Watermark errors are recognised as of major importance. They comprise stamps intended to be on unwatermarked paper but issued watermarked by mistake, or stamps printed on paper with the wrong watermark. Varieties showing letters omitted from the watermark are also included, but broken or deformed bits on the dandy roll are not listed unless they represent repairs.

Watermark positions. The diagram shows how watermark position is described in the Catalogue. Paper has a side intended for printing and watermarks are usually impressed so that they read normally when looked through from that printed side. However, since philatelists customarily detect watermarks by looking at the back of the stamp the watermark diagram also makes clear what is actually seen.

Illustrations in the Catalogue are of watermarks in normal positions (from the front of the stamps) and are actual size where possible.

Differences in watermark position are collectable varieties. This Catalogue now lists inverted, sideways inverted and reversed watermark varieties on Commonwealth stamps from the 1860s onwards except where the watermark position is completely haphazard.

Great Britain inverted and sideways inverted watermarks can be found in the *Great Britain Specialised Catalogue* and the *Great Britain Concise Catalogue*.

Where a watermark comes indiscriminately in various positions our policy is to cover this by a general note: we do not give separate listings because the watermark position in these circumstances has no particular philatelic importance.

AS DESCRIBED (Read through front of stamp)		AS SEEN DURING WATERMARK DETECTION (Stamp face down and back examined
GvR	Normal	GvR
GvR	Inverted	GvR
GvR	Reversed	GvR
GvR	Reversed and Inverted	GvR
GvR	Sideways	GvR
GvR	Sideways Inverted	GvR

Standard types of watermark. Some watermarks have been used generally for various British possessions rather than exclusively for a single colony. To avoid repetition the Catalogue classifies 11 general types, as under, with references in the headings throughout the listings being given either in words or in the form ("W w **9**") (meaning "watermark type w **9**"). In those cases where watermark illustrations appear in the listings themselves, the respective reference reads, for example, W **153**, thus indicating that the watermark will be found in the normal sequence of illustrations as (type) **153**.

The general types are as follows, with an example of each quoted.

W	*Description*	*Example*
w **1**	Large Star	St. Helena No. 1
w **2**	Small Star	Turks Is. No. 4
w **3**	Broad (pointed) Star	Grenada No. 24
w **4**	Crown (over) CC, small stamp	Antigua No. 13
w **5**	Crown (over) CC, large stamp	Antigua No. 31
w **6**	Crown (over) CA, small stamp	Antigua No. 21
w **7**	Crown CA (CA over Crown), large stamp	Sierra Leone No. 54
w **8**	Multiple Crown CA	Antigua No. 41
w **9**	Multiple Script CA	Seychelles No. 158
w **9*a***	do. Error	Seychelles No. 158a
w **9*b***	do. Error	Seychelles No. 158b
w **10**	V over Crown	N.S.W. No. 327
w **11**	Crown over A	N.S.W. No. 347

CC in these watermarks is an abbreviation for "Crown Colonies" and CA for "Crown Agents". Watermarks w **1**, w **2** and w **3** are on stamps printed by Perkins, Bacon; w **4** onwards on stamps from De La Rue and other printers.

w **1**
Large Star

w **2**
Small Star

w **3**
Broad-pointed Star

Watermark w **1**, *Large Star*, measures 15 to 16 mm across the star from point to point and about 27 mm from centre to centre vertically between stars in the sheet. It was made for long stamps like Ceylon 1857 and St. Helena 1856.

Watermark w **2**, *Small Star* is of similar design but measures 12 to 13½mm from point to point and 24 mm from centre to centre vertically. It was for use with ordinary-size stamps such as Grenada 1863–71.

When the Large Star watermark was used with the smaller stamps it only occasionally comes in the centre of the paper. It is frequently so misplaced as to show portions of two stars above and below and this eccentricity will very often help in determining the watermark.

Watermark w **3**, *Broad-pointed Star*, resembles w **1** but the points are broader.

w **4**
Crown (over) CC

w **5**
Crown (over) CC

Two *Crown (over) CC* watermarks were used: w **4** was for stamps of ordinary size and w **5** for those of larger size.

w **6**
Crown (over) CA

w **7**
CA over Crown

Two watermarks of *Crown CA* type were used, w **6** being for stamps of ordinary size. The other, w **7**, is properly described as *CA over Crown*. It was specially made for paper on which it was intended to print long fiscal stamps: that some were used postally accounts for the appearance of w **7** in the Catalogue. The watermark occupies twice the space of the ordinary Crown CA watermark, w **6**. Stamps of normal size printed on paper with w **7** watermark show it *sideways*; it takes a horizontal pair of stamps to show the entire watermark.

w **8**
Multiple Crown CA

w **9**
Multiple Script CA

Multiple watermarks began in 1904 with w **8**, *Multiple Crown CA*, changed from 1921 to w **9**, *Multiple Script CA*. On stamps of ordinary size portions of two or three watermarks appear and on the large-sized stamps a greater number can be observed. The change to letters in script character with w **9** was accompanied by a Crown of distinctly different shape.

It seems likely that there were at least two dandy rolls for each Crown Agents watermark in use at any one time with a reserve roll being employed when the normal one was withdrawn for maintenance or repair.

Both the Mult Crown CA and the Mult Script CA types exist with one or other of the letters omitted from individual impressions. It is possible that most of these occur from the reserve rolls as they have only been found on certain issues. The MCA watermark experienced such problems during the early 1920s and the Script over a longer period from the early 1940s until 1951.

During the 1920s damage must also have occurred on one of the Crowns as a substituted Crown has been found on certain issues. This is smaller than the normal and consists of an oval base joined to two upright ovals with a circle positioned between their upper ends. The upper line of the Crown's base is omitted, as are the left and right-hand circles at the top and also the cross over the centre circle.

Substituted Crown

The *Multiple Script CA* watermark, w **9**, is known with two errors, recurring among the 1950–52 printings of several territories. In the first a crown has fallen away from the dandy-roll that impresses the watermark into the paper pulp. It gives w **9a**, *Crown missing*, but this omission has been found in both "Crown only" (*illustrated*) and "Crown CA" rows. The resulting faulty paper was used for Bahamas, Johore, Seychelles and the postage due stamps of nine colonies

w **9a**: Error, Crown missing

w **9b**: Error, St. Edward's Crown

When the omission was noticed a second mishap occurred, which was to insert a wrong crown in the space, giving w 9b, St. Edward's Crown. This produced varieties in Bahamas, Perlis, St. Kitts-Nevis and Singapore and the incorrect crown likewise occurs in (Crown only) and (Crown CA) rows.

w **10**
V over Crown

w **11**
Crown over A

Resuming the general types, two watermarks found in issues of several Australian States are: w **10**, *V over Crown*, and w **11**, *Crown over A*.

w **12**
Multiple St. Edward's Crown Block CA

The *Multiple St. Edward's Crown Block CA* watermark, w **12**, was introduced in 1957 and besides the change in the Crown (from that used in Multiple Crown Script CA, w **9**) the letters reverted to block capitals. The new watermark began to appear sideways in 1966 and these stamps are generally listed as separate sets.

w **14**
Multiple Crown CA Diagonal

By 1974 the two dandy-rolls (the "upright" and the "sideways") for w **12** were wearing out; the Crown Agents therefore discontinued using the sideways watermark one and retained the other only as a stand-by. A new dandy-roll with the pattern of w **14.** *Multiple Crown CA Diagonal,* was introduced and first saw use with some Churchill Centenary issues.

The new watermark has the design arranged in gradually spiralling rows. It is improved in design to allow smooth passage over the paper (the gaps between letters and rows had caused jolts in previous dandy-rolls) and the sharp corners and angles, where fibres used to accumulate, have been eliminated by rounding.

This watermark has no "normal" sideways position amongst the different printers using it. To avoid confusion our more specialised listings do not rely on such terms as "sideways inverted" but describe the direction in which the watermark points.

w **16**
Multiple Crown Script CA Diagonal

A new Crown Agents watermark was introduced during 1985, w **16**, *Multiple Crown Script CA Diagonal.* This was very similar to the previous w **14**, but showed "CA" in script rather than block letters. It was first used on the omnibus series of stamps commemorating the Life and Times of Queen Elizabeth the Queen Mother.

6. Colours

Stamps in two or three colours have these named in order of appearance, from the centre moving outwards. Four colours or more are usually listed as multicoloured.

In compound colour names the second is the predominant one, thus:

orange-red = a red tending towards orange;

red-orange = an orange containing more red than usual.

Standard colours used. The 200 colours most used for stamp identification are given in the Stanley Gibbons Stamp Colour Key. The Catalogue has used the Stamp Colour Key as standard for describing new issues for some years. The names are also introduced as lists are rewritten, though exceptions are made for those early issues where traditional names have become universally established.

Determining colours. When comparing actual stamps with colour samples in the Stamp Colour Key, view in a good north daylight (or its best substitute; fluorescent "colour matching" light). Sunshine is not recommended. Choose a solid portion of the stamp design; if available, marginal markings such as solid bars of colour or colour check dots are helpful. Shading lines in the design can be misleading as they appear lighter than solid colour. Postmarked portions of a stamp appear darker than normal. If more than one colour is present, mask off the extraneous ones as the eye tends to mix them.

Errors of colour. Major colour errors in stamps or overprints which qualify for listing are: wrong colours; one colour inverted in relation to the rest; albinos (colourless impressions), where these have Expert Committee certificates; colours completely omitted, but only on unused stamps (if found on used stamps the information is footnoted) and with good credentials, missing colours being frequently faked.

Colours only partially omitted are not recognised, Colour shifts, however spectacular, are not listed.

Shades. Shades in philately refer to variations in the intensity of a colour or the presence of differing amounts of other colours. They are particularly significant when they can be linked to specific printings. In general, shades need to be quite marked to fall within the scope of this Catalogue; it does not favour nowadays listing the often numerous shades of a stamp, but chooses a single applicable colour name which will indicate particular groups of outstanding shades. Furthermore, the listings refer to colours as issued; they may deteriorate into something different through the passage of time.

Modern colour printing by lithography is prone to marked differences of shade, even within a single run, and variations can occur within the same sheet. Such shades are not listed.

Aniline colours. An aniline colour meant originally one derived from coal-tar; it now refers more widely to colour of a particular brightness suffused on the surface of a stamp and showing through clearly on the back.

Colours of overprints and surcharges. All overprints and surcharges are in black unless stated otherwise in the heading or after the description of the stamp.

7. Specimen Stamps

Originally, stamps overprinted SPECIMEN were circulated to postmasters or kept in official records, but after the establishment of the Universal Postal Union supplies were sent to Berne for distribution to the postal administrations of member countries.

During the period 1884 to 1928 most of the stamps of British Crown Colonies required for this purpose were overprinted SPECIMEN in various shapes and sizes by their printers from typeset formes. Some locally produced provisionals were handstamped locally, as were sets prepared for presentation. From 1928 stamps were punched with holes forming the word SPECIMEN, each firm of printers using a different machine or machines. From 1948 the stamps supplied for UPU distribution were no longer punctured.

Stamps of some other Commonwealth territories were overprinted or handstamped locally, while stamps of Great Britain and those overprinted for use in overseas postal agencies (mostly of the higher denominations) bore SPECIMEN overprints and handstamps applied by the Inland Revenue or the Post Office.

De La Rue & Co. Ltd.

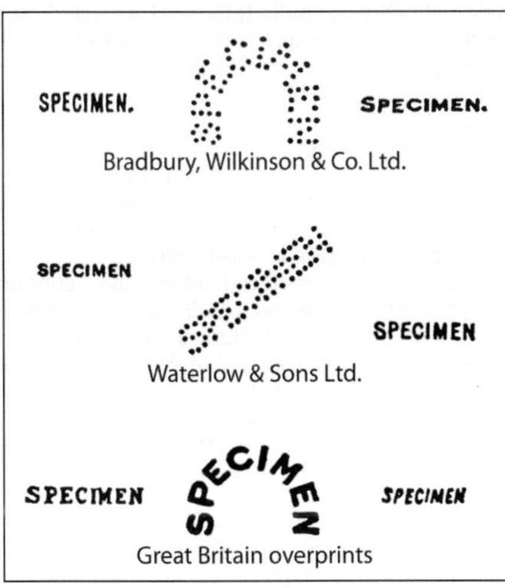

Bradbury, Wilkinson & Co. Ltd.

Waterlow & Sons Ltd.

Great Britain overprints

Some of the commoner types of overprints or punctures are illustrated here. Collectors are warned that dangerous forgeries of the punctured type exist.

The *Stanley Gibbons Commonwealth Catalogues* record those Specimen overprints or perforations intended for distribution by the UPU to member countries. In addition the Specimen overprints of Australia and its dependent territories, which were sold to collectors by the Post Office, are also included.

Various Perkins Bacon issues exist obliterated with a "CANCELLED" within an oval of bars handstamp.

Perkins Bacon "CANCELLED" Handstamp

This was applied to six examples of those issues available in 1861 which were then given to members of Sir Rowland Hill's family. 75 different stamps (including four from Chile) are recorded with this handstamp although others may possibly exist. The unauthorised gift of these "CANCELLED" stamps to the Hill family was a major factor in the loss of the Agent General for the Crown Colonies (the forerunner of the Crown Agents) contracts by Perkins Bacon in the following year. Where examples of these scarce items are known to be in private hands the catalogue provides a price.

For full details of these stamps see *CANCELLED by Perkins Bacon* by Peter Jaffé (published by Spink in 1998).

All other Specimens are outside the scope of this volume.

Specimens are not quoted in Great Britain as they are fully listed in the Stanley Gibbons *Great Britain Specialised Catalogue*.

In specifying type of specimen for individual high-value stamps, "H/S" means handstamped, "Optd" is overprinted and "Perf" is punctured. Some sets occur mixed, e.g. "Optd/Perf". If unspecified, the type is apparent from the date or it is the same as for the lower values quoted as a set.

Prices. Prices for stamps up to £1 are quoted in sets; higher values are priced singly. Where specimens exist in more than one type the price quoted is for the cheapest. Specimen stamps have rarely survived even as pairs; these and strips of three, four or five are worth considerably more than singles.

8. Coil Stamps

Stamps issued only in coil form are given full listing. If stamps are issued in both sheets and coils the coil stamps are listed separately only where there is some feature (e.g. perforation or watermark sideways) by which singles can be distinguished. Coil stamps containing different stamps *se-tenant* are also listed.

Coil join pairs are too random and too easily faked

to permit of listing; similarly ignored are coil stamps which have accidentally suffered an extra row of perforations from the claw mechanism in a malfunctioning vending machine.

9. Stamp Booklets

Stamp booklets are now listed in this catalogue.

Single stamps from booklets are listed if they are distinguishable in some way (such as watermark or perforation) from similar sheet stamps.

Booklet panes are listed where they contain stamps of different denominations *se-tenant*, where stamp-size labels are included, or where such panes are otherwise identifiable. Booklet panes are placed in the listing under the lowest denomination present.

Particular perforations (straight edges) are covered by appropriate notes.

10. Miniature Sheets and Sheetlets

We distinguish between "miniature sheets" and "sheetlets" and this affects the catalogue numbering. An item in sheet form that is postally valid, containing a single stamp, pair, block or set of stamps, with wide, inscribed and/or decorative margins, is a miniature sheet if it is sold at post offices as an indivisable entity. As such the Catalogue allots a single **MS** number and describes what stamps make it up. The sheetlet or small sheet differs in that the individual stamps are intended to be purchased separately for postal purposes. For sheetlets, all the component postage stamps are numbered individually and the composition explained in a footnote. Note that the definitions refer to post office sale—not how items may be subsequently offered by stamp dealers.

11. Forgeries and Fakes

Forgeries. Where space permits, notes are considered if they can give a concise description that will permit unequivocal detection of a forgery. Generalised warnings, lacking detail, are not nowadays inserted, since their value to the collector is problematic.

Fakes. Unwitting fakes are numerous, particularly "new shades" which are colour changelings brought about by exposure to sunlight, soaking in water contaminated with dyes from adherent paper, contact with oil and dirt from a pocketbook, and so on. Fraudulent operators, in addition, can offer to arrange: removal of hinge marks; repairs of thins on white or coloured papers; replacement of missing margins or perforations; reperforating in true or false gauges; removal of fiscal cancellations; rejoining of severed pairs, strips and blocks; and (a major hazard) regumming. Collectors can only be urged to purchase from reputable sources and to insist upon Expert Committee certification where there is any kind of doubt.

The Catalogue can consider footnotes about fakes where these are specific enough to assist in detection.

Abbreviations

Printers

A.B.N. Co.	American Bank Note Co, New York.
B.A.B.N.	British American Bank Note Co. Ottawa
B.W.	Bradbury Wilkinson & Co, Ltd.
C.B.N.	Canadian Bank Note Co, Ottawa.
Continental B.N. Co.	Continental Bank Note Co.
Courvoisier	Imprimerie Courvoisier S.A., La-Chaux-de-Fonds, Switzerland.
D.L.R.	De La Rue & Co, Ltd, London.
Enschedé	Joh. Enschedé en Zonen, Haarlem, Netherlands.
Harrison	Harrison & Sons, Ltd. London
P.B.	Perkins Bacon Ltd, London.
Waterlow	Waterlow & Sons, Ltd, London.

General Abbreviations

Alph	Alphabet
Anniv	Anniversary
Comp	Compound (perforation)
Des	Designer; designed
Diag	Diagonal; diagonally
Eng	Engraver; engraved
F.C.	Fiscal Cancellation
H/S	Handstamped
Horiz	Horizontal; horizontally
Imp, Imperf	Imperforate
Inscr	Inscribed
L	Left
Litho	Lithographed
mm	Millimetres
MS	Miniature sheet
N.Y.	New York
Opt(d)	Overprint(ed)
P or P-c	Pen-cancelled
P, Pf or Perf	Perforated
Photo	Photogravure
Pl	Plate
Pr	Pair
Ptd	Printed
Ptg	Printing
R	Right
R.	Row
Recess	Recess-printed
Roto	Rotogravure
Roul	Rouletted
S	Specimen (overprint)
Surch	Surcharge(d)
T.C.	Telegraph Cancellation
T	Type
Typo	Typographed
Un	Unused
Us	Used
Vert	Vertical; vertically
W or wmk	Watermark
Wmk s	Watermark sideways

(†) = Does not exist

(–) (or blank price column) = Exists, or may exist, but no market price is known.

/ between colours means "on" and the colour following is that of the paper on which the stamp is printed.

Colours of Stamps

Bl (blue); blk (black); brn (brown); car, carm (carmine); choc (chocolate); clar (claret); emer (emerald); grn (green); ind (indigo); mag (magenta); mar (maroon); mult (multicoloured); mve (mauve); ol (olive); orge (orange); pk (pink); pur (purple); scar (scarlet); sep (sepia); turq (turquoise); ultram (ultramarine); verm (vermilion); vio (violet); yell (yellow).

Colour of Overprints and Surcharges

(B.) = blue, (Blk.) = black, (Br.) = brown, (C.) = carmine, (G.) = green, (Mag.) = magenta, (Mve.) = mauve, (Ol.) = olive, (O.) = orange, (P.) = purple, (Pk.) = pink, (R.) = red, (Sil.) = silver, (V.) = violet, (Vm.) or (Verm.) = vermilion, (W.) = white, (Y.) = yellow.

Arabic Numerals

As in the case of European figures, the details of the Arabic numerals vary in different stamp designs, but they should be readily recognised with the aid of this illustration.

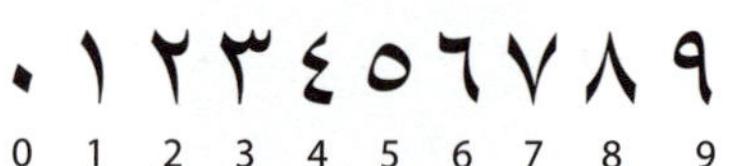

ACKNOWLEDGMENT

We are grateful to individual collectors, members of the philatelic trade and specialist societies and study circles for their assistance in improving and extending the the Stanley Gibbons range of catalogues. The addresses of societies and study circles relevant to this volume are:

Bechauanland and Botswana Society
Membersip Secretary — Mr N. Midwood
69 Porlock Lane, Furzton,
Milton Keynes MK4 1JY

Cape and Natal Study Circle
Secretary — Mr. J. Dickson, Lismore House,
Great Lane, Shepton Beauchamp,
Someset TA19 0LJ

Orange Free State Study Circle
Secretary — Mr J. Stroud
28 Oxford Street,
Burnham-on-Sea,
Somerset TA 1LQ

South African Collectors' Society
General Secretary — Mr C. Oliver
Telephone 020 8940 9833

Transvaal Study Circle
Secretary — Mr J. Woolgar
132 Dale Street,
Chatham, Kent
ME4 6QH

International Philatelic Glossary

English	French	German	Spanish	Italian
Agate	Agate	Achat	Agata	Agata
Air stamp	Timbre de la poste aérienne	Flugpostmarke	Sello de correo aéreo	Francobollo per posta aerea
Apple Green	Vert-pomme	Apfelgrün	Verde manzana	Verde mela
Barred	Annulé par barres	Balkenentwertung	Anulado con barras	Sbarrato
Bisected	Timbre coupé	Halbiert	Partido en dos	Frazionato
Bistre	Bistre	Bister	Bistre	Bistro
Bistre-brown	Brun-bistre	Bisterbraun	Castaño bistre	Bruno-bistro
Black	Noir	Schwarz	Negro	Nero
Blackish Brown	Brun-noir	Schwärzlichbraun	Castaño negruzco	Bruno nerastro
Blackish Green	Vert foncé	Schwärzlichgrün	Verde negruzco	Verde nerastro
Blackish Olive	Olive foncé	Schwärzlicholiv	Oliva negruzco	Oliva nerastro
Block of four	Bloc de quatre	Viererblock	Bloque de cuatro	Bloco di quattro
Blue	Bleu	Blau	Azul	Azzurro
Blue-green	Vert-bleu	Blaugrün	Verde azul	Verde azzuro
Bluish Violet	Violet bleuâtre	Bläulichviolett	Violeta azulado	Violtto azzurrastro
Booklet	Carnet	Heft	Cuadernillo	Libretto
Bright Blue	Bleu vif	Lebhaftblau	Azul vivo	Azzurro vivo
Bright Green	Vert vif	Lebhaftgrün	Verde vivo	Verde vivo
Bright Purple	Mauve vif	Lebhaftpurpur	Púrpura vivo	Porpora vivo
Bronze Green	Vert-bronze	Bronzegrün	Verde bronce	Verde bronzo
Brown	Brun	Braun	Castaño	Bruno
Brown-lake	Carmin-brun	Braunlack	Laca castaño	Lacca bruno
Brown-purple	Pourpre-brun	Braunpurpur	Púrpura castaño	Porpora bruno
Brown-red	Rouge-brun	Braunrot	Rojo castaño	Rosso bruno
Buff	Chamois	Sämisch	Anteado	Camoscio
Cancellation	Oblitération	Entwertung	Cancelación	Annullamento
Cancelled	Annulé	Gestempelt	Cancelado	Annullato
Carmine	Carmin	Karmin	Carmín	Carminio
Carmine-red	Rouge-carmin	Karminrot	Rojo carmín	Rosso carminio
Centred	Centré	Zentriert	Centrado	Centrato
Cerise	Rouge-cerise	Kirschrot	Color de ceresa	Color Ciliegia
Chalk-surfaced paper	Papier couché	Kreidepapier	Papel estucado	Carta gessata
Chalky Blue	Bleu terne	Kreideblau	Azul turbio	Azzurro smorto
Charity stamp	Timbre de bienfaisance	Wohltätigkeitsmarke	Sello de beneficenza	Francobollo di beneficenza
Chestnut	Marron	Kastanienbraun	Castaño rojo	Marrone
Chocolate	Chocolat	Schokolade	Chocolate	Cioccolato
Cinnamon	Cannelle	Zimtbraun	Canela	Cannella
Claret	Grenat	Weinrot	Rojo vinoso	Vinaccia
Cobalt	Cobalt	Kobalt	Cobalto	Cobalto
Colour	Couleur	Farbe	Color	Colore
Comb-perforation	Dentelure en peigne	Kammzähnung, Reihenzähnung	Dentado de peine	Dentellatura e pettine
Commemorative stamp	Timbre commémoratif	Gedenkmarke	Sello conmemorativo	Francobollo commemorativo
Crimson	Cramoisi	Karmesin	Carmesí	Cremisi
Deep Blue	Blue foncé	Dunkelblau	Azul oscuro	Azzurro scuro
Deep bluish Green	Vert-bleu foncé	Dunkelbläulichgrün	Verde azulado oscuro	Verde azzurro scuro
Design	Dessin	Markenbild	Diseño	Disegno
Die	Matrice	Urstempel. Type, Platte	Cuño	Conio, Matrice
Double	Double	Doppelt	Doble	Doppio
Drab	Olive terne	Trüboliv	Oliva turbio	Oliva smorto
Dull Green	Vert terne	Trübgrün	Verde turbio	Verde smorto
Dull purple	Mauve terne	Trübpurpur	Púrpura turbio	Porpora smorto
Embossing	Impression en relief	Prägedruck	Impresión en relieve	Impressione a relievo
Emerald	Vert-eméraude	Smaragdgrün	Esmeralda	Smeraldo
Engraved	Gravé	Graviert	Grabado	Inciso
Error	Erreur	Fehler, Fehldruck	Error	Errore
Essay	Essai	Probedruck	Ensayo	Saggio
Express letter stamp	Timbre pour lettres par exprès	Eilmarke	Sello de urgencia	Francobollo per espresso
Fiscal stamp	Timbre fiscal	Stempelmarke	Sello fiscal	Francobollo fiscale
Flesh	Chair	Fleischfarben	Carne	Carnicino
Forgery	Faux, Falsification	Fälschung	Falsificación	Falso, Falsificazione
Frame	Cadre	Rahmen	Marco	Cornice
Granite paper	Papier avec fragments	Faserpapier	Papel con filamentos	Carto con fili di seta

English	*French*	*German*	*Spanish*	*Italian*
	de fils de soie			
Green	Vert	Grün	Verde	Verde
Greenish Blue	Bleu verdâtre	Grünlichblau	Azul verdoso	Azzurro verdastro
Greenish Yellow	Jaune-vert	Grünlichgelb	Amarillo verdoso	Giallo verdastro
Grey	Gris	Grau	Gris	Grigio
Grey-blue	Bleu-gris	Graublau	Azul gris	Azzurro grigio
Grey-green	Vert gris	Graugrün	Verde gris	Verde grigio
Gum	Gomme	Gummi	Goma	Gomma
Gutter	Interpanneau	Zwischensteg	Espacio blanco entre dos grupos	Ponte
Imperforate	Non-dentelé	Geschnitten	Sin dentar	Non dentellato
Indigo	Indigo	Indigo	Azul indigo	Indaco
Inscription	Inscription	Inschrift	Inscripción	Dicitura
Inverted	Renversé	Kopfstehend	Invertido	Capovolto
Issue	Émission	Ausgabe	Emisión	Emissione
Laid	Vergé	Gestreift	Listado	Vergato
Lake	Lie de vin	Lackfarbe	Laca	Lacca
Lake-brown	Brun-carmin	Lackbraun	Castaño laca	Bruno lacca
Lavender	Bleu-lavande	Lavendel	Color de alhucema	Lavanda
Lemon	Jaune-citron	Zitrongelb	Limón	Limone
Light Blue	Bleu clair	Hellblau	Azul claro	Azzurro chiaro
Lilac	Lilas	Lila	Lila	Lilla
Line perforation	Dentelure en lignes	Linienzähnung	Dentado en linea	Dentellatura lineare
Lithography	Lithographie	Steindruck	Litografía	Litografia
Local	Timbre de poste locale	Lokalpostmarke	Emisión local	Emissione locale
Lozenge roulette	Percé en losanges	Rautenförmiger Durchstich	Picadura en rombos	Perforazione a losanghe
Magenta	Magenta	Magentarot	Magenta	Magenta
Margin	Marge	Rand	Borde	Margine
Maroon	Marron pourpré	Dunkelrotpurpur	Púrpura rojo oscuro	Marrone rossastro
Mauve	Mauve	Malvenfarbe	Malva	Malva
Multicoloured	Polychrome	Mehrfarbig	Multicolores	Policromo
Myrtle Green	Vert myrte	Myrtengrün	Verde mirto	Verde mirto
New Blue	Bleu ciel vif	Neublau	Azul nuevo	Azzurro nuovo
Newspaper stamp	Timbre pour journaux	Zeitungsmarke	Sello para periódicos	Francobollo per giornali
Obliteration	Oblitération	Abstempelung	Matasello	Annullamento
Obsolete	Hors (de) cours	Ausser Kurs	Fuera de curso	Fuori corso
Ochre	Ocre	Ocker	Ocre	Ocra
Official stamp	Timbre de service	Dienstmarke	Sello de servicio	Francobollo di
Olive-brown	Brun-olive	Olivbraun	Castaño oliva	Bruno oliva
Olive-green	Vert-olive	Olivgrün	Verde oliva	Verde oliva
Olive-grey	Gris-olive	Olivgrau	Gris oliva	Grigio oliva
Olive-yellow	Jaune-olive	Olivgelb	Amarillo oliva	Giallo oliva
Orange	Orange	Orange	Naranja	Arancio
Orange-brown	Brun-orange	Orangebraun	Castaño naranja	Bruno arancio
Orange-red	Rouge-orange	Orangerot	Rojo naranja	Rosso arancio
Orange-yellow	Jaune-orange	Orangegelb	Amarillo naranja	Giallo arancio
Overprint	Surcharge	Aufdruck	Sobrecarga	Soprastampa
Pair	Paire	Paar	Pareja	Coppia
Pale	Pâle	Blass	Pálido	Pallido
Pane	Panneau	Gruppe	Grupo	Gruppo
Paper	Papier	Papier	Papel	Carta
Parcel post stamp	Timbre pour colis postaux	Paketmarke	Sello para paquete postal	Francobollo per pacchi postali
Pen-cancelled	Oblitéré à plume	Federzugentwertung	Cancelado a pluma	Annullato a penna
Percé en arc	Percé en arc	Bogenförmiger Durchstich	Picadura en forma de arco	Perforazione ad arco
Percé en scie	Percé en scie	Bogenförmiger Durchstich	Picado en sierra	Foratura a sega
Perforated	Dentelé	Gezähnt	Dentado	Dentellato
Perforation	Dentelure	Zähnung	Dentar	Dentellatura
Photogravure	Photogravure, Heliogravure	Rastertiefdruck	Fotograbado	Rotocalco
Pin perforation	Percé en points	In Punkten durchstochen	Horadado con alfileres	Perforato a punti
Plate	Planche	Platte	Plancha	Lastra, Tavola
Plum	Prune	Pflaumenfarbe	Color de ciruela	Prugna
Postage Due stamp	Timbre-taxe	Portomarke	Sello de tasa	Segnatasse
Postage stamp	Timbre-poste	Briefmarke, Freimarke, Postmarke	Sello de correos	Francobollo postale
Postal fiscal stamp	Timbre fiscal-postal	Stempelmarke als Postmarke verwendet	Sello fiscal-postal	Fiscale postale
Postmark	Oblitération postale	Poststempel	Matasello	Bollo
Printing	Impression, Tirage	Druck	Impresión	Stampa, Tiratura
Proof	Épreuve	Druckprobe	Prueba de impresión	Prova
Provisionals	Timbres provisoires	Provisorische Marken. Provisorien	Provisionales	Provvisori
Prussian Blue	Bleu de Prusse	Preussischblau	Azul de Prusia	Azzurro di Prussia

English	*French*	*German*	*Spanish*	*Italian*
Purple	Pourpre	Purpur	Púrpura	Porpora
Purple-brown	Brun-pourpre	Purpurbraun	Castaño púrpura	Bruno porpora
Recess-printing	Impression en taille douce	Tiefdruck	Grabado	Incisione
Red	Rouge	Rot	Rojo	Rosso
Red-brown	Brun-rouge	Rotbraun	Castaño rojizo	Bruno rosso
Reddish Lilac	Lilas rougeâtre	Rötlichlila	Lila rojizo	Lilla rossastro
Reddish Purple	Poupre-rouge	Rötlichpurpur	Púrpura rojizo	Porpora rossastro
Reddish Violet	Violet rougeâtre	Rötlichviolett	Violeta rojizo	Violetto rossastro
Red-orange	Orange rougeâtre	Rotorange	Naranja rojizo	Arancio rosso
Registration stamp	Timbre pour lettre chargée (recommandée)	Einschreibemarke	Sello de certificado lettere	Francobollo per raccomandate
Reprint	Réimpression	Neudruck	Reimpresión	Ristampa
Reversed	Retourné	Umgekehrt	Invertido	Rovesciato
Rose	Rose	Rosa	Rosa	Rosa
Rose-red	Rouge rosé	Rosarot	Rojo rosado	Rosso rosa
Rosine	Rose vif	Lebhaftrosa	Rosa vivo	Rosa vivo
Roulette	Percage	Durchstich	Picadura	Foratura
Rouletted	Percé	Durchstochen	Picado	Forato
Royal Blue	Bleu-roi	Königblau	Azul real	Azzurro reale
Sage green	Vert-sauge	Salbeigrün	Verde salvia	Verde salvia
Salmon	Saumon	Lachs	Salmón	Salmone
Scarlet	Écarlate	Scharlach	Escarlata	Scarlatto
Sepia	Sépia	Sepia	Sepia	Seppia
Serpentine roulette	Percé en serpentin	Schlangenliniger Durchstich	Picado a serpentina	Perforazione a serpentina
Shade	Nuance	Tönung	Tono	Gradazione de colore
Sheet	Feuille	Bogen	Hoja	Foglio
Slate	Ardoise	Schiefer	Pizarra	Ardesia
Slate-blue	Bleu-ardoise	Schieferblau	Azul pizarra	Azzurro ardesia
Slate-green	Vert-ardoise	Schiefergrün	Verde pizarra	Verde ardesia
Slate-lilac	Lilas-gris	Schierferlila	Lila pizarra	Lilla ardesia
Slate-purple	Mauve-gris	Schieferpurpur	Púrpura pizarra	Porpora ardesia
Slate-violet	Violet-gris	Schieferviolett	Violeta pizarra	Violetto ardesia
Special delivery stamp	Timbre pour exprès	Eilmarke	Sello de urgencia	Francobollo per espressi
Specimen	Spécimen	Muster	Muestra	Saggio
Steel Blue	Bleu acier	Stahlblau	Azul acero	Azzurro acciaio
Strip	Bande	Streifen	Tira	Striscia
Surcharge	Surcharge	Aufdruck	Sobrecarga	Soprastampa
Tête-bêche	Tête-bêche	Kehrdruck	Tête-bêche	Tête-bêche
Tinted paper	Papier teinté	Getöntes Papier	Papel coloreado	Carta tinta
Too-late stamp	Timbre pour lettres en retard	Verspätungsmarke	Sello para cartas retardadas	Francobollo per le lettere in ritardo
Turquoise-blue	Bleu-turquoise	Türkisblau	Azul turquesa	Azzurro turchese
Turquoise-green	Vert-turquoise	Türkisgrün	Verde turquesa	Verde turchese
Typography	Typographie	Buchdruck	Tipografia	Tipografia
Ultramarine	Outremer	Ultramarin	Ultramar	Oltremare
Unused	Neuf	Ungebraucht	Nuevo	Nuovo
Used	Oblitéré, Usé	Gebraucht	Usado	Usato
Venetian Red	Rouge-brun terne	Venezianischrot	Rojo veneciano	Rosso veneziano
Vermilion	Vermillon	Zinnober	Cinabrio	Vermiglione
Violet	Violet	Violett	Violeta	Violetto
Violet-blue	Bleu-violet	Violettblau	Azul violeta	Azzurro violetto
Watermark	Filigrane	Wasserzeichen	Filigrana	Filigrana
Watermark sideways	Filigrane couché liegend	Wasserzeichen	Filigrana acostado	Filigrana coricata
Wove paper	Papier ordinaire, Papier uni	Einfaches Papier	Papel avitelado	Carta unita
Yellow	Jaune	Gelb	Amarillo	Giallo
Yellow-brown	Brun-jaune	Gelbbraun	Castaño amarillo	Bruno giallo
Yellow-green	Vert-jaune	Gelbgrün	Verde amarillo	Verde giallo
Yellow-olive	Olive-jaunâtre	Gelboliv	Oliva amarillo	Oliva giallastro
Yellow-orange	Orange jaunâtre	Gelborange	Naranja amarillo	Arancio giallastro
Zig-zag roulette	Percé en zigzag	Sägezahnartiger Durchstich	Picado en zigzag	Perforazione a zigzag

Botswana

formerly Bechuanaland

Before the 1880s the only Europeans in the area which became Bechuanaland were scattered hunters and traders, together with the missionaries who were established at Kuruman as early as 1816.

Tribal conflicts in the early years of the decade led to the intervention of Boers from the Transvaal who established the independent republics of Goshen and Stellaland.

STELLALAND

The Boer republic of Stellaland was proclaimed towards the end of 1882. A postal service was organised from the capital, Vryburg, and stamps were ordered from a firm in Cape Town. These were only valid within the republic. Until June 1885 mail to other parts of South Africa was sent through Christiana, in the Transvaal, and was franked with both Stellaland and Transvaal stamps.

No date stamps or obliterators were used by the Stellaland Post Office. Stamps were pen-cancelled with the initials of a postal official and the date.

PRICES FOR STAMPS ON COVER

The issues of Stellaland are very rare on cover.

1 Arms of the Republic

(Litho by Van der Sandt, de Villiers & Co., Cape Town)

1884 (29 Feb). P 12.

1	1	1d. red	£180	£325
		a. Imperf between (horiz pair)	£3750	
		b. Imperf between (vert pair)	£4000	
2		3d. orange	22·00	£325
		a. Imperf between (horiz pair)	£750	
		b. Imperf between (vert pair)	£1700	
		c. Imperf vert (horiz pair)	£1100	
3		4d. olive-grey	21·00	£350
		a. Imperf between (horiz pair)	£650	
		b. Imperf between (vert pair)	£1800	
4		6d. lilac-mauve	22·00	£350
		a. Imperf between (horiz pair)	£1300	
		b. Imperf between (vert pair)	£1500	
5		1s. green	60·00	£650

In 1884 the British Government, following appeals from local chiefs for protection, decided to annex both Goshen and Stellaland. A force under Sir Charles Warren from the Cape reached Vryburg on 7 February 1885 and continued to Mafeking, the principal town of Goshen.

On 30 September 1885 Stellaland and other territory to the south of the Molopo River was constituted the Crown Colony of British Bechuanaland. A protectorate was also proclaimed over a vast tract of land to the north of the Molopo.

Stellaland stamps continued to be used until 2 December 1885 with external mail, franked with Stellaland and Cape of Good Hope stamps, postmarked at Barkly West and Kimberley in Griqualand West.

1885 (Oct). *Handstamped "Twee" sideways in violet-lake.*

6	1	2d. on 4d. olive-grey	£3500

On 2 December 1885 Cape of Good Hope stamps overprinted "British Bechuanaland" were placed on sale at the Vryburg post office.

BRITISH BECHUANALAND

CROWN COLONY

PRICES FOR STAMPS ON COVER

Nos. 1/8	*from* × 12
No. 9	*from* × 80
Nos. 10/21	*from* × 8
Nos. 22/8	*from* × 10
No. 29	*from* × 10
No. 30	*from* × 10
Nos. 31/2	*from* × 12
Nos. 33/7	*from* × 20
Nos. 38/9	*from* × 25

British
Bechuanaland
(1)

BRITISH
BECHUANALAND
(2)

1885 (2 Dec)–**87**. *Stamps of Cape of Good Hope ("Hope" seated) optd with T* **1**, *by W. A. Richards & Sons, Cape Town.*

(*a*) Wmk Crown CC (No. 3) or Crown CA (others).

1	½d. grey-black (No. 40*a*) (R.)	18·00	25·00
	a. Opt in lake	£3500	£4000
	b. Opt double (Lake+Black)	£750	
2	3d. pale claret (No. 43)	35·00	48·00
	a. No dot to 1st "i" of "British"	£375	
3	4d. dull blue (No. 30) (6.87)	60·00	70·00

(*b*) Wmk Anchor (Cape of Good Hope. Type **13**).

4	½d. grey-black (No. 48*a*) (3.87)	8·00	15·00
	a. Error. "ritish"	£2250	
	b. Opt double	£3250	
5	1d. rose-red (No. 49)	14·00	9·00
	a. Error. "ritish"	£3750	£2250
	b. No dot to 1st "i" of "British"	£180	£170
	c. Opt double	†	£2000
6	2d. pale bistre (No. 50)	35·00	8·00
	a. Error. "ritish"	£6500	£3750
	b. No dot to 1st "i" of "British"	£375	£160
	c. Opt double	†	£1800
7	6d. reddish purple (No. 52)	£120	38·00
	a. No dot to 1st "i" of "British"	£1200	£500
8	1s. green (No. 53) (11.86)	£275	£160
	a. Error. "ritish"	£18000	£12000

Nos. 1/8 were overprinted from settings of 120. The missing "B" errors are believed to have occurred on one position for one of these settings only. The 'No dot to 1st "i"' variety occurs on R. 10/3 of the left pane.

Overprints with stop after "Bechuanaland" are forged.

1887 (1 Nov). *No. 197 of Great Britain optd with T* **2**, *by D.L.R.*

9	½d. vermilion	1·25	1·25
	a. Opt double	£2250	
	s. Handstamped "Specimen"	85·00	

3

4

5

(Typo D.L.R.)

1887 (1 Nov).

(*a*) Wmk Orb (Great Britain Type **48**). P 14.

10	3	1d. lilac and black	15·00	1·75
11		2d. lilac and black	75·00	1·75
		a. Pale dull lilac and black	60·00	23·00
12		3d. lilac and black	3·75	5·50
		a. Pale reddish lilac and black	65·00	21·00
13		4d. lilac and black	50·00	2·25
14		6d. lilac and black	60·00	2·50

(*b*) Wmk Script "V R" (sideways, reading up). P 13½.

15	4	1s. green and black	29·00	6·50
16		2s. green and black	50·00	40·00
17		2s.6d. green and black	60·00	60·00
18		5s. green and black	90·00	£150
19		10s. green and black	£180	£350

(*c*) Two Orbs (sideways). P 14×13½.

20	5	£1 lilac and black	£800	£750
21		£5 lilac and black	£3000	£1500
10s/21s		H/S "Specimen" *Set of* 12	£900	

Nos. 10/21 were produced by overprinting a series of "Unappropriated Die" designs originally produced by the Board of Inland Revenue for use as Great Britain fiscal stamps.

Several values are known on blued paper. No. 11*a* is the first printing of the 2d. (on safety paper?) and has a faded appearance.

When purchasing Nos. 20/21 in used condition beware of copies with fiscal cancellations cleaned off and bearing forged postmarks.

For No. 15 surcharged "£5" see No. F2.

1d.
(6)

1s.
(7)

Curved foot to "2"

1888 (7 Aug). *Nos. 10/11 and 13/15 surch as T* **6** *or* **7**, *by P. Townshend & Co., Vryburg.*

22	3	1d. on 1d. lilac and black	7·50	6·50
23		2d. on 2d. lilac and black (R.)	27·00	3·00
		a. Pale dull lilac and black (No. 11a)	90·00	48·00
		b. Curved foot to "2"	£275	£150
		c. Surch in green	†	£3500
25		4d. on 4d. lilac and black (R.)	£325	£425
26		6d. on 6d. lilac and black	£120	11·00
		a. Surch in blue	†	£12000
28	4	1s. on 1s. green and black	£180	85·00

Nos. 23c and 26a are from two sheets of surcharge trials subsequently put into stock and used at Vryburg (2d.) or Mafeking (6d.) during 1888–89.

It should be noted that, in addition to its curved foot, the "2" on No. 23b is distinctly shorter than the "d".

One
Half-
Penny
(8)

1888 (7 Dec). *No. 12a surch with T* **8**, *by P. Townshend & Co, Vryburg.*

29	3	½d. on 3d. pale reddish lilac and black	£170	£190
		a. Broken "f" in "Half"	£7000	

No. 29 was produced from a setting of 60 (12×5).

No. 29a shows the letter "f" almost completely missing and occurs on R. 5/11 of the setting. Five examples are known, one being in the Royal Collection.

Errors of spelling on this surcharge are bogus.

British
Bechuanaland.
(9)

British
Bechuanaland.
(10)

BRITISH
BECHUANALAND
(11)

1889 (Jan). *No. 48a of Cape of Good Hope* (wmk Anchor) *optd with T* **9**, *by P. Townshend & Co, Vryburg.*

30	½d. grey-black (G.)	3·25	27·00
	a. Opt "Bechuanaland British"	£1500	
	ab. "British" omitted	£4500	
	b. Opt double, one inverted, inverted opt "Bechuanaland British"	£1700	
	ba. Opt double, one inverted, inverted "British" omitted	£3500	
	c. Opt double, one vertical	£800	
	ca. *Se-tenant* with stamp without opt	£6000	

No. 30 was produced using a setting of 30 (6×5).

The overprint was misplaced upwards on at least one pane, giving the overprint "Bechuanaland British" (No. 30a) on rows 1 to 4 and "British" omitted on row 5 (No. 30ab). "British" was also omitted on R. 5/1 of the setting on some sheets only.

On one pane on which the overprint was applied double, one inverted, the inverted overprint was misplaced downwards, giving No. 30ba on rows 7 to 10 and "British" omitted (No. 30bb) on row 6.

n
Normal "n"

u
Inverted "u"

1891 (Nov). *Nos. 49/50 of Cape of Good Hope* (wmk Anchor), *optd with T* **10**, *reading upwards.*

31	1d. rose-red	10·00	9·50
	a. Horiz pair, one without opt		
	b. "British" omitted	—	£2250
	c. "Bechuanaland" omitted	£2250	
	d. Inverted "u" for 2nd "n"	£150	£150
32	2d. pale bistre	3·25	2·25
	a. No stop after "Bechuanaland"	£275	£325
	b. Inverted "u" for 2nd "n"		
31s/2s	H/S "Specimen" *Set of* 2	£130	

The overprint on Nos. 31 and 32 was of 120 impressions in two panes of 60 (6×10). That on No. 32 was applied both by a stereo plate and by a forme made up from loose type. No. 31 was overprinted only with the latter. No. 32a is from the stereo overprinting (left pane, R. 3/3), 31d and 32b are from the typeset overprinting (left pane, R. 10/4).

See also Nos. 38 and 39.

1891 (1 Dec)–**1904**. *Nos. 172, 200, 205, 208 and 211 of Great Britain optd with T* **11**, *by D.L.R.*

33	1d. lilac	6·00	1·50
34	2d. grey-green and carmine	13·00	4·00
35	4d. green and purple-brown	2·50	60
	a. Bisected (2d.) (on cover) (11.99)	†	£2500
36	6d. purple/*rose-red*	3·50	2·00
37	1s. dull green (7.94)	13·00	16·00
	a. Bisected (6d.) (on cover) (12.04)	†	—
33/7	*Set of* 5	35·00	22·00
33s/6s	H/S "Specimen" *Set of* 4	£170	

No. 35a was used at Palapye Station and No. 37a at Kanye, both in the Protectorate.

1893 (Dec)–**95**. *As Nos. 31/2, but T* **10** *reads downwards.*

38	1d. rose-red	2·25	2·25
	a. Pair, one without opt		
	b. "British" omitted	£3250	
	c. Optd "Bechuanaland. British"	£1300	£1400
	d. Inverted "u" for 2nd "n"	£120	£130
	e. No dots to "i" of "British"	£120	£130
	f. "s" omitted	£275	£275
	g. Opt reading up, no dots to "i" of "British"	£2750	
39	2d. pale bistre (12.3.95)	4·75	2·25
	a. Opt double	£1300	£650
	b. "British" omitted	£700	£500
	c. "Bechuanaland" omitted	—	£500
	d. Optd "Bechuanaland. British"	£400	£225
	e. Inverted "u" for 2nd "n"	£170	£130
	f. No dots to "i" of "British"	£170	£130
	g. Opt reading up, no dots to "i" of "British"		

The same typeset overprint was used for Nos. 38 and 39 as had been employed for Nos. 31 and 32 but applied the other way up; the inverted "u" thus falling on the right pane, R. 1/3. The no dots to "i" variety only occurs on this printing (right pane, R. 1/4). Some sheets of both values were overprinted the wrong way up, resulting in Nos. 38f. and 39g.

No. 38g. developed gradually on right pane R. 10/8. The variety is not known on Nos. 31, 32 or 39.

On 16 November 1895 British Bechuanaland was annexed to the Cape of Good Hope and ceased to have its own stamps, but they remained in use in the Protectorate until superseded in 1897. The Postmaster-General of Cape Colony had assumed control of the Bechuanaland postal service on 1 April 1893 and the Cape, and subsequently the South African, postal authorities continued to be responsible for the postal affairs of the Bechuanaland Protectorate until 1963.

BECHUANALAND PROTECTORATE

PRICES FOR STAMPS ON COVER TO 1945

Nos. 40/51	*from* × 10
Nos. 52/71	*from* × 6
Nos. 72/82	*from* × 5
Nos. 83/98	*from* × 4
Nos. 99/110	*from* × 6
Nos. 111/17	*from* × 10
Nos. 118/28	*from* × 4
Nos. 129/31	*from* × 10

PRICES FOR STAMPS ON COVER TO 1945

Nos. D1/3	*from* × 50
Nos. D4/6	*from* × 60
No. F1	*from* × 5
No. F2	—
No. F3	*from* × 5

This large area north of the Molopo River was proclaimed a British Protectorate on 30 September 1885 at the request of the native chiefs.

A postal service using runners was inaugurated on 9 August 1888 and Nos. 40 to 55 were issued as a temporary measure with the object of assessing the cost of this service

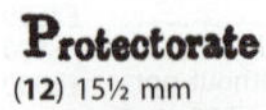
(**12**) 15½ mm

(**13**)

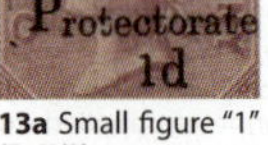
13a Small figure "1" (R. 7/2)

13b Small figure "1" (R. 10/2)

1888 (7 Aug). *No. 9 optd with T* **12** *and Nos. 10/19 surch or optd only as T* **13** *by P. Townshend & Co. Vryburg.*

40 – ½d. vermilion 5·50 35·00
a. "Protectorate" double £325
s. Handstamped "Specimen" 85·00
41 3 1d. on 1d. lilac and black 8·50 15·00
a. Small figure "1" (R. 7/2, 10/2) £425 £475
b. Space between "1" and "d" (R. 10/9) £550
42 2d. on 2d. lilac and black 29·00 17·00
b. Curved foot to "2" £700 £475
43 3d. on 3d. pale reddish lilac and black £130 £180
44 4d. on 4d. lilac and black £375 £400
a. Small figure "4" £4000 £4000
45 6d. on 6d. lilac and black 70·00 45·00
46 4 1s. green and black 90·00 50·00
a. First "o" omitted £5500 £3000
s. Handstamped "Specimen" £110
47 2s. green and black £600 £900
a. First "o" omitted £16000
48 2s.6d. green and black £550 £800
a. First "o" omitted £13000
49 5s. green and black £1200 £2000
a. First "o" omitted £20000
50 10s. green and black £4000 £6000
a. First "o" omitted £28000

Nos. 40/5 were produced from a basic setting of 120 (12×10) on which a faulty first "o" in "Protectorate" occurred on R. 5/12. For Nos. 46/50 the setting was reduced to 84 (12×7) and on many sheets the first "o" on R. 5/12 failed to print.

There are a number of smaller than normal "1"s in the setting, usually identifiable by the upper serif of the "1" which is pointed and slopes sharply downwards at the left. R. 7/2 and 10/2 are quite distinct and are as shown.

The normal space between "1" and "d" measures 1 mm. On No. 41b it is 1.7 mm.

It should be noted that, like No. 23b, the "2" on No. 42b is distinctly shorter than the "d".

See also Nos. 54/5.

1888 (Dec). *No. 25 optd with T* **12** *by P. Townshend & Co., Vryburg.*

51 3 4d. on 4d. lilac and black 80·00 42·00

Bechuanaland

Protectorate.
(**14**)

Protectorate
Fourpence
(**15**)

1889 (Jan). *No. 48a of Cape of Good Hope (wmk Anchor), optd with T* **14** *by P. Townshend & Co., Vryburg.*

52 ½d. grey-black (G.) 3·00 48·00
a. Opt double £475 £700
ab. Ditto, one reading "Protectorate Bechuanaland" £1100
ac. Ditto, one reading "Bechuanaland" only £2250
b. "Bechuanaland" omitted £1700
c. Optd "Protectorate Bechuanaland" £800 £900

1889 (Mar). *No. 9 surch with T* **15** *by P. Townshend & Co., Vryburg.*

53 4d. on ½d. vermilion 27·00 4·00
a. "rpence" omitted (R. 9/2) † £6000
b. "ourpence" omitted (R. 9/2) £10000
c. Surch (T **15**) inverted † £4000
cb. Ditto. "ourpence" omitted † £15000
s. Handstamped "Specimen" £130

The lines of the surcharge are normally 6 mm apart, but 5 mm and 4.5 mm spacings are known.

Examples of No. 53c are postmarked "679" (Tati).

Protectorate
(**16**) 15 mm

Protectorate
(**17**)

1890. *No. 9 optd.*

54 16 ½d. vermilion £160 £170
a. Type **16** inverted 75·00 95·00
b. Type **16** double £110 £160
c. Type **16** double and inverted £600 £650
d. Optd "Portectorate" inverted £17000
w. Wmk inverted
55 17 ½d. vermilion £190 £350
a. Type **17** double £1500
b. Optd "Protectorrte"
c. Optd "Protectorrte" double £17000

These were trial printings made in 1888 which were subsequently issued.

In June 1890 the Bechuanaland Protectorate and the Colony of British Bechuanaland came under one postal administration and the stamps of British Bechuanaland were used in the Protectorate until 1897.

BRITISH
BECHUANALAND
(**18**)

BECHUANALAND
PROTECTORATE
(**19**)

1897. *No. 61 of Cape of Good Hope* (wmk Anchor), *optd as T* **18**.

(a) Lines 13 mm apart, bottom line 16 mm long, by Taylor & Marshall, Cape Town.

56 ½d. yellow-green (July?) 2·50 13·00

(b) Lines 13½ mm apart bottom line 15 mm long, by P. Townshend & Co, Vryburg.

57 ½d. yellow-green (April) 23·00 80·00
a. Opt double, one albino inverted £225

(c) Lines 10½ mm apart, bottom line 15 mm long, by W. A. Richards & Sons, Cape Govt Printers.

58 ½d. yellow-green (July?) 10·00 50·00

Although issued only in the Protectorate, the above were presumably overprinted "BRITISH BECHUANALAND" because stamps bearing this inscription were in use there at the time.

1897 (Oct)–**1902**. *Nos. 172, 197, 200, 202, 205 and 208 of Great Britain (Queen Victoria) optd with T* **19** *by D.L.R.*

59 ½d. vermilion 1·25 2·25
60 ½d. blue-green (25.2.02) 1·40 3·50
61 1d. lilac 4·00 75
62 2d. grey-green and carmine 4·50 3·50
63 3d. purple/*yellow* (12.97) 5·50 8·50
64 4d. green and purple-brown 16·00 15·00
65 6d. purple/*rose-red* 23·00 11·00
59/65 *Set of 7* 50·00 40·00
59s/65s Optd or H/S (No. 60s) "Specimen" *Set of 7* £225

BECHUANALAND

PROTECTORATE
(**20**)

BECHUANALAND
PROTECTORATE
(**21**)

1904 (29 Nov)–**13**. *Nos. 216, 218/19, 230 and 313/14 (Somerset House ptgs) of Great Britain (King Edward VII) optd with T* **20**, *by D.L.R.*

66 ½d. blue-green (3.06) 2·00 2·00
67 ½d. yellowish green (11.08) 3·75 3·50
68 1d. scarlet (4.05) 7·50 30
s. Optd "Specimen" 60·00
69 2½d. ultramarine 7·50 5·00
a. Stop after "P" in "PROTECTORATE" £950 £1200
70 1s. deep green and scarlet (10.12) 42·00 £140
a. Opt double, one albino £200
71 1s. green and carmine (1913) 45·00 £120
s. Optd "Specimen" 95·00

No. 69a occurs on R. 5/9 of the lower pane.

1912 (Sept)–**14**. *No. 342 of Great Britain (King George V, wmk Crown) optd with T* **20**.

72 1d. scarlet 2·00 60
a. No cross on crown £150 75·00
b. Aniline scarlet (No. 343) (1914) £140 80·00

1913 (1 July)–**24**. *Stamps of Great Britain (King George V) optd.*

(a) Nos. 351, 357, 362, 367, 370/1, 376, 379, 385 and 395 (wmk Simple Cypher, T **100***) optd with T* **20**.

73 ½d. green (*shades*) 1·25 1·75
74 1d. scarlet (*shades*) (4.15) 2·75 75
a. Carmine-red (1922) 27·00 2·50
75 1½d. red-brown (12.20) 4·50 3·00
76 2d. reddish orange (Die I) 6·00 3·25
a. Orange (Die I) (1921) 17·00 3·00
aw. Wmk inverted
77 2d. orange (Die II) (1924) 38·00 2·75
78 2½d. cobalt-blue 3·50 23·00
a. Blue (1915) 13·00 23·00
79 3d. bluish violet 6·00 12·00
80 4d. grey-green 6·50 24·00
81 6d. reddish purple (*shades*) 7·50 18·00
a. Opt double, one albino
82 1s. bistre 12·00 25·00
a. Bistre-brown (1923) 27·00 32·00
s. Optd "Specimen" 75·00
73/82 *Set of 9* 45·00 £100

(b) With T **21**.

(i) *Waterlow printings (Nos. 399 and 401)* (1914–15).

83 2s.6d. deep sepia-brown (1.15) £130 £250
a. Re-entry (R. 2/1) £1100 £1700
b. Opt double, one albino £300
84 5s. rose-carmine (1914) £160 £375
a. Opt double, one albino £375
83s/4s Optd "Specimen" *Set of 2* £275

(ii) *D.L.R. printings (Nos. 407/8 and 409)* (1916–19).

85 2s.6d. pale brown (7.16) £120 £250
a. Re-entry (R. 2/1) £1100 £1700
86 2s.6d. sepia (1917) £130 £225
a. Opt treble, two albino
b. Re-entry (R. 2/1) £1300
87 5s. bright carmine (8.19) £300 £425
a. Opt double, one albino £450

(iii) *B.W. printings (Nos. 414 and 416)* (1920–23).

88 2s.6d. chocolate-brown (7.23) 85·00 £160
a. Major re-entry (R. 1/2) £2000
b. Opt double, one albino £550
c. Opt treble, two albino £500
89 5s. rose-red (7.20) £110 £275
a. Opt treble, two albino £375
b. Opt double, one albino

Examples of Nos. 83/9 are known showing a forged Lobatsi postmark dated "6 MAY 35" or "6 MAY 39".

1925 (July)–**27**. *Nos. 418/19, 421, 423/4, 426/a and 429 of Great Britain (wmk Block Cypher, T* **111***) optd with T* **20**.

91 ½d. green (1927) 1·50 1·75
92 1d. scarlet (8.25) 2·00 70
w. Wmk inverted
93 2d. orange (Die II) 1·75 1·00
94 3d. violet (10.26) 4·75 21·00
a. Opt double, one albino £200
w. Wmk inverted £200
95 4d. grey-green (10.26) 4·75 42·00
a. Printed on the gummed side
96 6d. reddish purple (*chalk-surfaced paper*) (12.25) 45·00 75·00
97 6d. purple (*ordinary paper*) (1926) 48·00 50·00
98 1s. bistre-brown (10.26) 9·00 24·00
w. Wmk inverted £325 £300
91/8 *Set of 8* £100 £190

No. 94w. also shows the variety, opt double, one albino.

22 King George V, Baobab Tree and Cattle drinking

22a Windsor Castle

(Des from photo by Resident Commissioner, Ngamiland, Recess Waterlow)

1932 (12 Dec). Wmk Mult Script CA. P 12½.

99 22 ½d. green 1·50 30
a. Imperf between (horiz pair) £20000
100 1d. scarlet 1·00 25
101 2d. brown 1·00 30
102 3d. ultramarine 1·75 3·00
103 4d. orange 1·75 7·00
104 6d. purple 2·75 5·00
105 1s. black and olive-green 3·00 7·00
106 2s. black and orange 24·00 48·00
107 2s.6d. black and scarlet 19·00 35·00
108 3s. black and purple 35·00 48·00
109 5s. black and ultramarine 75·00 80·00
110 10s. black and brown £150 £160
99/110 *Set of 12* £275 £350
99s/110s Perf "Specimen" *Set of 12* £275

Examples of most values are known showing a forged Lobatsi postmark dated "6 MAY 35" or "6 MAY 39".

Extra flagstaff (Plate "1" R. 9/1)

Short extra flagstaff (Plate "2" R. 2/1)

Lightning conductor (Plate "3" R. 2/5)

Flagstaff on right-hand turret (Plate "5" R. 7/1)

Double flagstaff (Plate "6" R. 5/2)

(Des H. Fleury. Recess B.W)

1935 (4 May). *Silver Jubilee.* Wmk Mult Script CA. P 11×12.

111 22a 1d. deep blue and scarlet 50 4·25
a. Extra flagstaff £250
b. Short extra flagstaff £400
c. Lightning conductor £350
d. Flagstaff on right-hand turret £350
e. Double flagstaff £350
112 2d. ultramarine and grey-black 1·25 4·25
a. Extra flagstaff £100 £160
b. Short extra flagstaff £150 £180
c. Lightning conductor £120 £170
113 3d. brown and deep blue 2·75 4·50
a. Extra flagstaff £140 £200
b. Short extra flagstaff £180
c. Lightning conductor £160 £200
114 6d. slate and purple 5·50 4·50
a. Extra flagstaff £130
b. Short extra flagstaff £160
c. Lightning conductor £160 £170
111/14 *Set of 4* 9·00 16·00
111s/14s Perf "Specimen" *Set of 4* £100

22b King George VI and Queen Elizabeth

23 King George VI, Baobab Tree and Cattle drinking

(Des and recess D.L.R.)

1937 (12 May). *Coronation.* Wmk Mult Script CA. P 14.

115	**22b**	1d. scarlet	45	40
116		2d. yellow-brown	60	1·00
117		3d. bright blue	60	1·25
115/17 *Set of 3*			1·50	2·40
115s/17s Perf "Specimen" *Set of 3*			85·00	

(Recess Waterlow)

1938 (1 Apr)–**52**. Wmk Mult Script CA. P 12½.

118	**23**	½d. green	2·00	3·00
		a. Light yellowish green (1941)	8·00	7·50
		b. Yellowish green (4.43)	7·50	4·25
		c. Deep green (4.49)	3·50	9·00
119		1d. scarlet	75	50
120		1½d. dull blue	9·50	2·00
		a. Light blue (4.43)	1·00	1·00
121		2d. chocolate-brown	75	50
122		3d. deep ultramarine	1·00	2·50
123		4d. orange	2·00	3·50
124		6d. reddish purple	4·75	3·00
		a. Purple (1944)	4·00	2·50
		ab. "A" of "CA" missing from wmk	†	—
125		1s. black and brown-olive	4·00	6·50
		a. Grey-black & olive-green (21.5.52)	17·00	26·00
126		2s.6d. black and scarlet	14·00	14·00
127		5s. black and deep ultramarine	30·00	21·00
		a. Grey-black & dp ultram (10.46)	75·00	50·00
128		10s. black and red-brown	17·00	24·00
118/28 *Set of 11*			70·00	70·00
118s/28s Perf "Specimen" *Set of 11*			£225	

Bechuanaland

(**24**)

1945 (3 Dec). *Victory. Stamps of South Africa optd with T* **24**. *Inscr alternately in English and Afrikaans.*

129	**55**	1d. brown and carmine	50	1·00
130	**56**	2d. slate-blue and violet	50	1·25
131	**57**	3d. deep blue and blue	50	1·25
		a. Opt omitted (in vert pair with normal)	£10000	
129/31 *Set of 3*			1·40	3·25

No. 131a comes from a sheet on which the overprint was displaced downwards so that it is omitted from stamps in the top row and shown on the sheet margin at foot.

24a King George VI

24b King George VI and Queen Elizabeth

24c Queen Elizabeth II as Princess and Princess Margaret

24d The Royal Family

(Recess Waterlow)

1947 (17 Feb). *Royal Visit.* Wmk Mult Script CA. P 12½.

132	**24a**	1d. scarlet	10	10
133	**24b**	2d. green	10	10
134	**24c**	3d. ultramarine	10	10
135	**24d**	1s. mauve	10	10
132/5 *Set of 4*			35	30
132s/5s Perf "Specimen" *Set of 4*			90·00	

24e King George VI and Queen Elizabeth

24f

(Des and photo Waterlow (T **24e**) Design recess; name typo B.W. (T **24f**)

1948 (1 Dec). *Royal Silver Wedding.* Wmk Mult Script CA.

136	**24e**	1½d. ultramarine (P 14×15)	30	10
137	**24f**	10s. black (P 11½×11)	30·00	38·00

24g Hermes Globe and Forms of Transport

24h Hemispheres Jet-powered Vickers Viking airliner and Steamer

24i Hermes and Globe

24j UPU Monument

(Recess Waterlow (T **24g**, **24j**). Designs recess name Typo B.W. (T **24h**, **24i**))

1949 (10 Oct). *75th Anniv of Universal Postal Union.* Wmk Mult Script CA.

138	**24g**	1½d. blue (P 13×14)	30	1·25
139	**24h**	3d. deep blue (P 11×11½)	1·25	2·50
140	**24i**	6d. magenta (P 11×11½)	45	2·50
141	**24j**	1s. olive (P 13½×14)	45	1·50
138/41 *Set of 4*			2·25	7·00

24k Queen Elizabeth II

25 Queen Elizabeth II, Baobab Tree and Cattle drinking

(Des and eng B.W. Recess D.L.R.)

1953 (3 June). *Coronation.* Wmk Mult Script CA. P 13½×13.

142	**24k**	2d. black and brown	60	30

(Des from photo by Resident Commissioner, Ngamiland. Recess Waterlow)

1955 (3 Jan)–**58**. Wmk Mult Script CA. P 13½×14.

143	**25**	1½d. green	50	30
144		1d. rose-red	80	10
145		2d. red-brown	1·25	30
146		3d. ultramarine	3·00	1·50
		a. Bright ultramarine (16.1.57)	8·50	3·00
146*b*		4d. red-orange 11.12.58)	6·50	8·50
147		4½d. blackish blue	1·50	35
148		6d. purple	1·25	60
149		1s. black and brown-olive	1·25	80
150		1s.3d. black and lilac	14·00	9·50
151		2s.6d. black and rose-red	11·00	9·50
152		5s. black and violet-blue	15·00	8·50
153		10s. black and red-brown	30·00	15·00
143/53 *Set of 12*			75·00	48·00

26 Queen Victoria, Queen Elizabeth II and Landscape

(Photo Harrison)

1960 (21 Jan). *75th Anniv of Bechuanaland Protectorate.* W w **12**. P 14½×14.

154	**26**	1d. sepia and black	40	50
155		3d. magenta and black	40	30
156		6d. bright blue and black	40	50
154/6 *Set of 3*			1·10	1·10

(New Currency. 100 cents = 1 rand)

1c (**27**) 1c (I) 1c (II) 2½c (I) 2½c (II)

3 (I) 3 (II) 3 (III) 5c (I) 5c (II) R1 (I) R1 (II)

2½c

Spaced "c" (R. 10/3)

1961. *Nos. 144/6a and 148/53 surch as T* **27** *by South African Govt Printer, Pretoria.*

157	**25**	1c. on 1d. rose-red (Type I)	30	10
		a. Type II (6 June)	40	10
158		2c. on 2d. red-brown	20	10
159		2½c. on 2d. red-brown (Type I)	30	10
		a. Type II (26 July)	85	1·00
		b. Vert pair, one without surch	£4000	
160		2½c. on 3d. bright ultramarine	2·00	5·00
		a. Spaced "c" (R. 10/3)	48·00	

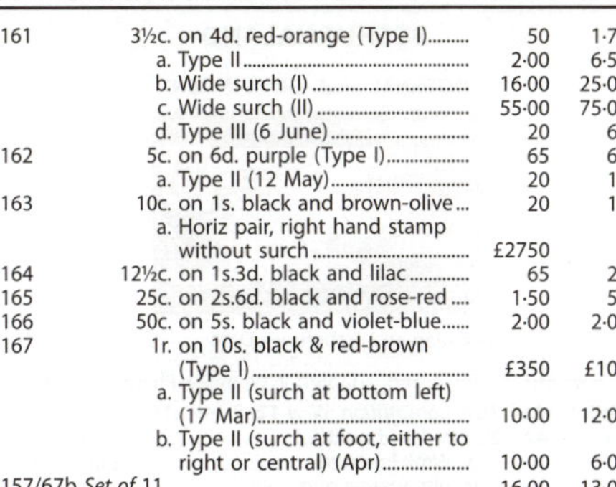

161	3½c. on 4d. red-orange (Type I)	50	1·75
	a. Type II	2·00	6·50
	b. Wide surch (I)	16·00	25·00
	c. Wide surch (II)	55·00	75·00
	d. Type III (6 June)	20	60
162	5c. on 6d. purple (Type I)	65	60
	a. Type II (12 May)	20	10
163	10c. on 1s. black and brown-olive	20	10
	a. Horiz pair, right hand stamp without surch	£2750	
164	12½c. on 1s.3d. black and lilac	65	20
165	25c. on 2s.6d. black and rose-red	1·50	50
166	50c. on 5s. black and violet-blue	2·00	2·00
167	1r. on 10s. black & red-brown (Type I)	£350	£100
	a. Type II (surch at bottom left) (17 Mar)	10·00	12·00
	b. Type II (surch at foot, either to right or central) (Apr)	10·00	6·00
157/67b *Set of 11*		16·00	13·00

Nos. 161/c occur from the same printing each sheet containing thirty-three examples of Type I, five of Type I with wide spacing, nineteen of Type II and three of Type II with wide spacing. The wide surcharge measures 9½ mm overall (with "c" spaced 1½ mm from "½") and comes on 8 of the 10 stamps in the last vertical row. The surcharge on the remainder of the sheet varies between 8½ and 9½ mm.

No. 163a was caused by a shift of the surcharge so that the last vertical row on the sheet is without "10c".

A later printing of the 12½c. on 1s.3d. was from a fresh setting of type, but is insufficiently different for separate listing. Later printings of the 10c. and 25c. were identical with the originals.

28 African Golden Oriole

29 Bechuana Ox

(Des P. Jones (1c. to 12½c.). Photo Harrison)

1961 (2 Oct). *T* **28**, **29** *and similar designs.* W w **12**. P 14½×14 (25, 50c.) or 14×14½ (others).

168	1c. yellow, red, black and lilac	1·50	40
169	2c. orange, black and yellow-olive	2·00	3·50
170	2½c. carmine, green, black and bistre	1·75	10
171	3½c. yellow, black, sepia and pink	2·50	3·50
172	5c. yellow, blue, black and buff	3·25	1·00
173	7½c. brown, red, black and apple-green	2·25	2·25
174	10c. red, yellow, sepia & turquoise-green	2·25	60
175	12½c. buff, blue, red and grey-black	18·00	5·50
176	20c. yellow-brown and drab	2·50	2·50
177	25c. deep brown and lemon	3·00	1·50
178	35c. deep blue and orange	2·50	2·75
179	50c. sepia and olive	1·75	2·25
180	1r. black and cinnamon	5·50	2·50
181	2r. brown and turquoise-blue	18·00	9·00
168/81 *Set of 14*		60·00	32·00

Designs: *Vert*—2c. Hoopoe; 2½c. Scarlet-chested Sunbird; 3½c. Yellow-rumped Bishop; 5c. Swallow-tailed Bee Eater; 7½c. African Grey Hornbill; 10c. Red-headed Weaver; 12½c. Brownhooded Kingfisher; 20c. Woman musician; 35c. Woman grinding maize; 1r. Lion; 2r. Police camel patrol. *Horiz*—25c. Baobab Tree.

30 Protein Foods

(Des M. Goaman. Photo Harrison)

1963 (4 June). *Freedom from Hunger.* W w **12**. P 14×14½.

182	**30**	12½c. bluish green	30	15

31 Red Cross Emblem

(Des V. Whiteley. Litho B.W.)

1963 (2 Sept). *Red Cross Centenary.* W w **12**. P 13½.

183	**31**	2½c. red and black	20	10
184		12½c. red and blue	40	50

32 Shakespeare and Memorial Theatre, Stratford-upon-Avon

(Des R. Granger Barrett. Photo Harrison)

1964 (23 April). *400th Birth Anniv of William Shakespeare.* W w **12**. P 14×14½

185	**32**	12½c. light brown	15	15

BECHUANALAND

INTERNAL SELF-GOVERNMENT

42 Map and Gaberones Dam

(Des Mrs. M. Townsend, adapted V. Whiteley. Photo Harrison)

1965 (1 Mar). *New Constitution.* W w **12**. P 14½×14.

186	**42**	2½c. red and gold	20	10
		w. Wmk inverted	15·00	3·75
187		5c. ultramarine and gold	20	40
188		12½c. brown and gold	30	40
189		25c. green and gold	40	55
186/9 *Set of 4*			1·00	1·25

42a ITU Emblem

(Des M. Goaman. Litho Enschedé)

1969 (17 May). *I.T.U. Centenary.* W w **12**. P 11×11½.

190	**42a**	2½c. red and bistre-yellow	20	10
191		12½c. mauve and brown	45	30

42b ICY Emblem

(Des V. Whiteley. Litho Harrison)

1965 (25 Oct). *International Co-operation Year.* W w **12**. P 14½.

192	**42b**	1c. reddish purple and turquoise-green	10	20
193		12½c. deep bluish green and lavender	60	55

42c Sir Winston Churchill and St. Paul's Cathedral in wartime

(Des Jennifer Toombs. Photo Harrison)

1966 (24 Jan). *Churchill Commemoration. Printed in black, cerise and gold and with background in colours stated.* W w **12**. P 14.

194	**42c**	1c. new blue	15	80
195		2½c. deep green	35	10
196		12½c. brown	70	30
197		20c. bluish violet	75	50
194/7 *Set of 4*			1·75	1·50

43 Haslar Smoke Generator

(Des V. Whiteley. Photo Harrison)

1966 (1 June). *Bechuanaland Royal Pioneer Corps. T* **43** *and similar horiz designs.* W w **12**. P 14½.

198	2½c. Prussian blue, red and light emerald	25	10
199	5c. brown and light blue	25	20
200	15c. Prussian blue, rosine and emerald	30	25
201	35c. buff, blackish brown, red and green	30	1·00
198/201 *Set of 4*		1·00	1·25

Designs:—5c. Bugler; 15c. Gun-site; 35c. Regimental cap badge.

Bechuanaland became the independent republic of Botswana, within the Commonwealth, on 30 September 1966.

INDEPENDENCE

47 National Assembly Building

(Des R. Granger Barrett. Photo Harrison)

1966 (30 Sept). *Independence. T* **47** *and similar horiz designs. Multicoloured.* P 14½.

202	2½c. Type **47**	15	10
	a. Imperf (pair)	£250	
203	5c. Abattoir, Lobatsi	20	10
204	15c. National Airways Douglas DC-3	65	20
205	35c. State House, Gaberones	40	30
202/5 *Set of 4*		1·25	55

REPUBLIC OF BOTSWANA

(51)

52 Golden Oriole

1966 (30 Sept). *Nos. 168/81 optd as T* **51**.

206	1c. yellow, red, black and lilac	25	10
207	2c. orange, black and yellow-olive	30	1·75
208	2½c. carmine, green, black and bistre	30	10
209	3½c. yellow, black, sepia and pink	1·00	20
	a. Yellow, black, sepia and flesh	1·25	1·00
210	5c. yellow, blue, black and buff	1·00	1·50
211	7¼c. brown, red, black and apple-green	50	1·75
	a. Blue-green omitted		
212	10c. red, yellow, sepia and turquoise-green	1·00	20
213	12½c. buff, blue, red and grey-black	2·00	2·75
214	20c. yellow-brown and drab	20	1·00
215	25c. deep brown and lemon	20	2·00
216	35c. deep blue and orange	30	2·25
217	50c. sepia and olive	20	70
218	1r. black and cinnamon	40	1·25
219	2r. brown and turquoise-blue	60	2·50
206/19 *Set of 14*		8·00	16·00

No. 209*a* was a special printing produced to make up quantities. It does not exist without the overprint.

No. 211a shows the background in yellow instead of apple-green, the blue-green overlay being omitted.

(Des D. M. Reid-Henry. Photo Harrison)

1967 (3 Jan). *Birds. Vert designs as T* **52**. *Multicoloured.* P 14×14.

220	1c. Type **52**	30	15
	a. Error. Wmk **105** of Malta	†	£700
221	2c. Hoopoe	60	70
222	3c. Groundscraper Thrush	55	10
223	4c. Cordon-bleu ("Blue Waxbill")	55	10
224	5c. Secretary Bird	55	10
225	7c. Yellow-billed Hornbill	60	1·00
226	10c. Burchell's Gonolek ("Crimson-breasted Shrike")	60	15
227	15c. Malachite Kingfisher	7·50	3·00
228	20c. African Fish Eagle	7·50	2·00
229	25c. Go-away Bird ("Grey Loerie")	4·00	1·50
230	35c. Scimitar-bill	6·00	2·25
231	50c. Comb Duck	2·75	2·75
232	1r. Levaillant's Barbet	5·00	3·50
233	2r. Didric Cuckoo	7·00	16·00
220/33 *Set of 14*		38·00	30·00

A used copy of the 20c. has been seen with the pale brown colour missing, resulting in the value (normally shown in white) being omitted.

The 1, 2, 4, 7 and 10c. values exist with PVA gum as well as gum arabic.

66 Students and University

(Des V. Whiteley. Photo Harrison)

1967 (7 Apr). *First Conferment of University Degrees.* P 14×14½.

234	**66**	3c. sepia, ultramarine & lt orange-yell	10	10
235		7c. sepia, ultram & lt greenish bl	10	10
236		15c. sepia, ultramarine and rose	10	10
237		35c. sepia, ultramarine and light violet	20	20
234/7 *Set of 4*			30	30

67 Bushbuck

(Des G, Vasarhelyi. Photo Harrison)

1967 (2 Oct). *Chobe Game Reserve. T* **67** *and similar horiz designs. Multicoloured.* P 14.

238	3c. Type **67**	10	20
239	7c. Sable Antelope	15	30
240	35c. Fishing on Chobe River	80	1·10
238/40 *Set of 3*		90	1·40

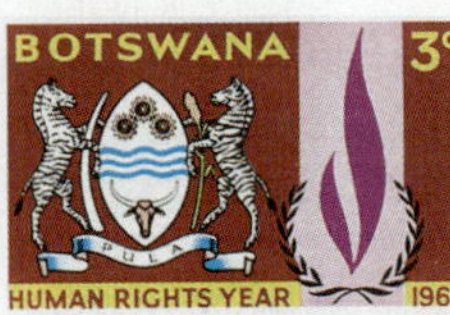

70 Arms of Botswana and Human Rights Emblem

(Litho D.L.R.)

1968 (8 Apr). *Human Rights Year. T* **70** *and similar horiz designs showing Anniv of Botswana and Human Rights emblem arranged differently.* P 13½×13.

241	3c. multicoloured	10	10
242	15c. multicoloured	25	45
243	25c. multicoloured	25	60
241/3 *Set of 3*		50	1·00

73 Eland and Giraffe Rock Paintings, Tsodilo Hills

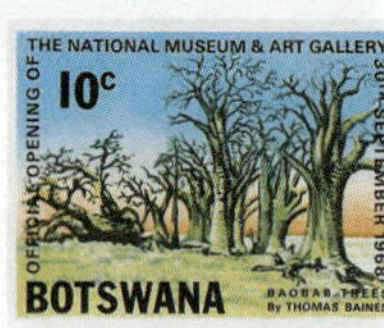

75 "Baobab Trees" (Thomas Baines)

76 National Museum and Art Gallery

(Litho D.L.R.)

1968 (30 Sept). *Opening of National Museum and Art Gallery. T* **73/6** *and similar multicoloured design.* P 12½ (7c.), 12½×13½ (15c.), or 13×13½ (others).

244	3c. Type **73**	20	20
245	7c. Girl wearing ceremonial beads (30×48 *mm*)	25	40
246	10c. Type **75**	25	30
247	15c. Type **76**	40	1·50
244/7 *Set of 4*		1·00	2·25
MS248 132×82 mm. Nos. 244/7. P 13		1·00	2·25

77 African Family, and Star over Village

(Des Mrs M. E. Townsend, adapted J. Cooter. Litho Enschedé)

1968 (11 Nov). *Christmas.* P 13×14.

249	**77**	1c. multicoloured	10	10
250		2c. multicoloured	10	10
251		5c. multicoloured	10	10
252		25c. multicoloured	15	50
249/52 *Set of 4*			30	70

78 Scout, Lion and Badge in Frame

(Des D.L.R. Litho Format)

1969 (21 Aug). *22nd World Scout Conference, Helsinki. T* **78** *and similar multicoloured designs.* P 13½.

253	3c. Type **78**	30	30
254	15c. Scouts cooking over open fire (*vert*)	35	1·00
255	25c. Scouts around camp fire	35	1·00
253/5 *Set of 3*		90	2·00

81 Woman, Child and Christmas Star

82 Diamond Treatment Plant, Orapa

(Des A. Vale, adapted V. Whiteley. Litho Harrison)

1969 (6 Nov). *Christmas.* P 14½×14.

256	**81**	1c. pale blue and chocolate	10	10
257		2c. pale yellow-olive and chocolate	10	10
258		4c. yellow and chocolate	10	10
259		35c. chocolate and bluish violet	20	20
256/9 *Set of 4*			30	30
MS260 86×128 mm. Nos. 256/9. P 14½ (*shades*)			70	1·10

(Des J.W. Litho Harrison)

1970 (23 Mar). *Developing Botswana. T* **82** *and similar designs. Multicoloured.* P 14½×14 (3c., 7c.) or 14×14½ (others).

261	3c. Type **82**	70	20
262	7c. Copper-nickel mining	95	20
263	10c. Copper-nickel mine, Selebi-Pikwe (*horiz*)	1·25	15

264 35c. Orapa diamond mine, and diamonds (*horiz*) 2·75 1·25
261/4 *Set of 4* 5·00 1·60

83 Mr. Micawber (*David Copperfield*)

(Des V. Whiteley. Litho Walsall)

1970 (6 July). *Death Centenary of Charles Dickens. T* **83** *and similar horiz designs. Multicoloured.* P 11.

265 3c. Type **83** 25 10
266 7c. Scrooge (*A Christmas Carol*) 25 10
267 15c. Fagin (*Oliver Twist*) 45 40
268 25c. Bill Sykes (*Oliver Twist*) 70 60
265/8 *Set of 4* 1·50 1·00
MS269 114×81 mm. Nos. 265/8 2·75 4·00

84 U.N. Building and Emblem

(Des J. Cooter. Litho Walsall)

1970 (24 Oct). *25th Anniv of United Nations.* P 11.

270 **84** 15c. bright blue, chestnut and silver 70 30

85 Crocodile

(Des A. Vale. Litho Questa)

1970 (3 Nov). *Christmas. T* **85** *and similar horiz designs. Multicoloured.* P 14.

271 1c. Type **85** 10 10
272 2c. Giraffe 10 10
273 7c. Elephant 15 15
274 25c. Rhinoceros 60 80
271/4 *Set of 4* 80 1·00
MS275 128×90 mm. Nos. 271/4 1·00 3·00

86 Sorghum

(Des J. W. Litho Questa)

1971 (6 April). *Important Crops. T* **86** *and similar horiz designs. Multicoloured.* P 14.

276 3c. Type **86** 15 10
277 7c. Millet 20 10
278 10c. Maize 20 10
279 35c. Groundnuts 70 1·00
276/9 *Set of 4* 1·10 1·10

87 Map and Head of Cow

88 King bringing Gift of Gold

(Des A. Vale, adapted L. Curtis. Litho Harrison)

1971 (30 Sept). *Fifth Anniv of Independence. T* **87** *and similar vert designs inscr "PULA" (local greeting).* P 14½×14.

280 3c. black, brown and apple-green 10 10
281 4c. black, new blue and pale blue 10 10
282 7c. black and red-orange 20 15
283 10c. multicoloured 20 15
284 20c. multicoloured 55 2·50
280/4 *Set of 5* 1·00 2·75

Designs:—4c. Map and cogs; 7c. Map and zebra; 10c. Map and sorghum stalk crossed by tusk; 20c. Arms and map of Botswana.

(Des A. Vale. Litho Questa)

1971 (11 Nov). *Christmas. T* **88** *and similar vert designs. Multicoloured.* P 14.

285 2c. Type **88** 10 10
286 3c. King bearing frankincense 10 10
287 7c. King bearing myrrh 10 10
288 20c. Three Kings behold the star 35 65
285/8 *Set of 4* 45 75
MS289 85×128 mm. Nos. 285/8 1·00 3·50

89 Orion

90 Postmark and Map

(Des R. Granger Barrett. Litho Questa)

1972 (24 Apr). *"Night Sky". T* **89** *and similar vert designs.* P 14.

290 3c. turquoise-blue, black and red 75 30
291 7c. dull blue, black and yellow 1·10 80
292 10c. dull green, black and orange 1·25 85
293 20c. deep violet-blue, black and blue-green 1·75 3·25
290/3 *Set of 4* 4·25 4·75

Constellations:—7c. The Scorpion; 10c. The Centaur; 20c. The Cross.

(Des M. Bryan. Litho A. & M.)

1972 (21 Aug). *Mafeking–Gubulawayo Runner Post. T* **90** *and similar vert designs. Multicoloured.* P 13½×13.

294 3c. Type **90** 30 10
a. Imperf (vert pair) £500
295 4c. Bechuanaland stamp and map 30 35
296 7c. Runners and map 45 50
297 20c. Mafeking postmark and map 1·10 1·50
294/7 *Set of 4* 2·00 2·25
MS298 84×216 mm. Nos. 294/7 vertically *se-tenant*, forming a composite map design 11·00 15·00
a. Pale buff (background) omitted £700

For these designs redrawn smaller with changed inscriptions see Nos. 652/6.

91 Cross, Map and Bells **92** Thor

(Des M. Bryan. Litho Questa)

1972 (6 Nov). *Christmas. Vert designs each with Cross and Map as T* **91**. *Multicoloured.* P 14.

299 2c. Type **91** 10 75
300 3c. Cross, map and candle 10 10
301 7c. Cross, map and Christmas tree 15 25
302 20c. Cross, map, star and holly 40 85
299/302 *Set of 4* 60 1·75
MS303 936×119 mm. Nos. 299/302 1·25 3·25

(Des Edna Elphick. Litho Questa)

1973 (23 Mar). *IMO/WMO Centenary. T* **92** *and similar designs showing Norse myths. Multicoloured.* P 14.

304 3c. Type **92** 20 10
305 4c. Sun God's chariot (*horiz*) 25 15
306 7c. Ymir, the frost giant 30 15
307 20c. Odin and Sleipnir (*horiz*) 75 70
304/7 *Set of 4* 1·40 1·00

93 Livingstone and River Scene

(Des G. Vasarhelyi. Litho Walsall)

1973 (10 Sept). *Death Centenary of Dr. Livingstone. T* **93** *and similar horiz designs. Multicoloured.* P 13½.

308 3c. Type **93** 20 10
309 20c. Livingstone meeting Stanley 90 90

94 Donkey and Foal at Village Trough **95** Gaborone Campus

(Des M. Bryan. Litho Questa)

1973 (3 Dec). *Christmas. T* **94** *and similar multicoloured designs.* P 14.

310 3c. Type **94** 10 10
311 4c. Shepherd and flock (*horiz*) 10 10
312 7c. Mother and child 10 10
313 20c. Kgotla meeting (*horiz*) 40 85
310/13 *Set of 4* 55 1·00

(Des M. Bryan, adapted P. Powell. Litho Questa)

1974 (8 May). *Tenth Anniv of University of Botswana, Lesotho and Swaziland. T* **95** *and similar horiz designs. Multicoloured.* P 14.

314 3c. Type **95** 10 10
315 7c. Kwaluseni Campus 10 10
316 20c. Roma Campus 15 20
317 35c. Map and flags of the three countries 20 35
314/17 *Set of 4* 35 55

96 Methods of Mail Transport

(Des. M. Bryan. Litho J. W.)

1974 (29 May). *Centenary of Universal Postal Union. T* **96** *and similar horiz designs. Multicoloured.* P 14.

318 2c. Type **96** 55 35
319 3c. Post Office, Palapye, circa 1889 55 35
320 7c. Bechuanaland Police Camel Post, circa 1900 95 70
321 20c. Hawker Siddeley H.S.748 and De Havilland D.H.9 mail planes of 1920 and 1974 2·75 2·50
318/21 *Set of 4* 4·25 3·50

97 Amethyst

98 *Stapelia variegata*

(Des M. Bayliss, adapted PAD Studio. Photo Enschedé)

1974 (1 July). *Botswana Minerals. T* **97** *and similar horiz designs. Multicoloured.* P 14×13.

322 1c. Type **97** 60 2·00
323 2c. Agate—"Botswana Pink" 60 2·00
324 3c. Quartz 65 80
325 4c. Copper nickel 70 60
326 5c. Moss agate 70 1·00
327 7c. Agate 80 1·25
328 10c. Stilbite 1·60 65
329 15c. Moshaneng Banded Marble 2·00 4·00
330 20c. Gem diamonds 4·00 4·50
331 25c. Chrysotile 5·00 2·50
332 35c. Jasper 5·00 5·50
333 50c. Moss quartz 4·50 7·00
334 1r. Citrine 7·50 10·00
335 2r. Chalcopyrite 20·00 20·00
322/35 *Set of 14* 48·00 55·00

(Des M. Bryan. Litho Questa)

1974 (4 Nov). *Christmas. T* **98** *and similar vert designs showing flowers. Multicoloured.* P 14.

336 2c. Type **98** 20 40
337 7c. *Hibiscus lunarifolius* 30 20
338 15c. *Ceratotheca triloba* 45 1·00
339 20c. *Nerine laticoma* 60 1·25
336/9 *Set of 4* 1·40 2·50
MS340 85×130 mm. Nos. 336/9 2·00 4·25

99 President Sir Seretse Khama **100** Ostrich

(Des M. Bryan, adapted G. Vasarhelyi. Photo Enschedé)

1975 (24 Mar). *Tenth Anniv of Self-Government.* P 13½×13.

341 **99** 4c. multicoloured 10 10
342 10c. multicoloured 15 10
343 20c. multicoloured 25 25
344 35c. multicoloured 45 50
341/4 *Set of 4* 85 85
MS345 93×130 mm. Nos. 341/4 1·00 1·50

(Des M. Bryan. Litho Questa)

1975 (23 June). *Rock Paintings, Tsodilo Hills. T* **100** *and similar horiz designs. Multicoloured.* P 14.

346 4c. Type **100** 60 10
347 10c. White Rhinoceros 1·00 10
348 25c. Spotted Hyena 2·00 55
349 35c. Scorpion 2·00 1·10
346/9 *Set of 4* 5·00 1·60
MS350 150×150 mm. Nos. 346/9 12·00 7·50

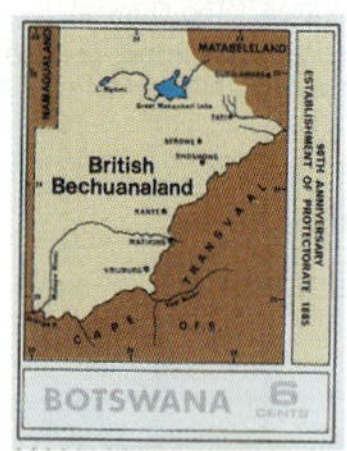

101 Map of British Bechuanaland, 1885 **102** *Aloe marlothii*

(Des M. Bryan, adapted G. Vasarhelyi. Litho Harrison)

1975 (13 Oct). *Anniversaries. T* **101** *and similar multicoloured designs.* P 14×14½ (25c.) or 14½×14 (others).

351 6c. Type **101** 30 20
352 10c. Chief Khama, 1875 .... 40 15
353 25c. Chiefs Sebele, Bathoen and Khama, 1895 (*horiz*) 80 75
51/3 *Set of 3* .... 1·40 1·00

Events:—6c. 90th Anniv of Protectorate; 10c. Centenary of Khama's Accession; 25c. 80th Anniv of Chiefs' visit to London.

(Des M. Bryan. Litho Questa)

1975 (3 Nov). *Christmas. T* **102** *and similar vert designs showing aloes. Multicoloured.* P 14½.

354 3c. Type **102** 20 10
355 10c. *Aloe lutescens* 40 20
356 15c. *Aloe zebrine* .... 60 1·50
357 25c. *Aloe littoralis* .... 75 2·50
354/7 *Set of 4* .... 1·75 3·75

103 Drum

(Des M. Bryan. Litho Questa)

1976 (1 Mar). *Traditional Musical Instruments. T* **103** *and similar horiz designs. Multicoloured.* P 14.

358 4c. Type **103** 15 10
359 10c. Hand Piano 20 10
360 15c. Segankuru (violin) 25 50
361 25c. Kudu Signal Horn .... 30 1·25
358/61 *Set of 4* .... 80 1·75

104 One Pula Note

(Des M. Bryan from banknotes by D.L.R. Litho Questa)

1976 (28 June). *First National Currency. T* **104** *and similar horiz designs. Multicoloured.* P 14.

362 4c. Type **104** 15 10
363 10c. Two pula note 20 10
364 15c. Five pula note 35 20
365 25c. Ten Pula note 45 45
362/5 *Set of 4* .... 1·00 70
MS366 163×107 mm. Nos. 362/5 .... 1·00 3·50

(New Currency. 100 thebe = 1 pula)

1t (Type I)	1t (Type II)
2t (I)	2t (II)
4t (I)	4t (II)
5t (I)	5t (II)
15t (I)	15t (II)
20t (I)	20t (II)

(Surch in letterpress by Govt Printer, Pretoria (Type I), or in lithography by Enschedé (Type II))

1976 (23 Aug)–**77**. *Nos. 322/35 surch as T* **105**.

367 1t. on 1c. Type **97** (I) .... 2·00 70
a. Type II Surch (15.7.77) .... 2·50 80
368 2t. on 2c. Agate—"Botswana Pink" (I) .. 2·00 1·75
a. Type II Surch (15.7.77) .... 2·50 80
369 3t. on 3c. Quartz (surch at top right) (Gold) .... 1·50 60
a. Surch at bottom right (17.10.77) .... 50·00 15·00
370 4t. on 4c. Copper nickel (I) .... 2·50 40
a. Type II Surch (15.7.77) .... 2·75 80
371 5t. on 5c. Moss agate (I) .... 2·50 40
a. Type II Surch (15.7.77) .... 2·75 70
372 7t. on 7c. Agate (surch at top right) .... 1·25 2·75
a. Surch at bottom right (10.10.77) .... 60·00 20·00
373 10t. on 10c. Stilbite .... 1·25 80
374 15t. on 15c. Moshaneng Banded Marble (I) (Gold) .... 4·25 3·25
a. Type II Surch (15.7.77) .... 7·00 1·50
375 20t. on 20c. Gem diamonds (I) .... 7·50 80
a. Type II Surch (15.7.77) .... 9·00 1·50
376 25t. on 25c. Chrysotile .... 5·00 1·25
377 35t. on 35c. Jasper .... 4·00 5·00
378 50t. on 50c. Moss quartz (surch at top right) .... 5·50 9·00
a. Surch at bottom right (17.10.77) .... £250 65·00
379 1p. on 1r. Citrine (surch at top right) .... 6·00 9·50
a. Surch at bottom left (10.10.77) .... 80·00 40·00
380 2p. on 2r. Chalcopyrite (Gold) .... 8·00 11·00
367/80 *Set of 14* .... 48·00 42·00
367a/75a *Set of 6* .... 24·00 5·50

Nos. 369a, 372a, 378a and 379a come from a second Pretoria printing on a small stock returned from the Crown Agents. By the time the stamps arrived in Pretoria the surcharge type for the 3t., 7t., 50t. and 1p. had been dispersed and when it was reset the position of the value figures was changed.

No 368 with a much larger "2t" surcharge is believed to be a postal forgery.

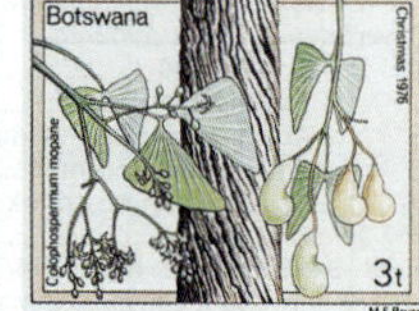

106 Botswanan Cattle **107** *Colophospermum mopane*

(Des M. Bryan. Litho Questa)

1976 (30 Sept). *Tenth Anniv of Independence. T* **106** *and similar multicoloured designs.* P 14.

381 4t. Type **106** 15 10
382 10t. Antelope, Okavango Delta (*vert*) 20 10
383 15t. Schools and pupils 20 40
384 25t. Rural weaving (*vert*) 20 50
385 35t. Miner (*vert*) 75 85
381/5 *Set of 5* .... 1·40 1·75

Nos. 381/5 were printed on sand-grained paper which has an uneven surface.

(Des M. Bryan. Litho J. W.)

1976 (1 Nov). *Christmas. T* **107** *and similar horiz designs showing trees. Multicoloured.* P 13.

386 3t. Type **107** 15 10
387 4t. *Baikiaea plurijuga* 15 10
388 10t. *Sterculia rogersii* 20 10
389 25t. *Acacia nilotica* 45 50
390 40t. *Kigelia africana* .... 75 1·25
386/90 *Set of 5* .... 1·50 1·75

108 Coronation Coach

(Des M. Bryan, adapted G. Vasarhelyi. Litho Cartor)

1977 (7 Feb). *Silver Jubilee. T* **108** *and similar horiz designs. Multicoloured.* P 12.

391 4t. Queen and Sir Seretse Khama 10 10
392 25t. Type **108** 20 15
393 40t. The Recognition 35 90
391/3 *Set of 3* .... 60 1·00

Nos. 391/3 have matt, almost invisible gum.

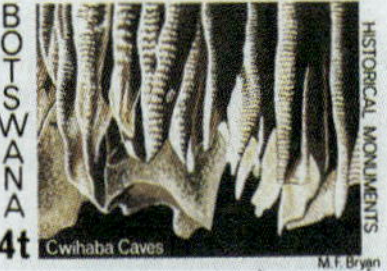

109 African Clawless Otter **110** Cwihaba Caves

(Des M. Bryan. Litho Questa)

1977 (7 June). *Diminishing Species. T* **109** *and similar horiz designs. Multicoloured.* P 14.

394 3t. Type **109** .... 4·25 40
395 4t. Serval .... 4·25 40
396 10t. Bat-eared Fox .... 4·75 40
397 25t. Temminck's Ground Pangolin .... 11·00 2·00
398 40t. Brown Hyena .... 13·00 7·50
394/8 *Set of 5* .... 32·00 9·50

(Des M. Bryan. Litho J. W.)

1977 (22 Aug). *Historical Monuments. T* **110** *and similar horiz designs. Multicoloured.* P 14.

399 4t. Type **110** 20 10
400 5t. Khama Memorial 20 10
401 15t. Green's Tree 30 40
402 20t. Mmajojo Ruins 30 45
403 25t. Ancient morabaraba board 30 50
404 35t. Matsieng's footprint 40 60
399/404 *Set of 6* .... 1·50 2·00
MS405 154×105 mm. Nos. 399/404 .... 2·50 3·25

111 *Hypoxis nitida* **112** Little Black Bustard

(Des M. Bryan. Litho Questa)

1977 (7 Nov). *Christmas. T* **111** *and similar vert designs showing lilies. Multicoloured.* P 14.

406 3t. Type **111** 15 10
407 5t. *Haemanthus magnificus* 15 10
408 10t. *Boophane disticha* 20 10
409 25t. *Vellozia retinervis* 40 55
410 40t. *Ammocharis coranica* .... 55 1·25
406/10 *Set of 5* .... 1·25 1·75

(Des M. Bryan. Photo Harrison)

1978 (3 July). *Birds. Vert designs as T* **112**. *Multicoloured.* P 14×14½ (1 to 20t.) or 14 (25t. to 5p.).

411 1t. Type **112** .... 70 1·25
412 2t. Marabou Stork .... 90 1·25
413 3t. Green Wood Hoopoe 70 85
414 4t. Carmine Bee Eater .... 1·00 1·00
415 5t. African Jacana .... 1·00 40
416 7t. African Paradise Flycatcher .... 1·00 3·00
417 10t. Bennett's Woodpecker .... 2·00 60
418 15t. Red Bishop .... 1·50 3·00
419 20t. Crowned Plover .... 1·75 2·00
420 25t. Giant Kingfisher .... 70 3·00
421 30t. White-faced Whistling Duck 70 70
422 35t. Green Heron .... 70 3·25
423 45t. Black-headed Heron .... 1·00 3·00
424 50t. Spotted Eagle Owl .... 5·00 4·50
425 1p. Gabar Goshawk .... 2·50 4·50
426 2p. Martial Eagle .... 3·00 8·00
427 5p. Saddle-bill Stork .... 6·50 16·00
411/27 *Set of 17* .... 27·00 48·00

113 Tawana making Karos

(Des M. Bryan. Litho Questa)

1978 (11 Sept). *Okavango Delta. T* **113** *and similar horiz designs. Multicoloured.* P 14.

428 4t. Type **113** 10 30
429 5t. Tribe localities 10 10
430 15t. Bushmen collecting roots 25 40
431 20t. Herero woman milking 35 70
432 25t. Yei poling "mokoro" (canoe) 40 60
433 35t. Mbukushu fishing .... 45 1·75
428/33 *Set of 6* .... 1·50 3·25
MS434 150×98 mm. Nos. 428/33 .... 1·50 3·75

Nos. 428/34 were printed on sand-grained paper which has an uneven surface.

114 *Caralluma lutea* **115** Sip Well

(Des M. Bryan. Litho J. W.)

1978 (6 Nov). *Christmas. Flowers. T* **114** *and similar vert designs. Multicoloured.* P 14.

435 5t. Type **114** 35 10
436 10t. *Hoodia lugardii* 50 15
437 15t. *Ipomoea transvaalensis* 90 55
438 25t. *Ansellia gigantea* .... 1·10 70
435/8 *Set of 4* .... 2·50 1·40

(Des M. Bryan. Litho Questa)

1979 (30 Mar). *Water Development. T* **115** *and similar vert designs. Multicoloured.* P 14.

439 3t. Type **115** 10 10
440 5t. Watering pit 10 10
441 10t. Hand dug well 15 10
442 25t. Windmill 20 30
443 40t. Modern drilling rig 40 55
439/43 *Set of 5* .... 80 1·00

116 Pottery **117** 1885 British Bechuanaland 1d. Stamp and Sir Rowland Hill

(Des M. Bryan. Litho Questa)

1979 (11 June). *Handicrafts. T* **116** *and similar vert designs. Multicoloured.* P 14½×14.

No.	Description	Unused	Used
444	5t. Type **116**	10	10
445	10t. Clay modelling	10	10
446	25t. Basketry	20	25
447	40t. Beadwork	40	50
444/7	*Set of 4*	70	80
MS448	123×96 mm. Nos. 444/7	1·00	2·50

(Des M. Bryan. Litho Secura, Singapore)

1979 (27 Aug). *Death Centenary of Sir Rowland Hill. T* **117** *and similar horiz designs showing stamps and Sir Rowland Hill. Multicoloured.* P 13½.

No.	Description	Unused	Used
449	5t. Type **117**	20	10
450	25t. 1932 Bechuanaland Protectorate 2d.	45	50
451	45t. 1967 2c. definitive	55	1·25
449/51	*Set of 3*	1·10	1·60

118 Children Playing

119 *Ximenia caffra*

(Des K. Mosinyi (5t.), M. Bryan (10t.). Litho Questa)

1979 (24 Sept). *International Year of the Child. T* **118** *and similar multicoloured design.* P 14.

No.	Description	Unused	Used
452	5t. Type **118**	20	10
453	10t. Child playing with doll (*vert*)	30	20

(Des M. Bryan. Litho Questa)

1979 (12 Nov). *Christmas. Fruit. T* **119** *and similar vert designs. Multicoloured.* P 14.

No.	Description	Unused	Used
454	5t. Type **119**	10	10
455	10t. *Sclerocarya caffra*	20	20
456	15t. *Hexalobus monopetalus*	35	35
457	25t. *Ficus soldanella*	45	45
454/7	*Set of 4*	1·00	1·00

120 Flap-necked Chameleon

121 Rock Breaking

(Des M. Bryan. Litho Security Printers (M), Malaysia)

1980 (3 Mar). *Reptiles. T* **120** *and similar horiz designs. Multicoloured.* P 13½.

No.	Description	Unused	Used
458	5t. Type **120**	30	10
459	10t. Leopard Tortoise	30	15
460	25t. Puff Adder	50	65
461	40t. White-throated Monitor	60	2·50
458/61	*Set of 4*	1·50	3·00

(Des M. Bryan. Litho Secura, Singapore)

1980 (7 July). *Early Mining. T* **121** *and similar horiz designs. Multicoloured.* P 13½.

No.	Description	Unused	Used
462	5t. Type **121**	25	15
463	10t. Ore hoisting	30	15
464	15t. Ore transport	70	60
465	20t. Ore crushing	75	90
466	25t. Smelting	80	90
467	35t. Tools and products	1·00	1·75
462/7	*Set of 6*	3·50	4·00

122 "Chiwele and the Giant"

(Des W. Battiss. Litho Questa)

1980 (8 Sept). *Folktales. T* **122** *and similar multicoloured designs.* P 14 (5t.), 14×13½ (45t.) or 14½×14 (others).

No.	Description	Unused	Used
468	5t. Type **122** (35×22 mm)	10	10
469	10t. "Kgori is not deceived" (28×37 mm)	15	10
470	30t. "Nyambi's wife and Crocodile" (28×37 mm)	45	45
471	45t. "Clever Hare" (44×27 mm)	60	60
468/71	*Set of 4*	1·10	1·10

123 Game watching. Makgadikgadi Pans

(Des M. Bryan. Litho Govt Printer, Pretoria)

1980 (6 Oct). *World Tourism Conference, Manila.* P 14.

No.	Type	Description	Unused	Used
472	**123**	5t. multicoloured	45	20

124 *Acacia gerrardii*

125 Heinrich von Stephan with Bechuanaland 1949 3d. and Botswana 1974 3c. UPU Anniversary Commemoratives

(Des M. Bryan. Litho Govt Printer, Pretoria)

1980 (3 Nov). *Christmas. Flora. T* **124** *and similar vert designs. Multicoloured.* P 14×13½.

No.	Description	Unused	Used
473	5t. Type **124**	10	10
474	10t. *Acacia nilotica*	20	10
475	25t. *Acacia erubescens*	45	30
476	40t. *Dichrostachys cinerea*	70	70
473/6	*Set of 4*	1·25	1·00

(Des M. Bryan. Litho Govt Printer, Pretoria)

1981 (7 Jan). *150th Birth Anniv of Heinrich von Stephan (founder of UPU). T* **125** *and similar horiz design showing Von Stephan and UPU anniversary commemoratives. Multicoloured.* P 14.

No.	Description	Unused	Used
477	6t. Type **125**	50	30
478	20t. Bechuanaland 1949 6d. and Botswana 1974 7c.	1·25	2·25

126 *Anax imperator* (dragonfly)

127 Camphill Community Ramkoromane, Otse

(Des M. Bryan. Litho Govt Printer, Pretoria)

1981 (23 Feb). *Insects. T* **126** *and similar vert designs. Multicoloured.* P 14.

No.	Description	Unused	Used
479	6t. Type **126**	15	10
480	7t. *Sphodromantis gastrica* (mantid)	15	20
481	10t. *Zonocerus elegans* (grasshopper)	15	20
482	20t. *Kheper nigroaeneus* (beetle)	25	50
483	30t. *Papilio demodocus* (butterfly)	35	70
484	45t. *Acanthocampa belina* (moth larva)	40	1·10
479/84	*Set of 6*	1·25	2·50
MS485	180×89 mm. Nos. 479/84	3·00	8·50

(Des M. Bryan. Litho Govt Printer, Pretoria)

1981 (6 Apr). *International Year for Disabled Persons. T* **127** *and similar horiz designs. Multicoloured.* P 14.

No.	Description	Unused	Used
486	6t. Type **127**	20	10
487	20t. Resource Centre for the Blind, Mochudi	55	35
488	30t. Tlamelong Rehabilitation Centre, Tlokweng	75	45
486/8	*Set of 3*	1·40	80

128 Woman reading Letter

129 Sir Seretse Khama and Building

(Des Petra Rouendaal. Litho Govt Printer, Pretoria)

1981 (8 June). *Literacy Programme. T* **128** *and similar vert designs. Multicoloured.* P 14.

No.	Description	Unused	Used
489	6t. Type **128**	20	10
490	7t. Man filling in form	20	15
491	20t. Boy reading newspaper	60	35
492	30t. Child being taught to read	80	45
489/92	*Set of 4*	1·60	90

(Des G. Vasarhelyi. Litho Format)

1981 (13 July). *First Death Anniv of President Sir Seretse Khama. T* **129** *and similar horiz designs. Multicoloured.* P 14.

No.	Description	Unused	Used
493	6t. Type **129**	15	10
494	10t. Seretse Khama and building (*different*)	25	15
495	30t. Seretse Khama and Botswana flag	40	45
496	45t. Seretse Khama and building (*different*)	55	70
493/6	*Set of 4*	1·25	1·25

(**130**)

131 Traditional Ploughing

1981 (1 Sept). *Nos. 417 and 422 surch as T* **130**.

No.	Description	Unused	Used
497	25t. on 35t. Green Heron	3·00	2·00
498	30t. on 10t. Bennett's Woodpecker	3·00	2·00

(Des K. Mosinyi. Litho Format)

1981 (21 Sept). *Cattle Industry. T* **131** *and similar horiz designs. Multicoloured.* P 14½.

No.	Description	Unused	Used
499	6t. Type **131**	10	10
500	20t. Agricultural show	30	50
501	30t. Botswana Meat Commission	35	60
502	45t. Vaccine Institute, Botswana	50	1·00
499/502	*Set of 4*	1·10	2·00

132 *Nymphaea caerulea*

133 "Cattle Post Scene" (Boitumelo Golaakwena)

(Des M. Bryan. Litho Govt Printer, Pretoria)

1981 (11 Nov). *Christmas. Flowers. T* **132** *and similar vert designs. Multicoloured.* P 14.

No.	Description	Unused	Used
503	6t. Type **132**	20	10
504	10t. *Nymphoides indica*	25	10
505	25t. *Nymphaea lotus*	60	90
506	40t. *Ottelia kunenensis*	80	2·25
503/6	*Set of 4*	1·60	3·00

(Litho Govt Printer, Pretoria)

1982 (15 Feb). *Children's Art. T* **133** *and similar horiz designs. Multicoloured.* P 14.

No.	Description	Unused	Used
507	6t. Type **133**	40	10
508	10t. "Kgotla Meeting" (Reginald Klinck)	50	15
509	30t. "Village Water Supply" (Keromemang Matswiri)	1·75	1·25
510	45t. "With the Crops" (Kennedy Balemoge)	1·75	2·75
507/10	*Set of 4*	4·00	3·75

134 Common Type

135 African Masked Weaver

(Des K. Mosinyi and V. Moremi. Litho Govt Printer, Pretoria)

1982 (3 May). *Traditional Houses. T* **134** *and similar horiz designs. Multicoloured.* P 14.

No.	Description	Unused	Used
511	6t. Type **134**	40	15
512	10t. Kgatleng type	50	15
513	30t. North Eastern type	2·00	1·10
514	45t. Sarwa type	2·00	3·00
511/14	*Set of 4*	4·50	4·00

(Des M. Bryan. Photo Harrison)

1982 (2 Aug). *Birds. T* **135** *and similar multicoloured designs.* P 14×14½ (1t. to 10t.) or 14½×14 (others).

No.	Description	Unused	Used
515	1t. Type **135**	80	1·50
516	2t. Lesser Double-collared Sunbird	90	1·60
517	3t. Red-throated Bee Eater	1·00	1·60
518	4t. Ostrich	1·00	1·60
519	5t. Grey-headed Gull	1·00	1·60
520	6t. African Pygmy Goose	1·00	40
521	7t. Cattle Egret	1·00	15
522	8t. Lanner Falcon	2·50	1·50
523	10t. Yellow-billed Stork	1·00	20
524	15t. Red-billed Pintail (*horiz*)	2·75	25
525	20t. Barn Owl (*horiz*)	5·50	3·50
526	25t. Hammerkop (*horiz*)	3·25	70
527	30t. South African Stilt (*horiz*)	3·75	90
528	35t. Blacksmith Plover (*horiz*)	3·75	80
529	45t. Senegal Wattled Plover (*horiz*)	3·75	1·75
530	50t. Helmet Guineafowl (*horiz*)	4·75	2·50
531	1p. Cape Vulture (*horiz*)	9·00	12·00
532	2p. Augur Buzzard (*horiz*)	11·00	16·00
515/32	*Set of 18*	48·00	42·00

136 *Coprinus comatus*

137 President Quett Masire

(Des Gillian Condy. Litho Mardon Printers Ltd, Zimbabwe)

1982 (2 Nov). *Christmas. Fungi. T* **136** *and similar vert designs. Multicoloured.* P 14½.

No.	Description	Unused	Used
533	7t. Type **136**	2·50	20
534	15t. *Lactarius deliciosus*	3·75	65
535	35t. *Amanita pantherina*	6·00	2·00
536	50t. *Boletus edulis*	7·50	8·00
533/6	*Set of 4*	18·00	9·75

(Des G. Vasarhelyi. Litho Questa)

1983 (14 Mar). *Commonwealth Day. T* **137** *and similar horiz designs. Multicoloured.* P 14.

No.	Description	Unused	Used
537	7t. Type **137**	10	10
538	15t. Native dancers	15	20

539	35t. Melbourne conference centre	45	55
540	45t. Meeting of Heads of State, Melbourne	55	80
537/40	*Set of 4*	1·00	1·50

138 Wattled Crane

139 Wooden Spoons

(Des Petra Rouendaal (50t.), Gillian Condy (others). Litho Mardon Printers Ltd, Zimbabwe)

1983 (19 Apr). *Endangered Species. T* **138** *and similar vert designs. Multicoloured.* P 14×14½.

541	7t. Type **138**	3·00	55
542	15t. *Aloe lutescens*	2·50	80
543	35t. Roan Antelope	3·00	3·25
544	50t. Ivory Palm (*Hyphaene ventricosa*)	3·50	7·00
541/4	*Set of 4*	11·00	10·50

(Des M. Bryan. Litho Mardon Printers Ltd, Zimbabwe)

1983 (20 July). *Traditional Artifacts. T* **139** *and similar vert designs. Multicoloured.* P 14½.

545	7t. Type **139**	25	10
546	15t. Personal ornaments	45	30
547	35t. Ox-hide milk bag	75	65
548	50t. Decorated knives	1·00	1·10
545/8	*Set of 4*	2·25	1·90
MS549	115×102 mm. Nos. 545/8	4·25	5·00

140 *Pantala flavescens*

141 Sorting Diamonds

(Des Beverley Boudreau. Litho Mardon Printers Ltd, Zimbabwe)

1983 (7 Nov). *Christmas. Dragonflies. T* **140** *and similar horiz designs. Multicoloured.* P 14½×14.

550	6t. Type **140**	85	10
551	15t. *Anax imperator*	1·75	50
552	25t. *Trithemis arteriosa*	2·00	85
553	45t. *Chlorolestes elegans*	2·75	4·75
550/3	*Set of 4*	6·50	5·50

(Des M. Kahn. Litho Mardon Printers Ltd, Zimbabwe)

1984 (19 Mar). *Mining Industry. T* **141** *and similar multicoloured designs.* P 14½.

554	7t. Type **141**	2·00	50
555	15t. Lime kiln	2·00	75
556	35t. Copper-nickel smelter plant (*vert*)	3·25	3·25
557	50t. Stockpiled coal (*vert*)	3·75	10·00
554/7	*Set of 4*	10·00	12·00

142 Riding Cattle

143 Avro 504 Aircraft

(Des S. Mogotsi. Litho Mardon Printers Ltd, Zimbabwe)

1984 (18 June). *Traditional Transport. T* **142** *and similar horiz designs. Multicoloured.* P 14½×14.

558	7t. Type **142**	20	10
559	25t. Sledge	65	60
560	35t. Wagon	85	1·50
561	50t. Two wheeled donkey cart	1·25	4·50
558/61	*Set of 4*	2·75	6·00

(Des V. Larsson. Litho Mardon Printers Ltd, Zimbabwe)

1984 (8 Oct). *40th Anniv of International Civil Aviation Organization. T* **143** *and similar horiz designs, each with ICAO emblem. Multicoloured.* P 14½×14.

562	7t. Type **143**	75	20
563	10t. Westland Wessex trimotor	1·00	35
564	15t. Junkers Ju 52/3m	1·40	95
565	25t. De Havilland D.H.89B Dominie	2·00	1·75
566	35t. Douglas DC-3	2·25	3·50
567	50t. Fokker F.27 Friendship	2·50	7·00
562/7	*Set of 6*	9·00	12·00

144 *Papilio demodocus*

145 Seswaa (meat dish)

(Des M. Kahn. Litho Mardon Printers Ltd, Zimbabwe)

1984 (5 Nov). *Christmas. Butterflies. T* **144** *and similar horiz designs. Multicoloured.* P 14½×14.

568	7t. Type **144**	2·00	30
569	25t. *Byblia anvatara*	3·25	1·50
570	35t. *Danaus chrysippus*	3·50	3·00
571	50t. *Graphium taboranus*	4·75	11·00
568/71	*Set of 4*	12·00	14·00

No. 570 is incorrectly inscribed "Hypolimnas misippus".

(Des K. Mosinyi. Litho Mardon Printers Ltd, Zimbabwe)

1985 (18 Mar). *5th Anniv of Southern African Development Co-ordination Conference. Traditional Foods. T* **145** *and similar vert designs. Multicoloured.* P 14½.

572	7t. Type **145**	50	10
573	15t. Bogobe (cereal porridge)	75	35
574	25t. Madila (soured coagulated cows milk)	1·00	55
575	50t. Phane (caterpillars)	1·50	2·25
572/5	*Set of 4*	3·25	2·75
MS576	117×103 mm. Nos. 572/5	7·00	10·00

146 1885 British Bechuanaland Overprint on Cape of Good Hope ½d.

147 Bechuanaland Border Police, 1885–95

(Des D. Finlay and J. Hodgson. Litho Mardon Printers Ltd, Zimbabwe)

1985 (24 June). *Centenary of First Bechuanaland Stamps. T* **146** *and similar designs.* P 14½.

577	7t. black, grey-black and orange-vermilion	1·00	20
578	15t. black, deep brown and greenish yellow	1·75	50
579	25t. black and bright scarlet	2·25	80
580	35t. black, ultramarine and gold	2·50	2·00
581	50t. multicoloured	2·75	3·75
577/81	*Set of 5*	9·00	6·50

Designs: Vert—15t. 1897 Bechuanaland Protectorate overprint on G.B. 3d.; 25t. Bechuanaland Protectorate 1932 1d. definitive. Horiz—35t. Bechuanaland 1965 Internal Self-Government 5c.; 50t. Botswana 1966 Independence 2½c.

(Des V. Larsson. Litho Mardon Printers Ltd, Zimbabwe)

1985 (5 Aug). *Centenary of Botswana Police. T* **147** *and similar horiz designs. Multicoloured.* P 14½×14.

582	7t. Type **147**	2·25	50
583	10t. Bechuanaland Mounted Police, 1895–1902	2·50	50
584	25t. Bechuanaland Protectorate Police, 1903–66	3·50	2·00
585	50t. Botswana Police, from 1966	5·50	7·50
582/5	*Set of 4*	12·00	9·50

148 *Cucumis metuliferus*

149 Mr. Shippard and Chief Gaseitsiwe of the Bangwaketse

(Des Audrey Renew. Litho Mardon Printers Ltd, Zimbabwe)

1985 (4 Nov). *Christmas. Edible Wild Cucumbers. T* **148** *and similar horiz designs. Multicoloured.* P 14½×14.

586	7t. Type **148**	1·25	10
587	15t. *Acanthosicyos naudinianus*	2·25	70
588	25t. *Coccinia sessifolia*	3·50	1·25
589	50t. *Momordica balsamina*	5·00	9·50
586/9	*Set of 4*	11·00	10·50

(Des A. Campbell. Litho Mardon Printers Ltd. Zimbabwe)

1985 (30 Dec). *Centenary of Declaration of Bechuanaland Protectorate. T* **149** *and similar vert designs. Multicoloured.* P 14×14½.

590	7t. Type **149**	35	10
591	15t. Sir Charles Warren and Chief Sechele of the Bakwena	70	45
592	25t. Revd. Mackenzie and Chief Khama of the Bamangwato	1·25	85
593	50t. Map showing Protectorate	2·75	6·50
590/3	*Set of 4*	4·50	7·00
MS594	130×133 mm. Nos. 590/3	12·00	14·00

150 Halley's Comet over Serowe

151 Milk Bag

(Des L. Hutchings. Litho Mardon Printers Ltd, Zimbabwe)

1986 (24 Mar). *Appearance of Halley's Comet. T* **150** *and similar horiz designs. Multicoloured.* P 14½×14.

595	7t. Type **150**	80	15
596	15t. Comet over Bobonong at sunset	1·50	70
597	35t. Comet over Gomare at dawn	2·00	1·50
598	50t. Comet over Thamaga and Letlhakeng	2·25	3·75
595/8	*Set of 4*	6·00	5·50

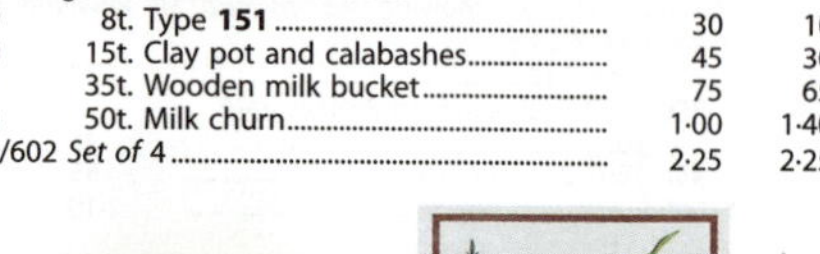

(Des B. Mazebedi. Litho Mardon Printers Ltd, Zimbabwe)

1986 (23 June). *Traditional Milk Containers. T* **151** *and similar vert designs. Multicoloured.* P 14½.

599	8t. Type **151**	30	10
600	15t. Clay pot and calabashes	45	30
601	35t. Wooden milk bucket	75	65
602	50t. Milk churn	1·00	1·40
599/602	*Set of 4*	2·25	2·25

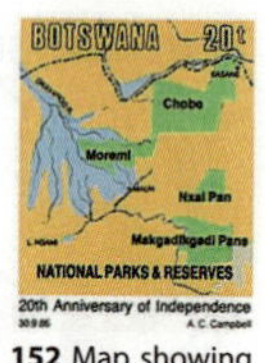

152 Map showing National Parks and Reserves

153 *Ludwigia stogonifera*

(Des K. Bogatsu, A. Campbell, I. Marshall and K. Mosinyi. Litho Govt Printer, Pretoria)

1986 (30 Sept). *20th Anniv of Independence. Sheet 100×120 mm, containing T* **152** *and similar vert designs. Multicoloured.* P 14.

MS603	20t. Type **152**; 20t. Morupule Power Station; 20t. Cattle breeding in Kgalagadi; 20t. National Assembly Building	3·75	2·50

(Des Julia Cairns. Litho Mardon Printers Ltd, Zimbabwe)

1986 (3 Nov). *Christmas. Flowers of Okavango. T* **153** *and similar vert designs. Multicoloured.* P 14×14½.

604	8t. Type **153**	1·25	10
605	15t. *Sopubia mannii*	2·25	1·10
606	35t. *Commelina diffusa*	3·50	3·00
607	50t. *Hibiscus diversifolius*	4·00	12·00
604/7	*Set of 4*	10·00	14·00

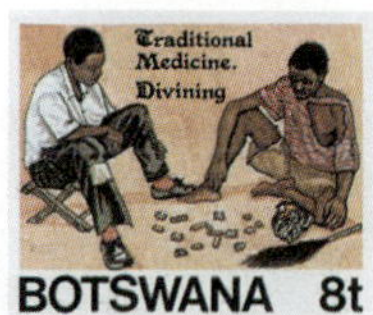

154 Divining

(155)

156 Oral Rehydration Therapy

(Des K. Mosinyi. Litho Mardon Printers Ltd, Zimbabwe)

1987 (2 Mar). *Traditional Medicine. T* **154** *and similar horiz designs. Multicoloured.* P 14½×14.

608	8t. Type **154**	80	10
609	15t. Lightning prevention	1·50	80
610	35t. Rain making	2·25	2·50
611	50t. Blood letting	2·75	8·50
608/11	*Set of 4*	6·50	10·50

1987 (1 Apr). *Nos. 520, 523 and 530 surch as T* **155**.

612	3t. on 6t. African Pygmy Goose	1·75	60
613	5t. on 10t. Yellow-billed Stork	1·75	60
614	20t. on 50t. Helmet Guineafowl (*horiz*)	3·25	1·40
612/14	*Set of 3*	6·00	2·40

(Des A. Nunoo. Litho Govt Printer, Pretoria)

1987 (1 June). *UNICEF Child Survival Campaign. T* **156** *and similar vert designs. Multicoloured.* P 14.

615	8t. Type **156**	35	10
616	15t. Growth monitoring	60	55
617	35t. Immunization	1·25	2·00
618	50t. Breast feeding	1·50	5·00
615/18	*Set of 4*	3·25	7·00

157 Cape Fox

158 *Cyperus articulatus*

(Des P. Huebsch. Photo Harrison)

1987 (3 Aug). *Animals. T* **157** *and similar horiz designs. Multicoloured.* P 14.

619	1t. Type **157**	10	1·00
620	2t. Lechwe	50	1·50
621	3t. Zebra	15	1·00
622	4t. Duiker	15	1·75
623	5t. Banded Mongoose	20	1·75
624	6t. Rusty-spotted Genet	20	1·75
625	8t. Hedgehog	30	10
626	10t. Scrub Hare	30	10
627	12t. Hippopotamus	3·00	3·50
628	15t. Suricate	2·50	2·25
629	20t. Caracal	70	65
630	25t. Steenbok	70	1·50
631	30t. Gemsbok	1·50	1·50
632	35t. Square-lipped Rhinoceros	2·00	2·50

633	40t. Mountain Reedbuck	1·75	1·50
634	50t. Rock Dassie	90	1·75
635	1p. Giraffe	2·50	3·75
636	2p. Tsessebe	2·50	5·50
637	3p. Side-striped Jackal	3·75	7·00
638	5p. Hartebeest	6·00	9·00
619/38	*Set of* 20	25·00	45·00

(Des Julia Cairns. Litho National Printing & Packaging, Zimbabwe)

1987 (26 Oct). *Christmas. Grasses and Sedges of Okavango. T* **158** *and similar vert designs. Multicoloured.* P 14×14½.

639	8t. Type **158**	40	10
640	15t. Broomgrass	60	40
641	30t. *Cyperus alopurcides*	1·25	75
642	1p. Bulrush Sedge	2·50	5·75
639/42	*Set of* 4	4·25	6·25
MS643	88×99 mm. Nos. 639/42	4·25	5·75
	a. 30t. value imperf vert	40·00	

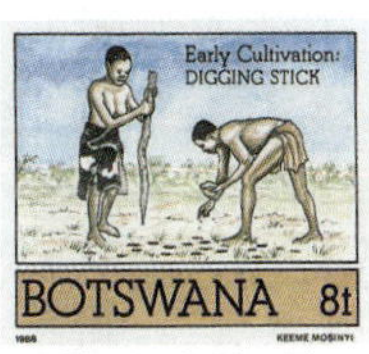

159 Planting Seeds with Digging Stick

160 Red Lechwe at Water-hole

(Des K. Mosinyi. Litho National Printing & Packaging, Zimbabwe)

1988 (14 Mar). *Early Cultivation. T* **159** *and similar horiz designs. Multicoloured.* P 14½×14.

644	8t.Type **159**	40	10
645	15t.Using iron hoe	60	35
646	35t.Wooden ox-drawn plough	1·00	1·00
647	50t.Villagers working on lesotla (Communal field)	1·40	2·00
644/7	*Set of* 4	3·00	3·00

(Des P. Augustinus. Litho National Printing & Packaging, Zimbabwe)

1988 (6 June). *Red Lechwe. T* **160** *and similar horiz designs. Multicoloured.* P 14½×14.

648	10t. Type **160**	90	15
649	15t. Red Lechwe and early morning sun	1·75	65
650	35t. Female and calf	2·50	1·75
651	75t. Herd on the move	3·75	8·50
648/51	*Set of* 4	8·00	10·00

161 Gubulawayo Postmark and Route Southwards to Tati

162 Pope John Paul II and Outline Map of Botswana

(Des M. Bryan, adapted Lucy Phalayagae. Litho National Printing & Packaging, Zimbabwe)

1988 (22 Aug). *Centenary of Mafeking-Gubulawayo Runner Post. Designs as Nos. 294/8, but redrawn smaller with changed inscription as in T* **161**. *Multicoloured.* P 14½.

652	10t. Type **161**	35	10
653	15t. Bechuanaland 1888 6d. on 6d. stamp and route from Tati southwards	55	30
654	30t. Runners and twin routes south from Shoshong	95	75
655	60t. Mafeking postmark and routes to Bechuanaland and Transvaal	1·60	2·75
652/5	*Set of* 4	3·00	3·50
MS656	81×151 mm. Nos. 652/5 vertically *se-tenant*, forming a composite map design	6·00	6·50

(Des P. Lodoen. Litho National Printing & Packaging, Zimbabwe)

1988 (13 Sept). *Visit of Pope John Paul II. T* **162** *and similar vert designs. Multicoloured.* P 14×14½.

657	10t. Type **162**	2·00	20
658	15t. Pope John Paul II	2·25	30
659	30t. Pope giving blessing and outline map	2·75	70
660	80t. Pope John Paul II (*different*)	3·50	2·75
657/60	*Set of* 4	9·50	3·50

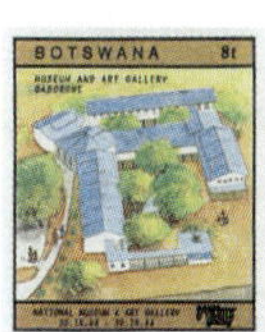

163 National Museum and Art Gallery

164 *Grewia flava*

(Des G. Mattsson and T. Sandberg (8t.), A. Campbell (15t.), K. Bogatsu (30t.), T. Sandberg (60t.). Litho National Printing & Packaging, Zimbabwe)

1988 (30 Sept). *20th Anniv of National Museum and Art Gallery, Gaborone. T* **163** *and similar vert designs. Multicoloured.* P 14½.

661	8t. Type **163**	15	10
662	15t. Pottery	20	25
663	30t. Blacksmith's buffalo bellows	35	40
664	60t. Children and mobile museum van	70	1·00
661/4	*Set of* 4	1·25	1·60

(Des Verena Blomberg-Ermatinger. Litho National Printing & Packaging, Zimbabwe)

1988 (31 Oct). *Flowering Plants of South-eastern Botswana. T* **164** *and similar vert designs. Multicoloured.* P 14×14½.

665	8t. Type **164**	20	10
666	15t. *Cienfuegosia digitata*	30	25
667	40t. *Solanum seaforthianum*	60	55
668	75t. *Carissa bispinosa*	1·00	1·40
665/8	*Set of* 4	1·90	2·00

165 Basket Granary

166 Female Red-throated Heron with Eggs

(Des K. Mosinyi. Litho National Printing & Packaging, Zimbabwe)

1989 (13 Mar). *Traditional Grain Storage. T* **165** *and similar vert designs. Multicoloured.* P 14×14½.

669	8t. Type **165**	75	10
670	15t. Large letlole granary	1·25	40
671	30t. Pot granary	1·75	60
672	60t. Two types of serala	2·50	2·25
669/72	*Set of* 4	5·50	3·00

The use of different paper stocks led to a wide range of shades in this issue.

(Des P. Augustinus. Litho Harrison)

1989 (5 July). *Slaty Egret. T* **166** *and similar horiz designs. Multicoloured.* P 15×14.

673	8t. Type **166**	55	15
674	15t. Chicks in nest	75	40
675	30t. Red-throated Heron in flight	1·00	75
676	60t. Pair building nest	1·40	1·60
673/6	*Set of* 4	3·25	2·50
MS677	119×89 mm. Nos. 673/6	3·25	2·75

167 "My Work at Home" (Ephraim Seeletso)

168 *Eulophia angolensis*

(Litho Govt Printer, Pretoria)

1989 (4 Sept). *Children's Paintings. T* **167** *and similar multicoloured designs.* P 14.

678	10t. Type **167**	35	10
679	15t. "My Favourite Game" (hopscotch) (Neelma Bhatia) (*vert*)	50	35
680	30t. "My Favourite Toy" (clay animals) (Thabo Habana)	75	70
681	1p. "My School Day" (Thabo Olesitse)	2·00	3·25
678/81	*Set of* 4	3·25	4·00

(Des Julia Cairns. Litho Govt Printer, Pretoria)

1989 (30 Oct). *Christmas. Orchids. T* **168** *and similar vert designs. Multicoloured.* P 14.

682	8t. Type **168**	90	10
683	15t. *Eulophia hereroensis*	1·50	60
684	30t. *Eulophia speciosa*	2·00	1·00
685	60t. *Eulophia petersii*	3·50	7·00
682/5	*Set of* 4	7·00	8·00

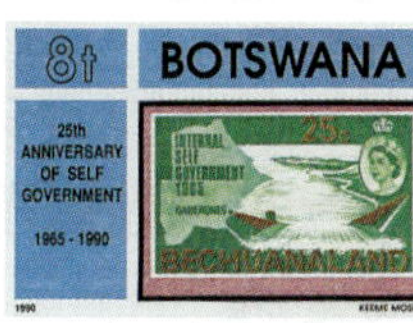

169 Bechuanaland 1965 New Constitution 25c. Stamp (25th anniv of Self-Government)

10t
(170)

(Des K. Mosinyi. Litho National Printing & Packaging, Zimbabwe)

1990 (5 Mar). *Anniversaries. T* **169** *and similar horiz designs.* P 14½.

686	8t. multicoloured	70	15
687	15t. multicoloured	75	50
688	30t. multicoloured	3·75	1·60
689	60t. black, new blue and yellow-ochre	3·75	7·00
686/9	*Set of* 4	8·00	8·25

Designs:—15t. Casting vote in ballot box (25th anniv of First Elections); 30t. Outline map and flags of Southern African Development Coordination Conference countries (10th anniv); 60t. Penny Black (150th anniv of first postage stamp).

1990 (27 Apr). *Nos. 619, 624 and 627 surch as T* **170**.

690	10t. on 1t. Type **157**	45	20
	a. Surch double	†	—
691	20t. on 6t. Rusty-spotted Genet	60	80
692	50t. on 12t. Hippopotamus	2·00	3·50
690/2	*Set of* 3	2·75	4·00

See also Nos. 725/8.

171 Telephone Engineer

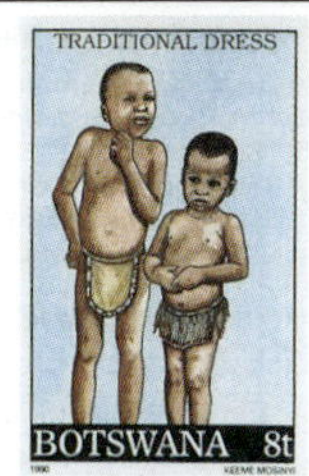

172 Young Children

(Des M. Kahn. Litho National Printing & Packaging, Zimbabwe)

1990 (3 May). *"Stamp World London 90" International Stamp Exhibition. T* **171** *and similar vert designs. Multicoloured.* P 14½.

693	8t. Type **171**	35	10
694	15t. Transmission pylon	65	40
695	30t. Public telephone	1·00	75
696	2p. Testing circuit board	3·00	6·50
693/6	*Set of* 4	4·50	7·00

(Des K. Mosinyi. Litho National Printing & Packaging, Zimbabwe)

1990 (1 Aug). *Traditional Dress. T* **172** *and similar vert designs. Multicoloured.* P 14½.

697	8t. Type **172**	35	10
698	15t. Young woman	65	40
699	30t. Adult man	1·00	70
700	2p. Adult woman	3·00	6·50
697/700	*Set of* 4	4·50	7·00
MS701	104×150 mm. Nos. 697/700	5·00	7·50
	a. 30t. and 2p. imperf vert		

173 *Acacia nigrescens*

174 Children running in front of Car

(Des Gillian Condy. Litho National Printing & Packaging, Zimbabwe)

1990 (30 Oct). *Christmas. Flowering Trees. T* **173** *and similar vert designs. Multicoloured.* P 14×14½.

702	8t. Type **173**	60	10
703	15t. *Peltophorum africanum*	95	35
704	30t. *Burkea Africana*	1·75	75
705	2p. *Pterocarpus angolensis*	3·75	7·50
702/5	*Set of* 4	6·25	8·00

(Des B. Heman-Ackah. Litho National Printing & Packaging, Zimbabwe)

1990 (7 Dec). *First National Road Safety Day. T* **174** *and similar horiz designs. Multicoloured.* P 14½.

706	8t. Type **174**	2·50	30
707	15t. Careless overtaking	3·00	1·00
708	30t. Cattle on road	3·75	2·75
706/8	*Set of* 3	8·25	3·50

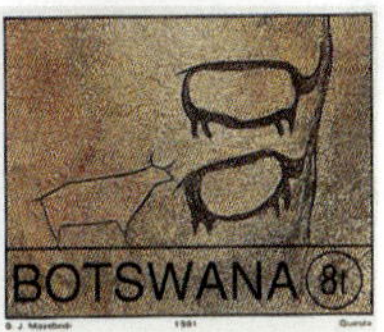

175 Cattle

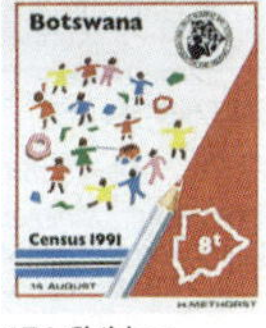

176 Children

(Des B. Mazebedi. Litho Questa)

1991 (4 Mar). *Rock Paintings. T* **175** *and similar horiz designs. Multicoloured.* P 14.

709	8t. Type **175**	2·25	40
710	15t. Cattle, drying frames and tree	2·75	85
711	30t. Animal hides	3·25	1·50
712	2p. Family herding cattle	6·00	10·00
709/12	*Set of* 4	13·00	11·50

Nos. 709/12 were printed on sand-grained paper which has an uneven surface.

(Des H. Methorst. Litho National Printing & Packaging, Zimbabwe)

1991 (3 June). *National Census. T* **176** *and similar vert designs. Multicoloured.* P 14.

713	8t. Type **176**	1·50	20
	a. Perf 14½	4·50	10
714	15t. Village	3·25	60
	a. Perf 14½	2·00	55
715	30t. School	2·25	1·00
	a. Perf 14½	2·25	90
716	2p. Hospital	8·00	11·00
	a. Perf 14½	8·00	9·50
713/16	*Set of* 4	12·50	10·00

177 Tourists viewing Elephants

178 *Harpagophytum procumbens*

(Des P. Lodoen. Litho Govt Printer, Pretoria)

1991 (30 Sept). *African Tourism Year. Okavango Delta. T* **177** *and similar multicoloured designs.* P 14 (2p.) or 14×14½ (others)

717 8t. Type **177** 1·50 70
718 15t. Crocodiles basking on river bank 1·75 90
719 35t. African Fish Eagles and De Havilland D.H.C.7 Dash Seven aircraft 3·50 3·25
720 2p. Okavango wildlife (*26×44 mm*) 5·50 9·00
717/20 *Set of 4* 11·00 12·50

(Des Gillian Condy. Litho Govt Printer, Pretoria)

1991 (4 Nov). *Christmas. Seed Pods. T* **178** *and similar vert designs. Multicoloured.* P 14.

721 8t. Type **178** 60 10
722 15t. *Tylosema esculentum* 1·00 40
723 30t. *Abrus precatorius* 1·75 80
724 2p. *Kigelia africana* 4·50 8·50
721/4 *Set of 4* 7·00 8·75

1992 (9 Mar). *Nos. 621, 624 and 627 surch as T* **170**.

725 8t. on 12t. Hippopotamus 1·25 70
a. Surch triple † —
726 10t. on 12t. Hippopotamus 1·25 70
727 25t. on 6t. Rusty-spotted Genet 1·25 1·50
728 40t. on 3t. Zebra 2·25 4·00
725/8 *Set of 4* 5·50 6·25

179 *Cacosternum boettgeri* **180** Air-conditioned Carriages

(Des Julia Cairns. Litho Govt Printer, Pretoria)

1992 (23 Mar). *Climbing Frogs. T* **179** *and similar multicoloured designs.* P 14.

729 8t. Type **179** 75 30
730 10t. *Hyperolius marmoratus angolensis* (*vert*) 75 30
731 40t. *Bufo fenoulheti* 2·50 1·50
732 1p. *Hyperolius sp* (*vert*) 5·00 7·00
729/32 *Set of 4* 8·00 8·25

(Des P. Lodoen. Litho Harrison)

1992 (29 June). *Deluxe Railway Service. T* **180** *and similar multicoloured designs.* P 14.

733 10t. Type **180** 1·50 40
734 25t. Diesel locomotive No. BD001 (*vert*) 2·25 80
735 40t. Carriage interior (*vert*) 2·50 1·25
736 2p. Diesel locomotive No. BD028 3·75 7·50
733/6 *Set of 4* 9·00 9·00
MS737 127×127 mm. Nos. 733/6 12·00 12·00

181 Cheetah **182** Boxing

(Des Judith Penny. Photo Harrison)

1992 (3 Aug). *Animals. T* **181** *and similar horiz designs. Multicoloured.* P 14½×14.

738 1t. Type **181** 30 1·75
739 2t. Spring Hare 30 1·75
740 4t. Blackfooted Cat 40 1·75
741 5t. Striped Mouse 40 1·50
742 10t. Oribi 55 10
743 12t. Pangolin 1·00 2·50
744 15t. Aardwolf 1·00 40
745 20t. Warthog 1·00 40
746 25t. Ground Squirrel 1·00 20
747 35t. Honey Badger 1·25 30
748 40t. Common Mole Rat 1·25 30
749 45t. Wild Dog 1·25 30
750 50t. Water Mongoose 1·25 35
751 80t. Klipspringer 1·75 1·75
752 1p. Lesser Bushbaby 1·75 1·75
753 2p. Bushveld Elephant Shrew 2·50 4·00
754 5p. Zorilla 4·25 7·00
755 10p. Vervet Monkey 6·50 10·00
738/55 *Set of 18* 25·00 32·00

(Litho Harrison)

1992 (7 Aug). *Olympic Games, Barcelona. T* **182** *and similar vert designs. Multicoloured.* P 14×15.

756 10t. Type **182** 60 10
757 50t. Running 1·50 50
758 1p. Boxing (*different*) 2·00 2·50
759 2p. Running (*different*) 2·50 5·00
756/9 *Set of 4* 6·00 7·25
MS760 87×117 mm. Nos. 756/9 5·50 8·00

183 *Adiantum incisum* **184** Helping Blind Person (Lions Club International)

(Des Gillian Condy. Litho National Printing & Packaging, Zimbabwe)

1992 (23 Nov). *Christmas. Ferns. T* **183** *and similar vert designs. Multicoloured.* P 14½.

761 10t. Type **183** 40 10
762 25t. *Actiniopteris radiata* 70 35
763 40t. *Ceratopteris cornuta* 1·00 55
764 1p.50 *Pellaea calomelanos* 3·00 7·00
761/4 *Set of 4* 4·50 7·25

(Des Ann Nilsson. Litho National Printing & Packaging, Zimbabwe)

1993 (29 Mar). *Charitable Organizations in Botswana. T* **184** *and similar multicoloured designs.* P 14.

765 10t. Type **184** 80 20
766 15t. Nurse carrying child (Red Cross Society) (*horiz*) 90 40
767 25t. Woman watering seedling (Ecumenical Decade) 90 50
768 35t. Deaf children (Round Table) (*horiz*) 1·25 1·50
769 40t. Crowd of people (Rotary International) 1·25 1·75
770 50t. Hands at prayer (Botswana Christian Council) (*horiz*) 1·50 2·50
765/70 *Set of 6* 6·00 6·25

185 Bechuanaland Railways Class "6" Locomotive No. 1 **186** Long-crested Eagle

(Des P. Lodoen. Litho Harrison)

1993 (24 May). *Railway Centenary. T* **185** *and similar horiz designs. Multicoloured.* P 15×14.

771 10t. Type **185** 75 40
772 40t. Class "19" locomotive No. 317 1·40 75
773 50t. Class "12" locomotive No. 256 1·40 90
774 1p.50 Class "7" locomotive No. 71 2·00 5·00
771/4 *Set of 4* 5·00 6·25
MS775 190×100 mm. Nos. 771/4 5·00 6·00

(Des J. Leath. Litho National Printing & Packaging, Zimbabwe)

1993 (30 Aug). *Endangered Eagles. T* **186** *and similar vert designs. Multicoloured.* P 14½.

776 10t. Type **186** 70 35
777 25t. Short-toed Eagle 1·25 65
778 50t. Bateleur 1·60 1·75
779 1p.50 Secretary Bird 2·50 6·50
776/9 *Set of 4* 5·50 8·25

187 *Aloe zebrina* **188** Boy with String Puppet

(Des Gillian Condy. Litho National Printing & Packaging, Zimbabwe)

1993 (25 Oct). *Christmas. Flora. T* **187** *and similar vert designs. Multicoloured.* P 14×14½.

780 12t. Type **187** 40 10
781 25t. *Croton megalobotrys* 60 25
782 50t. *Boophane disticha* 85 70
783 1p. *Euphoria davyi* 1·25 3·50
780/3 *Set of 4* 2·75 4·00

(Des K. Mosinyi. Litho National Printing & Packaging Zimbabwe)

1994 (28 Mar). *Traditional Toys. T* **188** *and similar horiz designs. Multicoloured.* P 14½.

784 10t. Type **188** 20 10
785 40t. Boys with clay cattle 45 30
786 50t. Boy with spinner 50 50
787 1p. Girls playing in make-believe houses 1·10 3·00
784/7 *Set of 4* 2·00 3·50

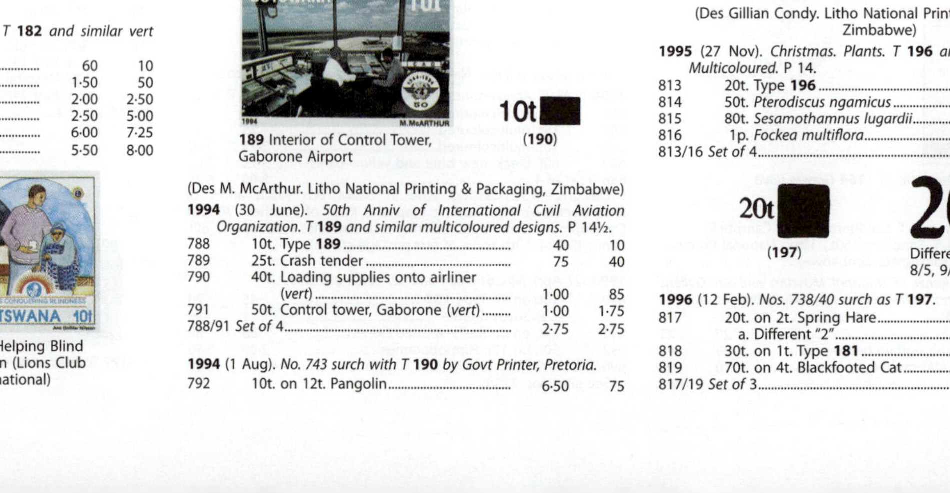

189 Interior of Control Tower, Gaborone Airport (**190**)

(Des M. McArthur. Litho National Printing & Packaging, Zimbabwe)

1994 (30 June). *50th Anniv of International Civil Aviation Organization. T* **189** *and similar multicoloured designs.* P 14½.

788 10t. Type **189** 40 10
789 25t. Crash tender 75 40
790 40t. Loading supplies onto airliner (*vert*) 1·00 85
791 50t. Control tower, Gaborone (*vert*) 1·00 1·75
788/91 *Set of 4* 2·75 2·75

1994 (1 Aug). *No. 743 surch with T* **190** *by Govt Printer, Pretoria.*

792 10t. on 12t. Pangolin 6·50 75

191 Lesser Flamingos at Sua Pan **192** *Ziziphus mucronata*

(Des P. Lodoen. Litho National Printing & Packaging, Zimbabwe)

1994 (26 Sept). *Environment Protection. Makgadikgadi Pans. T* **191** *and similar multicoloured designs.* P 14×14½ (*vert*) or 14½×14 (*horiz*).

793 10t. Type **191** 1·00 40
794 35t. Baobab trees (*horiz*) 50 40
795 50t. Zebra and palm trees 65 80
796 2p. Map of area (*horiz*) 3·00 6·00
793/6 *Set of 4* 4·75 6·75

(Des Gillian Condy. Litho National Printing & Packaging, Zimbabwe)

1994 (24 Oct). *Christmas. Edible Fruits. T* **192** *and similar vert designs. Multicoloured.* P 14×14½.

797 10t. Type **192** 25 10
798 25t. *Strychnos cocculoides* 40 30
799 40t. *Bauhinia petersiana* 60 70
800 50t. *Schinziphyton rautoneii* 70 1·40
797/800 *Set of 4* 1·75 2·25

193 Fisherman with Bow and Arrow **194** Boys watering Horses (FAO)

(Des B. Mazebedi. Litho National Printing & Packaging, Zimbabwe)

1995 (3 Apr). *Traditional Fishing. T* **193** *and similar horiz designs. Multicoloured.* P 14½.

801 15t. Type **193** 35 20
802 40t. Men in canoe and boy with fishing rod 60 45
803 65t. Fisherman with net 80 90
804 80t. Fisherman with basket fish trap 1·00 2·00
801/4 *Set of 4* 2·50 3·25

(Des M. McArthur. Litho National Printing & Packaging Zimbabwe)

1995 (16 Oct). *50th Anniv of United Nations. T* **194** *and similar vert designs. Multicoloured.* P 14½.

805 20t. Type **194** 20 10
806 50t. Schoolchildren queuing for soup (WFP) 35 30
807 80t. Policeman carrying out hut census (UNDP) 1·00 1·00
808 1p. Weighing baby (UNICEF) 70 2·00
805/8 *Set of 4* 2·00 3·00

195 Brown Hyena **196** *Adenia glauca*

(Des Judith Penny. Litho Questa)

1995 (6 Nov). *Endangered Species. Brown Hyena. T* **195** *and similar horiz designs. Multicoloured.* P 14½.

809 20t. Type **195** 45 60
a. Strip of 4. Nos. 809/12 3·00
810 50t. Pair of Hyenas 65 75
811 80t. Hyena stealing ostrich eggs 1·10 1·50
812 1p. Adult Hyena and cubs 1·25 2·25
809/12 *Set of 4* 3·00 4·50

In addition to separate sheets of 50 Nos. 809/12 were also available in sheets of 16 (4×4) with the stamps arranged *se-tenant* both horizontally and vertically.

(Des Gillian Condy. Litho National Printing & Packaging, Zimbabwe)

1995 (27 Nov). *Christmas. Plants. T* **196** *and similar vert designs. Multicoloured.* P 14.

813 20t. Type **196** 35 10
814 50t. *Pterodiscus ngamicus* 60 30
815 80t. *Sesamothamnus lugardii* 1·00 1·00
816 1p. *Fockea multiflora* 1·10 2·00
813/16 *Set of 4* 2·75 3·00

(**197**) Different "2" (R. 7/5, 8/5, 9/5)

1996 (12 Feb). *Nos. 738/40 surch as T* **197**.

817 20t. on 2t. Spring Hare 1·00 30
a. Different "2" 6·50 2·00
818 30t. on 1t. Type **181** 1·25 30
819 70t. on 4t. Blackfooted Cat 2·00 3·25
817/19 *Set of 3* 3·75 3·50

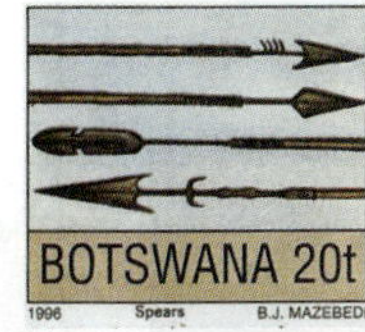

198 Spears

(Des B. Mazebedi. Litho National Printing & Packaging, Zimbabwe)

1996 (25 Mar). *Traditional Weapons. T* **198** *and similar horiz designs. Multicoloured. P* 14½×14.

820 20t. Type **198** ... 20 10
821 50t. Axes ... 35 30
822 80t. Shield and knobkerries ... 55 65
823 1p. Knives and sheaths ... 60 1·50
820/3 *Set of* 4 ... 1·50 2·25

199 Child with Basic Radio

200 Olympic Flame, Rings and Wreath

(Des P. Lodoen. Litho National Printing & Packaging, Zimbabwe)

1996 (3 June). *Centenary of Radio. T* **199** *and similar vert designs. Multicoloured.* P 14×14½.

824 20t. Type **199** ... 25 10
825 50t. Radio Botswana's mobile transmitter ... 40 30
826 80t. Police radio control ... 1·50 1·10
827 1p. Listening to radio ... 70 1·75
824/7 *Set of* 4 ... 2·50 3·00

(Des R. Andersson. Litho Govt Printer, Pretoria)

1996 (19 July). *Centenary of Modern Olympic Games. T* **200** *and similar vert designs. Multicoloured.* P 14.

828 20t. Type **200** ... 30 10
829 50t. Pierre de Coubertin (founder of modern Olympics) ... 45 30
830 80t. Map of Botswana with flags and athletes ... 90 90
831 1p. Ruins of ancient stadium at Olympia ... 90 1·60
828/31 *Set of* 4 ... 2·25 2·50

201 Family Planning Class (Botswana Family Welfare Association)

202 *Adansonia digitata* Leaf and Blossom

(Des K. Mosinyi. Litho National Printing and Packaging, Zimbabwe)

1996 (23 Sept). *Local Charities. T* **201** *and similar vert designs. Multicoloured.* P 14½.

832 20t. Type **201** ... 20 10
833 30t. Blind workers (Pudulogong Rehabilitation Centre) ... 20 15
834 50t. Collecting seeds (Forestry Association of Botswana) ... 30 30
835 70t. Secretarial class (YWCA) ... 40 70
836 80t. Children's day centre (Botswana Council of Women) ... 50 80
837 1p. Children's village, Tlokweng (SOS Children's village) ... 60 1·50
832/7 *Set of* 6 ... 2·00 3·25

(Des Gillian Condy. Litho National Printing and Packaging, Zimbabwe)

1996 (4 Nov). *Christmas. T* **202** *and similar vert designs showing parts of life cycle for Adansonia digitata. Multicoloured.* P 14.

838 20t. Type **202** ... 25 10
839 50t. Fruit ... 40 25
840 80t. Tree in leaf ... 60 75
841 1p. Tree with bare branches ... 70 1·60
838/41 *Set of* 4 ... 1·75 2·40

203 Tati Hotel

204 Steam Locomotive, Bechuanaland Railway, 1897

(Des M. Smith. Litho National Printing and Packaging, Zimbabwe)

1997 (21 Apr). *Francistown Centenary. T* **203** *and similar horiz designs. Multicoloured.* P 14½×14.

842 20t. Type **203** ... 15 10
843 50t. Railway Station ... 75 35
844 80t. Company Manager's House ... 60 80
845 1p. Monarch Mine ... 1·00 1·60
842/5 *Set of* 4 ... 2·25 2·50

(Des P. Lodoen. Litho National Printing and Packaging, Zimbabwe)

1997 (12 July). *Railway Centenary. T* **204** *and similar vert designs. Multicoloured.* P 14×14½.

846 35t. Type **204** ... 40 20
847 50t. Elephants crossing railway line ... 60 35
848 80t. First locomotive in Bechuanaland, 1897 ... 70 45
849 1p. Beyer-Garratt type steam locomotive No. 352 ... 75 75
850 2p. Diesel locomotive No. BD339 ... 1·00 1·75
851 2p.50 Fantuzzi container stacker ... 1·25 2·25
846/51 *Set of* 6 ... 4·25 5·25

205 Pel's Fishing Owl

205a Prince Philip with carriage

(Des Helena Schüssel. Litho Enschedé)

1997 (4 Aug). *Birds. T* **205** *and similar multicoloured designs.* P 13½×13 (*vert*) or 13×13½ (*horiz*).

852 5t. Type **205** ... 50 75
853 10t. Gymnogene (*horiz*) ... 50 75
854 15t. Meyer's Parrot ... 50 60
855 20t. Harlequin Quail (*horiz*) ... 60 60
856 25t. Marico Sunbird (*horiz*) ... 60 60
857 30t. Kurrichane Thrush (*horiz*) ... 65 60
858 40t. Redheaded Finch ... 70 60
859 50t. Buffalo Weaver ... 80 40
860 60t. Sacred Ibis (*horiz*) ... 90 70
861 70t. Cape Shoveler (*horiz*) ... 90 80
862 80t. Greater Honeyguide (*horiz*) ... 90 70
863 1p. Woodland Kingfisher (*horiz*) ... 1·10 80
864 1p.25 Purple Heron ... 1·40 1·40
865 1p.50 Yellow-billed Oxpecker (*horiz*) ... 1·40 1·75
866 2p. Shaft-tailed Whydah ... 1·60 2·00
867 2p.50 White Stork ... 1·75 2·00
868 5p. Sparrowhawk ... 2·25 2·75
869 10p. Spotted Crake ... 3·25 4·50
852/69 *Set of* 18 ... 18·00 20·00

No. 861 is inscribed "Shoveller" in error.

(Des N. Shewring (No. **MS**876), D. Miller (others). Litho Questa (No. **MS**876), Cartor (others))

1997 (22 Sept). *Golden Wedding of Queen Elizabeth and Prince Philip. Multicoloured T* **205a** *and similar vert designs.* W w **14**. P 13.

870 35t. Type **205a** ... 20 55
a. *Horiz pair.* Nos. 870/1 ... 40 1·10
871 35t. Queen Elizabeth with binoculars ... 20 55
872 2p. Queen Elizabeth with horse team ... 90 1·50
a. *Horiz pair.* Nos. 872/3 ... 1·75 3·00
873 2p. Prince Philip and horse ... 90 1·50
874 2p.50 Queen Elizabeth and Prince Philip ... 1·10 1·50
a. *Horiz pair.* Nos. 874/5 ... 2·10 3·00
875 2p.50 Princess Anne and Prince Edward ... 1·10 1·50
870/5 *Set of* 6 ... 4·00 6·25

MS876 110×70 mm. 10p. Queen Elizabeth and Prince Philip in landau (*horiz*). Wmk sideways. P 14×14½ ... 4·00 5·50

Nos. 870/1, 872/3 and 874/5 were each printed together, *se-tenant*, in horizontal pairs throughout the sheets.

206 *Combretum zeyheri*

207 Baobab Trees

(Des Gillian Condy. Litho National Printing and Packaging, Zimbabwe)

1997 (10 Nov). *Christmas. Plants. T* **206** *and similar vert designs. Multicoloured.* P 14.

877 35t. Type **206** ... 45 10
878 1p. *Combretum apiculatum* ... 1·00 35
879 2p. *Combretum molle* ... 1·75 1·90
880 2p.50 *Combretum imberbe* ... 2·00 2·50
877/80 *Set of* 4 ... 4·75 4·25

(Des A. Campbell. Litho National Printing and Packaging, Zimbabwe)

1998 (23 Mar). *Tourism (1st series). T* **207** *and similar multicoloured designs.* P 14½.

881 35t. Type **207** ... 25 15
882 1p. Crocodile ... 50 45
883 2p. Stalactites (*vert*) ... 85 1·10
884 2p.50 Tourists and rock paintings (*vert*) ... 1·10 1·60
881/4 *Set of* 4 ... 2·40 3·00

See also Nos. 899/902.

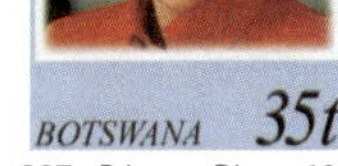

207a Princess Diana, 1990

208 "Village Life" (tapestry)

(Des D. Miller. Litho Cartor)

1998 (1 June). *Diana, Princess of Wales Commemoration. T* **207a** *and similar vert designs. Multicoloured.* W w **14**. P 13.

885 35t. Type **207a** ... 25 15
886 1p. In green hat, 1992 ... 40 35
887 2p. In white blouse, 1993 ... 75 1·10
888 2p.50 With crowd, Cambridge, 1993 ... 90 1·50
885/8 *Set of* 4 ... 2·10 2·75

MS889 145×70 mm. As Nos. 885/8, but each with a face value of 2p.50 ... 4·50 3·75

(Des M. McArthur. Litho Enschedé)

1998 (28 Sept). *Botswana Weavers. T* **208** *and similar multicoloured designs.* P 14×13½.

890 35t. Type **208** ... 30 15
891 55t. Weaver dyeing threads ... 40 20
892 1p. "African wildlife" (tapestry) ... 1·40 1·00
893 2p. Weaver at loom ... 1·50 2·25
890/3 *Set of* 4 ... 3·25 3·25

MS894 68×58 mm. 2p.50, "Elephants" (tapestry) (*horiz*). P 13½×14 ... 3·00 3·25

209 *Ficus ingens*

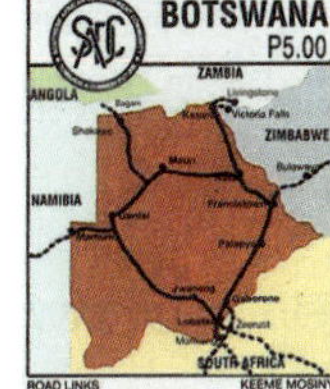

210 Road Map

(Des Gillian Condy. Litho Oriental Press, Bahrain)

1998 (30 Nov). *Christmas. Plants. T* **209** *and similar vert designs. Multicoloured.* P 13×13½.

895 35t. Type **209** ... 40 10
896 55t. *Ficus pygmaea* ... 60 20
897 1p. *Ficus abutilifolia* ... 1·00 55
898 2p.50 *Ficus sycomorus* ... 1·90 2·75
895/8 *Set of* 4 ... 3·50 3·25

(Des A. Campbell. Litho Enschedé)

1999 (24 May). *Tourism (2nd series). Multicoloured designs as T* **207**. P 13½×14 (*horiz*) or 14×13½ (*vert*).

899 35t. Rock painting of men and cattle ... 70 25
900 55t. Expedition at salt pan ... 1·00 30
901 1p. Rock painting of elephant and antelope (*vert*) ... 1·40 1·40
902 2p. Tourists under Baobab tree (*vert*) ... 1·60 2·25
899/902 *Set of* 4 ... 4·25 3·75

(Des K. Mosinyi. Litho National Printing and Packaging, Harare)

1999 (17 Aug). *Southern African Development Community Day. Sheet* 77×84 *mm.* P 14½.

MS903 **210** 5p. multicoloured ... 3·50 3·75

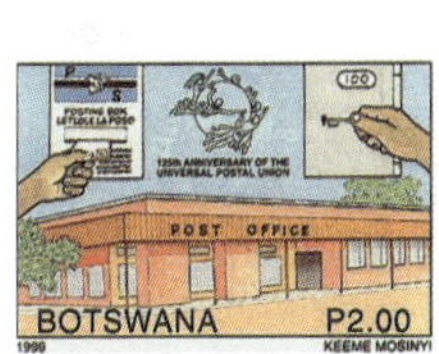

211 Modern Post Office

212 Mpule Kwelagobe winning Contest

(Des K. Mosinyi. Litho National Printing and Packaging, Zimbabwe)

1999 (9 Oct). *125th Anniv of Universal Postal Union.* P 14½.

904 **211** 2p. multicoloured ... 1·50 1·50

(Des Seasky Design Studio. Litho Southern Colour Print, Dunedin)

1999 (1 Dec). *Mpule Kwelagobe ("Miss Universe 1999"). T* **212** *and similar multicoloured designs.* P 14½.

905 35t. Type **212** ... 35 10
906 1p. In traditional dress (*horiz*) ... 75 30
907 2p. In traditional dancing costume with lion ... 1·10 60
908 2p.50 Wearing "Botswana" sash (*horiz*) ... 1·25 75
909 15p. With leopard in background (*horiz*) ... 7·00 11·00
905/9 *Set of* 5 ... 9·50 11·50

MS910 175×80 mm. Nos. 905/9 ... 9·50 12·00

213 Saddle-bill Stork and Limpopo River

(Des SeaSky Design. Litho Southern Colour Print, Dunedin)

2000 (5 Apr). *Scenic Rivers. T* **213** *and similar multicoloured designs.* P 14.

911 35t. Type **213** ... 40 20
912 1p. Hippopotamuses in water lilies (*vert*) ... 70 60
913 2p. African Skimmer and makoro (dugout canoe) ... 1·25 1·50
914 2p.50 African elephant at sunset, Chobe River (*vert*) ... 1·40 2·00
911/14 *Set of* 4 ... 3·25 3·75

214 Mopane Moth

(Des Donna McKenna. Litho Cartor)

2000 (19 July). *Moths.* *T* **214** *and similar diamond-shaped designs. Multicoloured.* P 12½.

915 35t. Type **214** ... 15 10
916 70t. Wild Silk Moth ... 25 20
917 1p. Crimson Speckled Footman ("Tiger Moth") ... 35 30
918 2p. African Lunar Moth ... 65 60
919 15p. Speckled Emperor Moth ... 4·75 8·00
915/19 *Set of 5* ... 5·50 8·25
MS920 175×135 mm. Nos. 915/19 ... 7·50 9·50

No. **MS**920 is in the shape of a moth.

215 Mother reading Medicine Label with Child ("Protect Your Children") **216** Pres. Sir Seretse Khama

(Des B. Pearce and K. Mosinyi. Litho Southern Colour Print, Dunedin)

2000 (23 Aug). *United Nations Literacy Decade.* *T* **215** *and similar horiz designs. Multicoloured.* P 12.

921 35t. Type **215** ... 20 10
922 70t. Adult literacy class ("Never Too Old To Learn") ... 30 20
923 2p. Man smoking next to petrol pump ("Be Aware Of Danger") ... 75 1·10
924 2p.50 Man at Automatic Teller Machine ("Be Independent") ... 90 2·00
921/4 *Set of 4* ... 1·90 3·00

Nos. 921/4 were each printed with *se-tenant* label (45×10 mm) at foot inscribed with the Botswana Post logo and the theme of the stamp.

(Des Karen Odiam. Litho and embossed Southern Colour Print, Dunedin)

2000 (29 Sept). *Chiefs and Presidents.* *T* **216** *and similar designs.* P 14.

925 35t. black, orange-red and gold ... 40 10
926 1p. multicoloured ... 65 40
927 2p. multicoloured ... 1·00 1·10
928 2p.50 multicoloured ... 1·25 2·00
925/8 *Set of 4* ... 3·00 3·25

Designs: *Horiz* (60×40 mm)—35t. Chiefs Sebele I of Bakwena, Bathoen I of Bangwaketse and Khama III of Bangato, 1895 *Vert* (as T **216**)—2p. Pres. Sir Ketumile Masire; 2p.50, Pres. Festus Mogae.

217 Doctor giving Eye Test **218** Hippopotamus

(Des C. Abbott. Litho Cartor)

2000 ((3 Nov)). *Airborne Medical Service.* *T* **217** *and similar vert designs. Multicoloured.* P 13×13½.

929 35t. Type **217** ... 30 10
a. Horiz strip of 4. Nos. 929/32 plus label ... 3·25
930 1p. Medical team and family ... 65 40
931 2p. Aircraft over canoes ... 1·25 1·40
932 2p.50 Donkeys and mule cart on airstrip ... 1·50 2·25
929/32 *Set of 4* ... 3·25 3·75

Nos. 929/32 were printed either in sheets of one value or as *se-tenant* horizontal strips of four stamps with a central label showing the flight network. The borders along the bottom of the strip form a composite design.

(Des G. Ryan. Litho Enschedé)

2000 (6 Dec). *Wetlands (1st series) Okavango Delta.* *T* **218** *and similar multicoloured designs.* P 13½×14 (*horiz*) or 14×13½ (*vert*).

933 35t. Type **218** ... 50 20
934 1p. Tiger Fish and Tilapia ... 55 30
935 1p.75 Painted Reed Frog and Wattled Crane (*vert*) ... 1·50 1·50
936 2p. Pels Fishing Owl and Vervet Monkey (*vert*) ... 1·75 1·75
937 2p.50 Nile Crocodile, Sitatunga and Red Lechwe ... 1·75 1·75
933/7 *Set of 5* ... 5·50 5·00
MS938 175×80 mm. Nos. 933/7. P 13½ ... 5·50 5·50

See also Nos. 958/63, 994/9 and 1009/14.

2001 (1 Feb). *"HONG KONG 2001" Stamp Exhibition. No.* **MS**938 *optd with exhibition logo on sheet margin.*

MS939 175×80 mm. Nos. 933/7 ... 6·00 7·00

219 Diamonds

(Des D. Gunson. Litho Southern Colour Print, Dunedin)

2001 (1 Feb). *Diamonds.* *T* **219** *and similar diamond-shaped designs. Multicoloured. Self-adhesive.* Roul 9 (die-cut perf 10 around designs).

940 35t. Type **219** ... 55 20
941 1p.75 JCB in open-cast mine ... 1·50 1·60
942 2p. Quality inspector ... 1·75 1·90
943 2p.50 Diamonds in jewellery ... 2·00 2·25
940/3 *Set of 4* ... 5·25 5·25

220 African Pygmy Falcon **221** Shallow Basket

(Des Karen Odiam. Litho Cartor)

2001 (12 May). *Kgalagadi Transfrontier Wildlife Park. Joint Issue with South Africa.* *T* **220** *and similar horiz designs. Multicoloured.* P 13.

944 35t. Type **220** ... 85 35
945 1p. Leopard ... 1·00 70
946 2p. Gemsbok ... 1·40 1·60
947 2p. Bat-eared Fox ... 1·60 2·25
944/7 *Set of 4* ... 4·25 4·50
MS948 115×80 mm. Nos. 945 and 947 ... 2·50 3·00

(Des C. Abbott. Litho Enschedé)

2001 (30 July). *Traditional Baskets.* *T* **221** *and similar vert designs. Multicoloured.* P 13½.

949 35t. Type **221** ... 20 15
950 1p. Tall basket ... 35 25
951 2p. Woman weaving ... 60 85
952 2p.50 Spherical basket ... 65 95
949/52 *Set of 4* ... 1·60 2·00
MS953 177×92 mm. Nos. 949/52 ... 2·00 3·00

222 Boys by River at Sunset

(Des Typeface. Litho B.D.T)

2001 (28 Sept). *Scenic Skies.* *T* **222** *and similar horiz designs. Multicoloured.* P 13½.

954 50t. Type **222** ... 25 15
955 1p. Woman with baby at sunset ... 50 25
956 2p. Girls carrying firewood at sunset ... 75 75
957 10p. Traditional village at sunset near huts ... 2·50 3·50
954/7 *Set of 4* ... 3·50 4·25

(Des G. Ryan. Litho Enschedé)

2001 (12 Dec). *Wetlands (2nd series). Chobe River. Multicoloured designs as T* **218**. P 13½×14 (*horiz*) or 14×13½ (*vert*).

958 50t. Water Moniter and Carmine Bee-eater ... 65 20
959 1p.75 Buffalo ... 75 60
960 2p. Savanna Baboons (*vert*) ... 90 1·00
961 2p. Lion (*vert*) ... 1·10 1·40
962 3p. African Elephants in river ... 2·25 2·25
958/62 *Set of 5* ... 5·00 5·00
MS963 175×80 mm. Nos. 958/62. P 13½ ... 5·00 5·00

223 Black Mamba **224** Mbukushu Pots

(Des P. Lodoen. Litho Enschedé)

2002 (22 Mar). *Snakes.* *T* **223** *and similar multicoloured designs.* P 14×13½ (*horiz*) or 13½×14 (*vert*).

964 50t. Type **223** ... 45 15
965 1p.75 Spitting Cobra (*vert*) ... 70 45
966 2p.50 Puff Adder ... 80 1·25
967 3p. Boomslang (*vert*) ... 1·00 1·50
964/7 *Set of 4* ... 2·75 3·00

(Des B. Mazebedi. Litho B.D.T.)

2002 (31 May). *Botswana Pottery.* *T* **224** *and similar horiz designs. Multicoloured.* P 13½.

968 50t. Type **224** ... 45 10
969 2p. Sekgatla pots ... 80 75
970 2p.50 Setswana pots ... 90 1·10
971 3p. Kalanga pots ... 1·10 1·50
968/71 *Set of 4* ... 3·00 3·00

225 Queen Elizabeth in Evening Dress and Commonwealth Emblem **226** Tree Squirrel

(Litho Cartor)

2002 (25 July). *Golden Jubilee.* *T* **225** *and similar multicoloured design.* P 13.

972 55t. Type **225** ... 65 15
973 2p. Queen Elizabeth with bouquet (*vert*) ... 1·75 2·00

(Des Judith Greenwood Penny. Photo Enschedé)

2002 (5 Aug). *Mammals.* *T* **226** *and similar multicoloured designs. Glazed, ordinary paper.* P 13½.

974 5t. Type **226** ... 10 10
975 10t. Black-backed Jackal ... 10 10
976 20t. African Wild Cat ... 10 10
977 30t. Slender Mongoose (*horiz*) ... 15 10
978 40t. African Civet (*horiz*) ... 25 20
a. Chalk-surfaced paper (20.11.05) ... 15 10
979 55t. Elephant ... 20 15
980 90t. Reedbuck ... 30 25
981 1p. Kudu ... 35 35
982 1p.45 Waterbuck ... 50 50
983 1p.95 Sable (*horiz*) ... 60 65
984 2p.20 Sitatunga (*horiz*) ... 70 75
985 2p.75 Porcupine (*horiz*) ... 80 85
986 3p.30 Serval (*horiz*) ... 95 1·00
987 4p. Antbear (*horiz*) ... 1·25 1·40
988 5p. Bushpig (*horiz*) ... 1·40 1·50
989 15p. Chakma Baboon ... 3·50 3·75
974/89 Set of 16 ... 10·00 10·00

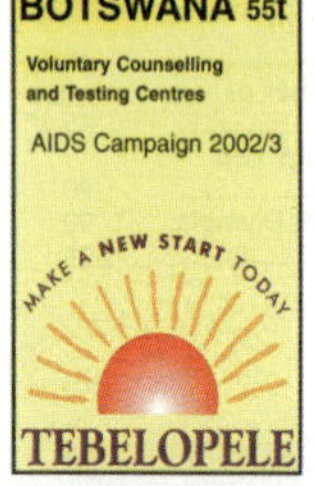

227 Tebelopele (councelling and testing centres) Symbol **228** Lentswe la Baratani ("Hill of Lovers")

(Des B. Mazebede. Litho Govt Printer, Pretoria)

2002 (1 Dec). *AIDS Awareness.* *T* **227** *and similar vert designs. Multicoloured.* P 14.

990 55t. Type **227** ... 60 15
991 1p.10 AIDS ribbon and mother and baby badge ... 1·10 40
992 2p.75 Hands and male gender symbol ... 1·75 1·90
993 3p.30 Orphans with foster parent ... 1·90 2·25
990/3 *Set of 4* ... 4·75 4·25

(Des G. Ryan. Litho Enschedé)

2002 (18 Dec). *Wetlands (3rd series). The Makgadikgadi Pans. Multicoloured designs as T* **218**. P 13½×14 (*horiz*) or 14×13½ (*vert*).

994 55t. Aardwolf ... 50 15
995 1p.10 Blue Wildebeest and Zebra ... 85 30
996 2p.50 Zebra (*vert*) ... 1·40 1·40
997 2p.75 Flamingo (*vert*) ... 1·75 1·90
998 3p.30 Pelican in flight ... 1·90 2·25
994/8 *Set of 5* ... 5·75 5·50
MS999 175×80 mm. Nos. 994/8. P 13½ ... 5·75 5·75

(Des U. Nermark. Litho Enschedé)

2003 (27 Mar). *Natural Places of Interest.* *T* **228** *and similar multicoloured designs.* P 13½.

1000 55t. Type **228** ... 35 15
1001 2p.20 Sand dunes ... 1·00 90
1002 2p.75 Moremi Waterfalls (*vert*) ... 1·50 1·50
1003 3p.30 Gcwihaba Cave ... 1·75 1·90
1000/3 Set of 4 ... 4·25 4·00

229 Ngwale **230** San People with Birds (Cg' Ose Ntcox'o)

(Des Dr. M. Sctshogo. Litho Cartor)

2003 (12 Nov). *Beetles.* *T* **229** *and similar horiz designs. Multicoloured.* P 13.

1004 55t. Type **229** ... 40 15
1005 2p.20 Kgomo-ya-buru ... 1·10 70
1006 2p.75 Kgomo-ya-pula ... 1·40 1·50
1007 3p.30 Lebitse ... 1·75 1·90
1004/7 *Set of 4* ... 4·25 3·75
MS1008 69×59 mm. 5p.50 Kgaladuwa ... 3·00 3·50

(Des G. Ryan. Litho Enschedé)

2003 (23 Dec). *Wetlands (4th series). The Limpopo River. Multicoloured designs as T* **218**. P 13½×14 (*horiz*) or 14×13½ (*vert*).

1009 55t. Giraffe ... 70 35
1010 1p.45 Black Eagle and Nile Crocodile (*vert*) ... 1·50 85
1011 2p.50 Ostrich (*vert*) ... 2·00 1·50
1012 2p.75 Klipspringer ... 1·60 1·75
1013 3p.30 Serval Cat ... 1·90 2·25
1009/13 *Set of 5* ... 7·00 6·00
MS1014 175×80 mm. Nos. 1009/13. P 13½ ... 7·00 7·00

(Litho Enschedé)

2004 (29 Apr). *Kuru Art Project. T* **230** *and similar vert designs. Multicoloured.* P 14.

1015 55t. Type **230** ... 35 20
1016 1p.45 Tree with gum (Nxaedom Qhomatca) ... 75 55
1017 2p.75 Tree with berries (Nxaedom Qhomatca) ... 1·10 1·40
1018 3p.30 Snake (Qgoma Ncokg'o) ... 1·50 1·75
1015/18 *Set of 4* ... 3·25 3·50

231 Masimo (working the land)

232 Child posting Letter

(Des K. Mosinyi. Litho B.D.T)

2004 (30 June). *Traditional Life Styles. T* **231** *and similar horiz designs. Multicoloured.* P 14.

1019 80t. Type **231** ... 50 25
1020 2p.10 Kgotla (village meeting place) ... 1·25 85
1021 3p.90 Moraka (cattle post) ... 1·75 1·90
1022 4p.70 Legae (compound within village) ... 2·25 2·50
1019/22 *Set of 4* ... 5·25 5·00

(Des P. Lodoen. Litho B.D.T)

2004 (9 Oct). *World Post Day. T* **232** *and similar vert designs. Multicoloured.* P 14×14½.

1023 80t. Type **232** ... 45 25
1024 2p.10 Children sharing a letter ... 1·00 85
1025 3p.90 Post man ... 1·60 1·90
1026 4p.70 Woman reading letter ... 2·00 2·50
1023/6 *Set of 4* ... 4·50 5·00

233 Peregrine Falcon (Angola)

234 *Pterodiscus speciosus*

(Des Anja Denker. Litho Enschedé)

2004 (9 Oct). *First Joint Issue of Southern Africa Postal Operators Association Members. Sheet 170×95 mm containing T* **233** *and similar hexagonal designs showing national birds of Association Members. Multicoloured.* P 14.

MS1027 40t. Type **233**; 50t. Two African Fish Eagles in flight (Zambia); 60t. Two African Fish Eagles perched (Zimbabwe); 70t. Bar-tailed Trogon (Malawi) (inscribed "apaloderma vittatum"); 80t. Purple-crested Turaco ("Lourie") (Swaziland); 1p. African Fish Eagle (Namibia); 2p. Stanley ("Blue") Crane (South Africa); 5p. Cattle Egret (Botswana) ... 7·00 7·50

The 70t. value stamp is not inscribed with the country of which the bird is a national symbol.

(Litho Cartor)

2004 (8 Dec). *Christmas. Flowers. T* **234** *and similar vert designs. Multicoloured.* P 13.

1028 80t. Type **234** ... 45 25
1029 2p.10 *Bulbine narcissifolia* ... 85 60
1030 3p.90 *Bulbiana hypogea* ... 1·60 1·90
1031 4p.70 *Hibiscus micranthus* ... 2·00 2·50
1028/31 *Set of 4* ... 4·50 4·75

235 Blackbeard's Store, Phalatswe

236 Cowpeas ("beans")

(Des Mike Smith. Litho BDT)

2005 (21 Mar). *Historical Buildings. T* **235** *and similar horiz designs. Multicoloured.* P 15×14.

1032 80t. Type **235** ... 45 25
1033 2p.10 Primary School ... 85 60
1034 3p.90 Telegraph Office, Phalatswe ... 1·60 1·90
1035 4p.70 Magistrate's Court, Phalatswe ... 2·00 2·50
1032/5 *Set of 4* ... 4·50 4·75

(Des Ann Gollifer. Litho Enschedé)

2005 (15 June). *Edible Crops. T* **236** *and similar vert designs. Multicoloured.* P 14.

1036 80t. Type **236** ... 40 20
1037 2p.10 Pearl millet ... 80 55
1038 3p.90 Sorghum ... 1·40 1·60
1039 4p.70 Watermelon ... 1·75 2·00
1036/9 *Set of 4* ... 4·00 4·00

237 Black-footed Cat with Prey

238 Namaqua Dove

(Des Roger Gorringe. Litho Cartor)

2005 (25 Oct). *Endangered Species. Black-footed Cat* (*Felis nigripes*). *T* **237** *and similar horiz designs. Multicoloured.* P 13½.

1040 80t. Type **237** ... 45 20
1041 2p.10 Black-footed cat ... 85 60
1042 3p.90 With cub ... 1·60 1·75
1043 4p.70 In close-up ... 2·00 2·25
1040/3 *Set of 4* ... 4·50 4·25
MS1044 160×185 mm. Nos. 1040/3, each ×2 ... 7·00 7·50

(Des Anja Denker. Litho BDT)

2005 (20 Dec). *Christmas. Doves and Pigeons. T* **238** *and similar vert designs. Multicoloured.* P 14½×15.

1045 80t. Type **238** ... 45 20
1046 2p.10 Red-eyed dove ... 85 60
1047 3p.90 Laughing doves (pair) ... 1·60 1·75
1048 4p.70 Green pigeons (pair) ... 2·00 2·25
1045/8 *Set of 4* ... 4·50 4·25

(238a) **(238b)**

2006 (26 Apr). *Nos. 980 and 983 surch as T* **238a/b**.

1048a 80t. on 90t. Reedbuck ... 30 25
1048b 2p.10 on 1p.95 Sable (*horiz*) ... 70 75

239 Nembwe

240 Oxen

(Des Tim Liversedge. Litho Enschedé)

2006 (30 May). *Okavango Fish. T* **239** *and similar horiz designs. Multicoloured.* P 13½×14.

1049 80t. Type **239** ... 25 30
1050 2p.10 Tiger fish ... 65 70
1051 3p.90 Pike ... 1·10 1·25
1052 4p.70 Spotted squeaker ... 1·50 1·75
1049/52 *Set of 4* ... 3·25 3·50

(Des Keeme Mosinyi. Litho Enschedé)

2006 (4 Sept). *Tswana Cattle. T* **240** *and similar vert designs. Multicoloured.* P 14×13½.

1053 1p.10 Type **240** ... 40 35
1054 2p.60 Cows and calves ... 85 75
1055 4p.10 Bulls ... 1·25 1·40
1056 4p.90 Horn shapes ... 1·50 1·75
1053/6 *Set of 4* ... 3·50 3·75

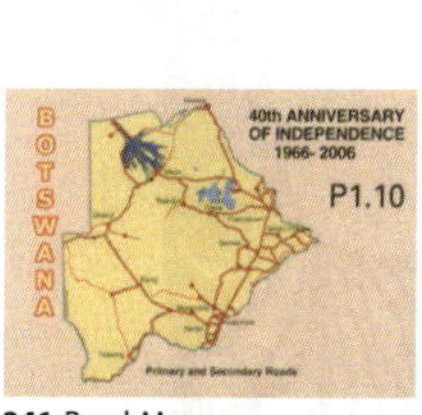

241 Road Map

242 *Hyphaene petersiana*

(Des Lucy Phalaagae. Litho Enschedé)

2006 (19 Oct). *40th Anniv of Independence. T* **241** *and similar horiz designs showing maps of Botswana. Multicoloured.* P 13½×14.

1057 1p.10 Type **241** ... 45 30
1058 2p.60 Population distribution ... 85 75
1059 4p.10 Mines and coal resources ... 1·50 1·60
1060 4p.90 National parks and game reserves ... 1·75 1·90
1057/60 *Set of 4* ... 4·00 4·00
MS1061 109×85 mm. Nos. 1057/60 ... 4·00 4·25

Nos. 1057/**MS**1061 were expected to be issued on 29 September 2006, but did not go on sale at post offices until 19 October. First day covers, prepared in advance, were cancelled with the original date.

(Des Gillian Condy. Litho Enschedé)

2006 (1 Dec). *Christmas. Trees. T* **242** *and similar vert designs. Multicoloured.* P 14×13½.

1062 1p.10 Type **242** ... 35 30
1063 2p.60 *Phoenix reclinata* ... 80 70
1064 4p.10 *Hyphaene petersiana* ... 1·25 1·40
1065 4p.90 *Phoenix reclinata* ... 1·50 2·00
1062/5 *Set of 4* ... 3·50 4·00

STAMP BOOKLETS

BOTSWANA
POSTAL SERVICES
THIS BOOKLET CONTAINS
20 × 2t stamps
PRICE
40t

B **1**

1989 (1 Dec)–**92**. *Covers as Type* B **1** *printed in blue on coloured card, each showing different stamp and postal logo. Stapled.*

SB1 20t. booklet containing 2t. (No. 620) in block of 10 (white cover) ... 75
SB2 40t. booklet containing 2t. (No. 620) in block of 20 (white cover) ... 1·00
SB3 50t. booklet containing 5t. (No. 623) in block of 10 (claret cover) ... 1·00
SB4 80t. booklet containing 8t. (No. 625) in block of 10 (grey cover) ... 1·40
a. Containing 8t. on 12t. (No. 725) (1992) ...
SB5 1p. booklet containing 5t. (No. 623) in block of 20 (claret cover) ... 1·50
SB6 1p. booklet containing 10t. (No. 626) in block of 10 (cinnamon cover) ... 1·50
a. Containing 10t. on 1t. (No. 690) (1990) ...
b. Containing 10t. on 12t. (No. 726) (1992) ...
SB7 1p.50 booklet containing 15t. (No. 628) in block of 10 (pink cover) ... 2·25
SB8 1p.60 booklet containing 8t. (No. 625) in block of 20 (grey cover) ... 2·50
a. Containing 8t. on 12t. (No. 725) (1992) ...
SB9 2p. booklet containing 10t. (No. 626) in block of 20 (cinnamon cover) ... 2·75
a. Containing 10t. on 1t. (No. 690) (1990) ...
b. Containing 10t. on 12t. (No. 726) (1992) ...
SB10 2p. booklet containing 20t. (No. 629) in block of 10 (pale blue cover) ... 2·75
a. Containing 20t. on 6t. (No. 691) (1990) ...
SB11 3p. booklet containing 15t. (No. 628) in block of 20 (pink cover) ... 3·75
SB12 3p. booklet containing 30t. (No. 631) in block of 10 (lemon cover) ... 3·75
SB13 4p. booklet containing 20t. (No. 629) in block of 20 (pale blue cover) ... 4·00
SB14 4p. booklet containing 40t. (No. 633) in block of 10 (pale green cover) ... 4·00
a. Containing 40t. on 3t. (No. 728) (1992) ...
b. Error. Containing 50t. on 12t. (No. 692) (1990) ...
SB15 6p. booklet containing 30t. (No. 631) in block of 20 (lemon cover) ... 6·00
SB16 8p. booklet containing 40t. (No. 633) in block of 20 (pale green cover) ... 8·00
a. Containing 40t. on 3t. (No. 728) (1992) ...

The booklets of twenty are larger, 81×69 mm.

No. SB14b, which was produced in error, has the face value of the booklet amended in manuscript.

This booklet contains
10 × 10t stamps
BOTSWANA POSTAL SERVICES
PRICE
P1.00

B **2**

1993 (4 Oct)–**94**. *Covers as Type* B **2** *printed in black on coloured card, each showing different stamp with postal logo. Stapled.*

SB17 1p. booklet containing 10t. (No. 742) in strip of 10 (yellow cover) ... 1·00
a. Containing 10t. on 12t. (No. 792)(1994) ... 1·00
SB18 1p.20 booklet containing 12t. (No. 743) in strip of 10 (pale orange cover) ... 1·25
SB19 1p.50 booklet containing 15t. (No. 744) in strip of 10 (orange cover) ... 1·40
SB20 2p. booklet containing 10t. (No. 742) in block of 20 (yellow cover) ... 1·75
a. Containing 10t. on 12t. (No. 792) (1994) ... 1·75
SB21 2p. booklet containing 20t. (No. 745) in strip of 10 (white cover) ... 1·75
SB22 2p.40 booklet containing 12t. (No. 743) in block of 20 (pale orange cover) ... 8·00
SB23 2p.50 booklet containing 25t. (No. 746) in strip of 10 (pink cover) ... 2·00
SB24 3p. booklet containing 15t. (No. 744) in block of 20 (orange cover) ... 2·25
SB25 3p.50 booklet containing 35t. (No. 747) in strip of 10 (green cover) ... 3·50
SB26 4p. booklet containing 20t. (No. 745) in block of 20 (white cover) ... 3·00
SB27 4p. booklet containing 40t. (No. 748) in strip of 10 (blue cover) ... 3·00
SB28 4p.50 booklet containing 45t. (No. 749) in strip of 10 (pale rose-lilac cover) ... 3·25
SB29 5p. booklet containing 25t. (No. 746) in block of 20 (pink cover) ... 3·50
SB30 5p. booklet containing 50t. (No. 750) in strip of 10 (grey cover) ... 3·50
SB31 7p. booklet containing 35t. (No. 747) in block of 20 (green cover) ... 4·25

SB32 8p. booklet containing 40t. (No. 748) in block of 20 (blue cover) 4·50
SB33 9p. booklet containing 45t. (No. 749) in block of 20 (pale rose-lilac cover) 5·00
SB34 10p. booklet containing 50t. (No. 750) in block of 20 (grey cover) 5·50

The booklets of twenty are larger, 75×80 mm.

1996. *Covers as Nos. SB17 and SB21 cut down to 75×40 mm. Stamps attached by selvedge.*

SB35 1p. booklet containing 5t. and 15t. (Nos. 741 and 744) each in strip of 5 (yellow cover)....
SB36 1p. booklet containing 20t. (No. 809) in strip of 5 (white cover)

Nos. SB35/6 were issued from machines at Gaborone and Francistown Main Post Offices. They were subsequently replaced by booklets with plain white covers containing 1p. worth of current stamps attached by the selvedges.

B 3

2002 (29 Apr)–**04**. *Covers as Type* B **3**. *Stamps attached by selvedge.*

SB37 5p. booklet containing 50t. (No. 954) in strip of 10 40·00
SB38 5p. booklet containing 50t. (No. 958) in strip of 10 40·00
SB39 5p. booklet containing 50t. (No. 964) in strip of 10 40·00
SB40 5p. booklet containing 50t. (No. 968) in strip of 10 40·00
SB41 5p. booklet containing 55t. (No. 972) in strip of 10 40·00
SB42 5p. booklet containing 55t. (No. 979) in strip of 10 40·00
SB43 5p. booklet containing 55t. (No. 990) in strip of 10 40·00
SB44 5p. booklet containing 55t. (No. 994) in strip of 10 40·00
SB45 5p. booklet containing 55t. (No. 1000) in strip of 10 (2003) 40·00
SB46 5p. booklet containing 55t. (No. 1004) in block of 10 (2003) 40·00
SB47 5p. booklet containing 55t. (No. 1009) in strip of 10 (2003) 40·00
SB48 5p. booklet containing 55t. (No. 1015) in strip of 10 (2004) 40·00

Nos. SB41/8 sold for 5p.50.

POSTAGE DUE STAMPS

BECHUANALAND PROTECTORATE
(D 1)

BECHUANALAND PROTECTORATE
(D 2)

1926 (Jan). *Nos. D9/10 and D13 of Great Britain, optd with Types* D **1** *or* D **2** *(2d.).*

D1 ½d. emerald (No. D10) 6·50 90·00
D2 1d. carmine (No. D9) 6·50 55·00
D3 2d. agate (No. D13) 6·00 85·00
D1/3 *Set of 3* 17·00 £200

D 3

2d Normal

2d Large "d." (R. 9/6, 10/6)

Serif on "d" (R. 1/6)

(Typo D.L.R.)

1932 (12 Dec)–**58**. *Ordinary paper. Wmk Mult Script CA.* P 14.

D4 D **3** ½d. sage-green 6·00 50·00
D5 1d. carmine 7·00 9·00
a. Chalk-surfaced paper (27.11.58) 1·50 22·00
D6 2d. violet 9·00 50·00
a. Large "d" £120
b. Serif on "d" £170

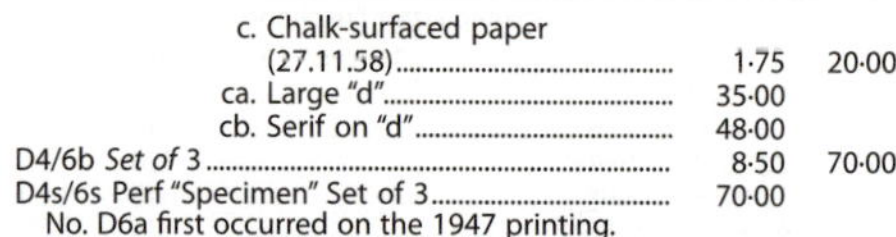

c. Chalk-surfaced paper (27.11.58) 1·75 20·00
ca. Large "d" 35·00
cb. Serif on "d" 48·00
D4/6b *Set of 3* 8·50 70·00
D4s/6s Perf "Specimen" Set of 3 70·00

No. D6a first occurred on the 1947 printing.

1c (I) (Small)

1c (II) (Large)

1961 (14 Feb). *Surch as T* **27**. *Chalk-surfaced paper (Nos. D7/8).*

D7 D **3** 1c. on 1d. (Type I) 25 50
a. Type II (Apr) 15 1·75
ab. Double surch £180
ac. Ordinary paper 16·00 50·00
D8 2c. on 2d. (Type I) 25 1·50
a. Large "d" 7·50
b. Serif on "d" 11·00
c. Type II 15 2·00
ca. Large "d" 4·75
cb. Serif on "d" 8·00
d. Ordinary paper. Type II £100 £110
da. Large "d" £400
D9 5c. on ½d. 20 60
D7/9 *Set of 3* 45 2·40

1961 (15 Nov). *As Type* D **3** *but values in cents. Chalk-surfaced paper. Wmk Mult Script CA.* P 14.

D10 1c. carmine 20 2·00
D11 2c. violet 20 2·00
D12 5c. green 40 2·00
D10/12 *Set of 3* 70 5·50

REPUBLIC OF BOTSWANA
(D 4)

D **5** African Elephant

D **6** Common Zebra

1967 (1 Mar). *Nos. D10/12 optd with Type* D **4**.

D13 1c. carmine 15 1·75
D14 2c. violet 15 1·75
D15 5c. green 20 1·75
D13/15 *Set of 3* 45 4·75

(Des and litho B.W.)

1971 (9 June). P 13½.

D16 D **5** 1c. carmine 1·10 3·25
D17 2c. bluish violet 1·40 3·50
D18 6c. sepia 1·75 5·50
D19 14c. blue-green 2·00 7·50
D16/19 *Set of 4* 5·50 18·00

(Des M. Bryan. Litho Govt Printer, Pretoria)

1977 (18 Apr)–**84**. P 12½.

D20 D **6** 1t. black and vermilion (1978) 1·25 2·75
a. Black and bright orange (1980) 1·75 2·75
b. Perf 14 (1982?) 1·00 2·75
D21 2t. black and emerald 40 3·00
a. Perf 14 (5.8.81*) 1·00 3·00
D22 4t. black and red 40 3·00
a. Perf 14 (28.9.81*) 1·00 3·00
D23 10t. black and deep ultramarine 40 2·75
a. Perf 14 (7.3.84) 1·00 2·75
D24 16t. black and chestnut 65 3·50
a. Perf 14 (7.3.84) 1·25 3·50
D20/24 *Set of 5* 2·75 13·50
D20b/24a *Set of 5* 4·75 13·50

*First supplies of Nos. D20b, D21a and D22a were sent to Botswana in June 1981. The dates quoted for the 2t. and 4t. are earliest known dates of use. Early use of the 1t. has yet to be identified.

Nos. D20b/4a are on white paper. A subsequent printing in September 1988 was on poorer grade paper. Stamps perforated 14 measure 24 mm across from perforation to perforation.

Type I

Type II

Two Types of Nos. D25/9 (Zimbabwe ptgs):—

Type I. Grass sparse. No shading dots on zebra. Zebra's right ear has right edge missing.

Type II. Grass thicker. Shading dots on zebra. Right ear almost complete.

(Litho National Printing & Packaging, Zimbabwe)

1989 (1 Apr)–**96**. P 14½.

D25 D **6** 1t. black and reddish orange (I) 30 1·00
a. Type II. Perf 14 (1993) 40 1·25
ab. Perf 14½ 10 10
D26 2t. black and emerald (I) 30 1·00
a. Type II. Perf 14 (1993) 40 1·25
ab. Perf 14½ 10 10
D27 4t. black and bright scarlet (I) 30 1·00
a. Type II. Perf 14 (1993) 40 1·25
ab. Perf 14½ 10 10
D28 10t. black and deep ultramarine (I) 35 1·00
a. Type II. Perf 14 (1993) 40 1·25
ab. Perf 14½ 10 10
D29 16t. black and reddish brown (I) 50 1·25
a. Type II. Perf 14 (1993) 50 1·50
ab. Perf 14½ 10 10
D25/9 *Set of 5* 1·60 4·75
D25a/9a *Set of 5* 1·90 5·75

Nos. D25a/9a measure 26 mm across from perforation to perforation.

POSTAL FISCAL STAMPS

The following stamps issued for fiscal purposes were each allowed to be used for postal purposes for a short time. No. F2 was used by the public because the word "POSTAGE" had not been obliterated and No. F3 because the overprint did not include the words "Revenue only" as did the contemporary fiscal overprints for Basutoland and Swaziland.

Bechuanaland Protectorate
(F 1)

£5
(F 2)

Bechuanaland Protectorate.
(F 3)

1910 (July). *No. 266a of Transvaal optd with Type* F **1** *by Transvaal Govt Ptg Wks, Pretoria.*

F1 6d. black and brown-orange (Bl-Blk) £160 £325

No. F1 was supplied to Assistant Commissioners in January 1907 for revenue purposes. The "POSTAGE" inscription was not obliterated, however, and the stamp is known postally used for a period of a year from July 1910.

1918. *No. 15 surch with Type* F **2** *at top.*

F2 **4** £5 on 1s. green and black (F.C. £650) £12000

1921. *No. 4b of South Africa optd with Type* F **3**, *in varying positions.*

F3 1d. scarlet 42·00 £130
a. Opt double, one albino £160

Lesotho
formerly Basutoland

Stamps of CAPE OF GOOD HOPE were used in Basutoland from about 1876, initially cancelled by upright oval with framed number type postmarks of that colony. Cancellation numbers known to have been used in Basutoland are 133 (Quthing), 156 (Mafeteng), 210 (Mohaleshoek), 277 (Morija), 281 (Maseru), 317 (Thlotse Heights) and 688 (Teyateyaneng).

From 1910 until 1933 the stamps of SOUTH AFRICA were in use. Stamps of the Union provinces are also known used in Basutoland during the early years of this period and can also be found cancelled-to-order during 1932–33.

The following post offices and postal agencies existed in Basutoland before December 1933. Stamps of Cape of Good Hope or South Africa with recognisable postmarks from them are worth a premium. For a few of the smaller offices or agencies there are, as yet, no actual examples recorded. Dates given are those generally accepted as the year in which the office was first opened.

Bokong (1931)	Motsekuoa (1915)
Butha Buthe (1907)	Mount Morosi (1918)
Jonathan's (1927)	Mphotos (1914)
Khabos (1927)	Peka (1908)
Khetisas (1930)	Phamong (1932)
Khukhune (1933)	Pitseng (1921)
Kolonyama (1914)	Qachasnek (1895)
Kueneng (1914)	Qalo (1923?)
Leribe (1890)	Quthing (1882)
Mafeteng (1874)	Rankakalas (1933)
Majara (1912)	Roma Mission (1913)
Makhoa (1932)	Sebapala (1930)
Makoalis (1927)	Seforong (1924)
Mamathes (1919)	Sehlabathebe (1921)
Mapoteng (1925)	Sekake (1931)
Marakabeis (1932)	Teyateyaneng (1886)
Maseru (1872)	Thaba Bosigo (1913)
Maseru Rail (1915?)	Thabana Morena (1922)
Mashai (1929)	Thabaneng (1914)
Matsaile (1930)	Thaba Tseka (1929)
Mekading (1914)	Thlotse Heights (1872)
Mofokas (1915)	Tsepo (1923)
Mohaleshoek (1873)	Tsoelike (1927)
Mokhotlong (1921)	Tsoloane (1918)
Morija (1884)	

For further details of the postal history of Basutoland see *The Cancellations and Postal Markings of Basutoland/Lesotho* by A. H. Scott, published by Collectors Mail Auctions (Pty) Ltd, Cape Town, from which the above has been, with permission, extracted.

PRICES FOR STAMPS ON COVER TO 1945

Nos. 1/19	*from* × 5
Nos. 11/14	*from* × 6
Nos. 15/17	*from* × 10
Nos. 18/28	*from* × 6
Nos. 29/31	*from* × 10
Nos. O1/4	*from* × 4
Nos. D1/2	*from* × 25

CROWN COLONY

1 King George V, Nile Crocodile and Mountains

(Recess Waterlow)

1933 (1 Dec). Wmk Mult Script CA. P 12½.

No.	Type	Description	Unused	Used
1	**1**	½d. emerald	1·00	1·75
2		1d. scarlet	75	1·25
3		2d. bright purple	1·00	80
4		3d. bright blue	75	1·25
5		4d. grey	2·00	7·00
6		6d. orange-yellow	2·25	1·75
7		1s. red-orange	2·25	4·50
8		2s.6d. sepia	23·00	45·00
9		5s. violet	50·00	70·00
10		10s. olive-green	£140	£150
1/10 *Set of* 10			£200	£250
1s/10s Perf "Specimen" *Set of* 10			£300	

Diagonal line by turret (Plate 2A R. 10/1 and 10/2)

Dot to left of chapel (Plate 2B R. 8/3)

Dot by flagstaff (Plate 4 R. 8/4)

Dash by turret (Plate 4 R. 3/6)

1935 (4 May). *Silver Jubilee. As Nos. 11/14 of Botswana.* P 13½×14.

No.	Description	Unused	Used
11	1d. deep blue and carmine	55	2·00
	f. Diagonal line by turret	£100	£140
12	2d. ultramarine and grey	65	2·00
	f. Diagonal line by turret	90·00	£150
	g. Dot to left of chapel	£140	£180
13	3d. brown and deep blue	3·75	5·00
	g. Dot to left of chapel	£180	
	h. Dot by flagstaff	£225	
	i. Dash by turret	£250	
14	6d. slate and purple	3·75	5·00
	g. Dot to left of chapel	£250	
	h. Dot by flagstaff	£250	£300
	i. Dash by turret	£250	
11/14 *Set of* 4		8·00	12·50
11s/14s Perf "Specimen" *Set of* 4		£110	

1937 (12 May). *Coronation. As Nos. 115/17 of Botswana.* P 14.

No.	Description	Unused	Used
15	1d. scarlet	35	1·25
16	2d. bright purple	50	1·25
17	3d. bright blue	60	1·25
15/17 *Set of* 3		1·25	3·25
15s/17s Perf "Specimen" *Set of* 3		80·00	

2 King George VI, Nile Crocodile and Mountains

Tower flaw (R. 2/4)

(Recess Waterlow)

1938 (1 Apr). Wmk Mult Script CA. P 12½.

No.	Type	Description	Unused	Used
18	**2**	½d. green	30	1·25
19		1d. scarlet	50	70
		a. Tower flaw	£140	
20		1½d. light blue	40	50
21		2d. bright purple	30	60
22		3d. bright blue	30	1·25
23		4d. grey	1·50	3·50
24		6d. orange-yellow	1·25	1·50
25		1s. red-orange	1·25	1·00
26		2s.6d. sepia	12·00	8·50
27		5s. violet	29·00	9·50
28		10s. olive-green	29·00	17·00
18/28 *Set of* 11			70·00	40·00
18s/28s Perf "Specimen" *Set of* 11			£250	

Basutoland
(**3**)

1945 (3 Dec). *Victory. Stamps of South Africa, optd with T* **3**, *inscr alternately in English and Afrikaans.*

No.	Type	Description	*Un pair*	*Used pair*	*Used Single*
29	**55**	1d. brown and carmine	40	60	10
30	**56**	2d. slate-blue and violet	40	50	10
31	**57**	3d. deep blue and blue	40	70	15
29/31 *Set of* 3			1·10	1·75	30

1947 (17 Feb). *Royal Visit. As Nos. 132/5 of Botswana.*

No.	Type	Description	Unused	Used
32	**4**	1d. scarlet	10	10
33	**5**	2d. green	10	10
34	**6**	3d. ultramarine	10	10
35	**7**	1s. mauve	15	10
32/5 *Set of* 4			40	30
32s/5s Perf "Specimen" *Set of* 4			90·00	

1948 (1 Dec). *Royal Silver Wedding. As Nos. 136/7 of Botswana.*

No.	Description	Unused	Used
36	1½d. ultramarine	20	10
37	10s. grey-olive	35·00	35·00

1949 (10 Oct). *75th Anniv of Universal Postal Union. As Nos. 138/41 of Botswana.*

No.	Description	Unused	Used
38	1½d. blue	20	1·50
39	3d. deep blue	1·75	2·00
40	6d. orange	1·00	3·50
41	1s. red-brown	50	1·25
38/41 *Set of* 4		3·00	7·50

1953 (3 June). *Coronation. As No. 142 of Botswana.*

No.	Description	Unused	Used
42	2d. black and reddish purple	40	30

8 Qiloane

9 Mohair (Shearing Angora Goats)

(Recess D.L.R.)

1954 (18 Oct)–**58**. *Designs as T* **8/9**. Wmk Mult Script CA. P 11½ (10s.) or 13½ (others).

No.	Description	Unused	Used
43	½d. grey-black and sepia	10	10
44	1d. grey-black and bluish green	10	10
45	2d. deep bright blue and orange	60	10
46	3d. yellow-green and deep rose-red	80	30
	a. Yellow-green and rose (27.11.58)	8·50	1·75
47	4½d. indigo and deep ultramarine	70	15
48	6d. chestnut and deep grey-green	1·25	15
49	1s. bronze-green and purple	1·25	30
50	1s.3d. brown and turquoise-green	20·00	6·00
51	2s.6d. deep ultramarine and crimson	20·00	8·00
	a. Brt ultram & crimson-lake (27.11.58)	60·00	18·00
52	5s. black and carmine-red	5·50	8·50
53	10s. black and maroon	27·00	23·00
43/53 *Set of* 11		70·00	42·00

Designs: *Horiz as T* **8**—1d. Orange River; 2d. Mosuto horseman; 3d. Basuto household; 4½d. Maletsunyane Falls; 6d. Herd-boy playing lesiba; 1s. Pastoral scene; 1s.3d. Aeroplane over Lancers Gap; 2s.6d. Old Fort Leribe; 5s. Mission Cave House.

½d. ▬
(**19**)

20 "Chief Moshoeshoe I" (engraving by Delangle)

1959 (1 Aug). *No. 45 surch with T* **19**, *by South African Govt Ptr, Pretoria.*

No.	Description	Unused	Used
54	½d. on 2d. deep bright blue and orange	10	15

(Des from drawings by James Walton. Recess Waterlow)

1959 (15 Dec). *Basutoland National Council. T* **20** *and similar vert designs.* W w **12**. P 13×13½.

No.	Description	Unused	Used
55	3d. black and yellow-olive	30	10
56	1s. carmine and yellow-green	30	10
57	1s.3d. ultramarine and red-orange	50	45
55/7 *Set of* 3		1·00	55

Designs:—1s. Council house; 1s.3d. Mosuto horseman.

(New Currency. 100 cents = 1 rand)

½c. (**23**) 1c. (**24**) 2c (**25**)

2½c (I) 2½c (II) 3½c (I) 3½c (II)

5c (I) 5c (II) 10c (I) 10c (II)

12½c (I) 12½c (II) 50c (I) 50c (II)

25c (I) 25c (I) 25c (II)

R1 (I) R1 (II) R1 (III)

1961 (14 Feb). *Nos. 43/53 surch with T* **23** *(½c.),* **24** *(1c.) or as T* **25** *(others) by South African Govt Printer, Pretoria.*

No.	Description	Unused	Used
58	½c. on ½d. grey-black and sepia	10	10
	a. Surch double	£450	
59	1c. on 1d. grey-black and bluish green	10	10
60	2c. on 2d. deep bright blue and orange	10	10
	a. Surch inverted	£130	
61	2½c. on 3d. yellow-green and rose (Type I)	10	10
	a. Type II	10	10
	b. Type II inverted	†	£1500
62	3½c. on 4½d. indigo & deep ultram (Type I)	10	10
	a. Type II	1·50	4·75
63	5c. on 6d. chestnut & dp grey-green (Type I)	10	10
	a. Type II	15	10
64	10c. on 1s. bronze-green and purple (Type I)	10	10
	a. Type II	95·00	£110
65	12½c. on 1s.3d. brown & turq-green (Type I)	3·50	1·00
	a. Type II	2·75	75
66	25c. on 2s.6d. bright ultramarine and crimson-lake (Type I)	30	60
	a. Type II	30·00	9·00
	b. Type III	30	60
67	50c. on 5s. black and carmine-red (Type I)	1·25	1·40
	a. Type II	1·50	2·25
68	1r. on 10s. black and maroon (Type I)	29·00	16·00
	a. Type II	15·00	35·00
	b. Type III	15·00	16·00
58/68b *Set of* 11		18·00	17·00

There were two printings of the 2½c. Type II, differing in the position of the surcharge on the stamps.

Examples of the 2c. surcharge are known in a fount similar to Type **24** (*Price* £150, *unused*).

26 Basuto Household

(Recess D.L.R.)

1961–63. *As Nos. 43/53 but values in cents as in T* **26**. Wmk Mult Script CA. P 13½ or 11½ (1r.).

69 ½c. grey-black and sepia (as ½d.) (25.9.62) 10 20
a. Imperf (pair) £275
70 1c. grey-blk & bluish grn (as 1d.) (25.9.62) 10 40
71 2c. dp but blue & orange (as 2d.) (25.9.62) 50 1·40
72 2½c. yellow-green & deep rose-red (14.2.61) 80 20
a. Pale yellow-green & rose-red (22.5.62) 12·00 1·50
73 3½c. indigo & dp ultram (as 4½d.) (25.9.62) 30 1·50
74 5c. chestnut and deep grey-green (as 6d.) (10.8.62) 60 75
75 10c. bronze-green & pur (as 1s.) (22.10.62) 30 40
76 12½c. brown and turquoise-green (as 1s.3d.) (17.12.62) 17·00 7·50
77 25c. deep ultramarine and crimson (as 2s.6d.) (25.9.62) 6·50 6·50
78 50c. black & carmine-red (as 5s.) (22.10.62) 18·00 15·00
79 1r. black and maroon (as 10s.) (4.2.63) 40·00 15·00
a. Black and light maroon (16.12.63) 60·00 24·00
69/79 *Set of 11* 75·00 45·00

1963 (4 June). *Freedom from Hunger. As No. 182 of Botswana.*
80 12½c. reddish violet 40 15

1963 (2 Sept). *Red Cross Centenary. As Nos. 183/4 of Botswana.*
81 2½c. red and black 20 10
82 12½c. red and blue 80 60

1964. *As Nos. 70, 72, 74, 76 and 78, but W w* **12**.
84 1c. grey-black and bluish green (11.8.64) 10 20
86 2½c. pale yellow-green and rose-red (10.3.64) 15 15
88 5c. chestnut and deep grey-green (10.11.64) 30 40
90 12½c. brown and turquoise-green (10.11.64) 4·25 1·50
92 50c. black and carmine-red (29.9.64) 7·25 11·00
84/92 *Set of 5* 10·50 12·00

SELF-GOVERNMENT

28 Mosotho Woman and Child

29 Maseru Border Post

1965 (10 May). *New Constitution. T* **28/9** *and similar horiz designs. Multicoloured.* W w **12**. P 14×13½.
94 2½c. Type **28** 20 10
w. Wmk inverted 24·00 15·00
95*a* 3½c. Type **29** 25 20
96 5c. Mountain scene 25 20
w. Wmk inverted 24·00 15·00
97 12½c. Legislative Buildings 45 70
94/7 *Set of 4* 1·10 1·10

1965 (17 May). *I.T.U. Centenary. As Nos. 190/1 of Botswana.*
98 1c. orange-red and bright purple 15 10
99 20c. light blue and orange-brown 50 30

1965 (25 Oct). *International Co-operation Year. As Nos. 192/3 of Botswana.*
100 ½c. reddish purple & turquoise-green 10 10
101 12½c. deep bluish green and lavender 45 35

1966 (24 Jan). *Churchill Commemoration. As Nos. 194/7 of Botswana.*
102 1c. new blue 15 50
103 2½c. deep green 40 10
104 10c. brown 65 30
105 22½c. bluish violet 1·00 70
102/5 *Set of 4* 2·00 1·40

Basutoland attained independence on 4 October 1966 as the Kingdom of Lesotho.

INDEPENDENT KINGDOM

King Moshoeshoe II,
4 October 1966–November 1990 (deposed)

33 Moshoeshoe I and Moshoeshoe II

(Des and photo Harrison)

1966 (4 Oct). *Independence.* P 12½×13.
106 **33** 2½c. light brown, black and red 10 10
107 5c. light brown, black and new blue 10 10
108 10c. light brown, black and emerald 15 10
109 20c. light brown, black and bright purple 20 15
106/9 *Set of 4* 45 30

LESOTHO
(34)

35 "Education Culture and Science"

1966 (1 Nov). *Stamps of Basutoland optd as T* **34**.

A. On Nos. 69/71 and 73/9 (Script CA wmk)
110A ½c. grey-black and sepia 10 10
111A 1c. grey-black and bluish green 10 10
112A 2c. deep bright blue and orange 60 10
114A 3½c. indigo and deep ultramarine 30 10
115A 5c. chestnut and deep grey-green 10 10
116A 10c. bronze-green and purple 10 10
117A 12½c. brown and turquoise-green 4·50 35
118A 25c. deep ultramarine and crimson 30 20
119A 50c. black and carmine-red 80 80
120A 1r. black and maroon 75 3·50
a. "LSEOTHO" 60·00
b. Opt double £110
ba. Ditto. "LSEOTHO"
110A/20A *Set of 10* 6·50 4·50

B. On Nos. 84/92 and unissued 1r. (wmk w **12**).
111B 1c. grey-black and bluish green 10 10
113B 2½c. pale yellow-green and rose-red 50 10
115B 5c. chestnut and deep grey-green 20 10
117B 12½c. brown and turquoise-green 30 20
119B 50c. black and carmine-red 70 50
120B 1r. black and maroon 65 75
a. "LSEOTHO" 42·00 50·00
111B/20B *Set of 6* 2·00 1·40

(Des V. Whiteley. Litho D.L.R.)

1966 (1 Dec). *20th Anniv of U.N.E.S.C.O.* P 14½×14.
121 **35** 2½c. orange-yellow and emerald-green 10 10
122 5c. light green and olive 15 10
123 12½c. light blue and red 35 15
124 25c. red-orange and deep greenish blue 60 75
121/4 *Set of 4* 1·10 50

36 Maize

37 Moshoeshoe II

(Des and photo Harrison)

1967 (1 Apr). *Designs as T* **36/7**. No wmk. P 14½×13½ (2r.) or 13½×14½ (others).
125 ½c. bluish green and light bluish violet 10 10
126 1c. sepia and rose-red 10 10
127 2c. orange-yellow and light green 10 50
128 2½c. black and ochre 10 10
129 3½c. chalky blue and yellow 10 20
130 5c. bistre and new blue 20 10
131 10c. yellow-brown and bluish grey 10 10
132 12½c. black and red-orange 20 10
133 25c. black and bright blue 55 20
134 50c. black, new blue and turquoise 4·50 1·50
135 1r. multicoloured 65 75
136 2r. black, gold and magenta 1·00 1·75
125/36 *Set of 12* 6·25 4·50

Designs: *Horiz as T* **36**—1c. Cattle; 2c. Agaves (wrongly inscr "Aloes"); 2½c. Basotho Hat; 3½c. Merino Sheep ("Wool"); 5c. Basotho Pony; 10c. Wheat; 12½c. Angora Goat ("Mohair"); 25c. Maletsunyane Falls; 50c. Diamonds; 1r. Arms of Lesotho.

See also Nos. 147/59 and 191/203.

46 Students and University

(Des V. Whiteley. Photo Harrison)

1967 (7 Apr). *First Conferment of University Degrees.* P 14×14½.
137 **46** 1c. sepia, ultramarine and light yellow-orange 10 10
138 2½c. sepia, ultramarine and light greenish blue 10 10
139 12½c. sepia, ultramarine and rose 10 10
140 25c. sepia, ultramarine and light violet 15 15
137/40 *Set of 4* 30 30

47 Statue of Moshoeshoe I

(Des and photo Harrison)

1967 (4 Oct). *First Anniv of Independence. T* **47** *and similar triangular designs.* P 14½×14.
141 2½c. black and light yellow-green 10 10
142 12½c. multicoloured 25 15
143 25c. black, green and light ochre 35 25
141/3 *Set of 3* 65 40

Designs:—12½c. Lesotho flag; 25c. Crocodile (national emblem).

50 Lord Baden-Powell and Scout Saluting

(Des V. Whiteley. Photo Harrison)

1967 (1 Nov). *60th Anniv of Scout Movement.* P 14×14½.
144 **50** 15c. multicoloured 20 10

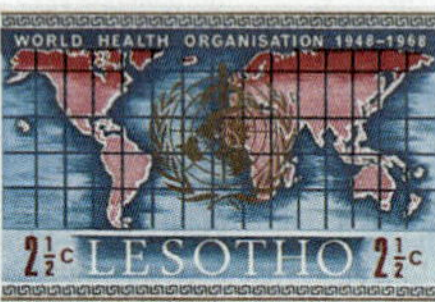

51 W.H.O. Emblem and World Map

(Des G. Vasarhelyi. Photo Harrison)

1968 (7 Apr). *20th Anniv of World Health Organization. T* **51** *and similar horiz design.* P 14×14½.
145 2½c. blue, gold and carmine-red 15 10
a. Gold (emblem) omitted
146 25c. multicoloured 45 60

Design:—25c. Nurse and child.

53 Basotho Hat

54 Sorghum

1968–69. *As Nos. 125/36 and T* **54**, but wmk **53** (sideways on 2r.).
147 ½c. bluish green and light bluish violet (26.11.68) 10 10
a. Blue-green and violet (30.9.69) 1·50 1·50
148 1c. sepia and rose-red (26.11.68) 10 10
149 2c. orange-yellow and light green (26.11.68) 10 10
a. Orange-yellow and yellow-green (30.9.69) 1·00 1·00
150 2½c. black and ochre (21.10.68) 15 10
a. Black and yellow-ochre (30.9.69) 1·00 1·00
151 3c. chocolate, green and yellow-brown (1.8.68) 15 15
152 3½c. chalky blue and yellow (26.11.68) 15 10
153 5c. bistre and new blue (22.7.68) 60 10
154 10c. yellow-brown and pale bluish grey (26.11.68) 15 10
155 12½c. black and red-orange (30.9.69) 60 35
156 25c. black and bright blue (30.9.69) 1·50 1·00
157 50c. black, new blue and turquoise (30.9.69) 11·00 3·25
158 1r. multicoloured (26.11.68) 1·50 2·75
159 2r. black, gold and magenta (30.9.69) 8·00 13·00
147/59 *Set of 13* 21·00 18·00

55 Running Hunters

(Des Jennifer Toombs. Photo Harrison)

1968 (1 Nov). *Rock Paintings. T* **55** *and similar designs.* W **53** (sideways on 5c., 15c.). P 14×14½ (5c., 15c.) or 14½×14 (others).
160 3c. yellow-brown, light blue-green and blackish green 25 10
161 3½c. greenish yellow, yellow-olive and sepia 30 10
162 5c. Venetian red, yellow-ochre and blackish brown 35 10
163 10c. yellow, rose and deep maroon 45 10
164 15c. light buff, pale olive-yellow and blackish brown 60 30
165 20c. yellow-green, greenish yellow and blackish brown 70 55
166 25c. yellow, orange-brown and black 80 75
160/6 *Set of 7* 3·00 1·75

Designs: *Horiz*—3½c. Baboons; 10c. Archers; 20c. Eland; 25c. Hunting scene. *Vert*—5c. Javelin throwing; 15c. Blue Cranes.

62 Queen Elizabeth II Hospital

(Des C. R. Househam and G. Drummond. Litho P.B.)

1969 (11 Mar). *Centenary of Maseru (capital). T* **62** *and similar horiz designs. Multicoloured.* W **53** (sideways). P 14×13½.

167	2½c. Type **62**	10	10
168	10c. Lesotho Radio Station	10	10
169	12½c. Leabua Jonathan Airport	35	10
170	25c. Royal Palace	25	15
167/70	*Set of 4*	65	30

66 Rally Car passing Mosotho Horseman

(Des P. Wheeler. Photo Harrison)

1969 (26 Sept). *Roof of Africa Car Rally. T* **66** *and similar horiz designs.* W **53**. P 14.

171	2½c. yellow, mauve and plum	15	10
172	12½c. cobalt, greenish yellow and olive-grey	20	10
173	15c. blue, black and mauve	20	10
174	20c. black, red and yellow	20	10
171/4	*Set of 4*	65	30

Designs:—12½c. Rally car on mountain road; 15c. Chequered flags and mountain scenery; 20c. Map of rally route and Rally Trophy.

71 Gryponyx and Footprints

75 Moshoeshoe I, when a Young Man

(Des Jennifer Toombs. Photo Harrison)

1970 (5 Jan). *Prehistoric Footprints (1st series). T* **71** *and similar designs.* W **53** (sideways*). P 14×14½ (3c.) or 14½×14 (others).

175	3c. pale brown, yellow-brown and sepia	90	70
176	5c. dull purple, pink and sepia	1·10	30
	w. Wmk hat pointing right	3·25	
177	10c. pale yellow, black and sepia	1·40	35
178	15c. olive-yellow, black and sepia	2·00	2·25
179	25c. cobalt and lack	2·75	2·25
175/9	*Set of 5*	7·25	5·25

Designs: (60×23 *mm*)—3c. Dinosaur footprints at Moyeni. (40×24 *mm*)—10c. Plateosauravus and footprints; 15c. Tritylodon and footprints; 25c. Massospondylus and footprints.

*The normal sideways watermark shows the hat pointing left, *when seen from the back of the stamp.*

See also Nos. 596/8.

(Des G. Vasarhelyi. Litho D.L.R.)

1970 (11 Mar). *Death Centenary of King Moshoeshoe I. T* **75** *and similar vert design.* W **53**. P 13½.

180	2½c. pale green and magenta	10	10
181	25c. pale blue and chesnut	20	20

Design:—25c. Moshoeshoe I as an old man.

77 U.N. Emblem and "25"

(Des V. Whiteley. Litho Questa)

1970 (26 June). *25th Anniv of United Nations. T* **77** *and similar horiz designs.* W **53** (sideways). P 14½×14.

182	2½c. light pink, light blue and maroon	10	10
183	10c. multicoloured	10	10
184	12½c. brown-red, cobalt and drab	10	25
185	25c. multicoloured	15	65
182/5	*Set of 4*	30	60

Designs:— 10c. U.N. Building; 12½c. "People of the World"; 25c. Symbolic Dove.

78 Basotho Hat Gift Shop, Maseru

(Des G. Drummond. Litho Questa)

1970 (27 Oct). *Tourism. T* **78** *and similar horiz designs. Multicoloured.* W **53** (sideways). P 14.

186	2½c. Type **78**	10	10
187	5c. Trout fishing	20	10
188	10c. Pony trekking	25	10
189	12½c. Skiing	50	10
190	20c. Holiday Inn, Maseru	40	50
186/90	*Set of 5*	1·25	70

79 Maize

80 Lammergeier

(Des Harrison. Litho Questa)

1971 (4 Jan–1Apr). *As Nos. 147/58 but in new format omitting portrait of Moshoeshoe II, as in T* **79**. *4c. and 2r. in new designs.* W **53** *(sideways* except 2r.).* P 14.

191	½c. blue-green and light bluish violet	10	10
192	1c. brown and orange-red	10	10
193	2c. yellow and green	10	10
	w. Wmk top of hat to right		
194	2½c. black, olive-green and yellow-ochre	10	10
195	3c. brown, green and yellow-ochre	10	10
196	3½c. indigo and yellow	10	10
196*a*	4c. multicoloured (1.4.71)	20	10
	aw. Wmk top of hat to right		
197	5c. yellow-brown and pale blue	15	10
198	10c. orange-brown and grey-blue	15	10
199	12½c. chocolate and yellow-orange	25	30
200	25c. slate and pale bright blue	60	40
201	50c. black, pale blue and turquoise-green	6·00	4·50
202	1r. multicoloured	1·25	1·75
203	2r. yellow-brown and ultramarine	70	2·25
191/203	*Set of 14*	8·50	8·50

Designs: *Horiz*—4c. National flag. *Vert*—2r. Statue of Moshoeshoe I.

*The normal sideways watermark shows top of hat to left, as seen from the back of the stamp.

For 2r. value without watermark see No. 401.

(Des R. Granger Barrett. Litho J.W.)

1971 (1 Mar). *Birds. T* **80** *and similar vert designs. Multicoloured.* W **53**. P 14.

204	2½c. Type **80**	2·50	20
205	5c. Bald Ibis	3·50	2·50
206	10c. Rufous Rockjumper	3·50	2·00
207	12½c. Blue Bustard	3·75	3·50
208	15c. Painted Snipe	4·25	4·50
209	20c. Golden-breasted Bunting	4·25	4·50
210	25c. Ground Woodpecker	4·75	4·50
204/10	*Set of 7*	24·00	19·00

81 Lionel Collett Dam

(Des G. Drummond. Litho J.W.)

1971 (15 July). *Soil Conservation. T* **81** *and similar horiz designs. Multicoloured.* W **53** (sideways). P 14.

211	4c. Type **81**	10	10
212	10c. Contour ridges	10	10
213	15c. Earth dams	25	10
214	25c. Beaver dams	35	35
211/14	*Set of 4*	70	50

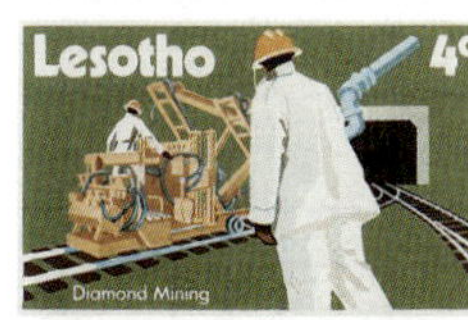

82 Diamond Mining

(Des J.W. Litho Questa)

1971 (4 Oct). *Development. T* **82** *and similar horiz designs. Multicoloured.* W **53** (sideways). P 14.

215	4c. Type **82**	75	40
216	10c. Pottery	30	10
217	15c. Weaving	45	60
218	20c. Construction	55	1·50
215/18	*Set of 4*	1·90	2·25

83 Mail Cart

84 Sprinting

(Des D. B. Picton-Phillips. Litho Questa)

1972 (3 Jan). *Post Office Centenary. T* **83** *and similar designs.* W **53** (sideways on 5, 10 and 20c.). P 14×13½ (15c.) or 13½×14 (others).

219	5c. pale pink and black	15	20
220	10c. multicoloured	15	10
221	15c. pale drab, light blue and black	20	15
222	20c. multicoloured	30	90
219/22	*Set of 4*	70	1·10

Designs: Horiz—10c. Postal bus; 20c. Maseru P.O. *Vert*—15c. Cape of Good Hope 4d. stamp of 1876.

(Des J.W. Litho Questa)

1972 (1 Sept). *Olympic Games, Munich. T* **84** *and similar vert designs. Multicoloured.* W **53**. P 14.

223	4c. Type **84**	15	10
	w. Wmk inverted		
224	10c. Shot putting	20	10
225	15c. Hurdling	30	10
226	25c. Long-jumping	35	55
223/6	*Set of 4*	90	70

85 "Adoration of the Shepherds" (Matthias Stomer)

(Des and litho J.W.)

1972 (1 Dec). *Christmas.* W **53** (sideways). P 14.

227	**85**	4c. multicoloured	10	10
228		10c. multicoloured	10	10
229		25c. multicoloured	15	20
227/9		*Set of 3*	30	30

86 WHO Emblem

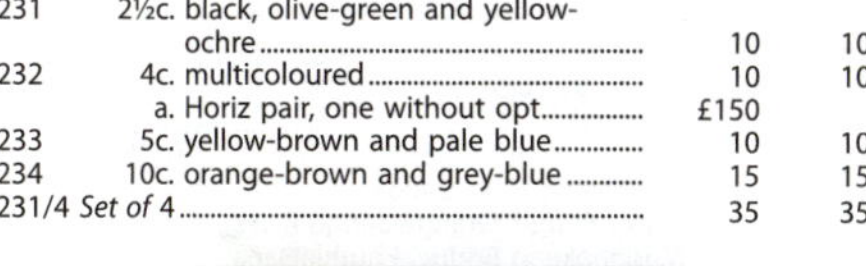

O.A.U.
10th Anniversary
Freedom in Unity
(87)

(Des J. Cooter. Litho Questa)

1973 (7 Apr). *25th Anniv of WHO.* W **53** (sideways). P 13½.

230	**86**	20c. greenish blue and yellow	30	30

1973 (25 May). *Tenth Anniv of OAU. Nos. 194 and 196a/8 optd with T* **87** *by Govt Printer, Maseru.*

231	2½c. black, olive-green and yellow-ochre	10	10
232	4c. multicoloured	10	10
	a. Horiz pair, one without opt	£150	
233	5c. yellow-brown and pale blue	10	10
234	10c. orange-brown and grey-blue	15	15
231/4	*Set of 4*	35	35

88 Basotho Hat and WFP Emblem

(Des locally; adapted J. Cooter. Litho Format)

1973 (1 June). *Tenth Anniv of World Food Programme. T* **88** *and similar horiz designs. Multicoloured.* W **53** (sideways). P 13½.

235	4c. Type **88**	10	10
236	15c. School feeding	20	15
237	20c. Infant feeding	20	20
	a. Imperf (pair)	£250	
238	25c. "Food for Work"	25	25
235/8	*Set of 4*	65	60

89 *Aeropetes tulbaghia*

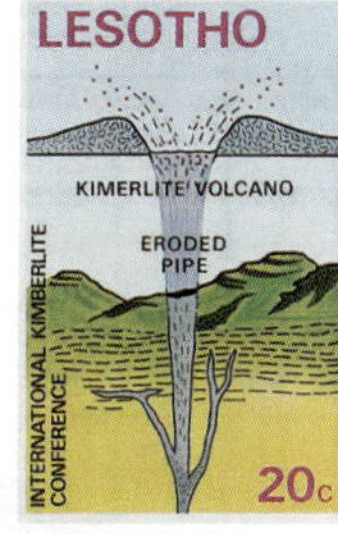

90 Kimberlite Volcano

(Des A. Mcleod; artwork G. Drummond. Litho Questa)

1973 (3 Sept). *Butterflies. T* **89** *and similar horiz designs. Multicoloured.* W **53** (sideways). P 14.

239	4c. Type **89**	75	10
240	5c. *Papilio demodocus*	85	50
241	10c. *Cynthia cardui*	1·25	50
242	15c. *Precis hierta*	2·25	1·75
243	20c. *Precis oenone*	2·25	1·75
244	25c. *Danaus chrysippus*	2·50	2·75
245	30c. *Colotis evenina*	2·50	3·75
239/45	*Set of 7*	11·00	10·00

(Des PAD Studio. Litho Questa)

1973 (1 Oct). *International Kimberlite Conference. T* **90** *and similar multicoloured designs.* W **53** (sideways on 10 and 15c.). P 13½.

246	10c. Map of diamond mines (*horiz*)	2·00	50
247	15c. Kimberlite-diamond rock (*horiz*)	2·25	2·25
248	20c. Type **90**	2·25	2·50
249	30c. Diamond prospecting	3·75	7·00
246/9 *Set of 4*		9·00	11·00

Type **90** is incorrectly inscribed "KIMERLITE VOLCANO".

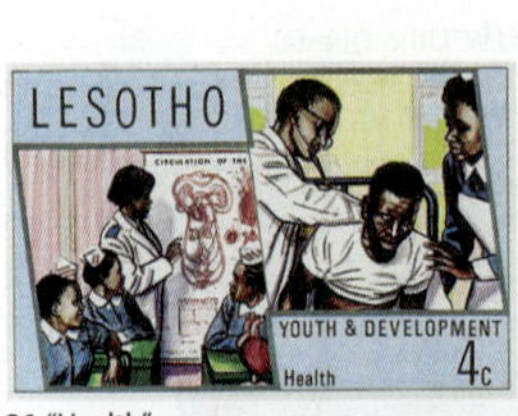

91 "Health"

92 Open Book and Wreath

(Des R. Granger Barrett. Litho Questa)

1974 (18 Feb). *Youth and Development. T* **91** *and similar horiz designs. Multicoloured.* W **53** (sideways). P 13½.

250	4c. Type **91**	10	10
251	10c. "Education"	15	10
252	20c. "Agriculture"	20	10
253	25c. "Industry"	30	20
254	30c. "Service"	30	25
250/4 *Set of 5*		85	55

(Des PAD Studio. Litho Questa)

1974 (8 Apr). *Tenth Anniv of U.B.L.S. T* **92** *and similar vert designs. Multicoloured.* W **53**. P 14.

255	10c. Type **92**	15	10
256	15c. Flags, mortar-board and scroll	20	20
257	20c. Map of Africa	25	25
258	25c. King Moshoeshoe II capping a graduate	25	65
255/8 *Set of 4*		75	1·00

93 Senqunyane River Bridge, Marakabei

(Des J. Cooter. Litho Questa)

1974 (26 June). *Rivers and Bridges. T* **93** *and similar horiz designs. Multicoloured.* W **53** (sideways). P 14½.

259	4c. Type **93**	10	10
260	5c. Tsoelike River and bridge	10	10
261	10c. Makhaleng River Bridge	20	10
262	15c. Seaka Bridge, Orange/Senqu River	35	35
263	20c. Masianokeng Bridge, Phuthiatsana River	40	40
264	25c. Mahobong Bridge, Hlotse River	45	45
259/64 *Set of 6*		1·50	1·25

94 UPU Emblem

(Des R. Granger Barrett. Litho Enschedé)

1974 (6 Sept). *Centenary of Universal Postal Union. T* **94** *and similar horiz designs.* W **53** (sideways). P 13½×13.

265	4c. light emerald and black	10	10
266	10c. orange, greenish yellow and black	15	10
267	15c. multicoloured	20	60
268	20c. multicoloured	45	85
265/8 *Set of 4*		80	1·40

Designs:—10c. Map of air-mail routes; 15c. Post Office H.Q., Maseru; 20c. Horseman taking rural mail.

On No. 266 the inscriptions for the airstrips at Mokhotlong and Mohlanapeng were transposed in error.

95 Siege of Thaba-Bosiu

(Des Jennifer Toombs. Litho Enschedé)

1974 (25 Nov). *150th Anniv of Establishment of Thaba-Bosiu as Capital. T* **95** *and similar multicoloured designs.* W **53** (sideways on 4 and 5c.). P 12½×12 (4 and 5c.) or 12×12½ (others).

269	4c. Type **95**	10	10
270	5c. The wreath-laying	10	10
271	10c. Moshoeshoe I (*vert*)	25	10
272	20c. Makoanyane, the warrior (*vert*)	90	55
269/72 *Set of 4*		1·25	65

96 Mamokhorong

(Des PAD Studio. Litho Questa)

1975 (25 Jan). *Basotho Musical Instruments. T* **96** *and similar horiz designs. Multicoloured.* W **53** (sideways). P 14.

273	4c. Type **96**	10	10
274	10c. Lesiba	10	10
275	15c. Setolotolo	15	20
276	20c. Meropa	15	20
273/6 *Set of 4*		40	45
MS277 108×92 mm. Nos. 273/6		1·00	2·00

97 Horseman in Rock Archway

98 Morena Moshoeshoe I

(Des J. Cooter. Litho Questa)

1975 (15 Apr). *Sehlabathebe National Park. T* **97** *and similar horiz designs. Multicoloured.* W **53** (sideways). P 14.

278	4c. Type **97**	30	10
279	5c. Mountain view through arch	30	10
280	15c. Antelope by stream	50	45
281	20c. Mountains and lake	50	50
282	25c. Tourists by frozen waterfall	65	75
278/82 *Set of 5*		2·00	1·60

(Des G. Vasarhelyi. Litho Questa)

1975 (10 Sept). *Leaders of Lesotho. T* **98** *and similar vert designs.* W **53**. P 14.

283	3c. black and light blue	10	10
284	4c. black and light mauve	10	10
285	5c. black and pink	10	10
286	6c. black and light grey-brown	10	10
287	10c. black and light claret	10	10
288	15c. black and light orange-red	20	20
289	20c. black and dull green	25	30
290	25c. black and azure	25	40
283/90 *Set of 8*		1·00	1·10

Designs:—4c. King Moshoeshoe II; 5c. Morena Letsie I; 6c. Morena Lerotholi; 10c. Morena Letsie II; 15c. Morena Griffith; 20c. Morena Seeiso Griffith Lerotholi; 25c. Mofumahali' Mantšebo Seeiso, OBE.

The 25c. also commemorates International Women's Year.

99 Mokhibo Dance

(Des PAD Studio. Litho Questa)

1975 (17 Dec). *Traditional Dances. T* **99** *and similar horiz designs. Multicoloured.* W **53** (sideways). P 14×14½.

291	4c. Type **99**	15	10
292	10c. Ndlamo	20	10
293	15c. Baleseli	35	75
294	20c. Mohobelo	40	1·25
291/4 *Set of 4*		1·00	1·75
MS295 111×100 mm. Nos. 291/94		3·75	3·50

100 Enrolment

(Des L. Curtis. Litho Questa)

1976 (20 Feb). *25th Anniv of the Lesotho Red Cross. T* **100** *and similar horiz designs. Multicoloured.* W **53** (sideways). P 14.

296	4c. Type **100**	50	10
297	10c. Medical aid	70	10
298	15c. Rural service	1·00	1·25
299	25c. Relief supplies	1·40	2·50
296/9 *Set of 4*		3·25	3·50

101 Tapestry

102 Football

(Des V. Whiteley Studio. Litho Format)

1976 (2 June). *Multicoloured designs as T* **101**. W **53** (sideways* on 2 to 50c.). P 14.

300	2c. Type **101**	10	35
	w. Wmk top of hat to right	—	40·00
301	3c. Mosotho horseman	20	30
302	4c. Map of Lesotho	1·50	10
	w. Wmk top of hat to right		
303	5c. Lesotho Brown diamond	75	1·00
	w. Wmk top of hat to right		
304	10c. Lesotho Bank	30	10
305	15c. Lesotho and OAU flags	2·00	1·00
306	25c. Sehlabathebe National Park	60	35
307	40c. Pottery	60	1·00
308	50c. Prehistoric rock art	2·75	2·00
309	1r. King Moshoeshoe II (*vert*)	60	1·75
300/9 *Set of 10*		8·00	7·00

*The normal sideways watermark shows top of hat to left when seen from the back of the stamp.

For 25c., 40c.and 50c. values on unwatermarked paper, see Nos. 398/400.

(Des P. Powell. Litho Questa)

1976 (9 Aug). *Olympic Games, Montreal. T* **102** *and similar vert designs. Multicoloured.* W **53**. P 14.

310	4c. Type **102**	15	10
311	10c. Weightlifting	15	10
312	15c. Boxing	35	35
313	25c. Throwing the discus	50	80
310/13 *Set of 4*		1·00	1·25

103 "Rising Sun"

104 Telephones, 1876 and 1976

(Des L. Curtis. Litho Questa)

1976 (4 Oct). *Tenth Anniv of Independence. T* **103** *and similar vert designs. Multicoloured.* W **53**. P 14.

314	4c. Type **103**	10	10
315	10c. Open gates	10	10
316	15c. Broken chains	40	20
317	25c. Britten Norman Islander aircraft over hotel	50	35
314/17 *Set of 4*		1·00	55

(Des and litho J.W.)

1976 (6 Dec). *Telephone Centenary. T* **104** *and similar horiz designs. Multicoloured.* W **53** (sideways). P 13.

318	4c. Type **104**	10	10
319	10c. Early handset and telephone-user, 1976	15	10
320	15c. Wall telephone and telephone exchange	25	20
321	25c. Stick telephone and Alexander Graham Bell	45	50
318/21 *Set of 4*		85	75

105 *Aloe striatula*

106 Large-toothed Rock Hyrax

(Des D. Findlay. Litho Walsall)

1977 (14 Feb). *Aloes and Succulents. T* **105** *and similar vert designs. Multicoloured.* W **53** (inverted). P 14.

322	3c. Type **105**	25	10
323	4c. *Aloe aristata*	25	10
324	5c. *Kniphofia caulescens*	25	10
325	10c. *Euphorbia pulvinata*	35	10
326	15c. *Aloe saponaria*	1·00	30
327	20c. *Caralluma lutea*	1·00	50
328	25c. *Aloe polyphylla*	1·25	70
322/8 *Set of 7*		4·00	1·60

(Des D. Findlay. Litho Questa)

1977 (25 Apr). *Endangered Species. T* **106** *and similar horiz designs. Multicoloured.* W **53** (sideways). P 14.

329	4c. Type **106**	3·50	30
330	5c. Cape Porcupine	3·50	75
331	10c. Zorilla (polecat)	3·50	30
332	15c. Klipspringer	11·00	2·50

333 25c. Chacma Baboon 12·00 3·75
329/33 *Set of 5* 30·00 6·75

107 "Rheumatic Man"

108 Small-mouthed Yellowfish

(Des C. Abbott. Litho Questa)

1977 (4 July). *World Rheumatism Year. T* **107** *and similar vert designs showing the "Rheumatic Man".* W **53**. P 14.

334 4c. yellow and red 10 10
335 10c. new blue and deep blue 15 10
336 15c. yellow and blue-green 30 10
337 25c. orange-red and black 40 45
334/7 *Set of 4* 85 55

Designs:—10c. Man surrounded by "pain"; 15c. Man surrounded by "chain"; 25c. Man supporting globe.

(Des D. Findlay. Litho Questa)

1977 (28 Sept). *Fish. T* **108** *and similar horiz designs. Multicoloured.* W **53** (sideways). P 14.

338 4c. Type **108** 30 10
339 10c. Mudfish 45 10
340 15c. Rainbow Trout 1·00 35
341 25c. Barnard's Mudfish 1·10 60
338/41 *Set of 4* 2·50 1·00

(109)

110 Black and White Heads

1977 (7 Dec*). *No. 198 surch with T* **109** *by Govt Printer, Maseru.*

342 3c. on 10c. yellow-brn & pale bluish grey 1·00 1·00
a. Top obliterating bar short at left (R.2/5) 14·00
b. Top obliterating bar short at right (R.5/5) 14·00
w. Wmk top of hat to right

*Earliest known date of use.

Nos. 342a/b occur on the upper pane.

(Des Jennifer Toombs. Litho Walsall)

1977 (12 Dec). *Decade for Action to Combat Racism. T* **110** *and similar vert designs.* W **53**. P 14.

343 4c. chocolate and mauve 10 10
344 10c. chocolate and light new blue 10 10
345 15c. chocolate and light orange 15 15
346 25c. chocolate and light turquoise-green 25 25
343/6 *Set of 4* 55 45

Designs:—10c. Jigsaw pieces; 15c. Cogwheels; 25c. Handshake.

(Des D. Findlay. Litho Questa)

1978 (13 Feb). *Flowers. Vert designs similar to T* **105**. *Multicoloured.* W **53**. P 14.

347 2c. *Papaver aculeatum* 10 50
348 3c. *Diascia integerrima* 10 50
349 4c. *Helichrysum trilineatum* 10 10
350 5c. *Zaluzianskya maritima* 10 10
351 10c. *Gladiolus natalensis* 15 10
352 15c. *Chironia krebsii* 20 40
353 25c. *Wahlenbergia undulata* 35 1·00
354 40c. *Brunsvigia radulosa* 65 2·00
347/54 *Set of 8* 1·50 4·00

111 Edward Jenner performing Vaccination

112 Tsoloane Falls

(Des G. Hutchins. Litho J.W.)

1978 (8 May). *Global Eradication of Smallpox. T* **111** *and similar vert design. Multicoloured.* W **53**. P 13.

355 5c. Type **111** 25 35
356 25c. Head of child and WHO emblem 75 90
w. Wmk inverted 5·00

(Des Kobus De Beer Art Studio. Litho Questa)

1978 (28 July). *Waterfalls. T* **112** *and similar vert designs. Multicoloured.* W **53**. P 14.

357 4c. Type **112** 15 10
358 10c. Qiloane Falls 25 10
359 15c. Tsoelikana Falls 35 60
360 25c. Maletsunyane Falls 55 1·75
357/60 *Set of 4* 1·10 2·25

113 Wright Flyer III, 1903

114 *Orthetrum farinasum*

(Des L. Curtis. Litho Harrison)

1978 (9 Oct). *75th Anniv of Powered Flight. T* **113** *and similar horiz design.* W **53** (sideways). P 14½×14.

361 5c. black, brown-ochre and new blue 15 30
362 25c. multicoloured 40 60

Design:—25c. Wilbur and Orville Wright.

(Des D. Findlay. Litho Questa)

1978 (18 Dec). *Insects. T* **114** *and similar vert designs. Multicoloured.* W **53**. P 14.

363 4c. Type **114** 10 10
364 10c. *Phymateus viridipes* 20 10
365 15c. *Belonogaster lateritis* 30 55
366 25c. *Sphodromantis gastrica* 50 90
363/6 *Set of 4* 1·00 1·40

115 Oudehout branch in flower

116 Mampharoane

(Des D. Findlay. Litho Questa)

1979 (26 Mar). *Trees. T* **115** *and similar vert designs showing branches in flower. Multicoloured.* W **53**. P 14.

367 4c. Type **115** 15 10
368 10c. Wild Olive 20 10
369 15c. Blinkblaar 35 80
370 25c. Cape Holly 70 1·50
367/70 *Set of 4* 1·25 2·25

(New Currency. 100 lisente = 1(ma)loti)

(Des D. Findlay. Litho Questa)

1979 (1 June). *Reptiles. T* **116** *and similar horiz designs. Multicoloured.* P 14.

A. No wmk.

371A 4s. Type **116** 10 10
372A 10s. Qoaane 20 10
373A 15s. Leupa 30 70
374A 25s. Masumu 60 1·40
371A/4A *Set of 4* 1·10 2·00

B. W **53** *(sideways).*

371B 4s. Type **116** 10 10
372B 10s. Qoaane 20 10
373B 15s. Leupa 30 70
374B 25s. Masumu 60 1·50
371B/4B *Set of 4* 1·10 2·10

117 Basutoland 1933 1d. Stamp

118 Detail of painting "Children's Games" by Breughel

(Des J.W. Litho Format)

1979 (22 Oct). *Death Centenary of Sir Rowland Hill. T* **117** *and similar vert designs showing stamps.* P 14.

375 4s. multicoloured 10 10
376 15s. multicoloured 30 20
377 25s. black, yellow-orange and olive-bistre 40 30
375/7 *Set of 3* 70 50
MS378 118×95 mm. 50s. multicoloured 60 80

Designs:—15s. Basutoland 1962 ½c. definitive; 25s. Penny Black; 50s. 1972 15c. Post Office Centenary commemorative.

(Des C. Abbott. Litho Questa)

1979 (10 Dec). *International Year of the Child. T* **118** *and similar vert designs showing details of the painting "Children's Games" by Brueghel.* W **53**. P 14.

379 4s. multicoloured 10 10
380 10s. multicoloured 10 10
381 15s. multicoloured 15 15
379/81 *Set of 3* 30 30
MS382 113×88 mm. 25s. multicoloured (*horiz*) (wmk sideways) 55 45

119 Beer Strainer, Brooms and Mat

(Des Kobus de Beer Art Studio. Litho Walsall)

1980 (18 Feb). *Grasswork. T* **119** *and similar horiz designs. Multicoloured.* W **53** (sideways). P 14.

383 4s. Type **119** 10 10
384 10s. Winnowing Basket 10 10
385 15s. Basotho Hat 20 25
386 25s. Grain storage 35 40
383/6 *Set of 4* 60 70

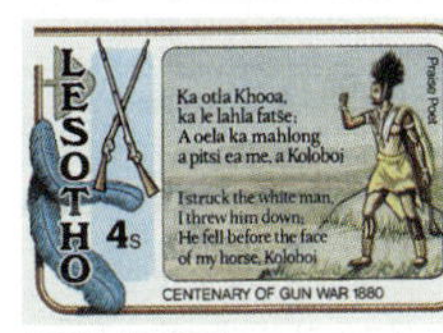

120 Praise Poet

(Des BG Studio. Litho Walsall)

1980 (6 May). *Centenary of Gun War. T* **120** *and similar horiz designs. Multicoloured.* P 14.

387 4s. Type **120** 15 10
388 5s. Lerotholi (commander of Basotho Army) 15 10
389 10s. Ambush at Qalabane 20 10
390 15s. Snider and Martini-Henry rifles 60 45
391 25s. Map showing main areas of action 70 55
87/91 *Set of 5* 1·60 1·10

121 Olympic Flame, Flags and Kremlin

(122)

(Des G. Vasarhelyi. Litho Format)

1980 (20 Sept). *Olympic Games, Moscow. T* **121** *and similar horiz designs. Multicoloured.* P 14½.

392 25s. Type **121** 25 25
a. Horiz strip of 5. Nos. 392/6 1·10
393 25s. Doves, flame and flags 25 25
394 25s. Football 25 25
395 25s. Running 25 25
396 25s. Opening ceremony 25 25
392/6 *Set of 5* 1·10 1·10
MS397 110×85 mm. 1m.40, Ancient and modern athletes carrying Olympic torch 1·10 1·25

Nos. 392/6 were printed together, *se-tenant*, in horizontal strips of 5 throughout the sheet.

A further series for the Moscow Olympics, printed by Walsall, showing 4s. Javelin, 10s. Sprinting, 15s. Marathon and 25s. Football, was prepared, but not issued.

1980. *As Nos. 203 and 306/8, but without wmk.*

398 25c. Sehlabathebe National Park 75 1·40
399 40c. Pottery 2·00 5·00
400 50c. Prehistoric rock art 2·75 5·00
401 2r. Statue of Moshoeshoe I (yellow-brown and ultramarine) 70 2·25
398/401 *Set of 4* 5·50 12·00

Two opt types of No. 409:

Type I. Cancelling bars centred on depth of "M1" (stamps surcharged in individual panes of 25 and from the righthand panes of those surcharged in sheets of 50 (2 panes 5×5)).

Type II. Lower cancelling bar aligns with foot of "M1" (stamps from left hand panes of those surcharged in sheets of 50).

1980 (20 Oct)–**81**. *As Nos. 300/5, 309 and 398/401 surch as T* **122** *or with new figures of value (5s. (No. 410A), 6, 75s., 1 and 2m.). A. By typo (locally). (a) W* **53** *(sideways on 2, 3, 6, 10, 40, 60 and 75s.).*

402A 2s. on 2c. Type **101** 10 10
w. Wmk top of hat to right 5·50
403A 3s. on 3c. Mosotho horseman 20 10
404A 6s. on 4c. Map of Lesotho 1·00 10
a. Surch double † —
b. Albino surch † —
405A 10s. on 10c. Lesotho Bank 80 10
405cA 25s. on 25c. Sehlabathebe National Park 3·25 4·50
406A 40s. on 40c. Pottery 45 50
407A 50s. on 50c. Prehistoric rock art 2·50 1·75
408A 75s. on 15c. Lesotho and OAU flags 80 75
409A 1m. on 1r. King Moshoeshoe II (I) (Sil.) 80 1·00
a. Surch double
b. Surch inverted
c. Surch double, one inverted 55·00
d. Opt Type II 3·75 4·00

(b) No wmk.

410A 5s. on 5c. Lesotho Brown diamond 1·50 10
a. Third surch (Basotho hat and "5s.") double 35·00
b. Basotho hat and "5s." surch albino 25·00
c. Basotho hat and "5s." omitted 25·00
d. Basotho hat and "5s." surch treble 40·00
e. Basotho hat and "5s." surch treble, one inverted 45·00
f. Second surch ("6s." and bars) albino 20·00

412A 25s. on 25c. Sehlabathebe National Park ... 25 30
a. Surch double ... 12·00
b. Surch triple ...
c. Surch quadruple ...
413A 40s. on 40c. Pottery ... 2·50 4·25
414A 50s. on 50c. Prehistoric rock art ... 2·00 55
a. Surch double, one inverted ... 30·00
b. Surch quadruple, one inverted ... 35·00
c. Surch omitted (in pair with normal) ...
417A 2m. on 2r. Statue of Moshoeshoel ... 80 1·40
402A/17A *Set of 14* ... 15·00 14·00

B. By Litho (London). (a) W **53** *(sideways on 2, 3, 6, 10, 40, 50 and 75s.).*

402B 2s. on 2c. Type **101** ... 10 10
403B 3s. on 3c. Mosotho horseman ... 20 10
404B 6s. on 4c. Map of Lesotho ... 1·00 10
405B 10s. on 10c. Lesotho Bank ... 5·00 5·50
406B 40s. on 40c. Pottery ... 45 50
407B 50s. on 50c. Prehistoric rock art ... 1·25 55

(b) No wmk.

410B 5s. on 5c. Lesotho Brown diamond ... 60 10
411B 10s. on 10c. Lesotho Bank ... 10 10
412B 25s. on 25c. Sehlabathebe National Park ... 25 30
415B 75s. on 15c. Lesotho and OAU flags ... 1·50 75
416B 1m. on 1r. King Moshoeshoe II (Blk. and Sil.) ... 80 1·00
417B 2m. on 2r. Statue of Moshoeshoe I ... 80 1·40
402B/17B *Set of 12* ... 11·00 9·00

No. 410A is a further surcharge on No. 410B. Initially sheets of No. 410B were locally surcharged "6s.", but this was later obliterated by a Basotho hat emblem and a further "5s." surcharge added, both in typography.

The surcharge on No. 416 is similar to that on No. 409 but has the cancelling bars printed in black and the new face value in silver.

On each value except the 5s. and 1m. stamps, the design of the surcharge on the local printing is identical to that on the London printing. Stamps from the local printing can easily be identified from those of the London printing as indentations are clearly visible on the reverse of stamps with the typographed surcharge.

It is believed that the local surcharges were not placed on general sale before 1 December 1980. No. 410A did not appear until 20 January 1981.

Nos. 412Ab/c occurred in the same sheet which contained 5 examples of the triple surcharge, 5 of a partial quadruple surcharge and 40 with complete quadruple surcharge.

123 Beer Mug

124 Queen Elizabeth the Queen Mother and Prince Charles

(Des G. Vasarhelyi (No. **MS**422), Kobus de Beer Art Studio (others). Litho Format (No. **MS**422), Questa (others))

1980 (20 Nov). *Pottery. T* **123** *and similar horiz designs. Multicoloured.* W **53** (sideways). P 14.

418 4s. Type **123** ... 10 10
419 10s. Beer brewing pot ... 10 10
420 15s. Water pot ... 15 15
421 25s. Pot shapes ... 25 30
418/21 *Set of 4* ... 50 50
MS422 150×110 mm. 40s.×4 Wedgwood plaques of Prince Philip; Queen Elizabeth II; Prince Charles; Princess Anne (each 22×35 mm). P 14×14½ ... 50 90

No. **MS**422 was issued to commemorate the 250th birth anniversary of Josiah Wedgwood.

(Des G. Vasarhelyi. Litho Format)

1980 (1 Dec). *80th Birthday of Queen Elizabeth the Queen Mother. T* **124** *and similar multicoloured designs.* P 14½.

423 5s. Type **124** ... 25 25
a. Horiz strip of 3. Nos. 423/5 ... 1·25
424 10s. Queen Elizabeth the Queen Mother ... 25 25
425 1m. Basutoland 1947 Royal Visit 2d. commemorative and flags (54×44 mm) ... 90 90
423/5 *Set of 3* ... 1·25 1·25

Nos. 423/5 were printed together, *se-tenant*, in horizontal strips of 3 throughout small sheets of nine stamps.

125 Lesotho Evangelical Church, Morija

(Des G. Vasarhelyi. Litho Format (75s., 1m.50), Harrison (others))

1980 (8 Dec). *Christmas. T* **125** *and similar horiz designs. Multicoloured. No wmk (75s.) or W* **53** *(others).* P 14×14½.

426 4s. Type **125** ... 10 10
427 15s. St. Agnes' Anglican Church, Teyateyaneng ... 10 10
428 25s. Cathedral of Our Lady of Victories, Maseru ... 15 10
429 75s. University Chapel, Roma ... 45 50
426/9 *Set of 4* ... 65 60
MS430 110×85 mm. 1m.50, Nativity scene (43×29 mm). No wmk. P 14½ ... 50 80

126 "Voyager" Satellite and Jupiter

127 Greater Kestrel

(Des G. Vasarhelyi. Litho Format)

1981 (15 Mar). *Space Exploration. T* **126** *and similar horiz designs. Multicoloured.* P 13½×14.

431 25s. Type **126** ... 30 25
a. Horiz strip of 5. Nos. 431/5 ... 1·40
432 25s. "Voyager" and Saturn ... 30 25
433 25s. "Voyager" passing Saturn ... 30 25
434 25s. "Space Shuttle" releasing satellite ... 30 25
435 25s. "Space Shuttle" launch ... 30 25
431/5 *Set of 5* ... 1·40 1·10
MS436 111×85 mm. 1m.40, Saturn ... 1·40 1·00

Nos. 431/5 were printed together, *se-tenant*, in horizontal strips of 5 throughout the sheet.

No. **MS**436 exists imperforate from stock dispersed by the liquidator of Format International Security Printers Ltd.

(Des G. Vasarhelyi. Litho Format)

1981 (20 Apr). *Birds. Multicoloured designs as T* **127**. *With imprint date.* P 14½.

437 1s. Type **127** ... 15 40
a. Perf 13 (12.81) ... 55 30
438 2s. Speckled Pigeon (*horiz*) ... 15 40
a. Perf 13 (12.81) ... 65 30
439 3s. South African Crowned Crane ... 20 40
440 5s. Bokmakierie Shrike ... 20 40
a. Perf 13 (12.81) ... 90 30
441 6s. Cape Robin Chat ... 30 10
442 7s. Yellow Canary ... 30 10
443 10s. Red-billed Pintail (*horiz*) ... 40 10
a. Perf 13 (12.81) ... 90 30
444 25s. Malachite Kingfisher ... 1·00 15
445 40s. Yellow-tufted Malachite Sunbird (*horiz*) ... 1·25 55
446 60s. Cape Longclaw (*horiz*) ... 1·50 1·00
447 75s. Hoopoe (*horiz*) ... 1·50 85
448 1m. Red Bishop (*horiz*) ... 1·50 75
449 2m. Egyptian Goose (*horiz*) ... 1·00 1·50
450 5m. Lilac-breasted Roller (*horiz*) ... 1·25 4·00
437/50 *Set of 14* ... 9·75 9·50

Imprint dates: "1981", Nos. 437/50; "1982", Nos. 437/41, 443.

Nos. 437/50 exist imperforated and as progressive proofs from stock dispersed by the liquidator of Format International Security Printers Ltd.

For these stamps watermarked w **14** see Nos. 500/13.

128 Wedding Bouquet from Lesotho

(Des J.W. Litho Format)

1981 (22 July). *Royal Wedding. T* **128** *and similar vert designs. Multicoloured.* P 14.

451 25s. Type **128** ... 10 10
a. Booklet pane. No. 451×3plus printed label ... 50
b. Booklet pane. Nos. 451/3 plus printed label ... 50
452 50s. Prince Charles riding ... 20 25
a. Booklet pane. No. 452×3 plus printed label ... 55
453 75s. Prince Charles and Lady Diana Spencer ... 30 50
a. Booklet pane. No. 453×3 plus printed label ... 70
451/3 *Set of 3* ... 55 75

Nos. 451/3 also exist imperforate from a restricted printing (price for set of 3 £5.50 mint).

Booklet panes Nos. 451a/3a exist part perforated from stock dispersed by the liquidator of Format International Security Printers Ltd.

129 Prince Charles and Lady Diana Spencer

(Des G. Vasarhelyi. Litho Format)

1981 (5 Sept). *Royal Wedding (2nd issue). Sheet 115×90 mm.* P 14½.

MS454 **129** 1m.50 multicoloured ... 1·00 1·25

No. **MS**454 also exists imperforate from a restricted printing (price £4 mint).

130 "Santa planning his Annual Visit"

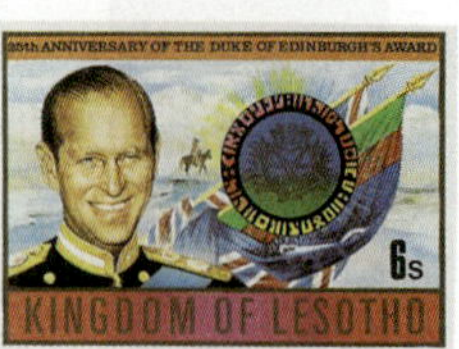

131 Duke of Edinburgh, Award Scheme Emblem and Flags

(Des G. Vasarhelyi. Litho Format)

1981 (5 Oct). *Christmas. Paintings by Norman Rockwell (6 to 60s.) or Botticelli (1m.25). T* **130** *and similar multicoloured designs.* P 13½.

455 6s. Type **130** ... 15 10
456 10s. "Santa reading his Mail" ... 25 10
457 15s. "The Little Spooners" ... 30 20
458 20s. "Raleigh Rockwell Travels" ... 30 25
459 25s. "Ride 'em Cowboy" ... 30 30
460 60s. "The Discovery" ... 50 1·00
455/60 *Set of 6* ... 1·60 1·75
MS461 111×85 mm. 1m.25, "Mystic Nativity" (48×31 mm). P 13½×14 ... 1·10 1·10

(Des G. Vasarhelyi. Litho Format)

1981 (5 Nov). *25th Anniv of Duke of Edinburgh Award Scheme. T* **131** *and similar multicoloured designs.* P 14½.

462 6s. Type **131** ... 10 10
463 7s. Tree planting ... 10 10
464 25s. Gardening ... 25 20
465 40s. Mountain climbing ... 40 40
466 75s. Award Scheme emblem ... 70 75
462/6 *Set of 5* ... 1·40 1·40
MS467 111×85 mm. 1m.40, Duke of Edinburgh (45×30 mm) ... 1·25 1·25

132 Wild Cat

(Des G. Vasarhelyi. Litho Format)

1982 (15 Jan). *Wildlife. T* **132** *and similar multicoloured designs.* P 13½ (6, 25s.) or 14½ (others).

468 6s. Type **132** ... 1·25 30
469 20s. Chacma Baboon (44×31 mm) ... 2·00 70
470 25s. Eland ... 2·50 75
471 40s. Cape Porcupine (44×31 mm) ... 3·25 1·75
472 50s. Oribi (44×31 mm) ... 3·25 1·75
468/72 *Set of 5* ... 11·00 4·75
MS473 111×85 mm. 1m.50, Black-backed Jackal (47×31 mm). P 13½×14 ... 2·75 1·90

No. **MS**473 exists imperforate from stock dispersed by the liquidator of Format International Security Printers Ltd.

133 Scout Bugler

(Des G. Vasarhelyi. Litho Format)

1982 (5 Mar). *75th Anniv of Boy Scout Movement. T* **133** *and similar horiz designs. Multicoloured.* P 13½.

474 6s. Type **133** ... 30 25
a. Booklet pane. Nos. 474/8×2 and **MS**479 ... 5·00
475 30s. Scouts hiking ... 35 50
476 40s. Scout sketching ... 40 60
477 50s. Scout with flag ... 40 65
478 75s. Scouts saluting ... 45 80
474/8 *Set of 5* ... 1·75 2·50
MS479 117×92 mm. 1m.50, Lord Baden-Powell ... 1·00 2·00

Nos. 474/9 exist imperforate from stock dispersed by the liquidator of Format International Security Printers Ltd.

134 Jules Rimet Trophy with Footballers and Flags of 1930 Finalists (Argentina and Uruguay)

(Des G. Vasarhelyi. Litho Format)

1982 (14 Apr). *World Cup Football Championship, Spain. T* **134** *and similar horiz designs showing World Football Cup with players and flags of countries in past finals (Nos. 480/90). Multicoloured.* P 14½.

480	15s. Type **134**	25	25
	a. Sheetlet. Nos. 480/91	2·50	
481	15s. Jules Rimet Trophy with Czechoslovakia and Italy, 1934	25	25
482	15s. Jules Rimet Trophy with Hungary and Italy, 1938	25	25
483	15s. Jules Rimet Trophy with Brazil and Uruguay, 1950	25	25
484	15s. Jules Rimet Trophy with Hungary and West Germany, 1954	25	25
485	15s. Jules Rimet Trophy with Sweden and Brazil, 1958	25	25
486	15s. Jules Rimet Trophy with Czechoslovakia and Brazil, 1962	25	25
487	15s. Jules Rimet Trophy with West Germany and England, 1966	25	25
488	15s. Jules Rimet Trophy with Italy and Brazil, 1970	25	25
489	15s. World Cup with Holland and West Germany, 1974	25	25
490	15s. World Cup with Holland and Argentina, 1978	25	25
491	15s. World Cup and map of World on footballs	25	25
480/91 *Set of 12*		2·50	2·50

MS492 118×93 mm. 1m.25, Bernabeu Stadium, Madrid (47×35 mm). P 13½ ... 1·10 1·25

Nos. 480/91 were printed together, *se-tenant*, in sheetlets of 12.

Nos. 480/92 exist imperforate from stock dispersed by the liquidator of Format International Security Printers Ltd.

135 Portrait of George Washington

136 Lady Diana Spencer in Tetbury, May 1981

(Des G. Vasarhelyi. Litho Format)

1982 (7 June). *250th Birth Anniv of George Washington. T* **135** *and similar horiz designs. Multicoloured.* P 14×13½.

493	6s. Type **135**	10	10
494	7s. Washington with step-children and dog	10	10
495	10s. Washington with Indian chief	15	10
496	25s. Washington with troops	30	30
497	40s. Washington arriving in New York	40	40
498	1m. Washington on parade	1·00	1·10
493/8 *Set of 6*		1·80	1·90

MS499 117×92 mm. 1m.25, Washington crossing the Delaware ... 1·00 1·00

No. **MS**499 exists imperforate from stock dispersed by the liquidator of Format International Security Printers Ltd.

1982 (14 June). *As Nos. 437/50 but W w* **14** *(sideways on Nos. 500, 502/5 and 507). "1982" imprint date.*

500	1s. Type **127**	20	50
501	2s. Speckled Pigeon (*horiz*)	20	50
502	3s. South African Crowned Crane	30	50
503	5s. Bokmakierie Shrike	30	40
504	6s. Cape Robin Chat	30	10
505	7s. Yellow Canary	30	10
506	10s. Red-billed Pintail (*horiz*)	30	10
507	25s. Malachite Kingfisher	80	30
508	40s. Yellow-tufted Malachite Sunbird (*horiz*)	1·00	45
509	60s. Cape Longclaw (*horiz*)	1·25	90
510	75s. Hoopoe (*horiz*)	1·50	90
511	1m. Red Bishop (*horiz*)	1·75	2·75
512	2m. Egyptian Goose (*horiz*)	1·75	5·00
513	5m. Lilac-breasted Roller (*horiz*)	2·25	12·00
500/13 *Set of 14*		11·00	22·00

Nos. 500/13 exist imperforate from stock dispersed by the liquidator of Format International Security Printers Ltd.

(Des Jennifer Toombs. Litho Format)

1982 (1 July). *21st Birthday of Princess of Wales. T* **136** *and similar vert designs. Multicoloured.* W w **14**. P 13½.

514	30s. Lesotho coat of arms	60	60
	a. Perf 13½×14	40	40
515	50s. Type **136**	60	60
	a. Perf 13½×14	1·25	1·25
516	75s. Wedding picture at Buckingham Palace	80	1·00
	a. Perf 13½×14	1·00	1·00
517	1m. Formal portrait	1·25	1·40
	a. Perf 13½×14	1·40	1·40
514/17 *Set of 4*		3·00	3·25
514a/17a *Set of 4*		3·50	3·50

Nos. 514/17 exist imperforate from stock dispersed by the liquidator of Format International Security Printers Ltd.

137 Mosotho reading Sesotho Bible

138 Birthday Greetings

(Des G. Vasarhelyi. Litho Format)

1982 (20 Aug). *Centenary of Sesotho Bible. T* **137** *and similar multicoloured designs.* P 14½.

518	6s. Type **137**	15	20
	a. Horiz strip of 3. Nos. 518/20	75	
519	15s. Sesotho Bible and Virgin Mary holding infant Jesus	20	25
520	1m. Sesotho Bible and Cathedral (62×42 mm)	50	75
518/20 *Set of 3*		75	1·10

Nos. 518/20 were printed together, *se-tenant*, in horizontal strips of 3 throughout the sheet.

(Des G. Vasarhelyi. Litho Questa)

1982 (30 Sept). *Birth of Prince William of Wales. T* **138** *and similar vert design. Multicoloured.* P 14×13½.

521	6s. Type **138**	2·25	2·75
	a. Sheetlet. No. 521 and 522×5	6·50	
522	60s. Princess Diana and Prince William of Wales	1·00	1·00

Nos. 521/2 come from sheetlets of 6 containing one 6s. and five 60s. stamps.

139 "A Partridge in a Pear Tree"

(Litho Format)

1982 (1 Dec). *Christmas. "The Twelve Days of Christmas". T* **139** *and similar horiz designs depicting Walt Disney cartoon characters. Multicoloured.* P 11.

523	2s. Type **139**	10	10
	a. Horiz pair. Nos. 523/4	10	10
524	2s. "Two turtle doves"	10	10
525	3s. "Three French hens"	10	10
	a. Horiz pair. Nos. 525/6	10	10
526	3s. "Four calling birds"	10	10
527	4s. "Five golden rings"	10	10
	a. Horiz pair. Nos. 527/8	15	15
528	4s. "Six geese a-laying"	10	10
529	75s. "Seven swans a-swimming"	1·40	1·75
	a. Horiz pair. Nos. 529/30	2·75	3·50
530	75s. "Eight maids a-milking"	1·40	1·75
523/30 *Set of 8*		2·75	3·50

MS531 126×101 mm. 1m.50, "Nine ladies dancing, ten lords a-leaping, eleven pipers piping, twelve drummers drumming". P 13½ ... 2·40 2·75

Nos. 523/4, 525/6, 527/8 and 529/30 were each printed in horizontal *se-tenant* pairs throughout the sheet.

140 *Lepista caffrorum*

(Des G. Vasarhelyi. Litho Format)

1983 (11 Jan). *Fungi. T* **140** *and similar horiz designs. Multicoloured.* P 14½.

532	10s. Type **140**	15	10
	a. Tête-bêche (vert pair)	30	30
	b. Booklet pane. Nos. 532/5	2·50	
	c. Booklet pane. Nos. 532/3	3·25	
533	30s. *Broomeia congregata*	30	40
	a. Tête-bêche (vert pair)	60	80
534	50s. *Afroboletus luteolus*	60	90
	a. Tête-bêche (vert pair)	1·10	1·75
535	75s. *Lentinus tuber-regium*	90	1·40
	a. Tête-bêche (vert pair)	1·75	2·75
532/5 *Set of 4*		1·75	2·50

Nos. 532/5 were each printed in sheets of 36 stamps plus 4 labels as the fourth horizontal row.

The stamps in horizontal rows two, six, eight and ten were inverted, forming vertical tête-bêche pairs.

Nos. 532/5 exist imperforate from stock dispersed by the liquidator of Format International Security Printers Ltd.

141 Ba-Leseli Dance

(Des J.W. Litho Format)

1983 (14 Mar). *Commonwealth Day. T* **141** *and similar multicoloured designs.* P 14½.

536	5s. Type **141**	10	10
537	30s. Tapestry weaving	20	30
538	60s. Queen Elizabeth II (*vert*)	35	65
539	75s. King Moshoeshoe II (*vert*)	40	80
536/9 *Set of 4*		90	1·60

Nos. 536/9 exist imperforate from stock dispersed by the liquidator of Format International Security Printers Ltd.

142 "Dancers in a Trance" (rock painting from Ntloana-Tšoana)

(Des G. Drummond. Litho Format)

1983 (20 May). *Rock Paintings. T* **142** *and similar multicoloured designs.* P 14½.

540	6s. Type **142**	20	10
541	25s. "Baboons", Sehonghong	55	35
542	60s. "Hunters attacking Mountain Reedbuck", Makhetha	60	1·10
543	75s. "Eland", Lehaha-la-Likhomo	65	1·60
540/3 *Set of 4*		1·75	2·75

MS544 166×84 mm. Nos. 540/3 and 10s. "Cattle herding", Sehonghong (52×52 mm) ... 1·25 3·50

Nos. 540/4 exist imperforate from stock dispersed by the liquidator of Format International Security Printers Ltd.

143 Montgolfier Balloon, 1783

(Des J.W. Litho Format)

1983 (11 July). *Bicentenary of Manned Flight. T* **143** *and similar multicoloured designs.* P 14½.

545	7s. Type **143**	15	10
	a. Booklet pane. Nos. 545/8	2·75	
546	30s. Wright brothers and Flyer I	30	40
547	60s. First airmail flight	50	1·25
548	1m. Concorde	2·25	2·50
545/8 *Set of 4*		2·75	3·75

MS549 180×92 mm. Nos. 545/8 and 6s. Dornier Do-28D Skyservant of Lesotho Airways (60×60 mm) ... 2·75 2·75

Nos. 545/9 exist imperforate from stock dispersed by the liquidator of Format International Security Printers Ltd.

144 Rev. Eugène Casalis

(Des G. Vasarhelyi. Litho Questa)

1983 (5 Sept). *150th Anniv of Arrival of the French Missionaries. T* **144** *and similar horiz designs. Multicoloured.* P 13½×14.

550	6s. Type **144**	10	10
	a. Tête-bêche (vert pair)	10	15
551	25s. The founding of Morija	10	10
	a. Tête-bêche (vert pair)	15	20
552	40s. Baptism of Libe	10	15
	a. Tête-bêche (vert pair)	20	30
553	75s. Map of Lesotho	20	25
	a. Tête-bêche (vert pair)	40	50
550/3 *Set of 4*		40	60

Nos. 550/3 were each issued in sheets of 20 containing two panes (2×5) separated by a vertical gutter. Within these sheets horizontal rows two and four are inverted forming tête-bêche vertical pairs.

145 Mickey Mouse and Pluto Greeted by Friends

(Litho Questa)

1983 (18 Oct). *Christmas. T* **145** *and similar horiz designs showing Disney cartoon characters in scenes from "Old Christmas" (Washington Irving's sketchbook). Multicoloured.* P 14×13½.

554	1s. Type **145**	10	10
555	2s. Donald Duck and Pluto	10	10
556	3s. Donald Duck with Huey, Dewey and Louie	10	10
557	4s. Goofy, Donald Duck and Mickey Mouse	10	10
558	5s. Goofy holding turkey, Donald Duck and Mickey Mouse	10	10
559	6s. Goofy and Mickey Mouse	10	10

560	75s. Donald and Daisy Duck	2·00	2·40
561	1m. Goofy and Clarabell	2·50	2·75
554/61	*Set of 8*	4·50	5·00
MS562	132×113 mm. 1m.75, Scrooge McDuck, Pluto and Donald Duck	3·25	4·50

146 *Danaus chrysippus*

(Des and litho Format)

1984 (20 Jan). *Butterflies. T* **146** *and similar horiz designs. Multcoloured.* P 14.

563	1s. *Type 146*	30	40
564	2s. *Aeropetes tulbaghia*	30	40
565	3s. *Colotis evenina*	35	40
566	4s. *Precis oenone*	35	40
567	5s. *Precis hierta*	35	40
568	6s. *Catopsilia florella*	35	10
569	7s. *Phalanta phalantha*	35	10
570	10s. *Acraea stenobea*	40	10
571	15s. *Cynthia cardui*	75	10
572	20s. *Colotis subfasciatus*	75	10
573	30s. *Charaxes jasius*	75	30
574	50s. *Terias brigitta*	75	40
575	60s. *Pontia helice*	75	50
576	75s. *Colotis regina*	75	50
577	1m. *Hypolimnas misippus*	75	1·50
578	5m. *Papilio demodocus*	1·50	7·50
563/78	*Set of 16*	8·50	11·50

Nos. 563/78 exist imperforate and as progressive proofs from stock dispersed by the liquidator of Format International Security Printers Ltd.

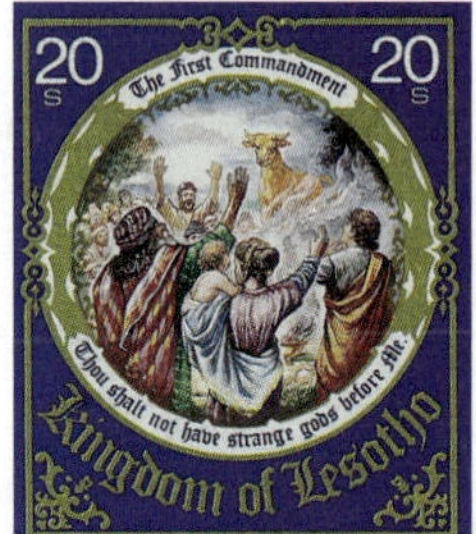

147 "Thou Shalt not have Strange Gods before Me"

(Des G. Vasarhelyi. Litho Format)

1984 (30 Mar). *Easter. The Ten Commandments. T* **147** *and similar vert designs. Multicoloured.* P 13½×14.

579	20s. Type **147**	30	30
	a. Sheetlet. Nos. 579/88	2·75	
580	20s. "Thou shalt not take the name of the Lord thy God in vain"	30	30
581	20s. "Remember thou keep holy the Lord's Day"	30	30
582	20s. "Honour thy father and mother"	30	30
583	20s. "Thou shalt not kill"	30	30
584	20s. "Thou shalt not commit adultery"	30	30
585	20s. "Thou shalt not steal"	30	30
586	20s. "Thou shalt not bear false witness against thy neighbour"	30	30
587	20s. "Thou shalt not covet thy neighbour's wife"	30	30
588	20s. Thou shalt not covet thy neighbour's goods"	30	30
579/88	*Set of 10*	2·75	2·75
MS589	102×73 mm. 1m.50, Moses with Tablets (45×28 mm). P 14	1·00	2·25

Nos. 579/88 were printed together in small sheets of 12 including 2 *se-tenant* stamp-size labels.

The second Commandment, "Thou shalt not make any graven image", was omitted and the tenth divided between Nos 587 and 588.

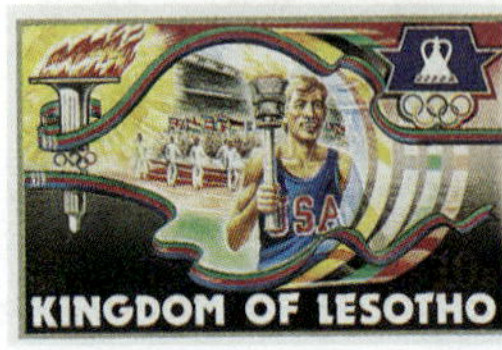

148 Torch Bearer

(Des G. Vasarhelyi. Litho Format)

1984 (3 May). *Olympic Games, Los Angeles. T* **148** *and similar horiz designs. Multicoloured.* P 13½×14.

590	10s. Type **148**	10	10
591	30s. Horse-riding	10	10
592	50s. Swimming	15	20
593	75s. Basketball	20	25
594	1m. Running	25	30
590/4	*Set of 5*	70	80
MS595	101×72 mm. 1m.50, Olympic Flame & flags	1·25	2·50

Nos. 590/4 exist imperforate from stock dispersed by the liquidator of Format International Security Printers Ltd.

149 Sauropodomorph Footprints

(Des G. Drummond. Litho Format)

1984 (2 July). *Prehistoric Footprints (2nd series). T* **149** *and similar horiz designs. Multicoloured.* P 13½×14.

596	10s. Type **149**	50	30
597	30s. Lesothosaurus footprints	60	1·25
598	50s. Footprint of carnivorous dinosaur	70	2·00
596/8	*Set of 3*	1·60	3·25

Nos. 596/8 exist imperforate from stock dispersed by the liquidator of Format International Security Printers Ltd.

150 Wells Fargo Coach, 1852

(Des G. Vasarhelyi. Litho Format)

1984 (5 Sept). *"Ausipex" International Stamp Exhibition, Melbourne, and Bicentenary of First Mail Coach Run. T* **150** *and similar horiz designs. Multicoloured.* P 14.

599	6s. Type **150**	10	10
	a. Sheetlet. Nos. 599×4 and No. 603	70	
600	7s. Basotho mail cart, circa 1900	10	10
	a. Sheetlet. No. 600×4 and No. 603	80	
601	10s. Bath mail coach, 1784	10	10
	a. Sheetlet. No. 601×4 and No. 603	90	
602	30s. Cobb coach, 1853	15	15
	a. Sheetlet. No. 602×4 and No. 603	1·00	
603	50s. Exhibition logo and Royal Exhibition Buildings, Melbourne (82×25 mm)	50	80
599/603	*Set of 5*	75	1·10
MS604	147×98 mm. 1m.75, G.B. Penny Black, Basutoland 1934 "OFFICIAL" optd 6d. and Western Australia 1854 4d. with frame inverted (82×25 mm)	2·25	3·75

In addition to the listed sheetlets, Nos. 599/602 also exist in separate sheets of 50. No. 603 only comes from the sheetlets.

Nos. 599/602 exist imperforate from stock dispersed by the liquidator of Format International Security Printers Ltd.

151 "The Orient Express" (1900)

(Des Walsall. Litho Format)

1984 (5 Nov). *Railways of the World. T* **151** *and similar horiz designs. Multicoloured.* P 14×13½.

605	6s. Type **151**	30	15
606	15s. Class 05 streamlined steam locomotive No. 001, Germany (1935)	30	30
607	30s. Caledonian Railway steam locomotive Cardean (1906)	35	60
608	60s. Atchison, Topeka & Santa Fe "Super Chief" express (1940)	40	1·75
609	1m. LNER "Flying Scotsman" (1934)	40	2·00
605/9	*Set of 5*	1·60	4·25
MS610	108×82 mm. 2m. South African Railways "The Blue Train" (1972)	1·00	2·50

No. 607 exists imperforate from stock dispersed by the liquidator of Format International Security Printers Ltd.

152 Eland Calf

153 Crown of Lesotho

(Des G. Drummond. Litho Format)

1984 (20 Dec). *Baby Animals. T* **152** *and similar horiz designs. Multicoloured.* P *14×13½ (1m.) or 15 (others).*

611	15s. Type **152**	35	20
612	20s. Young Chacma Baboons	35	25
613	30s. Oribi calf	35	40
614	75s. Young Natal Red Hares	50	1·60
615	1m. Black-backed Jackal pups (46×27 mm)	50	2·00
611/15	*Set of 5*	1·75	4·00

No. 615 exists imperforate from stock dispersed by the liquidator of Format International Security Printers Ltd.

(Des G. Vasarhelyi. Litho Format)

1985 (30 Jan). *Silver Jubilee of King Moshoeshoe II. T* **153** *and similar vert designs. Multicoloured.* P *15.*

616	6s. Type **153**	10	10
617	30s. King Moshoeshoe in 1960	20	30
618	75s. King Moshoeshoe in traditional dress, 1985	50	75
619	1m. King Moshoeshoe in uniform, 1985	70	1·10
616/19	*Set of 4*	1·25	2·00

154 Christ condemned to Death

(Des G. Vasarhelyi. Litho Format)

1985 (8 Mar). *Easter. The Stations of the Cross. T* **154** *and similar vert designs. Multicoloured.* P 11.

620	20s. Type **154**	25	35
	a. Sheetlet. Nos. 620/33	3·25	
621	20s. Christ carrying the Cross	25	35
622	20s. Falling for the first time	25	35
623	20s. Christ meets Mary	25	35
624	20s. Simon of Cyrene helping to carry the Cross	25	35
625	20s. Veronica wiping the face of Christ	25	35
626	20s. Christ falling a second time	25	35
627	20s. Consoling the women of Jerusalem	25	35
628	20s. Falling for the third time	25	35
629	20s. Christ being stripped	25	35
630	20s. Christ nailed to the Cross	25	35
631	20s. Dying on the Cross	25	35
632	20s. Christ taken down from the Cross	25	35
633	20s. Christ being laid in the sepulchre	25	35
620/33	*Set of 14*	3·25	4·50
MS634	138×98 mm. 2m. "The Crucifixion" (Mathias Grünewald). P 13½×14	1·50	3·50

Nos. 620/33 were printed together, *se-tenant*, in a sheetlet of 14 stamps with one stamp-sized label which appears in the central position.

155 Duchess of York with Princess Elizabeth, 1931

(Des G. Vasarhelyi. Litho Format)

1985 (30 May). *Life and Times of Queen Elizabeth the Queen Mother. T* **155** *and similar multicoloured designs.* P 13½×14.

635	10s. Type **155**	25	10
636	30s. The Queen Mother in 1975	70	50
637	60s. Queen Mother with Queen Elizabeth and Princess Margaret, 1980	80	90
638	2m. Four generations of Royal Family at Prince Henry's christening, 1984	1·25	2·50
635/8	*Set of 4*	2·75	3·50
MS639	139×98 mm. 2m. Queen Elizabeth with the Princess of Wales and her children at Prince Henry's christening (37×50 mm)	2·25	2·75

156 B.M.W. "732i"

157 American Cliff Swallow

(Litho Format)

1985 (10 June). *Century of Motoring. T* **156** *and similar multicoloured designs.* P 14×13½.

640	6s. Type **156**	25	15
641	10s. Ford "Crown Victoria"	35	15
642	30s. Mercedes-Benz "500SE"	75	50
643	90s. Cadillac "Eldorado Biarritz"	1·50	2·50
644	2m. Rolls-Royce "Silver Spirit"	2·00	4·00
640/4	*Set of 5*	4·25	6·50
MS645	139×98 mm. 2m. Rolls-Royce "Silver Ghost Tourer", 1907 (37×50 mm). P 13½×14	4·00	6·00

Nos. 640/5 exist imperforate from stock dispersed by the liquidator of Format International Security Printers Ltd.

(Litho Format)

1985 (5 Aug). *Birth Bicentenary of John J. Audubon (ornithologist). T* **157** *and similar multicoloured designs showing original paintings.* P 15.

646	5s. Type **157**	40	30
647	6s. Great Crested Grebe (*horiz*)	40	30
648	10s. Vesper Sparrow (*horiz*)	55	30
649	30s. Greenshank (*horiz*)	1·25	75
650	60s. Stilt Sandpiper (*horiz*)	1·75	2·75
651	2m. Glossy Ibis (*horiz*)	2·50	6·00
646/51 *Set of 6*		6·25	9·25

Nos. 646/51 were reissued in February 1986 in sheetlets containing five stamps and one label.

158 Two Youths Rock-climbing

159 UN (New York) 1951 1c. Definitive and UN Flag

(Des Walsall. Litho Format)

1985 (26 Sept). *International Youth Year and 75th Anniv of Girl Guide Movement. T* **158** *and similar vert designs. Multicoloured.* P 15.

652	10s. Type **158**	20	10
653	30s. Young technician in hospital laboratory	50	40
654	75s. Three guides on parade	1·00	1·25
655	2m. Guide saluting	1·75	3·00
652/5 *Set of 4*		3·00	4·25
MS656 138×98 mm. 2m. "Olave, Lady Baden Powell" (Grace Wheatley) (37×50 mm). P 13½×14		2·40	2·75

(Des G. Vasarhelyi. Litho Format)

1985 (15 Oct). *40th Anniv of United Nations Organization. T* **159** *and similar designs.* P 15.

657	10s. multicoloured	25	10
658	30s. multicoloured	60	35
659	50s. multicoloured	95	85
660	2m. black and bronze-green	5·00	6·50
657/60 *Set of 4*		6·25	7·00

Designs: *Vert*—30s. Ha Sofonia Earth Satellite Station; 2m. Maimonides (physician, philosopher and scholar). Horiz -50s. Lesotho Airways Fokker F.27 Friendship at Maseru Airport.

160 Cosmos

160a Mrs. Jumbo and Baby Dumbo

(Des D. Drummond. Litho Format)

1985 (11 Nov). *Wild Flowers. T* **160** *and similar vert designs. Multicoloured.* P 15.

661	6s. Type **160**	40	15
662	10s. Small Agapanthus	55	15
663	30s. Pink Witchweed	1·10	70
664	60s. Small Iris	1·50	2·00
665	90s. Wild Geranium or Cranesbill	1·75	3·00
666	1m. Large Spotted Orchid	3·00	5·00
661/6 *Set of 6*		7·50	10·00

(Des Walt Disney Productions. Litho Questa)

1985 (2 Dec). *150th Birth Anniv of Mark Twain. T* **160a** *and similar vert designs showing Walt Disney cartoon characters illustrating various Mark Twain quotations. Multicoloured.* P 11.

667	6s. Type **160a**	50	15
668	50s. Uncle Scrooge and Goofy reading newspaper	1·50	1·00
669	90s. Winnie the Pooh, Tigger, Piglet and Owl	2·00	2·00
670	1m.50 Goofy at ship's wheel	3·00	3·00
667/70 *Set of 4*		6·25	5·50
MS671 127×102 mm. 1m.25, Mickey Mouse as astronaut. P 13½×14		4·75	3·75

No. 669 was printed in sheetlets of 8 stamps.

160b Donald Duck as the Tailor

161 Male Lammergeier on Watch

(Des Walt Disney Productions. Litho Format)

1985 (2 Dec). *Birth Bicentenaries of Grimm Brothers (folklorists). T* **160b** *and similar vert designs showing Walt Disney cartoon characters in scenes from "The Wishing Table". Multicoloured.* P 11.

672	10s. Type **160b**	50	20
673	60s. The second son (Dewey) with magic donkey and gold coins	1·50	1·50
674	75s. The eldest son (Huey) with wishing table laden with food	1·75	1·75
675	1m. The innkeeper stealing the third son's (Louie) magic cudgel	2·00	2·75
672/5 *Set of 4*		5·25	5·50
MS676 127×102 mm. 1m.50, The tailor and eldest son with wishing table. P 13½×14		4·75	5·50

No. 673 was printed in sheetlets of 8 stamps.

(Des G. Drummond. Litho Format)

1986 (20 Jan). *Flora and Fauna of Lesotho. T* **161** *and similar vert designs. Multicoloured.* P 15.

677	7s. Type **161**	1·75	65
678	9s. Prickly Pear	70	20
679	12s. Stapelia	70	20
680	15s. Pair of Lammergeiers	2·50	60
681	35s. Pig's Ears	1·10	60
682	50s. Male Lammergeier in flight	3·75	2·75
683	1m. Adult and juvenile Lammergeiers	3·75	4·75
684	2m. Columnar cereus	3·75	6·50
677/84 *Set of 8*		16·00	14·50
MS685 125×106 mm. 2m. Verreaux's Eagle		8·50	12·00

162 Two Players chasing ball

162a Galileo and 200-inch Hale telescope at Mt. Palomer Observatory, California

(Des Lori Anzalone. Litho Questa)

1986 (17 Mar). *World Cup Football Championship, Mexico. T* **162** *and similar vert designs. Multicoloured.* P 14.

686	35s. Type **162**	1·25	50
687	50s. Goalkeeper saving goal	1·75	1·25
688	1m. Three players chasing ball	3·00	2·75
689	2m. Two players competing for ball	5·00	5·00
686/9 *Set of 4*		10·00	8·50
MS690 104×74 mm. 3m. Player heading ball		9·00	8·50

(Des W. Hanson. Litho Questa)

1986 (5 Apr). *Appearance of Halley's Comet. T* **162a** *and similar horiz designs. Multicoloured.* P 14.

691	9s. Type **162a**	50	15
692	15s. Halley's Comet and "Pioneer Venus 2" spacecraft	75	20
693	70s. Halley's Comet of 684 A.D. (from Nuremberg Chronicle, 1493)	1·40	1·40
694	3m. Comet and landing of William the Conqueror, 1066	4·00	5·50
691/4 *Set of 4*		6·25	6·50
MS695 101×70 mm. 4m. Halley's Comet over Lesotho		6·50	7·00

Nos. 691/3 show the face value followed by "S". Examples of these stamps without this currency abbreviation were prepared, but not issued.

163 International Year of the Child Gold Coin

163a Princess Elizabeth in Pantomime

(Litho Format)

1986 (Apr). *First Anniv of New Currency (1980). T* **163** *and similar horiz designs. Multicoloured.* P 13½×14.

696	30s. Type **163**	4·00	6·50
	a. Horiz strip of 5. Nos. 696/700	18·00	
697	30s. Five maloti banknote	4·00	6·50
698	30s. Fifty lisente coin	4·00	6·50
699	30s. Ten maloti banknote	4·00	6·50
700	30s. One sente coin	4·00	6·50
696/700 *Set of 5*		18·00	29·00

Nos. 696/700 were printed together, *se-tenant*, in horizontal strips of 5 throughout the sheet.

These stamps were prepared in 1980, but were not issued at that time. Due to increased postal rates a severe shortage of 30s. stamps occurred in 1986 and Nos. 696/700 were sold for postal purposes from mid-April until early August.

(Des L. Nardo. Litho Questa)

1986 (21 Apr). *60th Birthday of Queen Elizabeth II. T* **163a** *and similar vert designs.* P 14.

701	90s. black and yellow	50	60
702	1m. multicoloured	55	65
703	2m. multicoloured	90	1·40
701/3 *Set of 3*		1·75	2·40
MS704 119×85 mm. 4m. black and grey-brown		1·75	3·25

Designs:—1m. Queen at Windsor Horse Show, 1971; 2m. At Royal Festival Hall, 1971; 4m. Princess Elizabeth in 1934.

163b Statue of Liberty and Bela Bartok (composer)

(Des J. Iskowitz. Litho Questa)

1986 (5 May). *Centenary of Statue of Liberty. T* **163b** *and similar horiz designs showing the Statue of Liberty and immigrants to the USA. Multicoloured.* P 14.

705	15s. Type **163b**	85	30
706	35s. Felix Adler (philosopher)	85	30
707	1m. Victor Herbert (composer)	3·00	2·00
708	3m. David Niven (actor)	4·25	4·25
705/8 *Set of 4*		8·00	6·25
MS709 103×74 mm. 3m. Statue of Liberty (*vert*)		3·50	5·00

163c Mickey Mouse and Goofy as Japanese Mail Runners

(Des Walt Disney Productions. Litho Format)

1986 (25 May). *"Ameripex" International Stamp Exhibition, Chicago. T* **163c** *and similar horiz designs showing Walt Disney cartoon characters delivering mail. Multicoloured.* P 11.

710	15s. Type **163c**	80	20
711	35s. Mickey Mouse and Pluto with mail sledge	1·25	30
712	1m. Goofy as postman riding Harley Davidson motorcycle	2·50	2·75
713	2m. Donald Duck operating railway mailbag apparatus	2·75	4·00
710/13 *Set of 4*		6·50	6·50
MS714 127×101 mm. 4m. Goofy driving mail to aircraft. P 14×13½		6·50	7·00

9s (164) 9s (165) 15s (166) 35s (167) 35s (167a)

15s Extra bar (R.2/5) 9s Long bars R. 3/8 35s Small "s"

Nos. 720a, 720bb, 721a, 721ca, 730ba. Occurs eleven times in the sheet of 40 on R. 1/5, 1/6, 1/8, 1/9, 2/6, 2/7, 2/8, 3/5, 4/4, 4/6 and 4/8 for Nos. 720a, 720bb and 730bc or R. 1/4, 2/4, 4/4, 5/4, 6/4, 7/1, 7/4, 9/1, 9/3, 10/1 and 10/2 for Nos. 721a and 721ca.

No. 728a. Occurs thirteen times in the sheet of 49 on R. 6/2 to 7 and on all positions in Row 7.

9s (168) 35s (169) 20s (170)

1986 (6 June)–**88**. *Various stamps surch (a) As T 164/7a by Lesotho Ads, Maseru. (i) On Nos. 440, 447, 500/1, 506/7 and 509.*

715	9s. on 10s. Red-billed Pintail (*horiz*) (No. 506) (Type 164)	3·50	1·25
	a. Surch on No. 443 ("1982" imprint date)	2·25	2·25
	b. Surch double	†	—
	c. Surch inverted		
	d. Surch double, one inverted	†	—
716	15s. on 1s. Type **127** (No. 500) (22.8.86)	7·00	3·00
	a. Extra bar b. Surch on No. 437 ("1982" imprint date)	£110	
	c. Surch on No. 437a	5·00	6·00
	ca. Extra bar cb. Surch double		
717	15s. on 2s. Speckled Pigeon (*horiz*) (22.8.86)	4·00	4·50
	a. Surch double	60·00	
	b. Surch triple		
	c. Surch omitted (in horiz pair with normal)		
718	15s. on 5s. Bokmakierie Shrike ("1982" imprint date) (2.11.87)	2·00	35
	a. Surch double	50·00	
719	15s.. on 60s. Cape Longclaw (*horiz*) (No. 509) (22.8.86)	20	10
	a. Surch on No. 446	60	30
720	35s. on 25s. Malachite Kingfisher (No. 507) (9.87)	17·00	20·00
	a. Small "s"	32·00	35·00
	b. Surch on No. 444	50·00	50·00
	ba. Surch double	£100	
	bb. Surch inverted		
	bc. Small "s"	£100	£100
721	35s. on 75s. Hoopoe (*horiz*) (No. 447) (Type 167) (9.87)	16·00	15·00
	a. Small "s"	32·00	32·00
	b. Surch double	55·00	
	c. Surch on No 510	£110	95·00
	ca. Small "s"	£200	

721*d* 35s. on 75s. Hoopoe (*horiz*) (No. 447) (Type 167a) (1.88) 75·00

(ii) On Nos. 563/5, 567, 573 and 575/6.

722 9s. on 30s. Charaxes jasius (Type 164) (1.7.86) 15 10
a. Surch with Type **165** 6·50 4·50
ab. Surch double † —
ac. Surch double (in horiz pair with normal)
ad. Surch omitted (in horiz pair with normal) 75·00
ae. Surch triple
b. Surch omitted (in horiz pair with misplaced surch)

723 9s. on 60s. Pontia helice (Type **165**) (1.7.86) 3·25 4·00
a. Surch double 50·00
b. Surch double, one inverted 50·00
c. Surch inverted d. Surch triple

724 15s. on 1s. Type **146** (25.6.86) 2·00 2·25
a. Surch double b. Surch omitted (in horiz pair with normal)

725 15s. on 2s. Aeropetes tulbaghia (25.6.86) 20 20
726 15s. on 3s. Colotis evenina (25.6.86) 20 20
a. Surch omitted (in horiz pair with normal)

727 15s. on 5s. Precis hierta (14.8.87) 20 20
a. Surch double 32·00
b. Surch omitted (in horiz pair with normal) 30·00
c. Surch triple

728 35s. on 75s. Colotis regina (15.8.86) 35 35
a. Small "s" 1·50 1·50

*(b) As T **168/170** by Epic Printers, Maseru.*

(i) On Nos. 440 and 444.

729 9s. on 5s. Bokmakierie Shrike ("1982" imprint date) (30.12.87) 75 20
a. Long bars

730 16s. on 25s. Malachite Kingfisher (No. 444) (3.88) 2·75 1·00
a. Surch on No. 507 £225

730b 16s. on 35s. on 25s. (No. 720) 90·00
ba. Small "s" in surch T **167** £170
c. Surch on No. 720b † —

731 35s. on 25s. Malachite Kingfisher (No. 444) (15.12.87) 1·50 60
a. Surch on No. 507 13·00 10·00

(ii) On Nos. 566 and 569.

732 20s. on 4s. *Precis oenone* (30.12.87) 10 10
a. Surch double
b. Surch double, one inverted 12·00 9·00

733 40s.. on 7s. *Phalanta phalantha* (30.12.87). 15 20

(iii) On No. 722.

734 3s. on 9s. on 30s. *Charaxes jasius* (2.2.88) 1·00 1·00
a. Surch Type **164** † —
b. "3s" surch double
c. Additionally Surch 7s. (as No. 735)..

735 7s. on 9s. on 30s. *Charaxes jasius* (2.2.88) 1·25 1·00

715/35 *Set of 21* 55·00 50·00

Some examples of Nos. 722a and 723 show thicker figures due to the method used to construct the artwork for the surcharge.

Nos. 730b/ba show a 16s. surcharge as T **168** applied to stamps previously surcharged with T **167**.

170a Prince Andrew and Miss Sarah Ferguson

171 Basotho Pony and Rider

(Des D. Miller. Litho Questa)

1986 (23 July). *Royal Wedding. T **170a** and similar vert designs. Multicoloured.* P 14.

736 50s. Type **170a** 40 40
737 1m. Prince Andrew 70 80
738 3m. Prince Andrew piloting helicopter 2·75 2·25
736/8 *Set of 3* 3·50 3·00
MS739 88×88 mm. 4m. Prince Andrew and Miss Sarah Ferguson (different) 3·50 4·50

(Des B. Bundock. Litho Format)

1986 (3 Oct). *20th Anniv of Independence. T **171** and similar horiz designs. Multicoloured.* P 15.

740 9s. Type **171** 40 10
741 15s. Basotho woman spinning mohair 40 15
742 35s. Crossing river by rowing boat 50 30
743 3m. Thaba-Tseka Post Office 1·00 3·00
740/3 *Set of 4* 2·10 3·25
MS744 109×78 mm. 4m. King Moshoeshoe I 4·75 8·00

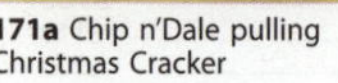

171a Chip n'Dale pulling Christmas Cracker

172 Rally car

(Des Walt Disney Co. Litho Format)

1986 (4 Nov). *Christmas. T **171a** and similar vert designs showing Walt Disney cartoon characters. Multicoloured.* P 11.

745 15s. Type **171a** 80 20
746 35s. Mickey and Minnie Mouse 1·10 30
747 1m. Pluto pulling Christmas taffy 1·90 2·75
748 2m. Aunt Matilda baking 2·25 4·00
745/8 *Set of 4* 5·50 6·50
MS749 126×102 mm. 5m. Huey and Dewey with gingerbread house. P 13½×14 5·50 7·00

(Litho Questa)

1987 (28 Apr). *Roof of Africa Motor Rally. T **172** and similar vert designs. Multicoloured.* P 14.

750 9s. Type **172** 30 10
751 15s. Motorcyclist 35 15
752 35s. Motorcyclist (different) 55 35
753 4m. Rally car (different) 3·00 5·00
750/3 Set of 4 3·75 5·00

173 Lawn Tennis

174 Isaac Newton and Reflecting Telescopelsaac Newton and Reflecting Telescope

(Des Y. Berry. Litho Questa)

1987 (29 May). *Olympic Games, Seoul (1988) (1st issue). T **173** and similar vert designs. Multicoloured.* P 14.

754 9s. Type **173** 70 10
755 15s. Judo 70 15
756 20s. Athletics 75 20
757 35s. Boxing 85 30
758 1m. Diving 1·10 1·75
759 3m. Ten-pin bowling 2·75 5·50
754/9 *Set of 6* 6·25 7·25
MS760 Two sheets, each 75×105 mm. (a) 2mLawn tennis (different). (b) 4m. Football *Set of $1 sheets* 6·00 5·00

Nos. 754/60 incorrectly show the Lesotho flag with white field and emblem at top right.

Similar stamps, with face values of 5, 10, 25, 40, 50s., 3m.50 and a 4m. miniature sheet showing the correct flag with white field and emblem at top left, were placed on philatelic sale from 30 November 1987. They were not, however, according to the Lesotho Philatelic Bureau, sold through post offices and agencies for postal purposes (Price for set of 6 £3, mint; miniature sheet £2.75 mint).

See also Nos. 838/42.

(Des Mary Walters. Litho Format)

1987 (30 June). *Great Scientific Discoveries. T **174** and similar horiz designs. Multicoloured.* P 15.

761 5s. Type **174** 30 10
762 9s. Alexander Graham Bell and first telephone 30 15
763 75s. Robert Goddard and liquid fuel rocket 80 75
764 4m. Chuck Yeager and Bell XS-1 rocket plane 2·75 4·50
761/4 *Set of 4* 3·50 5·00
MS765 98×68 mm. 4m. "Mariner 10" spacecraft 2·75 3·00

175 Grey Rhebuck

176 Scouts hiking

(Des G. Drummond. Litho Format)

1987 (14 Aug). *Flora and Fauna. T **175** and similar multicoloured designs.* P 15.

766 5s. Type **175** 40 15
767 9s. Cape Clawless Otter 40 15
768 15s. Cape Grey Mongoose 55 20
769 20s. Free State Daisy (*vert*) 60 20
770 35s. River Bells (*vert*) 75 30
771 1m. Turkey Flower (*vert*) 1·75 2·50
772 2m. Sweet Briar (*vert*) 2·25 3·75
773 3m. Mountain Reedbuck 2·75 5·00
766/73 *Set of 8* 8·50 11·00
MS774 114×98 mm. (a) 2m. Pig-Lily (*vert*). (b) 4m. Cape Wildebeest. *Set of $1 sheets* 5·50 9·00

(Des Mary Walters. Litho Questa)

1987 (10 Sept). *World Scout Jamboree, Australia. T **176** and similar vert designs. Multicoloured.* P 14.

775 9s. Type **176** 60 20
776 15s. Scouts playing football 65 20
777 35s. Kangaroos 80 50
778 75s. Scout saluting 1·75 1·25
779 4m. Australian scout windsurfing 3·75 6·50
775/9 *Set of 5* 6·75 7·75
MS780 96×66 mm. 4m. Outline map and flag of Australia 3·25 4·00

177 Spotted Trunkfish and Columbus' Fleet

178 "Madonna and Child" (detail)

(Des I. MacLaury. Litho Questa)

1987 (14 Dec). *500th Anniv of Discovery of America by Columbus (1992). T **177** and similar horiz designs. Multicoloured.* P 14.

781 9s. Type **177** 65 20
782 15s. Green Turtle and ships 80 20
783 35s. Columbus watching Common Dolphins from ship 1·00 40
784 5m. White-tailed Tropic Bird and fleet at sea 6·50 8·00
781/4 *Set of 4* 8·00 8·00
MS785 105×76 mm. 4m. Santa Maria and Cuban Amazon in flight 5·00 4·00

No. 782 is inscribed "Carribbean" in error.

(Litho Questa)

1987 (21 Dec). *Christmas. T **178** and similar vert designs showing religious paintings by Raphael. Multicoloured.* P 14.

786 9s. Type **178** 30 10
787 15s. "Marriage of the Virgin" 45 15
788 35s. "Coronation of the Virgin" (detail) 90 40
789 90s. "Madonna of the Chair" 2·00 3·50
786/9 *Set of 4* 3·25 3·75
MS790 75×100 mm. 3m. "Madonna and Child enthroned with Five Saints" (detail) 3·00 3·00

179 Lesser Pied Kingfisher

40TH WEDDING ANNIVERSARY
H.M. QUEEN ELIZABETH II
H.R.H. THE DUKE OF EDINBURGH
(180)

(Des G. Drummond. Litho Format)

1988 (5 Apr). *Birds. T **179** and similar horiz designs. Multicoloured. "1988" imprint date, but no printer's imprint.* P 15.

791 2s. Type **179** 20 30
792 3s. Three-banded Plover 20 30
793 5s. Spur-winged Goose 20 30
794 10s. Clapper Lark 20 20
795 12s. Red-eyed Bulbul 30 10
796 16s. Cape Weaver 30 10
797 20s. Paradise Sparrow ("Red-headed Finch") 30 10
798 30s. Mountain Chat 35 20
799 40s. Stonechat 40 20
800 55s. Pied Barbet 50 25
801 60s. Red-shouldered Glossy Starling 55 50
802 75s. Cape Sparrow 60 60
803 1m. Cattle Egret 60 80
804 3m. Giant Kingfisher 90 2·50
805 10m. Helmet Guineafowl 1·90 7·00
791/805 *Set of 15* 6·75 12·00

For these stamps showing Questa imprint at bottom left see Nos. 887/99.

1988 (3 May). *Royal Ruby Wedding. Nos. 701/4 optd with T **180** in silver.*

806 90s. black and yellow 90 65
807 1m. multicoloured 1·00 80
808 2m. multicoloured 1·75 1·40
806/8 *Set of 3* 3·25 2·50
MS809 119×85 mm. 4m. black and grey-brown 3·00 2·75

*Nos. 806/9 were not available in Lesotho until the middle of 1990.

181 Mickey Mouse and Goofy outside Presidential Palace, Helsinki

(Des Walt Disney Co. Litho Questa)

1988 (2 June). *"Finlandia '88" International Stamp Exhibition, Helsinki. T **181** and similar horiz designs showing Walt Disney cartoon characters in Finland. Multicoloured.* P 14×13½.

810 1s. Type **181** 10 10
811 2s. Goofy and Mickey Mouse in sauna 10 10
812 3s. Goofy and Mickey Mouse fishing in lake 10 10
813 4s. Mickey and Minnie Mouse and Finlandia Hall, Helsinki 10 10
814 5s. Mickey Mouse photographing Goofy at Sibelius Monument, Helsinki 10 10
815 10s. Mickey Mouse and Goofy pony trekking 10 10
816 3m. Goofy, Mickey and Minnie Mouse at Helsinki Olympic stadium 4·50 3·00
817 5m. Mickey Mouse and Goofy meeting Santa at Arctic Circle 5·50 4·00
810/17 *Set of 8* 9·50 6·75

MS818 Two sheets, each 127×102 mm. (a) 4m. Mickey Mouse and nephew as Lapps. (b) 4m. Daisy Duck, Goofy, Mickey and Minnie Mouse by fountain, Helsinki. *Set of* $1 *sheets* 5·50 7·00

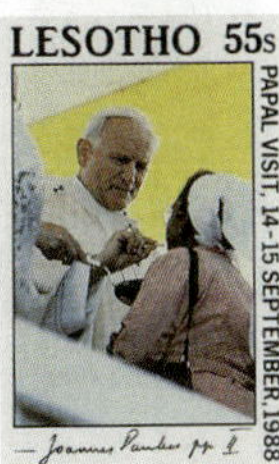

182 Pope John Paul II giving Communion

183 Large-toothed Rock Hyrax

(Litho Questa)

1988 (1 Sept). *Visit of Pope John Paul II. T* **182** *and similar multicoloured designs.* P 14.

819 55s. Type **182** 40 25
820 2m. Pope leading procession 1·25 1·50
821 3m. Pope at airport 1·75 2·00
822 4m. Pope John Paul II 2·25 2·75
819/22 *Set of* 4 5·00 6·00
MS823 98×79 mm. 5m. Archbishop Morapeli (*horiz*) 5·00 4·50

(Des L. Watkins. Litho B.D.T.)

1988 (13 Oct). *Small Mammals of Lesotho. T* **183** *and similar vert designs. Multicoloured.* P 14.

824 16s. Type **183** 55 15
825 40s. Ratel and Black-throated Honeyguide (bird) 1·75 55
826 75s. Small-spotted Genet 1·50 85
827 3m. Yellow Mongoose 3·25 5·50
824/7 *Set of* 4 6·25 6·25
MS828 110×78 mm. 4m. Meerkat 3·25 4·00

184 "Birth of Venus" (detail) (Botticelli)

(Litho Questa)

1988 (17 Oct). *Famous Paintings. T* **184** *and similar vert designs. Multicoloured.* P 13½×14.

829 15s. Type **184** 30 15
830 25s. "View of Toledo" (El Greco) 35 20
831 40s. "Maids of Honour" (detail) (Velasquez) 45 25
832 50s. "The Fifer (Manet) 55 30
833 55s. "Starry Night" (detail) (Van Gogh) 55 30
834 75s. "Prima Ballerina" (Degas) 70 70
835 2m. "Bridge over Water Lilies" (Monet) 1·75 2·25
836 3m. "Guernica" (detail) (Picasso) 1·75 2·75
829/36 *Set of* 8 5·75 6·25
MS837 Two sheets, each 110×95 mm. (a) 4m. "The Presentation of the Virgin in the Temple" (Titian). (b) 4m. "The Miracle of the Newborn Infant" (Titian) *Set of* $1 *sheets* 4·00 4·50

185 Wrestling

(Des J. Martin. Litho B.D.T.)

1988 (11 Nov). *Olympic Games, Seoul (2nd issue). T* **185** *and similar multicoloured designs.* P 14.

838 12s. Type **185** 10 10
839 16s. Show jumping (*vert*) 10 10
840 55s. Shooting 20 30
841 3m.50 As 16s. (*vert*) 1·40 2·00
838/41 *Set of* 4 1·50 2·25
MS842 108×77 mm. 4m. Olympic flame (*vert*) 2·75 3·50

A similar set of three values and a miniature sheet, with fencing instead of show jumping on the 16s., exists, but was not issued, possibly because the 55s., 3m.50 and miniature sheet show the obsolete Lesotho flag.

186 Yannick Noah and Eiffel Tower, Paris

186a "The Averoldi Polyptych" (detail) (Titian)

(Des J. McDaniels. Litho Questa)

1988 (18 Nov). *75th Anniv of International Tennis Federation. T* **186** *and similar multicoloured designs.* P 14.

843 12s. Type **186** 60 25
844 20s. Rod Laver and Sydney Harbour Bridge and Opera House 1·00 30
845 30s. Ivan Lendl and Prague 65 25
846 65s. Jimmy Connors and Tokyo (*vert*) 80 40
847 1m. Arthur Ashe and Barcelona (*vert*) 1·25 60
848 1m.55 Althea Gibson and New York (*vert*). 1·25 90
849 2m. Chris Evert and Vienna (*vert*) 1·50 1·25
850 2m.40 Boris Becker and Houses of Parliament, London (*vert*) 1·75 1·75
851 3m. Martina Navratilova and Golden Gate Bridge, San Francisco 2·00 2·00
843/51 *Set of* 9 9·75 7·00
MS852 98×72 mm. 4m. Steffi Graf and Berlin 3·00 3·75

No. 844 is inscribed "SIDNEY" in error.

(Litho Questa)

1988 (1 Dec). *Christmas. 500th Birth Anniv of Titian (artist). T* **186a** *and similar multicoloured designs.* P 13½×14.

853 12s. Type **186a** 20 10
854 20s. "Christ and the Adulteress" (detail). 20 10
855 35s. "Christ and the Adulteress" (different detail) 30 20
856 45s. "Angel of the Annunciation" 40 30
857 65s. "Saint Dominic" 55 50
858 1m. "The Vendramin Family" (detail) 75 80
859 2m. "Mary Magdalen" 1·25 1·75
860 3m. "The Tribute Money" 1·75 2·50
853/60 *Set of* 8 4·75 5·50
MS861 (a) 94×110 mm. 5m. "Mater Doloroso". P 13½×14. (b) 110×94 mm. 5m. "Christ and the Woman taken in Adultery" (*horiz*). P 14×13½ *Set of* $1 *sheets* 6·00 8·00

187 Pilatus PC-6 Turbo Porter

(Des K. Gromell. Litho Questa)

1989 (30 Jan). *125th Anniv of International Red Cross. Aircraft. T* **187** *and similar multicoloured designs.* P 14.

862 12s. Type **187** 50 10
863 20s. Unloading medical suppliesfrom Cessna 208 Caravan I 60 20
864 55s. De Havilland D.H.C.6 Twin Otter 200/300 90 50
865 3m. Douglas DC-3 2·75 3·50
862/5 *Set of* 4 4·25 3·75
MS866 109×80 mm. 4m. Red Cross logo and Douglas DC-3 (*vert*) 6·50 3·75

187a "Dawn Mist at Mishima" (Hiroshige)

(Litho Questa)

1989 (19 June). *Japanese Art. Paintings by Hiroshige. T* **187a** *and similar horiz designs. Multicoloured.* P 14×13½.

867 12s. Type **187a** 30 10
868 16s. "Night Snow at Kambara" 35 10
869 20s. "Wayside Inn at Mariko Station" 35 10
870 35s. "Shower at Shono" 55 10
871 55s. "Snowfall on the Kisokaido near Oi" 65 40
872 1m. "Autumn Moon at Seba" 85 85
873 3m.20 "Evening Moon at Ryogoku Bridge" 2·25 3·00
874 5m. "Cherry Blossoms at Arashiyama" 2·75 3·75
867/74 *Set of* 8 7·25 7·50
MS875 Two sheets, each 102×76 mm. (a) 4m. "Listening to the Singing Insects at Dokanyama". (b) 4m. "Moonlight, Nagakubo" *Set of* $1 *sheets* 6·00 7·00

Nos. 867/74 were each printed in sheetlets of 10 containing two horizontal strips of 5 stamps separated by printed labels commemorating Emperor Hirohito.

188 Mickey Mouse as General

189 *Paxillus involutus*

(Des Walt Disney Company. Litho Questa)

1989 (10 July). *"Philexfrance 89" International Stamp Exhibition, Paris. T* **188** *and similar multicoloured designs showing Walt Disneycartoon characters in French military uniforms of the Revolutionary period.* P 13½×14.

876 1s. Type **188** 10 10
877 2s. Ludwig von Drake as infantryman 10 10
878 3s. Goofy as grenadier 10 10
879 4s. Horace Horsecollar as cavalryman 10 10
880 5s. Pete as hussar 10 10
881 10s. Donald Duck as marine 10 10
882 3m. Gyro Gearloose as National Guard 3·25 3·25
883 5m. Scrooge McDuck as admiral 4·00 4·25
876/83 *Set of* 8 6·75 7·00
MS884 Two sheets, each 127×102 mm. (a) 4m. Mickey and Minnie Mouse as King Louis XVI and Marie Antoinette with Goofy as a National Guard (*horiz*). P 14×13½. (b) 4m. Mickey Mouse as drummer. P 13½×14. *Set of* $1 *sheets* 7·50 9·00

No. 879 is inscribed "CALVARYMAN" in error.

(Litho Questa)

1989 (31 Aug)–**91**. *As Nos. 793, 795/7 and 803/5, but "1989" imprint date and with printer's imprint at bottom left.* P 14.

887 5s. Spur-winged Goose (18.1.90) 55 70
889 12s. Red-eyed Bulbul 60 15
890 16s. Cape Weaver (11.11.89) 60 15
891 20s. Paradise Sparrow ("Red-headed Finch") (2.12.89) 60 15
897 1m. Cattle Egret (1991) 1·75 1·10
898 3m. Giant Kingfisher (1991) 2·75 3·50
899 10m. Helmet Guineafowl (1991) 7·00 8·00
887/99 *Set of* 7 12·00 12·00

This issue is also known perforated 12, but there is no evidence that stamps in this perforation were used for postal purposes in Lesotho.

(Des S. Wood. Litho Questa)

1989 (8 Sept). *Fungi. T* **189** *and similar vert designs. Multicoloured.* P 14.

900 12s. Type **189** 20 10
901 16s. *Ganoderma applanatum* 20 15
902 55s. *Suillus granulatus* 45 35
903 5m. *Stereum hirsutum* 3·25 4·50
900/3 *Set of* 4 3·75 4·50
MS904 96×69 mm. 4m. *Scleroderma cepa* ("*flavidum*") 5·00 5·50

190 Basotho Huts

191 Marsh Sandpiper

(Des S. Wood. Litho Questa)

1989 (18 Sept). *Maloti Mountains. T* **190** *and similar vert designs. Multicoloured.* P 14.

905 1m. Type **190** 70 1·00
a. Horiz strip of 4. Nos. 905/8 2·50
906 1m. American Aloe and mountains 70 1·00
907 1m. River valley with waterfall 70 1·00
908 1m. Mosotho man on ledge 70 1·00
905/8 *Set of* 4 2·50 3·50
MS909 86×117 mm. 4m. Spiral Aloe 3·00 4·00

Nos. 905/8 were printed together, *se-tenant*, in horizontal strips of 4 throughout the sheet forming a composite design.

(Des Tracy Pedersen. Litho Questa)

1989 (18 Sept). *Migrant Birds. T* **191** *and similar multicoloured designs.* P 14.

910 12s. Type **191** 80 30
911 65s. Little Stint 1·50 70
912 1m. Ringed Plover 2·00 1·50
913 4m. Curlew Sandpiper 3·50 5·50
910/13 *Set of* 4 7·00 7·25
MS914 97×69 mm. 5m. Ruff (*vert*) 8·50 9·00

192 Launch of "Apollo 11"

193 English Penny Post Paid Mark, 1680

(Des G. Welker. Litho Questa)

1989 (6 Nov). *20th Anniv of First Manned Landing on Moon. T* **192** *and similar multicoloured designs.* P 14.

915 12s. Type **192** 25 10
916 16s. Lunar module Eagle landing on Moon (*horiz*) 25 15
917 40s. Neil Armstrong leaving Eagle 45 25
918 55s. Edwin Aldrin on Moon (*horiz*) 50 30
919 1m. Aldrin performing scientific experiment (*horiz*) 85 85
920 2m. Eagle leaving Moon (*horiz*) 1·50 1·75
921 3m. Command module Columbia in Moon orbit (*horiz*) 2·00 2·25
922 4m. Command module on parachutes 2·50 2·75
915/22 *Set of* 8 7·50 7·50
MS923 81×111 mm. 5m. Astronaut on Moon 5·00 6·00

(Des U. Purins. Litho B.D.T)

1989 (17 Nov). *"World Stamp Expo '89" International Stamp Exhibition, Washington (1st issue). Stamps and Postmarks. T* **193** *and similar horiz designs.* P 14.

924 75s. brown-lake, black and stone 80 80
a. Sheetlet. Nos. 924/32 6·50
925 75s. black, grey and rosine 80 80
926 75s. dull violet, black and cinnamon 80 80
927 75s. red-brown, black and cinnamon 80 80
928 75s. black and olive-yellow 80 80
929 75s. multicoloured 80 80
930 75s. black and bright brown-lilac 80 80
931 75s. black, bright carmine and pale brown 80 80
932 75s. brt carmine, black & greenish yellow 80 80
924/32 *Set of* 9 6·50 6·50

Designs:—No. 925, German postal seal and feather, 1807; 926, British Post Offices in Crete 1898 20pa. stamp; 927, Bermuda 1848 Perot 1d. provisional; 928, USA Pony Express cancellation, 1860; 929, Finland 1856 5k. stamp; 930, Fiji 1870 Fiji Times 1d. stamp, 1870; 931, Sweden newspaper wrapper handstamp, 1823; 932, Bhor 1879 ½a. stamp.

Nos. 924/32 were printed together, *se-tenant*, in sheetlets of 9.

193a Cathedral Church of St. Peter and St. Paul, Washington

193b "The Immaculate Conception" (Valazquez)

(Des Design Element. Litho Questa)

1989 (17 Nov). *"World Stamp Expo '89" International Stamp Exhibition, Washington (2nd issue). Sheet 78×61 mm.* P 14.

MS933 **193a** 4m. multicoloured 2·50 3·00

(Litho Questa)

1989 (18 Dec). *Christmas. Paintings by Velazquez. T* **193b** *and similar vert designs. Multicoloured.* P 14.

934 12s. Type **193b** 10 10
935 20s. "St. Anthony Abbot and St. Paul the Hermit" 15 10
936 35s. "St. Thomas the Apostle" 25 25
937 55s. "Christ in the House of Martha and Mary" 35 35
938 1m. "St. John writing The Apocalypse on Patmos" 60 75
939 3m. "The Virgin presenting the Chasuble to St. Ildephonsus" 1·60 2·25
940 4m. "The Adoration of the Magi" 2·00 2·75
934/40 *Set of* 7 4·50 6·00
MS941 71×96 mm. 5m. "The Coronation of the Virgin" 6·50 7·50

194 Scene from 1966 World Cup Final, England

(Des G. Vasarhelyi. Litho Questa)

1989 (27 Dec). *World Cup Football Championship, Italy. T* **194** *and similar horiz designs showing scenes from past finals. Multicoloured.* P 14.

942 12s. Type **194** 50 10
943 16s. 1970 final, Mexico 50 15
944 55s. 1974 final, West Germany 1·00 40
945 5m. 1982 final, Spain 3·75 5·50
942/5 Set of 4 5·25 5·50
MS946 106×85 mm. 4m. Player's legs and symbolic football 6·00 7·00

16 s (**195**) 16 s (**196**) 16 s Long bars (R. 6/3) 16 s (**196a**)

1990 (22 Feb)–**91**. *Nos. 795, 798/9 and 889 surch with T* **195**/**196a** *by Lesotho Ads.*

947 16s. on 12s. Red-eyed Bulbul (No. 795) (T **195**) 6·00 1·25
948 16s. on 12s. Red-eyed Bulbul (No. 889) (T **196**) 1·75 20
a. Surch inverted 40·00
b. Surch double 60·00
c. Long bars d. Surch with Type **195**
948*e* 16s. on 30s. Mountain Chat (No. 798) (T **196a**) (18.1.91) 75 15
ea. Surch inverted eb. Lower bar omitted
948*f* 16s. on 40s. Stonechat (No. 799) (T **196a**) (18.1.91) 75 15
fa. Lower bar omitted
947/8f *Set of* 4 8·25 1·60

The lower cancelling bar is frequently completely omitted from Type **196a** on R. 4/4, although on occasions traces of it do remain.

197 *Byblia anvatara*

198 *Satyrium princeps*

(Des L Nelson. Litho Questa)

1990 (26 Feb). *Butterflies. T* **197** *and similar vert designs. Multicoloured.* P 14.

949 12s. Type **197** 80 15
950 16s. *Cynthia cardui* 90 15
951 55s. *Precis oenone* 1·40 40
952 65s. *Pseudacraea boisduvali* 1·40 65
953 1m. *Precis orithya* 2·25 1·25
954 2m. *Precis sophia* 3·25 2·50
955 3m. *Danaus chrysippus* 4·25 4·25
956 4m. *Druryia antimachus* 5·00 6·50
949/56 *Set of* 8 17·00 14·00
MS957 105×70 mm. 5m. *Papilio demodocus* 7·50 9·00

(Des B. Tear. Litho Questa)

1990 (12 Mar). *"EXPO 90" International Garden and Greenery Exhibition, Osaka. Local Orchids. T* **198** *and similar horiz designs. Multicoloured.* P 14.

958 12s. Type **198** 55 15
959 16s. *Huttonaea pulchra* 60 15
960 55s. *Herschelia graminifolia* 1·25 30
961 1m. *Ansellia gigantea* 1·75 75
962 1m.55 *Polystachya pubescens* 2·00 1·75
963 2m.40 *Penthea filicornis* 2·00 2·25
964 3m. *Disperis capensis* 2·25 3·25
965 4m. *Disa uniflora* 3·00 4·00
958/65 *Set of* 8 12·00 11·50
MS966 95×68 mm. 5m. *Stenoglottis longifolia* 7·50 9·00

198a Lady Elizabeth Bowes-Lyon and Brother in Fancy Dress

199 King Moshoeshoe II and Prince Mohato wearing Seana-Marena Blankets

(Des Young Phillips Studio. Litho Questa)

1990 (5 July)–**10**. *90th Birthday of Queen Elizabeth the Queen Mother. T* **198a** *and similar vert portraits, 1910–1919. P 14.*

967 1m.50 brownish black and bright magenta 1·25 1·25
a. Strip of 3. Nos. 967/9 3·25
968 1m.50 brownish black and bright magenta 1·25 1·25
969 1m.50 brownish black and bright magenta 1·25 1·25
967/9 *Set of* 3 3·25 3·25
MS970 90×75 mm. 5m. dull orange-brown, brownish black and bright magenta 4·00 4·00

Designs:—No. 967, Type **198a**; 968, Lady Elizabeth Bowes-Lyon in evening dress; 969, Lady Elizabeth Bowes-Lyon wearing hat; **MS**970, Lady Elizabeth Bowes-Lyon as a child.

Nos. 967/9 were printed together, horizontally and vertically *se-tenant*, in sheetlets of 9 (3×3).

(Litho B.D.T.)

1990 (17 Aug). *Traditional Blankets. T* **199** *and similar multicoloured designs.* P 14.

971 12s. Type **199** 10 10
972 16s. Prince Mohato wearing Seana-Marena blanket 10 10
973 1m. Pope John Paul II wearing Seana-Marena blanket 1·75 1·10
974 3m. Basotho horsemen wearing Matlama blankets 2·00 3·00
971/4 *Set of* 4 3·50 3·25
MS975 85×104 mm. 5m. Pope John Paul II wearing hat and Seana-Marena blanket (*horiz*) 4·50 4·75

200 Filling Truck at No. 1 Quarry

201 Mother breastfeeding Baby

(Litho B.D.T.)

1990 (24 Aug). *Lesotho Highlands Water Project. T* **200** *and similar vert designs. Multicoloured.* P 14.

976 16s. Type **200** 75 10
977 20s. Tanker lorry on Pitseng–Malibamatšo road 80 10
978 55s. Piers for Malibamatšo Bridge 90 30
979 2m. Excavating Mphosong section of Pitseng–Malibamatšo road 3·00 3·75
976/9 *Set of* 4 5·00 3·75
MS980 104×85 mm. 5m. Sinking blasting boreholes on Pitseng–Malibamatšo road 6·50 7·50

(Litho Questa)

1990 (26 Oct). *UNICEF Child Survival Campaign. T* **201** *and similar vert designs. Multicoloured.* P 14.

981 12s. Type **201** 60 10
982 55s. Baby receiving oral rehydration therapy 1·10 45
983 1m. Weight monitoring 1·75 2·75
981/3 *Set of* 3 3·00 3·00

King Letsie III,
November 1990–25 January 1995 (abdicated).

202 Men's Triple Jump

203 "Virgin and Child" (detail, Rubens)

(Des B. Grout. Litho Questa)

1990 (5 Nov). *Olympic Games, Barcelona (1992). T* **202** *and similar multicoloured designs.* P 14.

984 16s. Type **202** 65 10
985 55s. Men's 200 metres race 85 25
986 1m. Men's 5000 metres race 1·40 1·25
987 4m. Show jumping 4·00 6·00
984/7 *Set of* 4 6·25 6·75
MS988 100×70 mm. 5m. Olympic flame (*horiz*) 6·50 7·50

(Litho Questa)

1990 (5 Dec). *Christmas. Paintings by Rubens. T* **203** *and similar vert designs. Multicoloured.* P 13½×14.

989 12s. Type **203** 20 10
990 16s. "Adoration of the Magi" (detail) 20 10
991 55s. "Head of One of the Three Kings" 45 25
992 80s. "Adoration of the Magi" (different detail) 60 60
993 1m. "Virgin and Child" (different detail) 70 70
994 2m. "Adoration of the Magi" (different detail) 1·25 1·75
995 3m. "Virgin and Child" (different detail) 2·00 2·50
996 4m. "Adoration of the Magi" (different detail) 2·25 3·25
989/96 *Set of* 8 7·00 8·25
MS997 71×100 mm. 5m. "Assumption of the Virgin" (detail) 4·00 5·50

204 Mickey Mouse at Nagasaki Peace Park

(Des Walt Disney Company. Litho Questa)

1991 (10 June). *"Phila Nippon '91" International Stamp Exhibition, Tokyo. T* **204** *and similar horiz designs showing Walt Disney cartoon characters in Japan. Multicoloured.* P 14×13½.

998 20s. Type **204** 80 15
999 30s. Mickey Mouse on Kamakura Beach 85 20
1000 40s. Mickey and Donald Duck with Bunraku puppet 95 25
1001 50s. Mickey and Donald eating soba 1·00 35
1002 75s. Mickey and Minnie Mouse at tea house 1·40 70
1003 1m. Mickey running after "Hikari" express train 1·40 1·00
1004 3m. Mickey Mouse with deer at Todaiji Temple, Nara 3·25 3·50
1005 4m. Mickey and Minnie outside Imperial Palace 3·25 4·00

998/1005 *Set of 8* ... 11·50 9·00
MS1006 Two sheets, each 127×112 mm. (a) 5m. Mickey Mouse skiing; (b) 5m. Mickey and Minnie having a picnic *Set of $1 sheets* ... 7·00 8·00

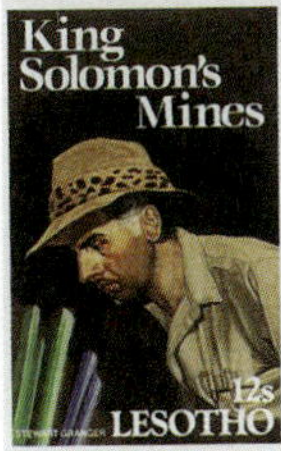

205 Stewart Granger (King Solomon's Mines)

206 Satyrus aello

(Des R. Jung. Litho Questa)

1991 (20 June). *Famous Films with African Themes. T* **205** *and similar vert designs. Multicoloured.* P 14.

1007 12s. Type **205** ... 35 20
1008 16s. Johnny Weissmuller (Tarzan the Ape Man) ... 35 20
1009 30s. Clark Gable with Grace Kelly (Mogambo) ... 50 35
1010 55s. Sigourney Weaver and male gorilla (Gorillas in the Mist) ... 75 55
1011 70s. Humphrey Bogart and Katharine Hepburn (The African Queen) ... 90 80
1012 1m. John Wayne and capture of rhinoceros (Hatari!) ... 1·25 1·00
1013 2m. Meryl Streep and De Havilland D.H.60G Gipsy Moth light aircraft (Out of Africa) ... 2·00 2·25
1014 4m. Arsenio Hall and Eddie Murphy (Coming to America) ... 2·75 3·50
1007/14 *Set of 8* ... 8·00 8·00
MS1015 108×77 mm. 5m. Elsa the lioness (Born Free) ... 3·75 4·50

(Des S. Heimann. Litho Cartor)

1991 (1 Aug)–**92**. *Butterflies. T* **216** *and similar horiz designs. Multicoloured.* P 14×13½.

A. Without imprint date.

1016cA 2s. Type **206** (p 13½) ... 30 30
1017cA 3s. *Erebia medusa* (p 13½) ... 30 30
1018A 5s. *Melanargia galathea* ... 10 30
1019A 10s. *Erebia aethiops* ... 30 30
1020A 20s. *Coenonympha pamphilus* ... 20 10
c. Perf 13½ ... 35 30
1021A 25s. *Pyrameis atalanta* ... 35 30
1022A 30s. *Charaxes jasius* ... 40 30
c. Perf 13½ ... 40 30
1023A 40s. *Colias palaeno* ... 40 30
1024A 50s. *Colias cliopatra* ... 45 40
1025A 60s. *Colias philodice* ... 60 60
1026A 70s. *Rhumni gonepterix* ... 75 75
1027cA 1m. *Colias caesonia* (p 13½) ... 75 75
1028A 2m. *Pyrameis cardui* ... 1·50 1·50
c. Perf 13½ ... 1·50 1·50
1029cA 3m. *Danaus chrysippus* (p 13½) ... 1·40 1·75
1030cA 10m. *Apatura iris* (p 13½) ... 4·50 5·50
1016cA/130cA *Set of 15* ... 12·00 13·00

B. With imprint date ("1992") at foot (4.92).

1016B 2s. Type **206** ... 10 10
1017B 3s. *Erebia medusa* ... 10 10
1018B 5s. *Melanargia galathea* ... 10 10
1019B 10s. *Erebia aethiops* ... 10 10
1020B 20s. *Coenonympha pamphilus* ... 10 10
c. Perf 13½ ... 10 10
1021B 25s. *Pyrameis atalanta* ... 20 10
1022B 30s. *Charaxes jasius* ... 20 10
c. Perf 13½ ... 25 10
1023B 40s. *Colias palaeno* ... 25 10
1024B 50s. *Colias cliopatra* ... 30 10
1025B 60s. *Colias philodice* ... 30 10
1026B 70s. *Rhumni gonepterix* ... 30 10
1027B 1m. *Colias caesonio* ... 50 25
1028B 2m. *Pyrameis cardui* ... 90 75
1029B 3in. *Danaus chrysippus* ... 1·40 1·75
1030B 10m. *Apatura iris* ... 1·75 1·90
1016B/30B *Set of 15* ... 5·50 4·75

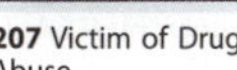

207 Victim of Drug Abuse

208 Wattled Cranes

(Litho Cartor)

1991 (23 Sept). *"Say No To Drugs" Campaign.* P 13½×14.

1031 **207** 16s. multicoloured ... 1·50 60

(Litho Cartor)

1991 (10 Oct). *Southern Africa Development Co-ordination Conference. Tourism Promotion. T* **208** *and similar horiz designs. Multicoloured.* P 14×13½.

1032 12s. Type **208** ... 1·50 1·00
1033 16s. Butterfly on flowers ... 1·50 1·00
1034 25s. Zebra and tourist bus at Mukurub (former rock formation), Namibia ... 2·00 60
1032/4 *Set of 3* ... 4·50 2·40
MS1035 75×117 mm. 3m. Basotho women in ceremonial dress. P 13×12 ... 3·75 4·50

209 De Gaulle in 1939

210 Prince and Princess of Wales

(Des D. Miller. Litho B.D.T.)

1991 (6 Dec). *Birth Centenary of Charles de Gaulle (French statesman). T* **209** *and similar vert designs.* P 14.

1036 20s. black and lake-brown ... 80 15
1037 40s. black and purple ... 1·00 1·25
1038 50s. black and yellow-olive ... 1·00 40
1039 60s. black and greenish blue ... 1·00 70
1040 4m. black and dull vermilion ... 3·50 4·50
1036/40 *Set of 5* ... 6·50 6·25

Designs:—40s. General De Gaulle as Free French leader; 50s. De Gaulle as provisional President of France, 1944–46; 60s. Charles de Gaulle in 1958; 4m. Pres. De Gaulle, 1969.

(Des D. Miller. Litho B.D.T.)

1991 (9 Dec). *10th Wedding Anniv of Prince and Princess of Wales. T* **210** *and similar horiz designs. Multicoloured.* P 14.

1041 50s. Type **210** ... 1·50 25
1042 70s. Prince Charles at polo and Princess Diana holding Prince Henry ... 1·50 45
1043 1m. Prince Charles with Prince Henry and Princess Diana in evening dress ... 1·60 70
1044 3m. Prince William and Prince Henry in school uniform ... 2·25 3·00
1041/4 *Set of 4* ... 6·25 4·00
MS1045 68×91 mm. 4m. Portraits of Prince with Princess and sons ... 5·50 4·25

211 "St. Anne with Mary and the Child Jesus" (Dürer)

212 Mickey Mouse and Pluto pinning the Tail on the Donkey

(Litho Walsall)

1991 (13 Dec). *Christmas. Drawings by Albrecht Dürer. T* **211** *and similar vert designs.* P 12.

1046 20s. black and bright magenta ... 60 10
1047 30s. black and new blue ... 75 20
1048 50s. black and yellowish green ... 90 25
1049 60s. black and vermilion ... 95 30
1050 70s. black and lemon ... 1·00 60
1051 1m. black and orange ... 1·25 1·10
1052 2m. black and bright purple ... 2·50 2·75
1053 4m. black and ultramarine ... 3·50 6·00
1046/53 *Set of 8* ... 9·50 10·00
MS1054 Two sheets, each 102×127 mm. (a) 5m. black and carmine-rose. (b) 5m. black and cobalt. P 14. *Set of $1 sheets* ... 6·00 7·50

Designs:—30s. "Mary on Grass Bench"; 50s. "Mary with Crown of Stars"; 60s. "Mary with Child beside Tree"; 70s. "Mary with Child beside Wall"; 1m. "Mary in Halo on Crescent Moon"; 2m. "Mary breastfeeding Child"; 4m. "Mary with Infant in Swaddling Clothes"; 5m. (No. **MS**1054a) "The Birth of Christ"; 5m. (No. **MS**1054b) "The Holy Family with Dragonfly".

(Des Walt Disney Co. Litho Questa)

1991 (16 Dec). *Children's Games. T* **212** *and similar vert designs showing Walt Disney cartoon characters. Multicoloured.* P 13½×14.

1055 20s. Type **212** ... 65 15
1056 30s. Mickey playing mancala ... 70 20
1057 40s. Mickey rolling hoop ... 80 20
1058 50s. Minnie Mouse hula-hooping ... 90 25
1059 70s. Mickey and Pluto throwing a frisbee ... 1·25 75
1060 1m. Donald Duck with a diabolo ... 1·60 1·40
1061 2m. Donald's nephews playing marbles ... 2·50 3·00
1062 3m. Donald with Rubik's cube ... 3·00 4·00
1055/62 *Set of 8* ... 10·50 9·00
MS1063 Two sheets, each 127×112 mm. (a) 5m. Donald's and Mickey's nephews playing tug-of-war; (b) 5m. Mickey and Donald mock fighting. *Set of $1 sheets* ... 8·00 9·00

213 Lanner Falcon

214 Queen Elizabeth II and Cooking at a Mountain Homestead

(Des Tracy Pedersen. Litho Questa)

1992 (10 Feb). *Birds. T* **213** *and similar vert designs. Multicoloured.* P 14½×14.

1064 30s. Type **213** ... 70 60
a. Sheetlet. Nos. 1064/83 ... 12·50
1065 30s. Bateleur ... 70 60
Paradise Sparrow ("Red-headed
1066 30s. Finch") ... 70 60
1067 30s. Lesser Striped Swallow ... 70 60
1068 30s. Alpine Swift ... 70 60
1069 30s. Didric Cuckoo ... 70 60
1070 30s. Yellow-tufted Malachite Sunbird ... 70 60
Burchell's Gonolek ("Crimson-
1071 30s. breasted Shrike") ... 70 60
1072 30s. Pin-tailed Whydah ... 70 60
1073 30s. Lilac-breasted Roller ... 70 60
1074 30s. Little Black Bustard ("Korhaan") ... 70 60
1075 30s. Black-collared Barbet ... 70 60
1076 30s. Secretary Bird ... 70 60
1077 30s. Red-billed Quelea ... 70 60
1078 30s. Red Bishop ... 70 60
1079 30s. Ring-necked Dove ... 70 60
1080 30s. Yellow Canary ... 70 60
1081 30s. Cape Longclaw ... 70 60
1082 30s. Cordon-bleu ("Blue Waxbill") ... 70 60
1083 30s. Golden Bishop ... 70 60
1064/83 *Set of 20* ... 12·50 11·00

Nos. 1064/83 were printed together, *se-tenant*, as a sheetlet of 20 with the backgrounds forming a composite design.

(Des D. Miller. Litho Questa)

1992 (2 Mar). *40th Anniv of Queen Elizabeth II's Accession. T* **214** *and similar horiz designs. Multicoloured.* P 14.

1084 20s. Type **214** ... 35 15
1085 30s. View of the Lowlands ... 35 20
1086 1m. Agaves and escarpment ... 1·00 65
1087 4m. Thaba-Bosiu ... 3·00 3·50
1084/7 *Set of 4* ... 4·25 4·00
MS1088 75×97 mm. 5m. Mountains at sunset ... 4·25 4·50

215 Minnie Mouse as Spanish Lady, 1540–1660

(Des Walt Disney Co. Litho Questa)

1992 (13 Apr). *International Stamp Exhibitions. T* **215** *and similar vert designs showing Walt Disney cartoon characters. Multicoloured.* P 13½×14.

(a) "Granada 92", Spain. Traditional Spanish Costumes.

1089 20s. Type **215** ... 90 20
1090 50s. Mickey Mouse as Don Juan at Lepanto, 1571 ... 1·10 40
1091 70s. Donald in Galician costume, 1880 ... 1·40 70
1092 2m. Daisy Duck in Aragonese costume, 1880 ... 2·75 3·25
1089/92 *Set of 4* ... 5·50 4·00
MS1093 127×112 mm. 5m. Goofy the Bullfighter ... 4·50 5·00

(b) "World Columbian Stamp Expo '92". Red Indian Life.

1094 30s. Donald Duck making arrowheads ... 70 30
1095 40s. Goofy playing lacrosse ... 75 40
1096 1m. Mickey Mouse and Donald Duck planting corn ... 1·25 1·10
1097 3m. Minnie Mouse doing bead work ... 2·75 3·25
1094/7 *Set of 4* ... 4·75 4·50
MS1098 127×112 mm. 5m. Mickey paddling canoe ... 4·50 5·00

216 Stegosaurus

217 Men's Discus

(Des D. Burkhart. Litho Questa)

1992 (9 June). *Prehistoric Animals. T* **216** *and similar horiz designs. Multicoloured.* P 14.

1099 20s. Type **216** ... 90 30
1100 30s. Ceratosaurus ... 1·00 35
1101 40s. Procompsognathus ... 1·25 45
1102 50s. Lesothosaurus ... 1·50 55
1103 70s. Plateosaurus ... 1·50 70
1104 1m. Gasosaurus ... 1·75 1·25
1105 2m. Massospondylus ... 2·25 2·75
1106 3m. Archaeopteryx ... 2·50 3·50
1099/106 *Set of 8* ... 11·00 9·00
MS1107 Two sheets, each 105×77 mm. (a) 5m. As 50s. (b) 5m. As 3m. *Set of $1 sheets* ... 11·00 9·50

(Litho Questa)

1992 (5 Aug). *Olympic Games, Albertville and Barcelona. T* **217** *and similar multicoloured designs.* P 14.

1108 20s. Type **217** ... 20 15
1109 30s. Men's long jump ... 25 15
1110 40s. Women's 4×100 metres relay ... 30 25
1111 70s. Women's 100 metres ... 50 50

1112 1m. Men's parallel bars 70 70
1113 2m. Men's double luge (*horiz*) 1·40 1·75
1114 3m. Women's 30k cross-country skiing (*horiz*) 1·75 2·50
1115 4m. Men's biathlon 2·00 2·75
1108/15 *Set of 8* 6·50 7·75
MS1116 Two sheets, each 100×70 mm. (a) 5m. Women's figure skating. (b) 5m. Ice hockey (*horiz*). *Set of 2 sheets* 6·75 7·50

218 "Virgin and Child" (Sasaetta)

219 World Trade Centre, New York

(Litho Questa)

1992 (2 Nov). *Christmas. Religious Paintings. T* **218** *and similar vert designs. Multicoloured.* P 13½×14.
1117 20s. Type **218** 45 15
1118 30s. "Coronation of the Virgin" (Master of Bonastre) 55 20
1119 40s. "Virgin and Child" (Master of SS. Cosmas and Damian) 65 25
1120 70s. "The Virgin of Great Panagia" (detail) (12th-century Russian school) 1·00 55
1121 1m. "Madonna and Child" (Vincenzo Foppa) 1·60 1·10
1122 2m. "Madonna and Child" (School of Lippo Memmi) 2·25 2·50
1123 3m. "Virgin and Child" (Barnaba da Modena) 2·75 3·25
1124 4m. "Virgin and Child with Saints" (triptych) (Simonedei Crocifissi) 3·00 3·50
1117/24 *Set of 8* 11·00 10·50
MS1125 Two sheets, each 76×102 mm. (a) 5m. "Virgin and Child with Saints"(different detail) (Simone dei Crocifissi). (b) 5m. "Virgin and Child enthroned and surrounded by Angels" (Cimabue). *Set of 2 sheets* 8·00 10·00

(Des Kerri Schiff. Litho Questa)

1992 (17 Nov). *Postage Stamp Mega Event, New York. Sheet 100×70 mm.* P 14.
MS1126 **219** 5m. multicoloured 5·50 6·50

220 Baby Harp Seal (Earth Summit '92, Rio)

(Des L. Birmingham. Litho Questa)

1993 (8 Feb). *Anniversaries and Events. T* **220** *and similar horiz designs. Multicoloured.* P 14.
1127 20s. Type **220** 1·00 40
1128 30s. Giant Panda (Earth Summit '92, Rio) 1·40 40
1129 40s. Airship LZ-127 Graf Zeppelin over globe (75th death anniv of Count Ferdinand von Zeppelin) 1·40 40
1130 70s. Woman grinding maize (International Conference on Nutrition, Rome) 60 45
1131 4m. Lt. Robinson's Royal Aircraft Factory B.E 2C shooting down Schutte Lanz SL-11 airship (75th death anniv of Count Ferdinand von Zeppelin) 3·75 4·50
1132 5m. Valentina Tereshkova and "Vostok 6" (30th anniv of first woman in space) 3·75 4·50
1127/32 *Set of 6* 9·75 9·50
MS1133 Two sheets, each 100×70 mm. (a) 5m. Dr. Ronald McNair (Challenger astronaut) (International Space Year). (b) 5m. South African Crowned Crane (Earth Summit '92, Rio). *Set of $1 sheets* 9·00 9·00

221 "Orpheus and Eurydice" (detail) (Poussin)

222 Aloe

(Litho Walsall)

1993 (19 Mar). *Bicentenary of the Louvre, Paris. T* **221** *and similar vert designs showing paintings. Multicoloured.* P 12.
1134 70s. Type **221** 80 80
a. Sheetlet. Nos. 1134/41 5·75
1135 70s. "Rape of the Sabine Women" (left detail) (Poussin) 80 80
1136 70s. "Rape of the Sabine Women" (right detail) (Poussin) 80 80
1137 70s. "The Death of Sapphira" (left detail) (Poussin) 80 80
1138 70s. "The Death of Sapphira" (right detail) (Poussin) 80 80
1139 70s. "Echo and Narcissus"(left detail) (Poussin) 80 80
1140 70s. "Echo and Narcissus" (right detail) (Poussin) 80 80
1141 70s. "Self-portrait" (Poussin) 80 80
1134/41 *Set of 8* 5·75 5·75
MS1142 70×100 mm. 5m. "The Money Lender and his Wife" (57×89 mm) (Metsys). P 14½ 4·75 5·00
Nos. 1134/41 were printed together, *se-tenant*, in sheetlets of 8 stamps and one centre label.

(Des Mary Walters. Litho B.D.T.)

1993 (1 June). *Flowers. T* **222** *and similar vert designs. Multicoloured.* P 14.
1143 20s. Type **222** 40 10
1144 30s. Calla Lily 45 15
1145 40s. Bird of Paradise plant 45 15
1146 70s. Amaryllis 75 40
1147 1m. Agapanthus 90 60
1148 2m. Crinum 3·25 2·25
1149 4m. Watsonia 2·50 3·25
1150 5m. Gazania 2·50 3·50
1143/50 *Set of 8* 10·00 9·50
MS1151 Two sheets, each 98×67 mm. (a) 7m. Plumbago. (b) 7m. Desert Rose. *Set of $1 sheets* 7·50 8·50

223 *Precis westermanni*

(Des L. Nelson. Litho B.D.T.)

1993 (30 June). *Butterflies. T* **223** *and similar horiz designs. Multicoloured.* P 14.
1152 20s. Type **223** 40 15
1153 40s. *Precis sophia* 50 20
1154 70s. *Precis terea* 65 45
1155 1m. *Byblia acheloia* 75 75
1156 2m. *Papilio antimachus* 1·25 1·50
1157 5m. *Pseudacraea boisduvali* 1·75 3·00
1152/7 *Set of 6* 4·75 5·50
MS1158 Two sheets, each 96×62 mm. (a)7m. Precis oenone. (b) 7m. *Precis octavia*. *Set of $1 sheets* 7·00 7·00
No. 1157 is inscribed "*Pesudacraea boisduvali*" in error.

224 Queen Elizabeth II at Coronation (photograph by Cecil Beaton)

(Des Kerri Schiff. Litho Questa)

1993 (30 July). *40th Anniv of Coronation. T* **224** *and similar designs.* P 13½×14.
1159 20s. multicoloured 90 90
a. Sheetlet. Nos. 1159/62×2 12·00
1160 40s. multicoloured 1·25 1·25
1161 1m. black and bottle-green 1·60 1·60
1162 5m. multicoloured 3·50 3·50
1159/62 *Set of 4* 6·50 6·50
MS1163 70×100 mm. 7m. multicoloured (42½×28½ mm). P 14 6·00 6·50
Designs: *Vert*—40s. St. Edward's Crown and Sceptre; 1m. Queen Elizabeth the Queen Mother; 5m. Queen Elizabeth II and family. Horiz—7m. "Conversation Piece at Royal Lodge, Windsor" (detail) (Sir James Gunn).
Nos. 1159/62 were printed in sheetlets of 8, containing two *se-tenant* blocks of 4.

225 East African Railways Vulcan Steam Locomotive, 1929

226 Court-house

(Des. G. Vasarhelyi. Litho B.D.T.)

1993 (31 Aug). *African Railways. T* **225** *and similar horiz designs. Multicoloured.* P 14.
1164 20s. Type **225** 75 25
1165 30s. Bayer-Garratt Class 15A steam locomotive, Zimbabwe Railways, 1952 85 30
1166 40s. Class (25) steam locomotive, South African Railways, 1953 90 30
1167 70s. Class A 58 steam locomotive, East African Railways 1·25 60
1168 1m. Class 9E electric locomotives,South African Railways 1·40 85
1169 2m. Class 87 diesel-electric locomotive No. 8737, East African Railways,1971 1·75 1·60
1170 3m. Class 92 diesel locomotive, East African Railways, 1971 2·00 2·25
1171 5m. Class 26 steam locomotive, No. 3450, South African Railways, 1982 2·50 3·50
1164/71 *Set of 8* 10·00 8·50
MS1172 Two sheets, each 104×82 mm. (a) 7m. Class 6E electric locomotive, South African Railways, 1969. (b) 7m. Class 231-132BT steam locomotive, Algerian Railways, 1937. *Set of 2 sheets* 10·00 10·00

(Des V. Seatile Nkhomo. Litho Government Printer, Pretoria)

1993 (24 Sept). *Traditional Houses. T* **226** *and similar horiz designs. Multicoloured.* P 14×14½.
1173 20s. Type **226** 50 10
1174 30s. House with reed fence 55 15
1175 70s. Unmarried girls' house 1·00 40
1176 4m. Hut made from branches 3·50 5·00
1173/6 *Set of 4* 5·00 5·00
MS1177 81×69 mm. 4m. Decorated houses 3·00 4·00

227 Black and White Shorthair

(Des V. Seatile Nkhomo. Litho Government Printer, Pretoria)

1993 (29 Oct). *Domestic Cats. T* **227** *and similar multicoloured designs.* P 14.
1178 20s. Type **227** 60 25
1179 30s. Shorthair Tabby lying down 60 25
1180 70s. Head of Shorthair Tabby 80 40
1181 5m. Black and White Shorthair with Shorthair Tabby 2·75 4·00
1178/81 *Set of 4* 4·25 4·50
MS1182 113×89 mm. 5m. Shorthair Tabby with rat (*vert*) 3·75 4·00

228 Pluto in Chung Cheng Park, Keelung

229 Tšeliso "Frisco" Khomari (Lesotho)

(Des Rosemary DeFiglio. Litho Questa)

1993 (15 Nov). *"Taipei '93" Asian International Stamp Exhibition, Taiwan. T* **228** *and similar multicoloured designs showing Walt Disney cartoon characters in Taiwan.* P 14×13½ (*horiz*) or 13½×14 (*vert*).
1183 20s. Type **228** 65 10
1184 30s. Donald Duck at Chiao-Tienkung Temple Festival 75 15
1185 40s. Goofy with lantern figures 85 20
1186 70s. Minnie Mouse shopping at temple festival 1·25 40
1187 1m. Daisy Duck at Queen's Head Rock, Yehliu (*vert*) 1·50 70
1188 1m.20 Mickey and Minnie at National Concert Hall (*vert*) 1·60 1·60
1189 2m. Donald at Chiang Kai-shek Memorial Hall (*vert*) 1·75 2·00
1190 2m.50 Donald and Daisy at the Grand Hotel, Taipei 2·00 2·75
1183/90 *Set of 8* 9·25 7·00
MS1191 Two sheets, each 128×102 mm. (a) 5m. Goofy over National Palace Museum, Taipei. (b) 6m. Mickey and Minnie at Presidential Palace Museum, Taipei (*vert*). *Set of 2 sheets* 8·50 8·50

(Des Rosemary DeFiglio. Litho Cartor)

1994 (1 Feb). *World Cup Football Championship '94, U.S.A. T* **229** *and similar multicoloured designs.* P 13½×14.
1192 20s. Type **229** 50 10
1193 30s. Thato "American Spoon" Mohale (Lesotho) 55 15
1194 40s. Jozic Davor (Yugoslavia) and Freddy Rincorn (Colombia) 65 20
1195 50s. Lefika "Mzee" Lekhotla (Lesotho) 70 25
1196 70s. Litšitso "House-on-fire" Khali (Lesotho) 85 55
1197 1m. Roger Milla (Cameroun) 1·00 85
1198 1m.20 David Platt (England) 1·50 2·00
1199 2m. Karl Heinz Rummenigge (Germany) and Soren Lerby (Denmark) 1·75 2·50
1192/9 *Set of 8* 6·75 6·00
MS1200 Two sheets, each 100×70 mm. (a) 6m. Klaus Lindenberger (Czechoslovakia). (b) 6m. Franco Baresi (Italy) and Ivan Hasek (Czechoslovakia) (*horiz*). P 13. *Set of 2 sheets* 8·50 8·50

230 King Letsie III signing the Oath of Office

231 Aquatic River Frog

(Litho Government Printer, Pretoria)

1994 (2 Apr). *1st Anniv of Restoration of Democracy. T* **230** *and similar multicoloured designs.* P 14.

1201 20s. Type **230** 20 15
1202 30s. Parliament building (*horiz*) 25 15
1203 50s. Swearing-in of Dr. Ntsu Mokhehle as Prime Minister (*horiz*) 40 20
1204 70s. Maj-Gen (P.) Ramaema handing Instruments of Government to Dr. Ntsu Mokhehle (*horiz*) 70 40
1201/4 *Set of 4* .... 1·40 80

(Des V. Seatile Nkhomo (Nos. 1205/8), R. Rundo (No. **MS**1209). Litho Questa)

1994 (16 Aug). *"Philakorea '94" International Stamp Exhibition, Seoul. Frogs and Toads. T* **231** *and similar multicoloured designs.* P 14×14½.

1205 35s. Type **231** 25 10
1206 50s. Bubbling Kassina 35 15
1207 1m. Guttural Toad 60 60
1208 1m.50 Common River Frog .... 80 1·25
1205/8 *Set of 4* .... 1·75 1·90
MS1209 Two sheets, each 102×72 mm. (a) 5m. Jade frog (sculpture). (b) 5m. Black Spotted Frog and Oriental White Eye (bird) (*vert*). P 14. *Set of $1 sheets* .... 8·50 8·50

232 De Havilland D.H.C.6 Twin Otter and Emblem

(Des V. Seatile Nkhomo. Litho Goverment Printer, Pretoria)

1994 (17 Nov). *50th Anniv of International Civil Aviation Organization. T* **232** *and similar horiz designs. Multicoloured.* P 14.

1210 35s. Type **232** 50 15
1211 50s. Fokker F.27 Friendship on runway... 65 20
1212 1m. Fokker F.27 Friendship over Moshoeshoe I International Airport .... 1·00 70
1213 1m.50 Cessna light aircraft over mountains .... 1·40 1·75
1210/13 *Set of 4* .... 3·25 2·50

King Moshoeshoe II, 25 January 1995 (restored)–15 January 1996

20s (233)

234 *Tagetes minuta*

1995 (3 Mar). *No. 1022Bc surch with T* **233** *by Mazenod Ptg Wks, Lesotho.*

1214 20s. on 30s. *Charaxes jasius* (p13½) .... 1·25 75
a. Perf 14×13½ (No. 1022B) .... 1·00 65

(Des V. Seatile Nkhomo. Litho Government Printer, Pretoria)

1995 (22 May). *Medicinal Plants. T* **234** *and similar vert designs. Multicoloured.* P 14.

1215 35s. Type **234** 30 10
1216 50s. *Plantago lanceolata* 35 15
1217 1m. *Amaranthus spinosus* 55 50
1218 1m.50 *Taraxacum officinale* .... 90 1·40
1215/18 *Set of 4* .... 1·90 1·90
MS1219 120×91 mm. 5m. *Datura stramonium* .... 2·00 2·25

235 Pius XII College, 1962

236 Qiloane Pinnacle, Thaba-Bosiu

(Des Sumitra Talukdar (2m.), D. Ambrose (others). Litho Government Printer, Pretoria)

1995 (26 July). *50th Anniv of University Studies in Lesotho. T* **235** *and similar horiz designs. Multicoloured.* P 14.

1220 35s. Type **235** 15 10
1221 50s. Campus, University of Basutoland, Bechuanaland and Swaziland, 1966 .... 20 15
1222 70s. Campus, University of Botswana, Lesotho and Swaziland, 1970 .... 30 15
1223 1m. Administration Block, University of Botswana, Lesotho andSwaziland, 1975 .... 45 40
1224 1m.50 Administration Block, National University of Lesotho, 1988 .... 65 85
1225 2m. Procession of Vice-Chancellors, National University of Lesotho, 1995 .... 80 1·40
1220/5 *Set of 6* .... 2·25 2·75

(Des M. Phakisi. Litho Government Printer, Pretoria)

1995 (28 Aug). *20th Anniv of World Tourism Organization. T* **236** *and similar multicoloured designs.* P 14.

1226 35s. Type **236** 25 10
1227 50s. Ha Mohalenyane rock formation 30 15
1228 1m. Botsoela Falls (*vert*) 55 45
1229 1m.50 Backpackers in Makhaleng River Gorge .... 80 1·25
1226/9 *Set of 4* .... 1·75 1·75
MS1230 143×88 mm. 4m. Red Hot Pokers (38×57 mm) .... 2·00 2·25
No. **MS**1230, which is inscribed "RED HOT PORKERS" in error, was withdrawn in Lesotho on 12 September.

237 "Peace"

238 "Sutter's Gold" Rose

(Des V. Seatile Nkhomo. Litho Government Printer, Pretoria)

1995 (26 Sept). *50th Anniv of United Nations. T* **237** *and similar multicoloured designs.* P 14.

1231 35s. Type **237** 30 10
1232 50s. "Justice" (scales) 40 20
1233 1m.50 "Reconciliation" (clasped hands) (*horiz*) .... 1·00 1·40
1231/3 *Set of 3* .... 1·50 1·40

(Des V. Seatile Nkhomo. Litho Government Printer, Pretoria)

1995 (1 Nov). *Christmas. Roses. T* **238** *and similar vert designs. Multicoloured.* P 14.

1234 35s. Type **238** 10 30
1235 50s. "Michele Meilland" 35 10
1236 1m. "J. Otto Thilow" 60 40
1237 2m. "Papa Meilland" .... 95 1·40
1234/7 *Set of 4* .... 1·75 2·00

King Letsie III. 15 January 1996 (restored)

239 Part of 1911 Map showing Lephaqhoa

240 Adding Salt to Cooking Pot

(Des D.Ambrose. Litho Government Printer, Pretoria)

1996 (17 June). *Completion of New Standard Map of Lesotho (1994). T* **239** *and similar horiz designs showing map sections of the Malibamatso Valley. Multicoloured.* P 14.

(a) 1911 Map.

1238 35s. Type **239** 30 30
a. Sheetlet. Nos. 1238/47 .... 2·75
1239 35s. Boritsa Tsuene 30 30
1240 35s. Molapo 30 30
1241 35s. Nkeu 30 30
1242 35s. Three rivers flowing east 30 30
1243 35s. Tibedi and Rafanyane 30 30
1244 35s. Two rivers flowing east 30 30
1245 35s. Madibatmatso River 30 30
1246 35s. Bokung River 30 30
1247 35s. Semena River 30 30

(b) 1978 Map.

1248 35s. Mountains and river valley 30 30
a. Sheetlet. Nos. 1248/57 .... 2·75
1249 35s. Pelaneng and Lepaqoa 30 30
1250 35s. Mamohau 30 30
1251 35s. Ha Lejone 30 30
1252 35s. Ha Thoora 30 30
1253 35s. Ha Mikia 30 30
1254 35s. Ha Kosetabole 30 30
1255 35s. Ha Seshote 30 30
1256 35s. Ha Rapooane 30 30
1257 35s. Bokong Ha Kennan 30 30

(c) 1994 Map.

1258 35s. Mafika-Lisiu Pass 30 30
a. Sheetlet. Nos. 1258/67 .... 2·75
1259 35s. Ha Lesaoana 30 30
1260 35s. Ha Masaballa 30 30
1261 35s. Ha Nkisi 30 30
1262 35s. Ha Rafanyane 30 30
1263 35s. Laitsoka Pass 30 30
1264 35s. "Katse Reservoir" 30 30
1265 35s. Seshote 30 30
1266 35s. Sephareng 30 30
1267 35s. Katse Dam 30 30
1238/67 *Set of 30* .... 8·00 8·00

Nos. 1238/47, 1248/57 and 1258/67 were printed together, *se-tenant*, in sheetlets of 10 (2×5) each forming composite designs.

Nos. 1238/67 were issued in conjunction with a schools campaign to promote use and understanding of maps.

(Des V. Seatile Nkhomo. Litho Government Printer, Pretoria)

1996 (30 July). *50th Anniv of UNICEF. T* **240** *and similar multicoloured designs.* P 14.

1268 35s. Type **240** 25 10
1269 50s. Herdboys with livestock (*horiz*) 35 20
1270 70s. Children in class (*horiz*) 45 20
1271 1m.50 Boys performing traditional dance (*horiz*) .... 90 1·25
1268/71 *Set of 4* .... 1·75 1·50

241 USA Basketball Team, 1936

(Des J. Puvillard. Litho Questa)

1996 (1 Aug). *Olympic Games, Atlanta. Previous Gold Medal Winners. T* **241** *and similar multicoloured designs.* P 14.

1272 1m. Type **241** 50 20
1273 1m.50 Brandenburg Gate and stadium, Berlin, 1936 .... 50 30
1274 1m.50 Glen Morris (USA) (decathlon, 1936) (*vert*) 50 50
a. Sheetlet. Nos. 1274/82 .... 4·00
1275 1m.50 Saidi Aouita (Morocco) (5000m running, 1984) (*vert*) 50 50
1276 1m.50 Arnie Robinson (USA) (long jump, 1976) (*vert*) 50 50
1277 1m.50 Hans Woellke (Germany) (shotput, 1936) (*vert*) 50 50
1278 1m.50 Renate Stecher (Germany) (100m running, 1972) (*vert*) 50 50
1279 1m.50 Evelyn Ashford (USA) (100m running, 1984) (*vert*) 50 50
1280 1m.50 Willie Davenport (USA) (110m hurdles, 1968) (*vert*) 50 50
1281 1m.50 Bob Beamon (USA) (long jump, 1968) (*vert*) 50 50
1282 1m.50 Heidi Rosendhal (Germany) (long jump, 1972) (*vert*) 50 50
1283 2m. Jesse Owens (USA) (track and field, 1936) (*vert*) 65 70
1284 3m. Speed boat racing .... 85 1·00
1272/84 *Set of 13* .... 6·25 6·00
MS1285 Two sheets, each 110×80 mm. (a) 8m. Michael Gross (Germany) (swimming, 1984) (*vert*). (b) 8m. Kornelia Ender (Germany) (swimming, 1976) (*vert*). *Set of 2 sheets* .... 6·50 7·00

No. 1273 is inscribed "BRANDEBOURG GATE" in error.

No. 1274 incorrectly identifies Glen Morris as the gold medal winner in the 1936 long jump.

Nos. 1274/82 were printed together, *se-tenant*, in sheetlets of 9, the backgrounds forming a composite design.

242 Class WP Steam Locomotive (India)

243 Mothers' Union Member, Methodist Church

(Des G. Bibi. Litho Questa)

1996 (2 Sept). *Trains of the World. T* **242** *and similar horiz designs. Multicoloured.* P 14.

1286 1m.50 Type **242** 75 75
a. Sheetlet. Nos. 1286/91 .... 4·00
1287 1m.50 Canadian Pacific steam locomotive No. 2471 (Canada) 75 75
1288 1m.50 The "Caledonian" (Great Britain) 75 75
1289 1m.50 Steam locomotive William Mason (USA) 75 75
1290 1m.50 "Trans-Siberian Express" (Russia) 75 75
1291 1m.50 Steam train (Switzerland) 75 75
1292 1m.50 ETR 450 high speed train (Italy) 75 75
a. Sheetlet. Nos. 1292/7 .... 4·00
1293 1m.50 TGV express train (France) 75 75
1294 1m.50 XPT hlgh speed train (Australia) 75 75
1295 1m.50 "Blue Train" (South Africa) 75 75
1296 1m.50 Intercity 225 express train (Great Britain) 75 75
1297 1m.50 "Hikari" express train (Japan) 75 75
1286/97 *Set of 12* .... 8·00 8·00
MS1298 Two sheets, each 98×68 mm. (a) 8m. Class 52 steam locomotive (Germany) (57×43 mm). (b) 8m. ICE high speed train (Germany) (57×43 mm). *Set of 2 sheets* .... 7·50 8·00

Nos. 1286/91 and 1292/7 were each printed together, *se-tenant*, in sheetlets of 6.

(Des V. Seatile Nkhomo. Litho Goverment Printer, Pretoria)

1996 (10 Dec). *Christmas. Mothers' Unions. T* **243** *and similar vert designs. Multicoloured.* P 14.

1299 35s. Type **243** 25 10
1300 50s. Roman Catholic Church 30 10
1301 1m. Lesotho Evangelical Church 55 35
1302 1m.50 Anglican Church .... 80 1·25
1299/1302 *Set of 4* .... 1·75 1·60

No. 1302 is inscribed "Anglian" in error.

244 Hand Clasp (Co-operation for Development) **245** Land Reclamation

(Des V. Seatile Nkhomo. Litho Government Printer, Pretoria)

1997 (21 Apr). *10th Anniv of Lesotho Highlands Water Project (1996). T* **244** *and similar horiz designs. Multicoloured.* P 14.

No.	Description	Unused	Used
1303	35s. Type **244**	25	10
1304	50s. Bearded Vulture and rock painting (Nature and Heritage)	50	20
1305	1m. Malibamatšo Bridge (Engineering)	60	40
1306	1m.50 Katse Valley in 1986 and 1996 (75×28 mm)	90	1·25
1303/6	*Set of 4*	2·00	1·75

No. 1305 is inscribed "Developement" in error.

(Des V. Seatile Nkhomo. Litho Government Printer, Pretoria)

1997 (30 June). *Environment Protection. T* **245** *and similar vert designs. Multicoloured.* P 14.

No.	Description	Unused	Used
1307	35s. Type **245**	25	10
1308	50s. Throwing rubbish into bin	30	15
1309	1m. Hands holding globe and tree	55	30
1310	1m.20 Recycling symbol and rubbish	65	65
1311	1m.50 Collecting rain water	75	85
1307/11	*Set of 5*	2·25	1·75

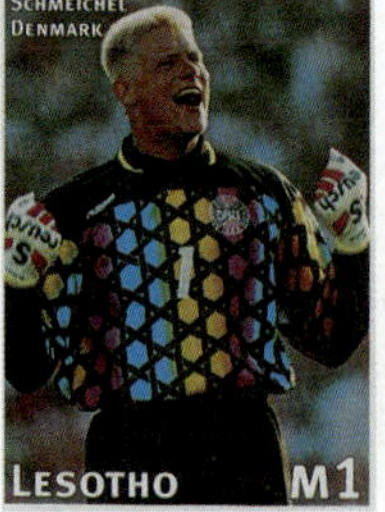

246 Schmeichel, Denmark **247** *Spalia spio*

(Litho Questa)

1997 (3 Nov). *World Cup Football Championship, France (1998). T* **246** *and similar multicoloured designs.* P 13½×14.

No.	Description	Unused	Used
1312	1m. Type **246**	40	20
1313	1m.50 Bergkamp, Netherlands	55	55
1314	1m.50 Argentine players celebrating	55	55
	a. Sheetlet. Nos. 1314/19	3·00	
1315	1m.50 Argentine and Dutch players competing for ball	55	55
1316	1m.50 Players heading ball	55	55
1317	1m.50 Goalkeeper deflecting ball	55	55
1318	1m.50 Goalmouth melee	55	55
1319	1m.50 Argentine player kicking ball	55	55
1320	2m. Southgate, England	70	70
1321	2m.50 Asprilla, Colombia	80	85
1322	3m. Gascoigne, England	90	95
1323	4m. Giggs, Wales	1·10	1·25
1312/23	*Set of 12*	7·00	7·00

MS1324 Two sheets, each 127×102 mm. (a) 8m. Littbarski, West Germany (*horiz*). P 14×13½. (b) 8m. Shearer, England. P 13½×14. *Set of* $1 *sheets* 6·50 7·00

Nos. 1314/19 were printed together, *se-tenant*, in sheetlets of 6 and show scenes from the Argentina v Netherlands final of 1978.

Although First Day Covers for Nos. 1312/24 are dated 31 October 1997, the stamps were not available from Lesotho post offices before 3 November.

(Des D. Burkhart. Litho Questa)

1997 (28 Nov). *Butterflies. T* **247** *and similar horiz designs. Multicoloured.* P 14.

No.	Description	Unused	Used
1325	1m.50 Type **247**	60	60
	a. Sheetlet. Nos. 1325/33	4·75	
1326	1m.50 *Leptotes pirithous*	60	60
1327	1m.50 *Acraea satis*	60	60
1328	1m.50 *Belenois aurota aurota*	60	60
1329	1m.50 *Spindasis natalensis*	60	60
1330	1m.50 *Torynesis orangica*	60	60
1331	1m.50 *Lepidochysops variabilis*	60	60
1332	1m.50 *Pinacopteryx eriphia*	60	60
1333	1m.50 *Anthene butleri livida*	60	60
1325/33	*Set of 9*	4·75	4·75

MS1334 Two sheets, each 106×76 mm. (a) 8m. *Bematistes aganice*. (b) 8m. *Papilio demodocus*. *Set of* $1 *sheets* 6·50 6·50

Nos. 1325/33 were printed together, *se-tenant*, in sheetlets of 9 with the backgrounds forming a composite design.

No. 1326 is inscribed "Cyclyrius pirithous", No. 1332 "Pinacopteryx eriphea" and No. **MS**1334(b) "Papalio demodocus", all in error.

248 Rock Paintings and Boy **249** Diana, Princess of Wales

(Des V. Seatile Nkhomo. Litho Government Printer, Pretoria)

1998 (30 Jan). *40th Anniv of Morija Museum and Archives. T* **248** *and similar multicoloured designs based on drawings by Frédéric Christol.* P 14½ (with two elliptical holes on the horiz sides (45s. and 2m.) or on the vert sides (others)).

No.	Description	Unused	Used
1335	35s. Type **248**	20	10
1336	45s. Hippopotamus and lower jaw bone (*horiz*)	20	10
1337	50s. Woman and cowhide skirt	20	10
1338	1m. Drum and "thomo" (musical bow)	30	30
1339	1m.50 Warrior with "khau" (gorget awarded for valour)	50	60
1340	2m. Herders with ox (*horiz*)	60	80
1335/40	*Set of 6*	1·80	1·80

(Litho Questa)

1998 (16 Mar). *Diana, Princess of Wales Commemoration. T* **249** *and similar vert designs. Multicoloured.* P 13½.

No.	Description	Unused	Used
1341	3m. Type **249**	1·10	1·25
	a. Sheetlet. Nos. 1341/6	6·00	
1342	3m. Wearing grey jacket	1·10	1·25
1343	3m. Wearing white polo-necked jumper	1·10	1·25
1344	3m. Wearing pearl necklace	1·10	1·25
1345	3m. Wearing white evening dress	1·10	1·25
1346	3m. Wearing pale blue jacket	1·10	1·25
1341/6	*Set of 6*	6·00	6·75

MS1347 70×100 mm. 9m. Accepting bouquet 6·50 6·50

Nos. 1341/6 were printed together, *se-tenant*, in sheetlets of 6.

250 Atitlan Grebe **251** Cape Vulture

(Des M. Leboeuf (Nos. 1368/76, **MS**1377d D. Burkhart (others). Litho Questa)

1998 (14 Apr). *Fauna of the World. T* **250** *and similar multicoloured designs.* P 14.

(a) Vert designs as T **250**.

No.	Description	Unused	Used
1348	1m. Type **250**	30	30
	a. Sheetlet. Nos. 1348/67	5·50	
1349	1m. Cabot's Tragopan	30	30
1350	1m. Spider Monkey	30	30
1351	1m. Dibatag	30	30
1352	1m. Right Whale	30	30
1353	1m. Imperial Parrot	30	30
1354	1m. Cheetah	30	30
1355	1m. Brown-eared Pheasant	30	30
1356	1m. Leatherback Turtle	30	30
1357	1m. Imperial Woodpecker	30	30
1358	1m. Andean Condor	30	30
1359	1m. Barbary Deer	30	30
1360	1m. Grey Gentle Lemur	30	30
1361	1m. Cuban Parrot	30	30
1362	1m. Numbat	30	30
1363	1m. Short-tailed Albatross	30	30
1364	1m. Green Turtle	30	30
1365	1m. White Rhinoceros	30	30
1366	1m. Diademed Sifaka	30	30
1367	1m. Galapagos Penguin	30	30

(b) Horiz designs, each 48×31 mm. P 13½×14.

No.	Description	Unused	Used
1368	1m.50 Impala	50	50
	a. Sheetlet. Nos. 1368/76	4·00	
1369	1m.50 Black Bear	50	50
1370	1m.50 American Buffalo	50	50
1371	1m.50 African Elephant	50	50
1372	1m.50 Kangaroo	50	50
1373	1m.50 Lion	50	50
1374	1m.50 Giant Panda	50	50
1375	1m.50 Tiger	50	50
1376	1m.50 Zebra	50	50
1348/76	*Set of 29*	9·50	9·50

MS1377 Four sheets, each 98×68 mm. (a) 8m. White-bellied Sunbird. P 14. (b) 8m. Golden-shouldered Parrot. P 14. (c) 8m. Snail Darter. P 14. (d) 8m. Monkey (47×31 mm). P 13½×14 *Set of 4 sheets* 8·50 8·50

Nos. 1348/67 and 1368/76 were each printed together, *se-tenant*, in sheetlets of 20 or 9.

(Des D. Burkhart. Litho Questa)

1998 (14 Apr). *Endangered Species. Cape Vulture. T* **251** *and similar horiz designs. Multicoloured.* P 14.

No.	Description	Unused	Used
1378	1m. Type **251**	50	50
	a. Horiz strip of 4. Nos. 1378/81	1·75	
1379	1m. Looking towards ground	50	50
1380	1m. Looking over shoulder	50	50
1381	1m. Facing right	50	50
1378/81	*Set of 4*	1·75	1·75

Nos. 1378/81 were printed together, *se-tenant*, in horizontal strips of 4 throughout the sheet.

252 Siamese

(Des D. Burkhart. Litho Questa)

1998 (4 May). *Cats of the World. T* **252** *and similar horiz designs. Multicoloured.* P 14.

No.	Description	Unused	Used
1382	70s. Type **252**	30	20
1383	1m. Chartreux	40	25
1384	2m. Korat	65	65
1385	2m. Japanese Bobtail	65	65
	a. Sheetlet. Nos. 1385/90	3·50	
1386	2m. British White	65	65
1387	2m. Bengal	65	65
1388	2m. Abyssinian	65	65
1389	2m. Snowshoe	65	65
1390	2m. Scottish Fold	65	65
1391	2m. Maine Coon	65	65
	a. Sheetlet. Nos. 1391/6	3·50	
1392	2m. Balinese	65	65
1393	2m. Persian	65	65
1394	2m. Javanese	65	65
1395	2m. Turkish Angora	65	65
1396	2m. Tiffany	65	65
1397	3m. Egyptian Mau	85	85
1398	4m. Bombay	95	1·10
1399	5m. Burmese	1·10	1·25
1382/99	*Set of 18*	11·00	11·00

MS1400 Two sheets, each 98×69 mm. (a) 8m. Tonkinese. (b) 8m. Singapura. *Set of 2 sheets* 5·50 6·00

Nos. 1385/90 and 1391/6 were each printed together, *se-tenant*, in sheetlets of 6 with the backgrounds forming composite designs.

253 *Laccaria laccata*

(Des Rina Lyamphe. Litho Questa)

1998 (2 June). *Fungi of the World. T* **253** *and similar horiz designs. Multicoloured.* P 14.

No.	Description	Unused	Used
1401	70s. Type **253**	30	20
1402	1m. *Mutinus caninus*	40	40
1403	1m. *Hygrophorus psittacinus*	40	40
	a. Sheetlet. Nos. 1403/14	4·25	
1404	1m. *Cortinarius obtusus*	40	40
1405	1m. *Volvariella bombycina*	40	40
1406	1m. *Cortinarius caerylescens*	40	40
1407	1m. *Laccaria amethystina*	40	40
1408	1m. *Tricholoma aurantium*	40	40
1409	1m. *Amanita excelsa* (spissa)	40	40
1410	1m. *Clavaria helvola*	40	40
1411	1m. Unidentified species (inscr "Cortinarius caerylescens")	40	40
1412	1m. *Russula queletii*	40	40
1413	1m. *Amanita phalloides*	40	40
1414	1m. *Lactarius deliciosus*	40	40
1415	1m.50 *Tricholoma lascivum*	55	55
1416	2m. *Clitocybe geotropa*	65	65
1417	3m. *Amanita excelsa*	85	90
1418	4m. *Red-capped Bolete*	95	1·10
1401/18	*Set of 18*	7·75	7·75

MS1419 Two sheets, each 98×68 mm. (a) 8m. *Amanita pantherina*. (b) 8m. *Boletus satanas*. *Set of 2 sheets* 5·50 6·00

Nos. 1403/14 were printed together, *se-tenant*, in sheetlets of 12.

Nos. 1406, 1407, 1414, 1416 and **MS**1419b are inscribed "*Continarius caerylescens*", "*Laccaria amethystea*", "*Lactarius delicious*", "*Clitocybe geotrapa*" and "*Boletys satanus*", all in error.

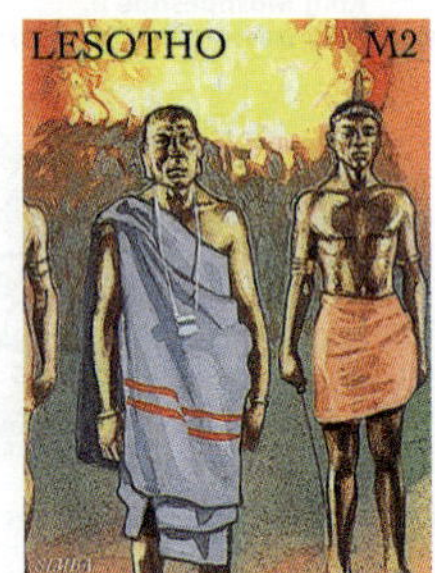

254 Simba

(Des Zina Saunders (Nos. 1420/7, **MS**1437a), J. Iskowitz (others). Litho B.D.T.)

1998 (14 July). *World Cinema. T* **254** *and similar multicoloured designs.* P 14.

(a) Films about Africa.

No.	Description	Unused	Used
1420	2m. Type **254**	60	60
	a. Sheetlet. Nos. 1420/7	4·25	
1421	2m. Call to Freedom	60	60
1422	2m. Cry the Beloved Country	60	60
1423	2m. King Solomon's Mines	60	60
1424	2m. Flame and the Fire	60	60
1425	2m. Cry Freedom	60	60
1426	2m. Bopha!	60	60
1427	2m. Zulu	60	60

(b) Japanese Film Stars.

No.	Description	Unused	Used
1428	2m. Takamine Hideko	60	60
	a. Sheetlet. Nos. 1428/36	4·75	
1429	2m. James Shigeta	60	60
1430	2m. Miyoshi Umeki	60	60
1431	2m. May Ishimara	60	60
1432	2m. Sessue Hayakawa	60	60
1433	2m. Miiko Taka	60	60
1434	2m. Mori Masayuki	60	60
1435	2m. Hara Setsuko	60	60
1436	2m. Kyo Machiko	60	60
1420/36	*Set of 17*	9·25	9·25

MS1437 Two sheets. (a) 68×98 mm. 10m. Lion cubs from Born Free (*horiz*). (b) 70×100 mm. 10m. Toshiro Mifune *Set of* $1 *sheets* 5·50 6·00

Nos. 1420/7 and 1428/36 were each printed together, *se-tenant*, in sheetlets of 8 or 9, with the backgrounds forming composite designs.

No. 1423 is inscribed "KING SOLOMAN'S MINES" in error.

255 Ceresiosaurus

(Des R. Rundo. Litho B.D.T.)

1998 (10 Aug). *Prehistoric Animals. T* **255** *and similar multicoloured designs.* P 14.

1438 2m. Type **255** ... 60 60
a. Sheetlet. Nos. 1438/46 ... 4·75
1439 2m. Rhomaleosaurus ... 60 60
1440 2m. Anomalocaris ... 60 60
1441 2m. Mixosaurus ... 60 60
1442 2m. Stethacanthus ... 60 60
1443 2m. Dunklosteus ... 60 60
1444 2m. Tommotia ... 60 60
1445 2m. Sanctacaris ... 60 60
1446 2m. Ammonites ... 60 60
1447 2m. Rhamphorhynchus ... 60 60
a. Sheetlet. Nos. 1447/55 ... 4·75
1448 2m. Brachiosaurus ... 60 60
1449 2m. Mamenchisaurus hochuanensis ... 60 60
1450 2m. Ceratosaurus nasicornis ... 60 60
1451 2m. Archaeopteryx ... 60 60
1452 2m. Leaellynasaura amicagraphica ... 60 60
1453 2m. Chasmosaurus belli ... 60 60
1454 2m. Deinonychus and Pachyrhinosaurus ... 60 60
1455 2m. Deinonychus ... 60 60
1456 2m. Nyctosaurus ... 60 60
a. Sheetlet. Nos. 1456/64 ... 4·75
1457 2m. Volcanoes ... 60 60
1458 2m. Eudimorphodon ... 60 60
1459 2m. Apatosaurus ... 60 60
1460 2m. Peteinosaurus ... 60 60
1461 2m. Tropeognathus ... 60 60
1462 2m. Pteranodon ingens ... 60 60
1463 2m. Ornithodesmus ... 60 60
1464 2m. Wuerhosaurus ... 60 60
1438/64 *Set of 27* ... 14·50 14·50

MS1465 Three sheets, each 100×70 mm.(a) 10m. Coelophysis (*vert*). (b) 10m. Tyrannosaurus (*vert*). (c) 10m. Woolly Rhinoceros. *Set of* $1 *sheets* ... 8·50 9·00

Nos. 1438/46, 1447/55 and 1456/64 were each printed together, *se-tenant*, in sheetlets of 9 with the backgrounds forming composite designs.

256 Treefish

(Des D. Burkhart. Litho Questa)

1998 (15 Oct). *Year of the Ocean. Fishes. T* **256** *and similar horiz designs. Multicoloured.* P 14.

1466 1m. Type **256** ... 30 30
1467 1m. Tigerbarb ... 30 30
1468 1m. Bandtail Puffer ... 30 30
1469 1m. Cod ... 30 30
1470 1m.50 Clown Loach ... 45 45
1471 1m.50 Christy's Lyretail ... 45 45
1472 1m.50 Filefish ... 45 45
1473 1m.50 Sicklefin Killie ... 45 45
1474 2m. Brook Trout ... 55 55
1475 2m. Emerald Betta ... 55 55
1476 2m. Pacific Electric Ray ... 55 55
1477 2m. Bighead Searobin ... 55 55
1478 2m. Weakfish ... 55 55
a. Sheetlet. Nos. 1478/85 ... 4·00
1479 2m. Red Drum ... 55 55
1480 2m. Blue Marlin ... 55 55
1481 2m. Yellowfin Tuna ... 55 55
1482 2m. Barracuda ... 55 55
1483 2m. Striped Bass ... 55 55
1484 2m. White Shark ... 55 55
1485 2m. Permit ... 55 55
1486 2m. Purple Firefish ... 55 55
a. Sheetlet. Nos. 1486/93 ... 4·00
1487 2m. Harlequin Sweetlips ... 55 55
1488 2m. Clown Wrasse ... 55 55
1489 2m. Bicolour Angelfish ... 55 55
1490 2m. False Cleanerfish ... 55 55
1491 2m. Mandarinfish ... 55 55
1492 2m. Regal Tang ... 55 55
1493 2m. Clownfish ... 55 55
1494 2m. Bluegill ... 55 55
a. Sheetlet. Nos. 1494/1501 ... 4·00
1495 2m. Grayling ... 55 55
1496 2m. Walleye ... 55 55
1497 2m. Brown Trout ... 55 55
1498 2m. Atlantic Salmon ... 55 55
1499 2m. Northern Pike ... 55 55
1500 2m. Large-mouth Bass ... 55 55
1501 2m. Rainbow Trout ... 55 55
1502 2m. Platy Variatus ... 55 55
a. Sheetlet. Nos. 1502/9 ... 4·00
1503 2m. Archerfish ... 55 55
1504 2m. Clown Knifefish ... 55 55
1505 2m. Angelicus ... 55 55
1506 2m. Black Arowana ... 55 55
1507 2m. Spotted Scat ... 55 55
1508 2m. Kribensis ... 55 55
1509 2m. Golden Pheasant ... 55 55
1510 3m. Harlequin Tuskfish ... 80 80
1511 4m. Half-moon Angelfish ... 90 90
1512 5m. Spotted Trunkfish ... 1·10 1·10
1513 6m. Wolf Eel ... 1·40 1·50
1514 7m. Cherubfish ... 1·50 1·60
1466/1514 *Set of 49* ... 26·00 26·00

MS1515 Four sheets, each 98×73 mm. (a) 12m. Common Carp. (b) 12m. Sockeye Salmon. (c) 12m. Winter Flounder. (d) 12m. Horn Shark. *Set of 4 sheets* ... 10·00 11·00

Nos. 1470/3 show the face value as "M1.5".

Nos. 1478/85, 1486/93, 1494/1501 and 1502/9 were each printed together, *se-tenant*, in sheetlets of 8.

Distribution of Nos. 1466/1515 and possibly also Nos. 1516/18, was delayed by unrest in Maseru.

257 Crowning of King Letsie III

(Des V. Seatile Nkhomo. Litho Government Printer, Pretoria)

1998 (31 Oct). *First Anniv of Coronation of King Letsie III. T* **257** *and similar horiz designs. Multicoloured.* P 14.

1516 1m. Type **257** ... 45 45
a. Horiz strip of 3. Nos. 1516/18 ... 1·25
1517 1m. King saluting Basotho nation ... 45 45
1518 1m. King Letsie in profile ... 45 45
1516/18 *Set of 3* ... 1·25 1·25

Nos. 1516/18 were printed together, *se-tenant*, in horizontal strips of 3.

258 *Pelargonium sidioides*

259 Japanese Akita

(Des Ina-Maria Harris. Litho Government Printer, Pretoria)

1998 (23 Nov). *Flowers. T* **258** *and similar vert designs. Multicoloured.* P 14.

1519 10s. Type **258** ... 10 10
1520 15s. *Aponogeton ranunculiflorus* ... 10 10
1521 20s. *Sebaea leiostyla* ... 10 10
1522 40s. *Sebaea grandis* ... 10 10
1523 50s. *Satyrium neglectum* ... 10 10
1524 60s. *Massonia jasminiflora* ... 10 10
1525 70s. *Ajuga ophrydis* ... 10 15
1526 80s. *Nemesia fruticans* ... 10 15
1527 1m. *Aloe broomii* ... 15 20
1528 2m. *Wahlenbergia androsacea* ... 25 30
1529 2m.50 *Phygelius capensis* ... 35 40
1530 3m. *Dianthus basuticus* ... 40 45
1531 4m.50 *Rhodohypoxis baurii* ... 60 65
1532 5m. *Turbina oblongata* ... 70 75
1533 6m. *Hibiscus microcarpus* ... 85 90
1534 10m. *Lobelia erinus* (Moraea stricta) ... 1·40 1·50
1519/34 *Set of 16* ... 5·00 5·50

(Des R. Francisco. Litho Questa)

1999 (18 May). *Dogs. T* **259** *and similar horiz designs. Multicoloured.* P 14.

1535 70s. Type **259** ... 40 20
1536 1m. Canaan dog ... 45 20
1537 2m. Husky ("ESKIMO DOG") ... 60 60
1538 2m. Cirneco dell' Etna ... 60 60
a. Sheetlet. Nos. 1538/43 ... 3·25
1539 2m. Afghan Hound ... 60 60
1540 2m. Finnish Spitz ... 60 60
1541 2m. Dalmatian ... 60 60
1542 2m. Basset Hound ... 60 60
1543 2m. Shar-pei ... 60 60
1544 2m. Boxer ... 60 60
a. Sheetlet. Nos. 1544/9 ... 3·25
1545 2m. Catalan Sheepdog ... 60 60
1546 2m. English Toy Spaniel ... 60 60
1547 2m. Greyhound ... 60 60
1548 2m. Keeshond ... 60 60
1549 2m. Bearded Collie ... 60 60
1550 4m.50 Norwegian Elkhound ... 1·50 1·60
1535/50 *Set of 16* ... 9·25 8·75

MS1551 Two sheets, each 98×69 mm. (a) 8m. Rough Collie. (b) 8m. Borzoi. *Set of 2 sheets* ... 6·50 6·50

Nos. 1538/43 and 1544/9 were each printed together, *se-tenant*, in sheetlets of 6 with the backgrounds forming composite designs.

260 Belted Kingfisher

261 *Cattleya dowiana*

(Des R. Rundo, Litho Questa)

1999 (28 June). *Birds. T* **260** *and similar multicoloured designs.* P 14.

1552 70s. Type **260** ... 45 20
1553 1m.50 Palm Cockatoo (*vert*) ... 60 45
1554 2m. Red-tailed Hawk ... 65 65
1555 2m. Evening Grosbeak ... 65 65
a. Sheetlet. Nos. 1555/63 ... 5·25
1556 2m. Lesser Blue-winged Pitta ... 65 65
1557 2m. Altamira Oriole ... 65 65
1558 2m. Rose-breasted Grosbeak ... 65 65
1559 2m. Yellow Warbler ... 65 65
1560 2m. Akiapolaau ... 65 65
1561 2m. American Goldfinch ... 65 65
1562 2m. Northern Flicker ... 65 65
1563 2m. Western Tanager ... 65 65
1564 2m. Blue Jay (*vert*) ... 65 65
a. Sheetlet. Nos. 1564/72 ... 5·25
1565 2m. Northern Cardinal (*vert*) ... 65 65
1566 2m. Yellow-headed Blackbird (*vert*) ... 65 65
1567 2m. Red Crossbill (*vert*) ... 65 65
1568 2m. Cedar Waxwing (*vert*) ... 65 65
1569 2m. Vermilion Flycatcher (*vert*) ... 65 65
1570 2m. Pileated Woodpecker (*vert*) ... 65 65
1571 2m. Western Meadowlark (*vert*) ... 65 65
1572 2m. Kingfisher (*vert*) ... 65 65
1573 3m. Tufted Puffin ... 85 85
1574 4m. Reddish Egret ... 95 1·00
1575 5m. Hoatzin (*vert*) ... 1·10 1·25
1552/75 *Set of 24* ... 13·00 13·00

MS1576 Two sheets. (a) 76×106 mm. 8m. Great Egret. (b) 106×76 mm. 8m. Chestnut-flanked White Eye (Zosterops erythropleura) *Set of* $1 *sheets* ... 7·00 7·00

No. 1553 shows the face value as "M1.5".

Nos. 1555/63 and 1564/72 were each printed together, *se-tenant*, in sheetlets of 9 with the backgrounds forming composite designs.

(Des D. Burkhart. Litho Questa)

1999 (30 July). *Orchids of the World. T* **261** *and similar vert designs. Multicoloured.* P 14.

1577 1m.50 Type **261** ... 60 30
1578 2m. *Cochleanthes discolor* ... 65 65
a. Sheetlet. Nos. 1578/86 ... 5·25
1579 2m. *Cischweinfia dasyandra* ... 65 65
1580 2m. *Ceratostylis retisquama* ... 65 65
1581 2m. *Comparettia speciosa* ... 65 65
1582 2m. *Cryptostylis subulata* ... 65 65
1583 2m. *Cycnoches ventricosum* ... 65 65
1584 2m. *Dactylorhiza maculata* ... 65 65
1585 2m. *Cypripedium calceolus* ... 65 65
1586 2m. *Cymbidium finlaysonianum* ... 65 65
1587 2m. *Apasia epidendroides* ... 65 65
a. Sheetlet. Nos. 1587/95 ... 5·25
1588 2m. *Barkaria lindleyana* ... 65 65
1589 2m. *Bifrenaria tetragona* ... 65 65
1590 2m. *Bulbophyllum graveolens* ... 65 65
1591 2m. *Brassavola flagellaris* ... 65 65
1592 2m. *Bollea lawrenceana* ... 65 65
1593 2m. *Caladenia carnea* ... 65 65
1594 2m. *Catasetum macrocarpum* ... 65 65
1595 2m. *Cattleya aurantiaca* ... 65 65
1596 2m. *Dendrobium bellatulum* ... 65 65
a. Sheetlet. Nos. 1596/1604 ... 5·25
1597 2m. *Dendrobium trigonopus* ... 65 65
1598 2m. *Dimerandra emarginata* ... 65 65
1599 2m. *Dressleria eburnea* ... 65 65
1600 2m. *Dracula tubeana* ... 65 65
1601 2m. *Disa kirstenbosch* ... 65 65
1602 2m. *Encyclia alata* ... 65 65
1603 2m. *Epidendrum pseudepidendrum* ... 65 65
1604 2m. *Eriopsis biloba* ... 65 65
1605 3m. *Diurus behrii* ... 85 85
1606 4m. *Ancistrochilus rothchildianus* ... 95 1·00
1607 5m. *Aerangis curnowiana* ... 1·10 1·25
1608 7m. *Arachnis flos-aeris* ... 1·50 1·75
1609 8m. *Aspasia principissa* ... 1·60 1·90
1577/1609 *Set of 33* ... 22·00 22·00

MS1610 Four sheets, each 110×82 mm. (a) 10m. *Paphiopedilum tonsum*. (b) 10m. *Ansellia africana*. (c) 10m. *Laelia rubescens*. (d) 10m. *Ophrys apifera*. *Set of 4 sheets* ... 11·00 12·00

Nos. 1578/86, 1587/95 and 1596/1604 were each printed together, *se-tenant*, in sheetlets of 9.

No. 1583 was inscribed "Cycnoches ventricsum" in error.

262 "Austerity" Type Series 52 Steam Locomotive, Frankfurt, 1939

(Des B. Pevsner. Litho Questa)

1999 (16 Aug). *"iBRA '99" International Stamp Exhibition, Nuremburg. Railway Locomotives. T* **262** *and similar horiz design. Multicoloured.* P 14×14½.

1611 7m. Type **262** ... 2·00 2·00
1612 8m. Adler and Brandenburg Gate, Berlin, 1835 ... 2·00 2·00

263 "View of Sumida River in Snow" (Hokusai)

264 African Boy

(Des. R. Sauber. Litho Questa)

1999 (16 Aug). *150th Death Anniv of Katsushika Hokusai (Japanese artist). T* **263** *and similar multicoloured designs.* P 14×13½.

1613 3m. Type **263** ... 75 75
a. Sheetlet. Nos. 1613/18 ... 4·00
1614 3m. "Two Carp" ... 75 75

1615 3m. "The Blind" (woman with eyes closed) 75 75
1616 3m. "The Blind" (woman with one eye open) 75 75
1617 3m. "Fishing by Torchlight" 75 75
1618 3m. "Whaling off the Goto Islands" 75 75
1619 3m. "Makamaro watching the Moon from a Hill" 75 75
a. Sheetlet. Nos. 1619/24 4·00
1620 3m. "Peonies and Butterfly" 75 75
1621 3m. "The Blind" (old man with open eyes) 75 75
1622 3m. "The Blind" (old man with one eye open) 75 75
1623 3m. "People crossing an Arched Bridge" (four people on bridge) 75 75
1624 3m. "People crossing an Arched Bridge" (two people on bridge) 75 75
1613/24 *Set of 12* 8·00 8·00
MS1625 Two sheets, each 102×72 mm. (a) 10m. "Bell-flower and Dragonfly" (*vert*). (b) 10m. "Moon above Yodo River and Osaka Castle" (*vert*). P 13½×14 *Set of $1 sheets* 4·25 4·75

Nos. 1613/18 and 1619/24 were each printed together, *se-tenant*, in sheetlets of 6.

(Des M. Harper. Litho Questa)

1999 (16 Aug). *10th Anniv of United Nations Rights of the Child Convention. T* **264** *and similar vert designs. Multicoloured.* P 14.
1626 2m. Type **264** 60 70
a. Sheetlet. Nos. 1626/8 1·60
1627 2m. Asian girl 60 70
1628 2m. European boy 60 70
1626/8 *Set of 3* 1·60 1·90

Nos. 1626/8 were printed together, *se-tenant*, in sheetlets of 3 with the backgrounds forming a composite design.

265 Mephistopheles appearing as Dog in Faust's study

266 "Water Lily at Night" (Pan Tianshou)

(Des J. Iskowitz. Litho Questa)

1999 (16 Aug). *250th Birth Anniv of Johann von Goethe (German writer). T* **265** *and similar designs.* P 14.
1629 6m. multicoloured 1·40 1·60
a. Sheetlet. Nos. 1629/31 3·75
1630 6m. deep ultramarine, slate-lilac and black 1·40 1·60
1631 6m. multicoloured 1·40 1·60
1629/31 *Set of 3* 3·75 4·25
MS1632 76×106 mm. 12m. bright crimson, reddish violet and black 2·75 3·00

Designs: Horiz—No. 1629, Type **265**; 1630, Von Goethe and Von Schiller; 1631, Mephistopheles disguised as a dog scorching the Earth. *Vert*—No. **MS**1632, Mephistopheles.

Nos. 1629/31 were printed together, *se-tenant*, in sheetlets of 3 with enlarged illustrated margins.

No. 1629, in addition to the normal country name, shows "GUYANA" twice in violet across the centre of the design.

(Litho Questa)

1999 (16 Aug). *"China '99" International Stamp Exhibition, Beijing. Paintings of Pan Tianshou (Chinese artist). T* **266** *and similar multicoloured designs.* P 13×13½.
1633 1m.50 Type **266** 40 50
a. Sheetlet. Nos. 1633/42 3·50
1634 1m.50 "Hen and Chicks" 40 50
1635 1m.50 "Plum Blossom and Orchid" 40 50
1636 1m.50 "Plum Blossom and Banana Tree" 40 50
1637 1m.50 "Crane and Pine" 40 50
1638 1m.50 "Swallows" 40 50
1639 1m.50 "Eagle on the Pine" (bird looking up) 40 50
1640 1m.50 "Palm Tree" 40 50
1641 1m.50 "Eagle on the Pine" (bird looking down) 40 50
1642 1m.50 "Orchids" 40 50
1633/42 *Set of 10* 3·50 4·50
MS1643 138×105 mm. 6m. "Sponge Gourd" (51×39 mm); 6m. "Dragonfly" (51×39 mm).P 13. 4·25 4·75

Nos. 1633/42 were printed together, *se-tenant*, in sheetlets of 10.

267 Queen Elizabeth, 1938

268 Chinese Soldier firing Rocket, 1150

(Litho Questa)

1999 (17 Aug). *"Queen Elizabeth the Queen Mother's Century". T* **267** *and similar vert designs.* P 14.
1644 5m. black and gold 1·50 1·50
a. Sheetlet. Nos. 1644/7 5·50
1645 5m. multicoloured 1·50 1·50
1646 5m. black and gold 1·50 1·50
1647 5m. multicoloured 1·50 1·50
1644/7 *Set of 4* 5·50 5·50
MS1648 153×152 mm. 15m. multicoloured. P 13½×14 3·75 4·00

Designs: (As Type **267**)—No. 1644 Type **267**; 1645, King George VI and Queen Elizabeth, 1948; 1646, Queen Mother wearing tiara, 1963; 1647, Queen Mother wearing blue hat, Canada, 1989. (37×50 mm)—No. **MS**1648, Queen Mother outside Clarence House.

Nos. 1644/7 were printed together, *se-tenant*, as a sheetlet of 4 stamps and a central label with inscribed and embossed margins.

No. **MS**1648 also shows the Royal Arms embossed in gold.

(Des L. Birmingham. Litho Cartor)

1999 (31 Dec). *New Millennium. Events of Second Half of 12th Century. T* **268** *and similar multicoloured designs.* P 12½.
1649 1m.50 Type **268** 45 50
a. Sheetlet. Nos. 1649/65 6·75
1650 1m.50 Burmese temple guardian, 1150 45 50
1651 1m.50 Troubadour serenading Lady, 1150 45 50
1652 1m.50 Abbot Sager (advisor to French Kings), 1150 45 50
1653 1m.50 Pope Adrian IV, 1154 45 50
1654 1m.50 Henry II of England, 1154 45 50
1655 1m.50 Bust of Frederick Barbarossa, King of Germany and Holy Roman Emperor, 1155 45 50
1656 1m.50 Shogun Yoritomo of Japan, 1156 45 50
1657 1m.50 Count and Countess of Vaudemont (Crusader monument), 1165 45 50
1658 1m.50 Ibn Rushd (Arab translator), 1169 45 50
1659 1m.50 Archbishop Thomas a Becket, 1170 45 50
1660 1m.50 Leaning Tower of Pisa, 1174 45 50
1661 1m.50 Pivot windmill, 1180 45 50
1662 1m.50 Saladin (Saracen general), 1187 45 50
1663 1m.50 King Richard the Lionheart of England, 1189 45 50
1664 1m.50 Moai (statues), Easter Island, 1150 (59×39 mm) 45 50
1665 1m.50 Crusader, 1189 45 50
1649/65 *Set of 17* 6·75 7·50

Nos. 1649/65 were printed together, *se-tenant*, in sheetlets of 17 including a central label (59×39 mm) and inscribed left margin.

269 U.S.S. New Jersey (battleship)

270 King Letsie III and Miss Karabo Anne Motšoeneng

(Des F. Rivera. Litho Questa)

1999 (31 Dec). *Maritime Development 1700–2000. T* **269** *and similar multicoloured designs.* P 14.
1666 4m. Type **269** 1·00 1·00
a. Sheetlet. Nos. 1666/71 5·50
1667 4m. *Aquila* (Italian aircraft carrier) 1·00 1·00
1668 4m. *De Zeven Provincien* (Dutch cruiser) 1·00 1·00
1669 4m. HMS *Formidable* (aircraft carrier) 1·00 1·00
1670 4m. *Vittorio Veneto* (Italian cruiser) 1·00 1·00
1671 4m. HMS *Hampshire* (destroyer) 1·00 1·00
1672 4m. *France* (French liner) 1·00 1·00
a. Sheetlet. Nos. 1672/7 5·50
1673 4m. *Queen Elizabeth 2* (liner) 1·00 1·00
1674 4m. *United States* (American liner) 1·00 1·00
1675 4m. *Queen Elizabeth* (liner) 1·00 1·00
1676 4m. *Michelangelo* (Italian liner) 1·00 1·00
1677 4m. *Mauretania* (British liner) 1·00 1·00
1678 4m. *Shearwater* (British hydrofoil ferry) 1·00 1·00
a. Sheetlet. Nos. 1678/83 5·50
1679 4m. British Class M submarine 1·00 1·00
1680 4m. SRN 130 hovercraft 1·00 1·00
1681 4m. Italian Second World War submarine 1·00 1·00
1682 4m. SRN 3 hovercraft 1·00 1·00
1683 4m. *Soucoupe Plongeante* (oceanographic submersible) 1·00 1·00
1684 4m. *James Watt* (early steamship) 1·00 1·00
a. Sheetlet. Nos. 1684/9 5·50
1685 4m. *Savannah* (steam/sail ship), 1819 1·00 1·00
1686 4m. *Amistad* (slave schooner) 1·00 1·00
1687 4m. American Navy brig 1·00 1·00
1688 4m. *Great Britain* (liner) 1·00 1·00
1689 4m. *Sirius* (paddle steamer) 1·00 1·00
1666/89 *Set of 24* 22·00 22·00
MS1690 Four sheets, each 106×76 mm. (a) 15m. U.S.S. *Enterprise* (aircraft carrier) (*vert*); (b) 15m. *Titanic* (liner); (c) 15m. German U-boat; (d) 15m. *E. W. Morrison* (Great Lakes schooner) (*vert*) *Set of 4 sheets* 15·00 16·00

Nos. 1666/71, 1672/7, 1678/83 and 1684/9 were each printed together, *se-tenant*, in sheetlets of 6 with enlarged illustrated and inscribed top margins.

No. 1686 is wrongly described as "ARMISTAD" and No. 1687 "BRICK", both on the sheetlet margin.

(Des M. Friedman. Litho Questa)

2000 (18 Feb). *Wedding of King Letsie III. T* **270** *and similar vert designs. Multicoloured.* P 14.
1691 1m. Type **270** 50 50
a. Sheetlet. Nos. 1691/4 1·80
1692 1m. Miss Karabo Anne Motšoeneng 50 50
1693 1m. King Letsie III 50 50
1694 1m. King Letsie III and Miss Karabo Motšoeneng in traditional dress 50 50
1691/4 *Set of 4* 1·80 1·80

Nos. 1691/4 were printed together, *se-tenant*, as a sheetlet of 4 stamps and a central label with enlarged illustrated margins.

271 "Appollo 18" and "Soyuz 19" docked in orbit

272 Gena Rowlands (actress), 1978

(Des G. Capasso. Litho B.D.T.)

2000 (12 June). *25th Anniv of "Apollo–Soyuz" Joint Project. T* **271** *and similar horiz designs. Multicoloured.* P 14.
1695 8m. Type **271** 2·00 2·00
a. Sheetlet. Nos. 1695/7 5·50
1696 8m. "Apollo 18" and docking module 2·00 2·00
1697 8m. "Soyuz 19" 2·00 2·00
1695/7 *Set of 3* 5·50 5·50
MS1698 106×76 mm. 15m. Docking module and "Soyuz 19" 4·00 4·25

Nos. 1695/7 were printed together, *se-tenant*, in sheetlets of 3 with enlarged illustrated and inscribed margins.

(Des R. Sauber. Litho B.D.T.)

2000 (12 June). *50th Anniv of Berlin Film Festival. T* **272** *and similar vert designs showing actors, directors and film scenes with awards. Multicoloured.* P 14.
1699 6m. Type **272** 1·25 1·40
a. Sheetlet. Nos. 1699/704 6·75
1700 6m. Vlastimil Brodsky (actor), 1975 1·25 1·40
1701 6m. Carlos Saura (director), 1966 1·25 1·40
1702 6m. Scene from La Collectionneuse, 1967 1·25 1·40
1703 6m. Scene from Le Depart, 1967 1·25 1·40
1704 6m. Scene from Le Diable Probablement, 1977 1·25 1·40
1699/1704 *Set of 6* 6·75 7·50
MS1705 97×103 mm. 15m. Scene from Stammeheim, 1986 3·75 4·00

Nos. 1699/1704 were printed together, *se-tenant*, in sheetlets of 6 with an enlarged illustrated and inscribed left margin showing the Silver Berlin Bear Award.

No. 1704 is inscribed LE DIIABLE PROBABLEMENT" in error.

273 George Stephenson Bach

274 Johann Sebastian

(Des J. Iskowitz. Litho B.D.T.)

2000 (12 June). *175th Anniv of Stockton and Darlington Line (first public railway). T* **273** *and similar horiz designs. Multicoloured.* P 14.
1706 8m. Type **273** 2·25 2·25
a. Sheetlet. Nos. 1706/8 6·00
1707 8m. Stephenson's Patent Locomotive 2·25 2·25
1708 8m. Robert Stephenson's Britannia Tubular Bridge, Menai Straits 2·25 2·25
1706/8 *Set of 3* 6·00 6·00

Nos. 1706/8 were printed together, *se-tenant*, in sheetlets of 3 with an enlarged illustrated and inscribed right margin.

(Des R. Rundo. Litho B.D.T.)

2000 (12 June). *250th Death Anniv of Johann Sebastian Bach (German composer). Sheet 105×101 mm.* P 14.
MS1709 **274** 15m. multicoloured 4·50 4·50

275 Albert Einstein

(Des R. Sauber. Litho B.D.T.)

2000 (12 June). *Election of Albert Einstein (mathematical physicist) as Time Magazine "Man of the Century". Sheet 117×91 mm.* P14.
MS1710 **275** 15m. multicoloured 3·75 4·00

276 Ferdinand Zeppelin and LZ-127 Graf Zeppelin, 1928

(Des G. Capasso. Litho B.D.T.)

2000 (12 June). *Centenary of First Zeppelin Flight. T* **276** *and similar horiz designs. Multicoloured.* P 14.

1711 8m. Type **276** ... 2·00 2·00
a. Sheetlet. Nos. 1711/13 ... 5·50
1712 8m. LZ-130 Graf Zeppelin II, 1938 ... 2·00 2·00
1713 8m. LZ-10 Schwaben, 1911 ... 2·00 2·00
1711/13 *Set of 3* ... 5·50 5·50
MS1714 83×119 mm. 15m. LZ-130 Graf Zeppelin II, 1938 (50×37 mm) ... 3·75 4·00

Nos. 1711/13 were printed together, *se-tenant*, in sheetlets of 3 with enlarged illustrated and inscribed margins.

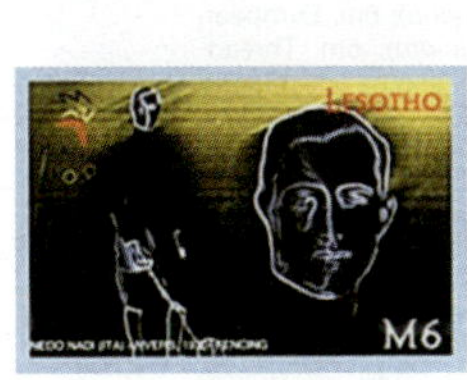

277 Nedo Nadi (Italian fencer), 1920

278 Prince William in Evening Dress

(Litho B.D.T.)

2000 (12 June). *Olympic Games, Sydney. T* **277** *and similar horiz designs. Multicoloured.* P 14.

1715 6m. Type **277** ... 1·40 1·50
a. Sheetlet. Nos. 1715/18 ... 5·00
1716 6m. Swimming (butterfly stroke) ... 1·40 1·50
1717 6m. Aztec Stadium, Mexico City, 1968 ... 1·40 1·50
1718 6m. Ancient Greek boxing ... 1·40 1·50
1715/18 *Set of 4* ... 5·00 5·50

Nos. 1715/18 were printed together, *se-tenant*, in sheetlets of 4 (2×2), with the horizontal rows separated by a gutter margin showing Sydney Opera House and athlete with Olympic Torch.

(Litho Questa)

2000 (21 June). *18th Birthday of Prince William. T* **278** *and similar vert designs. Multicoloured.* P 14.

1719 4m. Type **278** ... 1·25 1·25
a. Sheetlet. Nos. 1719/22 ... 4·50
1720 4m. Wearing coat and scarf ... 1·25 1·25
1721 4m. Wearing striped shirt and tie ... 1·25 1·25
1722 4m. Getting out of car ... 1·25 1·25
1719/22 *Set of 4* ... 4·50 4·50
MS1723 100×80 mm. 15m. Prince William (37×50 mm). P 13½×14 ... 4·50 4·50

Nos. 1719/22 were printed together, *se-tenant*, in sheetlets of 4 with illustrated margins.

279 Spotted-leaved Arum

280 Black Rhinoceros

(Des R. Matin. Litho Questa)

2000 (26 June). *African Flowers. T* **279** *and similar multicoloured designs.* P 14.

1724 3m. Type **279** ... 80 80
a. Sheetlet. Nos. 1724/9 ... 4·25
1725 3m. Christmas Bells ... 80 80
1726 3m. Lady Monson ... 80 80
1727 3m. Wild Pomegranate ... 80 80
1728 3m. Blushing Bride ... 80 80
1729 3m. Bot River Protea ... 80 80
1730 3m. Drooping Agapanthus ... 80 80
a. Sheetlet. Nos. 1730/5 ... 4·25
1731 3m. Yellow Marsh Afrikander ... 80 80
1732 3m. Weak-stemmed Painted Lady ... 80 80
1733 3m. Impala Lily ... 80 80
1734 3m. Beatrice Watsonia ... 80 80
1735 3m. Pink Arum ... 80 80
1736 3m. Starry Gardenia ... 80 80
a. Sheetlet. Nos. 1736/41 ... 4·25
1737 3m. Pink Hibiscus ... 80 80
1738 3m. Dwarf Poker ... 80 80
1739 3m. Coast Kaffirboom ... 80 80
1740 3m. Rose Cockade ... 80 80
1741 3m. Pride of Table Mountain ... 80 80
1742 4m. Moore's Crinum ... 95 95
1743 5m. Flame Lily ... 1·10 1·10
1744 6m. Cape Clivia ... 1·40 1·40
1745 8m. True Sugarbush ... 1·75 2·00
1724/45 *Set of 22* ... 18·00 18·00
MS1746 Two sheets, each 107×77 mm. (a) 15m. Red Hairy Erika (*horiz*). (b) 15m. Green Arum *Set of* $1 *sheets* ... 8·00 9·00

Nos. 1724/9, 1730/5 and 1736/41 were each printed together, *se-tenant*, in sheetlets of 6, with the backgrounds forming composite designs.

No. 1733 is inscribed "LIly", No. 1736 "Gardenia thumbergii" and No. 1741 "Disa unoflora", all in error.

(Des H. Friedman. Litho Questa)

2000 (10 Aug). *"The Stamp Show 2000" International Stamp Exhibition, London. Endangered Wildlife. T* **280** *and similar multicoloured designs.* P 14.

1747 4m. Type **280** ... 1·25 1·25
a. Sheetlet. Nos. 1747/52 ... 6·75
1748 4m. Leopard ... 1·25 1·25
1749 4m. Roseate Tern ... 1·25 1·25
1750 4m. Mountain Gorilla ... 1·25 1·25
1751 4m. Mountain Zebra ... 1·25 1·25
1752 4m. Zanzibar Red Colobus Monkey ... 1·25 1·25
1753 4m. Cholo Alethe ... 1·25 1·25
a. Sheetlet. Nos. 1753/8 ... 6·75
1754 4m. Temminck's Pangolin ... 1·25 1·25
1755 4m. Cheetah ... 1·25 1·25
1756 4m. African Elephant ... 1·25 1·25
1757 4m. Chimpanzee ... 1·25 1·25
1758 4m. Northern White Rhinoceros ... 1·25 1·25
1759 5m. Blue Wildebeest ... 1·25 1·25
a. Sheetlet. Nos. 1759/62 ... 5·00
1760 5m. Tree Hyrax ... 1·40 1·40
1761 5m. Red Lechwe ... 1·40 1·40
1762 5m. Eland ... 1·40 1·40
1747/62 *Set of 16* ... 19·00 19·00
MS1763 Two sheets, each 65×118 mm. (a) 15m. Dugong (*vert*). (b) 15m. West African Manatee (*vert*). *Set of 2 sheets* ... 8·00 9·00

Nos, 1747/52, 1753/8 and 1759/62 were each printed together, *se-tenant*, in sheetlets of 6 or 4 with the backgrounds forming composite designs and enlarged margins at top and bottom.

281 Cadillac Eldorado Seville (1960)

(Des F. Rivera. Litho Walsall)

2000 (1 Sept). *Classic Cars. T* **281** *and similar multicoloured designs.* P 14.

1764 3m. Type **281** ... 85 85
a. Sheetlet. Nos. 1764/9 ... 4·50
1765 3m. Citroen DS (1955–75) ... 85 85
1766 3m. Ford Zephyr Zodiac MK II (1961) ... 85 85
1767 3m. MG TF (1945–55) ... 85 85
1768 3m. Porsche 356 (1949–65) ... 85 85
1769 3m. Ford Thunderbird (1955) ... 85 85
1770 3m. Cisitalia 202 Coupe (1948–52) ... 85 85
a. Sheetlet. Nos. 1770/5 ... 4·50
1771 3m. Dodge Viper (1990s) ... 85 85
1772 3m. TVR Vixen SI (1968–69) ... 85 85
1773 3m. Lotus 7 (1957–70) ... 85 85
1774 3m. Ferrari 275 GTB/4 (1964–68) ... 85 85
1775 3m. Pegasus – Touring Spider (1951–58) ... 85 85
1776 4m. Fiat Type O (1913) ... 90 90
a. Sheetlet. Nos. 1776/81 ... 4·75
1777 4m. Stutz Bearcat (1914) ... 90 90
1778 4m. French Leyat (1924) ... 90 90
1779 4m. Benz gasoline-driven Motorwagon (1886) ... 90 90
1780 4m. Isotta Fraschini Type 8A (1925) ... 90 90
1781 4m. Markus Motor Carriage (1887) ... 90 90
1782 4m. Morris Minor (1951) ... 90 90
a. Sheetlet. Nos. 1782/7 ... 4·75
1783 4m. Hispano-Suiza Type **68** (1935) ... 90 90
1784 4m. MG TC (1949) ... 90 90
1785 4m. Morgan 4/4 (1955) ... 90 90
1786 4m. Jaguar XK120 (1950) ... 90 90
1787 4m. Triumph 1800/2000 Roadster (1946–49) ... 90 90
1764/87 *Set of 24* ... 19·00 19·00
MS1788 Four sheets. (a) 110×85 mm. 15m. AC ACE (1953–63). (b) 110×85 mm. 15m. Morris Minor 1000 (1948–71). (c) 85×110 mm. 15m. Ferrari F40 (*vert*). (d) 110×85 mm. 15m. Bersey Electric Cab (1896). *Set of 4 sheets* ... 15·00 16·00

Nos. 1764/9, 1770/5, 1776/81 and 1782/7 were each printed together, *se-tenant*, in sheetlets of 6 with either enlarged illustrated top or bottom margins.

282 Basotho Warrior fighting "AIDS"

(Des V. Seatile Nkhomo. Litho Questa)

2001 (22 Jan). *Anti-Aids Campaign. T* **282** *and similar horiz designs. Multicoloured.* P 14.

1789 70c. Type **282** ... 45 20
1790 1m. "Speed Kills So Does Aids" ... 60 30
1791 1m.50 Two women (*vert*) ... 75 60
1792 2m.10 "Even when you're off duty protect the nation" and symbols ... 90 90
1789/92 *Set of 4* ... 2·40 1·80

Nos. 1789/92 show the Aids emblem printed on the top (1m.50) or left sheet margin.

283 Great Orange Tip

(Des T. Wood. Litho Cartor)

2001 (30 Apr). *Butterflies. T* **283** *and similar horiz designs. Multicoloured.* P 13½.

1793 70s. Type **283** ... 40 20
1794 1m. Red-banded Pereute ... 45 20
1795 1m.50 Sword Grass Brown ... 60 45
1796 2m. Striped Blue Crow ... 65 65
1797 2m. Orange-banded Sulphur ... 65 65
a. Sheetlet. Nos. 1797/804 ... 4·75
1798 2m. Large Wood Nymph ... 65 65
1799 2m. The Postman ... 65 65
1800 2m. Palmfly ... 65 65
1801 2m. Gulf Fritillary ... 65 65
1802 2m. Cairns Birdwing ... 65 65
1803 2m. Common Morpho ... 65 65
1804 2m. Common Dotted Border ... 65 65
1805 2m. African Migrant ... 65 65
a. Sheetlet. Nos. 1805/12 ... 4·75
1806 2m. Large Oak Blue ... 65 65
1807 2m. The Wanderer ... 65 65
1808 2m. Tiger Swallowtail ... 65 65
1809 2m. Union Jack ... 65 65
1810 2m. Saturn ... 65 65
1811 2m. Broad-bordered Grass Yellow ... 65 65
1812 2m. Hewitson's Uraneis ... 65 65
1813 3m. Bertoni's Antwren Bird ... 85 85
a. Sheetlet. Nos. 1813/20 ... 6·00
1814 3m. Chlorinde ... 85 85
1815 3m. Iolas Blue ... 85 85
1816 3m. Mocker Swallowtail ... 85 85
1817 3m. Common Indian Crow ... 85 85
1818 3m. Grecian Shoemaker ... 85 85
1819 3m. Small Flambeau ... 85 85
1820 3m. Orchid Swallowtail ... 85 85
1821 3m. Alfalfa Butterfly ... 85 85
1822 4m. Doris Butterfly ... 95 95
1793/822 *Set of 30* ... 18·00 18·00
MS1823 Two sheets, each 70×100 mm. (a) 15m. Forest Queen. (b) 15m. Crimson Tip. *Set of 2 sheets* ... 9·00 9·50

Nos. 1797/804, 1805/12 and 1813/20 were each printed together, *se-tenant*, in sheetlets of 8 with the backgrounds forming composite designs.

284 Roman General and Soldiers from "Battle of Lepanto and Map of the World" (anon)

285 *Cortinarius violaceus*

(Litho Questa)

2001 (31 May). *"Philanippon 01" International Stamp Exhibition, Tokyo. Paintings from Momoyama Era. T* **284** *and similar vert designs. Multicoloured.* P 14 (5m.) or 13½×14 (others)

1824 1m.50 Type **284** ... 45 30
1825 2m. Pikemen and musketeers from "Battle of Lepanto and Map of the World" ... 60 40
1826 3m. Crane from "Birds and Flowers of the Four Seasons" (Kano Eitoku) ... 85 65
1827 4m. Travellers in the mountains from "Birds and Flowers of the Four Seasons" ... 1·00 1·00
1828 5m. "Portrait of a Lady" (24½×81½ mm) ... 1·00 1·00
a. Sheetlet. Nos. 1828/32 ... 4·50
1829 5m. "Honda Tadakatsu" (24½×81½ mm) ... 1·00 1·00
1830 5m. "Wife of Goto Tokujo" (24½×81½ mm) ... 1·00 1·00
1831 5m. "Emperor Go-Yozei (Kano Takanobu) (24½×81½ mm) ... 1·00 1·00
1832 5m. "Tenzuiin Hideyoshi's Mother, Hoshuku Sochin" (24½×81½ mm) ... 1·00 1·00
1833 6m. "Hosokawa Yusai" (Ishin Suden) (24½×81½ mm) ... 1·25 1·25
a. Sleetlet. Nos. 1833/7 ... 5·75
1834 6m. "Sen No Rikyu" (attr Hasegawa Tohaku) (24½×81½ mm) ... 1·25 1·25
1835 6m. "Oichi No Kata" (24½×81½ mm) ... 1·25 1·25
1836 6m. "Inaba Ittetsu" (attr Hasegawa Tohaku) (24½×81½ mm) ... 1·25 1·25
1837 6m. "Oda Nobunaga (Kokei Sochin) (24½×81½ mm) ... 1·25 1·25
1838 7m. "Viewing the Maples at Mount Takao" ... 1·40 1·60
1839 8m. "The Four Accomplishments" (Kaiho Yusho) ... 1·50 1·75
1824/39 *Set of 16* ... 15·50 15·50
MS1840 Two sheets. (a) 98×131 mm. 15m. "Tokugawa Ieyasu". (b) 114×134 mm. 15m. "Toyotomi Hideyoshi". *Set of* $1 *sheets* ... 8·00 9·00

Nos. 1828/32 and 1833/7 were each printed together, *se-tenant*, in sheetlets of 5 with inscribed top and bottom margins.

(Des Irina Lyampe. Litho B.D.T.)

2001 (29 June). *"Belgica 2001" International Stamp Exhibition, Brussels. African Fungi. T* **285** *and similar multicoloured designs.* P 14.

1841 3m. Type **285** ... 85 85
a. Sheetlet. Nos. 1841/6 ... 4·50
1842 3m. *Pleurocybella Porrigens* ... 85 85
1843 3m. *Collybia velutibes* ... 85 85
1844 3m. *Lentinellus cochleatus* ... 85 85
1845 3m. *Anthurua aseroiformis* ... 85 85
1846 3m. Caesar's Mushroom ... 85 85
1847 4m. *Cortinarius traganus* ... 95 95
a. Sheetlet. Nos. 1847/52 ... 5·25
1848 4m. *Peziza sarcosphaera* ... 95 95
1849 4m. *Russula emetica* ... 95 95
1850 4m. *Stropharia ambigua* ... 95 95
1851 4m. *Phologiotis helvelliodes* ... 95 95
1852 4m. *Clitocybe odora* ... 95 95
1853 5m. Golden False Pholiota ... 1·10 1·10
1854 5m. *Coprinus micaceus* ... 1·10 1·10
1855 5m. *Hygrophorus camarophyllus* ... 1·10 1·10
1856 5m. *Panaeolus campanulatus* ... 1·10 1·10
1841/56 *Set of 16* ... 13·50 13·50

MS1857 Two sheets, each 75×55 mm. (a). 15m. *Boletus parasiticus* (*horiz*). (b) 15m. *Hygrophorus hygrocybe conicus* (*horiz*). *Set of 2 sheets* ...... 9·00 9·50

Nos. 1841/6 and 1847/52 were each printed together, *se-tenant*, in sheetlets of 6, with illustrated margins.

No. 1841 is inscribed "violaceys", No. 1842 "Pleyrocybella", No. 1844 "Cochleathus", No. 1852 "Clitoeybe" and No. 1856 "Panaelus companulatus", all in error.

286 "Woman with Baby in Sunset" (Leila Hall)

287 Black Kite

(Litho Questa)

2001 (20 Aug). *Winners of United Nations Children's Art Competiton. T* **286** *and similar multicoloured designs.* P. 14.

1858 70s. Type **286** 40 15
1859 1m. "Herdboy with Lamb" (Chambeli Ramathe) 50 20
1860 1m.50 "Girl with A.I.D.S. Ribbon" (Chambeli Ramathe) (*vert*) 65 50
1861 2m.10 "Satellite Dish and Map seen through Keyhole" (Mika Sejake) (*vert*) 80 80
1858/61 *Set of 4* ...... 2·10 1·50

(Des K. Maja. Litho Questa)

2001 (1 Oct). *Birds of Prey. T* **287** *and similar vert designs. Multicoloured.* P 14.

1862 70s. Type **287** 45 25
1863 1m. Martial Eagle 55 30
1864 1m.50 Bateleur 70 55
1865 2m.10 African Goshawk 85 85
1866 2m.50 Bearded Vulture 90 90
1867 3m. Jackal Buzzard ...... 1·00 1·00
1862/7 *Set of 6* ...... 4·00 3·50

No. 1865 is inscribed "GASHAWK" in error.

288 Grass Owl

(Des R. Martin. Litho Questa)

2001 (15 Oct). *Wildlife of Southern Africa. T* **288** *and similar multicoloured designs.* P14.

1868 1m. Type **288** 70 40
1869 2m.10 Klipspringer 75 50
1870 3m. Saddle-backed Jackal 85 65
1871 4m. Aardvark ...... 1·10 1·10
a. Sheetlet. Nos. 1871/6 ...... 6·00
1872 4m. Rock Kestrel ...... 1·10 1·10
1873 4m. Black-footed Cat ...... 1·10 1·10
1874 4m. Springhare ...... 1·10 1·10
1875 4m. Aardwolf ...... 1·10 1·10
1876 4m. Rock Hyrax ...... 1·10 1·10
1877 4m. Damara Zebra ...... 1·10 1·10
a. Sheetlet. Nos. 1877/82 ...... 6·00
1878 4m. Bontebok ...... 1·10 1·10
1879 4m. Eland ...... 1·10 1·10
1880 4m. Lion ...... 1·10 1·10
1881 4m. Saddled-backed Jackal ...... 1·10 1·10
1882 4m. Yellow-billed Kite ...... 1·10 1·10
1883 5m. Black Wildebeest ...... 1·25 1·25
1868/83 *Set of 16* ...... 15·00 14·50

MS1884 Two sheets, each 90×64 mm. (a). 15m. Black-shouldered Kite. (b) 15m. Caracal (*vert*). *Set of 2 sheets* ...... 10·00 10·00

Nos. 1871/6 and 1877/82 were each printed together, *se-tenant*, in sheetlets of 6, with the backgrounds forming composite designs which continue onto the sheetlet margins.

289 Queen Elizabeth wearing Purple Coat

290 Homer Wood (Rotary pioneer)

(Des D. Miller. Litho Questa)

2002 (3 June). *Golden Jubilee. T* **289** *and similar square designs. Multicoloured.* P 14½.

1885 8m. Type **289** ...... 2·50 2·50
a. Sheetlet. Nos. 1885/8 ...... 9·00
1886 8m. Queen Elizabeth with Duke of Edinburgh on launch ...... 2·50 2·50
1887 8m. Queen Elizabeth with mayor ...... 2·50 2·50
1888 8m. Duke of Edinburgh wearing sunglasses ...... 2·50 2·50
1885/8 *Set of 4* ...... 9·00 9·00

MS1889 76×108 mm. 20m. Queen Elizabeth inspecting R.A.F. guard of honour. P 14 ...... 6·50 7·00

Nos. 1885/8 were printed together, *se-tenant*, in sheetlets of 4, with an illustrated left margin.

(Des R. Rundo. Litho Questa)

2002 (13 Aug). *25th Anniv of Rotary International in Lesotho. T* **290** *and similar multicoloured designs.* P 14.

1890 8m. Type **290** ...... 2·00 2·00
1891 10m. Paul Harris (founder of Rotary International) ...... 2·25 2·25

MS1892 Two sheets. (a) 60×75 mm. 25m. Coloured globe and Rotary logo (*horiz*). *Set of 2 sheets* ...... 12·00 14·00

No. 1890 is inscribed "HORNER" in error.

291 Machache

(Des H. Friedman. Litho Questa)

2002 (13 Aug). *International Year of Mountains. T* **291** *and similar multicoloured designs showing Lesotho mountains. (except No.* **MS***1897).* P 14.

1893 8m. Type **291** ...... 2·00 2·00
a. Sheetlet. Nos. 1893/6 ...... 7·25
1894 8m. Thabana-li-Mèlè ...... 2·00 2·00
1895 8m. Qiloane ...... 2·00 2·00
1896 8m. Thaba-Bosiu ...... 2·00 2·00
1893/6 *Set of 6* ...... 7·25 7·25

MS1897 64×83 mm. 25m. The Matterhorn, Switzerland (*vert*) ...... 7·50 8·00

Nos. 1893/6 were printed together, *se-tenant*, in sheetlets of 4 with enlarged illustrated left and bottom margins. No. **MS**1897 is inscribed "Mount Rainer" in error.

292 Boys with Calf, Lithabaneng

(Des M. Friedman. Litho Questa)

2002 (13 Aug). *S.O.S. Children's Villages (Kinderdorf International).* P 14.

1898 **292** 10m. multicoloured ...... 2·50 2·50

293 Spiral Aloe

294 U.S. Flag as Statue of Liberty with Lesotho Flag)

(Des R. Rundo. Litho Questa)

2002 (13 Aug). *UN Year of Eco Tourism. T* **293** *and similar multicoloured designs.* P 14.

1899 6m. Type **293** ...... 1·40 1·50
a. Sheetlet. Nos. 1899/1904 ...... 7·50
1900 6m. *Anthrixia gerradii* (flower) ...... 1·40 1·50
1901 6m. Horseman and Packhorse ...... 1·40 1·50
1902 6m. Lion ...... 1·40 1·50
1903 6m. Frog ...... 1·40 1·50
1904 6m. Thatched building ...... 1·40 1·50
1899/904 *Set of 6* ...... 7·50 8·00

MS1905 77×83 mm. 20m. European Bee Eater (*vert*) ...... 7·00 7·50

Nos. 1899/1904 were printed together, *se-tenant*, in sheetlets of 6 with an enlarged illustrated bottom margin.

(Des M. Friedman. Litho Questa)

2002 (13 Aug). *"United We Stand". Support for Victims of 11 September 2001 Terrorist Attacks.* P 14.

1906 **294** 7m. multicoloured ...... 1·60 1·75

No. 1906 was printed in sheetlets of 4 with an illustrated left margin.

295 Sheet Bend Knot

296 Angel's Fishing Rod (*Dierama pulcherrimum*)

(Des H. Friedman. Litho Questa)

2002 (13 Aug). *20th World Scout Jamboree, Thailand. T* **295** *and similar horiz designs. Multicoloured.* P 14.

1907 9m. Type **295** ...... 2·00 2·25
a. Sheetlet. Nos. 1907/10 ...... 7·25
1908 9m. Pup and forester tents ...... 2·00 2·25
1909 9m. Scouts in canoe ...... 2·00 2·25
1910 9m. Life-saving ...... 2·00 2·25
1907/10 *Set of 4* ...... 7·25 8·00

MS1911 75×59 mm. 25m. Scouts asleep in tent ...... 7·00 8·00

Nos. 1907/10 were printed together, *se-tenant*, in sheetlets of 4 with enlarged illustrated left and top margins.

(Des R. Rundo. Litho Walsall)

2003 (13 Jan). *Flowers, Orchids and Insects. T* **296** *and similar multicoloured designs.* P 14.

MS1912 100×180 mm. 6m. Type **296**; 6m. Marigold (*Calendula officinalis*); 6m. Dianthus "Joan's Blood", 6m. Mule Pink (*Dianthus plumarius*) ; 6m. Tiger Lily (*Lilium lancifolium*); 6m. *Clematis viticella* "Comtesse de Bouchaud" ...... 8·50 9·00

MS1913 180×100 mm. 6m. Leaf Grasshopper (*Brochopeplus exalatus*); 6m. Golden-ringed Dragonfly (*Cordulegaster boltoni*); 6m. Weevel-hunting Wasp (*Cerceris arenaria*); 6m. European Grasshopper (*Oedipoda miniata*); 6m. Thread-waisted Wasp (*ammophilia alberti*) 6m. Mantid (*Mantis acontista*) (all horiz) ...... 8·50 9·00

MS1914 95×103 mm. 6m. *Phragmipedium besseae*; 6m. *Cypripedium calceolus*; 6m. Cattleya "Louise Georgiana"; 6m. *Brassocattleya binosa*; 6m. *Laelia gouldiana*; 6m. *Paphiopedilum maudiae* "Alba" ...... 8·50 9·00

MS1915 Three sheets. (a) 63×75 mm. 20m. Bleeding Heart (*Dicentra spectabilis*). (b) 75×63 mm. 20m. Orb Web Spider (*Argiope bruennichi*). (c) 75×63 mm. 20m. *Brassavola tuberculata*. *Set of 3 sheets* ...... 16·00 18·00

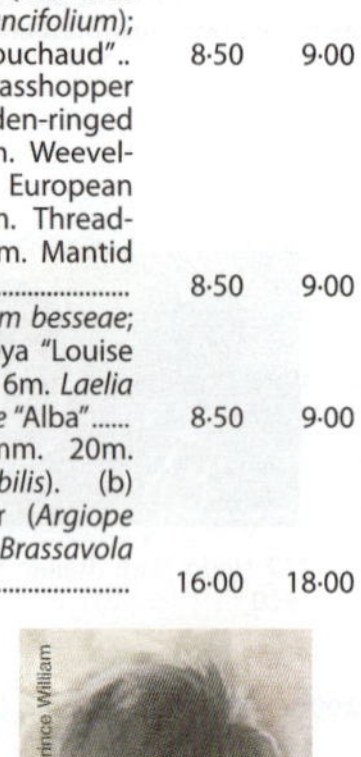

297 Blériot's Canard at Bagatelle, 1906

298 Prince William

(Des J. Iskowiz. Litho BDT)

2004 (17 May). *Centenary of Powered Flight. T* **297** *and similar horiz designs. Multicoloured.* P 14.

MS1916 177×97 mm. 6m. Type **297**; 6m. Blériot's Double-winged Libellule, 1907; 6m. Blériot's No. VIII in Touy–Artenay cross-country flight, 1908; 6m. Blériot's XII Test Flight, 1909 ...... 5·00 5·50

MS1917 66×97 mm. 15m. Louis Blériot's No. XI ...... 4·00 4·25

(Des R. Rundo. Litho BDT)

2004 (17 May). *21st Birthday of Prince William. T* **298** *and similar vert designs. Multicoloured.* P 14.

MS1918 77×148 mm. 8m. Type **298**; 8m. Wearing grey suit and tie; 8m. Wearing yellow polo shirt ...... 6·50 7·00

MS1919 98×68 mm. 15m. Young Prince William ...... 4·25 4·50

299 Queen Elizabeth II

300 *Acraea rabbaiae*

(Des R. Rundo. Litho BDT)

2004 (17 May). *50th Anniv (2003) of Coronation. T* **299** *and similar vert designs. Multicoloured.* P 14.

MS1920 148×85 mm. 8m. Wearing ivory suit and hat; 8m. Wearing royal uniform ...... 6·50 7·00

MS1921 68×97 mm. 15m. Queen Elizabeth II ...... 4·25 4·50

(Des R. Rundo. Litho BDT)

2004 (17 May). *Butterflies. T* **300** *and similar horiz designs. Multicoloured.* P 14.

1922 1m.50 Type **300** 60 40
1923 2m.10 *Alaena margaritacea* 70 55
1924 4m. *Bematistes aganice* ...... 1·10 1·25
1925 6m. *Acraea quirina* ...... 1·50 1·75
1922/5 *Set of 4* ...... 3·50 3·50

MS1926 117×116 mm. 6m. *Bematistes excisa* (male) 6m. *Bematistes excisa* (female); 6m. *Bematistes epiprotea*; 6m. *Bematiste poggei* ...... 7·50 8·00

MS1927 67×98 mm. 15m. *Acraea satis* ...... 4·25 4·50

301 Secretary Bird

302 Bald Ibis

(Des R. Rundo. Litho BDT)

2004 (17 May). *Birds. T* **301** *and similar vert designs. Multicoloured.* P 14.

1928 1m.50 Type **301** 60 40
1929 2m.10 South African Crowned Crane ("Gray-crowned Crane") 70 55

1930 3m. Pied Avocet .... 1·00 1·00
1931 5m. Common Kestrel .... 1·40 1·50
1928/31 *Set of 14* .... 3·25 3·00
MS1932 108×136 mm. 6m. European Roller; 6m. European Cuckoo ("Common Cuckoo"); 6m. Great Spotted Cuckoo; 6m. Pel's Fishing Owl .... 7·50 8·00
MS1933 68×97 mm. 15m. Kori Bustard .... 4·25 4·50

(Des Irina Lyampe. Litho BDT)

2004 (17 May). *Endangered Species. Bald Ibis. T* **302** *and similar horiz designs.*
1934 3m. Type **302** .... 1·10 1·10
a. Strip of 4. Nos. 1934/7 .... 4·00
1935 3m. Bald Ibis at rest .... 1·10 1·10
1936 3m. Bald Ibis on nest .... 1·10 1·10
1937 3m. Bald Ibis in flight (facing right) .... 1·10 1·10
1934/7 *Set of 4* .... 4·00 4·00
MS1938 207×132 mm. Designs as Nos. 1934/6 and1937 (Bald Ibis facing left), each ×2 .... 8·00 8·50

Nos. 1934/7 were printed together, *se-tenant*, in horizontal and vertical strips of 4 in sheets of 16.

No. **MS**1938 contained two strips of four stamps separated by an enlarged illustrated gutter showing a Bald Ibis.

303 Cape Porcupine

304 *Sparaxis grandiflora*

(Litho BDT)

2004 (17 May). *Animals. T* **303** *and similar multicoloured designs.* P 14.
1939 1m. Type **303** 35 20
1940 1m.50 Brown rat 45 30
1941 2m.10 Springhare (*vert*) 60 55
1942 5m. South African galago (*vert*) .... 1·25 1·50
1939/42 *Set of 4* .... 2·40 2·30
MS1943 117×136 mm. 5m. Striped grass mouse; 5m. Greater galago; 5m. Ground pangolin; 5m. Banded mongoose .... 4·50 5·00
MS1944 68×98 mm. 15m. Egyptian rousette (*vert*) .... 3·75 4·00

(Litho BDT)

2004 (17 May). *Flowers. T* **304** *and similar vert designs. Multicoloured.* P 14.
1945 1m.50 Type **304** 45 30
1946 2m.10 *Agapanthus africanus* 60 50
1947 3m. *Protea linearis* 85 85
1948 5m. *Nerine cultivars* .... 1·25 1·50
1945/8 *Set of 4* .... 2·75 2·75
MS1949 104×117 mm. 5m. *Kniphofia uvaria*; 5m. *Amaryllis belladonna*; 5m. *Gazania Splendens*; 5m. *Erica coronata* .... 4·50 5·00
MS1950 68×98 mm. 15m. *Saintpaulia cultivars* .... 3·75 4·00

305 Qiloane Falls

2004 (17 May). *International Year of Freshwater. T* **305** *and similar horiz designs. Multicoloured. Litho.* P 14.
MS1951 85×167 mm. 8m. Type **305**, 8m. Halfway down Qiloane Falls; 8m. Base of Qiloane Falls .... 6·00 6·50
MS1952 118×84 mm. 15m. Orange River .... 3·75 4·00

306 Mokhoro (Round House and Cooking Hut)

(Des Makhabane C. Moshoeshoe. Litho BDT)

2005 (21 Feb). *Basotho Houses. T* **306** *and similar horiz designs. Multicoloured.* P 14.
1953 70s. Type **306** 25 10
1954 1m. Heisi (Rectangular house) 35 20
1955 1m.50 Typical homestead 45 35
1956 2m.10 Mathule (Round house with porch) 60 50
1953/6 *Set of 4* .... 1·50 1·00

No. 1953 is inscribed "70L" and No. 1956 "Mohlongoa-fat'se", both in error.

307 *Journey to the Centre of the Earth*

(Litho State Ptg Wks, Beijing)

2005 (22 Aug). *Death Centenary of Jules Verne (writer). T* **307** *and similar multicoloured designs.* P 13.
1957 8m. Type **307** .... 2·00 2·00
a. Sheetlet. Nos. 1957/9 .... 5·50
1958 8m. Jules Verne and "100 YEARS" .... 2·00 2·00
1959 8m. *20,000 Leagues under the Sea* .... 2·00 2·00
1957/9 *Set of 3* .... 5·50 5·50
MS1960 107×83 mm. 15m. Jules Verne (*vert*) .... 3·75 4·00

308 USS *Arizona* (battleship)

309 US Troops land on Omaha Beach

(Litho State Ptg Wks, Beijing)

2005 (22 Aug). *60th Anniv of Victory in Japan. T* **308** *and similar vert designs. Multicoloured.* P 13.
1961 4m. Type **308** .... 1·10 1·10
a. Sheetlet. Nos. 1961/5 .... 5·00
1962 4m. Bunker at Chula Beach, Tinian Island .... 1·10 1·10
1963 4m. Flight crew of *Bockscar* (B-29 aircraft) .... 1·10 1·10
1964 4m. Men showing newspaper headline. .... 1·10 1·10
1965 4m. Marker of second atomic bomb loading pit, Tinian Island .... 1·10 1·10
1961/5 *Set of 5* .... 5·00 5·00

Nos. 1961/5 were printed together, *se-tenant*, in sheetlets of five stamps with an enlarged, illustrated top margin.

(Litho State Ptg Wks, Beijing)

2005 (22 Aug). *60th Anniv of Victory in Europe. T* **309** *and similar vert designs. Multicoloured.* P 13.
1966 4m. Type **309** .... 1·10 1·10
a. Sheetlet. Nos. 1966/70 .... 5·00
1967 4m. General George C. Marshall .... 1·10 1·10
1968 4m. Field Marshall Wilhelm Keitel .... 1·10 1·10
1969 4m. General Dwight D. Eisenhower and Lt. General George S. Patton .... 1·10 1·10
1970 4m. Soldiers searching through rubble .... 1·10 1·10
1966/70 *Set of 5* .... 5·00 5·00

Nos. 1966/70 were printed together, *se-tenant*, in sheetlets of five stamps with an enlarged, illustrated top margin.

310 Pope John Paul II

311 Albert Einstein

(Litho State Ptg Wks, Beijing)

2005 (22 Aug). *Pope John Paul II Commemoration.* P 13.
1971 **310** 10m. multicoloured .... 2·75 2·75

No. 1971 was printed in sheetlets of four stamps with an enlarged, illustrated left margin.

(Litho State Ptg Wks, Beijing)

2005 (22 Aug). *50th Death Anniv of Albert Einstein (physicist). T* **311** *and similar multicoloured designs.* P 13.
1972 8m. Wearing glasses .... 2·00 2·00
a. Sheetlet. Nos. 1972/4 .... 5·50
1973 8m. With Nikola Tesla (inscr "Testa") and Charles Steinmetz .... 2·00 2·00
1974 8m. Type **311** .... 2·00 2·00
1972/4 *Set of 3* .... 5·50 5·50
MS1975 100×70 mm. 15m. On the cover of *Time* magazine (*vert*) .... 3·75 4·00

Nos. 1972/4 were printed together, *se-tenant*, in sheetlets of three stamps with an enlarged illustrated top margin.

312 Uruguay Football Team, 1930

(Litho State Ptg Wks, Beijing)

2005 (22 Aug). *75th Anniv of First World Cup Football Championship, Uruguay. T* **312** *and similar multicoloured designs.* P 12.
1976 8m. Type **312** .... 2·00 2·00
a. Sheetlet. Nos. 1976/8 .... 5·50
1977 8m. Opposing players and referee .... 2·00 2·00
1978 8m. German team .... 2·00 2·00
1976/8 *Set of 3* .... 5·50 5·50
MS1979 105×70 mm. 15m. Bodo Illgner (Germany) (*vert*) .... 3·75 4·00

Nos. 1976/8 were printed together, *se-tenant*, in sheetlets of three stamps with illustrated and inscribed margins.

313 Child eating

314 Hans Christian Andersen (statue)

(Litho State Ptg Wks, Beijing)

2005 (22 Aug). *Centenary of Rotary International. T* **313** *and similar vert designs. Multicoloured.* P 13.
1980 8m. Type **313** .... 2·00 2·00
a. Sheetlet. Nos. 1980/2 .... 5·50
1981 8m. Classroom scene .... 2·00 2·00
1982 8m. Children .... 2·00 2·00
1980/2 *Set of 3* .... 5·50 5·50

Nos. 1980/2 were printed together, *se-tenant*, in sheetlets of three stamps with enlarged, illustrated and inscribed top and left margins.

(Litho State Ptg Wks, Beijing)

2005 (22 Aug). *Birth Bicentenary of Hans Christian Andersen (writer). T* **314** *and similar vert designs. Multicoloured.* P 13.
1983 8m. Type **314** .... 2·00 2·00
a. Sheetlet. Nos. 1983/5 .... 5·50
1984 8m. Former home of Hans Christian Andersen, Odense .... 2·00 2·00
1985 8m. "The Steadfast Tin Soldier" .... 2·00 2·00
1983/5 *Set of 3* .... 5·50 5·50
MS1986 75×82 mm. 15m. "The Little Mermaid" .... 3·75 4·00

Nos. 1983/5 were printed together, *se-tenant*, in sheetlets of three stamps with illustrated and inscribed margins.

315 HMS *Victory*

(Litho State Ptg Wks, Beijing)

2005 (22 Aug). *Bicentenary of the Battle of Trafalgar. T* **315** *and similar horiz designs. Multicoloured.* P 13.
1987 8m. Type **315** .... 2·50 2·50
a. Sheetlet. Nos. 1987/90 .... 9·00
1988 8m. Admiral Lord Horatio Nelson .... 2·50 2·50
1989 8m. Admiral Nelson fatally wounded .... 2·50 2·50
1990 8m. Ships engaged in battle .... 2·50 2·50
1987/90 *Set of 4* .... 9·00 9·00
MS1991 70×100 mm. 25m. Admiral Lord Horatio Nelson and crew (50×38 mm). P 12 .... 8·00 8·50

Nos. 1987/90 were printed together, *se-tenant*, in sheetlets of four stamps with an enlarged, illustrated right margin.

316 Brownies

317 Herdboy riding Calf

(Litho BDT)

2005 (12 Dec). *80th Anniv of Lesotho Girl Guides Association. T* **316** *and similar multicoloured designs.* P 14.
1992 70l. Type **316** 30 15
1993 1m. Procession of rangers and guides 45 30
1994 1m.50 Rangers recycling tin cans (*vert*) 60 50
1995 2m.10 Ranger and guides at Lesotho Girl Guides Headquarters 80 80
1992/5 *Set of 4* .... 1·90 1·60
MS1996 66×98 mm. 10m. Queen 'Mamohato Seeiso (patron 1966–2003) .... 2·50 2·75

(Des Vincent Seatile Nkhomo. Litho BDT)

2006 (13 Mar). *Herdboys. T* **317** *and similar vert designs. Multicoloured.* P 14.
1997 70l. Type **317** 25 10
1998 1m. Feeding cattle 35 20
1999 1m.50 Three herdboys playing morabaraba and grazing cattle 50 50
2000 2m. Carrying newborn lamb on shoulders 60 60
1997/2000 *Set of 4* .... 1·50 1·30
MS2001 95×65 mm. 10m. Herdboys dancing ndlamo and practicing stick fighting .... 2·50 2·75

318 Woman carrying Thatching Grass

319 Grass work

(Des Vincent Seatile Nkhomo. Litho BDT)

2006 (19 June). *Basotho women carrying goods on their heads. T* **318** *and similar vert designs. Multicoloured.* P 14.

2002	70l. Type **318**	25	10
2003	1m. Carrying iron cooking pot on head	35	20
2004	1m.50 Carrying clay water pot on head	50	50
2005	2m.10 Carrying basket of pumpkins, maize and sorghum	70	70
2002/5	*Set of 4*	1·60	1·30
MS2006	96×67 mm. 10m. Girl carrying basket of maize flour on head	2·50	2·75

(Des Roman Francisco. Litho Questa)

2006 (9 Oct). *Handicrafts. T* **319** *and similar multicoloured designs. Litho.* P 14.

2007	70l. Type **319**	20	10
2008	1m. Tapestry weaving (vert)	35	20
2009	1m.50 Pottery	50	50
2010	2m.10 Horn work	70	70
2007/10	*Set of 4*	1·60	1·30
MS2011	96×65 mm. 10m. Young girl dressed in beads (*vert*)	2·50	2·75

STAMP BOOKLETS

1981 (20 Apr). *Multicoloured cover, 165×100 mm, showing Hoopoe (bird) on front and Lesotho village scene on back. Stapled.*

SB1 4m.30 booklet containing 5s., 6s., 7s. and 25s. (Nos. 440, 441/2, 444) in blocks of 10 ... 9·00

1981 (22 July). *Royal Wedding. Multicoloured cover, 150×100 mm, showing Prince Charles and Lady Diana Spencer on front and Ba-Leseli dance on back. Stitched.*

SB2 6m. booklet containing four different panes of 3 stamps and 1 label (Nos. 451a/b, 452a, 453a) ... 2·00
a. Stapled ...

1982 (5 Mar). *75th Anniv of Boy Scout Movement. Multicoloured cover, 170×98 mm, showing Lord Baden-Powell on front and Scout with flag on back. Pane attached by selvedge.*

SB3 5m.52 booklet containing *se-tenant* pane of 10 stamps and one miniature sheet (No. 474a) ... 5·00

1982 (14 Apr). *World Cup Football Championship, Spain. Multicoloured cover, 170×102 mm, showing Championship emblems. Stamps attached by selvedge.*

SB4 4m.85 booklet containing twenty-four 15s. (Nos. 480/91) in blocks of 12 and one miniature sheet (No. **MS**492) ... 6·00

1982 (14 June). *Multicoloured cover as No. SB1. Stapled.*

SB5 4m.30 booklet containing 5s., 6s., 7s. and 25s. (Nos. 503/5, 507) in blocks of 10 ... 8·50

1983 (11 Jan). *Fungi. Multicoloured cover, 155×80 mm, showing fungi on front and with biography of G. L. Vasarhelyi on back. Panes attached by selvedge.*

SB6 3m.70 booklet containing two *se-tenant* panes of 4 stamps and 1 label (No. 532b) and one *se-tenant* pane of 2 stamps and 1 label (No. 532c) ... 7·50

1983 (11 July). *Bicentenary of Manned Flight. Multicoloured cover, 211×100 mm, showing Montgolfier balloon. Panes attached by selvedge.*

SB7 4m. booklet containing *se-tenant* pane of 4 stamps and 1 label (No. 545a) and one miniature sheet (No. **MS**549) ... 5·25

OFFICIAL STAMPS

OFFICIAL

(O **1**)

1934 (Feb). *Nos. 1/3 and 6 optd with Type* O **1**, *by Govt printer, Pretoria.*

O1	**1**	½d. emerald	£10000	£6000
O2		1d. scarlet	£2500	£2250
O3		2d. bright purple	£2750	£800
O4		6d. orange-yellow	£11000	£4750
O1/4		*Set of 4*	£24000	£12500

Collectors are advised to buy these stamps only from reliable sources. They were not sold to the public.

300 of each value were supplied in January 1934 for use by the Secretariat in Maseru. Limited usage is recorded between 28 Feb 1934 and 8 June 1934. The issue was then withdrawn and the remainders destroyed. Only the following numbers appear to have been issued: ½d. 24, 1d. 34, 2d. 54, 6d. 27, from which a maximum of ten mint sets exist.

POSTAGE DUE STAMPS

D **1**

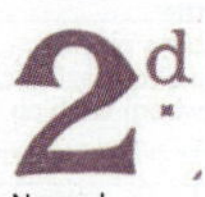

Normal

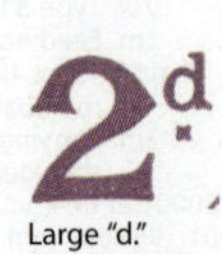

Large "d." (R. 9/6, 10/6)

(Typo D.L.R.)

1933 (1 Dec)–**52**. *Ordinary paper.* Wmk Mult Script CA. P 14.

D1	D **1**	1d. carmine	1·75	9·00
		a. Scarlet (1938)	38·00	45·00
		b. Chalk-surfaced paper. *Deep carmine* (24.10.51)	1·50	3·00
		ba. Error. Crown missing, W **9***a*	£200	
		bb. Error. St. Edward's Crown, W **9***b*	90·00	
D2		2d. violet	7·50	18·00
		a. Chalk-surfaced paper (6.11.52)	30	15·00
		ab. Error. Crown missing, W **9***a*	£225	
		ac. Error. St. Edward's Crown, W **9***b*	95·00	
		ad. Large "d"	6·00	
D1s/2s		Perf "Specimen" *Set of 2*	45·00	

D **2**

(Typo D.L.R.)

1956 (1 Dec). *Wmk Mult Script CA.* P 14.

D3	D **2**	1d. carmine	30	3·00
D4		2d. deep reddish violet	30	6·00

5c (I) **5c** (II)

1961 (14 Feb). *Surch as T* **24**, *but without stop.*

D5	D **2**	1c. on 1d. carmine	10	35
D6		1c. on 2d. deep reddish violet	10	1·00
D7		5c. on 2d. deep reddish violet (Type I)	15	45
		a. Type II	12·00	42·00
D5/7		*Set of 3*	30	1·60

1961 (1 June). *No. D2a surch as T* **24** *(without stop).*

D8	D **1**	5c. on 2d. violet	1·00	6·50
		a. Error. Missing Crown, W **9**a	£1300	
		b. Error. St. Edward's Crown, W **9**b	£250	
		c. Large "d"	15·00	

1964. *As No. D3/4 but values in cents and W w* **12** *(sideways on 1c.).*

D9	D **2**	1c. carmine	2·75	18·00
D10		5c. deep reddish violet	2·75	18·00

1966 (1 Nov). *Nos. D9/10 of Basutoland optd as T* **34** *but smaller.*

D11	D **2**	1c. carmine	30	75
		a. "LSEOTHO" (R. 4/7)	25·00	
D12		5c. deep reddish violet	30	90
		a. "LSEOTHO" (R. 4/7)	45·00	

No. D11 exists with the overprint centred near the foot of the stamp (just above "POSTAGE DUE") (price £50 mint). It is believed that this comes from a proof sheet which was issued in the normal way. It contains the "LSEOTHO" error, which only occurred in the first printing.

D **3**

D **4**

(Litho B.W.)

1967 (18 Apr). *No wmk.* P 13½.

D13	D **3**	1c. blue	15	3·00
D14		2c. brown-rose	15	3·50
D15		5c. emerald	20	3·50
D13/15		*Set of 3*	45	9·00

1976 (30 Nov). W **53** (sideways). P 13½.

D17	D **4**	2c. rose-red	1·50	6·00
D18		5c. emerald	1·75	6·00

(Des G. Vasarhelyi. Litho Format)

1986. No wmk. P 13×13½.

D19	D **4**	2s. light green	20	1·25
D20		5s. new blue	20	1·25
D21		25s. violet	70	1·50
D19/21		*Set of 3*	1·00	3·50

Nos. D19/21 exist imperforate from stock dispersed by the liquidator of Format International Security Printers Ltd.

POSTAL FISCAL

In July 1961 the 10s. stamp, T **9**, surcharged "R1 Revenue", was used for postage at one post office at least, but such usage was officially unauthorised.

Appendix

The following stamps have either been issued in excess of postal needs, or have not been made available to the public in reasonable quantities at face value. Miniature sheets, imperforate stamps etc., are excluded from this section.

1981–83.

15th Anniv of Independence. Classic Stamps of the World. 10m.×40, each embossed on gold foil.

Namibia

formerly South West Africa

SOUTH WEST AFRICA

The stamps of Germany were used in the colony from July 1886 until the introduction of issues for GERMAN SOUTH-WEST AFRICA in May 1897. Following occupation by South African forces in 1914–15 the issues of SOUTH AFRICA were used, being replaced by the overprinted issues in 1923.

Walvis (or Walfish) Bay, the major anchorage on the South West Africa coast, was claimed by Great Britain as early as 1796. In 1878 the 430 sq mile area around the port, together with a number of offshore islands, was annexed to Cape Province, passing to the Union of South Africa in 1910.

Stamps of the Cape of Good Hope and South Africa were used at Walfish Bay, often cancelled with numeral obliterator 300, until the enclave was transferred to the South West Africa administration on 1 October 1922.

The Walfish Bay territory reverted to South Africa on 30 August 1977 and from that date the stamps of South Africa were, once again, in use.

PRICES FOR STAMPS ON COVER TO 1945

Nos. 1/40*a*	*from* × 6
Nos. 41/133	*from* × 2
Nos. D1/5	*from* × 10
Nos. D6/51	*from* × 20
Nos. O1/4	*from* × 3
Nos. O5/20	*from* × 15
No. O21	*from* × 2
No. O22	*from* × 15

INSCRIPTIONS. Most of the postage stamps up to No. 140 are inscribed alternately in English and Afrikaans throughout the sheets and the same applies to all the Official stamps and to Nos. D30/33.

PRICES for Nos. 1/140 are for unused horizontal pairs, used horizontal pairs or used singles (either inscr), *unless otherwise indicated.*

OVERPRINT SETTINGS. Between 1923 and 1928 the King George V definitives of South Africa, Types **2** and **3**, and the various postage due stamps were issued overprinted for use in South West Africa. A number of overprint settings were used:

Setting – Overprint Types **1** and **2** ("Zuid-West Afrika"). 14 mm between lines of overprint. See Nos. 1/12 and D1/9

Setting – As Setting I, but 10 mm between lines of overprint. See Nos. 13/15 and D10/13

Setting – Overprint Types **3** ("Zuidwest Afrika") and **4**. "South West" 14 mm long. "Zuidwest" 11 mm long. 14 mm between lines of overprint. See Nos. 16/27 and D14/17

Setting – As Setting III, but "South West" 16 mm long, "Zuidwest" 12 mm long and 14 mm between lines of overprint. See Nos. 28 and D17*a*/20

Setting – As Setting IV, but 12 mm between lines of overprint. See Nos. D21/4

Setting – As Setting IV, but 9½ mm between lines of overprint. See Nos. 29/40 and D25/32.

South West Africa. (1) Zuid-West Afrika. (2)

1923 (1 Jan–17 June). *Nos. 3/4, 6 and 9/17 of South Africa optd alternately with T* **1** *and* **2** *by typography.*

(a) Setting I (14 mm between lines of opt).

		Un pair	*Us pair*	*Us single*
1	½d. green	2·50	9·00	1·00
	a. "Wes" for "West" (R. 20/8)	90·00	£140	
	b. "Afr ica" (R. 20/2)	£120		
	c. Litho opt in shiny ink (17 June)	9·50	55·00	4·75
2	1d. rose-red	3·50	9·00	1·00
	a. Opt inverted	£500		
	b. "Wes" for "West" (R. 12/2)	£170		
	c. "Af.rica" for "Africa" (R. 20/6)	£170	£275	
	d. Opt double	£900		
	e. "Afr ica" (R. 20/2)	£120		
	f. "Afrika" without stop (R. 17/8)	£275		
3	2d. dull purple	4·50	12·00	1·50
	a. Opt inverted	£600	£700	
	b. "Wes" for "West" (R. 20/8)	£250		
	c. Litho opt in shiny ink (30 Mar)	45·00	£110	10·00
4	3d. ultramarine	7·50	16·00	2·75
5	4d. orange-yellow and sage-green	13·00	45·00	4·00
	a. Litho opt in shiny ink (19 Apr)	35·00	70·00	8·00
6	6d. black and violet	8·00	45·00	4·00
	a. Litho opt in shiny ink (19 Apr)	30·00	75·00	7·50
7	1s. orange-yellow	18·00	48·00	5·00
	a. Litho opt in shiny ink (19 Apr)	60·00	£120	11·00
	b. "Afrika" without stop (R. 17/8)			
8	1s.3d. pale violet	30·00	55·00	5·50
	a. Opt inverted	£375		
	b. Litho opt in shiny ink (19 Apr)	75·00	£140	14·00
9	2s.6d. purple and green	60·00	£130	18·00
	a. Litho opt in shiny ink (19 Apr)	£130	£275	35·00
10	5s. purple and blue	£150	£350	50·00
11	10s. blue and olive-green	£1300	£2750	£400
12	£1 green and red	£700	£1900	£250
1/12 *Set of 12*		£2000	£4750	£650
1s/12s Optd "Specimen" *Set of 12 singles*		£1400		

Nos. 1/12 were overprinted in complete sheets of 240 (4 panes 6×10).

No. 3b shows traces of a type spacer to the right of where the "t" should have been. This spacer is not visible on Nos. 1a and 2b.

Minor varieties, such as broken "t" in "West", were caused by worn type. Stamps showing one line of overprint only or with the lower line above the upper line due to overprint misplacement may also be found. All values exist showing a faint stop after "Afrika" on R. 17/8, but only examples of the 1d. and 1s. have been seen with it completely omitted.

(b) Setting II (10 mm between lines of opt) (31 Mar).

13	5s. purple and blue	£140	£275	45·00
	a. "Afrika" without stop (R. 6/1)	£1000	£1300	£225
14	10s. blue and olive-green	£500	£850	£140
	a. "Afrika" without stop (R. 6/1)	£2250	£2750	£550
15	£1 green and red	£1000	£1400	£200
	a. "Afrika" without stop (R. 6/1)	£4000	£5000	£1000
13/15 *Set of 3*		£1500	£2250	£350

Nos. 13/15 were overprinted in separate panes of 60 (6×10).

Examples of most values are known showing a forged Windhoek postmark dated "30 SEP 24".

Zuidwest Afrika. (3) South West Africa. (4)

1923 (15 July)–**26**. *Nos. 3/4, 6 and 9/17 of South Africa optd as T* **3** *("Zuidwest" in one word, without hyphen) and* **4** *alternately.*

(a) Setting III ("South West" 14 mm long, "Zuidwest" 11 mm long, 14 mm between lines of opt).

16	½d. green (5.9.24)	8·00	35·00	3·75
	a. "outh" for "South" (R. 1/1)	£1700		
17	1d. rose-red (28.9.23)	5·50	9·00	1·40
	a. "outh" for "South" (R. 1/1)	£1600		
18	2d. dull purple (28.9.23)	7·50	9·00	1·25
	a. Opt double	£1000		
19	3d. ultramarine	5·00	10·00	1·25
20	4d. orange-yellow and sage-green	6·00	21·00	2·75
	w. Wmk inverted	†	†	—
21	6d. black and violet (28.9.23)	12·00	45·00	5·00
22	1s. orange-yellow	12·00	45·00	5·00
23	1s.3d. pale violet	22·00	45·00	5·50
24	2s.6d. purple and green	45·00	85·00	10·00
25	5s. purple and blue	60·00	£140	18·00
26	10s. blue and olive-green	£160	£250	40·00
27	£1 green and red (28.9.23)	£300	£400	60·00
16/27 *Set of 12*		£600	£1000	£140

Nos. 16/27 were overprinted in complete sheets of 240 (4 panes 6×10).

Two sets may be made with this overprint, one with bold lettering, and the other from September 1924, with thinner lettering and smaller stops.

(b) Setting IV ("South West" 16 mm long, "Zuidwest" 12 mm long, 14 mm between lines of opt).

28	2s.6d. purple and green (29.6.24)	80·00	£160	28·00

No. 28 was overprinted on two panes of 60 horizontally side by side.

(c) Setting VI ("South West" 16 mm long, "Zuidwest" 12 mm long, 9½ mm between lines of opt).

29	½d. green (16.12.25)	7·00	40·00	5·00
30	1d. rose-red (9.12.24)	3·25	10·00	1·40
	a. Opt omitted (in pair with normal)	£1500		
31	2d. dull purple (9.12.24)	4·00	22·00	1·75
32	3d. ultramarine (31.1.26)	4·50	29·00	2·75
	a. Deep bright blue (20.4.26)	42·00	£100	12·00
33	4d. orge-yellow & sage-grn (9.12.24)	5·50	45·00	4·00
34	6d. black and violet (9.12.24)	9·00	48·00	5·00
35	1s. orange-yellow (9.12.24)	8·50	48·00	5·00
36	1s.3d. pale violet (9.12.24)	11·00	48·00	5·00
37	2s.6d. purple and green (9.12.24)	30·00	75·00	10·00
38	5s. purple and blue (31.1.26)	45·00	£120	14·00
39	10s. blue and olive-green (9.12.24)	80·00	£160	20·00
40	£1 green and red (9.1.26)	£250	£400	55·00
	a. Pale olive-green and red (8.11.26)	£250	£450	65·00
29/40*a Set of 12*		£400	£900	£120
35s, 39s/40s H/S "Specimen" *Set of 3*		£500		

Nos. 29/40 were overprinted in complete sheets of 240 (4 panes of 6×10) with, initially, "South West Africa" 16½ mm long on the upper two panes and 16 mm long on the lower two. This order was subsequently reversed. For printings from 8 November 1926 all four panes showed the 16½ mm measurement. No. 40a only comes from this printing.

Examples of most values are known showing a forged Windhoek postmark dated "30 SEP 24".

Suidwes Afrika. (5) South West Africa. (6)

1926 (1 Jan–1 May). *Nos. 30/2 of South Africa optd with T* **5** *(on stamps inscr in Afrikaans) and* **6** *(on stamps inscr in English) sideways, alternately in black.*

41	½d. black and green	4·25	9·00	1·00
42	1d. black and carmine	3·50	8·00	80
43	6d. green and orange (1 May)	22·00	48·00	7·00
41/3 *Set of 3*		26·00	60·00	8·00

SOUTH WEST AFRICA (7) SUIDWES-AFRIKA (8)

1926. *No. 33 of South Africa, imperf optd.*

(a) With T **7** *(English).*

			Single stamps
44A	4d. grey-blue	75	3·00

(b) With T **8** *(Afrikaans).*

44B	4d. grey-blue	75	3·00

1927. *As Nos. 41/3, but Afrikaans opt on stamp inscr in English and vice versa.*

45	½d. black and green	2·00	7·00	80
	a. "Africa" without stop (R. 13/8)	£160		
46	1d. black and carmine	2·50	2·50	50
	a. "Africa" without stop (R. 13/8)	£300		
47	6d. green and orange	9·00	30·00	3·00
	a. "Africa" without stop (R. 13/8)	£180		
45/7 *Set of 3*		12·00	35·00	3·75

SOUTH WEST AFRICA (9) S.W.A. (10) S.W.A. (11)

1927. *As No. 44A, but overprint T* **9**.

			Single stamps
48	4d. grey-blue	6·00	19·00
	s. Handstamped "Specimen"	70·00	

1927 (Apr). *Nos. 34/9 of South Africa optd alternately as T* **5** *and* **6**, *in blue, but with lines of overprint spaced 16 mm.*

49	2d. grey and purple	4·75	16·00	1·75
50	3d. black and red	4·75	28·00	2·50
51	1s. brown and blue	15·00	32·00	4·00
52	2s.6d. green and brown	35·00	95·00	13·00
53	5s. black and green	75·00	£190	20·00
54	10s. blue and bistre-brown	65·00	£160	20·00
49/54 *Set of 6*		£180	£475	50·00
49s/51s, 54s H/S "Specimen" *Set of 4*		£375		

A variety of Nos. 49, 50, 51 and 54 with spacing 16½ mm between lines of overprint, occurs in the third vertical row of each sheet.

1927. *As No. 44, but perf 11½ by John Meinert Ltd, Windhoek.*

(a) Optd with T **7** *(English).*

			Single stamps
55A	4d. grey-blue	1·00	4·75
	a. Imperf between (pair)	35·00	70·00
	s. Handstamped "Specimen"	70·00	

(b) Optd with T **8** *(Afrikaans).*

55B	4d. grey-blue	1·00	4·75
	a. Imperf between (pair)	35·00	70·00
	s. Handstamped "Specimen"	70·00	

1927 (Aug)–**30**. *Optd with T* **10**.

(a) On Nos. 13 and 17a of South Africa.

56	1s.3d. pale violet	1·25	6·50
	a. Without stop after "A" (R. 3/4)	£100	
	s. Handstamped "Specimen"	75·00	
57	£1 pale olive-green and red	90·00	£160
	a. Without stop after "A" (R. 3/4)	£1500	£2250

(b) On Nos. 30/2 and 34/9 of South Africa.

58	½d. black and green	2·50	6·50	80
	a. Without stop after "A"	40·00	75·00	
	b. "S.W.A." opt above value	2·75	16·00	2·25
	c. As b, in vert pair, top stamp without opt	£550		
59	1d. black and carmine	1·25	3·75	55
	a. Without stop after "A"	40·00	75·00	
	b. "S.W.A." opt at top (30.4.30)	1·75	14·00	1·60
	c. As b, in vert pair, top stamp without opt	£600		
60	2d. grey and maroon	9·00	28·00	1·50
	c. Perf 14×13½	16·00	40·00	
	ca. Without stop after "A"	85·00	£140	
	cb. Opt double, one inverted	£750	£1000	
61	3d. black and red	5·00	23·00	3·25
	a. Without stop after "A"	75·00	£120	
	b. Perf 14×13½	11·00	45·00	
	ba. Without stop after "A"	90·00	£160	
	bb. Without stop after "W"	£170		
62	4d. brown (4.28)	12·00	40·00	7·00
	a. Without stop after "A"	90·00	£140	
	b. Perf 14×13½	26·00	60·00	
63	6d. green and orange	8·50	24·00	2·75
	a. Without stop after "A"	£120		
64	1s. brown and deep blue	15·00	48·00	5·00
	b. Perf 14×13½	48·00	90·00	
	ba. Without stop after "A"	£1400	£1800	£350
65	2s.6d. green and brown	42·00	85·00	12·00
	a. Without stop after "A"	£160	£275	
	b. Perf 14×13½	75·00	£140	
	ba. Without stop after "A"	£225	£350	
66	5s. black and green	60·00	£120	18·00
	a. Without stop after "A"	£250	£375	
	b. Perf 14×13½	£100	£170	
	ba. Without stop after "A"	£275	£425	
67	10s. bright blue and brown	£100	£200	28·00
	a. Without stop after "A"	£375	£600	
58/67 *Set of 10*		£225	£500	70·00
58s/61s, 63s/7s H/S "Specimen" *Set of 9*		£600		

On the ½d., 1d. and 6d. the missing stop variety occurs three times on each sheet, R. 1/7, 13/4 and one position not yet identified. For the other values it comes on R. 2/3 of the right pane and, for the 2s.6d., 5s. and 10s., on R. 8/1 of the left pane.

The missing stop after "W" on the 3d. occurs on R. 10/5 of the right pane.

The overprint is normally found at the base of the ½d., 1d., 6d., 1s.3d. and £1 values and at the top of the remainder.

Examples of all values are known showing a forged Windhoek postmark dated "20 MAR 31".

1930–31. *Nos. 42 and 43 of South Africa (rotogravure printing) optd with T* **10**.

68	½d. black and green (1931)	11·00	30·00	2·75
69	1d. black and carmine	8·50	27·00	2·75

1930 (27 Nov–Dec). *Air. Nos. 40/1 of South Africa optd.*

(a) As T **10**.

70	4d. green (*first printing*)	8·00	28·00
	a. No stop after "A" of "S.W.A."	70·00	£140
	b. Later printings	5·00	28·00
71	1s. orange (*first printing*)	70·00	£120
	a. No stop after "A" of "S.W.A."	£450	£650
	b. Later printings	8·00	50·00

First printing: Thick letters, blurred impression. Stops with rounded corners.

Later printings: Thinner letters, clear impression. Clean cut, square stops.

(b) As T **11** *(12.30).*

		Un single	*Us single*
72	4d. green	1·25	6·00
	a. Opt double	£170	
	b. Opt inverted	£170	
73	1s. orange	3·25	15·00
	a. Opt double	£500	

12 Kori Bustard

13 Cape Cross

14 Bogenfels

15 Windhoek

16 Waterberg

17 Luderitz Bay

18 Bush Scene

19 Elands

20 Mountain Zebra and Blue Wildebeests

21 Herero Huts

22 Welwitschia Plant

23 Okuwahaken Falls

24 Monoplane over Windhoek

25 Biplane over Windhoek

(Recess B.W.)

1931 (5 Mar). *T* **12** *to* **25** *(inscr alternately in English and Afrikaans).* W **9** of South Africa. P 14×13½.

(a) Postage.

74	½d. black and emerald	2·75	2·50	10
75	1d. indigo and scarlet	2·25	2·50	10
76	2d. blue and brown	70	4·50	15
	w. Wmk inverted	£425		
77	3d. grey-blue and blue	70	4·25	15
78	4d. green and purple	1·50	7·00	20
79	6d. blue and brown	1·50	9·50	20
80	1s. chocolate and blue	2·25	12·00	25
81	1s.3d. violet and yellow	6·00	11·00	50
82	2s.6d. carmine and grey	20·00	24·00	1·75
83	5s. sage-green and red-brown	16·00	40·00	2·75
84	10s. red-brown and emerald	45·00	50·00	6·00
85	20s. lake and blue-green	70·00	80·00	10·00
	(b) Air.			
86	3d. brown and blue	26·00	32·00	2·50
87	10d. black and purple-brown	40·00	75·00	7·00
74/87 *Set of 14*		£200	£300	28·00

Examples of most values are known showing a forged Windhoek postmark dated "20 MAR 31".

26

(Recess B.W.)

1935 (1 May). *Silver Jubilee. Inscr bilingually.* W **9** of South Africa. P 14×13½.

			Un single	*Us single*
88	**26**	1d. black and scarlet	1·00	25
89		2d. black and sepia	1·00	25
90		3d. black and blue	7·50	23·00
91		6d. black and purple	3·00	12·00
88/91 *Set of 4*			11·00	32·00

1935–36. *Voortrekker Memorial Fund. Nos. 50/3 of South Africa optd with T* **10**.

92	½d. +½d.black and green	1·50	5·50	75
	a. Opt inverted	£275		
93	1d. +½d.grey-black and pink	1·50	3·25	40
	a. Blurred "SOUTH AFRICA" and red "comet" flaw	42·00		
94	2d. +1d.grey-green and purple	5·50	6·00	80
	a. Without stop after "A"	£200	£225	
	b. Opt double	£225		
95	3d. +1½d.grey-green and blue	16·00	32·00	4·00
	a. Without stop after "A"	£250	£325	
92/5 *Set of 4*		22·00	42·00	5·50

27 Mail Train

28

Re-entry (R. 6/3)

(Recess B.W.)

1937 (1 Mar). W **9** of South Africa. P 14×13½.

96	**27**	1½d. purple-brown	25·00	3·75	35

(Recess B.W.)

1937 (12 May). *Coronation.* W **9** of South Africa (sideways). P 13½×14.

97	**28**	½d. black and emerald	40	15	10
98		1d. black and scarlet	40	15	10
99		1½d. black and orange	40	15	10
100		2d. black and brown	40	15	10
101		3d. black and blue	50	15	10
102		4d. black and purple	50	20	10
		a. Re-entry	16·00	16·00	
103		6d. black and yellow	50	3·00	20
104		1s. black and grey-black	55	3·25	25
97/104 *Set of 8*			3·25	6·50	65

On. No. 102a the frame and leaves at lower left are doubled. The stamp is inscribed in Afrikaans.

1938 (14 Dec). *Voortrekker Centenary Memorial. Nos. 76/9 of South Africa optd as T* **11**.

105	½d. +½d.blue and green	9·50	22·00	1·75
106	1d. +1d.blue and carmine	24·00	17·00	1·00
107	1½d. +1½d. chocolate and blue-green	24·00	28·00	2·75
108	3d. +3d.bright blue	48·00	75·00	7·50
105/8 *Set of 4*		95·00	£130	11·50

1938 (14 Dec). *Voortrekker Commemoration. Nos. 80/1 of South Africa optd as T* **11**.

109	1d. blue and carmine	10·00	19·00	1·50
	a. Three bolts in wheel rim	55·00		
110	1½d. greenish blue and brown	15·00	24·00	2·00

1939 (17 July). *250th Anniv of Landing of Huguenots in South Africa and Huguenot Commemoration Fund. Nos. 82/4 of South Africa optd as T* **11**.

111	½d. +½d. brown and green	14·00	14·00	1·10
112	1d. +1d. green and carmine	19·00	14·00	1·25
113	1½d. +1½d. blue-green and purple	29·00	14·00	1·25
111/13 *Set of 3*		55·00	38·00	3·25

SWA	SWA	SWA	S W A
(29)	**(30)**	**(31)**	**(32)**

1941 (1 Oct)–**43**. *War Effort. Nos. 88/96 of South Africa optd with T* **29** *or* **30** *(3d. and 1s.).*

(a) Inscr alternately.

114	½d. green (1.12.41)	75	4·25	25
	a. Blue-green (1942)	65	2·50	15
115	1d. carmine (1.11.41)	55	3·25	15
	a. "Stain" on uniform	11·00		
116	1½d. myrtle-green (21.1.42)	55	3·50	15
117	3d. blue	22·00	23·00	1·00
	a. Cigarette flaw	75·00		
118	4d. orange-brown	6·50	16·00	1·00
	a. Red-brown	18·00	25·00	3·00
119	6d. red-orange	6·00	7·00	50
120	1s.3d. olive-brown (15.1.43)	13·00	21·00	1·25

(b) Inscr bilingually.

		Un single	*Us single*
121	2d. violet	50	1·50
122	1s. brown (17.11.41)	1·40	1·75
114/22 *Set of 7 pairs and 2 singles*		45·00	70·00

1943–44. *War Effort (reduced sizes). Nos. 97/104 of South Africa, optd with T* **29** *(1½d. and 1s., No. 130), or T* **31** *(others).*

(a) Inscr alternately.

		Un unit	*Us single*	*Us single*
123	½d. blue-green (T)	50	5·00	20
	a. Green	4·75	7·00	25
	b. Greenish blue	4·00	6·00	20
124	1d. carmine-red (T)	3·00	5·00	15
	a. Bright carmine	3·00	5·00	15
125	1½d. red-brown (P)	50	1·25	10
126	2d. violet (P)	7·50	5·00	10
	a. Reddish violet	10·00	5·00	10
	b. Apostrophe flaw	38·00		
127	3d. blue (T)	3·25	17·00	45
128	6d. red-orange (P)	6·00	2·75	30
	a. Opt inverted	£500		
	(b) Inscr bilingually.			
129	4d. slate-green (T)	2·00	20·00	55
	a. Opt inverted	£700	£425	55·00
130	1s. brown (opt T **29**) (P)	11·00	25·00	2·00
	a. Opt inverted	£500	£325	
	b. Opt T **31**(1944)	4·00	5·50	30
	c. Opt T **31** inverted	£450	£300	40·00
	d. "Bursting shell"	32·00		
	e. Smoking "L"	32·00		
123/30b *Set of 8*		23·00	55·00	1·75

The "units" referred to above consist of pairs (P) or triplets (T).

No. 128 exists with another type of opt as Type **31**, but with broader "s", narrower "w" and more space between the letters.

1945. *Victory. Nos. 108/10 of South Africa optd with T* **30**.

131	1d. brown and carmine	25	75	10
	a. Opt inverted	£300	£325	
132	2d. slate-blue and violet	30	75	10
133	3d. deep blue and blue	1·50	1·75	10
131/3 *Set of 3*		1·75	3·00	20

1947 (17 Feb). *Royal Visit. Nos. 111/13 of South Africa optd as T* **31**, *but 8½×2 mm.*

134	1d. black and carmine	10	10	10
135	2d. violet	10	60	10
	a. "Bird" on "2"	6·50		
136	3d. blue	15	40	10
	a. "Black-eyed Princess"	8·00		
134/6 *Set of 3*		30	1·00	15

1948 (26 Apr). *Royal Silver Wedding. No. 125 of South Africa, optd as T* **31**, *but 4×2 mm.*

137	3d. blue and silver	1·00	35	10

1949 (1 Oct). *75th Anniv of U.P.U. Nos. 128/30 of South Africa optd as T* **30**, *but 13×4 mm.*

138	½d. blue-green	75	2·25	25
139	1½d. brown-red	75	1·75	15
140	3d. bright blue	1·25	1·00	25
	a. Serif on "C"	38·00		
	b. "Lake" in East Africa	40·00		
138/40 *Set of 3*		2·50	4·50	60

1949 (1 Dec). *Inauguration of Voortrekker Monument, Pretoria. Nos. 131/3 of South Africa optd with T* **32**.

		Un single	*Us single*
141	1d. magenta	10	10
142	1½d. blue-green	10	10
143	3d. blue	15	60
141/3 *Set of 3*		30	70

1952 (14 Mar). *Tercentenary of Landing of Van Riebeeck. Nos. 136/40 of South Africa optd as T* **30**, *but 8×3½ mm (1d., 4½d.) or 11×4 mm (others).*

144	½d. brown-purple and olive-grey	10	50
145	1d. deep blue-green	10	10
146	2d. deep violet	50	10
147	4½d. blue	30	2·75
148	1s. brown	75	20
144/8 *Set of 5*		1·50	3·25

33 Queen Elizabeth II and *Catophracies alexandri*

1953 (2 June). *Coronation. T* **33** *and similar horiz designs.* W **9** of South Africa. P 14.

149	1d. bright carmine	40	10
150	2d. deep bluish green	40	10
151	4d. magenta	50	30
152	6d. dull ultramarine	50	60
153	1s. deep orange-brown	65	20
149/53 *Set of 5*		2·25	1·10

Designs:—2d. *Bauhinia macrantha*, 4d. *Caralluma nebrownii*, 6d. *Gloriosa virescens*, 1s. *Rhigozum trieholotum*.

34 "Two Bucks" (rock painting)

36 "Rhinoceros Hunt" (rock painting)

38 Karakul Lamb

39 Ovambo Woman blowing Horn

(Des O. Schroeder (1d. to 4d.), M. Vandenschen (4½d. to 10s.))

1954 (15 Nov). *T* **34**, **36**, **38/9** *and similar designs.* W **9** of South Africa (sideways* on vert designs). P 14.

154	1d. brown-red	30	10
	w. Wmk horns of springbok to right	15·00	7·00
155	2d. deep brown	35	10
156	3d. dull purple	1·25	10
157	4d. blackish olive	1·50	10
158	4½d. deep blue	70	40
159	6d. myrtle-green	70	70
	w. Wmk horns of springbok to right	65·00	32·00
160	1s. deep mauve	70	50
161	1s.3d. cerise	2·00	1·00
162	1s.6d. purple	2·00	50
163	2s.6d. bistre-brown	4·50	70
164	5s. deep bright blue	6·00	2·75
165	10s. deep myrtle-green	32·00	15·00
154/65 *Set of 12*		48·00	20·00

Designs: *Vert* (*as T* **34**)—2d. "White Lady" (rock painting). (*As T* **38**)—2s.6d. Lioness; 5s. Gemsbok; 10s. African Elephant. (*As T* **39**)—1s. Ovambo woman; 1s.3d. Herero woman 1s.6d. Ovambo girl. *Horiz* (*as T* **36**)—1d. "White Elephant and Giraffe (rock painting).

*The normal sideways watermark shows the horns of the springbok pointing left, *as seen from the back of the stamp.*

1960. *As Nos. 154/7,162, but* W **102** of South Africa (sideways on vert designs). P 14.

166	1d. brown-red	55	1·75
167	2d. deep brown	70	1·75
168	3d. dull purple	1·40	4·75
169	4d. blackish olive	3·50	4·75
169*a*	6d. myrtle-green	£750	£400
170	1s.6d. purple	23·00	15·00
166/70 (ex 169a) *Set of 5*		26·00	25·00

(New Currency. 100 cents = 1 South African rand)

46 G.P.O. Windhoek

47 Finger Rock

48 Mounted Soldier Monument

49 Quivertree

50 S.W.A. House, Windhoek

50a Greater Flamingoes and Swakopmund Lighthouse

51 Fishing Industry

52 Greater Flamingo

53 German Lutheran Church, Windhoek

54 Diamond

55 Fort Namutoni

55a Hardap Dam

56 Topaz

57 Tourmaline

58 Heliodor

1961 (14 Feb)–**63**. *Unsurfaced paper.* W **102** of South Africa (sideways on vert designs). P 14.

171	**46**	½c. brown and pale blue	60	10
172	**47**	1c. sepia and reddish lilac	15	10
173	**48**	1½c. slate-violet and salmon	20	10
174	**49**	2c. deep green and yellow	75	1·40
175	**50**	2½c. red-brown and light blue	35	10
176	**50a**	3c. ultramarine and rose-red (1.10.62)	4·50	40
177	**51**	3½c. indigo and blue-green	1·00	15
178	**52**	5c. scarlet and grey-blue	7·00	10
179	**53**	7½c. sepia and pale lemon	70	15
180	**54**	10c. blue and greenish yellow	1·75	60
181	**55**	12½c. indigo and lemon	60	40
182	**55a**	15c. chocolate and light blue (16.3.63)	14·00	3·25
183	**56**	20c. brown and red-orange	4·00	30
184	**57**	50c. deep bluish green and yellow-orange	6·00	1·50
185	**58**	1r. yellow, maroon and blue	10·00	15·00
171/185 *Set of 15*			45·00	21·00

See also Nos. 186/91, 202/16, 224/6 and 240.

1962–66. *As No. 171, etc., but without watermark.*

186	**46**	½c. brown and pale blue (8.62)	50	1·75
187	**48**	1½c. slate-violet and salmon (9.62)	5·00	45
188	**49**	2c. deep green and yellow (5.62)	3·50	4·00
189	**50**	2½c. red-brown and light blue (1964)	6·00	5·50
190	**51**	3½c. indigo and blue-green (1966)	13·00	4·50
191	**52**	5c. scarlet and grey-blue (9.62)	7·00	1·50
186/91 *Set of 6*			32·00	16·00

59 "Agricultural Development"

60 Centenary Emblem and Map

61 Centenary Emblem and part of Globe

1963 (16 Mar). *Opening of Hardap Dam.* W **102** of South Africa (sideways). P 14.

192	**59**	3c. chocolate and light green	30	15

1963 (30 Aug). *Centenary of Red Cross.* P 14.

193	**60**	7½c. red, black and light blue	4·00	5·00
194	**61**	15c. red, black and orange-brown	6·00	8·00

62 Interior of Assembly Hall

63 Calvin

1964 (14 May). *Opening of Legislative Assembly Hall, Windhoek.* W **102** of South Africa. P 14.

195	**62**	3c. ultramarine and salmon	50	30

1964 (1 Oct). *400th Death Anniv of Calvin (Protestant reformer).* P 14.

196	**63**	2½c. brown-purple and gold	50	15
197		15c. deep bluish green and gold	2·25	3·75

64 Mail Runner of 1890

65 Kurt yon Francois (founder)

66 Dr. H. Vedder

(Des D. Aschenborn)

1965 (18 Oct). *75th Anniv of Windhoek. Chalk-surfaced paper.* W **127** of South Africa (sideways). P 14.

198	**64**	3c. sepia and scarlet	50	15
199	**65**	15c. red-brown and blue-green	90	1·75

1966 (4 July). *90th Birth Anniv, of Dr. H. Vedder (philosopher and writer). Chalk-surfaced paper.* W **127** of South Africa (sideways). P 14.

200	**66**	3c. blackish green and salmon	30	15
201		15c. deep sepia and light blue	70	40

Nos. 200/1 exist on Swiss-made paper with *tête-bêche* watermark from a special printing made for use in presentation albums for delegates to the U.P.U. Congress in Tokyo in 1969, as supplies of the original Harrison paper were by then exhausted (*Set of 2 price* £22 *mint*).

1966–72. *As 1961–66 but chalk-surfaced paper and* W **127** of South Africa* (sideways† on vert designs).

202	**46**	½c. brown and pale blue (1967)	1·25	10
203	**47**	1c. sepia and light reddish lilac (1967)	1·50	10
		a. Grey-brown and lilac (9.72)	3·00	10
204	**48**	1½c. slate-violet and salmon (1968)	7·00	30
205	**49**	2c. deep bluish green and yellow	4·50	10
206	**50**	2½c. deep red-brown and light turquoise-blue	2·50	30
		a. Deep red-brown and pale blue (1967)	70	10
207	**50a**	3c. ultramarine and rose-red (1970)	8·50	1·25
208	**51**	3½c. indigo and blue-green (1967)	4·00	6·00
209	**50**	4c. deep red-brown and light turquoise-blue (1.4.71)	1·50	2·50
210	**52**	5c. scarlet and grey-blue (1968)	4·00	10
211	**53**	6c. sepia and greenish yellow (31.8.71)	7·00	9·00
212		7½c. sepia and pale lemon (1967)	3·50	30
		w. Wmk top of triangle to right	3·50	30
213	**55**	9c. indigo and greenish yellow (1.7.71)	8·50	11·00
214	**54**	10c. bright blue and greenish yellow (6.70)	18·00	1·75
		a. Whiter background** (9.72)	18·00	2·50
215	**55a**	15c. chocolate and light blue (1.72)	22·00	7·00
216	**56**	20c. brown and red-orange (1968)	18·00	1·75
202/16 *Set of 15*			95·00	35·00

*The watermark in this issue is indistinct but the stamps can be distinguished from the stamps without watermark by their shades and the chalk-surfaced paper which is appreciably thicker and whiter. The 1 1½, 3 4 5, 6, 9 10 15 and 20c. are known only with the watermark *tête-bêche* but the ½ c. and 2½ c. exist with both forms, the remainder being as illustrated.

†The normal sideways watermark shows top of triangle pointing to left, *as seen from the back of the stamp.*

**No. 214a, printed from sheets, has a much whiter background around the value and behind "SOUTH WEST AFRICA" compared with No. 214, which was issued in coils only.

See also Nos. 224/6 and 240.

67 Camelthorn Tree

(Des D. Aschenborn (2½ c., 3c.), Govt Printer, Pretoria (15c.))

1967 (6 Jan). *Verwoerd Commemoration. Chalk-surfaced paper. T* **67** *and similar designs.* W **127** of South Africa (sideways on vert designs). P 14.

217	2½c. black and emerald-green	15	10
218	3c. brown and new blue	15	10
219	15c. blackish brown and reddish purple	55	45
217/19 *Set of 3*		75	60

Designs: *Vert.*—3c. Waves breaking against rock; 15c. Dr. H. F. Verwoerd.

70 President Swart

71 President and Mrs. Swart

1968 (2 Jan). *Swart Commemoration. Chalk-surfaced paper.* W **127** of South Africa (tete-beche, sideways). P 14×15.

220	**70**	3c. orange-red, black and turquoise-blue		
		G. Inscribed in German	30	15
		A. Inscribed in Afrikaans	30	15
		E. Inscribed in English	30	15
221	**71**	15c. red, blackish olive and dull green		
		G. Inscribed in German	1·00	1·25
		A. Inscribed in Afrikaans	1·00	1·25
		E. Inscribed in English	1·00	1·25
		a. Red, brownish olive and bronze-green		
		G. Inscribed in German	3·00	2·25
		A. Inscribed in Afrikaans	3·00	2·25
		E. Inscribed in English	3·00	2·25
220/1 *Set of 2 values in strips of three*			11·00	9·00
Set of 6 singles			3·50	2·75

The three languages appear, *se-tenant*, both horizontally and vertically, throughout the sheet.

1970 (14 Feb). *Water 70 Campaign. As Nos. 299/300 of South Africa, but without phosphor band and inscr "SWA".*

222 2½c. green, bright blue and chocolate.... 50 30
223 3c. Prussian blue, royal blue and buff.. 50 30

72 GPO, Windhoek

73 "Red Sand-dunes, Eastern South West Africa"

1970–71. *As Nos. 202 and 204/5 but "POSGELD INKOMSTE" omitted and larger figure of value as in T* **72**. W **127** of South Africa (tête-bêche, sideways on 1½ and 2c.).

224 **72** ½c. brown and pale blue (6.70)....... 1·50 30
225 – 1½c. slate-violet and salmon (1.6.71)............ 13·00 16·00
226 – 2c. deep bluish green and lemon (11.70)............ 5·00 40
224/6 *Set of 3*............ 18·00 16·00

1970 (24 Aug). *150th Anniv of Bible Society of South Africa. As Nos. 301/2 of South Africa, but inscr "SWA".*

228 2½c. multicoloured............ 1·50 10
229 12½c. gold, black and blue............ 5·00 6·00

No. 228 has a phosphor frame, probably added in error.

A mint example of No. 229 exists with a second, blind, impression of the die-stamped features.

1971 (31 May). *"Interstex" Stamp Exhibition, Cape Town. As No. 303A of South Africa, but without phosphor frame and inscr "SWA".*

230 5c. light greenish blue, black and pale yellow............ 3·25 1·50

1971 (31 May). *Tenth Anniv of Antarctic Treaty. As No. 304 of South Africa, but without phosphor frame, and inscr "SWA".*

231 12½c. blue-black, greenish blue and orange-red............ 18·00 15·00

1971 (31 May). *Tenth Anniv of the South African Republic. As Nos. 305/6 of South Africa, but without phosphor frame, and inscr "SWA".*

232 2c. pale flesh and brown-red............ 3·25 75
233 4c. green and black............ 3·25 75

1972 (19 Sept). *Centenary of SPCA. As No. 312 of South Africa, but inscr "SWA".*

234 5c. multicoloured............ 3·00 1·25

WATERMARK. All issues from this date are on unwatermarked paper.

(Lettering by E. de Jong)

1973 (1 May). *Scenery. T* **73** *and similar multicoloured designs showing paintings by Adolph Jentsch.* P 11½×12½ (10 and 15c.) or 12½×11½ (others).

235 2c. Type **73**............ 75 75
236 4c. "After the Rain"............ 85 1·00
237 5c. "Barren Country"............ 1·00 1·25
238 10c. "Schaap River" (*vert*)............ 1·25 1·75
239 15c. "Namib Desert" (*vert*)............ 2·25 3·25
235/9 *Set of 5*............ 5·50 7·25

1973 (28 May). *As Nos. 207 but without wmk. Phosphorised paper.*

240 **50a** 3c. ultramarine and rose-red.......... 2·50 1·50

No. 240 is also distinguishable in that the lettering of "SOUTH WEST AFRICA" is whiter.

74 *Sarcocaulon rigidum*

75 *Euphorbia virosa*

(Des D. Findlay)

1973 (1 Sept)–**79**. *Succulents. Various multicoloured designs as T* **74/5**. *Phosphorised glossy paper (original printing of all values) or ordinary paper (1, 2, 3, 4, 5, 9, 10, 15, 20, 30, 50c.).*

(a) *As T* **74**. *P 12½.*

241 1c. Type **74**............ 15 10
a. Black (face value, etc.) omitted......... £250
242 2c. *Lapidaria margaretae*............ 1·00 75
a. Perf 14×13½ (4.8.79)............ 20 10
243 3c. *Titanopsis schwantesii*............ 20 10
a. Black (face value, etc.) omitted......... 80·00
b. Perf 14×13½ (8.8.79)............ 30 15
244 4c. *Lithops karasmontana*............ 25 10
245 5c. *Caralluma lugardii*............ 40 50
a. Black (face value, etc.) omitted......... £140
b. Perf 14×13½ (12.12.79)............ 50 20
246 6c. *Dinteranthus microspermus*............ 2·50 3·00
247 7c. *Conophytum gratum*............ 1·50 2·75
248 9c. *Huernia oculata*............ 1·00 2·50
249 10c. *Gasteria pillansii*............ 1·20 55
a. Black (face value, etc.) omitted......... £275
b. Perf 14×13½ (13.8.79)............ 40 30
250 14c. *Stapelia pedunculata*............ 2·00 3·00
251 15c. *Fenestraria aurantiaca*............ 65 30
252 20c. *Decabelone grandiflora*............ 5·00 3·50
253 25c. *Hoodia bainii*............ 5·00 3·00

(b) *As T* **75**. *P 11½×12½ (30c., 1r.) or 12½×11½ (50c.).*

254 30c. Type **75**............ 75 1·00
a. Perf 13½×14 (27.12.79)............ 70 90
255 50c. *Pachypodium namaquanum* (*vert*).... 1·00 2·25
a. Perf 14×13½ (18.12.79)............ 75 1·25
256 1r. *Welwitschia bainesii*............ 1·00 5·00
241/56 *Set of 16*............ 22·00 26·00

1973 (1 Sept)–**80**. *Coil stamps. As Nos. 241/2 and 245 but photo, colours changed.* P 14.

257 1c. black and light mauve............ 70 75
a. Chalk-surfaced paper (7.76)............ 1·00 40
b. Imperf×perf 14. Chalk-surfaced paper (1980)............ 4·75 5·50
258 2c. black and yellow............ 50 50
a. Chalk-surfaced paper (7.76?)............ 1·00 50
b. Imperf×perf 14. Chalk-surfaced paper (1.79)............ 1·00 40
259 5c. black and light rose-red............ 1·75 80
a. Imperf×perf 14. Chalk-surfaced paper (8.2.78)............ 1·00 80
257/9 *Set of 3*............ 2·00 1·50

Coils of Nos. 257b, 258b and 259a come with every fifth stamp numbered on the reverse.

76 Chat-shrike

77 Giraffe, Antelope and Spoor

(Des D. Findlay)

1974 (13 Feb). *Rare Birds. T* **76** *and similar vert designs. Multicoloured.* P 12½×11½.

260 4c. Type **76**............ 2·75 1·00
261 5c. Peach-faced Lovebirds............ 3·25 1·50
262 10c. Damaraland Rock Jumper............ 6·00 5·50
263 15c. Rüppell's Parrots............ 8·00 9·50
260/3 *Set of 4*............ 18·00 16·00

(Des O. Schröder)

1974 (10 Apr). *Twyfelfontein Rock-engravings. T* **77** *and similar multicoloured designs.* P 11½×12½ (15c.) or 12½ (others).

264 4c. Type **77**............ 1·00 50
265 5c. Elephant, hyena, antelope and spoor............ 1·00 80
a. Black (value and "SWA") omitted...... £1200
266 15c. Kudu cow (38×21 mm)............ 4·00 6·50
264/6 *Set of 3*............ 5·50 7·00

78 Cut Diamond

79 Wagons and Map of the Trek

(Des M. Barnett)

1974 (30 Sept). *Diamond Mining. T* **78** *and similar vert design. Multicoloured.* P 12½×11½.

267 10c. Type **78**............ 2·75 4·25
268 15c. Diagram of shore workings............ 2·75 4·25

(Des K. Esterhuysen)

1974 (13 Nov). *Centenary of Thirstland Trek.* P 11½×12½.

269 **79** 4c. multicoloured............ 75 1·00

80 Peregrine Falcon

81 Kolmannskop (ghost town)

(Des D. Findlay)

1975 (19 Mar). *Protected Birds of Prey. T* **80** *and similar vert designs. Multicoloured.* P 12½×11½.

270 4c. Type **80**............ 1·50 1·25
271 5c. Verreaux's Eagle............ 1·50 1·75
272 10c. Martial Eagle............ 3·75 4·75
273 15c. Egyptian Vulture............ 4·50 7·00
270/3 *Set of 4*............ 10·00 13·50

(Des A. H. Barrett)

1975 (23 July). *Historic Monuments. T* **81** *and similar horiz designs. Multicoloured.* P 11½×12½.

274 5c. Type **81**............ 15 15
275 9c. "Martin Luther" (steam tractor)......... 30 60
276 15c. Kurt von François and Old Fort, Windhoek............ 50 75
274/6 *Set of 3*............ 85 1·30

82 "View of Lüderitz"

(Des J. Hoekstra)

1975 (15 Oct). *Otto Schröder. T* **82** *and similar horiz designs showing his paintings. Multicoloured.* P 11½×12½.

277 15c. Type **82**............ 30 60
a. Block of 4. Nos. 277/80............ 1·10
278 15c. "View of Swakopmund"............ 30 60
279 15c. "Harbour Scene"............ 30 60
280 15c. "Quayside, Walvis Bay"............ 30 60
277/80 *Set of 4*............ 1·10 2·20
MS281 122×96 mm. Nos. 277/80............ 1·00 3·50

Nos. 277/80 were printed together, in *se-tenant* blocks of four within the sheet.

83 Elephants

(Des H. Pager)

1976 (31 Mar). *Prehistoric Rock Paintings. T* **83** *and similar horiz designs. Multicoloured.* P 11½×12½.

282 4c. Type **83**............ 30 15
283 10c. Rhinoceros............ 30 60
284 15c. Antelope............ 35 70
285 20c. Man with bow and arrow............ 40 1·00
282/5 *Set of 4*............ 1·25 2·20
MS286 121×95 mm. Nos. 282/5............ 1·25 3·50

84 Schwerinsburg

(Des H. Pager)

1976 (14 May). *Castles. T* **84** *and similar horiz designs. Multicoloured.* P 11½×12½.

287 10c. Type **84**............ 20 30
288 15c. Schloss Duwisib............ 30 50
289 20c. Heynitzburg............ 30 70
287/9 *Set of 3*............ 70 1·25

85 Large-toothed Rock Hyrax

(Des D. Findlay)

1976 (16 July). *Fauna Conservation. T* **85** *and similar horiz designs. Multicoloured.* P 11½×12½.

290 4c. Type **85**............ 30 20
291 10c. Kirk's Dik-Dik............ 50 75
292 15c. Kuhl's Tree Squirrel............ 75 1·60
290/2 *Set of 3*............ 1·40 2·25

86 The Augustineum, Windhoek

(Des H. Pager)

1976 (17 Sept). *Modern Buildings. T* **86** *and similar horiz design.* P 11½×12½.

293 15c. black and yellow............ 30 60
294 20c. black and light yellow............ 40 80

Design:—20c. Katutura Hospital, Windhoek.

87 Ovambo Water Canal System

(Des A. H. Barrett)

1976 (19 Nov). *Water and Electricity Supply. T* **87** *and similar horiz design. Multicoloured.* P 11½×12½.

295 15c. Type **87**............ 30 50
296 20c. Ruacana Falls Power Station............ 40 75

88 Coastline near Pomona

(Des A. H. Barrett)

1977 (29 Mar). *Namib Desert. T* **88** *and similar horiz designs. Multicoloured.* P 12½.

297 4c. Type **88**............ 15 15
298 10c. Bush and dunes, Sossusvlei............ 20 20
299 15c. Plain near Brandberg............ 35 35
300 20c. Dunes, Sperr Gebiet............ 40 40
297/300 *Set of 4*............ 1·00 1·00

89 Kraal

(Des A. H. Barrett)

1977 (15 July). *The Ovambo People. T* **89** *and similar horiz designs.* P 11½×12½.

301	4c. multicoloured	10	10
302	10c. black, dull orange and cinnamon	20	15
303	15c. multicoloured	25	20
304	20c. multicoloured	25	35
301/4	*Set of 4*	70	70

Designs—10c. Grain baskets; 15c. Pounding grain; 20c. Women in tribal dress.

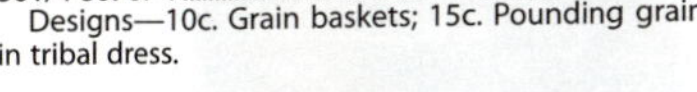

90 Terminal Buildings

(Des H. Pager and A. H. Barrett)

1977 (22 Aug). *J. G. Strijdom Airport, Windhoek.* P 12½.

305	**90**	20c. multicoloured	40	30

91 Drostdy, Lüderitz **92** Side-winding Adder

(Des A. H. Barrett)

1977 (4 Nov). *Historic Houses. T* **91** *and similar horiz designs. Multicoloured.* P 12×12½.

306	5c. Type **91**	15	10
307	10c. Woermannhaus, Swakopmund	25	30
308	15c. Neu-Heusis, Windhoek	30	35
309	20c. Schmelenhaus, Bethanie	40	40
306/9	*Set of 4*	1·00	1·00
MS310	122×96 mm. Nos. 306/9	1·00	2·00

(Des D. Findlay)

1978 (6 Feb). *Small Animals. T* **92** *and similar horiz designs Multicoloured.* P 12½.

311	4c. Type **92**	15	10
312	10c. Grant's Desert Golden Mole	25	20
313	15c. Palmato Gecko	25	25
314	20c. Namaqua Chameleon	25	25
311/14	*Set of 4*	80	70

93 Ostrich Hunting

(Des A. H. Barrett)

1978 (14 Apr). *The Bushmen. T* **93** *and similar horiz designs in light grey-brown, stone and black.* P 12×12½.

315	4c. Type **93**	30	10
316	10c. Woman carrying ostrich eggs	30	20
317	15c. Hunters kindling fire	40	20
318	20c. Woman with musical instrument	40	30
315/18	*Set of 4*	1·25	70

94 Lutheran Church, Windhoek

ALGEMENE STEMREG
(95)

(Des A. H. Barrett)

1978 (16 June). *Historic Churches. T* **94** *and similar horiz designs.* P 12½.

319	4c. grey-black and cinnamon	10	10
320	10c. grey-black and ochre	15	20
321	15c. grey-black and light brown-rose	20	25
322	20c. grey-black and light grey-blue	30	35
319/22	*Set of 4*	65	80
MS323	125×90 mm. Nos. 319/22	75	1·75

Designs:—10c. Lutheran Church, Swakopmund; 15c. Rhenish Mission Church, Otjimbingwe; 20c. Rhenish Missionary Church, Keetmanshoop.

1978 (1 Nov). *Universal Suffrage. Designs as Nos. 244/5, 249 and 251/3 optd with T* **95** *(or similar inscr in English or German).*

324	4c. *Lithops karasmontana*		
	A. Opt in Afrikaans	10	10
	E. Opt in English	10	10
	G. Opt in German	10	10
325	5c. *Caralluma lugardii*		
	A. Opt in Afrikaans	10	10
	E. Opt in English	10	10
	G. Opt in German	10	10
326	10c. *Gasteria pillansii*		
	A. Opt in Afrikaans	10	10
	E. Opt in English	10	10
	G. Opt in German	10	15
327	15c. *Fenestraria aurantiaca*		
	A. Opt in Afrikaans	10	15
	E. Opt in English	10	15
	G. Opt in German	10	15
328	20c. *Decabelone grandiflora*		
	A. Opt in Afrikaans	10	15
	E. Opt in English	10	15
	G. Opt in German	10	15
329	25c. *Hoodia bainii*		
	A. Opt in Afrikaans	15	15
	E. Opt in English	15	15
	G. Opt in German	15	15
324/9	*Set of 18 (6 strips of 3)*	1·25	1·50

Nos. 324A/G, 325A/G, 326A/G, 327A/G, 328A/G and 329A/G were each printed together, *se-tenant*, in horizontal and vertical strips of 3 throughout the sheets.

96 Greater Flamingo **97** Silver Topaz

(Des D. Findlay)

1979 (5 Apr). *Water Birds. T* **96** *and similar vert designs. Multicoloured.* P 14.

330	4c. Type **96**	20	10
331	15c. White-breasted Cormorant	35	25
332	20c. Chestnut-banded Sand Plover	35	35
333	25c. Eastern White Pelican	35	40
330/3	*Set of 4*	1·10	1·00

(Des H. Botha)

1979 (26 Nov). *Gemstones. T* **97** *and similar horiz designs. Multicoloured.* P 14.

334	4c. Type **97**	30	10
335	15c. Aquamarine	65	25
336	20c. Malachite	70	35
337	25c. Amethyst	70	40
334/7	*Set of 4*	2·10	1·00

98 Killer Whale **99** Impala

(Des A. H. Barrett)

1980 (25 Mar). *Whales. T* **98** *and similar multicoloured designs.* P 14.

338	4c. Type **98**	25	20
339	5c. Humpback Whale (38×22 mm)	25	20
340	10c. Black Right Whale (38×22 mm)	35	30
341	15c. Sperm Whale (58×22 mm)	45	75
342	20c. Fin Whale (58×22 mm)	55	90
343	25c. Blue Whale (88×22 mm)	65	1·25
338/43	*Set of 6*	2·25	3·25
MS344	202×95 mm. Nos. 338/43	2·75	5·00

(Des P. Bosman)

1980 (25 June). *25th Anniv of Division of Nature Conservation and Tourism. Antelopes. T* **99** *and similar horiz designs. Multicoloured.* P 14.

345	5c. Type **99**	15	10
346	10c. Topi	15	10
347	15c. Roan Antelope	25	15
348	20c. Sable Antelope	25	20
345/8	*Set of 4*	70	50

100 Black-backed Jackal **101** Meerkat

(Des Sheila Nowers (11, 12, 14, 16c.), P. Bosman (others))

1980 (1 Oct)–**89**. *Wildlife. Multicoloured designs as T* **100**. *Ordinary paper.* P 14.

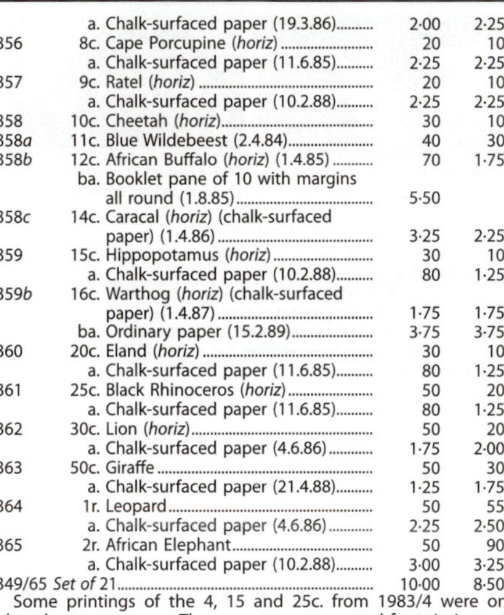

349	1c. Type **100**	15	10
	a. Chalk-surfaced paper (11.6.85)	1·00	1·00
350	2c. Hunting Dog	15	10
	a. Chalk-surfaced paper (4.6.86)	1·25	1·25
351	3c. Brown Hyena	15	10
	a. Chalk-surfaced paper (10.2.88)	80	1·00
352	4c. Springbok	15	10
	a. Chalk-surfaced paper (29.7.87)	80	1·00
353	5c. Gemsbok	15	10
	a. Chalk-surfaced paper (11.6.85)	1·75	1·75
354	6c. Greater Kudu	15	10
	a. Chalk-surfaced paper (8.8.88)	2·50	2·50
355	7c. Mountain Zebra (*horiz*)	40	20
	a. Chalk-surfaced paper (19.3.86)	2·00	2·25
356	8c. Cape Porcupine (*horiz*)	20	10
	a. Chalk-surfaced paper (11.6.85)	2·25	2·25
357	9c. Ratel (*horiz*)	20	10
	a. Chalk-surfaced paper (10.2.88)	2·25	2·25
358	10c. Cheetah (*horiz*)	30	10
358*a*	11c. Blue Wildebeest (2.4.84)	40	30
358*b*	12c. African Buffalo (*horiz*) (1.4.85)	70	1·75
	ba. Booklet pane of 10 with margins all round (1.8.85)	5·50	
358*c*	14c. Caracal (*horiz*) (chalk-surfaced paper) (1.4.86)	3·25	2·25
359	15c. Hippopotamus (*horiz*)	30	10
	a. Chalk-surfaced paper (10.2.88)	80	1·25
359*b*	16c. Warthog (*horiz*) (chalk-surfaced paper) (1.4.87)	1·75	1·75
	ba. Ordinary paper (15.2.89)	3·75	3·75
360	20c. Eland (*horiz*)	30	10
	a. Chalk-surfaced paper (11.6.85)	80	1·25
361	25c. Black Rhinoceros (*horiz*)	50	20
	a. Chalk-surfaced paper (11.6.85)	80	1·25
362	30c. Lion (*horiz*)	50	20
	a. Chalk-surfaced paper (4.6.86)	1·75	2·00
363	50c. Giraffe	50	30
	a. Chalk-surfaced paper (21.4.88)	1·25	1·75
364	1r. Leopard	50	55
	a. Chalk-surfaced paper (4.6.86)	2·25	2·50
365	2r. African Elephant	50	90
	a. Chalk-surfaced paper (10.2.88)	3·00	3·25
349/65	*Set of 21*	10·00	8·50

Some printings of the 4, 15 and 25c. from 1983/4 were on phosphorescent paper. The same paper was used for printings of the 1, 2, 3, 8, 9, 10, 16c. (No. 359ba), 20, 30c. and 1r. during 1989. For $1.20 design as No. 359b see No. **MS**675 and for $1.30 as No. 358c see No. **MS**685.

(Des P. Bosman. Photo)

1980 (1 Oct). *Coil stamps. Wildlife. Vert designs as T* **101**. Imperf×perf 14.

366	1c. yellow-brown	20	20
367	2c. deep dull blue	20	20
368	5c. yellow-olive	30	30
366/8	*Set of 3*	65	65

Designs:—2c. Savanna Monkey; 5c. Chacma Baboon.

102 Von Bach

(Des A. H. Barrett)

1980 (25 Nov). *Water Conservation. Dams. T* **102** *and similar horiz designs. Multicoloured.* P 14.

369	5c. Type **102**	10	10
370	10c. Swakoppoort	15	10
371	15c. Naute	15	20
372	20c. Hardap	15	25
369/72	*Set of 4*	50	60

103 View of Fish River Canyon **104** *Aloe erinacea*

(Des A. H. Barrett)

1981 (20 Mar). *Fish River Canyon. T* **103** *and similar horiz designs showing various views of canyon.* P 14.

373	5c. multicoloured	10	10
374	15c. multicoloured	15	20
375	20c. multicoloured	20	25
376	25c. multicoloured	20	30
373/6	*Set of 4*	60	75

(Des D. Findlay)

1981 (14 Aug). *Aloes. T* **104** *and similar vert designs. Multicoloured.* P 14×13½.

377	5c. Type **104**	15	10
378	15c. *Aloe viridiflora*	25	25
379	20c. *Aloe pearsonii*	35	25
380	25c. *Aloe littoralis*	35	30
377/80	*Set of 4*	1·00	80

105 Paul Weiss-Haus

(Des A. H. Barrett)

1981 (16 Oct). *Historic Buildings of Lüderitz. T* **105** *and similar horiz designs. Multicoloured.* P 14.

381	5c. Type **105**	10	10
382	15c. Deutsche Afrika Bank	15	20
383	20c. Schroederhaus	20	30
384	25c. Altes Postamt	20	35
381/4	*Set of 4*	60	85
MS385	125×90 mm. Nos. 381/4	65	1·00

106 Salt Pan

107 Kalahari Starred Tortoise (Psammobates oculifer)

(Des A. H. Barrett)

1981 (4 Dec). *Salt Industry. T* **106** *and similar horiz designs Multicoloured.* P 14.

386 5c. Type **106** 10 10
387 15c. Dumping and washing 20 20
388 20c. Loading by conveyor 25 30
389 25c. Dispatch to refinery 30 35
386/9 *Set of* 4 75 85

(Des A. H. Barrett)

1982 (12 Mar). *Tortoises. T* **107** *and similar horiz designs. Multicoloured.* P 14.

390 5c. Type **107** 15 10
391 15c. Leopard Tortoise (*Geochelone pardalis*) 25 25
392 20c. Angulate Tortoise (*Chersina angulata*) 30 35
393 25c. Speckled Padloper (*Homopus signatus*) 40 45
390/3 *Set of* 4 1·00 1·00

108 Mythical Sea-monster

(Des Sheila Nowers)

1982 (28 May). *Discoverers of South West Africa. (1st series). Bartolomeu Dias. T* **108** *and similar horiz designs. Multicoloured.* P 14.

394 15c. Type **108** 20 20
395 20c. Bartolomeu Dias and map of Africa showing voyage 40 30
396 25c. Dias' caravel 65 40
397 30c. Dias erecting commemorative cross, Angra das Voltas, 25 July 1488 70 45
394/7 *Set of* 4 1·75 1·25

See also Nos. 455/8.

109 Brandberg

110 Otjikaeva Head-dress of Herero Woman

(Des A. H. Barrett)

1982 (3 Aug). *Mountains of South West Africa. T* **109** *and similar horiz designs. Multicoloured.* P 13½×14.

398 6c. Type **109** 10 10
399 15c. Omatako 20 20
400 20c. Die Nadel 25 30
401 25c. Spitzkuppe 30 35
398/401 *Set of* 4 75 85

(Des A. H. Barrett)

1982 (15 Oct). *Traditional Head-dresses of South West Africa (1st series). T* **110** *and similar vert designs. Multicoloured.* P 14.

402 6c. Type **110** 10 10
403 15c. Ekori head-dress of Himba 20 35
404 20c. Oshikoma hair-piece and iipando plaits of Ngandjera 25 45
405 25c. Omhatela head-dress of Kwanyama 25 60
402/5 *Set of* 4 70 1·25

See also Nos. 427/30.

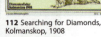

111 Fort Vogelsang

112 Searching for Diamonds, Kolmanskop, 1908

(Des J. van Ellinckhuijzen)

1983 (16 Mar). *Centenary of Lüderitz. T* **111** *and similar designs.* P 14.

406 6c. brownish black and deep carmine-red 10 10
407 20c. brownish black and yellow-brown 15 20
408 25c. brownish black and chestnut 20 25
409 30c. brownish black and brown-purple 20 30
410 40c. brownish black and bright green 25 50
406/10 *Set of* 5 80 1·25

Designs: Vert (23×29 mm)—20c. Chief Joseph Fredericks; 30c. Heinrich Vogelsang (founder); 40c. Adolf Lüderitz (colonial promoter). Horiz (As T **111**)—25c. Angra Pequena.

(Des J. van Ellinckhuijzen)

1983 (8 June). *75th Anniv of Discovery of Diamonds. T* **112** *and similar designs.* P 13½×14 (10, 20c.) or 14×13½ (others).

411 10c. deep brown and pale stone 15 15
412 20c. maroon and pale stone 30 40
413 25c. Prussian blue and pale stone 35 45
414 40c. brownish black and pale stone 55 85
411/14 *Set of* 4 1·25 1·75

Designs: Horiz (34×19 mm)—20c. Digging for diamonds, Kolmanskop, 1908. Vert (19×26 mm)—25c. Sir Ernest Oppenheimer (industrialist); 40c. August Stauch (prospector).

113 "Common Zebras drinking"

114 The Rock Lobster

(Des J. van Ellinckhuijzen)

1983 (1 Sept). *Painters of South West Africa. T* **113** *and similar horiz designs. Multicoloured.* P 13½×14.

415 10c. Type **113** 15 15
416 20c. "Rossing Mountain" (H. Henckert) 20 30
417 25c. "Stampeding African Buffalo" (F. Krampe) 20 35
418 40c. "Erongo Mountains" (J. Blatt) 30 55
415/18 *Set of* 4 75 1·25

(Des J. van Ellinckhuijzen)

1983 (23 Nov). *Lobster Industry. T* **114** *and similar horiz designs Multicoloured.* P 13½×14.

419 10c. Type **114** 15 15
420 20c. Mother ship and fishing dinghies 20 30
421 25c. Netting lobsters from dinghy 20 35
422 40c. Packing lobsters 30 55
419/22 *Set of* 4 75 1·25

115 Hohenzollern House

(Des A. H. Barrett)

1984 (8 Mar). *Historic Buildings of Swakopmund. T* **115** *and similar horiz designs.* P 14.

423 10c. grey-black and orange-brown 15 15
424 20c. grey-black and new blue 20 25
425 25c. grey-black and yellow-green 20 30
426 30c. grey-black and ochre 25 30
423/6 *Set of* 4 70 90

Designs:—20c. Railway Station; 25c. Imperial District Bureau; 30c. Ritterburg.

(Des A. H. Barrett)

1984 (25 May). *Traditional Head-dresses of South West Africa (2nd series). Multicoloured designs as T* **110**. P 14.

427 11c. Eendjushi head-dress of Kwambi 15 15
428 20c. Bushman woman 20 25
429 25c. Omulenda head-dress of Kwaluudhi 20 35
430 30c. Mbukushu women 20 35
427/30 *Set of* 4 70 1·00

116 Map and German Flag

117 Sweet Thorn

(Des J. van Ellinckhuijzen)

1984 (7 Aug). *Centenary of German Colonisation. T* **116** *and similar horiz designs. Multicoloured.* P 14×14½.

431 11c. Type **116** 35 15
432 25c. Raising the German flag, 1884 65 50
433 30c. German Protectorate boundary marker 65 60
434 45c. Elizabeth and Leipzig (German corvettes) 1·40 1·75
431/4 *Set of* 4 2·75 2·75

(Des Eva-Maria Linsmayer)

1984 (22 Nov). *Spring in South West Africa. T* **117** *and similar vert designs. Multicoloured.* P 14.

435 11c. Type **117** 15 15
436 25c. Camel Thorn 20 35
437 30c. Hook Thorn 20 35
438 45c. Candle-pod Acacia 25 50
435/8 *Set of* 4 70 1·25

118 Head of Ostrich

(Des J. van Ellinckhuijzen)

1985 (15 Mar). *Ostriches. T* **118** *and similar horiz designs. Multicoloured.* P 14.

439 11c. Type **118** 40 10
440 25c. Ostrich on eggs 60 30
441 30c. Newly-hatched chick and eggs 70 50
442 50c. Mating dance 90 75
439/42 *Set of* 4 2·40 1·50

119 Kaiserstrasse

(Des A. H. Barrett)

1985 (6 June). *Historic Buildings of Windhoek. T* **119** *and similar horiz designs.* P 14.

443 12c. black and brown-ochre 15 10
444 25c. black and grey-olive 20 25
445 30c. black and brown 20 30
446 50c. black and yellow-brown 25 70
443/6 *Set of* 4 70 1·25

Designs:—25c. Turnhalle; 30c. Old Supreme Court Building; 50c. Railway Station.

120 Zwilling Locomotive

121 Lidumu-dumu instrument) (keyboard)

(Des J. van Ellinckhuijzen)

1985 (2 Aug). *Narrow-gauge Railway Locomotives. T* **120** *and similar horiz designs. Multicoloured.* P 14.

447 12c. Type **120** 25 10
448 25c. Feldspur side-tank locomotive 45 25
449 30c. Jung and Henschel side-tank locomotive 40 35
450 50c. Henschel Hd locomotive 60 60
447/50 *Set of* 4 1·50 1·20

(Des J. van Ellinckhuijzen)

1985 (17 Oct). *Traditional Musical Instruments. T* **121** *and similar horiz designs. Multicoloured.* P 14.

451 12c. Type **121** 10 10
452 25c. Ngoma (drum) 15 20
453 30c. Okambulumbumbwa (stringed instrument) 20 25
454 50c. Gwashi (stringed instrument) 25 35
451/4 *Set of* 4 60 80

122 Erecting Commemorative Pillar at Cape Cross, 1486

123 Ameib, Erongo Mountains

(Des J. van Ellinckhuijzen)

1986 (24 Jan). *Discoverers of South West Africa (2nd series). Diogo Coa. T* **122** *and similar horiz designs.* P 14.

455 12c. black, brownish grey and deep dull green 35 10
456 20c. black, brownish grey and pale red-brown 55 25
457 25c. black, brownish grey and dull blue 75 35
458 30c. black, brownish grey and dull reddish purple 80 60
455/8 *Set of* 4 2·25 1·10

Designs:—20c. Diogo Cao's coat of arms; 25c. Caravel; 30c. Diogo Cao.

(Des J. van Niekerk)

1986 (24 Apr). *Rock Formations. T* **123** *and similar horiz designs Multicoloured.* P 14.

459 14c. Type **123** 35 15
460 20c. Vingerklip, near Outjo 40 25
461 25c. Petrified sand dunes, Kuiseb River 45 40
462 30c. Orgelpfeifen, Twyfelfontein 50 55
459/62 *Set of* 4 1·50 1·25

PHILATELIC FOUNDATION MINIATURE SHEETS. These miniature sheets were issued by the Philatelic Foundation of Southern Africa and not the postal administration. They could be purchased by post or from a limited number of philatelic offices, mainly in South Africa, at a premium in aid of various national and international stamp exhibitions.

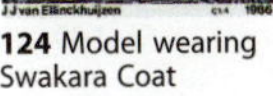

124 Model wearing Swakara Coat   **125** Pirogue, Lake Liambezi

(Des J. van Ellinckhuijzen)

1986 (10 July). *Karakul Industry. T* **124** *and similar vert designs. Multicoloured.* P 14.

463		14c. Type **124**	15	15
464		20c. Weaving karakul wool carpet	25	30
465		25c. Flock of karakul ewes on Veld	25	45
466		30c. Karakul rams	30	60
463/6 *Set of 4*			85	1·40

The 30c. value exists as a Philatelic Foundation miniature sheet.

1986 (6 Nov). *Life in the Caprivi Strip. T* **125** *and similar horiz designs. Multicoloured.* P 14.

467		14c. Type **125**	30	15
468		20c. Ploughing with oxen	50	80
469		25c. Settlement in Eastern Caprivi	60	1·25
470		30c. Map of Caprivi Strip	1·00	2·00
467/70 *Set of 4*			2·25	3·75

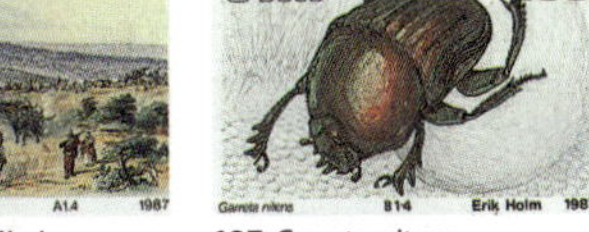

126 "Gobabis Mission Station", 1863   **127** *Garreta nitens* (beetle)

1987 (19 Feb). *Paintings by Thomas Baines. T* **126** *and similar horiz designs. Multicoloured.* P 14.

471		14c. Type **126**	30	15
472		20c. "Outspan at Koobie", 1861	55	80
473		25c. "Outspan under Oomahaama Tree", 1862	70	1·50
474		30c. "Swakop River", 1861	80	2·25
471/4 *Set of 4*			2·10	4·25

The 25c. value exists as a Philatelic Foundation miniature sheet.

(Des E. Holm)

1987 (7 May). *Useful Insects. T* **127** *and similar horiz designs Multicoloured.* P 14.

475		16c. Type **127**	40	15
476		20c. *Alcimus stenurus* (fly)	60	80
477		25c. *Anthophora caerulea* (bee)	75	1·50
478		30c. *Hemiempusa capensis* (mantid)	1·10	2·00
475/8 *Set of 4*			2·50	4·00

128 Okaukuejo

(Des J. van Niekerk)

1987 (23 July). *Tourist Camps. T* **128** *and similar horiz designs Multicoloured.* P 14½×14.

479		16c. Type **128**	25	15
480		20c. Daan Viljoen	40	55
481		25c. Ai-Ais	45	1·25
482		30c. Hardap	50	1·40
479/82 *Set of 4*			1·40	3·00

129 Wreck of Hope (Dutch whaling schooner), 1804   **130** Bartolomeu Dias

(Des Sheila Nowers)

1987 (15 Oct). *Shipwrecks. T* **129** *and similar horiz designs Multicoloured.* P 14.

483		16c. Type **129**	50	15
484		30c. Tilly (brig), 1885	75	80
485		40c. Eduard Bohlen (steamer), 1909	1·00	2·00
486		50c. Dunedin Star (liner), 1942	1·25	2·50
483/6 *Set of 4*			3·25	5·00

(Des Sheila Nowers)

1988 (7 Jan). *500th Anniv of Discovery of Cape of Good Hope by Bartolomeu Dias. T* **130** *and similar vert designs. Multicoloured.* P 14.

487		16c. Type **130**	35	15
488		30c. Caravel	70	55
489		40c. Map of South West Africa, c. 1502	80	70
490		50c. King João II of Portugal	80	75
487/90 *Set of 4*			2·40	1·90

131 *Sossusvlei*

(Des J. van Niekerk)

1988 (3 Mar). *Landmarks of South West Africa. T* **131** *and similar horiz designs. Multicoloured.* P 14.

491		16c. Type **131**	30	15
492		30c. Sesriem Canyon	60	65
493		40c. Hoaruseb "clay castles"	70	1·25
494		50c. Hoba meteorite	80	1·50
491/4 *Set of 4*			2·25	3·25

132 First Postal Agency, Otyimbingue, 1888   **133** Herero Chat

(Des H. Pulon)

1988 (7 July). *Centenary of Postal Service in South West Africa. T* **132** *and similar horiz designs. Multicoloured.* P 14.

495		16c. Type **132**	30	15
496		30c. Post Office, Windhoek, 1904	60	55
497		40c. Mail-runner and map	70	75
498		50c. Camel mail, 1904	80	1·00
495/8 *Set of 4*			2·25	2·25

The 50c. value exists as a Philatelic Foundation miniature sheet.

(Des G. Arnott)

1988 (3 Nov). *Birds of South West Africa. T* **133** *and similar vert designs. Multicoloured.* P 14.

499		16c. Type **133**	80	25
500		30c. Gray's Lark	1·25	80
501		40c. Rüppell's Bustard	1·40	1·25
502		50c. Monteiro's Hornbill	1·40	1·40
499/502 *Set of 4*			4·25	3·25

134 Dr. C. H. Hahn and Gross-Barmen Mission   **135** Beech Commuter 1900

(Des H. Pulon)

1989 (16 Feb). *Missionaries. T* **134** *and similar horiz designs Multicoloured.* P 14.

503		16c. Type **134**	20	10
504		30c. Revd. J. G. Krönlein and Berseba Mission	35	60
505		40c. Revd. F. H. Kleinschmidt and Rehoboth Mission	40	70
506		50c. Revd. J. H. Schmelen and Bethanien Mission	40	85
503/6 *Set of 4*			1·25	2·00

(Des M. Botha)

1989 (18 May). *75th Anniv of Aviation in South West Africa. T* **135** *and similar horiz designs. Multicoloured.* P 14.

507		18c. Type **135**	55	20
508		30c. Ryan Navion	90	60
509		40c. Junkers F-13	1·00	65
510		50c. Pfalz Otto biplane	1·25	85
507/10 *Set of 4*			3·25	2·10

The 50c. value exists as a Philatelic Foundation miniature sheet.

136 Barchan Dunes

(Des A. H. Barrett)

1989 (14 Aug). *Namib Desert Sand Dunes. T* **136** *and similar horiz designs. Multicoloured.* P 14.

511		18c. Barchan dunes	20	15
512		30c. Star dunes (36×20 mm)	30	40
513		40c. Transverse dunes	35	60
514		50c. Crescentic dunes (36×20 mm)	40	80
511/14 *Set of 4*			1·10	1·75

137 Ballot Box and Outline Map of South West Africa

1989 (24 Aug). *South West Africa Constitutional Election.* P 14.

515	**137**	18c. purple-brown and salmon	15	15
516		35c. deep grey-blue and pale emerald	25	40
517		45c. plum and lemon	35	60
518		60c. dull green and deep yellow-ochre	45	80
515/18 *Set of 4*			1·10	1·75

138 Gypsum   **139** Oranjemund Alluvial Diamond Field

(Des J. van Niekerk)

1989 (16 Nov)–**90**. *Minerals. T* **138/9** *and similar multicoloured designs. Phosphorised paper (25c.) or chalk-surfaced paper (30, 35, 50c., 1r.).* P 14.

519		1c. Type **138**	15	30
520		2c. Fluorite	20	30
521		5c. Mimetite	30	30
522		7c. Cuprite	45	45
523		10c. Azurite	50	20
524		18c. Boltwoodite (inscr "K" (H30) (U02) (Si04)")	70	10
		a. Formula corrected to "K2 (U02) 2 (Si03) 2 (OH) 2 5 H20" (25.10.90)	11·00	2·00
525		20c. Dioptase	75	15
526		25c. Type **139**	1·25	15
527		30c. Tsumeb lead and copper complex	1·00	20
528		35c. Rosh Pinah zinc mine	1·00	20
529		40c. Diamonds	1·25	30
530		45c. Wulfenite	1·00	30
531		50c. Uis tin mine	1·25	40
532		1r. Rössing uranium mine	1·75	1·00
533		2r. Gold	2·75	2·00
519/33 *Set of 15*			13·00	5·75

The 1, 2, 5, 7, 10, 18, 20, 40, 45c. and 2r. are vertical as T **138**, and the 25, 30, 35, 50c. and 1r. horizontal as T **139**.

140 Arrow Poison

(Des Eva-Maria Linsmayer)

1990 (1 Feb). *Flora. T* **140** *and similar vert designs. Multicoloured.* P 14.

534		18c. Type **140**	20	10
535		35c. Baobab flower	35	40
536		45c. Sausage Tree flowers	40	50
537		60c. Devil's Claw	45	90
534/7 *Set of 4*			1·25	1·75

The 60c. value exists as a Philatelic Foundation miniature sheet.

NAMIBIA

South West Africa became independent, as Namibia, on 21 March 1990. The Walvis Bay Territory was ceded by South Africa to Namibia on 1 March 1994.

PRINTERS. The following stamps were printed in lithography by the Government Printer, Pretoria, South Africa.

141 Pres. Sam Nujoma, Map of Namibia and National Flag   **142** Fish River Canyon

(Des T. Marais)

1990 (21 Mar). *Independence. T* **141** *and similar multicoloured designs.* P 14.

538		18c. Type **141**	20	15
539		45c. Hands releasing dove and map of Namibia (*vert*)	50	75
540		60c. National flag and map of Africa	1·00	1·50
538/40 *Set of 3*			1·50	2·25

(Des J. van Ellinckhuijzen)

1990 (26 Apr). *Namibia Landscapes. T* **142** *and similar horiz designs. Multicoloured.* P 14.

541		18c. Type **142**	25	20
542		35c. Quiver-tree forest, Keetmanshoop	50	35
543		45c. Tsaris Mountains	60	55
544		60c. Dolerite boulders, Keetmanshoop	70	65
541/4 *Set of 4*			1·90	1·60

The 60c. value exists as a Philatelic Foundation miniature sheet.

143 Stores on Kaiser Street, c. 1899

144 Maizefields

(Des J. van Ellinckhuijzen)

1990 (26 July). *Centenary of Windhoek. T* **143** *and similar horiz designs. Multicoloured.* P 14.

545 18c. Type **143** 20 20
546 35c. Kaiser Street, 1990 30 35
547 45c. City Hall, 1914 40 65
548 60c. City Hall, 1990 50 1·00
545/8 *Set of* 4 1·25 2·00

1990 (11 Oct). *Farming. T* **144** *and similar horiz designs. Multicoloured.* P 14.

549 20c. Type **144** 15 20
550 35c. Sanga bull 30 35
551 50c. Damara ram 40 45
552 65c. Irrigation in Okavango 50 60
549/52 *Set of* 4 1·25 1·40

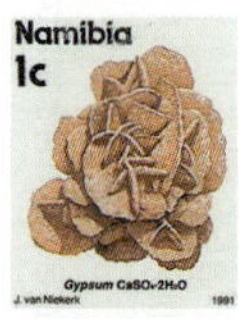

145 Gypsum

146 Radiosonde Weather Balloon

(Des J. van Niekerk)

1991 (2 Jan). *Minerals. Designs as Nos. 519/21 and 523/33, some with values changed, and new design (5r.), inscr "Namibia" as T* **145**. *Multicoloured. Chalk-surfaced paper (25, 30, 35, 50c., 1r.).* P 14.

553 1c. Type **145** 15 10
554 2c. Fluorite 25 10
555 5c. Mimetite 30 10
556 10c. Azurite 40 10
557 20c. Dioptase 50 10
558 25c. Type **139** 50 15
a. Ordinary paper (14 June) 55 15
559 30c. Tsumeb lead and copper complex 70 20
560 35c. Rosh Pinah zinc mine 70 20
561 40c. Diamonds 90 25
562 50c. Uis tin mine 75 25
563 65c. Boltwoodite 75 35
564 1r. Rössing uranium mine 80 50
565 1r.50 Wulfenite 1·10 70
566 2r. Gold 1·75 1·10
567 5r. Willemite (vert as T 145) 3·00 2·75
553/67 *Set of* 15 12·00 6·00

Printings of the 5c. and 10c. in 1992 were on phosphorescent paper.

(Des L. Kriedemann)

1991 (1 Feb). *Centenary of Weather Service. T* **146** *and similar horiz designs. Multicoloured.* P 14.

568 20c. Type **146** 20 20
569 35c. Sunshine recorder 35 30
570 50c. Measuring equipment 45 50
571 65c. Meteorological station, Gobabeb 50 60
568/71 *Set of* 4 1·40 1·40

147 Herd of Zebras

148 Karas Mountains

1991 (18 Apr). *Endangered Species. Mountain Zebra. T* **147** *and similar horiz designs. Multicoloured.* P 14.

572 20c. Type **147** 1·10 60
573 25c. Mare and foal 1·25 70
574 45c. Zebras and foal 2·00 1·75
575 60c. Two zebras 2·50 3·00
572/5 *Set of* 4 6·00 5·50

The 45c. value exists as a Philatelic Foundation miniature sheet.

(Des A. H. Barrett)

1991 (18 July). *Mountains of Namibia. T* **148** *and similar horiz designs. Multicoloured.* P 14.

576 20c. Type **148** 20 20
577 25c. Gamsberg Mountains 30 30
578 45c. Mount Brukkaros 45 70
579 60c. Erongo Mountains 65 1·00
576/9 *Set of* 4 1·50 2·00

149 Bernabe de la Bat Camp

150 Artist's Pallet

(Des J. van Niekerk)

1991 (24 Oct). *Tourist Camps. T* **149** *and similar horiz designs Multicoloured.* P 14.

580 20c. Type **149** 45 30
581 25c. Von Bach Dam Recreation Resort 55 45
582 45c. Gross Barmen Hot Springs 85 65
583 60c. Namutoni Rest Camp 1·00 1·00
580/3 *Set of* 4 2·50 2·25

(Des H. Pulon)

1992 (30 Jan). *21st Anniv of Windhoek Conservatoire. T* **150** *and similar horiz designs. Multicoloured.* P 14.

584 20c. Type **150** 20 15
585 25c. French horn and cello 25 20
586 45c. Theatrical masks 50 60
587 60c. Ballet dancers 65 1·00
584/7 *Set of* 4 1·40 1·75

151 Mozambique Mouthbrooder

152 Old Jetty

(Des B. Jackson)

1992 (16 Apr). *Freshwater Angling. T* **151** *and similar horiz designs. Multicoloured.* P 14.

588 20c. Type **151** 40 20
589 25c. Large-mouthed Yellowfish 45 20
590 45c. Common Carp 85 50
591 60c. Sharp-toothed Catfish 95 65
588/91 *Set of* 4 2·40 1·40

The 45c. value exists as a Philatelic Foundation miniature sheet.

1992 (2 July). *Centenary of Swakopmund. T* **152** *and similar horiz designs. Multicoloured.* P 14.

592 20c. Type **152** 25 25
593 25c. Recreation centre 25 25
594 45c. State House and lighthouse 80 60
595 60c. Sea front 85 75
592/5 *Set of* 4 1·90 1·60
MS596 118×93 mm. Nos. 592/5 3·00 3·00

153 Running

154 Wrapping English Cucumbers

(Des B. Jackson)

1992 (24 July). *Olympic Games, Barcelona. T* **153** *and similar horiz designs. Multicoloured.* P 14.

597 20c. Type **153** 25 20
598 25c. Map of Namibia, Namibian flag and Olympic rings 30 20
599 45c. Swimming 50 40
600 60c. Olympic Stadium, Barcelona 65 55
597/600 *Set of* 4 1·50 1·25
MS601 115×75 mm. Nos. 597/600 (sold at 2r.) 2·25 2·75

1992 (10 Sept). *Integration of the Disabled. T* **154** *and similar horiz designs. Multicoloured.* P 14.

602 20c. Type **154** 20 15
603 25c. Weaving mats 20 15
604 45c. Spinning thread 40 30
605 60c. Preparing pot plants 55 50
602/5 *Set of* 4 1·25 1·00

155 Elephants in Desert

156 Herd of Simmentaler Cattle

(Des D. Murphy)

1993 (25 Feb). *Namibia Nature Foundation. Rare and Endangered Species. T* **155** *and similar horiz designs. Multicoloured.* P 14.

606 20c. Type **155** 40 20
607 25c. Sitatunga in swamp 30 20
608 45c. Black Rhinoceros 65 50
609 60c. Hunting Dogs 65 60
606/9 *Set of* 4 1·75 1·40
MS610 217×59 mm. Nos. 606/9 (sold at 2r.50) 3·75 3·50

(Des Carola Kronsbein-Goldbeck)

1993 (16 Apr). *Centenary of Simmentaler Cattle in Namibia. T* **156** *and similar horiz designs. Multicoloured.* P 14.

611 20c. Type **156** 30 10
612 25c. Cow and calf 30 15
613 45c. Bull 60 40
614 60c. Cattle on barge 85 75
611/14 *Set of* 4 1·90 1·25

The 45c. value exists as a Philatelic Foundation miniature sheet.

157 Sand Dunes, Sossusvlei

158 Smiling Child

(Des J. van Ellinckhuijzen)

1993 (4 June). *Namib Desert Scenery. T* **157** *and similar horiz designs. Multicoloured.* P 14.

615 30c. Type **157** 25 20
616 40c. Blutkuppe 25 20
617 65c. River Kuiseb, Homeb 40 45
618 85c. Desert landscape 60 65
615/18 *Set of* 4 1·40 1·40

(Des J. van Ellinckhuijzen)

1993 (6 Aug). *S.O.S. Child Care in Namibia. T* **158** *and similar horiz designs. Multicoloured.* P 14.

619 30c. Type **158** 20 20
620 40c. Family 25 20
621 65c. Modern house 45 55
622 85c. Young artist with mural 65 80
619/22 *Set of* 4 1·40 1·60

(New Currency. 100 cents = 1 Namibia dollar)

159 *Charaxes jasius*

160 White Seabream

(Des A. Ainslie)

1993 (1 Oct). *Butterflies. T* **159** *and similar vert designs. Multicoloured.* P 14.

623 5c. Type **159** 20 20
624 10c. *Acraea anemosa* 20 20
625 20c. *Papilio nireus* 30 10
626 30c. *Junonia octavia* 30 10
627 40c. *Hypolimnus misippus* 30 10
628 50c. *Physcaeneura panda* 40 20
629 65c. *Charaxes candiope* 40 30
630 85c. *Junonia hierta* 50 40
631 90c. *Colotis cellmene* 50 40
632 $1 *Cacyreus dicksoni* 55 35
633 $2 *Charaxes bohemani* 80 80
634 $2.50 *Stugeta bowkeri* 1·00 1·10
635 $5 *Byblia anvatara* 1·50 1·75
623/35 *Set of* 13 6·25 5·50

For similar design inscribed "STANDARDISED MAIL" see No. 648. For 5c. and 50c. with elliptical perforations see Nos. 707/8.

(Des B. Jackson)

1994 (4 Feb). *Coastal Angling. T* **160** *and similar horiz designs Multicoloured.* P 14.

636 30c. Type **160** 25 25
637 40c. Kob 25 25
638 65c. West Coast Steenbras 40 40
639 85c. Galjoen 60 60
636/9 *Set of* 4 1·40 1·40
MS640 134×89 mm. Nos. 636/9 (sold at $2.50) 2·00 2·50

161 Container Ship at Wharf

162 *Adenolobus pechuelii*

(Des Liza van der Wal (85c.))

1994 (1 Mar). *Incorporation of Walvis Bay Territory into Namibia. T* **161** *and similar vert designs. Multicoloured.* P 14.

641 30c. Type **161** 40 30
642 65c. Aerial view of Walvis Bay 60 80
643 85c. Map of Namibia 95 1·25
641/3 *Set of* 3 1·75 2·10

(Des Auriol Batten)

1994 (8 Apr). *Flowers. T* **162** *and similar vert designs. Multicoloured.* P 14.

644 35c. Type **162** 25 25
645 40c. *Hibiscus elliottiae* 25 25
646 65c. *Pelargonium cortusifolium* 40 40
647 85c. *Hoodia macrantha* 50 60
644/7 *Set of* 4 1·25 1·40

1994 (8 Apr). *Butterflies. Vert design as T* **159**, *but inscr "STANDARDISED MAIL". Multicoloured.* P 14.

648 35c. Graphium antheus 20 20

No. 648 was initially sold at 35c., but this was subsequently increased to reflect changes in postal rates.

163 Yellow-billed Stork

164 Steam Railcar, 1908

(Des A. Barrett)

1994 (3 June). *Storks. T* **163** *and similar vert designs. Multicoloured.* P 14.

649 35c. Type **163** ... 50 30
650 40c. Abdim's Stork ... 50 30
651 80c. African Open-bill Stork ... 80 50
652 $1.10 White Stork ... 1·00 65
649/52 *Set of 4* ... 2·50 1·60

(Des H. Botha)

1994 (5 Aug). *Steam Locomotives. T* **164** *and similar horiz designs. Multicoloured.* P 14.

653 35c. Type **164** ... 45 30
654 70c. Krauss side-tank locomotive No. 106, 1904 ... 70 50
655 80c. Class 24 locomotive, 1948 ... 75 55
656 $1.10 Class 7C locomotive, 1914 ... 1·10 80
653/6 *Set of 4* ... 2·75 1·90

The 80c. value exists as a Philatelic Foundation miniature sheet.

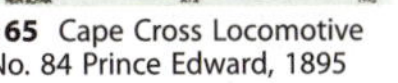

165 Cape Cross Locomotive No. 84 Prince Edward, 1895

166 National Arms

(Des H. Botha)

1995 (8 Mar). *Centenary of Railways in Namibia. T* **165** *and similar horiz designs. Multicoloured.* P 14.

657 35c. Type **165** ... 45 25
658 70c. Steam locomotive, German South West Africa ... 70 35
659 80c. South African Railways Class 8 steam locomotive ... 75 40
660 $1.10 Trans-Namib Class 33-400 diesel electric locomotive ... 1·10 55
657/60 *Set of 4* ... 2·75 1·40
MS661 101×94 mm. Nos. 657/60 ... 2·75 2·50
a. Optd "November 1995" on sheet margin (1 Nov) ... 3·25 3·00

(Des B. Wepener)

1995 (21 Mar). *5th Anniv of Independence.* P 14.

662 **166** 35c. multicoloured ... 40 30

No. 662 is inscribed "STANDARDISED MAIL" and was initially sold for 35c., but this was subsequently increased to reflect changes in postal rates.

167 Living Tortoise and *Geochelone stromeri* (fossil)

168 Martii Rautanen and Church

(Des L. Kriedemann)

1995 (24 May). *Fossils. T* **167** *and similar vert designs. Multicoloured.* P 14.

663 40c. Type **167** ... 65 25
664 80c. Ward's Diamond Bird and *Diamantornis wardi* (fossil eggs) ... 1·00 70
665 90c. Hyraxes and *Prohyrax hendeyi* skull ... 1·10 80
666 $1.20 Crocodiles and *Crocodylus lloydi* skull ... 1·40 1·40
663/6 *Set of 4* ... 3·75 2·75

The 80c. value exists as a Philatelic Foundation miniature sheet.

(Des H. Pulon)

1995 (10 July). *125th Anniv of Finnish Missionaries in Namibia. T* **168** *and similar horiz designs. Multicoloured.* P 14.

667 40c. Type **168** ... 25 20
668 80c. Albin Savola and hand printing press ... 50 50
669 90c. Karl Weikkolin and wagon ... 60 65
670 $1.20 Dr. Selma Rainio and Onandjokwe Hospital ... 85 95
667/70 *Set of 4* ... 2·00 2·10

169 Ivory Buttons

170 UN Flag

(Des H. Pulon)

1995 (16 Aug). *Personal Ornaments. T* **169** *and similar vert designs. Multicoloured.* P 14.

671 40c. Type **169** ... 20 20
672 80c. Conus shell pendant ... 45 45
673 90c. Cowrie shell headdress ... 55 55
674 $1.20 Shell button pendant ... 85 95
671/4 *Set of 4* ... 1·90 2·00

(Des Sheila Nowers)

1995 (1 Sept). *"Singapore '95" International Stamp Exhibition. Sheet, 110×52 mm, containing design as No. 359b with altered face value and inscription.* P 14.

MS675 $1.20 multicoloured ... 1·10 1·20

No. **MS**675 shows the exhibition emblem printed on the sheet margin.

(Des J. van Niekerk)

1995 (24 Oct). *50th Anniv of the United Nations.* P 14.

676 **170** 40c. new blue and black ... 20 20

171 Bogenfels Arch

172 Sister Leoni Kreitmeier and Döbra Education and Training Centre

(Des Christine Marais. Litho Harrison)

1996 (1 Apr). *Tourism. T* **171** *and similar horiz designs. Multicoloured.* P 15×14.

677 45c. Type **171** ... 15 15
678 90c. Ruacana Falls ... 30 30
679 $1 Epupa Falls ... 30 30
680 $1.30 Herd of wild horses ... 35 50
677/80 *Set of 4* ... 1·00 1·10

No. 677 is inscribed "Standardised Mail" and was initially sold at 45c.

(Des J. van Niekerk. Litho Harrison)

1996 (27 May). *Centenary of Catholic Missions in Namibia. T* **172** *and similar horiz designs. Multicoloured.* P 15×14.

681 50c. Type **172** ... 20 20
682 95c. Father Johann Malinowski and Heirachabis Mission ... 30 40
683 $1 St. Mary's Cathedral, Windhoek ... 30 40
684 $1.30 Archbishop Joseph Gotthardt and early church, Ovamboland ... 35 80
681/4 *Set of 4* ... 1·00 1·60

(Des Sheila Nowers)

1996 (8 June). *"CAPEX '96" International Stamp Exhibition, Toronto. Sheet, 105×45 mm, containing design similar to No. 358c with new face value and inscription.* P 14½×14.

MS685 $1.30 multicoloured ... 1·00 1·40

173 Children and UNICEF Volunteer

(Des A. Ainslie. Litho Harrison)

1996 (14 June). *50th Anniv of UNICEF. T* **173** *and similar horiz design. Multicoloured.* P 15×14.

686 50c. Type **173** ... 15 15
687 $1.30 Girls in school ... 60 60

No. 686 is inscribed "STANDARD POSTAGE" and was initially sold at 50c.

174 Boxing

175 Scorpius

(Des B. Jackson. Litho Harrison)

1996 (27 June). *Centennial Olympic Games, Atlanta. T* **174** *and similar horiz designs. Multicoloured.* P 15×14.

688 50c. Type **174** ... 15 15
689 90c. Cycling ... 50 40
690 $1 Swimming ... 30 40
691 $1.30 Running ... 30 55
688/91 *Set of 4* ... 1·10 1·40

No. 688 is inscribed "Standard Postage" and was initially sold at 50c.

(Des J. van Ellinckhuijzen. Litho Harrison)

1996 (12 Sept). *Stars in the Namibian Sky. T* **175** *and similar horiz designs. Multicoloured.* P 15×14.

692 50c. Type **175** ... 15 15
693 90c. Sagittarius ... 25 30
694 $1 Southern Cross ... 30 30
695 $1.30 Orion ... 40 50
692/5 *Set of 4* ... 1·00 1·10
MS696 100×80 mm. No. 694 ... 1·50 1·75

No. 692 is inscribed "Standard Postage" and was initially sold at 50c. For No. **MS**696 revalued to $3.50 see No. **MS**706.

176 Urn-shaped Pot

177 Khauxainas Ruins

(Des Sheila Nowers. Litho Harrison)

1996 (17 Oct). *Early Pottery. T* **176** *and similar vert designs Multicoloured.* P 14×15.

697 50c. Type **176** ... 15 15
698 90c. Decorated storage pot ... 30 40
699 $1 Reconstructed cooking pot ... 30 40
700 $1.30 Storage pot ... 35 70
697/700 *Set of 4* ... 1·00 1·50

No. 697 is inscribed "Standard Postage" and was initially sold at 50c.

(Des J. van Ellinckhuijzen. Litho Harrison)

1997 (6 Feb). *Khauxainas Ruins. T* **177** *and similar horiz designs showing different views.* P 15×14.

701 50c. multicoloured ... 35 20
702 $1 multicoloured ... 75 55
703 $1.10 multicoloured ... 85 75
704 $1.50 multicoloured ... 1·40 1·75
701/4 *Set of 4* ... 3·00 3·00

No. 701 is inscribed "Standard postage" and was initially sold at 50c.

178 Ox

179 Heinrich von Stephan

(Des J. van Ellinckhuijzen. Litho Harrison)

1997 (12 Feb). *"HONG KONG '97" International Stamp Exhibition and Chinese New Year ("Year of the Ox"). Sheet 103×67 mm.* P 15×14.

MS705 **178** $1.30 multicoloured ... 1·10 1·40

1997 (12 Feb). *Support for Organised Philately. No.* **MS**696 *with margin additionally inscr "Reprint February 17 Sold in aid of organized Philately N$3.50".*

MS706 $1 Southern Cross (sold at $3.50) ... 2·00 2·25

(Litho Harrison)

1997 (26 Mar). *As Nos. 623 and 628, but P 14½ (with two elliptical holes on each vertical side).*

707 5c. Type **159** ... 25 25
708 50c. Physcaeneura panda ... 75 75

(Des J. van Ellinckhuijzen. Litho Harrison)

1997 (8 Apr). *Death Centenary of Heinrich von Stephan (founder of UPU).* P 14×15.

709 **179** $2 multicoloured ... 1·00 1·00

180 Cinderella Waxbill

182 Jackass Penguins calling

(Des Julia Birkhead. Photo Harrison)

1997 (6 May). *Waxbills. T* **180** *and similar horiz design. Multicoloured.* P 14×14½ (with one elliptical hole on each horizontal side).

710 50c. Type **180** ... 20 20
a. Booklet pane. Nos. 710/11, each×5 ... 2·00
711 60c. Black-cheeked Waxbill ... 20 20

Nos. 710/11 were only issued in $5.50 stamp booklets.

181 Helmet Guineafowl

(Des Isabel van der Ploeg. Photo Enschedé)

1997 (6 May). *Greetings Stamp.* P 15×14.

712 **181** $1.20 multicoloured ... 1·00 1·00

For similar designs see Nos. 743/6.

183 Caracal

(Des D. Thorpe. Litho Harrison)

1997 (15 May). *Endangered Species. Jackass Penguin. T* **182** *and similar vert designs. Multicoloured.* P 14×15.

713 50c. Type **182** ... 35 30
714 $1 Incubating egg ... 55 40

715 $1.10 Adult with chick 60 50
716 $1.50 Penguins swimming 75 60
713/16 *Set of 4* ..... 1·90 1·50
MS717 101×92 mm. As Nos. 713/16, but without the WWF symbol (sold at $5) ..... 1·90 1·50

No. 713 is inscribed "STANDARD POSTAGE" and was initially sold for 50c.

(Des Sheila Nowers. Litho Harrison)

1997 (12 June). *Wildcats. T* **183** *and similar horiz designs Multicoloured.* P 15×14.

718 50c. Type **183** 20 20
719 $1 *Felis lybica* 40 30
720 $1.10 *Serval* 50 40
721 $1.50 Black-footed Cat 60 55
718/21 *Set of 4* ..... 1·50 1·25
MS722 100×80 mm. $5 As No. 721 ..... 2·00 2·25

No. 718 is inscribed "STANDARD POSTAGE" and was initially sold at 50c. No. **MS**722 was sold in aid of organised philately in Southern Africa.

184 *Catophractes alexandri*

185 Collecting Bag

(Des T. Breckwoldt (Nos. 723/7), Isabel van der Ploeg (others). Litho Enschedé)

1997 (27 June). *Greeting Stamps. Flowers and Helmet Guineafowl. T* **184** *and similar horiz designs. Multicoloured.* P 14×13½.

723 50c. Type **184** 30 30
a. Booklet pane. Nos. 723/7, each ×2, and (10) labels ..... 2·75
724 50c. *Crinum paludosum* 30 30
725 50c. *Gloriosa superba* 30 30
726 50c. *Tribulus zeyheri* 30 30
727 50c. *Aptosimum pubescens* 30 30
728 50c. Helmet Guineafowl raising hat 30 30
a. Booklet pane. Nos. 728/32, each ×2, and (10) labels ..... 4·00
729 50c. Holding bouquet 30 30
730 50c. Ill in bed 30 30
731 $1 With heart round neck 50 60
732 $1 With suitcase and backpack 50 60
723/32 *Set of 10* ..... 3·00 3·25

These stamps only come from $5 (Nos. 723/7) or $7 (Nos. 728/32) stamp booklets where they occur in panes of 10 (5×2) with margins all round and greetings labels at top and bottom. Nos. 723/7 are inscribed "Standard Postage" and were initially sold at 50c. each.

(Des J. van Niekerk. Litho Harrison)

1997 (8 July). *Basket Work. T* **185** *and similar vert designs. Multicoloured.* P 14×15.

733 50c. Type **185** 20 20
734 90c. Powder basket 30 30
735 $1.20 Fruit basket 35 35
736 $2 Grain basket 70 75
733/6 *Set of 4* ..... 1·40 1·40

186 Veterinary Association Coat of Arms

(Litho Harrison)

1997 (12 Sept). *50th Anniv of Namibian Veterinary Association.* P 14×14½.

737 **186** $1.50 multicoloured 50 50
a. Tête-bêche pair ..... 1·00 1·00

No. 737 was issued in sheets of 10 containing one row of tête-bêche pairs.

187 Head of Triceratops

188 German South West Africa Postman

(Des J. van Ellinckhuijzen. Litho Enschedé)

1997 (27 Sept). *Youth Philately. Dinosaurs. Sheet 82×56 mm.* P 12½×13.

MS738 **187** $5 multicoloured ..... 1·50 1·75

(Des J. Madisia. Litho Enschedé)

1997 (9 Oct). *World Post Day.* P 14×15.

739 **188** 50c. multicoloured 20 20

No. 739 is inscribed "STANDARD POSTAGE" and was initially sold at 50c.

189 False Mopane

190 Flame Lily

(Des Auriol Batten. Litho Enschedé)

1997 (10 Oct). *Trees. T* **189** *and similar vert designs. Multicoloured.* P 14×15.

740 50c. Type **189** 15 20
741 $1 Ana Tree 30 40
742 $1.10 Shepherd's Tree 35 55
743 $1.50 Kiaat 50 70
740/3 *Set of 4* ..... 1·10 1·60

No. 740 is inscribed "STANDARD POSTAGE" and was initially sold at 50c.

(Des Isabel van der Ploeg. Litho Enschedé)

1997 (3 Nov). *Christmas. Multicoloured designs as T* **181** *showing Helmet Guineafowl, each with festive frame.* P 13×12½.

744 50c. Guineafowl facing right 20 20
745 $1 Guineafowl in grass 35 30
746 $1.10 Guineafowl on rock 35 40
747 $1.50 Guineafowl in desert 50 55
744/7 *Set of 4* ..... 1·25 1·25
MS748 110×80 mm. $5 Helmet Guineafowl (*vert*). P 12½×13 ..... 2·75 2·75

No. 744 is inscribed "standard postage" and was initially sold at 50c.

(Des D. Murphy. Litho Enschedé)

1997 (3 Nov). *Flora and Fauna. T* **190** *and similar vert designs. Multicoloured.*

(a) P 13½.

749 5c. Type **190** 10 10
a. Perf 14×13½ 10 10
ab. Booklet pane. Nos. 749a/66a with margins all round ..... 6·25
750 10c. Bushman Poison 10 10
a. Perf 14×13½ 10 10
751 20c. Camel's Foot 10 10
a. Perf 14×13½ 10 10
752 30c. Western Rhigozum 15 10
a. Perf 14×13½ 15 10
753 40c. Blue-cheeked Bee-eater 15 15
a. Perf 14×13½ 15 10
754 50c. Laughing Dove 15 15
a. Perf 14×13½ 15 10
755 50c. Peach-faced Lovebird 15 10
a. Perf 14×13½ 10 10
ab. Booklet pane. No. 755a ×10 with margins all round ..... 1·50
756 60c. Lappet-faced Vulture 20 10
a. Perf 14×13½ 20 10
757 90c. Yellow-billed Hornbill 25 20
a. Perf 14×13½ 25 20
758 $1 Lilac-breasted Roller 30 25
a. Perf 14×13½ 30 25
759 $1.10 Hippopotamus 35 25
a. Perf 14×13½ 35 25
760 $1.20 Giraffe 40 25
a. Perf 14×13½ 40 25
761 $1.20 Leopard 30 25
a. Perf 14×13½ 20 25
ab. Booklet pane. No. 761a ×10 with margins all round ..... 2·50
762 $1.50 Elephant 40 30
a. Perf 14×13½ 40 30
763 $2 Lion 45 40
a. Perf 14×13½ 45 40
764 $4 Buffalo 80 70
a. Perf 14×13½ 80 75
765 $5 Black Rhinoceros ..... 1·10 1·00
a. Perf 14×13½ ..... 1·10 1·00
766 $10 Cheetah ..... 1·75 2·00
a. Perf 14×13½ ..... 1·75 2·00
749/66 *Set of 18* ..... 6·25 5·50

(b) Self-adhesive. P 12×12½.

767 50c. As No. 755 ..... 10 20
768 $1 As No. 758 ..... 20 30
769 $1.20 As No. 761 ..... 20 35
767/9 *Set of 3* 50 85

Nos. 755a and 767 are inscribed "standard postage" and were each initially sold at 50c., Nos. 761a and 769 are inscribed "postcard rate" and were each initially sold at $1.20.

Stamps perforated 14×13½ (13.8×13.3) come from the three booklets only. They show 20 teeth along the top and the bottom instead of the 19 on the sheet stamps (13.3).

191 John Muafangejo

192 Gabriel B. Taapopi

(Des J. van Ellinckhuijzen. Litho Harrison)

1997 (27 Nov). *10th Death Anniv of John Muafangejo (artist).* P 14×15.

770 **191** 50c. multicoloured 40 40

No. 770 is inscribed "STANDARD POSTAGE" and was initially sold at 50c.

(Des J. van Ellinckhuijzen. Litho Enschedé)

1998 (15 Jan). *Gabriel B. Taapopi (educator) Commemoration.* P 14×15.

771 **192** 50c. silver and reddish brown 40 40

No. 771 is inscribed "STANDARD POSTAGE" and was sold for 50c.

193 Year of the Tiger

(Litho Enschedé)

1998 (19 Jan). *International Stamp and Coin Exhibition 1997, Shanghai. Sheets, 165×125 mm or 97×85 mm, containing multicoloured designs as T* **193**.

(a) Lunar New Year

MS772 165×125 mm. $2.50×6. Type **193**; Light green tiger and circular symbol; Yellow tiger and head symbol; Blue tiger and square symbol; Emerald tiger and square symbol; Mauve tiger and triangular symbol (61×29 mm). P13½×12½ ..... 2·50 3·25
MS773 97×85 mm. $6 Symbolic tiger designs(71×40 mm). P 12½ ..... 1·25 1·40

(b) Chinese Calendar

MS774 165×125 mm. $2.50×6. Various calendar symbols (24×80 mm). P 14×13½ ..... 2·50 3·25
MS775 97×85 mm. $6 Soft toy tigers (71×36 mm). P 12½ ..... 1·25 1·40

(c) 25th Anniv of Shanghai Communique

MS776 165×125 mm. $3.50×4. Pres. Nixon's visit to China, 1972; Vice Premier Deng Xiaoping's visit to U.S.A., 1979; Pres. Reagan's visit to China, 1984; Pres. Bush's visit to China, 1989 (61×32 mm). P 13½×12½ ..... 2·50 3·00
MS777 97×85 mm. $6 China-U.S.A. Communique, 1972 (69×36 mm). P 14½×13 ..... 1·25 1·40

(d) Pres. Deng Xiaoping's Project for Unification of China

MS778 165×125 mm. $3.50×4. Beijing as national capital; Return of Hong Kong; Return of Macao; Links with Taiwan (37×65 mm). P 14×13 ..... 2·50 3·00
MS779 97×85 mm. $6 Reunified China (71×41 mm). P 12½ ..... 1·25 1·40

(e) Return of Macao to China, 1999

MS780 Two sheets, each 165×120 mm. (a) $4.50×3 Carnival dragon and modern Macao (44×33 mm). P 13½. (b) $4.50×3 Ruins of St. Paul's Church, Macao (62×29 mm). P 13½×12½. *Set of 2 sheets* ..... 4·00 5·50
MS781 Two sheets, each 97×85 mm. (a) $6 Carnival dragon and modern Macao (62×32 mm). P 13½×12½. (b) $6 Deng Xiaoping and ruins of St. Paul's Church, Macao (71×36 mm). P 12½. *Set of 2 sheets* ..... 2·00 2·75

194 Leopard

195 Narra Plant

(Des Sheila Nowers. Litho Enschedé)

1998 (26 Jan). *Large Wild Cats. T* **194** *and similar horiz designs. Multicoloured.* P 13×12½.

782 $1.20 Type **194** 50 25
783 $1.90 Lioness and cub 70 65
784 $2 Lion 70 80
785 $2.50 Cheetah ..... 80 1·10
782/5 *Set of 4* ..... 2·40 2·50
MS786 112×98 mm. Nos. 782/5 ..... 3·25 3·25

(Des Christine Marais. Litho Enschedé)

1998 (9 Feb). *Narra Cultivation.* P 12½.

787 **195** $2.40 multicoloured 45 45

196 Collecting Rain Water

197 White-faced Scops Owl

(Des J. van Ellinckhuijzen. Litho Enschedé)

1998 (23 Mar). *World Water Day.* P 14×15.

788 **196** 50c. multicoloured 40 40

No. 788 is inscribed "STANDARD POSTAGE" and was initially sold at 50c. On 1 April 1998 the standard postage rate was increased to 55c.

(Des D. Miller. Litho Questa)

1998 (31 Mar). *Diana, Princess of Wales Commemoration. Sheet, 145×70 mm, containing vert designs as T* **91** *of Kiribati. Multicoloured.* P 14½×14.

MS789 $1 Princess Diana wearing protective mask; $1 Wearing Red Cross badge; $1 Wearing white shirt; $1 Comforting crippled child ..... 1·60 1·75

(Des H. Denker. Litho Enschedé)

1998 (1 Apr). *Owls of Namibia. T* **197** *and similar multicoloured designs.* P 13½×12½.

790	55c. Black-tailed Tree Rat (20×24 mm)	30	30
	a. Booklet pane. Nos. 790/4	3·25	
791	$1.50 Type **197**	70	75
792	$1.50 Barred Owl	70	75
793	$1.90 Spotted Eagle Owl	90	1·00
794	$1.90 Barn Owl (61×24 mm)	90	1·00
790/4	*Set of 5*	3·25	3·50

Nos. 790/4 were only issued in $7.35 stamp booklets. For miniature sheet containing $11 as No. 794 see No. **MS**850.

198 *Patella ganatina* (Limpet)

(Des Mary Volkmann. Litho Enschedé)

1998 (14 May). *Shells. T* **198** *and similar horiz designs. Multicoloured.* P 13×12½.

795	55c. Type **198**	25	10
796	$1.10 *Cymatium cutaceum africanum* (Triton)	55	30
797	$1.50 *Conus mozambicus* (Cone)	75	65
798	$6 *Venus verrucosa* (Venus Clam)	2·50	3·00
795/8	*Set of 4*	3·50	3·50
MS799	109×84 mm. Nos. 795/8	4·00	5·00

No. 795 is inscribed "Standard Postage" and was initially sold at 55c.

199 Underwater Diamond Excavator

200 "Chinga" (cheetah)

(Des S. Williams. Litho Questa)

1998 (18 May). *Marine Technology. Sheet 70×90 mm.* P 14½×14.

MS800	**199** $2.50 multicoloured	1·75	1·75

(Litho Enschedé)

1998 (5 June). *Wildlife Conservation. "Racing for Survival" (Olympic sprinter Frank Frederiks v cheetah). Sheet 108×80 mm.* P 13.

MS801	**200** $5 multicoloured	1·75	2·00

201 Namibian Beach

202 Two Footballers

(Litho Cartor)

1998 (5 June). *World Environment Day. T* **201** *and similar horiz designs. Multicoloured.* P 13×13½.

802	55c. Type **201**	15	10
803	$1.10 Okavango sunset	30	25
804	$1.50 Sossusvlei	45	50
805	$1.90 African Moringo tree	55	65
802/5	*Set of 4*	1·40	1·40

No. 802 is inscribed "STANDARD POSTAGE" and was initially sold at 55c.

(Des J. Madisia. Litho Enschedé)

1998 (15 June). *World Cup Football Championship, France. Sheet 80×56 mm.* P 14×13½.

MS806	**202** $5 multicoloured	1·25	1·50

203 Chacma Baboon

204 Carmine Bee-eater

(Des D. Murphy. Litho Cartor)

1998 (18 June). *Animals with their Young. Sheet, 176×60 mm, containing T* **203** *and similar vert designs.* P 13½×13.

MS807	$1.50 Type **203**; $1.50 Blue Wildebeest; $1.50 Meercat(suricate); $1.50 African Elephant; $1.50 Burchell's Zebra	1·50	1·75

(Des Mary Volkmann. Litho Cartor)

1998 (26 Sept). *Wildlife of the Caprivi Strip. T* **204** *and similar multicoloured designs.* P 12½.

808	60c. Type **204**	60	50
	a. Sheetlet. Nos. 808/17	5·50	
809	60c. Sable Antelope (40×40 mm)	60	50
810	60c. Lechwe (40×40 mm)	60	50
811	60c. Woodland Waterberry	60	50
812	60c. Nile Monitor (40×40 mm)	60	50
813	60c. African Jacana	60	50
814	60c. African Fish Eagle	60	50
815	60c. Woodland Kingfisher	60	50
816	60c. Nile Crocodile (55×30 mm)	60	50
817	60c. Black Mamba (32×30 mm)	60	50
808/17	*Set of 10*	5·50	4·50

Nos. 808/17 were printed together, *se-tenant*, in sheetlets of 10 with the backgrounds forming a composite design.

205 Black Rhinoceros and Calf

(Des H. Denker. Litho Cartor)

1998 (20 Oct). *"ILSAPEX '98" International Stamp Exhibition, Johannesburg. Sheet 103×68 mm.* P 13.

MS818	**205** $5 multicoloured	1·50	1·75

206 Blue Whale

207 Damara Dik-dik

(Des Mary Butterfield. Litho Questa)

1998 (23 Oct). *Whales of the Southern Oceans (joint issue with Norfolk Island and South Africa). Sheet 103×70 mm.* P 13½×14.

MS819	**206** $5 multicoloured	1·75	2·00

(Des L. Voight. Litho Enschedé)

1999 (18 Jan). *"Fun Stamps for Children". Animals. T* **207** *and similar multicoloured design.* P 14×13½ ($1.80) or 13½×14 ($2.65).

820	$1.80 Type **207**	1·50	1·25
821	$2.65 Striped Tree Squirrel (26×36 mm)	2·75	2·50

208 Yoka perplexed

209 Windhuk (liner)

(Des J. van Ellinckhuijzen. Litho Enschedé)

1999 (1 Feb). *"Yoka the Snake" (cartoon) (1st series). T* **208** *and similar multicoloured designs. Self-adhesive.* P 5.

822	$1.60 Type **208**	35	40
	a. Booklet pane. Nos. 822/31	3·00	
823	$1.60 Yoka under attack (33×27 mm)	35	40
824	$1.60 Yoka caught on branch	35	40
825	$1.60 Yoka and wasps (33×27 mm)	35	40
826	$1.60 Yoka and footprint	35	40
827	$1.60 Yoka and tail of red and white snake	35	40
828	$1.60 Mouse hunt (33×27 mm)	35	40
829	$1.60 Snakes entwined	35	40
830	$1.60 Red and white snake singing	35	40
831	$1.60 Yoka sulking (33×27 mm)	35	40
822/31	*Set of 10*	3·00	3·50

Nos. 822/31 were only printed, *se-tenant*, in $16 stamp booklets on which the backing paper forms the cover. See also Nos. **MS**835 and **MS**877.

(Litho German State Ptg Wks, Berlin)

1999 (18 Mar). *Windhuk (liner) Commemoration. Sheet 110×90 mm.* P 14.

MS832	**209** $5.50, multicoloured	1·25	1·50

210 Zögling Glider, 1928

211 Yoka the Snake with Toy Zebra

(Des D. Bagnall. Litho Cartor)

1999 (13 Apr). *Gliding in Namibia. T* **210** *and similar horiz design. Multicoloured.* P 13.

833	$1.60 Type **210**	40	50
834	$1.80 Schleicher glider, 1998	60	70

(Des J. van Ellinckhuijzen. Litho German State Ptg Wks, Berlin)

1999 (27 Apr). *"iBRA '99" International Stamp Exhibition, Nuremberg. Sheet 110×84 mm.* P 14.

MS835	**211** $5.50 multicoloured	1·25	1·50

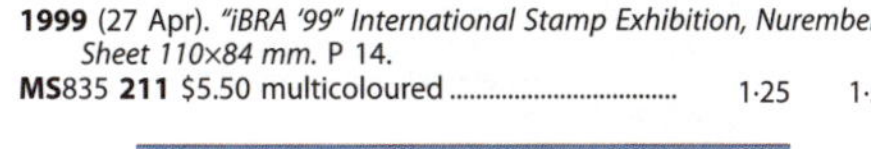

212 Greater Kestrel

(Des H. Denker. Litho Cartor)

1999 (18 May). *Birds of Prey. T* **212** *and similar horiz designs. Multicoloured.* P 13½.

836	60c. Type **212**	50	25
837	$1.60 Common Kestrel ("Rock Kestrel")	1·00	70
838	$1.80 Red-headed Falcon	1·00	85
839	$2.65 Lanner Falcon	1·75	2·25
836/9	*Set of 4*	3·75	3·50

213 Wattled Crane

214 *Termitomyces schimperi* (fungus)

(Des C. van Rooyen. Litho Enschedé)

1999 (28 June). *Wetland Birds. T* **213** *and similar horiz designs. Multicoloured.* P 13×12½.

840	$1.60 Type **213**	75	55
841	$1.80 Variegated Sandgrouse ("Burchell's Sandgrouse")	85	70
842	$1.90 Pratincole	85	70
843	$2.65 Eastern White Pelican	1·40	1·60
840/3	*Set of 4*	3·50	3·25

(Des C. van Rooyen. Litho Enschedé)

1999 (2 July). *"PhilexFrance '99" International Stamp Exhibition, Paris. Sheet 79×54 mm.* P 14×13½.

MS844	**214** $5.50 multicoloured	1·50	1·60

215 *Eulophia hereroensis* (orchid)

216 Johanna Gertze

(Des Mary Volkmann. Litho and embossed Cartor)

1999 (21 Aug). *"China '99" International Philatelic Exhibition, Beijing. Orchids. T* **215** *and similar diamond-shaped designs. Multicoloured.* P 12½.

845	$1.60 Type **215**	60	50
846	$1.80 *Ansellia africana*	70	60
847	$2.65 *Eulophia leachii*	95	95
848	$3.90 *Eulophia speciosa*	1·25	1·50
845/8	*Set of 4*	3·25	3·25
MS849	72×72 mm. $5.50 *Eulophia walleri*	1·75	2·00

(Des H. Denker. Litho Cartor)

1999 (30 Sept). *Winning entry in 5th Stamp World Cup, France. Sheet 120×67 mm design as No. 794, but with changed face value. Multicoloured.* P 13½×12½.

MS850	$11 Barn Owl (61×24 mm)	4·50	4·50

(Des Inge Madlé. Litho Enschedé)

1999 (1 Oct). *Johanna Gertze Commemoration.* P 12½×13.

851	**216** $20 Indian red, flesh and bright new blue	4·00	4·50

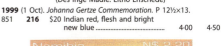

217 Sunset over Namibia

(Des J. van Ellinckhuijzen. Litho Enschedé)

1999 (31 Dec)–**2002**. *New Millennium. T* **217** *and similar multicoloured designs.* P 13½.

852	$2.20 Type **217**	70	80
853	$2.40 Sunrise over Namibia (1.1.2000)	90	1·10
MS854	77×54 mm. $9 Globe (hologram) (37×44 mm). P 14×13½	2·75	3·00

218 South African Shelduck

(219) standard postage

(Des P. Huebsch. Litho Enschedé)

2000 (18 Feb). *Ducks of Namibia. T* **218** *and similar horiz designs. Multicoloured.* P 13.

855	$2 Type **218**	70	55
856	$2.40 White-faced Whistling Duck	80	70

857 $3 Comb Duck ("Knobbilled duck") 90 90
858 $7 Cape Shoveler 2·00 2·50
855/8 *Set of 4* 4·00 4·25
No. 858 is inscribed "Cape shoveller" in error.

2000 (1 Mar). *Nos. 749/52 optd as T* **219**.
859 65c. on 5c. Type **190** 30 15
860 $1.80 on 30c Western Rhigozum 65 40
861 $3 on 10c. Bushman Poison 85 90
862 $6 on 20c. Camel's Foot 1·50 1·75
859/62 *Set of 4* 3·00 3·00
No. 859 was initially sold at 65c. The other surcharges show face values.

220 Namibian Children

221 Actor playing Jesus wearing Crown of Thorns

(Des Saatchi and Saatchi. Litho Enschedé)

2000 (21 Mar). *10th Anniv of Independence. T* **220** *and similar square design. Multicoloured.* P 13½×14.
863 65c. Type **220** 40 15
864 $3 Namibian flag 1·00 1·10

(Des J. van Ellinckhuijzen. Litho Enschedé)

2000 (1 Apr). *Easter Passion Play. T* **221** *and similar horiz design. Multicoloured.* P 13½×14.
865 $2.10 Type **221** 60 60
866 $2.40 On the way to Calvary 65 65

222 Tenebrionid Beetle

223 *Welwitschia mirabilis*

(Des Mary Volkmann. Litho SNP Ausprint, Australia)

2000 (22 May). *"The Stamp Show 2000" International Stamp Exhibition, London. Wildlife of Namibian Dunes. Sheet 165×73 mm containing T* **222** *and similar multicoloured designs.* P 14½.
MS867 $2 Type **222**; $2 Namib Golden Mole; $2 Brown Hyena; $2 Shovel-snouted Lizard (49×30 mm); $2 Dune Lark (25×36 mm); $6 Namib Side-winding Adder (25×36 mm) 5·00 5·50
No. **MS**867 shows the dunes, animal tracks and vegetation highlighted in varnish and phosphor ink.

(Des H. Denker. Litho Enschedé)

2000 (21 June). *Welwitschia mirabilis (prehistoric plant). T* **223** *and similar vert designs. Multicoloured.* P 14×13½.
868 65c. Type **223** 30 15
869 $2.20 *Welwitschia mirabilis* from above 70 50
870 $3 Seed pods 90 90
871 $4 Flats covered by *Welwitschia mirabilis* plants 1·10 1·25
868/71 *Set of 4* 2·75 2·50
No. 868 is inscribed "Standard inland mail" and was sold for 65c.

224 High Energy Stereoscopic System Telescopes

(Des K. van Ellinckhuijzen. Litho Enschedé)

2000 (7 July). *High Energy Stereoscopic System Telescopes Project, Namibian Khomas Highlands. Sheet 100×70 mm.* P 13½×14.
MS872 **224** $11 multicoloured 4·50 4·50

225 Jackal-berry Tree

(Des H. Denker. Litho Enschedé)

2000 (16 Aug). *Trees with Nutritional Value. T* **225** *and similar horiz designs. Multicoloured.* P 13½×14.
873 65c. Type **225** 35 25
874 $2 Sycamore Fig 65 65
875 $2.20 Bird Plum 70 70
876 $7 Marula 1·75 2·25
873/6 *Set of 4* 3·00 3·50
No. 873 is inscribed "Standard inland mail" and was sold for 65c.

226 Yoka and Nero the Elephant

227 Striped Anemone

(Des K. van Ellinckhuijzen. Litho Enschedé)

2000 (1 Sept). *"Yoka the Snake" (cartoon) (2nd series). Sheet 103×68 mm.* P 13.
MS877 **226** $11 multicoloured 4·00 4·25

(Des Anja Denker. Litho Enschedé)

2001 (18 Apr). *Sea Anemone. T* **227** *and similar vert designs. Multicoloured.* P 13½.
878 (70c.) Type **227** 30 15
879 $2.45 Violet-spotted Anemone 70 55
880 $3.50 Knobbly Anemone 90 90
881 $6.60 False Plum Anemone 1·60 1·90
878/81 *Set of 4* 3·25 3·25
No. 878 is inscribed "Standard inland mail" and was originally sold for 70c.

228 Cessna 210 Turbo Aircraft

229 Wood-burning Stove

(Des D. Bagnall. Litho Enschedé)

2001 (9 May). *Civil Aviation. T228 and similar horiz designs. Multicoloured.* P 13½.
882 (70c.) Type **228** 40 15
883 $2.20 Douglas DC-6B airliner 70 50
884 $2.50 Pitts S2A bi-plane 75 55
885 $13.20 Bell 407 helicopter 4·00 4·25
882/5 *Set of 4* 5·25 5·00
No. 882 is inscribed "Standard inland mail" and was originally sold for 70c.

(Des J. van Ellinckhuijzen. Litho Enschedé)

2001 (15 Aug). *Renewable Energy Sources. T* **229** *and similar square designs. Multicoloured.* P 13½×14.
886 ($1.10) Type **229** 40 45
a. Sheetlet. Nos. 886/95 6·00
887 ($1) Biogas digester 40 45
888 ($1) Solar cooker 40 45
889 ($1) Re-cycled tyre 40 45
890 ($1) Solar water pump 40 45
891 $3.50 Solar panel above traditional hut 90 1·00
892 $3.50 Solar street light 90 1·00
893 $3.50 Solar panels on hospital building 90 1·00
894 $3.50 Solar telephone 90 1·00
895 $3.50 Wind pump 90 1·00
886/95 *Set of 10* 6·00 6·50
Nos. 886/95 were printed together, *se-tenant*, in sheetlets of 10 with the backgrounds forming a composite design which extends onto the sheetlet margins Nos. 886/90 are inscribed "Standard Mail" and were originally sold for $1 each.

230 Ruppell's Parrot

231 Plaited Hair, Mbalantu

(Des H. Denker. Litho Cartor)

2001 (5 Sept). *Flora and Fauna from the Central Highlands. T* **230** *and similar multicoloured designs.* P 12½.
896 ($1) Type **230** 40 45
a. Sheetlet. Nos. 896/905 6·00
897 ($1) Flap-necked Chameleon (40×30 mm) 40 45
898 ($1) Klipspringer (40×30 mm) 40 45
899 ($1) Rockrunner (40×30 mm) 40 45
900 ($1) Pangolin (40×40 mm) 40 45
901 $3.50 Camel Thorn (55×30 mm) 90 1·00
902 $3.50 Berg Aloe (40×30 mm) 90 1·00
903 $3.50 Kudu (40×40 mm) 90 1·00
904 $3.50 Rock Agama (40×40 mm) 90 1·00
905 $3.50 Armoured Ground Cricket (40×30 mm) 90 1·00
896/905 *Set of 10* 6·00 6·50
Nos. 896/905 were printed together, *se-tenant*, in sheetlets of 10 with the backgrounds forming a composite design which extends onto the sheetlet margins. Nos. 896/900 are inscribed "Standard Mail" and were originally sold for $1 each.

(Des Mary Volkmann. Litho Cartor)

2002 (20 Mar). *Traditional Women's Hairstyles and Headdresses. T* **231** *and similar vert designs. Multicoloured.* P 13.
906 ($1) Type **231** 40 45
a. Sheetlet. Nos. 906/11 2·25
907 ($1) Cloth headdress, Damara 40 45
908 ($1) Beaded hair ornaments, San 40 45
909 ($1) Leather ekori headdress, Herero 40 45
910 ($1) Bonnet, Baster 40 45
911 ($1) Seed necklaces, Mafue 40 45
912 ($1) Thihukeka hairstyle, Mbukushu 40 45
a. Sheetlet. Nos. 912/17 2·25
913 ($1) Triangular cloth headress, Herero 40 45
914 ($1) Goat-skin headdress Himba 40 45
915 ($1) Horned headdress Kwanyama 40 45
916 ($1) Headscarf, Nama 40 45
917 ($1) Plaits and oshikoma Ngandjera/Kwaluudhi 40 45
906/17 *Set of 12* 4·25 4·75
Nos. 906/11 and 912/17, which were printed together, *se-tenant*, in sheetlets of 6 with illustrated margins, are inscribed "STANDARD MAIL" and were each originally sold for $1.

232 African Hoopoe

233 The Regular Floods of Kuiseb River

(Des Anja Denker. Litho Enschedé)

2002 (15 May). *Birds. T* **232** *and similar vert designs. Multicoloured.* P13½.
918 ($1) Type **232** 55 25
919 $2.20 Paradise Flycatcher 75 45
920 $2.60 Swallowtailed Bee-eater 90 90
921 $2.80 Malachite Kingfisher 1·10 1·25
918/21 *Set of 4* 3·00 2·50
No. 918 is inscribed "Standard Mail" and was originally sold for $1.

(Des H. Denker. Litho Cartor)

2002 (1 July). *Ephemeral Rivers. T* **233** *and similar multicoloured designs.* P 13 (922, 926), 13½×13 (924) or 13×13½ (923, 925).
922 ($1.30) Type **233** 50 25
923 $2.20 Tsauchab River after heavy rainfall (39×31 mm) 75 45
924 $2.60 Elephants in sandbed of the Hoarusib River (89×24 mm) 90 80
925 $2.80 Nossob River after heavy rainfall (39×32 mm) 1·00 1·00
926 $3.50 Fish River and birds (23×57 mm) 1·25 1·50
922/6 *Set of 5* 4·00 3·50
No. 922 is inscribed "Standard Mail" and was initially sold for $1.30.

234 Wall Mounted Telephone, 1958

standard postage

(**234a**)

(Des J. van Ellinckhuijzen. Litho Cartor)

2002 (26 Sept). *10th Anniv of Nampost and Telecommunication. T* **234** *and similar horiz designs. Multicoloured.* P 13.
MS927 102×171 mm. ($1.30) Type **234**; ($1.30) Courier van; ($1.30) Black wall mounted phone; ($1.30) Pillar box and envelope; ($1.30) Black desk top phone; ($1.30) Computer; ($1.30) Unplugged phone; ($1.30) Dolphin carrying envelope; ($1.30) Modern multi-function phone; ($1.30) Plane and envelopes 3·00 3·50
MS928 102×171 mm. ($1.30) Type **234** ×2; ($1.30) Black wall mounted phone ×2; ($1.30) Black desk top phone ×2; ($1.30) Unplugged phone ×2; ($1.30) Modern multi-function phone ×2 3·00 3·50
MS929 102×171 mm. ($1.30) Courier van ×2; ($1.30) Pillar box and envelope ×2; ($1.30) Computer ×2; ($1.30) Dolphin carrying envelope ×2; ($1.30) Plane and envelopes×2 3·00 3·50
The stamps in Nos. **MS**927/9 were all inscribed "Standard Mail" and were initially sold for $.30.

2002 (21 Oct). *Nos. 749/50 surch with T* **234a**.
930 ($1.30) Type **190** 50 40
931 ($1.30) Bushman Poison 50 40
Nos. 930/1 are surch "standard postage" and were initially sold for $1.30.

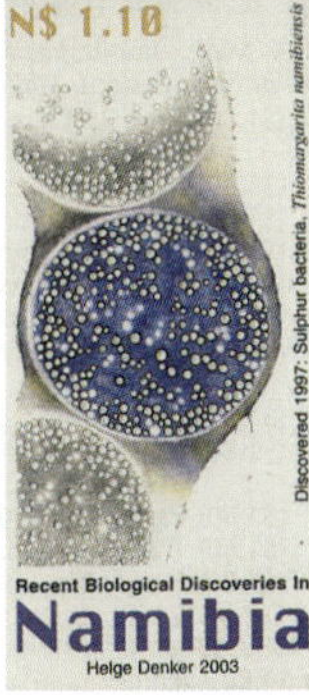

235 Black Cross **236** Sulphur Bacteria

(Des H. Denker. Litho Enschedé)

2002 (1 Dec). *Health care. AIDS Awareness.* T **235** *and similar vert designs. Multicoloured.* P 13½×13.

932	($1.30) Type **235**	35	25
933	$2.45 Blood cell	70	45
934	$2.85 Hand reaching to seated man	75	65
935	$11.50 Three test tubes	3·25	4·00
932/5	*Set of 4*	4·50	4·75

No. 932 was inscribed "Standard Mail" was initially sold for $1.30.

(Des H. Denker. Litho Enschedé)

2003 (22 Feb). *New Discoveries in Namibia.* T **236** *and similar multicoloured designs.* P 14×13½ (*vert*) or 13½×14 (*horiz*).

936	$1.10 Type **236**	30	20
937	$2.45 *Whiteheadia etesionamibensis*	65	45
938	$2.85 *Cunene Flathead (horiz)*	70	55
939	$3.85 Zebra Racer (*horiz*)	85	80
940	$20 Gladiator	4·50	5·50
936/40	*Set of 5*	6·25	6·75

237 Water and Electricity Supply

(Des H. Denker. Litho Enschedé)

2003 (17 Apr). *Rural Development.* T **237** *and similar horiz designs. Multicoloured.* P 13½×14.

941	$1.45 Type **237**	40	30
942	($2.75) Conservancy formation and land use diversification	60	50
943	$4.40 Education and health services	1·25	1·10
944	($11.50) Communication and road infrastructure	3·00	3·75
941/4	*Set of 4*	4·75	5·00

Nos. 942 and 944 were inscribed "Postcard Rate" (942) and "Registered Mail" (944) and were initially sold at $2.75 and $11.50 respectively.

238 Cattle Grazing and People Fishing at an Oshana

(Des H. Denker. Litho Enschedé)

2003 (6 June). *Cuvelai Drainage System.* T **238** *and similar horiz designs. Multicoloured.* P 13½×14.

945	$1.10 Type **238**	30	25
946	$2.85 Omadhiya Lakes	75	60
947	($3.85) Aerial view of Oshanas	1·00	1·50
945/7	*Set of 3*	1·90	2·10

No. 947 was inscribed "Non Standard Mail" and initially sold for $3.85.

239 Statue of Soldier and Obelisk

(Des Anja Denker. Litho Enschedé)

2003 (27 Aug). *National Monuments, Heroes Acre, Windhoek.* T **239** *and similar triangular designs. Multicoloured.* P 13½.

948	($1.45) Type **239**	60	50
	a. Tête bêche pair	1·20	1·20
949	($2.75) Statue of woman	90	75
	a. Tête bêche pair	1·75	1·50
950	($3.85) Stone monument	1·25	1·50
	a. Tête bêche pair	2·50	3·00
948/50	*Set of 3*	2·50	2·50

Nos. 948/50 were each printed as *se-tenant* tête bêche pairs. No. 948 was inscribed "Standard Mail" and sold for $1.45. No. 949 was inscribed "Postcard Rate" and sold for $2.75. No. 950 was inscribed "Non Standard Mail" and sold for $3.85.

240 Namibian Flag **241** Surveying Equipment

(Des J. van Ellinckhuijzen)

2003 (10 Sept). *25th Anniv of the Windhoek Philatelic Society. Sheet 67×57 mm. Litho.* P 13½×14.

MS951	**240** $10 multicoloured	3·75	3·75

(Des J. van Ellinckhuijzen)

2003 (10 Sept). *Centenary of Geological Survey. Sheet 67×57 mm. Litho.* P 13½×14.

MS952	**241** $10 multicoloured	3·75	3·75

(Des H. Denker)

2003 (8 Dec). *Winning Stamp of the Eighth Stamp World Cup. Sheet 140×80 mm. Multicoloured. Litho.* P 13½×13.

MS953	$3.15 As No. 924	2·50	2·50

242 Vervet Monkey **243** Honey Bees on Sickle Bush

(Des A. Lombard. Litho Cartor)

2004 (30 Jan). *Vervet Monkeys.* T **242** *and similar vert designs. Multicoloured.* P 13.

954	$1.60 Type **242**	50	30
955	$3.15 Two Monkeys in tree	95	90
956	$3.40 Adult monkey with offspring	1·00	90
957	($14.25) Monkey chewing twig	4·00	5·00
954/7	*Set of 4*	5·75	6·50
MS958	80×60 mm. $4.85 As. No. 957	1·50	1·60

No. 957 was inscribed "Inland Registered Mail Paid" and was initially sold for $14.25.

(Des Anja Denker. Litho Cartor)

2004 (30 Jan). *Honey Bees.* T **243** *and similar horiz designs. Multicoloured.* P 13 ×13½.

959	($1.60) Type **243**	50	30
960	$2.70 Bee on Daisy	80	75
961	($3.05) Bee on Aloe	85	80
962	$3.15 Bee on Cats Claw	90	85
963	($14.25) Bees on Edging Senecio	4·00	5·00
959/63	*Set of 5*	6·25	7·00
MS964	75×55 mm. $4.85 Bee on Pretty Lady (flower)	1·50	1·60

Nos. 959, 961 and 963 were each inscribed "standard mail" (959), "post card rate" (961) and "inland registered mail paid" (963) and were initially sold for $1.60, $3.05 and $14.25 respectively.

244 Dove

(Des H. Denker. Litho Cartor)

2004 (23 Mar). *Centenary of the War of Anti-Colonial Resistance.* T **244** *and similar horiz design.* P 13.

965	($1.60) Type **244**	55	40
MS966	105×70 mm. $5 As No. 965	1·50	1·60

No. 965 was inscribed "Standard Mail" and sold for $1.60 initially.

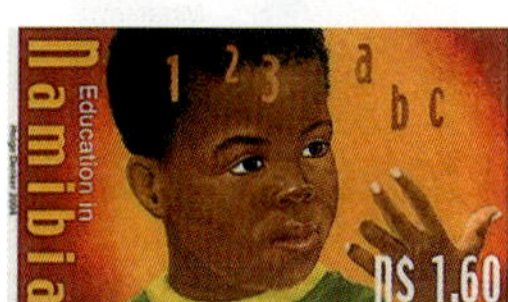

245 Boy and Pre-school Lessons

(Des H. Denker. Litho Enschedé)

2004 (19 Apr). *Education.* T **245** *and similar horiz designs. Multicoloured.* P 13½×14.

967	$1.60 Type **245**	50	30
968	$2.75 Teacher and primary and secondary school lessons	80	75
969	$4.40 Teacher and vocational lessons	1·10	95
970	($12.65) Teacher and life skill lessons	3·50	4·00
967/70	*Set of 4*	5·25	5·50

No. 970 was inscribed "Registered Mail" and sold for $12.65.

246 Loading Fish on Dockside

(Des L. Hess. Litho Enschedé)

2004 (22 June). *Fishing Industry.* T **246** *and similar horiz designs. Multicoloured.* P 13½×14.

971	$1.60 Type **246**	55	30
972	$2.75 Ship at dockside	90	75
973	$4.85 Preparing fish	1·40	2·00
971/3	*Set of 3*	2·50	2·75

247 Joseph Fredericks House

(Des P. Kiddo and A. Vogt. Litho Enschedé)

2004 (7 July). *Historical Buildings of Bethanie.* T **247** *and similar horiz designs. Multicoloured.* P 14×13½.

974	($1.60) Type **247**	50	30
975	($3.05) Schmelen House	80	75
976	($4.40) Rhenish Mission Church	1·00	95
977	($12.65) Stone Church	3·75	4·50
974/7	*Set of 4*	5·50	5·50

No. 974 was inscribed "Standard Mail" and sold for $1.60. No. 975 was inscribed "Postcard Rate" and sold for $3.05. No. 976 was inscribed "Non Standard Mail" and sold for $4.40. No. 977 was inscribed "Registered Mail" and sold for $12.65.

248 Wrestling

(Des H. Denker. Litho Enschedé)

2004 (3 Aug). *Olympic Games, Athens.* T **248** *and similar multicoloured designs.* P 14×13½ (*horiz*) or 13½×14 (*vert*).

978	($1.60) Type **248**	50	30
979	$2.90 Boxing (*vert*)	90	90
980	$3.40 Shooting	1·10	1·25
981	$3.70 Mountain biking (*vert*)	1·25	1·40
978/81	*Set of 4*	3·25	3·50

No. 978 was inscribed "Standard Mail" and sold for $1.60 No. 981 was also issued incorrectly inscribed XVIII Olympiad".

(Des Anja Denker. Litho Enschedé)

2004 (11 Oct). *First Joint Issue of Southern Africa Postal Operators Association Members. Sheet 170×95 mm containing hexagonal designs as* T **233** *of Botswana showing national birds of Association members. Multicoloured.* P. 14.

MS982	$3.40 African Fish Eagle (Namibia); $3.40 Two African Fish Eagles perched (Zimbabwe); $3.40 Peregrine Falcon (Angola); $3.40 Cattle Egret (Botswana); $3.40 Purple-crested Turaco ("Lourie") (Swaziland); $3.40 Stanley ("Blue") Crane (South Africa); $3.40 Bar-tailed Trogon (Malawi) (inscribed "apaloderma vittatum"); $3.40 Two African Fish Eagles in flight (Zambia)	7·25	7·50

The stamp depicting the Bar-tailed Trogon is not inscribed with the country of which the bird is a national symbol.

249 Gemsbok

(Des H. Denker)

2005 (23 Feb). *Centenary of Rotary International.* P 13×13½.

983	**249** $3.70 multicoloured	1·25	1·25

250 President Hifikepunye Pohamba **251** Mariqua ("Marico") Sunbird

(Litho Enschedé)

2005 (21 Mar). *Inauguration of Pres. Hifikepunye Pohamba.* P 13½×14.

984	**250** ($1.70) multicoloured	50	30

No. 984 was inscribed "Standard mail" and initially sold for $1.70.

(Litho Enschedé)

2005 (14 Apr). *Sunbirds.* T **251** *and similar multicoloured designs.* P 13½×14.

985	$2.90 Type **251**	1·00	70
986	$3.40 Dusky sunbird	1·25	80
987	($4.80) White-breasted ("bellied") sunbird	1·50	1·10
988	($15.40) Scarlet-chested sunbird	5·00	6·00
985/8	*Set of 4*	8·00	7·75
MS989	100×70 mm. $10 Amethyst sunbird. P 14×13½	3·50	3·75

No. 987 was inscribed "Non Standard Mail" and No. 988 "Registered Inland Postage Paid" and sold for $4.80 and $15.40 respectively.

Standard Mail
(252)

Standard Mail
(253)

N$2.90
(254)

N$2.90
(255)

Registered
Standard
Mail

N$2.90
(256)

(257)

N$50.00

(258)

2005 (10 June–10 Aug). *Nos. 750/1, 754, 757/8, 762 and 764/6 surch as Types* **252/8**.

990 ($1.70) on 10c. Bushman poison (flower) (T **252**) (10 Aug) ... 60·00 2·00
991 ($1.70) on 20c. Camel's foot (flower) (as T **253**, surch in two lines) (10 Aug) ... 60 30
992 ($1.70) on 20c. Camel's foot (T **252**) (10 Aug) ... 14·00 1·75
993 ($1.70) on 50c. Laughing dove (T **252**) (10 June) ... 75 30
994 ($1.70) on 90c. Yellow-billed hornbill (T **253**) (10 Aug) ... 75 30
995 ($1.70) on $1 Lilac-breasted roller (as T **253**) (10 Aug) ... 75 30
996 $2.90 on 20c. Camel's foot (T **254**) (17 June) ... 20·00 1·40
997 $2.90 on 20c. Camel's foot (T **255**) (17 June) ... 2·50 75
998 $2.90 on 90c. Yellow-billed hornbill (T **256**) (10 Aug) ... 2·50 1·00
999 ($4.80) on ($1.50) Elephant (as T **253**, surch in two lines) (10 Aug) ... 1·75 90
1000 ($4.80) on $4 Buffalo (as T **252**, surch in three lines) (17 June) ... 1·50 1·25
1001 $5.20 on 20c. Camel's foot (as T **255**) (10 Aug) ... 2·50 1·50
1002 $5.20 on 90c. Yellow-billed hornbill (as T **254**) (17 June) ... 2·75 1·50
1003 ($15.40) on $4 Buffalo (T **257**) (10 Aug) ... 3·25 2·50
1004 ($18.50) on $10 Cheetah (as T **257**, surch in two lines) (10 Aug) ... 4·50 4·00
1005 $25 on $5 Black rhinoceros (as T **255**) (10 Aug) ... 9·50 5·00
1006 $50 on $10 Cheetah (T **258**, surch at top right) (10 Aug) ... 14·00 7·00
1007 $50 on $10 Cheetah (as T **258**, surch at bottom right) (10 Aug) ... 60·00 10·00
991/1007 *Set of 18* ... £180 38·00

Nos. 990/5 are inscribed "Standard Mail" and were originally sold for $1.70. Nos. 999/1000 are inscribed "Non Standard Mail" and were originally sold for $4.80. No. 1003 is inscribed "Registered Standard Mail" and was originally sold for $15.40. No. 1004 is inscribed "Registered Non Standard Mail" and was originally sold for $18.50.

261 Nara (*Acanthosicyos horridus*)

262 Vegetables

(Des Anja Denker. Litho)

2005 (22 July). *Plants with Medicinal Value. T* **261** *and similar horiz designs. Multicoloured.* P 14×13½.

1013 ($1.70) Type **261** ... 55 30
1014 $2.90 Devil's claw ... 1·00 70
1015 ($3.10) *Hoodia gordonii* ... 1·10 75
1016 ($4.80) Tsamma ... 1·50 2·00
1013/16 *Set of 4* ... 3·75 3·50

No. 1013 is inscribed "Standard Mail", 1015 "Postcard Rate" and 1016 Non Standard Mail and they were originally sold for $1.70, $3.10 and $4.80 respectively.

(Litho Enschede)

2005 (2 Aug). *Crop Production in Namibia. T* **262** *and similar vert designs. Multicoloured.* P 13½×14.

1017 $2.90 Type **262** ... 90 60
1018 $3.40 Pearl millet ... 1·00 70
1019 ($13.70) Maize ... 4·25 4·75
1017/19 *Set of 3* ... 5·50 5·50

No. 1019 is inscribed "Registered Mail" and was originally sold for $13.70.

263 Cape Gull

(Des Anja Denker. Litho Enschede)

2006 (28 Feb). *Seagulls of Namibia. T* **263** *and similar horiz designs. Multicoloured.* P 14×13½.

1020 $3.10 Type **263** ... 1·25 65
1021 $4 Hartlaub's Gull ... 1·40 85
1022 $5.50 Sabine's Gull ... 1·50 1·10
1023 ($16.20) Grey-headed Gull ... 5·00 6·00
1020/3 *Set of 4* ... 8·25 7·75

No. 1023 is inscribed "Inland Registered Mail Paid" and was originally sold for $16.20.

N$3.10
(264)

N$3.10
(265)

N$3.10

(266)

2006 (13 Apr). *Nos. 933, 960 and 972 surch with T* **264/6**.

1024 $3.10 on $2.45 Blood cell ... 1·25 65
1025 $3.10 on $2.70 Bee on daisy ... 1·25 65
1026 $3.10 on $2.75 Ship at dockside ... 1·25 65
1024/6 *Set of 3* ... 3·50 1·75

267 Risso's Dolphin

(Des Helge Denker. Litho Cartor)

2006 (26 Apr). *Dolphins. T* **267** *and similar horiz designs. Multicoloured.* P 13×13½.

1027 ($1.80) Type **267** ... 55 20
1028 $3.10 Southern right-whale dolphin ... 95 65
1029 $3.70 Benguela dolphin ... 1·00 1·00
1030 $4 Common dolphin ... 1·10 1·25
1031 $5.50 Bottlenose dolphin ... 1·40 1·75
1027/31 *Set of 5* ... 4·50 4·25

No. 1027 is inscribed "Standard Mail" and was originally sold for $1.80.

268 Father with Young Child

(Des Helge Denker. Litho Cartor)

2006 (24 May). *Traditional Role of Men in Namibia. T* **268** *and similar horiz designs. Multicoloured.* P 13×13½.

1032 ($1.80) Type **268** ... 45 45
a. Sheetlet. Nos. 1032/7 ... 2·50
1033 ($1.80) Musicians ... 45 45
1034 ($1.80) Wood carver ... 45 45
1035 ($1.80) Shaman and rock painting ... 45 45
1036 ($1.80) Planter with ox-drawn plough ... 45 45
1037 ($1.80) Hunter with bow and arrow ... 45 45
1038 ($1.80) Leader speaking ... 45 45
a. Sheetlet. Nos. 1038/43 ... 2·50
1039 ($1.80) Blacksmith ... 45 45
1040 ($1.80) Warrior guarding houses ("protector") ... 45 45
1041 ($1.80) Pastoralist and cattle ... 45 45
1042 ($1.80) Trader ... 45 45
1043 ($1.80) Storyteller ... 45 45
1032/43 *Set of 12* ... 5·00 5·00

Nos. 1032/43 are all inscribed "standard mail" and were originally sold for $1.80 each.

Nos. 1032/7 and 1038/43 were each printed together, *se-tenant*, in sheetlets of six stamps.

Postcard Rate

(269)

2006 (20 June). *Nos. 758 and 760 surch with T* **269**.

1044 ($3.30) on $1 Lilac-breasted roller ... 1·50 65
1045 ($3.30) on $1.20 Giraffe ... 1·50 65

Nos. 1044/5 are surch "Postcard Rate" and were sold for $3.30 each.

270 Orange River in the Southern Namib

(Des Helge Denker. Litho Enschedé)

2006 (24 July). *Perennial Rivers of Namibia. T* **270** *and similar multicoloured designs.* P 13½ ($5.50) or 14×13½ (others).

1046 $3.10 Type **270** ... 1·00 50
1047 $5.50 Kunene River, northern Namib (24×58 mm) ... 1·60 1·25
1048 ($19.90) Zambezi River and African fish eagle (90×25 mm) ... 5·50 6·50
1046/8 *Set of 3* ... 7·25 7·50

No. 1048 is inscribed "Registered Non Standard Mail" and sold for $19.90 each.

271 Construction of OMEG Railway Line

272 Centenary Emblem and Cheetah

(Des Anja Denker. Litho Enschedé)

2006 (9 Aug). *Centenary of OMEG Railway Line. T* **271** *and similar horiz designs. Multicoloured.* P 15×14.

1049 $3.10 Type **271** ... 1·00 50
1050 $3.70 Henschel Class NG15 locomotive No. 41 ... 1·25 70
1051 $5.50 Narrow gauge Class Jung tank locomotive No. 9 pulling iron ore train ... 1·60 1·75
1049/51 *Set of 3* ... 3·50 2·75

(Des H. Mupotsa. Litho Austrian State Ptg Wks, Vienna)

2006 (17 Nov). *Centenary of Otjiwarongo.* P 14.

1052 **272** $1.90 multicoloured ... 60 60

No. 1052 was printed in sheetlets of ten with the two rows of five stamps separated by a horizontal central gutter.

273 Bullfrog (*Pyxicephalus adspersus*) and River

(Des Helge Denker. Litho Enschedé)

2007 (15 Feb). *Biodiversity. T* **273** *and similar horiz designs. Multicoloured.* P 14×13½.

1053	5c. Type **273**	10	10
1054	10c. Mesemb (*Namibia cinerea*) and desert landscape	10	10
1055	30c. Solifuge (*Ceroma inerme*) and seashore with shell, plover and seal	10	10
1056	40c. Jewel beetle (*Julodis egho*) and antelopes in desert	15	10
1057	60c. Compass jellyfish (*Chrysaora hysoscella*), turtle and seabirds	20	10
1058	($1.90) Web-footed gecko (*Palmatogecko rangei*) and sand dunes	60	20
1059	$2 Otjikoto tilapia (*Tilapia guinasana*)	70	30
1060	$6 Milkbush (*Euphorbia damarana*) and zebras in desert	1·75	70
1061	($6) African hawk-eagle with prey and landscape with trees	1·75	70
1062	$10 Black-faced impala and sandy river-bed	2·50	1·50
1063	$25 Lichens (*Santessonia* and *Xanthorea* sp.) on seashore rocks	5·50	4·50
1064	$50 Baobab, elephant and antelopes in bushveldt	9·00	9·00
1053/64	*Set of* 12	19·00	15·00

No. 1058 is inscr "Standard Mail" and sold for $1.90. No. 1061 is inscr "Non-Standard Mail" and sold for $6.

274 Caracal, Snake and Zebras, Otjovasandu Wilderness Area ("Conservation")

275 Red-billed Quelea

(Des Helge Denker)

2007 (22 Mar). *Centenary of Etosha National Park. Multicoloured.* P 14×13½.

(a) T **274** *and similar horiz designs. Litho and die-stamped Enschedé.*

1065	($1.90) Type **274**	60	20
1066	$3.40 Lions, elephants and gemsbok, Okaukuejo Waterhole and Resort ("Tourism")	1·10	60
1067	($17.20) Researcher and elephant herd ("Anthrax Research")	5·25	6·25
1065/7	Set of 3	6.25	6.25

(b) T **275** *and similar multicoloured designs. Litho Enschedé.*

MS1068 172×112 mm. ($2.25)×10 Gabar goshawk (29×29 mm); *Acacia tortillis* (umbrella thorn) (49×29 mm); Type **275**; Burchell's zebra; Elephant; Blue Wildebeest; *Salvadora persica* (mustard tree); *Anax tristis* (black emperor dragonfly) (39×40 mm); Springbok (39×40 mm); *Agama aculeata* (ground agama) (39×40 mm) .. 7·25 7·25

No. 1065 is inscr "Standard Mail" and sold for $1.90. No. 1067 is inscr "Inland Registered Mail Paid" and sold for $17.20.

The stamps within **MS**1068 are all inscr "Postcard Rate", and the miniature sheet sold for $22.50. The stamps and margins of **MS**1068 form a composite design showing wildlife at the Salvadora Waterhole.

276 *Anax imperator* (blue emperor)

(Des Anja Denker. Litho Enschedé)

2007 (16 Apr). *Dragonflies of Namibia. T* **276** *and similar horiz designs. Multicoloured. Litho.* P 13×14.

1069	($1.90) Type **276**	60	20
1070	$3.90 *Trithemis kirbyi ardens* (rock dropwing)	1·25	70
1071	$4.40 *Trithemis arteriosa* (red-veined dropwing)	1·50	1·75
1072	($6) *Trithemis stictica* (jaunty dropwing)	1·75	1·75
1069/72	*Set of* 4	4·50	4·00

MS1073 75×54 mm. $6 *Urothemis edwardsii* (blue basker) .. 1·75 1·75

No. 1069 is inscr "Standard Mail" and sold for $1.90. No. 1072 is inscr "Non Standard Mail Paid" and sold for $6.

MACHINE LABELS.

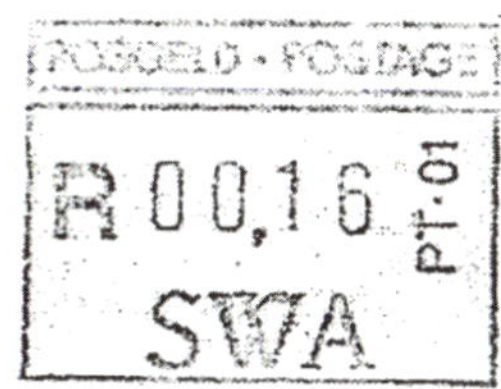

MACHINE LABELS. From 30 March 1988 gummed labels in the above design numbered "PT01", ranging in value from 1c. to 99r.99, were available from a machine located at the Windhoek Post Office. During 1989 three further machines at Windhoek Ausspanplatz (PT02) (6 March), Swakopmund (PT03) (10 March) and Keepmanshoop (PT04) (14 March) were added. Machines PT01/2 were withdrawn on 23 November 1990 and the other two followed four days later. A commemorative design, without code number, was used at the "OTYIMBINGUE 100" philatelic exhibition, Windhoek, between 7 and 9 July 1988.

STAMP BOOKLETS

B **1** Buffalo (Illustration further reduced. Actual size 125×74 mm)

1985 (1 Aug). *Multicoloured cover as Type* B **1**. *Pane attached by selvedge.*

SB1 1r.20 booklet containing pane of 10 12c. (No. 358ba) .. 5·50

1986 (1 Feb). *Multicoloured cover as Type* B **1** *but smaller, 125×70 mm, showing herd of buffaloes. Pane attached by selvedge.*

SB2 1r.20 booklet containing pane of 10 12c. (No. 358ba) .. 5·50

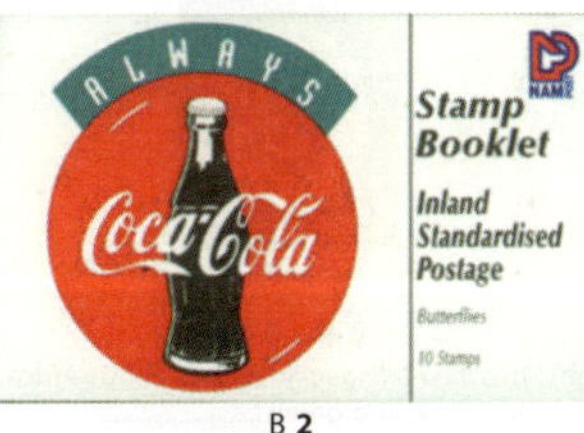

B **2**

1997 (1 Feb). *Multicoloured cover as Type* B **2**. *Stamps attached by selvedge.*

SB3 ($5) booklet containing block of 10 "STANDARDISED MAIL" (No. 648) .. 2·00

SB4 ($5) booklet containing two strips of 5 "STANDARDISED MAIL" (No. 662) .. 3·50

B **3**

1997 (6 May). *Waxbills. Multicoloured cover as Type* B **3**. *Stamps attached by selvedge.*

SB5 $5.50 booklet containing block of 10 (2×5) (No. 710a) .. 2·00

B **4** *Tribulus zeyheri* (Illustration further reduced. Actual size 132×80 mm)

1997 (27 June). *Greetings Stamps. Multicoloured covers as Type* B **4**. *Panes attached by selvedge.*

SB6 ($5) booklet containing pane of 10 (5×2) (No. 723a) (Type B **4**) .. 2·75

SB7 $7 booklet containing pane of 10 (5×2) (No. 728a) (cover showing Helmet Guineafowl and chicks) .. 4·00

B **5** Peach-faced Lovebird

1997 (3 Nov). *Flora and Fauna. Multicoloured covers as Type* B **5**. *Panes attached by selvedge.*

SB8 ($5) booklet containing pane of 10 (5×2) (No. 755ab) (cover showing Peach-faced Lovebird) .. 1·50

SB9 ($12) booklet containing pane of 10 (5×2) (No. 761ab) (cover showing Leopard) .. 2·50

SB10 ($30.55) booklet containing pane of 18 (9×2) (No. 749ab) (cover showing animals and birds) .. 6·25

B **6** Eagle Owl

1998 (1 Apr). *Owls of Namibia. Multicoloured cover as Type* B **6**. *Pane attached by selvedge.*

SB11 $7.35 booklet containing *se-tenant* pane (No. 790a) .. 3·25

B **7** Yoka the Snake

1999 (1 Feb). *Yoka the Snake. Multicoloured cover as Type* B **7**. *Self-adhesive.*

SB12 $16 booklet containing *se-tenant* pane (No. 822a) .. 3·00

POSTAGE DUE STAMPS

PRICES for Nos. D1/39 are for unused horizontal pairs, used horizontal pairs and used singles.

1923 (1 Jan–July). *Optd with T* **1** *and* **2** *alternately.*

(a) Setting I (14 mm between lines of overprint).

(i) On Nos. D5/6 of Transvaal.

		Un pair	Us pair	Us single
D1	5d. black and violet	4·00	50·00	11·00
	a. "Wes" for "West" (R. 8/6, 10/2 left pane)	£170		
	b. "Afrika" without stop (R. 6/1)	£110		
D2	6d. black and red-brown	17·00	50·00	11·00
	a. "Wes" for "West" (R. 10/2)	£350		
	b. "Afrika" without stop (R. 6/1, 7/2)	£190		
	c. 12 mm between lines of opt (R. 1/1)	£225		
	(ii) On Nos. D3/4 and D6 of South Africa (De La Rue printing).			
D3	2d. black and violet	32·00	50·00	10·00
	a. "Wes" for "West" (R. 10/2)	£225	£375	
	b. "Afrika" without stop (R. 6/1, 7/2)	£225		
D4	3d. black and blue	18·00	50·00	10·00
	a. "Wes" for "West" (R. 8/6, 10/2)	£160		
	b. "Africa" without stop (R. 9/1)	£275		
D5	6d. black and slate (20 Apr)	30·00	55·00	13·00
	a. "Wes" for "West" (R. 8/6)	£190		

(iii) On Nos. D9/10, D11 and D14 of South Africa (Pretoria printings).

D6 ½d. black and green (P 14) 6·00 29·00 5·50
 a. Opt inverted £500
 b. Opt double £1100 £1100
 c. "Wes" for "West" (R. 10/2) £100
 d. "Afrika" without stop (R. 6/1, 7/2) £100
D7 1d. black and rose (*roul*) 7·00 30·00 6·00
 a. "Wes" for "West" (R. 10/2) £110 £275
 b. "Afrika" without stop (R. 6/1) £110
 c. Imperf between (horiz pair) £1300
D8 1½d. black and yellow-brown (*roul*) 1·25 14·00 2·75
 a. "Wes" for "West" (R. 8/6, 10/2) 85·00
 b. "Afrika" without stop (R. 6/1) 90·00
D9 2d. black and violet (P 14) (21 June) 3·50 25·00 5·00
 a. "Wes" for "West" (R. 8/6) £100
 b. "Afrika" without stop (R. 6/1) £130

Nos. D1/9 were initially overprinted as separate panes of 60, but some values were later done as double panes of 120.

A variety of Nos. D1, D4/5 and D9 with 15 mm between the lines of overprint occurs on four positions in each pane from some printings.

(b) Setting II (10 mm between lines of overprint).

(i) On No. D5 of Transvaal.

D10 5d. black and violet (20 Apr) 55·00 £170

(ii) On Nos. D3/4 of South Africa (De La Rue printing).

D11 2d. black and violet (20 Apr) 17·00 45·00 9·00
 a. "Afrika" without stop (R. 6/1) £190
D12 3d. black and blue (20 Apr) 7·50 28·00 5·50
 a. "Afrika" without stop (R. 6/1) 95·00

(iii) On No. D9 of South Africa (Pretoria printing). Roul.

D13 1d. black and rose (July) £12000 — £1600

1923 (30 July)–**26**. *Optd as T* 3 *("Zuidwest" in one word without hyphen) and* **4**.

(a) Setting III ("South West" 14 mm long, "Zuidwest" 11 mm long and 14 mm between lines of overprint).

(i) On No. D6 of Transvaal.

D14 6d. black and red-brown 21·00 90·00 20·00

(ii) On Nos. D9 and D11/12 of South Africa (Pretoria printing).

D15 ½d. black and green (P 14) 13·00 32·00 5·50
D16 1d. black and rose (*roul*) 6·50 32·00 5·50
D17 1d. black and rose (P 14) (2.8.23) 21·00 32·00 5·50

(b) Setting IV ("South West" 16 mm long, "Zuidwest" 12 mm long and 14 mm between lines of overprint).

(i) On No. D5 of Transvaal.

D17*a* 5d. black and violet (1.7.24) £500 £1000

(ii) On Nos. D11/12 and D16 of South Africa (Pretoria printing). P 14.

D18 ½d. black and green (1.7.24) 7·50 29·00 5·50
D19 1d. black and rose (1.7.24) 7·50 29·00 5·50
D20 6d. black and slate (1.7.24) 2·25 42·00 9·00
 a. "Africa" without stop (R. 9/5) £120 £275

(c) Setting V (12 mm. between lines of overprint).

(i) On No. D5 of Transvaal.

D21 5d. black and violet (6.8.24) 5·00 50·00 9·00

(ii) On No. D4 of South Africa (De La Rue printing).

D22 3d. black and blue (6.8.24) 16·00 50·00 11·00

(iii) On Nos. D11 and D13 of South Africa (Pretoria printing). P 14.

D23 ½d. black and green (6.8.24) 3·00 29·00 6·50
D24 1½d. black & yellow-brown (6.8.24) 5·00 42·00 7·50

(d) Setting VI (9½ mm between lines of overprint).

(i) On No. D5 of Transvaal.

D25 5d. black and violet (7.9.24) 2·75 20·00 3·50
 a. "Africa" without stop (R. 9/5) 80·00

(ii) On No. D4 of South Africa (De La Rue printing).

D26 3d. black and blue (3.2.26) 8·50 55·00 11·00

(iii) On Nos. D11/16 of South Africa (Pretoria printing). P 14.

D27 ½d. black and green (1.3.26) 11·00 35·00 7·50
D28 1d. black and rose (16.3.25) 2·00 12·00 1·60
 a. "Africa" without stop (R. 9/5 right pane) 85·00
D29 1½d. black & yellow-brown (1.10.26) 4·50 32·00 6·50
 a. "Africa" without stop (R. 9/5 right pane) 90·00
D30 2d. black and violet (7.9.24) 2·50 18·00 3·50
 a. "Africa" without stop (R. 9/5) right pane) 75·00
D31 3d. black and blue (6.5.26) 4·50 19·00 3·75
 a. "Africa" without stop (R. 9/5) right pane) 80·00
D32 6d. black and slate (1.10.26) 11·00 50·00 14·00
 a. "Africa" without stop (R. 9/5 right pane) £150
D27/32 *Set of 6* 32·00 £150 32·00

For Setting VI the overprint was applied to sheets of 120 (2 panes of 60) of the 1d., 3d. and 6d., and to individual panes of 60 for the other values. The two measurements of "South West", as detailed under No. 40, also occur on the postage dues. Nos. D25 and D31/2 show it 16 mm long, No. 27 16½ mm long and the other stamps can be found with either measurement. In addition to the complete panes the 16½ mm long "South West" also occurs on R. 2/4 in the 16 mm left pane for Nos. D28 and D30/2.

Suidwes Afrika. (D 1)

South West Africa. (D 2)

1927 (14 May–27 Sept). *Optd as Types D* **1** *and D* **2**, *alternately, 12 mm between lines of overprint.*

(a) On No. D5 of Transvaal.

D33 5d. black and violet (27 Sept) 19·00 85·00 23·00

(b) On Nos. D13/16 of South Africa (Pretoria printing). P 14.

D34 1½d. black and yellow-brown 1·00 20·00 3·50
D35 2d. black and pale violet (27 Sept) 4·75 16·00 3·25
 a. Black and deep violet 8·00 17·00 3·50
D37 3d. black and blue (27 Sept) 13·00 45·00 11·00
D38 6d. black and slate (27 Sept) 8·00 35·00 8·50

(c) On No. D18 of South Africa (Pretoria printing). P 14.

D39 1d. black and carmine 1·00 11·00 2·25
D33/9 *Set of 6* 42·00 £200 45·00

No. D33 was overprinted in panes of 60 and the remainder as complete sheets of 120.

Examples of all values can be found with very small or very faint stops from various positions in the sheet.

1928–29. *Optd with T* **10**.

(a) On Nos. D15/16 of South Africa.

		Un single	Us single
D40	3d. black and blue	1·50	16·00
	a. Without stop after "A" (R. 3/6)	35·00	
D41	6d. black and slate	6·00	28·00
	a. Without stop after "A" (R. 3/6)	£130	

(b) On Nos. D17/21 of South Africa.

D42	½d. black and green	50	8·00
D43	1d. black and carmine	50	3·25
	a. Without stop after "A" (R. 3/6)	40·00	
D44	2d. black and mauve	50	4·50
	a. Without stop after "A" (R. 3/6)	55·00	
D45	3d. black and blue	2·25	26·00
D46	6d. black and slate	1·50	20·00
	a. Without stop after "A" (R. 3/6)	55·00	£190
D42/6	*Set of 5*	4·75	55·00

D 3

(Litho B.W.)

1931 (23 Feb). *Inscribed bilingually.* W **9** of South Africa. P 12.

D47	D **3** ½d. black and green	1·00	7·50
D48	1d. black and scarlet	1·00	1·25
D49	2d. black and violet	1·00	2·75
D50	3d. black and blue	4·25	13·00
D51	6d. black and slate	13·00	25·00
D47/51	*Set of 5*	18·00	45·00

PRINTER. The following issues have been printed by the South African Government Printer, Pretoria.

1959 (18 May). *Centre typo; frame roto. W* **9** *of South Africa.* P 15×14.

D52	D **4** 1d. black and scarlet	1·50	15·00
D53	2d. black and reddish violet	1·50	15·00
D54	3d. black and blue	1·50	15·00
D52/4	Set of 3	4·00	40·00

1960 (1 Dec). *As Nos. D52 and D54 but W* **102** *of South Africa.*

D55	1d. black and scarlet	1·50	3·00
D56	3d. black and blue	1·50	3·75

1961 (14 Feb). *As Nos. D52 etc, but whole stamp roto, and value in cents.* W **102** *of South Africa.*

D57	1c. black and blue-green	70	3·75
D58	2c. black and scarlet	70	3·75
D59	4c. black and reddish violet	70	6·00
D60	5c. black and light blue	1·00	4·25
D61	6c. black and green	1·25	6·50
D62	10c. black and yellow	4·00	9·00
D57/62	*Set of 6*	7·50	30·00

1972 (22 Mar). W **127** (sideways tête-bêche). Phosphorised chalk-surfaced paper. P 14×13½.

D63	D **5** 1c. emerald	75	5·00
D64	8c. ultramarine	3·00	8·50

The use of Postage Due stamps ceased in April 1975.

OFFICIAL STAMPS

OFFICIAL South West Africa. (O 1)

OFFISIEEL Suidwes Afrika. (O 2)

1926 (Dec). *Nos. 30, 31, 6 and 32 of South Africa optd with Type O* **1** *on English stamp and O* **2** *on Afrikaans stamp alternately.*

		Un pair	Us pair	Us single
O1	½d. black and green	75·00	£180	30·00
O2	1d. black and carmine	75·00	£180	30·00
O3	2d. dull purple	£170	£300	45·00
O4	6d. green and orange	95·00	£180	30·00
O1/4	*Set of 4*	£375	£750	£120

OFFICIAL S.W.A. (O 3)

OFFISIEEL S.W.A. (O 4)

1929 (May). *Nos. 30, 31, 32 and 34 of South Africa optd with Type O* **3** *on English stamp and O* **4** *on Afrikaans stamp.*

O5	½d. black and green	1·00	15·00	2·75
O6	1d. black and carmine	1·00	15·00	2·75
	w. Wmk inverted	£275		
O7	2d. grey and purple	1·50	20·00	3·50
	a. Pair, one stamp without stop after "OFFICIAL"	6·00	45·00	
	b. Pair, one stamp without stop after "OFFISIEEL"	6·00	45·00	
	c. Pair, comprising a and b	16·00	85·00	
O8	6d. green and orange	2·00	20·00	3·75
O5/8	*Set of 4*	5·00	65·00	11·50

Types O **3** and O **4** are normally spaced 17 mm between lines on all except the 2d. value, which is spaced 13 mm.

Except on No. O7, the words "OFFICIAL" or "OFFISIEEL" normally have no stops after them.

OFFICIAL S.W.A. (O 5)

OFFISIEEL S.W.A. (O 6)

OFFICIAL. S.W.A. (O 7)

OFFISIEEL. S.W.A. (O 8)

1929 (Aug). *Nos. 30, 31 and 32 of South Africa optd with Types O* **5** *and O* **6**, *and No. 34 with Types O* **7** *and O* **8**, *languages to correspond.*

O9	½d. black and green	75	15·00	2·75
O10	1d. black and carmine	1·00	15·00	2·75
O11	2d. grey and purple	1·00	15·00	3·25
	a. Pair, one stamp without stop after "OFFICIAL"	3·75	40·00	
	b. Pair, one stamp without stop after "OFFISIEEL"	3·75	40·00	
	c. Pair, comprising a and b	18·00	90·00	
O12	6d. green and orange	2·50	27·00	6·50
O9/12	*Set of 4*	4·75	65·00	13·50

Examples of Nos. O1/12 are known showing forged Windhoek postmarks dated "30 SEP 24" or "20 MAR 31".

OFFICIAL (O 9)

OFFISIEEL (O 10)

1931. *English stamp optd with Type O* **9** *and Afrikaans stamp with Type O* **10** *in red.*

O13	**12**	½d. black and emerald	11·00	20·00	3·50
O14	**13**	1d. indigo and scarlet	1·00	18·00	3·50
O15	**14**	2d. blue and brown	2·25	10·00	2·25
O16	**17**	6d. blue and brown	3·75	14·00	3·25
O13/16		*Set of 4*	16·00	55·00	11·50

OFFICIAL (O 11)

OFFISIEEL (O 12)

1938 (1 July). *English stamp optd with Type O* **11** *and Afrikaans with Type O* **12** *in red.*

O17	**27**	1½d. purple-brown	26·00	45·00	6·00

OFFICIAL (O 13)

OFFISIEEL (O 14)

1945–50. *English stamp optd with Type O* **13**, *and Afrikaans stamp with Type O* **14** *in red.*

O18	**12**	½d. black and emerald	13·00	29·00	5·00
O19	**13**	1d. indigo and scarlet (1950)	9·00	17·00	3·25
		a. Opt double	£475		
O20	**27**	1½d. purple-brown	35·00	48·00	6·50
O21	**14**	2d. blue and brown (1947?)	£600	£750	£100
O22	**17**	6d. blue and brown	22·00	55·00	7·00
O18/20, O22		*Set of 4*	70·00	£130	20·00

OFFICIAL (O 15)

OFFISIEEL (O 16)

1951 (16 Nov)–**52**. *English stamp optd with Type O* **15** *and Afrikaans stamp with Type O* **16**, *in red.*

O23	**12**	½d. black and emerald (1952)	16·00	23·00	4·50
		a. Opts transposed	—	£2000	
O24	**13**	1d. indigo and scarlet	5·00	17·00	1·75
		a. Opts transposed	90·00	£180	
O25	**27**	1½d. purple-brown	24·00	28·00	5·00
		a. Opts transposed	75·00	95·00	
O26	**14**	2d. blue and brown	2·50	20·00	3·50
		a. Opts transposed	60·00	£180	
O27	**17**	6d. blue and brown	2·75	45·00	7·50
		a. Opts transposed	25·00	£140	
O23/7		*Set of 5*	45·00	£120	20·00

The above errors refer to stamps with the English overprint on Afrikaans stamp and *vice versa*.

The use of official stamps ceased in January 1955.

South Africa

South Africa as a nation, rather than a geographical term, came into being with the creation of the Union of South Africa on 31 May 1910.

The development, both political and philatelic, of the area is very complex and the method adopted by the catalogue is to first list, in alphabetical order, the various colonies and republics which formed this federation, followed by stamps for the Union of South Africa.

The section is divided as follows:

I. CAPE OF GOOD HOPE. British Kaffraria. Mafeking Siege Stamps. Vryburg
II. GRIQUALAND WEST
III. NATAL
IV. NEW REPUBLIC
V. ORANGE FREE STATE. Orange River Colony
VI. TRANSVAAL. Pietersburg. Local British Occupation Issues
VII. ZULULAND
VIII. BRITISH ARMY FIELD OFFICES DURING SOUTH AFRICAN WAR
IX. UNION OF SOUTH AFRICA
X. REPUBLIC OF SOUTH AFRICA
XI. BOPHUTHATSWANA
XII. CISKEI
XIII. TRANSKEI
XIV. VENDA

I. CAPE OF GOOD HOPE

PRICES FOR STAMPS ON COVER

Nos. 1/4	from × 4
Nos. 5/14	from × 3
Nos. 18/21	from × 5
No. 22	—
Nos. 23/6	from × 5
Nos. 27/31	from × 8
Nos. 32/3	from × 10
No. 34	from × 25
No. 35	from × 20
No. 36	from × 10
Nos. 37/8	from × 25
Nos. 39/45	from × 10
Nos. 46/7	from × 12
Nos. 48/54	from × 10
Nos. 55/6	from × 25
No. 57	from × 50
Nos. 58/69	from × 10
Nos. 70/8	from × 6

PRICES. Our prices for early Cape of Good Hope are for stamps in very fine condition. Exceptional copies are worth more, poorer copies considerably less.

1 Hope

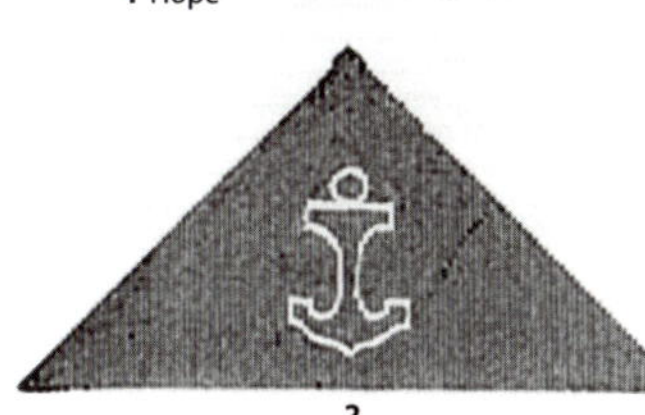

2

(Des Charles Bell, Surveyor-General. Eng W. Humphrys. Recess P.B.)

1853 (1 Sept). W **2**. Imperf.

(a) Paper deeply blued.

1	1	1d. pale brick-red	£3750	£300
		a. Deep brick-red	£5000	£325
		b. Wmk sideways	†	£400
2		4d. deep blue	£2250	£160
		a. Wmk sideways	£3000	£250

Plate proofs of the 4d. in a shade similar to the issued stamp exist on ungummed watermarked paper. (Price, £250) The blueing on the reverse of these proofs is uneven giving a blotchy appearance.

(b) Paper slightly blued (blueing not pronounced at back).

3	1	1d. brick-red	£3000	£200
		a. Brown-red	£3250	£225
		b. Wmk sideways	†	£325
4		4d. deep blue	£1300	£110
		a. Blue	£1400	£150
		b. Wmk sideways	†	£275

PERKINS BACON "CANCELLED". For notes on these handstamps showing "CANCELLED" between horizontal bars forming an oval, see Catalogue Introduction.

1855–63. W **2**.

(a) Imperf.

5	1	1d. brick-red/*cream toned paper* (1857)	£5000	£900
		a. Rose (1858) (H/S "CANCELLED" in oval £17000)	£450	£200
		ab. Wmk sideways	—	£425
		b. Deep rose-red	£650	£250
		ba. Wmk sideways	—	£425
6		4d. deep blue/*white paper* (1855)	£650	50·00
		a. Blue (H/S "CANCELLED" in oval £17000)	£475	50·00
		b. Bisected (on cover)	†	£35000
		c. Wmk sideways	†	£170
7		6d. pale rose-lilac/*white paper* (18.2.58) (H/S "CANCELLED" in oval £13000)	£800	£200
		a. Wmk sideways	†	£900
		b. Deep rose-lilac/white paper	£1700	£300
		c. Slate-lilac/blued paper (1862)	£4250	£450
		d. Slate-purple/blued paper (1863)	£3500	£1000
		e. Bisected (on cover)	†	—
8		1s. bright yellow-green/*white paper* (18.2.58) (H/S "CANCELLED" in oval £17000)	£2750	£180
		a. Wmk sideways	†	£1000
		b. Deep dark green (1859)	£275	£500

The method adopted for producing the plate of the 4d., 6d and 1s. stamps involved the use of two dies, so that there are two types of each of these values differing slightly in detail, but produced in equal numbers.

The 1d. value in dull rose on ungummed watermarked paper with the watermark sideways is a plate proof. (*Price* £250).

The 4d. is known bisected in 1858 and used with two other 4d. values to pay the inland registered fee. The 6d. is known bisected and used with 1d. for 4d. rate.

The paper of No. 5 is similar to that of Nos. 1/4, but is without the blueing. It is much thicker than the white paper used for later printings of the 1d. The evolution of the paper on these Cape of Good Hope stamps is similar to that on the line-engraved issues of Great Britain. Examples of the 6d. slate-lilac apparently on white paper have had the blueing washed out.

The 4d. value is known printed in black on white watermarked paper. Twelve authenticated copies have been recorded, the majority of which show cancellations or, at least, some indication that they have been used.

It was, at one time, believed that these stamps came from a small supply printed. in black to mark the death of the Prince Consort, but references to examples can be found in the philatelic press before news of this event reached Cape Town.

It is now thought that these stamps represent proof sheets, possibly pressed into service during a shortage of stamps in 1861.

There is, however, no official confirmation of this theory. (*Price £35000 un, £30000 with obliteration*).

(b) Unofficially rouletted.

9	1	1d. brick-red	†	£3000
10		4d. blue	†	£2250
11		6d. rose-lilac	†	£1500
12		1s. bright yellow-green	†	£3250
		a. Deep dark green	†	£3500

These rouletted stamps are best collected on cover.

3 Hope

(Local provisional (so-called "wood-block") issue. Engraved on steel by C. J. Roberts. Printed from stereotyped plates by Saul Solomon & Co, Cape Town)

1861 (Feb–Apr). *Laid paper.* Imperf.

13	3	1d. vermilion (27 February)	£14000	£2250
		a. Carmine (7 March)	£24000	£3000
		b. Brick-red (10 April)	£35000	£4250
		c. Error. Pale milky blue	£150000	£28000
		ca. Pale bright blue	—	£30000
14		4d. pale milky blue (23 February)	£20000	£1700
		aa. Retouch or repair to rt-hand corner	—	£6500
		a. Pale grey-blue (March?)	£21000	£1700
		b. Pale bright blue (March?)	£21000	£2000
		ba. Retouch or repair to rt-hand corner	—	£6500
		c. Deep bright blue (12 April)	£95000	£4500
		d. Blue	£25000	£3000
		e. Error. Vermilion	£150000	£40000
		ea. Carmine	—	£95000
		f. Sideways *tête-bêche* (pair)	†	£120000

Nos. 13/14 were each issued in *tête-bêche* pairs normally joined at edges bearing the same inscription ("POSTAGE" against "POSTAGE", etc). No. 14f, of which only one used example is known, comes from the first printing and shows the right-hand stamp misplaced so that "FOUR PENCE" adjoins "POSTAGE".

Nos. 13c/ca and 14e/ea were caused by the inclusion of incorrect clichés in the plates of the 1d. or 4d. values.

Both values were officially reprinted in March 1883, on wove paper. The 1d. is in deep red, and the 4d. in a deeper blue than that of the deepest shade of the issued stamp.

Specimens of the reprints have done postal duty, but their use thus was not intended. There are no reprints of the errors or of the retouched 4d.

Further reprints were made privately but with official permission, in 1940/41, in colours much deeper than those of any of the original printings, and on thick carton paper.

Examples of the 4d. are known unofficially rouletted.

Early in 1863, Perkins Bacon Ltd handed over the four plates used for printing the triangular Cape of Good Hope stamps to De La Rue & Co, Ltd, who made all the subsequent printings.

(Printed from the P.B. plates by D.L.R.)

1863–64. Imperf.

*(a) W **2**.*

18	1	1d. deep carmine-red (1864)	£170	£225
		a. Wmk sideways	£300	£300
		b. Deep brown-red	£375	£250
		ba. Wmk sideways	£500	£300
		c. Brownish red	£375	£225
		ca. Wmk sideways	£500	£275
19		4d. deep blue (1864)	£170	55·00
		a. Blue	£180	65·00
		b. Slate-blue	£2000	£500
		c. Steel-blue	£2000	£250
		d. Wmk sideways	£500	£180
20		6d. bright mauve (1864)	£225	£450
		a. Wmk sideways	†	£1200
21		1s. bright emerald-green	£400	£450
		a. Pale emerald-green	£1000	

(b) Wmk Crown CC (sideways).

22	1	1d. deep carmine-red	£22000	

No. 22 was a trial printing, and is only known unused.

Our prices for the 4d. blue are for stamps which are blue by comparison with the other listed shades. An exceptionally pale shade is recognised by specialists and is rare.

With the exception of the 4d., these stamps may be easily distinguished from those printed by Perkins Bacon by their colours, which are quite distinct.

The De La Rue stamps of all values are less clearly printed, the figure of Hope and the lettering of the inscriptions standing out less boldly, while the fine lines of the background appear blurred and broken when examined under a glass. The background as a whole often shows irregularity in the apparent depth of colour, due to wear of the plates.

For note regarding the two dies of the 4d., 6d., and 1s. values, see after No. 8.

All the triangular stamps were demonetised as from 1 October 1900.

4 "Hope" seated, with vine and ram. (With outer frame-line)

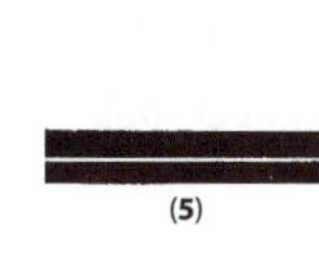

(5)

(Des Charles Bell. Die engraved on steel and stamps typo by D.L.R.)

1864–77. *With outer frame-line surrounding the design.* Wmk Crown CC. P 14.

23	4	1d. carmine-red (5.65)	85·00	26·00
		a. Rose-red	80·00	25·00
		w. Wmk inverted	£275	£130
24		4d. pale blue (8.65)	£100	3·50
		a. Blue	£100	3·50
		b. Ultramarine	£250	55·00
		c. Deep blue (1872)	£150	3·75
		w. Wmk inverted	£400	£150
25		6d. pale lilac (before 21.3.64)	£110	22·00
		a. Deep lilac	£200	7·00
		b. Violet (to bright) (1877)	£130	1·50
		w. Wmk inverted	†	£275
26		1s. deep green (1.64)	£500	18·00
		a. Green	£110	3·75
		ax. Wmk reversed		
		b. Blue-green	£120	4·75
		w. Wmk inverted	£600	£150

The 1d. rose-red, 6d. lilac, and 1s. blue-green are known imperf, probably from proof sheets.

The 1d. and 4d. stamps of this issue may be found with side and/or top outer frame-lines missing, due to wear of the plates.

See also Nos. 44 and 52/3.

(Surch by Saul Solomon & Co, Cape Town)

1868 (17 Nov). *No. 25a surch with T* **5**.

27	4	4d. on 6d. deep lilac (R.)	£250	16·00
		a. "Peuce" for "Pence"	£1800	£700
		b. "Fonr" for "Four"	—	£700
		w. Wmk inverted	—	£275

Specimens may also be found with bars omitted or at the top of the stamp, due to misplacement of the sheet.

The space between the words and bars varies from 12½ to 16 mm, stamps with spacing 15½ and 16 mm being rare. There were two printings, one of 120,000 in November 1868 and another of 1,000,000 in December. Stamps showing widest spacings are probably from the earlier printing.

6 (No outer frame-line)

(Die re-engraved. Typo D.L.R.)

1871–76. *Outer frame-line removed.* Wmk Crown CC. P 14.

28	6	½d. grey-black (*shades*) (12.75)	20·00	8·50
		w. Wmk inverted	—	£100
29		1d. carmine-red (*shades*) (2.72)	35·00	60
		w. Wmk inverted	£275	£120
30		4d. dull blue (*shades*) (12.76)	£100	75
		b. Ultramarine	£200	50·00
		w. Wmk inverted	£325	90·00
31		5s. yellow-orange (25.8.71)	£350	16·00
		w. Wmk inverted	†	£300

The ½d., 1d. and 5s. are known imperf, probably from proof sheets.

See also Nos. 36, 39, 40/3, 48/51, 54, 61/2 and 64/8.

ONE PENNY (7)

THREE PENCE (8)

HAVE YOU READ THE NOTES AT THE BEGINNING OF THIS CATALOGUE?
These often provide answers to the enquiries we receive

(Surch by Saul Solomon & Co, Cape Town)

1874–76. *Nos. 25a and 26a surch with T* **7**.

32	**4**	1d. on 6d. deep lilac (R.) (1.9.74)	£500	95·00
		a. "E" of "PENNY" omitted	—	£1000
33		1d. on 1s. green (11.76)	85·00	55·00

These provisionals are found with the bar only, either across the centre of the stamp or at top, with value only; or with value and bar close together, either at top or foot. Such varieties are due to misplacement of sheets during surcharging.

1879 (1 Nov). *No. 30 surch with T* **8**.

34	**6**	3d. on 4d. blue (R.)	£100	2·00
		a. "PENCB" for "PENCE"	£1700	£225
		b. "THE.EE" for "THREE"	£2000	£275
		c. Surch double	£9000	£3250
		d. Variety b. double		

The double surcharge must also have existed showing variety a. but only variety b. is known.

There are numerous minor varieties, including letters broken or out of alignment, due to defective printing and use of poor type.

The spacing between the bar and the words varies from 16½ to 18 mm.

THREEPENCE (9) 3 (10) 3 (11)

(Surch by D.L.R.)

1880 (Feb). *Special printing of the 4d. in new colour, surch, with T* **9**. Wmk Crown CC.

35	**6**	3d. on 4d. pale dull rose	70·00	2·00
		w. Wmk inverted	—	£200

A minor constant variety exists with foot of "P" in "PENCE" broken off, making the letter appear shorter.

1880 (1 July). Wmk Crown CC. P 14.

36	**6**	3d. pale dull rose	£190	26·00
		w. Wmk inverted	—	£300

(Surch by Saul Solomon & Co, Cape Town)

1880 (Aug). *No. 36 surch.*

37	**10**	"3" on 3d. pale dull rose	75·00	1·75
		a. Surch inverted	£900	40·00
		b. Vert pair. Nos. 37/8	£1000	£400
		w. Wmk inverted	—	£150
38	**11**	"3" on 3d. pale dull rose	£190	7·50
		a. Surch inverted	£8000	£950
		w. Wmk inverted	—	£400

The "3" (T **10**) is sometimes found broken. Vert pairs are known showing the two types of surcharge *se-tenant*, and vertical strips of three exist, the top stamp having surcharge T **10**, the middle stamp being without surcharge, and the lower stamp having surcharge T **11** (*Price for strip of 3 £4250 un.*).

1881 (Jan). Wmk Crown CC. P 14.

39	**6**	3d. pale claret	£140	3·00
		a. Deep claret	£110	2·75
		w. Wmk inverted		

This was a definite colour change made at the request of the Postmaster-General owing to the similarity between the colours of the 1d. stamp and the 3d. in pale dull rose. Imperf copies are probably from proof sheets.

Proofs of this value were printed in brown, on unwatermarked wove paper and imperf, but the colour was rejected as unsuitable.

1882 (July)–**83**. Wmk Crown CA. P 14.

40	**6**	½d. black (1.9.82)	26·00	2·50
		a. Grey-black	23·00	2·50
		w. Wmk inverted	—	£140
41		1d. rose-red	60·00	1·75
		a. Deep rose-red	55·00	1·75
		w. Wmk inverted	—	£170
42		2d. pale bistre (1.9.82)	95·00	75
		a. Deep bistre	£100	75
		w. Wmk inverted	—	£170
43		3d. pale claret	7·50	1·25
		a. Deep claret	12·00	75
		aw. Wmk inverted	—	£100
44	**4**	6d. mauve (to bright) (8.82)	90·00	80
45	**6**	5s. orange (8.83)	£800	£225

Imperf pairs of the ½d., 1d. and 2d. are known, probably from proof sheets.

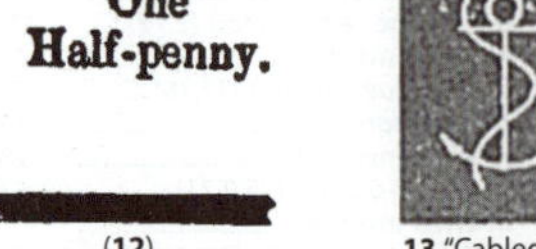

(12) **13** "Cabled Anchor"

(Surch by Saul Solomon & Co, Cape Town)

1882 (July). *Nos. 39a and 43a surch with T* **12**.

46	**6**	½d. on 3d. deep claret (Wmk CC)	£3250	£130
		a. Hyphen omitted	—	£3250
47		½d. on 3d. deep claret (Wmk CA)	30·00	4·00
		a. "p" in "penny" omitted	£2000	£700
		b. "y" in "penny" omitted	£1000	£600
		c. Hyphen omitted	£650	£350
		w. Wmk inverted	—	£300

Varieties also exist with broken and defective letters, and with the obliterating bar omitted or at the top of the stamp.

1884–90. W **13**. P 14.

48	**6**	½d. black (1.86)	5·50	10
		a. Grey-black	5·50	10
		w. Wmk inverted	—	£375
49		1d. rose-red (12.85)	6·50	10
		a. Carmine-red	6·50	10
		w. Wmk inverted	—	£170
50		2d. pale bistre (12.84)	26·00	1·25
		a. Deep bistre	7·50	10
		w. Wmk inverted	—	£130
51		4d. blue (6.90)	13·00	50
		a. Deep blue	13·00	50
52	**4**	6d. reddish purple (12.84)	60·00	1·60
		a. Purple (shades)	12·00	20
		b. Bright mauve	11·00	50
		w. Wmk inverted	—	£300
53		1s. green (12.85)	£140	5·00
		a. Blue-green (1889)	95·00	50
		w. Wmk inverted	—	£375
54	**6**	5s. orange (7.87)	95·00	6·00
48/54 *Set of 7*			£200	6·75

All the above stamps are known in imperf pairs, probably from proof sheets.

For later shade and colour changes, etc., see Nos. 61, etc.

2½d (14)

15

ONE PENNY. (16)

(Surch by D.L.R.)

1891 (Mar). *Special printing of the 3d. in new colour, surch with T* **14**.

55	**6**	2½d. on 3d. pale magenta	8·00	1·75
		a. Deep magenta	4·25	20
		b. "1" with horiz serif	55·00	32·00

No. 55b occurs on two stamps (Nos. 8 and 49) of the pane of 60.

Two types of "d" are found in the surcharge, one with square end to serif at top, and the other with pointed serif.

1892 (June). W **13**. P 14.

56	**15**	2½d. sage-green	13·00	10
		a. Olive-green	14·00	55

See also No. 63.

(Surch by W. A. Richards & Sons, Cape Town)

1893 (Mar). *Nos. 50/a surch with T* **16**.

57	**6**	1d. on 2d. pale bistre	6·00	1·75
		a. Deep bistre	3·50	50
		b. No stop after "PENNY"	55·00	13·00
		c. Surch double	—	£425

No. 57b occurs on stamp No. 42 of the upper left-hand pane, and on No. 6 of the lower right-hand pane.

Minor varieties exist showing broken letters and letters out of alignment or widely spaced. Also with obliterating bar omitted, due to misplacement of the sheet during surcharging.

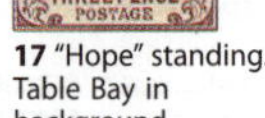

17 "Hope" standing. Table Bay in background

18 Table Mountain and Bay with Arms of the Colony

(Des Mr. Mountford. Typo D.L.R.)

1893 (Oct)–**1902**. W **13**. P 14.

58	**17**	½d. green (9.98)	3·50	10
59		1d. rose-red	4·50	1·75
		a. Carmine	1·25	10
		aw. Wmk inverted	†	£120
60		3d. magenta (3.02)	4·00	1·75

The 1d. is known in imperf pairs, probably from proof sheets.

1893–98. *New colours, etc.* W **13**. P 14.

61	**6**	½d. yellow-green (12.96)	1·50	50
		a. Green	2·75	50
62		2d. chocolate-brown (3.97)	2·00	1·00
63	**15**	2½d. pale ultramarine (3.96)	6·00	15
		a. Ultramarine	6·00	10
64	**6**	3d. bright magenta (9.98)	10·00	1·00
65		4d. sage-green (3.97)	5·00	2·50
66		1s. blue-green (12.93)	65·00	5·00
		a. Deep blue-green	80·00	9·50
67		1s. yellow-ochre (5.96)	11·00	1·75
68		5s. brown-orange (6.96)	75·00	3·50
61/8 *Set of 8*			£160	13·50

(Des E. Sturman. Typo D.L.R.)

1900 (Jan). W **13**. P 14.

69	**18**	1d. carmine	3·50	10
		w. Wmk inverted	—	£120

19

20

21

22 23

24

25

26

27

(Typo D.L.R.)

1902 (Dec)–**04**. W **13**. P 14.

70	**19**	½d. green	2·25	10
71	**20**	1d. carmine	2·00	10
		w. Wmk inverted		
		y. Wmk inverted and reversed		
72	**21**	2d. brown (10.04)	13·00	80
		w. Wmk inverted		
73	**22**	2½d. ultramarine (3.04)	2·75	6·50
74	**23**	3d. magenta (4.03)	8·00	1·00
75	**24**	4d. olive-green (2.03)	11·00	65
76	**25**	6d. bright mauve (3.03)	18·00	30
77	**26**	1s. yellow-ochre	14·00	80
78	**27**	5s. brown-orange (2.03)	90·00	19·00
70/8 *Set of 9*			£150	26·00

All values exist in imperf pairs, from proof sheets.

The ½d. exists from coils constructed from normal sheets for use in stamp machines introduced in 1911.

STAMP BOOKLET

1905 (Dec). *Black on red cover. Stapled.*

SB1	2s.7d. booklet containing thirty 1d. (No. 71) in blocks of 6	£2000

OFFICIAL STAMPS

The following stamps, punctured with a double triangle device, were used by the Stationery and Printed Forms Branch of the Cape of Good Hope Colonial Secretary's Department between 1904 and 1906. Later South Africa issues may have been similarly treated, but this has not been confirmed.

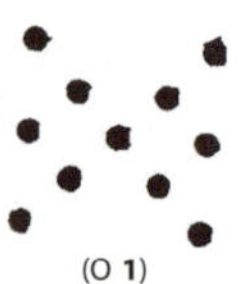

(O 1)

1904. *Various issues punctured as Type* O **1**.

		(a) Nos. 50 and 52a.	
O1	**6**	2d. pale bistre	18·00
O2	**4**	6d. purple	22·00
		(b) Nos. 58 and 60.	
O3	**17**	½d. green	24·00
O4		3d. magenta	18·00
		(c) Nos. 62 and 64/5.	
O5	**6**	2d. chocolate-brown	18·00
O6		3d. bright magenta	24·00
O7		4d. sage-green	24·00
		(d) No. 69.	
O8	**18**	1d. carmine	18·00
		(e) Nos. 70/2 and 74/8.	
O9	**19**	½d. green	24·00
O10	**20**	1d. carmine	14·00
O11	**21**	2d. brown	22·00
O12	**23**	3d. magenta	17·00
O13	**24**	4d. olive-green	18·00
O14	**25**	6d. bright mauve	19·00
O15	**26**	1s. yellow-ochre	24·00
O16	**27**	5s. brown-orange	60·00

Nos. O1/16 are only known used.

Cape of Good Hope became a province of the Union of South Africa on 31 May 1910.

BRITISH KAFFRARIA

The history of the Cape eastern frontier was punctuated by a series of armed conflicts with the native population, known as the Kaffir Wars. After a particularly violent outbreak in 1846 the Governor, Sir Harry Smith, advanced the line of the Cape frontier to the Keikama and Tyumie Rivers. In the area between the new frontier and the Kei River a buffer state, British Kaffraria, was established on 17 December 1847. This area was not annexed to the Cape, but was administered as a separate Crown dependency by the Governor of Cape Colony in his capacity as High Commissioner for South Africa.

The territory, with its administration based on King William's Town, used the stamps of the Cape of Good Hope from 1853 onwards, the mail being sent via Port Elizabeth or overland from the Cape. Covers from British Kaffraria franked with the triangular issues are rare.

The first postal marking known from British Kaffraria is the 1849 type octagonal numeral No 47 from Port Beaufort. Oval post-marks of the 1853 type were used at Alice, Aliwal North, Bedford, Fort Beaufort, King William's Town and Queenstown. In 1864 numeral cancellations were issued to all post offices within the Cape system and it is known that the following numbers were initially assigned to post towns in Kaffraria: 4 (King William's Town), 7 (Bedford), 11 (Queenstown), 29 (East London), 32 (Fort Beaufort), 38 (Aliwal North) and 104 (Cathcart).

It is believed that post offices may have also existed at Adelaide, Barkly East, Sterkstoom and Stutterheim, but, to date, no examples of handstamps or cancellations are known from them during the British Kaffraria period.

Following the decimation by famine of the Xhosa tribes in 1857 British Kaffraria was annexed to Cape Colony in 1865. The area eventually formed the basis of the Ciskei independent "homeland".

MAFEKING SIEGE STAMPS

PRICES FOR STAMPS ON COVER	
Nos. 1/16	from × 12
Nos. 17/18	from × 25
Nos. 19/20	from × 15
Nos. 21/2	from × 12

23 MARCH to 17 MAY 1900

There are numerous forgeries of the Mafeking overprints, many of which were brought home by soldiers returning from the Boer War.

MAFEKING,
3d.
BESIEGED.
(1)

MAFEKING
3d.
BESIEGED.
(2)

(Surcharged by Townsend & Co, Mafeking)

1900 (23 Mar–28 Apr). *Various stamps surch as T* **1** *and* **2**.

(a) Cape of Good Hope stamps surch as T **1** *(23 Mar).*

No.	Type	Description	Unused	Used
1	6	1d. on ½d. green	£200	65·00
2	17	1d. on ½d. green (24.3)	£250	75·00
3		3d. on 1d. carmine	£225	50·00
4	6	6d. on 3d. magenta (24.3)	£35000	£250
5		1s. on 4d. sage-green (24.3)	£6500	£350

A variety in the setting of each value exists without comma after "MAFEKING".

(b) Nos. 59 and 61/3 of Bechuanaland Protectorate (previously optd on Great Britain) surch as T **1**.

No.	Type	Description	Unused	Used
6		1d. on ½d. vermilion (28.3)	£200	60·00
		a. Surch inverted	†	£5500
		b. Vert pair, surch *tête-bêche*	†	£30000
7		3d. on 1d. lilac (4.4)	£850	90·00
		a. Surch double	†	£25000
8		6d. on 2d. green and carmine (6.4)	£1900	75·00
9		6d. on 3d. purple/*yellow* (30.3)	£5500	£275
		a. Surch inverted	†	£30000
		b. Surch double		

(c) Nos. 12 and 35 of British Bechuanaland (4d. previously optd on Great Britain) surch as T **1**.

No.	Type	Description	Unused	Used
10		6d. on 3d. lilac and black (27.3)	£375	65·00
11		1s. on 4d. green and purple-brown (29.3)	£1400	80·00
		a. Surch double (both Type **1**)	†	£23000
		ab. Surch double (Type **1** and Type **2**)	£10000	£6000
		b. Surch treble	†	£23000
		c. Surch double, one inverted	†	£23000

(d) Nos. 61/2 and 65 of Bechuanaland Protectorate (previously optd on Great Britain) surch as T **2**.

No.	Type	Description	Unused	Used
12		3d. on 1d. lilac (1 Apr)	£900	75·00
		a. Surch double	†	£9000
13		6d. on 2d. green and carmine (25 Apr)	£1100	75·00
14		1s. on 6d. purple/*rose-red* (12 Apr)	£5500	90·00

(e) Nos. 36/7 of British Bechuanaland (previously optd on Great Britain) surch as T **2**.

No.	Type	Description	Unused	Used
15		1s. on 6d. purple/*rose-red* (28 Apr)	£20000	£700
16		2s. on 1s. green (13 Apr)	£12000	£425

On the stamps overprinted "BECHUANALAND PROTECTORATE" and "BRITISH BECHUANALAND" the local surcharge is so adjusted as not to overlap the original overprint.

Two used examples of British Bechuanaland No. 37 are known surcharged 2s. as T1 but their status is uncertain. (*Price* £35,000).

3 Cadet Sergt.-major Goodyear

4 General Baden-Powell

(Des Dr. W. A. Hayes (T **3**), Capt. H. Greener (T **4**))

1900 (6–11 Apr). *Produced photographically by Dr. D. Taylor. Horiz laid paper with sheet wmk "OCEANA FINE". P 12.*

(a) 18½ mm wide. (b) 21 mm wide.

No.	Type	Description	Unused	Used
17	3	1d. pale blue/*blue* (7.4)	£850	£275
18		1d. deep blue/*blue*	£850	£275
19	4	3d. pale blue/*blue* (*a*)	£1200	£400
		a. Reversed design	£65000	£38000
20		3d. deep blue/*blue* (*a*)	£1200	£350
		a. Imperf between (horiz pair)	†	£65000
		b. Double print	†	£17000
21		3d. pale blue/*blue* (*b*) (11.4)	£9000	£850
		a. Vert laid paper	£13000	
22		3d. deep blue/*blue* (*b*) (11.4)	£10000	£1000

These stamps vary a great deal in colour from deep blue to pale grey.

No. 18 imperforate and without gum is believed to be a proof (*Price for unused pair* £18000).

No. 19a comes from a sheet of 12 printed in reverse of which nine, three mint and six used, are known to have survived.

VRYBURG

PRICES FOR STAMPS ON COVER	
Nos. 1/4	from × 5
Nos. 11/12	from × 2

BOER OCCUPATION

Vryburg was occupied by Boer forces on 15 October 1899. Unoverprinted stamps of Transvaal were used initially. Nos. 1/4 were only available from 24 to 29 November. The Boers evacuated the town on 7 May 1900.

½ PENCE
Z.A.R.
(1)

1899 (24 Nov). *Cape stamps surch as T* **1**. *Surch 12 mm high on No. 3 and 10 mm on all other values.*

No.	Type	Description	Unused	Used
1	6	½ PENCE green	£200	80·00
		a. Italic "Z"	£1700	£700
		b. Surch 12 mm high	£1700	£700
2	17	1 PENCE rose	£225	£100
		a. Italic "Z"	£1900	£800
		b. Surch 12 mm high	£1900	£800
		c. "I" for "1"	£1200	£500
3	4	2 PENCE on 6d. mauve	£2000	£500
		a. Italic "Z"	£10000	£4250
4	15	2½ PENCE on 2½d. blue	£1700	£425
		a. Italic "Z"	£10000	£4250
		b. Surch 12 mm high	£10000	£4250

The "2 PENCE" on 6d. shows the surcharge 12 mm high. It is possible that this was the first value surcharged as the remaining three show the height reduced to 10 mm with the exception of one position in the second vertical row of the setting. The italic "Z" occurs on one position in the sixth vertical row. It is believed that the setting was of 60 (6×10).

BRITISH REOCCUPATION

V. R.
SPECIAL
POST
(2)

1900 (16 May). *Provisionals issued by the Military Authorities. Stamps of Transvaal handstamped with T* **2**.

No.	Type	Description	Unused	Used
11	30	½d. green	—	£2250
11*a*		1d. rose-red (No. 206)		
12		1d. rose-red and green (No. 217)	£9000	£4250
13		2d. brown and green	†	£30000
14		2½d. dull blue and green	†	£30000

No. 11 is known used with double handstamp and Nos. 11/12 with the overprint reading downwards.

II. GRIQUALAND WEST

Griqualand West was situated to the North of Cape Colony, bounded on the north by what became British Bechuanaland and on the east by the Orange Free State.

The area was settled in the early nineteenth century by the Griqua tribal group, although many members of the tribe, including the paramount chief, migrated to Griqualand East (between Basutoland and the east coast of South Africa) in 1861–63. There was little European involvement in Griqualand West before 1866, but in that year the diamond fields along the Vaal River were discovered. Sovereignty was subsequently claimed by the Griqua Chief, the Orange Free State and the South African Republic (Transvaal). In 1871 the British authorities arbitrated in favour of the Griqua Chief who promptly ceded his territory to Great Britain. Griqualand West became a separate Crown Colony in January 1873.

During the initial stages of the prospecting boom, mail was passed via the Orange Free State, but a post office connected to the Cape Colony postal system was opened at Klip Drift (subsequently Barkly) in late 1870. Further offices at De Beer's New Rush (subsequently Kimberley), Douglas and Du Toit's Pan (subsequently Beaconsfield) were open by September 1873.

Cape of Good Hope stamps to the 5s. value were in use from October 1871, but those originating in Griqualand West can only be identified after the introduction of Barred Oval Diamond Numeral cancellations in 1873. Numbers known to have been issued in the territory are:

1	De Beers N.R. (New Rush) (subsequently Kimberley)
3	Junction R. & M. (Riet and Modder Rivers)
4	Barkly
6	or 9 Du Toit's Pan (subsequently Beaconsfield)
8	Langford (transferred to Douglas)
10	Thornhill

PRICES FOR STAMPS ON COVER. The stamps of Griqualand West are worth from ×10 the price quoted for used stamps, when on cover from the territory.

FORGED OVERPRINTS. Many stamps show forged overprints. Great care should be taken when purchasing the scarcer items.

***Stamps of the Cape of Good Hope,* Crown CC, perf 14, overprinted.**

1874 (Sept). *No. 24a of Cape of Good Hope surch "1d." in red manuscript by the Kimberley postmaster.*

No.	Type	Description	Unused	Used
1		1d. on 4d. blue	£1300	£2250

G. W.
(1)

1877 (Mar). *Nos. 29/30 of Cape of Good Hope optd with T* **1**.

No.	Type	Description	Unused	Used
2		1d. carmine-red	£500	85·00
		a. Opt double	†	£2000
3		4d. dull blue (R.)	£400	75·00
		w. Wmk inverted	£1300	£275

G (1a) G (2) G (3) G (4) G (5) G (6)
G (7) G (8) G (9) G (10) G (11)
G (12) G (13) G (14)

1877 (Mar)–**78**. *Nos. 24a, 25a, 26a and 28/31 Cape of Good Hope optd with capital "G".*

(a) First printing. Optd with T **1a/6** *and* **8** *in black (1d.) or red (others).*

No.	Type	Description	Unused	Used
4		½d. grey-black		
		a. Opt Type **1a**	25·00	28·00
		b. Opt Type **2**	60·00	75·00
		c. Opt Type **3**	32·00	40·00
		d. Opt Type **4**	60·00	75·00
		e. Opt Type **5**	70·00	85·00
		f. Opt Type **6**	29·00	35·00
		g. Opt Type **8**	£550	£600
5		1d. carmine-red		
		a. Opt Type **1a**	26·00	19·00
		b. Opt Type **2**	65·00	42·00
		c. Opt Type **3**	32·00	27·00
		d. Opt Type **4**	65·00	42·00
		e. Opt Type **5**	75·00	50·00
		f. Opt Type **6**	26·00	19·00
		g. Opt Type **8**	*	
6		4d. blue (with frame-line) (No. 24*a*)		
		a. Opt Type **1a**	£275	42·00
		b. Opt Type **2**	£700	£120
		c. Opt Type **3**	£450	60·00
		d. Opt Type **4**	£700	£120
		e. Opt Type **5**	£800	£150
		f. Opt Type **6**	£350	55·00
		g. Opt Type **8**	£2250	£700
7		4d. dull blue (without frame-line) (No. 30)		
		a. Opt Type **1a**	£190	27·00
		b. Opt Type **2**	£475	80·00
		c. Opt Type **3**	£325	35·00
		d. Opt Type **4**	£450	80·00
		e. Opt Type **5**	£550	£100
		f. Opt Type **6**	£300	32·00
		g. Opt Type **8**	£1800	£475
8		6d. deep lilac		
		a. Opt Type **1a**	£140	29·00
		b. Opt Type **2**	£325	85·00
		c. Opt Type **3**	£200	42·00
		cw. Wmk inverted	†	£325
		d. Opt Type **4**	£325	85·00
		e. Opt Type **5**	£400	£100
		f. Opt Type **6**	£180	40·00
		g. Opt Type **8**	£600	£600
9		1s. green		
		a. Opt Type **1a**	£170	25·00
		ab. Opt inverted	—	£500
		b. Opt Type **2**	£400	60·00
		ba. Opt inverted	—	£850
		c. Opt Type **3**	£300	32·00
		d. Opt Type **4**	£400	60·00
		da. Opt inverted	—	£850
		e. Opt Type **5**	£475	75·00
		f. Opt Type **6**	£275	28·00
		fa. Opt inverted	—	£600
		g. Opt Type **8**	£3000	£600
10		5s. yellow-orange		
		a. Opt Type **1a**	£650	30·00
		b. Opt Type **2**	£1000	70·00
		c. Opt Type **3**	£850	38·00
		cw. Wmk inverted	†	£800
		d. Opt Type **4**	£1000	70·00
		dw. Wmk inverted	†	£1100
		e. Opt Type **5**	£1500	85·00
		f. Opt Type **6**	£800	35·00
		g. Opt Type **8**	£3000	£750

*The 1d. with overprint Type **8** from this setting can only be distinguished from that of the second printing when *se-tenant* with overprint Type **3**.

Nos. 4/10 were overprinted by a setting of 120 covering two panes of 60 (6×10). This setting contained 41 examples of Type **1a**, 10 of Type **2**, 23 of Type **3**, 10 of Type **4**, 8 of Type **5**, 27 of Type **6** and 1 of Type **8**. Sub-types of Types **1a** and **2** exist. The single example of Type **8** occurs on R.7/4 of the right-hand pane.

It is believed that there may have been an additional setting used for the 5s. which was in considerable demand to cover the postage and registration on diamond consignments. It is also possible that single panes of this value and of the 1s. were overprinted using the right-hand half of the normal 120 setting.

(b) Second printing. Optd with T **6/14** *in black (1878).*

No.	Type	Description	Unused	Used
11		1d. carmine-red		
		a. Opt Type **6**	*	
		b. Opt Type **7**	28·00	19·00
		c. Opt Type **8**	60·00	32·00
		d. Opt Type **9**	29·00	20·00
		e. Opt Type **10**	80·00	70·00
		f. Opt Type **11**	70·00	45·00
		g. Opt Type **12**	75·00	65·00
		h. Opt Type **13**	£120	£100
		i. Opt Type **14**	£400	£325
12		4d. dull blue (without frame-line) (No. 30)		
		a. Opt Type **6**	£350	65·00
		b. Opt Type **7**	£130	25·00
		c. Opt Type **8**	£325	55·00
		d. Opt Type **9**	£150	26·00
		e. Opt Type **10**	£400	80·00
		f. Opt Type **11**	£350	70·00
		g. Opt Type **12**	£375	75·00
		h. Opt Type **13**	£550	£140
		i. Opt Type **14**	£1900	£450
13		6d. deep lilac		
		a. Opt Type **6**	£475	£100
		b. Opt Type **7**	£250	55·00
		ba. Opt double		
		c. Opt Type **8**	£450	90·00
		d. Opt Type **9**	£300	65·00
		da. Opt double	—	£850
		e. Opt Type **10**	£550	£140
		ea. Opt double	—	£1000
		f. Opt Type **11**	£475	£100
		g. Opt Type **12**	£475	£130
		h. Opt Type **13**	£750	£200
		i. Opt Type **14**	£2250	£600

*The 1d. with overprint Type **6** from this setting can only be distinguished from that of the first printing when *se-tenant* with Types **11**, **12** or **13**.

Nos. 11/13 were overprinted by another double-pane setting of 120 in which only Types **6** and **8** were repeated from that used for the first printing. The second printing setting contained 12 examples of Type **6**, 30 of Type **7**, 13 of Type **8**, 27 of Type **9**, 9 of Type **10**, 11 of Type **11**, 11 of Type **12**, 6 of Type **13** and 1 of Type **14**. Sub-types of Types **7** and **12** exist.

G (**15**) *G* (**16**) G (**17**)

1878 (June). *Nos. 24a, 25a and 28/30 of Cape of Good Hope optd with small capital "G", T* **15/16**.

No.	Type	Description	Unused	Used
14	**15**	½d. grey-black (R.)	13·00	13·00
		a. Opt inverted	15·00	15·00
		b. Opt double	50·00	65·00
		c. Opt double, both inverted	£100	£120
		d. Black opt	£200	£120
		da. Opt inverted	£225	
		db. Opt double, one inverted in red	£400	
		dc. Opt double, one inverted (Type **16**) in red	£190	
15	**16**	½d. grey-black (R.)	14·00	14·00
		a. Opt inverted	14·00	15·00
		b. Opt double	85·00	85·00
		c. Opt double, both inverted	70·00	80·00
		d. Black opt	50·00	50·00
		da. Opt inverted	£110	80·00
		db. Opt double, one inverted (Type **15**) in red	£190	
16	**15**	1d. carmine-red	14·00	11·00
		a. Opt inverted	14·00	14·00
		b. Opt double	£200	55·00
		c. Opt double, both inverted	£200	75·00
		d. Opt double, both inverted with one in red	42·00	45·00
		e. Opt double, both inverted with one (Type **16**) in red		
17	**16**	1d. carmine-red	14·00	13·00
		a. Opt inverted	90·00	32·00
		b. Opt double	—	95·00
		c. Opt double, both inverted	—	£120
		d. Opt double, both inverted with one in red	90·00	90·00
18	**15**	4d. blue (with frame-line) (No. 24a)	—	£160
19	**16**	4d. blue (with frame-line) (No. 24a)	—	£160
20	**15**	4d. dull blue (without frame-line) (No. 30)	£140	32·00
		a. Opt inverted	£225	90·00
		b. Opt double	—	£225
		c. Opt double, both inverted	—	£300
		d. Red opt	£350	£100
		da. Opt inverted	£400	85·00
21	**16**	4d. dull blue (without frame-line) (No. 30)	£160	14·00
		a. Opt inverted	£250	32·00
		b. Opt double	—	£200
		c. Opt double, both inverted	—	£275
		d. Red opt	—	90·00
		da. Opt inverted	£375	90·00
22	**15**	6d. deep lilac	£140	28·00
23	**16**	6d. deep lilac	—	28·00

Nos. 14/23 were also overprinted using a double-pane setting of 120. Based on evidence from surviving ½d. and 1d. sheets all overprints in the left-hand pane were roman, Type **15**, and all those in the right-hand pane italic, Type **16**, except for R.1/6, 4/5, 6/6, 7/6, 8/6, 9/6 and 10/6 which were Type **15**. There is considerable evidence to suggest that after the ½d. value had been overprinted the setting was amended to show a Type **15**, instead of a Type **16**, on R.10/5 of the right-hand pane. Two strikes of the setting were required to overprint the sheets of 240 and it would appear that on many sheets the bottom two panes had the overprints inverted.

1879. *Nos. 25b, 26b and 28/31 of Cape of Good Hope optd with small capital "G", T* **17**.

No.	Type	Description	Unused	Used
24		½d. grey-black	17·00	8·00
		a. Opt double	£400	£275
25		1d. carmine-red	18·00	6·00
		a. Opt inverted	—	90·00
		b. Opt double	—	£140
		c. Opt treble	—	£225
		w. Wmk inverted	†	£275
26		4d. dull blue	35·00	6·00
		a. Opt double	—	£120
27		6d. violet	£150	9·00
		a. Opt inverted	—	38·00
		b. Opt double	£700	£180
28		1s. green	£130	6·50
		a. Opt double	£375	95·00
29		5s. yellow-orange	£450	14·00
		a. Opt double	£600	85·00
		b. Opt treble	—	£300

Nos. 24/9 were also overprinted using a setting of 120 which contained a number of minor type varieties.

Griqualand West was merged with Cape Colony in October 1880. The remaining stock of the overprinted stamps was returned from Kimberley to Cape Town and redistributed among various post offices in Cape Colony where they were used as ordinary Cape stamps.

III. NATAL

PRICES FOR STAMPS ON COVER

Nos. 1/7	*from* × 2
Nos. 9/25	*from* × 3
Nos. 26/56	*from* × 4
Nos. 57/8	—
Nos. 59/73	*from* × 5
Nos. 76/84	*from* × 4
Nos. 85/93	*from* × 3
Nos. 96/103	*from* × 6
Nos. 104/5	*from* × 5
Nos. 106/25	*from* × 6
Nos. 127/42	*from* × 4

PRICES FOR STAMPS ON COVER

Nos. 143/5*a*	—
Nos. 146/57	*from* × 4
No. 162	—
Nos. 165/71	*from* × 3
No. F1	—
Nos. O1/6	*from* × 10

1 2 3 4 5

(Embossed in plain relief on coloured wove paper)

1857 (26 May)–**61**. Imperf.

No.	Type	Description	Unused	Used
1	**1**	1d. blue (9.59)	—	£1100
2		1d. rose (1859)	—	£1700
3		1d. buff (1861)	—	£1000
4	**2**	3d. rose	—	£400
		a. *Tête-bêche* (pair)	—	£35000
5	**3**	6d. green	—	£1100
6	**4**	9d. blue	—	£7000
7	**5**	1s. buff	—	£5500

All the above have been reprinted more than once, and the early reprints of some values cannot always be distinguished with certainty from originals.

Stamps on surface-coloured paper with higher face values and perforated 12½ are fiscals.

NOTE. The value of the above stamps depends on their dimensions, and the clearness of the embossing, but our prices are for fine used.

PERKINS BACON "CANCELLED". For notes on these handstamps showing "CANCELLED" between horizontal bars forming an oval, see Catalogue Introduction.

6

7

(Eng C. H. Jeens. Recess P.B.)

1859–60. No wmk. P 14.

No.	Type	Description	Unused	Used
9	**6**	1d. rose-red (1860) (H/S "CANCELLED" in oval £11000)	£130	70·00
10		3d. blue	£160	42·00
		a. Imperf between (vert pair)	†	£8000

No. 10a is only known from a cover of 1867 franked with two such pairs.

The 3d. also exists with "CANCELLED" in oval, but no examples are believed to be in private hands.

1861. No wmk. Intermediate perf 14 to 16.

No.	Type	Description	Unused	Used
11	**6**	3d. blue	£225	65·00

1861–62. No wmk. Rough perf 14 to 16.

No.	Type	Description	Unused	Used
12	**6**	3d. blue	£110	32·00
		a. Imperf between (horiz pair)	£4000	
		b. Imperf (pair)	—	£3750
13		6d. grey (1862)	£190	50·00

1862. Wmk Small Star. Rough perf 14 to 16.

No.	Type	Description	Unused	Used
15	**6**	1d. rose-red	£140	65·00

The 1d. without watermark and the 3d. watermark Small Star, both imperforate, are proofs.

(Recess D.L.R.)

1863. *Thick paper.* No wmk. P 13.

No.	Type	Description	Unused	Used
18	**6**	1d. lake	90·00	27·00
19		1d. carmine-red	90·00	27·00

1863–65. Wmk Crown CC. P 12½.

No.	Type	Description	Unused	Used
20	**6**	1d. brown-red	£140	38·00
		y. Wmk inverted and reversed	—	£100
21		1d. rose	90·00	35·00
		x. Wmk reversed	90·00	35·00
22		1d. bright red	90·00	38·00
		x. Wmk reversed	90·00	38·00
23		6d. lilac	70·00	17·00
24		6d. violet	55·00	28·00
		x. Wmk reversed	55·00	28·00

(Typo D.L.R.)

1867 (Apr). Wmk Crown CC. P 14.

No.	Type	Description	Unused	Used
25	**7**	1s. green	£170	32·00
		w. Wmk inverted	—	£275

POSTAGE (**7a**) Postage. (**7b**) Postage. (**7c**)

Postage. (**7d**) POSTAGE. (**7e**)

1869 (23 Aug). *Optd horiz in Natal.* No wmk (3d.), wmk Crown CC (others). P 14 or 14–16 (3d.), 12½ (1d., 6d) or 14 (1s.).

No.	Type	Description	Unused	Used
		(a) With T **7a** *(tall capitals without stop).*		
26	**6**	1d. rose	£375	80·00
		x. Wmk reversed	£375	80·00
27		1d. bright red	£325	70·00
		x. Wmk reversed	—	70·00
28		3d. blue (No. 10)	£2000	£600
28*a*		3d. blue (No. 11)	£650	£250
28*b*		3d. blue (No. 12)	£500	90·00
29		6d. lilac	£550	70·00
30		6d. violet	£475	80·00
		x. Wmk reversed	£475	80·00
31	**7**	1s. green	£7500	£1200
		(b) With T **7b** *(12¾ mm long).*		
32	**6**	1d. rose	£350	75·00
33		1d. bright red	£300	65·00
		a. Opt double	†	£1400
		x. Wmk reversed	£300	65·00
34		3d. blue (No. 10)	—	£300
34*a*		3d. blue (No. 11)	£550	£200
34*b*		3d. blue (No. 12)	£450	80·00
35		6d. lilac	£475	65·00
36		6d. violet	£400	75·00
		x. Wmk reversed	£400	75·00
37	**7**	1s. green	£5500	£900
		(c) With T **7c** *(13¾ mm long).*		
38	**6**	1d. rose	£700	£200
39		1d. bright red	£750	£180
		x. Wmk reversed	—	£180
40		3d. blue (No. 10)		
40*a*		3d. blue (No. 11)	—	£700
40*b*		3d. blue (No. 12)	£1500	£350
41		6d. lilac	£1600	£150
42		6d. violet	£1500	£140
		x. Wmk reversed	—	£160
43	**7**	1s. green	—	£1800
		(d) With T **7d** *(14½ to 15½ mm long).*		
44	**6**	1d. rose	£600	£170
45		1d. bright red	£600	£150
46		3d. blue (No. 10)		
46*a*		3d. blue (No. 11)	—	£450
46*b*		3d. blue (No. 12)	—	£275
47		6d. lilac	—	£100
48		6d. violet	£1200	95·00
49	**7**	1s. green	£14000	£1600
		(e) With T **7e** *(small capitals with stop).*		
50	**6**	1d. rose	£100	42·00
		x. Wmk reversed	£100	42·00
51		1d. bright red	£150	42·00
		x. Wmk reversed	£150	42·00
52		3d. blue (No. 10)	£300	75·00
53		3d. blue (No. 11)	£160	48·00
54		3d. blue (No. 12)	£180	42·00
		a. Opt double	†	£1100
54*b*		6d. lilac	£180	60·00
55		6d. violet	£140	50·00
		x. Wmk reversed	£140	50·00
56	**7**	1s. green	£200	65·00

It is believed that there were two settings of these overprints. The first setting, probably of 240, contained 60 examples of Type **7***a*, 72 of Type **7***b*, 20 of Type **7***c*, 28 of Type **7***d* and 60 of Type **7***e*. The second, probably of 60 (6×10), contained Type **7***e* only.

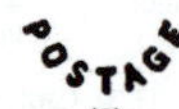

(**8**)

1870. *No. 25 optd with T* **8** *by De La Rue.*

No.	Type	Description	Unused	Used
57	**7**	1s. green (C.)	—	£3500
58		1s. green (Blk.)	£2500	£1200
		a. Opt double	—	£2500
59		1s. green (G.)	90·00	10·00

For 1s. orange, see No. 108.

POSTAGE POSTAGE (**9**) POSTAGE (**10**) POSTAGE POSTAGE (**11**)

1870–73. *Optd with T* **9** *by De La Rue.* Wmk Crown CC. P 12½.

No.	Type	Description	Unused	Used
60	**6**	1d. bright red	80·00	13·00
		x. Wmk reversed	80·00	13·00
61		3d. bright blue (R.) (1872)	85·00	13·00
		x. Wmk reversed	85·00	13·00
62		6d. mauve (1873)	£160	28·00
		x. Wmk reversed	£180	

1873 (July). *Fiscal stamp optd locally with T* **10**. Wmk Crown CC. P 14.

No.	Type	Description	Unused	Used
63	**7**	1s. purple-brown	£225	22·00
		w. Wmk inverted	—	£300

1874 (July). *No. 21 optd locally with T* **11**.

No.	Type	Description	Unused	Used
65	**6**	1d. rose	£250	75·00
		a. Opt double		
		x. Wmk reversed	—	75·00

12 13 14

15 16

(Typo D.L.R.)

1874 (Jan)–**99**. Wmk Crown CC (sideways on 5s.). P 14.

66 **12** 1d. dull rose ... 26·00 3·50
67 1d. bright rose ... 26·00 3·50
68 **13** 3d. blue ... £110 24·00
a. Perf 14×12½ ... £1600 £850
69 **14** 4d. brown (1878) ... £120 12·00
aw. Wmk inverted ... £350 £110
b. Perf 12½ ... £325 70·00
70 **15** 6d. bright reddish violet ... 60·00 7·50
w. Wmk inverted ... † £160
71 **16** 5s. maroon (1882) ... £200 55·00
a. Perf 15½×15 (1874) ... £375 95·00
72 5s. rose ... 85·00 35·00
73 5s. carmine (H/S S. £160) ... 80·00 32·00
a. Wmk upright (1899) ...

POSTAGE (17) POSTAGE (18) ½ HALF (19)

1875–76. Wmk Crown CC. P 14 (1s.) or 12½ (others).

(a) Optd locally with T **17**.

76 **6** 1d. rose ... £120 50·00
a. Opt double ... £1000 £450
x. Wmk reversed ... £120 50·00
77 1d. bright red ... £110 65·00
x. Wmk reversed ... £110 65·00

(b) Optd locally with T **18** *(14½ mm long, without stop).*

81 **6** 1d. rose (1876) ... 90·00 65·00
a. Opt inverted ... £1100 £450
x. Wmk reversed ... 90·00 65·00
82 1d. yellow (1876) ... 70·00 70·00
a. Opt double, one albino ... £200
x. Wmk reversed ... 80·00 80·00
83 6d. violet (1876) ... 60·00 8·00
a. Opt double ... — £650
b. Opt inverted ... £700 £150
w. Wmk inverted ... — £110
x. Wmk reversed ... 60·00 8·00
84 **7** 1s. green (1876) ... 90·00 7·50
a. Opt double ... — £325

TYPE 19. There are several varieties of this surcharge, of which T **19** is an example. They may be divided as follows:
(*a*) "½" 4½ mm high, "2" has straight foot.
(*b*) As last but "½" is 4 mm high.
(*c*) As last but "2" has curled foot.
(*d*) "½" 3½ mm. high, "2" has straight foot.
(*e*) As last but "2" has curled foot.
(*f*) As last but "2" smaller.

As the "½" and "HALF" were overprinted separately, they vary in relative position, and are frequently overlapping.

1877 (13 Feb). *No. 66 surch locally as T* **19**.

85 **12** ½d. on 1d. rose (*a*) ... 30·00 65·00
a. "½" double ...
86 ½d. on 1d. rose (*b*) ... £130
87 ½d. on 1d. rose (*c*) ... £110
88 ½d. on 1d. rose (*d*) ... 65·00 90·00
89 ½d. on 1d. rose (*e*) ... 70·00
90 ½d. on 1d. rose (*f*) ... 80·00

POSTAGE Half-penny (21)

23

ONE HALF-PENNY. (24)

1877 (7 Oct)–**79**. *T* **6** (wmk Crown CC. P 12½) *surch locally as T* **21**.

91 ½d. on 1d. yellow ... 8·50 16·00
a. Surch inverted ... £275 £190
b. Surch double ... £250 £180
c. Surch omitted (lower stamp, vertical pair) ... £2250 £1300
d. "POSTAGE" omitted (in pair with normal) ... £1600
e. "S" of "POSTAGE" omitted (R. 8/3) ... £250 £190
f. "T" of "POSTAGE" omitted ... £250 £250
x. Wmk reversed ... 8·50 16·00
92 1d. on 6d. violet (10.10.77) ... 50·00 11·00
a. "S" of "POSTAGE" omitted (R. 8/3) ... £375 £150
x. Wmk reversed ... — 11·00
93 1d. on 6d. rose (12.2.79) ... £100 48·00
a. Surch inverted ... £550 £300
b. Surch double ... — £250
c. Surch double, one inverted ... £250 £200
d. Surch four times ... £375 £200
e. "S" of "POSTAGE" omitted (R. 8/3) ... £500 £300
x. Wmk reversed ... — 48·00

No. 93c. is known with one surcharge showing variety "S" of "POSTAGE" omitted.
Other minor varieties exist in these surcharges.

(Typo D.L.R.)

1880 (13 Oct). Wmk Crown CC. P 14.

96 **23** ½d. blue-green ... 15·00 22·00
a. Imperf between (vert pair) ...

1882 (20 Apr)–**89**. Wmk Crown CA. P 14.

97 **23** ½d. blue-green (23.4.84) ... 95·00 16·00
a. Dull green (10.4.85) ... 3·75 1·25
aw. Wmk inverted ... £200
99 **12** 1d. rose (*shades*) (1.84) ... 3·50 25
a. Carmine ... 4·00 35
w. Wmk inverted ... † £160
100 **13** 3d. blue (23.4.84) ... £100 17·00
101 3d. grey (11.89) ... 5·00 2·50
102 **14** 4d. brown ... 7·00 1·50
103 **15** 6d. mauve ... 6·00 1·75
w. Wmk inverted ... † £110
97*a*/103 *Set of 6* ... £110 21·00
97*a*s, 99*a*s, 101s/3s H/S "Specimen" *Set of 5* ... £275

1885 (26 Jan). *No. 99 surch locally with T* **24**.

104 **12** ½d. on 1d. rose ... 16·00 11·00
a. No hyphen after "HALF" ... 70·00 42·00

TWO PENCE (25)

26

TWOPENCE HALFPENNY (27)

1886 (7 Jan). *No. 101 surch with T* **25** *by D.L.R.*

105 **13** 2d.. on 3d grey ... 19·00 5·50

(Typo D.L.R.)

1887 (Sept)–**89**. Wmk Crown CA. P 14.

106 **26** 2d. olive-green (Die I) ... 38·00 2·25
a. Top left triangle detached ... — £200
s. Optd "Specimen" ... 75·00
107 2d. olive-green (Die II) (1889) ... 3·50 1·40
s. Handstamped "Specimen" ... 60·00

The differences between Dies I and II are shown in the introduction.

1888 (16 Mar). *As No. 25, but colour changed and* wmk Crown CA, *optd with T* **8** *by D.L.R.*

108 **7** 1s. orange (C.) ... 5·50 1·75
a. Opt double ... — £1500
s. Handstamped "Specimen" ... £100

1891 (22 Apr). *Surch locally with T* **27**.

109 **14** 2½d. on 4d. brown ... 11·00 15·00
a. "TWOPENGE" ... 50·00
b. "HALFPENN" ... £250 £200
c. Surch double ... £275 £200
d. Surch inverted ... £375 £300
s. Handstamped "Specimen" ... 50·00

(28)

POSTAGE. Half-Penny (29)

POSTAGE. Varieties of long-tailed letters

(Typo D.L.R.)

1891 (June). Wmk Crown CA. P 14.

113 **28** 2½d. bright blue ... 6·50 1·50
s. Handstamped "Specimen" ... 60·00

1895 (12 Mar). *No. 24 surch locally with T* **29** *in carmine.*

114 ½d. on 6d. violet ... 2·25 4·50
a. "Ealf-Penny" ... 20·00 35·00
b. "Half-Pennv" and long "P" ... 18·00 35·00
ba. "Half Pennv" and long "T" and "A" ... 18·00 35·00
c. No stop after "POSTAGE" and long "P", "T" and "A" ... 18·00 35·00
d. Long "P" ... 2·50 6·00
e. Long "T" ... 2·50 6·00
f. Long "A" ... 3·50 8·00
g. Long "P" and "T" ... 2·50 6·00
h. Long "P" and "A" ... 2·50 6·00
i. Long "T" and "A" ... 3·00 7·50
k. Long "P", "T" and "A" ... 3·25 7·50
ka. Long "P", "T" and "A" with comma after "POSTAGE" ... 9·50 16·00
l. Surch double ... £250
la. Surch double, one vertical ... £250
m. "POSTAGE" omitted ... £1000
s. Handstamped "Specimen" ... 50·00
x. Wmk reversed ... 2·25 4·50

The surcharge was applied as a setting of 60 (12×5) which contained seventeen normals, one each of Nos. 114a, 114b, 114ba, 114c, six of No. 114d, six of 114e, three of 114f, six of 114g, seven of 114h, five of No. 114i, four of No. 114k and two of No. 114ka.

HALF (30)

31 32

1895 (18 Mar). *No. 99 surch locally with T* **30**.

125 HALF on 1d. rose (*shades*) ... 3·00 2·25
a. Surch double ... £350 £350
b. "H" with longer left limb ... 30·00
c. Pair, one without surcharge ...
s. Handstamped "Specimen" ... 50·00

No. 125b, in which the "A" also has a short right leg, occurs on the second, fourth, sixth etc., stamps of the first vertical column of the right-hand pane of the first printing only.

In the second printing what appears to be a broken "E" (with the top limb removed) was used instead of "L" in "HALF" on the last stamp in the sheet (*Price* £32), No. 125c also comes from this second printing.

(Typo D.L.R)

1902–03. *Inscr "POSTAGE REVENUE"*. Wmk Crown CA. P 14.

127 **31** ½d. blue-green ... 3·25 50
128 1d. carmine ... 9·00 15
129 1½d. green and black ... 4·00 2·75
130 2d. red and olive-green ... 2·75 25
131 2½d. bright blue ... 1·50 3·50
132 3d. purple and grey ... 1·25 1·75
133 4d. carmine and cinnamon ... 5·00 19·00
134 5d. black and orange ... 2·50 2·75
w. Wmk inverted ... £140 75·00
135 6d. green and brown-purple ... 2·50 3·25
136 1s. carmine and pale blue ... 3·00 3·50
137 2s. green and bright violet ... 50·00 9·00
138 2s.6d. purple ... 40·00 12·00
139 4s. deep rose and maize ... 70·00 75·00
a. Imperf between (horiz pair) ...
127/39 *Set of 13* ... £170 £120
127s/39s Optd "Specimen" *Set of 13* ... £170

No. 139a is also imperforate between stamp and left-hand margin.

(Typo D.L.R.)

1902. Wmk Crown CC. P 14.

140 **32** 5s. dull blue and rose ... 32·00 12·00
141 10s. deep rose and chocolate ... 70·00 27·00
142 £1 black and bright blue ... £180 55·00
143 £1. 10s green and violet ... £400 £100
s. Optd "Specimen" ... 75·00
144 £5 mauve and black ... £2750 £650
s. Optd "Specimen" ... £120
145 £10 green and orange ... £8000 £3000
as. Optd "Specimen" ... £200
145*b* £20 red and green ... £16000 £8000
bs. Optd "Specimen" ... £375
140s/2s Optd "Specimen" *Set of 3* ... £110

USED HIGH VALUES. Collectors are warned against fiscally used high value Natal stamps with penmarks cleaned off and forged postmarks added.

1904–08. *Chalk-surfaced paper (£1 10s.)*. Wmk Mult Crown CA. P 14.

146 **31** ½d. blue-green ... 6·50 15
147 1d. rose-carmine ... 6·50 15
a. Booklet pane of 6, one stamp optd "NOT FOR USE" (1907) ... £275
148 1d. deep carmine ... 9·00 30
w. Wmk inverted ... † 80·00
149 2d. red and olive-green ... 10·00 3·25
152 4d. carmine and cinnamon ... 2·75 1·25
153 5d. black and orange (1908) ... 4·25 4·00
155 1s. carmine and pale blue ... 80·00 7·00
156 2s. dull green and bright violet ... 55·00 40·00
157 2s.6d. purple ... 50·00 40·00
162 **32** £1 10s. brown-orange and deep purple (1908) ... £1200 £2000
s. Optd "Specimen" ... £200
146/57 *Set of 9* ... £200 80·00

1908–09. *Inscr "POSTAGE POSTAGE"*. Wmk Mult Crown CA. P 14.

165 **31** 6d. dull and bright purple ... 4·50 3·00
166 1s. black/*green* ... 6·00 3·00
167 2s. purple and bright blue/*blue* ... 15·00 3·00
168 2s.6d. black and red/*blue* ... 25·00 3·00
169 **32** 5s. green and red/*yellow* ... 23·00 28·00
170 10s. green and red/*green* ... 80·00 85·00
171 £1 purple and black/*red* ... £275 £250
165/71 *Set of 7* ... £375 £350
165s/71s Optd "Specimen" *Set of 7* ... £225

STAMP BOOKLETS

1906. *Black on red cover. Stapled.*

SB1 2s.7d. booklet containing thirty 1d. (No. 147) in blocks of 6 ... £2000

1907. *Black on red cover. Stapled.*

SB2 2s.6d. booklet containing thirty 1d. (No. 147) in blocks of 6 ... £2000

The first stamp of the first pane in No. SB2 was overprinted "NOT FOR USE" (No. 147a), the additional penny being used to defray the cost of production.

FISCALS USED FOR POSTAGE

1869. *Embossed on coloured wove, surfaced paper.* P 12½.

F1 **1** 1d. yellow ... 50·00 80·00

Examples of 1d. yellow and 6d. rose values as Type **6**, 1s. purple-brown as Type **7** and various values between 5s, and £10 in the design illustrated above are believed to exist postally used, but, as such use was not authorised, they are not now listed.

OFFICIAL STAMPS

OFFICIAL

(O **1**)

1904. *T* **31**, wmk Mult Crown CA, *optd with Type* O **1**. P 14.

No.	Description	Unused	Used
O1	½d. blue-green	3·00	35
O2	1d. carmine	5·00	80
O3	2d. red and olive-green	25·00	13·00
O4	3d. purple and grey	15·00	4·25
O5	6d. green and brown-purple	50·00	65·00
O6	1s. carmine and pale blue	£150	£200
O1/6	*Set of 6*	£225	£250

The use of stamps overprinted as above was discontinued after 30 May 1907. Stamps perforated with the letters "N.G.R." were for use on Government Railways.

Natal became a province of the Union of South Africa on 31 May 1910.

IV. NEW REPUBLIC

During the unrest following the death of Cetshwayo, the Zulu king, in 1884, a group of Boers from the Transvaal offered their support to his son, Dinizulu. The price for this support was the cession of a sizeable portion of Zulu territory to an independent Boer republic. The New Republic, centred on Vryheid, was proclaimed on 16 August 1884 with the remaining Zulu territory becoming a protectorate of the new administration. The first reference to an organised postal service occurs in December 1884.

Alarmed by these developments the British authorities annexed the southernmost part of the land grant, around St. Lucia Bay, to prevent access to the Indian Ocean. The remainder of the New Republic was, however, recognised as independent on 22 October 1886. Zululand was annexed by the British on 22 May 1887.

Difficulties beset the New Republic, however, and its Volksraad voted for union with the South African Republic (Transvaal). The two republics united on 21 July 1888. In 1903 the territory of the former New Republic was transferred to Natal.

Mail from Vryheid in 1884–85 was franked with issues of Transvaal (for dispatches made via Utrecht) or Natal (for those sent via Dundee from August 1885 onwards). Issues of the New Republic were never accepted as internationally valid by these administrations so that all external mail continued to show Transvaal or Natal stamps used in combination with those of the republic.

PRICES FOR STAMPS ON COVER

No. 1	—
Nos. 2/5	from × 50
Nos. 6/25	—
Nos. 26/9	from × 50
Nos. 30/47	—
Nos. 48/50	from × 50
No. 51	—
Nos. 52/3	from × 50
Nos. 72/5	from × 50
Nos. 76/7b	—
Nos. 78/80	from × 50
Nos. 81/95	—

1

Printed with a rubber handstamp on paper bought in Europe and sent out ready gummed and perforated.

1886 (7 Jan)–**87**. *Various dates indicating date of printing.* P 11½.

A. Without Arms. (i) Yellow paper.

No.	Type	Description	Unused	Used
1	1	1d. black (9.1.86)	—	£3000
2		1d. violet (9.1.86)	11·00	13·00
		a. "1d." omitted (in pair with normal) (24.4.86)	£2000	
3		2d. violet (9.1.86)	15·00	20·00
		a. "d" omitted (13.10.86)	£4000	
4		3d. violet (13.1.86)	30·00	35·00
		a. "d" omitted (13.10.86)	£4000	
		b. *Tête-bêche* (pair) (13.10.86)		
5		4d. violet (30.8.86)	45·00	
6		6d. violet (20.2.86)	40·00	45·00
		a. "6d." omitted (in pair with normal) (2.7.86)		
7		9d. violet (13.1.86)	75·00	
8		1s. violet (30.8.86)	75·00	
		a. "1s." omitted (in pair with normal) (6.9.86)		
9		1/s. violet (13.10.86)	£650	
10		1/6 violet (30.8.86)	80·00	
11		1s.6d. violet (13.1.86)	£450	
		a. *Tête-bêche* (pair) (6.9.86)		
		b. "d" omitted (13.10.86)	£100	
12		2s. violet (30.8.86)	42·00	
		a. *Tête-bêche* (pair) (6.9.86)	£750	
13		2/6 violet (13.1.86)	£150	
14		2s.6d. violet (1.86)	£120	
15		4/s. violet (17.1.87)	£450	
15*a*		4s. violet (17.1.87)		
16		5s. violet (1.86)	30·00	40·00
		a. "s" omitted (in pair with normal) (7.3.86)	£3000	
17		5/6 violet (20.2.86)	£140	
18		5s.6d. violet (13.1.86)	£300	
19		7/6 violet (13.1.86)	£180	
20		7s.6d. violet (24.5.86)	£120	
21		10s. violet (13.1.86)	£150	£160
		a. *Tête-bêche* (pair) (2.7.86)		
22		10s.6d. violet (1.86)	£170	
		a. "d" omitted (1.86)	£100	
23		13s. violet (24.11.86)	£450	
24		£1 violet (13.1.86)	£120	
		a. *Tête-bêche* (pair) (13.10.86)	£500	
25		30s. violet (13.1.86)	£100	
		a. *Tête-bêche* (pair) (24.11.86)	£500	

(ii) Blue granite paper.

No.	Type	Description	Unused	Used
26	1	1d. violet (20.1.86)	16·00	18·00
		a. "d" omitted (24.11.86)	£500	
		b. "1" omitted (in pair with normal) (24.11.86)		
27		2d. violet (24.1.86)	16·00	18·00
		a. "d" omitted (24.4.86)	£1000	
		b. "2d." omitted (in pair with normal) (24.4.86)		
28		3d. violet (30.8.86)	22·00	24·00
		a. *Tête-bêche* (pair) (13.10.86)	£300	
29		4d. violet (24.5.86)	30·00	35·00
30		6d. violet (20.2.86)	50·00	50·00
		a. "6" omitted in pair with normal (24.5.86)	£2000	
31		9d. violet (6.9.86)	£110	
32		1s. violet (1.86)	30·00	35·00
		a. *Tête-bêche* (pair) (21.5.86)	£325	
		b. "1s." omitted (in pair with normal) (29.4.86)	£2000	
33		1s.6d. violet (2.7.86)	£100	
		a. *Tête-bêche* (pair) (6.9.86)	£550	
		b. "d" omitted (13.10.86)		
34		1/6 violet (6.9.86)	£150	
35		2s. violet (21.5.86)	£120	
		a. "2s." omitted (in pair with normal) (24.5.86)	£2000	
36		2s.6d. violet (19.8.86)	£150	
37		2/6 violet (19.8.86)	£180	
38		4/s. violet (17.1.87)	£350	
39		5/6 violet (13.1.86)	£250	
		a. "/" omitted (13.1.87)		
40		5s.6d. violet (13.1.86)	£250	
41		7/6 violet (13.1.86)	£250	
41*a*		7s.6d. violet (13.1.86)	£300	
42		10s. violet (1.86)	£200	£200
		a. *Tête-bêche* (pair) (2.7.86)	£425	
		b. "s" omitted (13.1.86)		
43		10s.6d. violet (1.86)	£200	
		a. *Tête-bêche* (pair) (13.1.86)		
		b. "d" omitted (1.86)	£450	
44		12s. violet (13.1.86)	£300	
45		13s. violet (17.1.87)	£475	
46		£1 violet (13.1.86)	£275	
47		30s. violet (13.1.86)	£250	

B. With embossed Arms of New Republic.

(i) Yellow paper.

No.	Type	Description	Unused	Used
48	1	1d. violet (20.1.86)	14·00	16·00
		a. Arms inverted (20.1.86)	27·00	30·00
		b. Arms *tête-bêche* (pair) (14.4.86)	£100	£120
		c. *Tête-bêche* (pair) (3.11.86)	£800	
49		2d. violet (30.8.86)	16·00	18·00
		a. Arms inverted (24.11.86)	25·00	30·00
50		4d. violet (2.12.86)	50·00	60·00
		a. Arms inverted (12.86)	£100	70·00
		b. Arms *tête-bêche* (pair) (12.86)	£250	
51		6d. violet (2.12.86)	£200	

(ii) Blue granite paper.

No.	Type	Description	Unused	Used
52	1	1d. violet (20.1.86)	15·00	17·00
		a. Arms inverted (10.2.86)	38·00	42·00
		b. Arms *tête-bêche* (pair) (3.11.86)	£500	
53		2d. violet (24.5.86)	15·00	17·00
		a. Arms inverted (30.8.86)	50·00	60·00
		b. Arms *tête-bêche* (pair) (2.12.86)	£500	£500

Stamps as Type **1** were produced as and when stocks were required, each printing including in its design the date on which it was prepared. The dates quoted above for Nos. 1/53 are those on which the various stamps first appeared. Details of the various printing dates are given below. From these dates it can be seen that some values share common printing dates, and, it is believed, that the different values were produced *se-tenant* within the same sheet, at least in some instances. A reported proof sheet in the Pretoria Postal Museum, on yellow paper and embossed, contains 4 examples of the 6d. value and 3 each of the 3d., 4d., 9d., 1s., 1/6, 2/-, 2/6, 3s., 4s., 5s., 5/6, 7/6, 10/-, 10/6, £1 and 30/-.

The date on No. 1 measures 17 mm; on all others it is 15 mm.

The significance, if any, of the two coloured papers and the use of the embossing machine have never been satisfactorily explained. Both the different papers and the embossing machine were introduced in January 1886, and occur throughout the period that the stamps with dates were used.

PRINTINGS

Date	*Paper*	*Face value*	*Cat No.*	*Unused*	*Used*
Jan 86	*Yellow*	5s.	16	30·00	40·00
		10s.6d.	22	£200	
		10s.6	22a	£150	
	Blue	1s.	32		
		10s.	42	£200	£200
		10s.6d.	43	£200	
		10s.6	43b	£500	
7 Jan 86	*Yellow*	10s.6d.	22	£170	
	Blue	10s.	42		
		10s.6d.	43	£475	
9 Jan 86	*Yellow*	1d. blk	1	†	£3000
		1d. vio	2	11·00	13·00
		2d.	3	40·00	50·00
13 Jan 86	*Yellow*	1d.	2	38·00	
		2d.	3	35·00	38·00
		3d.	4	75·00	
		9d	7	£200	
		1s.6d.	11	£450	
		2/6	13	£160	
		2s.6d.	14	£200	
		5s.6d.	18		
		7/6	19	£180	
		10s.	21		
		£1	24	£150	
		30s.	25	£150	
	Blue	5/6	39	£250	
		5s.6d.	40	£250	
		7/6	41	£250	
		7s.6d.	41a	£300	
		10s.	42	£400	
		10s.	42b		
		10s.6d.	43	£200	
		10s.6d.	43a		
		12s.	44	£300	
		£1	46	£250	
		30s.	47	£250	
20 Jan 86	*Yellow*	1d.	2		
	Blue	1d.	26	£250	
	Yellow, embossed	1d.	48	75·00	
		1d.	48a	£100	
	Blue, embossed	1d.	52	£130	
Jan 20 86	*Blue*	1d.	26	25·00	
	Yellow, embossed	1d.	48a		
	Blue, embossed	1d.	52	£120	
24 Jan 86	*Blue*	1d.	26	30·00	
		2d.	27	50·00	
10 Feb 86	*Yellow*	1d.	2		
	Yellow, embossed	1d.	48		
		1d.	48a	75·00	
	Blue, embossed	1d.	52	£130	
		1d.	52a	45·00	
20 Feb 86	*Yellow*	6d.	6		
		1s.6d.	11		
		2s.6d.	14	£130	
		5/6	17	£140	
		5s.6d.	18		
	Blue	6d.	30		
7 Mar 86	*Yellow*	1d.	2	£110	
		2/6	13		
		2s.6d.	14	£120	
		5s.	16	£200	90·00
		5s.	16a	£3000	
		5/6	17	£140	
		5s.6d.	18	£300	
	Blue	2d.	27	£100	
		6d.	30		
		1s.	32		
17 Mar 86	*Yellow*	1d.	2	£100	
	Yellow, embossed	1d.	48	50·00	
	Blue, embossed	1d.	52	£130	
		1d.	52a	£110	
26 Mar 86	*Blue, embossed*	1d.	52a	£130	
14 Apr 86	*Yellow*	1d.	2		
	Yellow, embossed	1d.	48	30·00	
		1d.	48a	60.00	
		1d.	48b	£100	£120
	Blue, embossed	1d.	52	50·00	
		1d.	52a		
24 Apr 86	*Yellow*	1d.	2	£100	
		1d.	2a	£2000	
		5s.	16		
	Blue	2d.	27	75·00	
		2d.	27a	£1000	
		2d.	27b		
29 Apr 86	*Blue*	1s.	32	£110	
		1s.	32b		
21 May 86	*Yellow*	6d.	6	£130	
	Blue	1d.	26	90·00	
		1s.	32	30·00	35·00
		1s.	32a	£325	
		1s.	32b	£1500	
		2s.	35	£275	
23 May 86	*Blue, embossed*	1d.	52a	£100	
24 May 86	*Yellow*	1d.	2	£100	
		2d.	3	£120	
		5s.	16	£100	
		7/6	19	£180	
		7s.6d.	20	£120	
	Blue	1d.	26	35·00	38·00
		2d.	27	£300	£300
		4d.	29	£100	
		6d.	30	£120	
		6d.	30a	£2000	
		1s.	32	£200	
		1s.	32b	£2000	
		2s.	35	£150	
		2s.	35a	£2000	
	Blue, embossed	2d.	53	£100	
26 May 86	*Yellow*	1d.	2		
	Blue	1d.	26	£110	
	Yellow, embossed	1d.	48	£250	
		1d.	48a	£100	
	Blue, embossed	1d.	52	£130	
		1d.	52a	50·00	55·00
28 May 86	*Yellow, embossed*	1d.	48	£150	
Jun 30 86	*Blue*	1d.	26	16·00	18·00
	Yellow, embossed	1d.	48	18·00	20·00
		1d.	48a	27·00	30·00
		1d.	48b	£200	£225
	Blue, embossed	1d.	52	48·00	42·00
2 Jul 86	*Yellow*	6d.	6	£200	
		6d.	6a		
		9d	7	£200	£200
		10s.	21		
		10s.	21a		
	Blue	1s.6d.	33	£100	
		10s.	42	£200	
		10s.	42a	£425	
		10s.6d.	43		
		10s.6d.	43b	£450	
3 Jul 86	*Blue*	10s.	42		
Jul 7 86	*Yellow*	1d.	2		
	Blue	1d.	26		
	Yellow, embossed	1d.	48	75·00	
		1d.	48a	£100	£100
	Blue, embossed	1d.	52	18·00	20·00
		1d.	52a	60·00	42·00
4 Aug 86	*Yellow*	1d.	2		
	Yellow, embossed	1d.	48	60·00	
	Blue, embossed	1d.	52	60·00	
		1d.	52a		
19 Aug 86	*Yellow*	2/6	13		
		2s.6d.	14	£140	
	Blue	2s.6d.	36	£150	
		2/6	37	£180	
30 Aug 86	*Yellow*	1d.	2	11·00	13·00

Date	Paper	Face value	Cat No.	Unused	Used
		2d.	3	75·00	
		3d.	4	80·00	
		4d.	5	55·00	
		6d.	6	£100	
		9d.	7	75·00	
		1s.	8	75·00	
		1/6	10	80·00	
		2s.	12	£100	
		2/6	13	£150	
	Blue	2d.	27	16·00	18·00
		3d.	28		
	Yellow, embossed	2d.	49	£100	
	Blue, embossed	2d.	53	45·00	
		2d.	53a	£110	
6 Sep 86	*Yellow*	1d.	2	£100	
		2d.	3	35·00	40·00
		3d.	4	40·00	
		4d.	5	45·00	
		6d.	6	75·00	
		9d.	7	75·00	
		1s.	8	£100	
		1s.	8a		
		1/6	10	£140	
		1s.6d.	11	£450	
		1s.6d.	11a		
		2s.	12	£100	
		2s.	12a	£750	
		2/6	13	£150	
		2s.6d.	14		
		5s.	16	£140	
		7s.6d.	20	£200	
		10s.	21	£150	
		£1	24	£140	
	Blue	6d.	30	50·00	50·00
		9d.	31	£110	
		1s.	32	75·00	
		1s.6d.	33	£140	
		1s.6d.	33a	£550	
		1/6	34		
		2s.6d.	36		
		2/6	37	£400	
		7s.6d.	41a	£300	
		10s.6d.	43		
13 Sep 86	*Yellow*	1d.	2		
	Yellow, embossed	1d.	48	75·00	
		1d.	48a	75·00	
	Blue, embossed	1d.	52	£100	
6 Oct 86	*Yellow*	1d.	2		
	Blue	1d.	26	90·00	
	Yellow, embossed	1d.	48	75·00	60·00
		1d.	48a		
	Blue, embossed	1d.	52	48·00	20·00
		1d.	52a	90·00	
13 Oct 86	*Yellow*	1d.	2	25·00	25·00
		2d.	3	25·00	30·00
		2d.	3a	£4000	
		3d.	4	30·00	35·00
		3d.	4a	£4000	
		3d.	4b		
		4d.	5	50·00	
		6d.	6	40·00	45·00
		9d.	7	75.00	
		1s.	8	£150	
		1/s	9	£550	
		1/6	10	£150	
		1s 6.	11b	£100	
		2s.	12	42·00	
		2/6	13	£160	
		5s.	16	75·00	
		10s.	21	£150	£160
		10s.6.	22a	£100	
		£1	24	£120	
		£1	24a	£500	
	Blue	2d.	27	16·00	18·00
		3d.	28	22·00	24·00
		3d.	28a	£300	
		4d.	29	30·00	35·00
		1s.	32	50.00	
		1s 6.	33b		
		1/6	34	£150	
		2s.	35	£120	
3 Nov 86	*Yellow*	1d.	2	40·00	
	Blue	1d.	26		
	Yellow, embossed	1d.	48	14·00	16·00
		1d.	48a	27·00	30·00
		1d.	48b	£100	£120
		1d.	48c	£800	
	Blue, embossed	1d.	52	15·00	
		1d.	52a	38·00	42·00
		1d.	52b	£500	
13 Nov 86	*Yellow*	1d.	2	£120	
24 Nov 86	*Yellow*	1d.	2	£100	
		2d.	3	15·00	20·00
		3d.	4	35·00	40·00
		1/6	10	£150	
		10s.	21	£200	
		13s.	23	£450	
		30s.	25	£100	
		30s.	25a	£500	
	Blue	1d.	26	40·00	30·00
		1d.	26a	£500	
		1d.	26b		
		2d.	27	50·00	
		2d.	27a		
		4d.	29	30·00	35·00
		6d.	30	60·00	60·00
		9d.	31	£120	
		1s.	32	£100	£110
		1/6	34	£200	
		2s.	35	£150	
		2s.	35a	£3000	
	Yellow, embossed	2d.	49	£160	
		2d.	49a		
26 Nov 86	*Yellow*	1/6	10	£140	
2 Dec 86	*Yellow*	1d.	2		
		2d.	3		
	Blue	2d.	27		
	Yellow, embossed	1d.	48	25·00	30·00
		1d.	48a	£160	
		2d.	49	16·00	18·00
		2d.	49a	25·00	30·00
		4d.	50	£150	
		6d.	51	£150	
	Blue, embossed	1d.	52	35·00	
		1d.	52a	£160	
		2d.	53	15·00	17·00
		2d.	53a	50·00	60·00
		2d.	53b	£500	£500
3 Dec 86	*Yellow, embossed*	6d.	51		
Dec 86	*Yellow*	6d.	6		
	Blue	4d.	29		
	Yellow, embossed	4d.	50	50·00	60·00
		4d.	50a	£100	70·00
		4d.	50b	£250	
		6d.	51	£200	
4 Jan 87	*Yellow*	1d.	2	£100	
		2d.	3	40·00	
		13s.	23	£450	
	Blue	1d.	26	16·00	18·00
		2d.	27	20·00	20·00
	Blue, embossed	2d.	53	45·00	
13 Jan 87	*Yellow*	7/6	19		
	Blue	5/6	39	£450	
		5/6	39a		
		7/6	41	£500	
17 Jan 87	*Yellow*	1d.	2	75·00	
		2d.	3	75·00	
		3d.	4	75·00	
		4/s.	15	£450	
		4s.	15a		
	Blue	1d.	26	80·00	
		4/s.	38	£350	
		13s.	45	£475	
		30s.	47	£275	
20 Jan 87	*Blue*	2d.	27	38·00	
	Yellow, embossed	2d.	49	55·00	
		2d.	49a	£140	
	Blue, embossed	2d.	53	45·00	
		2d.	53a	£100	
Jan 20 87	*Yellow, embossed*	1d.	48a	£400	

1887 (Jan–Mar). *As T* **1**, *but without date. With embossed Arms.*

(a) Blue granite paper.

		Unused	Used
72	1d. violet	17·00	15·00
	b. Stamps *tête-bêche* (pair)	£475	
	c. Arms *tête-bêche* (pair)		
	d. Arms inverted	25·00	25·00
	e. Arms omitted	£110	£110
	f. Arms sideways		
73	2d. violet	10·00	10·00
	a. Stamps *tête-bêche* (pair)	£325	
	b. Arms inverted	28·00	28·00
	c. Arms omitted	£110	£100
	d. Arms *tête-bêche* (pair)		
74	3d. violet	17·00	17·00
	a. Stamps *tête-bêche* (pair)	£375	
	b. Arms *tête-bêche* (pair)		
	c. Arms inverted	50·00	50·00
75	4d. violet	14·00	14·00
	a. Stamps *tête-bêche* (pair)	£325	
	b. Arms *tête-bêche* (pair)	£275	
	c. Arms inverted	85·00	
76	6d. violet	17·00	17·00
	a. Arms inverted	85·00	
77	1/6 violet	24·00	22·00
	a. Arms inverted	£120	
	b. Arms *tête-bêche* (pair)	£400	
77*c*	2/6 violet	†	£750

(b) Yellow paper (March 1887).

		Unused	Used
78	2d. violet (*arms omitted*)	25·00	
79	3d. violet	16·00	17·00
	b. Stamps *tête-bêche* (pair)	£325	£375
	c. Arms *tête-bêche* (pair)	£200	
	d. Arms inverted	27·00	27·00
	e. Arms sideways	£300	
80	4d. violet	14·00	14·00
	a. Arms inverted	16·00	16·00
81	6d. violet	9·00	10·00
	a. Arms *tête-bêche* (pair)	£350	
	b. Arms inverted	45·00	45·00
	c. Arms omitted	80·00	
82	9d. violet	12·00	13·00
	a. Arms inverted	£200	
	b. Arms *tête-bêche* (pair)	£350	
83	1s. violet	12·00	12·00
	a. Arms inverted	70·00	
84	1/6 violet	22·00	20·00
85	2s. violet	19·00	18·00
	a. Arms inverted	55·00	50·00
	b. Arms omitted	£100	
86	2/6 violet	25·00	25·00
	a. Arms inverted	32·00	32·00
87	3s. violet	48·00	48·00
	a. Arms inverted	55·00	55·00
	b. Stamps *tête-bêche* (pair)	£450	
88	4s. violet	£300	
	a. Arms omitted		
88*b*	4/s violet	45·00	45·00
	ba. Arms omitted	£180	
89	5s. violet	40·00	40·00
	b. Arms inverted	—	£100
90	5/6 violet	16·00	17·00
91	7/6 violet	20·00	22·00
	a. Arms *tête-bêche* (pair)		
	b. Arms inverted	£100	
92	10s. violet	16·00	17·00
	b. Arms *tête-bêche* (pair)	£120	
	c. Arms inverted	27·00	
	d. Arms omitted	£100	48·00
93	10/6 violet	17·00	17·00
	b. Arms inverted	50·00	
94	£1 violet	55·00	55·00
	a. Stamps *tête-bêche* (pair)	£450	£500
	b. Arms inverted	60·00	
95	30s. violet	£140	

A £15 value as Nos. 78/95 exists, but is only known fiscally used (*Price* £4000).

Many values exist with double impressions of the handstamp.

New Republic united with the South African Republic (Transvaal) on 21 July 1888. In 1903 the territory of the former New Republic was transferred to Natal.

V. ORANGE FREE STATE

PRICES FOR STAMPS ON COVER	
Nos. 1/9	*from* × 20
Nos. 10/13	*from* × 30
Nos. 18/19	*from* × 20
No. 20	—
Nos. 21/42	*from* × 40
Nos. 48/51	*from* × 25
Nos. 52/138	*from* × 10
Nos. 139/51	*from* × 7
Nos. F1/17	—
Nos. PF1/3	*from* × 20
No. M1	*from* × 20

Supplies of Cape of Good Hope stamps were available at Bloemfontein and probably elsewhere in the Orange Free State, from mid-1856 onwards for use on mail to Cape Colony and beyond. Such arrangements continued after the introduction of Orange Free State stamps in 1868. It is not known if the dumb cancellations used on the few surviving covers were applied in the Free State or at Cape Town.

1

(Typo D.L.R.)

1868 (1 Jan)–**94**. P 14.

			Unused	Used
1	**1**	1d. pale brown	18·00	1·50
2		1d. red-brown	13·00	45
3		1d. deep brown	19·00	45
4		6d. pale rose (1868)	50·00	8·00
5		6d. rose (1871)	21·00	5·50
6		6d. rose-carmine (1891)	21·00	12·00
7		6d. bright carmine (1894)	13·00	2·00
8		1s. orange-buff	80·00	6·50
9		1s. orange-yellow	40·00	1·50
		a. Double print	—	£3000

4 4 4 4

(**2**) (*a*) (*b*) (*c*) (*d*)

1877. *No. 5 surcharged T* **2** *(a) to (d).*

			Unused	Used
10	**1**	4d. on 6d. rose (*a*)	£350	55·00
		a. Surch inverted	—	£550
		b. Surch double (*a* + *c*)		
		c. Surch double, one inverted (*a* + *c* inverted)	†	£2750
		d. Surch double, one inverted (*a* inverted + *c*)	†	£4500
11		4d. on 6d. rose (*b*)	£1200	£180
		a. Surch inverted	—	£1100
		b. Surch double (*b* + *d*)		
12		4d. on 6d. rose (*c*)	£180	28·00
		a. Surch inverted	—	£350
		b. Surch double		
13		4d. on 6d. rose (*d*)	£225	35·00
		a. Surch inverted	£1100	£375
		b. Surch double, one inverted (*d* + *c* inverted)	†	£3000

The setting of 60 comprised nine stamps as No. 10, four as No. 11, twenty-seven as No. 12 and twenty as No. 13.

1878 (July). P 14.

			Unused	Used
18	**1**	4d. pale blue	21·00	3·25
19		4d. ultramarine	4·00	2·50
20		5s. green	9·00	12·00

1d. 1d. 1d. 1d. 1d. 1d.

(**3**) (*a*) (*b*) (*c*) (*d*) (*e*) (*f*)

Type **3**: (*a*) Small "1" and "d." (*b*) Sloping serif. (*c*) Same size as (*b*), but "1" with straighter horizontal serif. (*d*) Taller "1" with horizontal serif and antique "d". (*e*) Same size as (*d*) but with sloping serif and thin line at foot. (*f*) as (*d*) but with Roman "d".

1881 (19 May). *No. 20 surch T* **3** *(a) to (f) with heavy black bar cancelling the old value.*

			Unused	Used
21	**1**	1d. on 5s. green (*a*)	95·00	22·00
22		1d. on 5s. green (*b*)	55·00	22·00
		a. Surch inverted	—	£800
		b. Surch double	—	£1100
23		1d. on 5s. green (*c*)	£200	75·00
		a. Surch inverted	—	£1200
		b. Surch double	—	£1400
24		1d. on 5s. green (*d*)	85·00	22·00
		a. Surch inverted	£1600	£800
		b. Surch double	—	£1100
25		1d. on 5s. green (*e*)	£500	£250
		a. Surch inverted	†	£2000
		b. Surch double	†	£2000
26		1d. on 5s. green (*f*)	80·00	22·00
		a. Surch inverted	—	£750
		b. Surch double	—	£800

No. 21 was the first printing in one type only. Nos. 22 to 25 constitute the second printing about a year later, and are all found on the same sheet; and No. 26 the third printing of which about half have the stop raised.

Owing to defective printing, examples of Nos. 22 and 24/5 may be found with the obliterating bar at the top of the stamps or, from the top row, without the bar.

½d

(**4**)

1882 (Aug). *No. 20 surch with T* **4** *and with a thin black line cancelling old value.*

			Unused	Used
36	**1**	½d. on 5s. green	18·00	3·75
		a. Surch double	£400	£325
		b. Surch inverted	£1200	£800

3d 3d 3d 3d 3d
(5) (a) (b) (c) (d) (e)

1882. *No. 19 surch with T* **5** *(a) to (e) with thin black line cancelling value.*

38 **1** 3d. on 4d. ultramarine (*a*) ... 80·00 26·00
a. Surch double ... † £1200
39 3d. on 4d. ultramarine (*b*) ... 80·00 18·00
a. Surch double ... † £1200
40 3d. on 4d. ultramarine (*c*) ... 35·00 17·00
a. Surch double ... † £1200
41 3d. on 4d. ultramarine (*d*) ... 80·00 19·00
a. Surch double ... † £1200
42 3d. on 4d. ultramarine (*e*) ... £200 65·00
a. Surch double ... † £2750

Examples of Nos. 39 and 41/2 exist without the cancelling bar due to the misplacement of the surcharge.

1883–84. P 14.

48 **1** ½d. chestnut ... 2·75 50
49 2d. pale mauve ... 15·00 75
50 2d. bright mauve ... 15·00 30
51 3d. ultramarine ... 3·25 2·00

For 1d. purple, see No. 68.

2d 2d 2d
(6) (a) (b) (c)

1888 (Sept–Oct). *No. 51 surch with T* **6** *(a), (b) or (c).*

(a) Wide "2". (b) Narrow "2".

52 **1** 2d. on 3d. ultramarine (*a*) (Sept) ... 55·00 9·00
a. Surch inverted ... — £750
53 2d. on 3d. ultramarine (*b*) ... 38·00 2·00
a. Surch inverted ... — £300
b. "2" with curved foot (*c*) ... £1200 £500

1d 1d 1d
(7) (a) (b) (c)

1890 (Dec)–**91**. *Nos. 51 and 19 surch with T* **7** *(a) to (c).*

54 **1** 1d. on 3d. ultramarine (*a*) ... 7·00 60
a. Surch double ... 80·00 70·00
c. "1" and "d" wide apart ... £140 £110
d. Dropped "d" (Right pane R. 5/6) ... £150 £120
55 1d. on 3d. ultramarine (*b*) ... 22·00 2·75
a. Surch double ... £250 £250
57 1d. on 4d. ultramarine (*a*) ... 28·00 6·50
a. Surch double ... £130 £110
b. Surch double (*a* + *b*) ... £375
c. Surch triple ... — £1500
d. Raised "1" (Left pane R. 3/1) ...
58 1d. on 4d. ultramarine (*b*) ... 75·00 50·00
a. Surch double ... £400 £325
59 1d. on 4d. ultramarine (*c*) ... £1400 £500
a. Surch double ...

The settings of the 1d. on 3d. and on 4d. are not identical. The variety (*c*) does not exist on the 3d.

2½d. 2½d.
(8) Printers leads after surcharge (Lower right pane No. 43)

1892 (Oct). *No. 51 surch with T* **8**.

67 **1** 2½d. on 3d. ultramarine ... 15·00 70
a. No stop after "d" ... 75·00 50·00
b. Printers leads after surcharge ... — 50·00

1894 (Sept). *Colour changed.* P 14.

68 **1** 1d. purple ... 3·25 30

½d ½d ½d
(9) (a) (b) (c)

½d ½d ½d ½d
(d) (e) (f) (g)

Types (*a*) and (*e*) differ from types (*b*) and (*f*) respectively, in the serifs of the "1", but owing to faulty overprinting this distinction is not always clearly to be seen.

1896 (Sept). *No. 51 surch with T* **9** *(a) to (g).*

69 **1** ½d. on 3d. ultramarine (*a*) ... 4·75 9·00
70 ½d. on 3d. ultramarine (*b*) ... 12·00 12·00
71 ½d. on 3d. ultramarine (*c*) ... 10·00 2·50
72 ½d. on 3d. ultramarine (*d*) ... 10·00 2·25
73 ½d. on 3d. ultramarine (*e*) ... 10·00 2·25
74 ½d. on 3d. ultramarine (*f*) ... 12·00 13·00
75 ½d. on 3d. ultramarine (*g*) ... 7·00 3·75
a. Surch double ... 13·00 10·00
b. Surch triple ... 70·00 70·00

The double and triple surcharges are often different types, but are always type (*g*), or in combination with type (*g*).

Double surcharges in the same type, but without the "d" and bar, also exist, probably from a trial sheet prepared by the printer. Both mint and used examples are known.

Halve Penny.

(10) 2½ (11)

1896. *No. 51 surch with T* **10**.

77 **1** ½d. on 3d. ultramarine ... 1·00 50

(i) Errors in setting.

78 **1** ½d. on 3d. (no stop) ... 16·00 28·00
79 ½d. on 3d. ("Peuny") ... 16·00 28·00

(ii) Surch inverted.

81 **1** ½d. on 3d. ... 55·00 60·00
81*a* ½d. on 3d. (no stop) ... £2000
81*b* ½d. on 3d. ("Peuny") ... £1500

(iii) Surch double, one inverted.

81*c* **1** ½d. on 3d. (Nos. 77 and 81) ... £180 £200
81*d* ½d. on 3d. (Nos. 77 and 81*a*) ... £750 £750
81*e* ½d. on 3d. (Nos. 77 and 81*b*) ... £850 £850
81*f* ½d. on 3d. (Nos. 81 and 78) ... — £850
82 ½d. on 3d. (Nos. 81 and 79) ... — £850

Examples from the top horizontal row can be found without the bar due to the surcharge being misplaced.

Nos. 69 to 75 also exist surcharged as last but they are considered not to have been issued with authority (*Prices from £30 each, unused*).

1897 (1 Jan). *No. 51 surch with T* **11**. *(a) As in illustration. (b) With Roman "1" and antique "2" in fraction.*

83 **1** 2½d. on 3d. ultramarine (*a*) ... 7·50 80
83*a* 2½d. on 3d. ultramarine (*b*) ... £160 90·00

1897. P 14.

84 **1** ½d. yellow (March) ... 2·00 35
85 ½d. orange ... 2·00 35
87 1s. brown (Aug) ... 22·00 1·50

The 6d. blue was prepared for use in the Orange Free State, but had not been brought into use when the stamps were seized in Bloemfontein. A few have been seen without the "V.R.I." overprint but they were not authorized or available for postage (*Price £60*).

BRITISH OCCUPATION

V. R. I. V. R. I. V. R. I.

4d ½d ½d
31 (Level stops) (**32**) Thin "V" (Raised stops) (**33**) Thick "V"

V. R. I.
Inserted "R"

(Surch by Curling & Co, Bloemfontein)

1900. *T* **1** *surch as T* **31/33** *(2½d. on 3d. optd "V.R.I." only).*

(a) First printings surch as T **31** *with stops level (March).*

101 ½d. on ½d. orange ... 3·25 3·75
a. No stop after "V" (R.10/3) ... 20·00 24·00
b. No stop after "I" (R.1/3) ... £160 £160
c. "½" omitted (R.7/5) ... £180 £180
d. "I" omitted ... £200 £200
e. "V.R.I." omitted ... £170
f. Value omitted ... £110
g. Small "½" ... 55·00 55·00
h. Surch double ... £180
102 1d. on 1d. purple ... 2·50 1·25
a. Surch on 1d. deep brown (No. 3) ... £600 £400
b. No stop after "V" (R. 10/3) ... 16·00 13·00
c. No stop after "R" ... £160 £170
d. No stop after "I" ...
e. "1" omitted (R. 7/5) ... £180 £190
f. "I" omitted (with strips present) ... £325 £325
g. "I" and stop after "R" omitted (R. 2/3) ... £250 £250
h. "V.R.I." omitted ... £160 £170
i. "d" omitted ... £325 £325
j. Value omitted ... 90·00 95·00
k. Inverted stop after "R" ... £225 £250
l. Wider space between "1" and "d" ... £100 £100
m. "V" and "R" close ... £160 £160
n. Pair, one without surch ... £475
o. "V" omitted ... £850
103 2d. on 2d. bright mauve ... 3·00 1·00
a. No stop after "V" (R. 10/3) ... 14·00 17·00
b. No stop after "R" ... £275 £275
c. No stop after "I" ... £275 £275
d. "V.R.I." omitted ... £300 £300
e. Value omitted ... £300
104 2½d. on 3d. ultramarine (*a*) ... 16·00 13·00
a. No stop after "V" (R. 10/3) ... 85·00 85·00
105 2½d. on 3d. ultramarine (*b*) ... £200 £200
106 3d. on 3d. ultramarine ... 2·50 2·50
a. No stop after "V" (R. 10/3) ... 19·00 19·00
b. Pair, one without surch ... £550
c. "V.R.I." omitted ... £250 £250
d. Value omitted ... £250 £250
107 4d. on 4d. ultramarine ... 8·00 16·00
a. No stop after "V" ... 60·00 70·00
108 6d. on 6d. bright carmine ... 40·00 35·00
a. No stop after "V" (R. 10/3) ... £250 £275
b. "6" omitted (R. 7/5) ... £300 £300
109 6d. on 6d. blue ... 9·00 4·00
a. No stop after "V" (R. 10/3) ... 40·00 42·00
b. "6" omitted (R. 7/5) ... 75·00 80·00
c. "V.R.I." omitted ... £500 £300
110 1s. on 1s. brown ... 7·00 2·75
a. Surch on 1s. orange-yellow (No. 9) ... £3500 £2500
b. No stop after "V" (R. 10/3) ... 45·00 32·00
c. "1" omitted ... £130 £130
ca. "1" inserted by hand ... † £1000
d. "1" omitted and spaced stop after "s" ... £140 £150
e. "V.R.I." omitted ... £190 £190
f. Value omitted ... £190 £190
g. Raised stop after "s" ... 17·00 11·00
h. Wider space between "1" and "s" ... £150 £150
111 5s. on 5s. green ... 22·00 45·00
a. No stop after "V" (R. 10/3) ... £250 £300
b. "5" omitted ... £950 £1000
c. Inverted stop after "R" ... £700 £700
d. Wider space between "5" and "s" ... £130 £140
e. Value omitted ... £375 £400

All values are found with a rectangular, instead of an oval, stop after "R". Misplaced surcharges (upwards or sideways) occur.

No. 110ca shows the missing "1" replaced by a handstamp in a different type face.

(b) Subsequent printings.

(i) Surch as T **32**.

112 ½d. on ½d. orange ... 30 20
a. Raised and level stops mixed ... 2·00 2·00
b. Pair, one with level stops ... 11·00 15·00
c. No stop after "V" ... 2·75 3·00
d. No stop after "I" ... 27·00 28·00
e. "V" omitted ... £550
f. Small "½" ... 15·00 17·00
g. As a, and small "½" ... 15·00 17·00
i. Space between "V" and "R" ... 20·00 22·00
j. Value omitted ... £120 £120
113 1d. on 1d. purple ... 30 20
a. Raised and level stops mixed ... 1·60 2·25
b. Pair, one with level stops ... 20·00 21·00
c. No stop after "V" ... 3·25 6·00
d. No stop after "R" ... 16·00 17·00
e. No stop after "I" ... 16·00 17·00
f. No stops after "V" and "I" ... £300
g. Surch inverted ... £375
h. Surch double ... £110 £100
i. Pair, one without surch ... £250
j. Short figure "1" ... £110 £110
k. Space between "V" and "R" ... 50·00 55·00
l. Space between "R" and "I" ... £120 £130
m. Space between "1" and "d" ... £190 £190
n. Inserted "R" ... £325 £325
o. Inserted "V" ... £700
p. Stamp doubly printed, one impression inverted ... £2500
114 2d. on 2d. bright mauve ... 1·25 30
a. Raised and level stops mixed ... 4·75 4·75
b. Pair, one with level stops ... 8·50 9·00
c. Surch inverted ... £325 £325
d. "1" raised ... 75·00 75·00
e. Pair, one without surch ... £325 £325
f. No stop after "V" ... £1000
g. No stop after "I" ...
115 2½d. on 3d. ultramarine (*a*) ... £200 £180
a. Raised and level stops mixed ... £600
116 2½d. on 3d. ultramarine (*b*) ... £1200
117 3d. on 3d. ultramarine ... 60 30
a. Raised and level stops mixed ... 7·00 7·00
b. Pair, one with level stops ... 18·00 19·00
c. No stop after "V" ... £140 £140
d. No stop after "R" ... £375 £450
e. "I" omitted ... £400 £425
f. Surch double ... £400
g. Surch double, one diagonal ... £375
h. Ditto, diagonal surch with mixed stops ... £6500
n. Inserted "R" ...
o. Space between "3" and "d" ... £140
118 4d. on 4d. ultramarine ... 3·25 2·75
a. Raised and level stops mixed ... 10·00 13·00
b. Pair, one with level stops ... 21·00 29·00
119 6d. on 6d. bright carmine ... 35·00 48·00
a. Raised and level stops mixed ... £140 £140
b. Pair, one with level stops ... £225 £275
120 6d. on 6d. blue ... 70 40
a. Raised and level stops mixed ... 8·00 8·00
b. Pair, one with level stops ... 20·00 22·00
c. No stop after "V" ... £500 £500
d. No stop after "R" ... £300
e. Value omitted ... £450
121 1s. on 1s. brown ... 5·00 45
a. Surch on 1s. orange-yellow (No. 9) ... £1300 £1300
b. Raised and level stops mixed ... 18·00 18·00
c. Pair, one with level stops ... 35·00 38·00
f. "s" omitted ... £250
g. "V.R.I." omitted ... £400
122 5s. on 5s. green ... 8·50 8·50
a. Raised and level stops mixed ... £325 £325
b. Pair, one with level stops ... £1000
c. Short top to "5" ... 60·00 70·00
s. Handstamped "Specimen" ... 50·00

(ii) Surch as T **33**.

123 ½d. on ½d. orange ... 4·25 3·00
124 1d. on 1d. purple ... 4·75 35
a. Inverted "1" for "I" ... 19·00 19·00
b. No stops after "R" and "I" ... 90·00 70·00
c. No stop after "R" ... 42·00 48·00
d. Surch double ... £325 £325
n. Inserted "R" ... £400 £400
p. Stamp doubly printed, one impression inverted ... £5500
125 2d. on 2d. bright mauve ... 10·00 11·00
a. Inverted "1" for "I" ... 27·00 30·00
126 2½d. on 3d. ultramarine (*a*) ... £650 £750
127 2½d. on 3d. ultramarine (*b*) ... £3750
128 3d. on 3d. ultramarine ... 5·50 12·00
a. Inverted "1" for "I" ... 65·00 75·00
b. Surch double ... £550
ba. Surch double, one diagonal ... £550
129 6d. on 6d. bright carmine ... £425 £425
130 6d. on 6d. blue ... 13·00 24·00
131 1s. on 1s. brown ... 22·00 8·00
132 5s. on 5s. green ... 50·00 48·00
s. Handstamped "Specimen" ... £150

Stamps with thick "V" occur in certain positions in *later* settings of the type with stops above the line (T **32**). *Earlier* settings with stops above the line have all stamps with thin "V".

Some confusion has previously been caused by the listing of certain varieties as though they occurred on stamps with thick "V" in fact they occur on stamps showing the normal thin "V", included in the settings which also contained the thick "V".

For a short period small blocks of unsurcharged Free State stamps could be handed in for surcharging so that varieties occur which are not found in the complete settings. Nos. 102a, 110a and 121a also occur from such stocks.

The inserted "R" variety occurs on positions 6 (T **32**) and 12 (T **33**) of the forme. The "R" of the original surcharge failed to print and the "R", but not the full stop, was added by the use of a handstamp. Traces of the original letter are often visible. The broken "V" flaw, also shown in the illustration, does not appear on No. 124n.

ORANGE RIVER COLONY

CROWN COLONY

ORANGE RIVER COLONY. (34) — 4d (35) — E. R. I. 6d (36)

1900 (10 Aug)–**02**. *Nos. 58a, 61a and 67 of Cape of Good Hope (wmk Cabled Anchor. P 14) optd with T* **34** *by W. A. Richards and Sons, Cape Town.*

133		½d. green (13.10.00)	50	10
		a. No stop	8·00	17·00
		b. Opt double	£650	£700
134		1d. carmine (May 1902)	1·75	10
		a. No stop	17·00	22·00
135		2½d. ultramarine	2·00	35
		a. No stop	65·00	75·00
133/5 *Set of 3*			3·75	50

In the ½d. and 2½d., the "no stop" after "COLONY" variety was the first stamp in the left lower pane. In the 1d. it is the twelfth stamp in the right lower pane on which the stop was present at the beginning of the printing but became damaged and soon failed to print.

1902 (14 Feb). *Surch with T* **35** *by "Bloemfontein Express".*

136		4d. on 6d. on 6d. blue (No. 120) (R.)	1·50	75
		a. No stop after "R"	35·00	40·00
		b. No stop after "I"	£1200	
		c. Surch on No. 130 (Thick "V")	2·00	6·00
		ca. Inverted "1" for "I"	6·00	16·00

1902 (Aug). *Surch with T* **36**.

137	1	6d. on 6d. blue	3·75	12·00
		a. Surch double, one inverted		
		b. Wide space between "6" and "d" (R. 4/2)	60·00	90·00

(37)

38 King Edward VII, Springbok and Gnu

1902 (Sept). *Surch with T* **37**.

138	1	1s. on 5s. green (O.)	7·50	15·00
		a. Thick "V"	15·00	38·00
		b. Short top to "5"	70·00	80·00
		c. Surch double		

(Typo D.L.R.)

1903 (3 Feb)–**04**. Wmk Crown CA. P 14.

139	**38**	½d. yellow-green (6.7.03)	9·00	1·25
		w. Wmk inverted	£150	85·00
140		1d. scarlet	5·50	10
		w. Wmk inverted	£150	75·00
141		2d. brown (6.7.03)	7·50	80
142		2½d. bright blue (6.7.03)	2·00	50
143		3d. mauve (6.7.03)	8·50	90
144		4d. scarlet and sage-green (6.7.03)	32·00	2·00
		a. "IOSTAGE" for "POSTAGE"	£800	£450
145		6d. scarlet and mauve (6.7.03)	8·50	1·00
146		1s. scarlet and bistre (6.7.03)	32·00	1·75
147		5s. blue and brown (31.10.04)	80·00	23·00
139/47 *Set of 9*			£170	28·00
139s/47s Optd "Specimen" *Set of 9*			£170	

No. 144a occurs on R. 10/2 of the upper left pane.

The 2d. exists from coils constructed from normal sheets for use in stamp machines introduced in 1911.

Several of the above values are found with the overprint "C.S.A.R.", in black, for use by the Central South African Railways. Examples also exist perforated "CSAR" or "NGR".

1905 (Nov)–**09**. Wmk Mult Crown CA. P 14.

148	**38**	½d. yellow-green (28.7.07)	9·00	50
149		1d. scarlet	9·00	30
150		4d. scarlet and sage-green (8.11.07)	4·50	3·00
		a. "IOSTAGE" for "POSTAGE"	£180	£150
151		1s. scarlet and bistre (2.09)	48·00	17·00
148/51 *Set of 4*			65·00	19·00

POSTCARD STAMPS

From 1889 onwards the Orange Free State Post Office sold postcards franked with adhesives as Type **1**, some subsequently surcharged, over which the State Arms had been overprinted.

There are five known dies of the Arms overprint which can be identified as follows:

(a) Shield without flags. Three cows (two lying down, one standing) at left. Point of shield complete.

(b) Shield with flags. Four cows (two lying down, two standing) at left (*illustrated*).

(c) Shield with flags. Three cows (one lying down, two standing) at left.

(d) Shield without flags. Three cows (one lying down, two standing) at left.

(e) Shield without flags. Three cows (two lying down, one standing) at left. Point of shield broken.

There are also other differences between the dies.

PRICES. Those in the left-hand column are for unused examples on complete postcard; those on the right for used examples off card. Examples used on postcard are worth more.

1889 (Feb). *No. 2 (placed sideways on card) optd Shield Type (a).*

P1	1	1d. red-brown	90·00	40·00
		a. Optd Shield Type (b)	32·00	7·00

1891 (Aug). *No. 48 optd Shield Type (b).*

P2	1	½d. chestnut	5·50	1·75
		a. Optd Shield Type (c)	13·00	4·25
		b. Optd Shield Type (d)	6·00	2·25
		c. Optd Shield Type (e)	14·00	5·00

1892 (June). *No. 54 optd Shield Type (b).*

P3	1	1d. on 3d. ultramarine	90·00	48·00
		a. Optd Shield Type (c)	15·00	3·00

1½d. (P 1) — 1½d. (P 2) — 1½d. (P 3)

1892 (Sept)–**95**. *Nos. 50/1 optd Shield Type (b) or (d) (No. P6) and surch with Types P* **1/3**.

P4	1	1½d. on 2d. bright mauve (Type P **1**) (11.92)	8·00	3·75
P5		1½d. on 2d. bright mauve (Type P **2**) (9.93)	6·00	1·75
		a. Surch inverted		
P6		1½d. on 2d. bright mauve (Type P **3**) (R.) (6.95)	13·00	4·25
P7		1½d. on 3d. ultramarine (Type P **1**)	7·50	2·25

No. P5a shows the stamp affixed to the card upside down with the surcharge correctly positioned in relation to the card.

½d. (P 4)

1895 (Aug). *No. 48 optd Shield Type (e) and surch with Type P* **4**.

P8	1	½d. on ½d. chestnut	13·00	2·75

1½d. (P 5) — 1½d. (P 6)

1895 (Dec)–**97**. *No. 50 optd Shield Type (e) and surch with Types P* **5/6**.

P9	1	1½d. on 2d. bright mauve (Type P **5**)	6·50	2·75
P10		1½d. on 2d. bright mauve (Type P **6**) (12.97)	7·50	3·25
P11		1½d. on 2d. bright mauve (as Type P **6**, but without stop) (12.97)	7·50	3·25

1897 (Mar). *No. 85 optd Shield Type (d).*

P12	1	½d. orange	13·00	1·75
		a. Optd Shield Type (e)	14·00	2·75

V.R.I. (P 7)

1900. *Nos. P10/11 optd as T* **31/2** *or with Type P* **7**.

P13	1	1½d. on 2d. bright mauve (No. P10) (T **31**)	28·00	5·50
P14		1½d. on 2d. bright mauve (No. P11) (T **31**)	28·00	5·50
P15		1½d. on 2d. bright mauve (No. P10) (T **32**)	28·00	5·50
P16		1½d. on 2d. bright mauve (No. P11) (T **32**)	28·00	5·50
P17		1½d. on 2d. bright mauve (No. P10) (Type P **7**)	40·00	10·00
P18		1½d. on 2d. bright mauve (No. P11) (Type P **7**)	40·00	10·00

POLICE FRANK STAMPS

The following frank stamps were issued to members of the Orange Free State Mounted Police ("Rijdende Dienst Macht") for use on official correspondence.

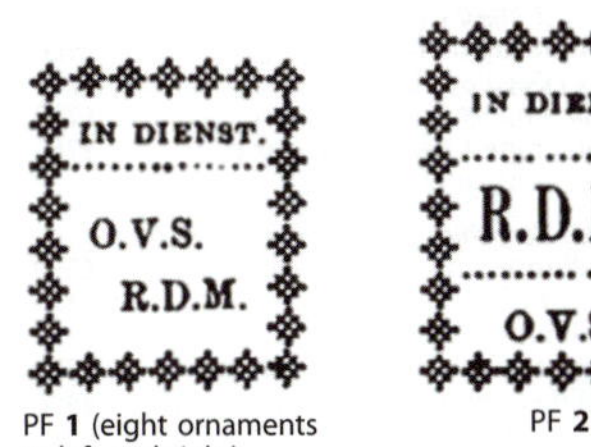

PF **1** (eight ornaments at left and right) — PF **2**

1896. P 12.

PF1	PF **1**	(–) Black	£225	£300

No. PF1 was printed in horizontal strips of 5 surrounded by wide margins.

1898. *As Type PF* **1**, *but with nine ornaments at left and right.* P 12.

PF2		(–) Black	£150	£200

No. PF2 was printed in blocks of 4 (2×2) surrounded by wide margins.

1899. P 12.

PF3	PF **2**	(–) Black/*yellow*	£130	£150
		a. No stop after "V"	£550	

No. PF3 was printed in sheets of 24 (6×4) with the edges of the sheet imperforate. It is believed that they were produced from a setting of 8 (2×4) repeated three times. No. PF3a occurs on R. 1/1 of the setting.

Examples of No. PF3 are known postmarked as late as 28 April 1900. The O.F.S. Mounted Police were disbanded by the British authorities at the end of the following month.

MILITARY FRANK STAMP

M **1**

(Typeset Curling & Co, Bloemfontein)

1899 (15 Oct). P 12.

M1	M **1**	(–) Black/*bistre-yellow*	19·00	55·00

Supplies of No. M1 were issued to members of the Orange Free State army on active service during the Second Boer War. To pass free through the O.F.S. fieldpost system, letters had to be franked with No. M1 or initialled by the appropriate unit commander. The franks were in use between October 1899 and February 1900.

No. M1 was printed in sheets of 20 (5×4) using a setting of five different types in a horizontal row. The colour in the paper runs in water.

Typeset forgeries can be identified by the appearance of 17 pearls, instead of the 16 of the originals, in the top and bottom frames. Forgeries produced by lithography omit the stops after "BRIEF" and "FRANKO".

FISCAL STAMPS USED FOR POSTAGE

The following were issued in December 1877 (Nos. F1 and F3 in 1882) and were authorised for postal use between 1882 and 1886.

F **1**

F **2**

F **3**

(Typo D.L.R.)

1882–**86**. P 14.

F1	F **1**	6d. pearl-grey	11·00	14·00
F2		6d. purple-brown	38·00	26·00
F3	F **2**	1s. purple-brown	12·00	19·00
F4		1s. pearl-grey	55·00	65·00
F5		1s.6d. blue	24·00	18·00
F6		2s. magenta	24·00	18·00
F7		3s. chestnut	29·00	65·00
F8		4s. grey		
F9		5s. rose	30·00	26·00
F10		6s. green	—	75·00
F11		7s. violet		
F12		10s. orange	65·00	42·00
F13	F **3**	£1 purple	75·00	42·00
		a. "VRY-STAAT" (R. 1/5)		
F14		£2 red-brown	85·00	95·00
		a. "VRY-STAAT" (R. 1/5)		
F14*b*		£4 carmine		
		ba. "VRY-STAAT" (R. 1/5)		
F15		£5 green	£120	65·00
		a. "VRY-STAAT" (R. 1/5)		

Die proofs of Type F **3** showed a hyphen in error between "VRY" and "STAAT". This was removed from each impression on the plate before printing, but was missed on R. 1/5.

A fiscally used example of No. F2 exists showing "ZES PENCE" double, one inverted.

The 8s. yellow was prepared but we have no evidence of its use postally without surcharge Type F **3**.

ZES PENCE. (F 4)

1886. *Surch with Type F* **4**.

F16	F **2**	6d. on 4s. grey		
F17		6d. on 8s. yellow	£300	

Postage stamps overprinted for use as Telegraph stamps and used postally are omitted as it is impossible to say with certainty which stamps were genuinely used for postal purposes.

Orange Free State became a province of the Union of South Africa on 31 May 1910.

VI. TRANSVAAL

(*formerly* South African Republic)

From 1852 mail from the Transvaal was forwarded to the Cape of Good Hope, via the Orange Free State, by a post office at Potchefstroom. In 1859 the Volksraad voted to set up a regular postal service and arrangements were made for letters sent to the Cape and for overseas to be franked with Cape of Good Hope stamps.

The Potchefstroom postmaster placed his first order for these on 23 August 1859 and examples of all four triangular values are known postmarked there. From 1868 mail via the Orange Free State required franking with their issues also.

A similar arrangement covering mail sent overseas via Natal was in operation from 9 July 1873 until the first British Occupation. Such letters carried combinations of Transvaal stamps, paying the rate to Natal, and Natal issues for the overseas postage. Such Natal stamps were sold, but not postmarked, by Transvaal post offices.

PRICES FOR STAMPS ON COVER

Nos. 1/6 are rare used on cover.	
Nos. 7/80	*from* × 20
Nos. 86/155	*from* × 3
Nos. 156/62	*from* × 6
Nos. 163/9	*from* × 5
Nos. 170/225	*from* × 10
Nos. 226/34	*from* × 20
Nos. 235/7	—
Nos. 238/43	*from* × 12
Nos. 244/55	*from* × 4
Nos. 256/7	*from* × 6
Nos. 258/9	—
Nos. 260/76	*from* × 20
Nos. F1/5	*from* × 5
Nos. D1/7	*from* × 20

The issues for Pietersburg, Lydenburg, Rustenburg, Schweizer Renecke and Wolmaransstad are very rare when on cover.

1 (Eagle with spread wings)

2

3

(Typo Adolph Otto, Gustrow, Mecklenburg-Schwerin)

1870 (1 May). *Thin paper, clear and distinct impressions.*

(a) Imperf.

No.	Type	Description	Unused	Used
1	1	1d. brown-lake	£425	
		a. Orange-red	£550	£550
2		6d. bright ultramarine	£180	£180
		a. Pale ultramarine	£200	£200
3		1s. deep green	£650	£650
		a. *Tête-bêche* (pair)		

(b) Fine roulette, 15½ to 16.

No.	Type	Description	Unused	Used
4	1	1d. brown-lake	£120	
		a. Brick-red	£100	
		b. Orange-red	£100	
		c. Vermilion	£100	
5		6d. bright ultramarine	90·00	90·00
		a. Pale ultramarine	£100	£100
6		1s. deep green	£180	£200
		a. Yellow-green	£150	£140
		b. Emerald-green	£110	£110

Examples of Nos. 1/6 may have been sold to dealers at some stage between their arrival in Transvaal during August 1869 and the sale of stamps to the public for postal purposes on 1 May 1870.

PLATES. The German printings of the 1d., 6d. and 1s. in Type **1** were from two pairs of plates, each pair printing sheets of 80 in two panes of five horizontal rows of eight.

One pair of plates, used for Nos. 4*a*, 4*c*, 5*a* and 6/*a*, produced stamps spaced 1¼ to 1½ mm apart with the rouletting close to the design on all four sides. The 1d. from these "narrow" plates shows a gap in the outer frame line at the bottom right-hand corner. The second pair, used for Nos. 1/3, 4, 4*b*, 5/*a* and 6*b*, had 2½ to 3½ mm between the stamps. These "wide" plates were sent to the Transvaal in 1869 and were used there to produce either single or double pane printings until 1883.

The 6d. and 1s. "wide" plates each had an inverted *cliché*. When printed these occurred on right-hand pane R. 4/1 of the 6d. and right-hand pane R. 1/1 of the 1s. These were never corrected and resulted in *tête-bêche* pairs of these values as late as 1883.

REPRINTS AND IMITATIONS. A number of unauthorised printings were made of these stamps by the German printer. Many of these can be identified by differences in the central arms, unusual colours or, in the case of the 1d., by an extra frame around the numeral tablets at top.

Genuine stamps always show the "D" of "EENDRAGT" higher than the remainder of the word, have no break in the border above "DR" and depict the flagstaff at bottom right, behind "MAGT", stopping short of the central shield. They also show the eagle's eye as a clear white circle. On the forgeries the eye is often blurred.

The most difficult of the reprints to detect is the 1s. yellow-green which was once regarded as genuine, but was subsequently identified, by J. N. Luff in *The Philatelic Record* 1911-12, as coming from an unauthorised plate of four. Stamps from this plate show either a white dot between "EEN" and "SHILLING" or a white flaw below the wagon pole.

(Typo M. J. Viljoen, Pretoria)

1870 (1 May–4 July).

I. Thin gummed paper from Germany. Impressions coarse and defective.

(a) Imperf.

No.	Type	Description	Unused	Used
8	1	1d. dull rose-red	90·00	
		a. Reddish pink	70·00	
		b. Carmine-red	60·00	70·00
9		6d. dull ultramarine	£300	70·00
		a. *Tête-bêche* (pair)		

(b) Fine roulette, 15½ to 16.

No.	Type	Description	Unused	Used
10	1	1d. carmine-red	£700	£275
11		6d. dull ultramarine	£200	90·00
		a. Imperf between (vert pair)	£750	

(c) Wide roulette, 6½.

No.	Type	Description	Unused	Used
12	1	1d. carmine-red	—	£950

II. Thick, hard paper with thin yellow smooth gum (No. 15) or yellow streaky gum (others).

(a) Imperf.

No.	Type	Description	Unused	Used
13	1	1d. pale rose-red	70·00	
		a. Carmine-red	70·00	80·00
14		1s. yellow-green	£110	£100
		a. *Tête-bêche* (pair)	£20000	
		b. Bisected (6d.) (on cover)	†	£1800

(b) Fine roulette, 15½ to 16.

No.	Type	Description	Unused	Used
15	1	1d. carmine-red (24 May)	90·00	
16		6d. ultramarine (10 May)	£100	£100
		a. *Tête-bêche* (pair)	£25000	£18000
17		1s. yellow-green	£650	£650

III. Medium paper, blotchy heavy printing and whitish gum. Fine roulette 15½ to 16 (4 July).

No.	Type	Description	Unused	Used
18	1	1d. rose-red	70·00	85·00
		a. Carmine-red	50·00	55·00
		b. Crimson. From over-inked plate	£140	£120
19		6d. ultramarine	90·00	70·00
		a. *Tête-bêche* (pair)		
		b. Deep ultramarine. From over-inked plate	£450	£160
20		1s. deep green	£130	75·00
		a. From over-inked plate	£500	£160

The rouletting machine producing the wide 6½ gauge was not introduced until 1875.

Nos. 18*b*, 19*b* and 20a were printed from badly over-inked plates giving heavy blobby impressions.

(Typo J. P. Borrius, Potchefstroom)

1870 (Sept)–**71**. *Stout paper, but with colour often showing through, whitish gum.*

(a) Imperf.

No.	Type	Description	Unused	Used
21	1	1d. black	£130	£110

(b) Fine roulette, 15½ to 16.

No.	Type	Description	Unused	Used
22	1	1d. black	18·00	27·00
		a. Grey-black	18·00	27·00
23		6d. blackish blue (7.71)	£140	60·00
		a. Dull blue	95·00	80·00

(Typo Adolph Otto, Gustrow, Mecklenburg-Schwerin)

1871 (July). *Thin paper, clear and distinct impressions. Fine roulette, 15½ to 16.*

No.	Type	Description	Unused	Used
24	2	3d. pale reddish lilac	80·00	90·00
		a. Deep lilac	90·00	£100
		b. Vert laid paper		

No. 24 and later printings in the Transvaal were produced from a pair of plates in the same format as the 1869 issue. All genuine stamps have a small dot on the left leg of the eagle.

Imperforate examples in the issued shade, without the dot on eagle's leg, had been previously supplied by the printer, probably as essays, but were not issued for postal purposes. (*Price* £550 *unused*). They also exist *tête-bêche* (*Price for un pair* £3250).

Imperforate and rouletted stamps in other colours are reprints.

(Typo J. P. Borrius, Potchefstroom)

1872–74. *Fine roulette, 15½ to 16.*

(a) Thin transparent paper.

No.	Type	Description	Unused	Used
25	1	1d. black	£190	£650
26		1d. bright carmine	£160	55·00
27		6d. ultramarine	£110	45·00
28		1s. green	£140	60·00

(b) Thinnish opaque paper, clear printing (Dec 1872).

No.	Type	Description	Unused	Used
29	1	1d. reddish pink	65·00	42·00
		a. Carmine-red	65·00	42·00
30	2	3d. grey-lilac	£100	50·00
31	1	6d. ultramarine	65·00	30·00
		a. Pale ultramarine	75·00	32·00
32		1s. yellow-green	80·00	42·00
		a. Green	80·00	42·00
		aa. Bisected (6d.) (on cover)	†	£1800

(c) Thickish wove paper (1873–74).

No.	Type	Description	Unused	Used
33	1	1d. dull rose	£400	75·00
		a. Brownish rose	£500	£120
		b. Printed on both sides		
34		6d. milky blue	£150	48·00
		a. Deep dull blue	90·00	42·00
		aa. Imperf (pair)	£700	
		ab. Imperf between (horiz pair)	£750	
		ac. Wide roulette 6½		

(d) Very thick dense paper (1873–74).

No.	Type	Description	Unused	Used
35		1d. dull rose	£550	£130
		a. Brownish rose	£425	£110
36		6d. dull ultramarine	£180	65·00
		a. Bright ultramarine	£200	65·00
37		1s. yellow-green	£850	£650

(Typo P. Davis & Son, Pietermaritzburg)

1874 (Sept). P 12½.

(a) Thin transparent paper.

No.	Type	Description	Unused	Used
38	1	1d. pale brick-red	£100	40·00
		a. Brownish red	£100	40·00
39		6d. deep blue	£140	60·00

(b) Thicker opaque paper.

No.	Type	Description	Unused	Used
40	1	1d. pale red	£160	75·00
41		6d. blue	£130	55·00
		a. Imperf between (pair)		
		b. Deep blue	£130	55·00

(Typo Adolph Otto, Gustrow, Mecklenburg-Schwerin)

1874 (Oct). *Thin smooth paper, clearly printed. Fine roulette 15½ to 16.*

No.	Type	Description	Unused	Used
42	3	6d. bright ultramarine	60·00	24·00
		a. Bisected (3d.) (on cover)	†	£1400

Stamps in other shades of blue, brown or red, often on other types of paper, are reprints.

(Typo J. F. Celliers on behalf of Stamp Commission, Pretoria)

1875 (29 Apr)–**77**.

I. Very thin, soft opaque (semi-pelure) paper.

(a) Imperf.

No.	Type	Description	Unused	Used
43	1	1d. orange-red	£130	50·00
		a. Pin-perf	£750	£350
44	2	3d. lilac	90·00	50·00
45	1	6d. blue	85·00	42·00
		a. Milky blue	£130	45·00
		aa. *Tête-bêche* (pair)	£15000	
		ab. Pin-perf	—	£350

(b) Fine roulette, 15½ to 16.

No.	Type	Description	Unused	Used
46	1	1d. orange-red	£500	£140
47	2	3d. lilac	£550	£150
48	1	6d. blue	£500	£140

(c) Wide roulette, 6½.

No.	Type	Description	Unused	Used
49	1	1d. orange-red	—	£200
50	2	3d. lilac	£700	£300
51	1	6d. blue	—	£150
		a. Bright blue	—	£150
		b. Milky blue	—	£150

II. Very thin, hard transparent (pelure) paper (1875–76).

(a) Imperf.

No.	Type	Description	Unused	Used
52	1	1d. brownish red	55·00	32·00
		a. Orange-red	45·00	25·00
		b. Dull red	50·00	50·00
		ba. Pin-perf	£600	£375
53	2	3d. lilac	50·00	42·00
		a. Pin-perf	—	£400
		b. Deep lilac	60·00	42·00
54	1	6d. pale blue	50·00	50·00
		a. Blue	50·00	42·00
		ab. *Tête-bêche* (pair)		
		ac. Pin-perf	—	£350
		b. Deep blue	55·00	45·00

(b) Fine roulette 15½ to 16.

No.	Type	Description	Unused	Used
55	1	1d. orange-red	£350	£120
		a. Brown-red	£350	£120
56	2	3d. lilac	£400	£130
57	1	6d. blue	£160	95·00
		a. Deep blue	£160	£110

(c) Wide roulette, 6½.

No.	Type	Description	Unused	Used
58	1	1d. orange-red	£1000	£200
		a. Bright red	—	£180
59	2	3d. lilac	£900	£250
60	1	6d. deep blue	£1000	£100

III. Stout hard-surfaced paper with smooth, nearly white, gum (1876).

(a) Imperf.

No.	Type	Description	Unused	Used
61	1	1d. bright red	24·00	18·00
62	2	3d. lilac	£375	£120
63	1	6d. bright blue	£100	24·00
		a. *Tête-bêche* (pair)		
		b. Pale blue	£100	24·00
		c. Deep blue (deep brown gum)	60·00	20·00
		ca. *Tête-bêche* (pair)	—	£17000

(b) Fine roulette, 15½ to 16.

No.	Type	Description	Unused	Used
64	1	1d. bright red	£400	£150
65	2	3d. lilac	£350	
66	1	6d. bright blue	£750	£110
		a. Deep blue (deep brown gum)	£600	£275

(c) Wide roulette, 6½.

No.	Type	Description	Unused	Used
67	1	1d. bright red	£600	£150
68		6d. pale blue	—	£200
		a. Deep blue (deep brown gum)	£650	£250

IV. Coarse, soft white paper (1876–77).

(a) Imperf.

No.	Type	Description	Unused	Used
69	1	1d. brick-red	£130	50·00
70		6d. deep blue	£200	£550
		a. Milky blue	£350	95·00
71		1s. yellow-green	£350	£110
		a. Bisected (6d.) (on cover)	†	£1600

(b) Fine roulette, 15½ to 16.

No.	Type	Description	Unused	Used
72	1	1d. brick-red	—	£375
73		6d. deep blue	—	£160
74		1s. yellow-green	£700	£350

(c) Wide roulette, 6½.

No.	Type	Description	Unused	Used
75	1	1d. brick-red	—	£450
76		6d. deep blue	—	£1100
77		1s. yellow-green	—	£1200

(d) Fine × wide roulette.

No.	Type	Description	Unused	Used
78	1	1d. brick-red	£700	£350

V. Hard, thick, coarse yellowish paper (1876–77).

No.	Type	Description	Unused	Used
79	1	1d. brick-red (imperf)	—	£300
80		1d. brick-red (wide roulette)	—	£400

The pin-perforated stamps have various gauges and were probably produced privately or by one or more post offices other than Pretoria.

On Nos. 63*c*/*ca*, 66*a* and 68*a* the brown gum used was so intense that it caused staining of the paper which is still visible on used examples.

See also Nos. 171/4.

FIRST BRITISH OCCUPATION

By 1876 conditions in the Transvaal had deteriorated and the country was faced by economic collapse, native wars and internal dissension. In early 1877 Sir Theophilus Shepstone, appointed Special Commissioner to the South African Republic by the British Government, arrived in Pretoria and on 12 April annexed the Transvaal with the acquiescence of at least part of the European population.

V. R.

TRANSVAAL.

(4)

V. R.

TRANSVAAL.

(5)

T **4** is the normal overprint, but Setting I No. 11 (R. 2/3) has a wider-spaced overprint as T **5**.

1877 (Apr). *Optd with T* **4** *in red.*

No.	Type	Description	Unused	Used
		(a) Imperf.		
86	2	3d. lilac (*semi-pelure*) (No. 44)	£1300	£300
		a. Opt Type **5**		
87		3d. lilac (*pelure*) (No. 53)	£1300	£180
		a. Opt Type **5**	£6500	£2500
		b. Opt on back	£3250	£3250
		c. Opt double, in red and in black	£6000	
88	1	6d. milky blue (No. 70)	£1600	£180
		a. Opt inverted	—	£5000
		b. Opt double	£4500	£1000
		c. Opt Type **5**	£7000	£3000
		d. Deep blue	—	£250
89		1s. yellow-green (No. 71)	£600	£180
		a. Bisected (6d.) (on cover)	†	£1800
		b. Opt inverted	—	£4500
		c. Opt Type **5**	£4500	£1500
		d. *Tête-bêche* (pair)		
		(b) Fine roulette, 15½ to 16.		
90	2	3d. lilac (*pelure*) (No. 56)	—	£1600
91	1	6d. deep blue (No. 73)	—	£1700
92		1s. yellow-green (No. 74)	£1600	£750
		a. Opt Type **5**		
		(c) Wide roulette, 6½.		
93	2	3d. lilac (*pelure*) (No. 59)	—	£2250
		a. Opt Type **5**		
94	1	6d. deep blue (No. 76)	—	£2250
		a. Opt Type **5**		
95		1s. yellow-green (No. 77)	£4000	£2000
		a. Opt inverted	—	£6000

Nos. 88a, 89b and 95a occurred on the inverted *cliché* of the basic stamps.

1877 (June). *Optd with T* **4** *in black.*

No.	Type	Description	Unused	Used
		I. Very thin, hard transparent (pelure) paper.		
96	1	1d. orange-red (imperf) (No. 52*a*)	£275	£100
97		1d. orange-red (*fine roulette*) (No. 55)	—	£1000
		II. Stout hard-surfaced paper with smooth, nearly white, gum.		
98	1	1d. bright red (imperf) (No. 61)	25·00	22·00
		a. Opt inverted	£550	£500
		b. Opt Type **5**	£750	£800
99		1d. bright red (*fine roulette*) (No. 64)	£160	50·00
		a. Opt inverted		
		b. Opt double	—	£1100
		c. Imperf between (horiz pair)	£750	
100		1d. bright red (*wide roulette*) (No. 67)	£650	£200
100*a*		1d. bright red (*fine × wide roulette*) (No. 78)		
		III. New ptgs on coarse, soft white paper.		
		(a) Imperf.		
101	1	1d. brick-red (5.77)	25·00	22·00
		a. Opt double	—	£1200
		b. Opt Type **5**	£800	
102	2	3d. lilac	80·00	42·00
		a. Opt inverted		
		b. Deep lilac	£170	85·00
103	1	6d. dull blue	90·00	32·00
		a. Opt double	£3500	£2000
		b. Opt inverted	£1400	£170
		d. Opt Type **5**	—	£1100
		da. Opt Type **5** inverted		
		e. Blue (bright to deep)	£160	30·00
		ea. Bright blue, opt inverted	—	£500
		f. Pin-perf	—	£600
104		1s. yellow-green	£100	50·00
		a. Opt inverted	£1200	£200
		b. *Tête-bêche* (pair)	£20000	£20000
		c. Opt Type **5**	£5000	£1500
		d. Bisected (6d.) (on cover)	†	£1500
		(b) Fine roulette, 15½ to 16.		
105	1	1d. brick-red	75·00	75·00
		a. Imperf horiz (vert strip of 3)		
		b. Imperf between (horiz pair)	†	£600
106	2	3d. lilac	£180	65·00
107	1	6d. dull blue	£200	55·00
		a. Opt inverted	—	£750
		b. Opt Type **5**	£5000	
108		1s. yellow-green	£200	90·00
		a. Opt inverted	£1100	£450
		b. Opt Type **5**	—	£2750
		(c) Wide roulette, 6½.		
109	1	1d. brick-red	£650	£150
		a. Opt Type **5**	—	£1000
110	2	3d. lilac	—	£750
111	1	6d. dull blue	—	£1200
		a. Opt inverted	—	£4000
112		1s. yellow-green	£475	£130
		a. Opt inverted	£1500	£600

1877 (31 Aug). *Optd with T* **4** *in black.*

No.	Type	Description	Unused	Used
113	1	6d. blue/*rose* (imperf)	85·00	48·00
		a. Bisected (3d.) (on cover)		
		b. Opt inverted	£110	48·00
		c. *Tête-bêche* (pair)		
		d. Opt omitted	£3500	£2500
114		6d. blue/*rose* (*fine roulette*)	£190	70·00
		a. Opt inverted	£550	70·00
		b. *Tête-bêche* (pair)		
		c. Opt omitted		
		d. Bisected (3d.) (on cover)		
115		6d. blue/*rose* (*wide roulette*)		
		a. Opt inverted	—	£650
		b. Opt omitted		

Nos. 113/15 were overprinted from a setting of 40 which was applied upright to one pane in each sheet and inverted on the other.

V. R.
Transvaal
(6)

V. R.
Transvaal
(7)

1877 (28 Sept)–**79**. *Optd with T* **6** *in black.*

No.	Type	Description	Unused	Used
		(a) Imperf.		
116	1	1d. red/*blue*	55·00	30·00
		a. "Transvral" (Right pane R. 2/3)	£5500	£2500
		b. Opt double	£4000	
		c. Opt inverted	£800	£400
		d. Opt omitted		
117		1d. red/*orange* (6.12.77)	20·00	20·00
		a. Pin-perf		
		b. Printed both sides		
		c. Opt double	£3500	
		d. Optd with Type **7** (15.4.78)	55·00	45·00
		e. Pair. Nos. 117 and 117d	£160	
118	2	3d. mauve/*buff* (24.10.77)	50·00	27·00
		a. Opt inverted	—	£750
		b. Pin-perf		
		c. Bisected (1½d) (on cover)	†	—
		d. Optd with Type **7** (15.4.78)	65·00	35·00
		da. Pin-perf	£750	£750
		e. Pair. Nos. 118 and 118d	£225	
119		3d. mauve/*green* (18.4.79)	£150	42·00
		a. Pin-perf		
		b. Opt inverted	—	£2000
		c. Opt double		
		d. Printed both sides	†	—
		e. Optd with Type **7**	£110	35·00
		ea. Opt inverted	—	£2000
		eb. Printed both sides	—	£1000
		f. Opt omitted	—	£3500
		g. Pair. Nos. 119 and 119e	£500	
120	1	6d. blue/*green* (27.11.77)	85·00	38·00
		a. Deep blue/green	£100	40·00
		b. Broken "Y" for "V" in "V.R." (Left pane R. 3/7)	—	£750
		c. Small "v" in "Transvaal" (Left pane R. 5/2)	—	£750
		d. "V..R." (Right pane R. 3/4)	—	£750
		e. *Tête-bêche* (pair)	—	£18000
		f. Opt inverted	—	£1100
		g. Pin-perf		
		h. Bisected (3d.) (on cover)	†	—
121		6d. blue/*blue* (20.3.78)	55·00	27·00
		a. *Tête-bêche* (pair)		
		b. Opt inverted	—	£1100
		c. Opt omitted	—	£2250
		d. Opt double	—	£3250
		e. Pin-perf		
		f. Bisected (3d.) (on cover)	†	£800
		g. Optd with Type **7**	£110	30·00
		ga. *Tête-bêche* (pair)	£15000	
		gb. Opt inverted	—	£700
		gc. Bisected (3d.) (on cover)	†	—
		h. Pair. Nos. 121 and 121g	£375	
		(b) Fine roulette, 15½ to 16.		
122	1	1d. red/*blue*	90·00	38·00
		a. "Transvral" (Right pane R. 2/3)	—	£3000
123		1d. red/*orange* (6.12.77)	32·00	27·00
		a. Imperf between (pair)	£600	
		b. Optd with Type **7** (15.4.78)	£140	£120
		c. Pair. Nos. 123 and 123b	£400	
124	2	3d. mauve/*buff* (24.10.77)	95·00	27·00
		a. Imperf horiz (vert pair)	£750	
		b. Opt inverted	—	£3000
		c. Optd with Type **7** (15.4.78)	£150	£110
		ca. Imperf between (pair)		
		d. Pair. Nos. 124 and 124c	£550	
125		3d. mauve/*green* (18.4.79)	£600	£150
		a. Optd with Type **7**	£600	£150
		b. Pair. Nos. 125 and 125a		
126	1	6d. blue/*green* (27.11.77)	85·00	27·00
		a. "V..R" (Right pane R. 3/4)	—	£1200
		b. *Tête-bêche* (pair)		
		c. Opt inverted	—	£650
		d. Opt omitted	—	£4000
		e. Bisected (3d.) (on cover)	†	£700
127		6d. blue/*blue* (20.3.78)	£225	55·00
		a. Opt inverted	—	£900
		b. Opt omitted	—	£3500
		c. Imperf between (pair)		
		d. Bisected (3d.) (on cover)	†	£750
		e. Optd with Type **7**	£375	£110
		ea. Opt inverted	—	£1100
		(c) Wide roulette, 6¼.		
128	1	1d. red/*orange* (15.4.78)	£250	£100
		a. Optd with Type **7**	—	£300
129	2	3d. mauve/*buff* (24.10.77)	—	£100
		a. Optd with Type **7** (15.4.78)	—	£350
130		3d. mauve/*green* (18.4.79)	£650	£275
		a. Optd with Type **7**	—	£300
131	1	6d. blue/*green* (27.11.77)	—	£1000
132		6d. blue/*blue* (20.3.78)	—	£300
		a. Opt inverted		
		b. Optd with Type **7**	—	£350
		ba. Opt inverted		
		(d) Fine × wide roulette.		
132*c*	1	1d. red/*orange*	£750	

Nos. 116/32c were overprinted from various settings covering sheets of 80 or panes of 40 (8×5). Initially these settings contained Type **6** only, but from March 1878 settings also contained examples of Type **7**. Details of these mixed settings are as follows:

1d. red/*orange* (sheets of 80): all Type **6** except for 16 Type **7**.
3d. mauve/*buff* (panes of 40): 16 Type **7**.
3d. mauve/*green* (panes of 40): uncertain, some panes at least contained 27 Type **7**.
6d. blue/*blue* (sheets of 80): either 24 or 27 Type **7**.

9

(Recess B.W.)

1878 (26 Aug)–**80**. P 14, 14½.

No.	Type	Description	Unused	Used
133	9	½d. vermilion (1.9.80)	23·00	80·00
134		1d. pale red-brown	13·00	4·25
		a. Brown-red	13·00	3·75
135		3d. dull rose (25 Nov)	16·00	5·00
		a. Claret	20·00	6·50
136		4d. sage-green	22·00	6·00
137		6d. olive-black (25 Nov)	12·00	4·50
		a. Black-brown	14·00	3·75
138		1s. green (25 Nov)	£120	40·00
139		2s. blue (25 Nov)	£160	75·00

The ½d. is printed on paper bearing the sheet watermark 'R TURNER/CHAFFORD MILLS' in double-lined block capitals. Other values are on unwatermarked paper.

The above prices are for specimens perforated on all four sides. Stamps from margins of sheets, with perforations absent on one or two sides, can be supplied for about 30% less.

The used price quoted for No. 139 is for an example with telegraphic cancel, a 23.5 mm circular datestamp of Pretoria (or more rarely Heidelberg or Standerton). Postally used examples are worth much more.

1 Penny (10) 1 Penny (11) 1 Penny (12)

1 Penny (13) 1 Penny (14)

1 PENNY (15) *1 Penny* (16)

1879 (22 Apr). *No. 137a surch with T* **10** *to* **16** *in black.*

No.	Type	Description	Unused	Used
140	**10**	1d. on 6d.	75·00	42·00
		a. Surch in red	£225	£150
141	**11**	1d. on 6d.	£180	80·00
		a. Surch in red	£550	£325
142	**12**	1d. on 6d.	£180	80·00
		a. Surch in red	£550	£325
143	**13**	1d. on 6d.	80·00	48·00
		a. Surch double		
		b. Surch in red	£275	£170
144	**14**	1d. on 6d.	£500	£160
		a. Surch in red	£5500	£1600
145	**15**	1d. on 6d.	40·00	23·00
		a. Surch in red	£140	75·00
146	**16**	1d. on 6d.	£170	75·00
		a. Surch in red	£475	£300

Nos. 140/6 were surcharged from a setting of 60 containing eleven examples of Type **10**, four of Type **11**, four of Type **12**, nine of Type **13**, two of Type **14** (although there may have been only one in the first two ptgs), twenty-five of Type **15** and five of Type **16**.

The red surcharges may have been produced first.

V. R.
Transvaal
(16a)

V. R.
Transvaal
Small "T" (R. 2/8, 3/8, 4/8, 5/8 on right pane of 1d. and left pane of 3d.)

1879 (Aug–Sept). *Optd with T* **16a** *in black.*

No.	Type	Description	Unused	Used
		(a) Imperf.		
147	1	1d. red/*yellow*	45·00	38·00
		a. Small "T"	£300	£200
		b. Red/orange	40·00	30·00
		ba. Small "T"	£250	£170
148	2	3d. mauve/*green* (Sept)	40·00	25·00
		a. Small "T"	£225	£100
149		3d. mauve/*blue* (Sept)	45·00	30·00
		a. Small "T"	£250	90·00
		(b) Fine roulette 15½ to 16.		
150	1	1d. red/*yellow*	£350	£200
		a. Small "T"	£1000	£650
		b. Red/orange	£750	£375
		ba. Small "T"	£2000	
151	2	3d. mauve/*green*	£750	£250
		a. Small "T"	—	£850
152		3d. mauve/*blue*	—	£180
		a. Small "T"	—	£650
		(c) Wide roulette 6½.		
153	1	1d. red/*yellow*	£650	£650
		a. Small "T"		
		b. Red/orange	—	£1200
154	2	3d. mauve/*green*	£1000	£650
		a. Small "T"		
155		3d. mauve/*blue*	—	£750
		(d) Pin-perf about 17.		
156	1	1d. red/*yellow*	—	£750
		a. Small "T"		
157	2	3d. mauve/*blue*	—	£850

SECOND REPUBLIC

Following the first Boer War the independence of the South African Republic was recognised by the Convention of Pretoria from 8 August 1881.

Nos. 133/9 remained valid and some values were available for postage until 1885.

EEN PENNY
(17)

1882 (11 Aug). *No. 136 surch with T* **17**.

No.	Type	Description	Unused	Used
170	9	1d. on 4d. sage-green	14·00	4·75
		a. Surch inverted	£300	£200

Used examples of a similar, but larger, surcharge (width 20 mm) are known. These were previously considered to be forgeries, but it is now believed that some, at least, may represent a trial printing of the "EEN PENNY" surcharge.

(Typo J. F. Celliers)

1883 (20 Feb–3 Aug). *Re-issue of T* **1** *and* **2**. P 12.

No.	Type	Description	Unused	Used
171	1	1d. grey (*to black*) (5 Apr)	5·50	2·00
		a. Imperf vert (horiz pair)	£275	
		b. Imperf horiz (vert pair)	£550	£350

172	2	3d. grey-black (*to* black)/*rose*	23·00	5·50
		a. Bisected (1d.) (on cover)	†	£600
173		3d. pale red (7 May)	11·00	2·50
		a. Bisected (1d.) (on cover)	†	£600
		b. Imperf horiz (vert pair)	†	£1000
		c. Chestnut	24·00	4·50
		ca. Imperf between (horiz pair)	†	—
		d. Vermilion	24·00	5·00
174	1	1s. green (*to* deep) (3 Aug)	55·00	4·25
		a. Bisected (6d.) (on cover)	†	£450
		b. *Tête-bêche* (pair)	£900	£150

Reprints are known of Nos. 172, 173, 173*b* and 173*c*. The paper of the first is *bright rose* in place of *dull rose*, and the impression is brownish black in place of grey-black to deep black. The reprints on white paper have the paper thinner than the originals, and the gum yellowish instead of white. The colour is a dull deep orange-red.

The used price quoted for No. 174b is for an example with telegraphic cancel. Postally used examples are worth much more. (See note below No. 139).

18

PERFORATIONS. Stamps perforated 11½×12 come from the first vertical row of sheets of the initial printing otherwise perforated 12½×12.

REPRINTS. Reprints of the general issues 1885–93, 1894–95, 1895–96 and 1896–97 exist in large quantities produced using the original plates from 1911 onwards. They cannot readily be distinguished from genuine originals except by comparison with used stamps, but the following general characteristics may be noted. The reprints are all perf 12½, large holes; the paper is whiter and thinner than that usually employed for the originals and their colours lack the lustre of those of the genuine stamps.

Forged surcharges have been made on these reprints.

(Des J. Vurtheim. Typo Enschedé)

1885 (13 Mar)–**93**. P 12½.

175	18	½d. grey (30.3.85)	1·00	10
		a. Perf 13½	5·00	1·00
		b. Perf 12½×12	2·25	10
		ba. Perf 11½×12	24·00	7·00
176		1d. carmine	80	10
		a. Perf 12½×12	1·00	10
		aa. Perf 11½×12	15·00	2·75
		b. Rose	80	10
		ba. Perf 12½×12	1·00	10
177		2d. brown-purple (P 12½×12) (9.85)	2·00	3·00
178		2d. olive-bistre (14.4.87)	1·50	10
		a. Perf 12½×12	3·75	10
179		2½d. mauve (*to* bright) (8.93)	2·50	50
180		3d. mauve (*to* bright)	2·75	1·50
		a. Perf 12½×12	6·00	1·40
		aa. Perf 11½×12	27·00	17·00
181		4d. bronze-green	4·00	1·00
		a. Perf 13½	8·00	1·25
		b. Perf 12½×12	14·00	1·00
		ba. Perf 11½×12	£200	80·00
182		6d. pale dull blue	3·75	2·75
		a. Perf 13½	5·50	1·00
		b. Perf 12½×12	7·00	30
		ba. Perf 11½×12		
183		1s. yellow-green	2·75	75
		a. Perf 13½	25·00	6·00
		b. Perf 12½×12	9·00	65
184		2s.6d. orange-buff (*to* buff) (2.12.85)	8·50	2·50
		a. Perf 12½×12	17·00	7·00
185		5s. slate (2.12.85)	8·00	4·50
		a. Perf 12½×12	35·00	7·50
186		10s. dull chestnut (2.12.85)	30·00	8·50
		a. Yellow-brown (1891)		
187		£5 deep green (3.92)* (Optd "Monster" £150)	£3250	£180

Singles of the 6d. pale dull blue imperforate have been reported used in 1893.

*Most examples of No. 187 on the market are either forgeries or reprints.

HALVE PENNY

(19)

1885 (22 May–Aug). *Surch with T* **19**. *Reading up or down.*

188	2	½d. on 3d. (No. 173)	6·00	10·00
189	1	½d. on 1s. (No. 174) (Aug)	23·00	50·00
		a. *Tête-bêche* (pair)	£800	£350

Nos. 188/9 were surcharged by a setting of 40. After the left pane had been surcharged reading down, the sheets were turned so that the right pane had the surcharges reading up.

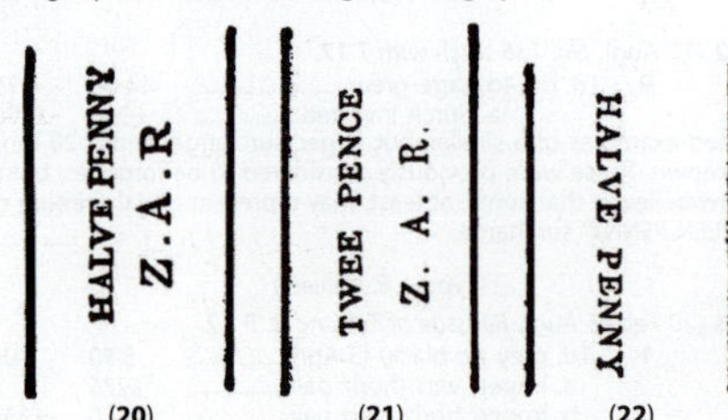

(20) (21) (22)

1885 (1 Sept). *No. 137a surch with T* **20/1** *in red.*

190	9	½d. on 6d. black-brown	60·00	90·00
191		2d.. on 6d black-brown	6·50	12·00

1885 (28 Sept). *No. 180a surch with T* **22**.

192	18	½d. on 3d. mauve	4·50	4·50
		a. "PRNNY" (R. 6/6)	42·00	60·00
		b. 2nd "N" inverted (R. 3/8)	90·00	£100
		c. Perf 11½×12	12·00	11·00

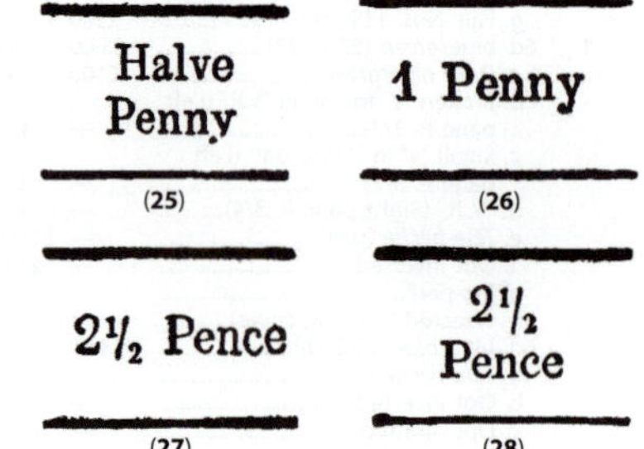

(23) (24)

1887 (15 Jan). *No. 180a surch with T* **23/4**.

193	18	2d. on 3d. mauve (Type **23**)	8·00	8·00
		a. Surch double	—	£275
		b. Perf 11½×12	24·00	12·00
194		2d. on 3d. mauve (Type **24**)	1·75	3·50
		a. Surch double	£180	£180
		b. Perf 11½×12	6·50	8·50

Nos. 193/4 were surcharged from the same setting of 60 (10×6) which showed Type **24** on the top five horizontal rows and Type **23** on the sixth horizontal row.

Halve Penny (25) 1 Penny (26)

2½ Pence (27) 2½ Pence (28)

Two types of surcharge:
A. Vertical distance between bars 12½ mm.
B. Distance 13½ mm.

1893. *T* **18** *surch.* P 12½.

(a) In red.

195	25	½d. on 2d. olive-bistre (A) (27 May)	80	2·00
		a. Surch inverted	2·50	2·50
		b. Surch Type B	1·50	2·75
		ba. Surch inverted	5·00	10·00

(b) In black.

196	25	½d. on 2d. olive-bistre (A) (2 July)	85	2·00
		a. Surch inverted	4·50	5·00
		b. Extra surch on back inverted	£160	
		c. Surch Type B	1·50	2·75
		ca. Surch inverted	20·00	15·00
		cb. Extra surch on back inverted	£275	
197	26	1d. on 6d. blue (A) (26 Jan)	1·00	1·00
		a. Surch double	55·00	45·00
		b. Surch inverted	1·75	2·25
		c. Surch treble		
		d. Surch Type B	1·75	1·75
		da. Surch inverted	5·00	4·00
		db. Surch double	—	80·00
		e. Pair, one without surch	£225	
198	27	2½d. on 1s. green (A) (2 Jan)	1·50	4·00
		a. "2/½d" for "2½" (R. 1/10)	35·00	65·00
		b. Surch inverted	6·50	7·50
		ba. Surch inverted and "2/½d" for "2½"	£350	£300
		c. Extra surch on back inverted	£450	£450
		d. Surch double, one inverted	£700	
		e. Surch Type B	2·50	5·50
		ea. Surch inverted	9·00	16·00
199	28	2½d. on 1s. green (A) (24 June)	5·50	4·50
		a. Surch double	45·00	40·00
		b. Surch inverted	7·50	7·50
		c. Surch Type B	8·50	9·00
		ca. Surch double	75·00	85·00
		cb. Surch inverted	19·00	19·00

Surcharge Types **25/8** all show a similar setting of the horizontal bars at top and bottom. On horizontal rows 1 to 4 and 6, the bars are 12½ mm apart and on row 5 the distance is 13½ mm.

29 (Wagon with shafts)

30 (Wagon with pole)

1894 (July). P 12½.

200	29	½d. grey	70	55
201		1d. carmine	1·50	10
202		2d. olive-bistre	1·50	10
203		6d. pale dull blue	2·25	40
204		1s. yellow-green	12·00	16·00

For note *re* reprints, see below T **18**.

1895 (16 Mar)–**96**. P 12½.

205	30	½d. pearl-grey (1895)	80	10
		a. Lilac-grey	80	10
206		1d. rose-red	80	10
207		2d. olive-bistre (1895)	1·00	15
208		3d. mauve (1895)	2·00	85
209		4d. olive-black (1895)	2·50	80
210		6d. pale dull blue (1895)	2·50	85
211		1s. yellow-green (18.3.95)	3·00	1·50
212		5s. slate (1896)	15·00	26·00
212*a*		10s. pale chestnut (1896)	15·00	5·50
205s/8s, 211s		Optd "Monster" *Set of* 5	£150	

For note *re* reprints, see below T **18**.

Halve Penny

(31)

1d. 1d.

(32—Round dot) (32*a*—Square dot)

1895 (July–Aug). *Nos. 211 and 179 surch with T* **31/2**.

213	30	½d. on 1s. green (R.)	1·00	25
		a. Surch spaced	2·00	1·50
		b. "Pennij" for "Penny" (R. 6/6)	50·00	60·00
		c. Surch inverted	4·00	4·50
		d. Surch double	65·00	90·00
214	18	1d. on 2½d. bright mauve (G.)	50	20
		a. Surch inverted	20·00	14·00
		b. Surch double	65·00	65·00
		c. Surch on back only	75·00	
		d. Surch Type **32***a*	1·50	1·25
		da. Surch inverted	65·00	
		e. Surch treble	£550	

The normal space between "Penny" and the bars is 3 mm. On No. 213a, which comes from the fifth horizontal row of the setting, this is increased to 4 mm. Copies may be found in which one or both of the bars have failed to print.

Type **32***a* with square stop occurred on R. 3/3-4, 3/6-8, 4/4-5, 4/7-8, 4/10, 6/3, 6/7-8 and 6/10 of the setting of 60.

33

34

1895 (July). *Fiscal stamp optd "*POSTZEGEL*".* P 11½.

215	33	6d. bright rose (G.)	1·75	1·75
		a. Imperf between (pair)		
		b. Opt inverted		

(Litho The Press Printing and Publishing Works, Pretoria)

1895 (6 Sept). *Introduction of Penny Postage.* P 11.

215*c*	34	1d. red (pale *to* deep)	1·75	2·00
		ca. Imperf between (pair)	95·00	£100
		cb. Imperf vert (horiz pair)		
		cc. Imperf (pair)		

1896–97. P 12½.

216	30	½d. green (1896)	80	10
217		1d. rose-red and green (1896)	80	10
218		2d. brown and green (2.97)	80	15
219		2½d. dull blue and green (6.96)	1·50	15
220		3d. purple and green (3.97)	2·00	2·25
221		4d. sage-green and green (3.97)	2·00	2·25
222		6d. lilac and green (11.96)	1·25	1·25
223		1s. ochre and green (3.96)	1·75	55
224		2s.6d. dull violet and green (6.96)	2·00	2·50

For note *re* reprints, see below T **18**.

SECOND BRITISH OCCUPATION

The Second Boer War began on 11 October 1899 and was concluded by the Peace of Vereeniging on 31 May 1902. Pretoria was occupied by the British on 5 June 1900 and a civilian postal service began operating thirteen days later.

FORGERIES. The forgeries of the "V.R.I." and "E.R.I." overprints most often met with can be recognised by the fact that the type used is perfect and the three stops are always in alignment with the bottom of the letters. In the genuine overprints, which were made from old type, it is impossible to find all three letters perfect and all three stops perfect and in exact alignment with the bottom of the letters.

V. R. I. (35) E. R. I. (36) E. R. I. Half Penny (37)

1900 (18 June). *Optd with T* **35**.

226	30	½d. green	30	30
		a. No stop after "V"	12·00	12·00
		b. No stop after "R"	9·00	9·00
		c. No stop after "I"	7·50	7·50
		d. Opt inverted	10·00	12·00
		e. Opt double		
		f. "V.I.R." (R. 4/4)	£550	
227		1d. rose-red and green	30	30
		a. No stop after "V"	12·00	12·00
		b. No stop after "R"	9·00	9·00
		c. No stop after "I"	6·00	6·00
		d. Opt inverted	10·00	17·00
		e. Opt double	70·00	85·00
		f. No stops after "R" and "I"	75·00	75·00
		g. Opt omitted (in pair with normal)	£250	
228		2d. brown and green	2·75	2·00
		a. No stop after "V"	27·00	29·00
		c. No stop after "I"	32·00	32·00
		d. Opt inverted	17·00	19·00
		e. Opt double		

f. "V.I.R." (R. 4/4) £550 £600
g. Opt albino
229 2½d. dull blue and green 1·00 2·00
a. No stop after "V" 19·00 23·00
b. No stop after "R" 45·00 55·00
c. No stop after "I" 15·00 18·00
d. Opt inverted 11·00 12·00
230 3d. purple and green 1·00 1·75
a. No stop after "V" 23·00 27·00
b. No stop after "R" 45·00 55·00
c. No stop after "I" 30·00 38·00
d. Opt inverted 70·00 80·00
231 4d. sage-green and green 2·75 1·50
a. No stop after "V" 42·00 42·00
b. No stop after "R" 55·00 55·00
c. No stop after "I" 38·00 38·00
d. Opt inverted 25·00 28·00
f. "V.I.R." (R. 4/4) £550
232 6d. lilac and green 2·75 1·75
a. No stop after "V" 21·00 21·00
b. No stop after "R" 27·00 27·00
c. No stop after "I" 27·00 27·00
d. Opt inverted 28·00 32·00
233 1s. ochre and green 2·75 3·25
a. No stop after "V" 21·00 24·00
b. No stop after "R" 21·00 24·00
c. No stop after "I" 38·00 42·00
d. Opt inverted 35·00 40·00
e. Opt double 75·00 85·00
234 2s.6d. dull violet and green 3·50 9·50
a. No stop after "V" 38·00
b. No stop after "R" 75·00
c. No stop after "I" — £425
235 5s. slate 6·50 12·00
a. No stop after "V" £100
236 10s. pale chestnut 8·50 14·00
a. No stop after "V" 90·00
c. No stop after "I" 90·00
237 18 £5 deep green* £2000 £800
a. No stop after "V"
234s/7s Optd "Specimen" *Set of 4* £200

*Many examples of No. 237 on the market are forgeries and the stamps should only be purchased if accompanied by a recent expert committee certificate.

The error "V.I.R." occurred on R. 4/4 in the first batch of stamps to be overprinted—a few sheets of the ½d., 2d. and 4d. The error was then corrected and stamps showing it are very rare.

A number of different settings were used to apply the overprint to Nos. 226/37. The missing stop varieties listed above developed during overprinting and occur on different positions in the various settings.

1901 (Jan)–**02**. *Optd with T* **36**.
238 **30** ½d. green 50 1·25
a. Opt double
239 1d. rose-red and green (20.3.01) 50 10
a. "E" of opt omitted 75·00
240 3d. purple and green (6.02) 2·25 3·00
241 4d. sage-green and green (6.02) 2·25 4·00
242 2s.6d. dull violet and green (10.02) 9·00 22·00

1901 (July). *Surch with T* **37**.
243 **30** ½d. on 2d. brown and green 65 65
a. No stop after "E" (R. 4/6) 50·00 55·00

38 (POSTAGE REVENUE) **39** (POSTAGE POSTAGE)

(Typo D.L.R.)

1902 (1 Apr–17 Dec). Wmk Crown CA. P 14.
244 **38** ½d. black and bluish green 1·75 20
w. Wmk inverted 85·00 60·00
245 1d. black and carmine 1·25 15
w. Wmk inverted 65·00 50·00
246 2d. black and purple 3·75 50
247 2½d. black and blue 8·00 1·25
w. Wmk inverted 60·00 35·00
248 3d. black and sage-green (17.12.02) 8·00 50
249 4d. black and brown (17.12.02) 6·50 1·25
250 6d. black and orange-brown 4·00 70
251 1s. black and sage-green 12·00 12·00
252 2s. black and brown 42·00 48·00
253 **39** 2s.6d. magenta and black 15·00 13·00
254 5s. black and purple/*yellow* 26·00 30·00
255 10s. black and purple/*red* 60·00 32·00
244/55 *Set of 12* £170 £120
244s/55s (*inc 247ws*) Optd "Specimen" *Set of 12* £140

The colour of the "black" centres varies from brownish grey or grey to black.

1903 (1 Feb). Wmk Crown CA. P 14.
256 **39** 1s. grey-black and red-brown 13·00 3·50
257 2s. grey-black and yellow 15·00 13·00
258 £1 green and violet £200 £130
259 £5 orange-brown and violet £1400 £650
256s/9s Optd "Specimen" *Set of 4* £200

1904–09. *Ordinary paper*. Wmk Mult Crown CA. P 14.
260 **38** ½d. black and bluish green 8·00 2·50
w. Wmk inverted £100 65·00
y. Wmk inverted and reversed 90·00 35·00
261 1d. black and carmine 5·00 30
262 2d. black and purple (*chalk-surfaced paper*) (1906) 10·00 1·50
263 2½d. black and blue (1905) 15·00 7·50
aw. Wmk inverted 90·00 70·00
b. Chalk-surfaced paper 13·00 3·50
264 3d. black and sage-green (*chalk-surfaced paper*) (1906) 3·50 50
265 4d. black and brown (*chalk-surfaced paper*) (1906) 4·75 70
w. Wmk inverted 90·00 60·00
266 6d. black and orange (1905) 9·00 1·50
a. Chalk-surfaced paper. *Black and brown-orange* (1906) 3·25 50
w. Wmk inverted £100 75·00
267 **39** 1s. black and red-brown (1905) 7·50 50
268 2s. black and yellow (1906) 22·00 7·50
269 2s.6d. magenta and black (1909) 48·00 6·00
270 5s. black and purple/*yellow* 22·00 1·50
271 10s. black and purple/*red* (1907) 55·00 2·75
272 £1 green and violet (1908) £225 30·00
a. Chalk-surfaced paper £200 16·00
260/72 *Set of 13* £375 40·00

There is considerable variation in the "black" centres as in the previous issue.

1905–09. Wmk Mult Crown CA. P 14.
273 **38** ½d. yellow-green 2·00 10
a. Deep green (1908) 2·50 20
w. Wmk inverted £120 75·00
274 1d. scarlet 1·25 10
aw. Wmk inverted — £275
b. Wmk Cabled Anchor, T **13** of Cape of Good Hope — £325
275 2d. purple (1909) 3·50 60
276 2½d. bright blue (1909) 14·00 6·00
273/6 *Set of 4* 19·00 6·00
273s/6s Optd "Specimen" *Set of 4* 70·00

A 2d. grey, T **38**, was prepared for use but not issued. It exists overprinted "Specimen", *price* £140.

The monocoloured ½d. and 1d. are printed from new combined plates. These show a slight alteration in that the frame does not touch the crown.

The ½d., 1d. and 2d. exist from coils constructed from normal sheets for use in stamp machines introduced in 1911. These coils were originally joined horizontally but the 1d. was subsequently issued joined vertically.

Many of the King's Head stamps are found overprinted or perforated "C.S.A.R.", for use by the Central South African Railways.

STAMP BOOKLETS

1905 (July). *Black on red cover showing arms. Stapled.*
SB1 2s.7d. booklet containing thirty 1d. (No. 261) in blocks of 6 £2000

1905. *Black on red cover. Stapled.*
SB2 2s.7d. booklet containing thirty 1d. (No. 274) in blocks of 6 £2250

1909. *Black on red cover. Stapled.*
SB3 2s.6d. booklet containing ten ½d. (No. 273) in block of 6 and block of 4, and twenty-four 1d. (No. 274) in blocks of 6 £2750

Stocks of No. SB3 were supplied containing twelve examples of the ½d., it being intended that the postal clerks would remove two stamps before the booklets were sold. In some instances this did not occur.

POSTAL FISCAL STAMPS

1900–02. *Fiscal stamps as in T* **33**, *but optd with T* **35**. P 11½.
F1 1d. pale blue — 45·00
F2 6d. dull carmine — 60·00
F3 1s. olive-bistre — 75·00
F4 1s.6d. brown — 90·00
F5 2s.6d. dull purple — £100

Nos. F1/5, previously listed as Nos. 1/5 of Volksrust, are fiscal issues which are known postally used from various Transvaal post offices between June 1900 and June 1902.

Other fiscal stamps are found apparently postally used, but these were used on telegrams not on postal matter.

POSTAGE DUE STAMPS

D **1**

Inverted "P" for "d" (Right pane R. 10/6)

(Typo D.L.R.)

1907. Wmk Mult Crown CA. P 14.
D1 D **1** ½d. black and blue-green 3·50 1·25
D2 1d. black and scarlet 4·00 85
D3 2d. brown-orange 4·75 1·25
D4 3d. black and blue 7·50 4·25
D5 5d. black and violet 2·00 12·00
a. Inverted "p" for "d" 50·00
D6 6d. black and red-brown 4·25 12·00
D7 1s. scarlet and black 11·00 8·50
D1/7 *Set of 7* 32·00 35·00

Transvaal became a province of the Union of South Africa on 31 May 1910.

PIETERSBURG

After the fall of Pretoria to the British in June 1900 the Transvaal government withdrew to the north of the country. Those post offices in areas not occupied by the British continued to function, but by early the following year supplies of stamps were exhausted. The following stamps were then authorised by the State Secretary and remained in use in some towns to early May 1901. Pietersburg itself was taken by British forces on 9 April.

PRICES. Genuinely used examples are very rare. Stamps cancelled by favour exist and are worth the same as the unused prices quoted.

The issued stamps are initialled by the Controller J. T. de V. Smit. All values exist without his signature and these are believed to come from remainders abandoned when the Boers evacuated Pietersburg.

P **1**

P **2**

P **3**

TYPES P 1/3. Each value was printed in sheets of 24 (6×4) of which the first two horizontal rows were as Type P **1** (Large "P" in "Postzegel" and large date), the third row as Type P **2** (Large "P" in "Postzegel" and small date) and the fourth as Type P **3** (Small "p" in "Postzegel" and small date). The stamps were issued to post offices in blocks of 12.

(Type-set *De Zoutpansberg Wachter* Press, Pietersburg)

1901 (20 Mar (1d.)–3 Apr (others)). A. Imperf.

(a) Controller's initials in black.
1 P **1** ½d. black/*green* 15·00
e. Controller's initials omitted 95·00
2 P **2** ½d. black/*green* 45·00
d. Controller's initials omitted 95·00
3 P **3** ½d. black/*green* 45·00
d. Controller's initials omitted 95·00
4 P **1** 1d. black/*red* 3·50
5 P **2** 1d. black/*red* 5·50
6 P **3** 1d. black/*red* 7·00
7 P **1** 2d. black/*orange* 6·00
8 P **2** 2d. black/*orange* 14·00
9 P **3** 2d. black/*orange* 22·00
10 P **1** 4d. black/*blue* 5·50
11 P **2** 4d. black/*blue* 9·50
12 P **3** 4d. black/*blue* 32·00
13 P **1** 6d. black/*green* 9·50
14 P **2** 6d. black/*green* 15·00
15 P **3** 6d. black/*green* 40·00
16 P **1** 1s. black/*yellow* 8·00
17 P **2** 1s. black/*yellow* 14·00
18 P **3** 1s. black/*yellow* 25·00

(b) Controller's initials in red.
19 P **1** ½d. black/*green* 15·00
20 P **2** ½d. black/*green* 35·00
21 P **3** ½d. black/*green* 40·00

B. P 11½.

(a) Controller's initials in red.
22 P **1** ½d. black/*green* 5·50
c. Imperf vert (horiz pair) 95·00
23 P **2** ½d. black/*green* 17·00
c. Imperf vert (horiz pair) £120
24 P **3** ½d. black/*green* 12·00
b. Imperf vert (horiz pair) £120

(b) Controller's initials in black.
25 P **1** 1d. black/*red* 2·00
m. Imperf vert (horiz pair) 55·00
n. Imperf between (vert pair: No. 25 + No. 26) 75·00
o. Imperf horiz (vert pair) 55·00
26 P **2** 1d. black/*red* 2·75
f. Imperf vert (horiz pair) 80·00
g. Imperf horiz (vert pair: No. 26 + No. 27) 60·00
27 P **3** 1d. black/*red* 4·00
f. Imperf vert (horiz pair) 80·00
28 P **1** 2d. black/*orange* 5·50
29 P **2** 2d. black/*orange* 8·00
30 P **3** 2d. black/*orange* 14·00

For the ½d. the First printing had initials in either black or red, those of the Second printing had them in black and all of the Third were in red.

CONSTANT VARIETIES

Rows 1 and 2 are as Type P **1**, *Row 3 as Type P* **2** *and Row 4 as Type P* **3**.

½d. value

First printing—Imperf

R.1/1 & 4 Top left "½" inverted, no stop after right "AFR" (No. 19c) 70·00
R.1/2 Top right "½" inverted (No. 19d) 90·00
R.1/3 "13" at lower right (No. 19e) 90·00
R.1/5 "POSTZFGEL" (No. 19f) 90·00
R.1/6 Left spray inverted, "AFB" at right (No. 19g) 90·00
R.2/1 "REB" at left, left side of inner frame 3 mm too high (No. 19h) 90·00
R.2/2 "BEP" at left (No. 19i) 90·00
R.2/3 "POSTZEOEL" (No. 19j) 90·00
R.2/4 "AER" at right, left side of inner frame 2 mm too high (No. 19k) 90·00
R.2/5 No stop after date (No. 19l) 90·00
R.2/6 No stop after "PENNY" (No. 19m)
R.3/1 "13" at top left, "PE" of "PENNY" spaced (No. 20c) 90·00
R.3/2 Right spray inverted (No. 20d) 90·00
R.3/3 Top left "½" inverted (No. 20e) 90·00
R.3/4 No stop after "2" at left (No. 20f)
R.3/5 Centre figures "½" level (No. 20g)
R.3/6 "POSTZEGFL", no stop after right "AFR" (No. 20h)
R.4/3 "13" at top right (No. 21b) 90·00

R.4/4	Lower left "½" inverted		(No. 21c)	90·00
R.4/5	"¼" at top left		(No. 21d)	90·00
R.4/6	Left spray inverted, "901" for "1901"		(No. 21e)	

This printing was produced first and was then adapted for the higher values.

Second printing

R.1/2	No stop after left "AFR"	Imperf	(No. 1a)	60·00
R.1/3	"13" at top left, no bar over lower right "½"	Imperf	(No. 1b)	60·00
R.1/6	No stop after date	Imperf	(No. 1c)	60·00
R.2/5	"BEP" at left, no stop after date	Imperf	(No. 1d)	60·00
R.3/3	"AFB" at left	Imperf	(No. 2a)	60·00
		Perf	(No. 23a)	
R.3/4	"POSTZEGEI"	Imperf	(No. 2b)	60·00
		Perf	(No. 23b)	
R.3/6	No bar over lower right "½"	Imperf	(No. 2c)	60·00
R.4/1	No stop after right "AFR"	Imperf	(No. 3a)	60·00
R.4/4	No stop after left "Z", no bar under top right "½"	Imperf	(No. 3b)	60·00
		Perf	(No. 23c)	
R.4/5	"POSTZECEL AER" at left	Imperf	(No. 3c)	60·00

Third printing

R.1/4	No stop after right "AFR"	Imperf	(No. 19a)	70·00
		Perf	(No. 22a)	40·00
R.2/1	Left side of inner frame too high	Imperf	(No. 19b)	70·00
		Perf	(No. 22b)	40·00
R.3/5	Centre figures "½" level	Imperf	(No. 20a)	70·00
		Perf	(No. 23d)	40·00
R.3/6	No stop after right "AFR"	Imperf	(No. 20b)	70·00
		Perf	(No. 23e)	40·00
R.4/6	Hyphen between right "AFR" and "REP"	Imperf	(No. 21a)	70·00
		Perf	(No. 24a)	40·00

1d. value

First printing

R.1/2	Inverted "1" at lower left, first "1" of date dropped	Imperf	(No. 4a)	35·00
		Perf	(No. 25a)	22·00
R.1/3	No bar under top left "1"	Imperf	(No. 4b)	35·00
		Perf	(No. 25b)	22·00
R.1/4	No bar over lower right "1".	Imperf	(No. 4c)	35·00
		Perf	(No. 25c)	22·00
R.1/5	"POSTZFGEL"	Imperf	(No. 4d)	35·00
		Perf	(No. 25d)	22·00
R.1/6	"AFB" at right	Imperf	(No. 4e)	35·00
		Perf	(No. 25e)	22·00
R.2/1	"REB" at left	Imperf	(No. 4f)	35·00
		Perf	(No. 25f)	22·00
R.2/2	"BEP" at left	Imperf	(No. 4g)	35·00
		Perf	(No. 25g)	22·00
R.2/3	"POSTZEOEL"	Imperf	(No. 4h)	35·00
		Perf	(No. 25h)	22·00
R.2/4	"AER" at right	Imperf	(No. 4i)	35·00
		Perf	(No. 25i)	22·00
R.2/5	No stop after date	Imperf	(No. 4j)	35·00
		Perf	(No. 25j)	22·00
R.2/6	No stop after "PENNY"	Imperf	(No. 4k)	35·00
		Perf	(No. 25k)	22·00
R.3/2	Right spray inverted	Imperf	(No. 5a)	35·00
		Perf	(No. 26a)	22·00
R.3/3	No bar over lower left "1"	Imperf	(No. 5b)	35·00
		Perf	(No. 26b)	22·00
R.3/4	No stop after left "Z"	Imperf	(No. 5c)	35·00
		Perf	(No. 26c)	22·00
R.3/6	"POSTZEGFL", no stop after right "AFR"	Imperf	(No. 5d)	35·00
		Perf	(No. 26d)	22·00
R.4/1	No stop after right "AFR"	Imperf	(No. 6a)	35·00
		Perf	(No. 27a)	22·00
R.4/2	& 6 Left spray inverted	Imperf	(No. 6b)	22·00
		Perf	(No. 27b)	13·00
R.4/3	"POSTZEGEI"	Imperf	(No. 6c)	35·00
		Perf	(No. 27c)	22·00
R.4/4	No bar under top right "1"	Imperf	(No. 6d)	35·00
		Perf	(No. 27d)	22·00

Second printing

R.1/2	First "1" in date dropped	Imperf	(No. 4l)	35·00
		Perf	(No. 25l)	22·00
R.3/6	No stop after right "AFR"	Imperf	(No. 5e)	35·00
		Perf	(No. 26e)	22·00
R.4/5	Dropped "P" in "PENNY"	Imperf	(No. 6e)	35·00
		Perf	(No. 27e)	22·00

It has been suggested that there may have been a third printing.

2d. value

First printing—Imperf

R.1/1	"1" at lower right	(No. 7a)	45·00
R.1/2	No stop after left "AFR" (*on small part of printing*)	(No. 7b)	90·00
R.1/3	No bar over lower right "2" (*on small part of printing*)	(No. 7c)	90·00
R.1/3	"PENNY" for "PENCE"	(No. 7d)	45·00
R.1/5	"POSTZFGEL"	(No. 7e)	45·00
R.1/6	"AFB" at right	(No. 7f)	45·00
R.2/1	"REB" at left	(No. 7g)	45·00
R.2/2	"AFB" at left	(No. 7h)	45·00
R.2/3	"POSTZEOEL"	(No. 7i)	45·00
R.2/4	"AER" at right	(No. 7j)	45·00
R.2/5	No stop after date	(No. 7k)	45·00
R.2/6	No stop after date, vertical line after "POSTZEGEL"	(No. 7l)	45·00
R.3/2	Right spray inverted	(No. 8a)	45·00
R.3/3	No bar over lower left "2"	(No. 8b)	45·00
R.3/4	Centre "2" inverted, no stop after left "Z"	(No. 8c)	45·00
R.3/6	"POSTZEGFL", no stop after right "AFR"	(No. 8d)	45·00
R.4/1	Centre "2" wider, no stop after right "AFR" (*occurs on second printing also*)	(No. 9a)	38·00
R.4/2	Centre "2" wider, left spray inverted	(No. 9b)	45·00
R.4/3	"POSTZEGEI"	(No. 9c)	45·00
R.4/4	No bar under top right "2"	(No. 9d)	45·00
R.4/5	"1" at lower left, "P" in "PENCE" dropped	(No. 9e)	45·00
R.4/6	Left spray inverted	(No. 9f)	45·00

Second printing

R.1/2	First "1" in date dropped	Imperf	(No. 7m)	45·00
		Perf	(No. 28a)	30·00
R.2/1	No stop after left "REP"	Imperf	(No. 7n)	45·00
		Perf	(No. 28b)	30·00
R.3/4	No stop after left "Z"	Imperf	(No. 8e)	45·00
R.3/6	No stop after right "AFR"	Imperf	(No. 8f)	45·00
		Perf	(No. 29a)	30·00
R.4/1	Centre 2 wider, no stop after right "AFR" (*occurs on first printing also*)	Imperf	(No. 9a)	38·00
		Perf	(No. 30a)	30·00
R.4/2	Centre "2" wider	Imperf	(No. 9g)	45·00
		Perf	(No. 30b)	30·00
R.4/5	"P" in "PENCE" dropped	Imperf	(No. 9h)	45·00
		Perf	(No. 30c)	30·00

It has been suggested that there was a third printing of this value.

4d. value

First printing

R.1/2	No stop after left "AFR"	(No. 10a)	45·00
R.1/3	No bar over lower right "4"	(No. 10b)	45·00
R.1/3	"PENNY" for "PENCE" (*on small part of printing*)	(No. 10c)	90·00
R.1/5	"POSTZFGEL"	(No. 10d)	45·00
R.1/6	"AFB" at right	(No. 10e)	45·00
R.2/1	"REB" at left	(No. 10f)	45·00
R.2/2	"AFB" at left	(No. 10g)	45·00
R.2/3	"POSTZEOEL"	(No. 10h)	45·00
R.2/4	"AER" at right	(No. 10i)	45·00
R.2/5	No stop after date	(No. 10j)	45·00
R.3/2	Right spray inverted	(No. 11a)	45·00
R.3/3	No bar over lower left "4" (*on small part of printing*)	(No. 11b)	90·00
R.3/4	No stop after left "Z"	(No. 11c)	45·00
R.3/6	"POSTZEGFL"	(No. 11d)	45·00
R.4/1	Centre "4" wider, no stop after right "AFR"	(No. 12a)	45·00
R.4/2	Centre "4" wider, left spray inverted	(No. 12b)	45·00
R.4/3	"POSTZEGEI"	(No. 12c)	45·00
R.4/4	No bar under top right "4"	(No. 12d)	45·00
R.4/5	"AER" at left, "P" in "PENCE" dropped	(No. 12e)	45·00
R.4/6	Left spray inverted	(No. 12f)	45·00

Second printing

R.2/1	Left inner frame too high	(No. 10k)	45·00
R.4/1–2	Centre "4" wider	(No. 12g)	35·00
R.4/5	"P" in "PENCE" dropped	(No. 12h)	45·00

6d. value

First printing

R.1/2	No stop after left "AFR"	(No. 13a)	55·00
R.1/3	No bar over lower right "6"	(No. 13b)	55·00
R.1/3	"PENNY" for "PENCE" (*on small part of printing*)	(No. 13c)	£100
R.1/5	"POSTZFGEL"	(No. 13d)	55·00
R.1/6	"AFB" at right	(No. 13e)	55·00
R.2/1	"REB" at left	(No. 13f)	55·00
R.2/2	"AFB" at left	(No. 13g)	55·00
R.2/3	"POSTZEOEL"	(No. 13h)	55·00
R.2/4	"AER" at right	(No. 13i)	55·00
R.2/5	No stop after date	(No. 13j)	55·00
R.3/2	Right spray inverted	(No. 14a)	55·00
R.3/4	Centre "6" inverted, no stop after left "Z" (*on small part of printing*)	(No. 14b)	£100
R.3/4	No stop after left "Z"	(No. 14c)	55·00
R.3/6	"POSTZEGFL"	(No. 14d)	55·00
R.4/1	Centre "6" wider, no stop after right "AFR"	(No. 15a)	55·00
R.4/2	Centre "6" wider, left spray inverted	(No. 15b)	55·00
R.4/3	"POSTZEGEI"	(No. 15c)	55·00
R.4/4	No bar under top right "6"	(No. 15d)	55·00
R.4/5	"AER" at left. "P" in "PENCE" dropped	(No. 15e)	55·00
R.4/6	Left spray inverted	(No. 15f)	55·00

Second printing

R.2/1	Left inner frame too high, no stop after left "REP"	(No. 13k)	55·00
R.4/1–2	Centre "6" wider	(No. 15g)	40·00
R.4/5	"P" in "PENCE" dropped	(No. 15h)	55·00

1s. value

R.1/2	No stop after left "AFR"	(No. 16a)	40·00
R.1/3	No bar over lower right "1"	(No. 16b)	40·00
R.2/5	No stop after date	(No. 16c)	40·00
R.3/3	Centre "1" inverted (*on small part of printing*)	(No. 17a)	
R.3/4	"POSTZEGEI", no stop after left "Z"	(No. 17b)	40·00
R.4/1	No stop after right "AFR"	(No. 18a)	40·00
R.4/4	No bar under top right "1"	(No. 18b)	40·00
R.4/5	"AER" at left	(No. 18c)	40·00

LOCAL BRITISH OCCUPATION ISSUES DURING THE SOUTH AFRICAN WAR 1900–2

Stamps of the Transvaal Republic, unless otherwise stated, variously overprinted or surcharged.

LYDENBURG

Lydenburg fell to the British on 6 September 1900.

V.R.I.
3d.
(L **1**)

1900 (Sept). *Nos. 215b and 217 surch as Type* L **1**, *others optd "V.R.I" only.*

1	**30**	½d. green	£120	£120
2		1d. rose-red and green	£110	£100
2*a*	**34**	1d. on 1d. red		
3	**30**	2d. brown and green	£1100	£800
4		2½d. blue and green	£2000	£850
5		3d. on 1d. rose-red and green	95·00	85·00
6		3d. purple and green		
7		4d. sage-green and green	£2750	£750
8		6d. lilac and green	£2250	£700
9		1s. ochre and green	£4000	£2500

The above were cancelled by British Army postal service postmarks. These overprints with Transvaal cancellations are believed to be forgeries.

RUSTENBURG

The British forces in Rustenburg, west of Pretoria, were besieged by the Boers during June 1900. When relieved on the 22 June 1900 no "V.R.I" stamps were available so a local handstamp was applied.

V.R.
(R **1**)

1900 (23 June). *Handstamped with Type* R **1** *in violet.*

1	**30**	½d. green	£140	£100
2		1d. rose-red and green	£100	80·00
3		2d. brown and green	£300	£120
4		2½d. blue and green	£170	£100
5		3d. purple and green	£225	£130
6		6d. lilac and green	£1100	£350
7		1s. ochre and green	£1600	£750
8		2s.6d. dull violet and green	£9000	£4500
		a. Handstamp in black	†	£8000

Nos. 2 and 5 exist with the handstamp inverted.

SCHWEIZER RENECKE

BESIEGED
(SR **1**)

1900 (Sept). *Handstamped with Type* SR **1** *in black, reading vert up or down.*

(a) On stamps of Transvaal.

1	**30**	½d. green	†	£250
2		1d. rose-red and green	†	£250
3		2d. brown and green	†	£325
4		6d. lilac and green	†	£900

(b) On stamps of Cape of Good Hope.

5	**17**	½d. green	†	£425
6		1d. carmine	†	£425

Schweizer Renecke, near the Bechuanaland border, was under siege from 1 August 1900 to 9 January 1901. The British commander authorised the above stamps shortly after 19 August. All stamps were cancelled with the dated circular town postmark ("Schweizer Renecke, Z.A.R."), usually after having been stuck on paper before use. Unused, without the postmark, do not exist.

No. 4 exists with double handstamp.

WOLMARANSSTAD

A British party occupied this town in the south-west of the Transvaal from 15 June to 27 July 1900. Transvaal stamps, to a face value of £5 2s.6d., were found at the local firm of Thos. Leask and Co. and surcharged as below. The first mail left on 24 June and the last on 21 July.

Cancelled **V-R-I.** (L **3**)

Cancelled **V-R-I.** (L **4**)

1900 (24 June). *Optd with Type* L **3**.

1	**30**	½d. green (B.)	£225	£350
		a. Opt inverted	£800	
		b. Opt in black		
1*c*		½d. on 1s. green (B.)		
2		1d. rose-red and green (B.)	£160	£250
		a. Opt in green	£1800	
		b. Opt in black		
3		2d. brown and green (B.)	£1800	£1800
		a. Opt in black	£3000	
4		2½d. blue and green (R.)	£1800	
		a. Opt in blue	£2750	£2750
		b. Opt in black		
5		3d. purple and green (B.)	£3000	£3250
6		4d. sage-green and green (B.)	£3750	£4250
7		6d. lilac and green (B.)	£4250	£4500
8		1s. ochre and green (B.)	—	£8500

The two lines of the overprint were handstamped separately. The ½d. exists with two impressions of the "Cancelled" handstamp, the 2½d. with two impressions of "V-R-I", one in red and one in blue and the 3d. with "Cancelled" in green and "V.R.I." in blue.

1900 (24 June). *Optd with Type* L **4**.

9	**34**	1d. red (B.)	£160	£275

The ½d., 1d. and 3d. in Type **30** are also known with this overprint.

VII. ZULULAND

Zululand remained an independent kingdom until annexed by Great Britain on 19 May 1887 when it was declared a Crown Colony.

The first European postal service was operated by a Natal postal agency at Eshowe opened in 1876 which cancelled Natal stamps with a "No. 56 P.O. Natal" postmark. The agency closed during the Zulu War of 1879 and did not re-open until 1885 when a Eshowe postmark was provided. "ZULULAND" was added to the cancellation in 1887 and stamps of Natal continued to be used until replaced by the overprinted series on 1 May 1888.

PRICES FOR STAMPS ON COVER

Nos. 1/2	*from* × 100
Nos. 3/10	*from* × 20
No. 11	—
Nos. 12/16	*from* × 20
Nos. 20/3	*from* × 30

PRICES FOR STAMPS ON COVER

No. 24	*from* × 20
Nos. 25/6	*from* × 12
Nos. 27/9	—
No. F1	*from* × 100

ZULULAND (1) ZULULAND. (2)

1888 (1 May)–**93**.

(a) Nos. 173, 180, 197, 200/2, 205a, 207a/8, 209 and 211 of Great Britain (Queen Victoria) optd with T **1** *by D.L.R.*

1	½d. vermilion (11.88)	4·25	2·50
2	1d. deep purple	27·00	4·00
3	2d. grey-green and carmine	17·00	30·00
4	2½d. purple/*blue* (9.91)	25·00	20·00
5	3d. purple/*yellow*	25·00	22·00
6	4d. green and deep brown	45·00	65·00
7	5d. dull purple and blue (3.93)	90·00	£120
	w. Wmk inverted	†	—
8	6d. purple/*rose-red*	14·00	17·00
9	9d. dull purple and blue (4.92)	95·00	95·00
10	1s. dull green (4.92)	£110	£130
11	5s. rose (4.92)	£550	£600
1/11 *Set of 11*		£900	£1000
1s/11s *(ex 1d.)* H/S "Specimen" *Set of 10*		£600	

(b) No. 97a of Natal optd with T **2** *at Pietermaritzburg*

12	½d. dull green (with stop) (7.88)	55·00	80·00
	a. Opt double	£1100	£1200
	b. Opt inverted	£1300	
	d. Opt omitted (vert pair with normal)	£6000	
13	½d. dull green (without stop)	25·00	40·00
	a. Opt double	£1500	£1500

1893 (29 Nov*). *T* **15** *of Natal optd with T* **1** *by D.L.R. (*Wmk Crown CA. P 14*).*

16	6d. dull purple	60·00	55·00

*Earliest known date of use. No. 16 was, apparently, originally supplied in 1889 for fiscal purposes.

3

4

Shaved "Z" (R. 4/3 and R. 6/3)

(Typo D.L.R.)

1894 (18 Apr)–**96**. Wmk Crown CA. P 14.

20	**3**	½d. dull mauve and green	3·50	4·75
		w. Wmk inverted	£150	£170
21		1d. dull mauve and carmine	5·00	2·50
		a. Shaved "Z"	60·00	38·00
22		2½d. dull mauve and ultramarine	14·00	8·50
23		3d. dull mauve and olive-brown	8·00	3·00
24	**4**	6d. dull mauve and black	20·00	20·00
25		1s. green	38·00	38·00
26		2s.6d. green and black (2.96)	75·00	85·00
27		4s. green and carmine	£110	£150
28		£1 purple/*red*	£450	£550
29		£5 purple and black/*red*	£4500	£1500
		s. Optd "Specimen"	£450	
20/8 *Set of 9*			£650	£750
20s/8s Optd "Specimen" *Set of 9*			£400	

Dangerous forgeries exist of the £1 and £5.

FISCAL STAMP USED FOR POSTAGE

ZULULAND

F **1**

1891 (5 May*). **F1**, *Fiscal stamp of Natal optd with T* **1**. Wmk Crown CA. P 14.

F1	1d. dull mauve	3·50	3·00
	a. Top left triangle detached	£140	£130
	s. Handstamped "Specimen"	60·00	

*Earliest known date of postal use. A proclamation published in the *Natal Government Gazette* on 27 June 1891 authorised the use of this stamp for postal purposes, but it is clear from the wording that such use had already commenced.

For illustration of "top left triangle detached" variety see above No. 21 of Antigua.

Other values, 1s. to £20 as No. F1 exist apparently with postmarks, but, as these were never authorised for postal use, they are no longer listed.

Zululand was annexed to Natal on 31 December 1897 and its stamps were withdrawn from sale on 30 June 1898.

VIII. BRITISH ARMY FIELD OFFICES DURING SOUTH AFRICAN WAR, 1899–1902

Z **1** Z **2**

Stamps of GREAT BRITAIN *used by British Army Field Offices in South Africa cancelled as Types* Z **1**, Z **2** *or similar postmarks.*

1881. *Stamp of Queen Victoria.*

Z1	1d. lilac (16 *dots*)	5·00

1883–84. *Stamps of Queen Victoria.*

Z1*a*	2s.6d lilac	£225
Z2	5s. rose	£250
Z2*a*	10s. ultramarine	£550

1887–92. *Stamps of Queen Victoria.*

Z3	½d. vermilion	6·00
Z4	1½d. dull purple and green	22·00
Z5	2d. grey-green and carmine	15·00
Z6	2½d. purple/*blue*	6·00
Z7	3d. purple/*yellow*	12·00
Z8	4d. green and brown	17·00
Z9	4½d. green and carmine	55·00
Z10	5d. dull purple and blue (Die II)	15·00
Z11	6d. purple/*rose-red*	12·00
Z12	9d. dull purple and blue	60·00
Z13	10d. dull purple and carmine	55·00
Z14	1s. dull green	80·00
Z15	£1 green	£850

1900. *Stamps of Queen Victoria.*

Z16	½d. blue-green	6·00
Z17	1s. green and carmine	£150

1902. *Stamps of King Edward VII.*

Z18	½d. blue-green	15·00
Z19	1d. scarlet	10·00
Z20	1½d. purple and green	
Z21	2d. yellowish green and carmine-red	
Z22	2½d. ultramarine	20·00
Z23	3d. purple/*orange-yellow*	
Z24	4d. green and grey-brown	
Z25	5d. dull purple and ultramarine	
Z26	6d. pale dull purple	35·00
Z27	9d. dull purple and ultramarine	
Z28	10d. dull purple and carmine	
Z29	1s. dull green and carmine	

ARMY OFFICIAL STAMPS

1896–1901. *Stamps of Queen Victoria optd "ARMY OFFICIAL".*

ZO1	½d. vermilion	£100
ZO2	½d. blue-green	£100
ZO3	1d. lilac (16 *dots*)	85·00
ZO4	6d. purple/*rose-red*	

IX. UNION OF SOUTH AFRICA

The province continued to use their existing issues until the introduction of Nos. 3/17. From 19 August 1910 the issues of any province were valid for use throughout the Union until they were demonetised on 31 December 1937.

PRICES FOR STAMPS ON COVER TO 1945	
Nos. 1/15	*from* × 4
Nos. 16/17	—
Nos. 18/21	*from* × 6
Nos. 26/32	*from* × 2
No. 33	*from* × 4
Nos. 34/110	*from* × 1
Nos. D1/7	*from* × 4
Nos. D8/33	*from* × 6
Nos. O1/33	*from* × 4

1

(Des H. S. Wilkinson. Recess D.L.R.)

1910 (4 Nov). *Opening of Union Parliament. Inscribed bilingually.* Wmk Multiple Rosettes. P 14.

1	1	2½d. deep blue	3·00	3·00
		s. Handstamped "Specimen"	£350	
2		2½d. blue	1·75	1·40

The deep blue shade is generally accompanied by a blueing of the paper.

No. 1s. has the overprint in italic capital and lower case letters which measure 12½ mm in length.

2

3

4 Springbok's Head

(Typo D.L.R.)

1913 (1 Sept)–**24**. *Inscribed bilingually.* W **4**.

(a) P 14.

3	2	½d. green	1·50	30
		a. Stamp doubly printed	£10000	
		b. Blue-green	2·00	20
		c. Yellow-green	2·50	80
		d. Printed on the gummed side	£700	
		w. Wmk inverted	2·00	80
4		1d. rose-red (*shades*)	1·75	10
		a. Carmine-red	2·25	10
		b. Scarlet (*shades*)	2·75	75
		c. Printed on the gummed side	£750	
		w. Wmk inverted	2·50	70
5		1½d. chestnut (*shades*) (23.8.20)	80	10
		a. *Tête-bêche* (pair)	1·75	18·00
		b. Printed on the gummed side	£800	
		c. Wmk sideways	†	£1500
		w. Wmk inverted	80	10
6	3	2d. dull purple	1·75	10
		a. Deep purple	2·50	10
		b. Printed on the gummed side	£800	
		w. Wmk inverted	3·25	1·75
7		2½d. bright blue	3·75	1·25
		a. Deep blue	5·50	3·00
		w. Wmk inverted	70·00	70·00
8		3d. black and orange-red	11·00	30
		a. Black and dull orange-red	10·00	70
		w. Wmk inverted	18·00	8·00
9		3d. ultramarine (*shades*) (4.10.22)	3·50	1·75
		w. Wmk inverted	9·50	5·50
10		4d. orange-yellow and olive-green	9·00	55
		a. Orange-yellow and sage-green	6·50	55
		w. Wmk inverted	8·00	85
11		6d. black and violet	5·50	60
		a. Black and bright violet	9·50	1·00
		aw. Wmk inverted	16·00	9·50
12		1s. orange	13·00	80
		a. Orange-yellow	20·00	1·00
		w. Wmk inverted	18·00	1·25
13		1s.3d. violet (*shades*) (1.9.20)	13·00	7·00
		w. Wmk inverted	£100	£150
14		2s.6d. purple and green	55·00	1·50
15		5s. purple and blue	£110	8·00
		a. Reddish purple and light blue	£110	8·50
		w. Wmk inverted	£4250	£2500
16		10s. deep blue and olive-green	£180	7·50
		w. Wmk inverted	£4000	£1800
17		£1 green and red (7.16)	£600	£350
		a. Pale olive-green and red (1924)	£800	£1200
3/17 *Set of 15*			£900	£350
3s/8s, 10s/17s Optd or H/S (1½d. and 1s.3d. in violet, £1 in green) "Specimen" *Set of 14*			£1300	

(b) Coil stamps. P 14×imperf.

18	2	½d. green	6·00	1·00
		w. Wmk inverted	£550	£325
19		1d. rose-red (13.2.14)	13·00	3·75
		a. Scarlet	17·00	8·50
		w. Wmk inverted	£550	£325
20		1½d. chestnut (15.11.20)	11·00	15·00
		w. Wmk inverted	†	—
21	3	2d. dull purple (7.10.21)	14·00	4·75
18/21 *Set of 4*			40·00	22·00

The 6d. exists with "Z" of "ZUID" wholly or partly missing due to wear of plate (*Price wholly missing, £80 un, £38 us*).

5 De Havilland D.H.9 Biplane

(Eng A. J. Cooper. Litho *Cape Times* Ltd)

1925 (26 Feb). *Air. Inscr bilingually.* P 12.

26	5	1d. carmine	4·00	10·00
27		3d. ultramarine	7·00	10·00
28		6d. magenta	9·00	11·00
29		9d. green	23·00	55·00
26/9 *Set of 4*			38·00	75·00

Beware of forgeries of all values perforated 11, 11½ or 13.

INSCRIPTIONS. From 1926 until 1951 most issues were inscribed in English and Afrikaans alternately throughout the sheets.

PRICES for Nos. 30/135 are for unused horizontal pairs, used horizontal pairs and used singles (either inscription), *unless otherwise indicated.* Vertical pairs are worth between 25% and 40% of the prices quoted for horizontal pairs.

6 Springbok

7 *Dromedaris* (Van Riebeeck's ship)

8 Orange Tree

9

(Typo Waterlow until 1927, thereafter Govt Printer, Pretoria)

1926 (2 Jan)–**27**. W **9**. P 14½×14.

			Un pair	*Used pair*	*Used single*
30	6	½d. black and green	3·00	4·00	10
		a. Missing "1" in "½"	£2000		
		b. Centre omitted (in pair with normal)	£1800		
		cw. Wmk inverted	4·25	4·50	20
		d. Frame printed double	£2500		
		e. Perf 13½×14 (1927)	70·00	70·00	4·00
		ea. *Tête-bêche* (pair)	£900		
		ew. Wmk inverted	65·00	65·00	4·00
31	7	1d. black and carmine	2·00	50	10
		a. Imperf (vert pair)*	£650		
		b. Imperf 3 sides (vert pair)*	£650	£700	
		cw. Wmk inverted	5·00	1·75	20
		d. Perf 13½×14 (1927)	95·00	80·00	4·00
		da. *Tête-bêche* (pair)	£1000		
		dw. Wmk inverted	95·00	80·00	4·00
		e. Wmk sideways	£2000	£2000	
32	8	6d. green and orange (1.5.26)	38·00	45·00	1·50
		w. Wmk inverted	70·00	75·00	
30/2 *Set of 3*			40·00	45·00	1·50

No. 30a exists in Afrikaans only. Nos. 30e and 31d were only issued in booklets.

No. 30d occurred on the bottom left-hand corner of one sheet and included the bottom four stamps in the first vertical row and the bottom two in the second. As listed No. 30d shows the left-hand stamp with the frame completely double and the right-hand stamp with two-thirds of the frame double.

*Both Nos. 31a and 31b occur in blocks of four with the other vertical pair imperforate at left.

For ½d. with pale grey centre, see No. 126.

For rotogravure printing see Nos. 42, etc.

10 "Hope"

(Recess B.W.)

1926 (2 Jan). *T* **10**. *Inscribed in English or Afrikaans.* W **9** (upright or inverted in equal quantities).

		Single stamps	
33	4d. grey-blue (English inscr) (*shades*)	1·75	1·25
	a. Inscr in Afrikaans	1·75	1·25

In this value the English and Afrikaans inscriptions are on separate sheets.

This stamp is known with private perforations or roulettes.

11 Union Buildings, Pretoria

12 Groot Schuur

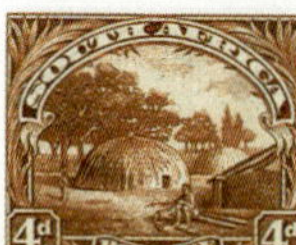

12a A Native Kraal

13 Black and Blue Wildebeest

14 Ox-wagon inspanned

15 Ox-wagon outspanned

16 Cape Town and Table Bay

(Recess B.W.)

1927 (1 Mar)–**30**. W **9**. P 14.

			Un pair	*Used pair*	*Used single*
34	11	2d. grey and maroon	11·00	23·00	60
		aw. Wmk inverted	£500	£550	30·00
		b. Perf 14×13½ (2.30)	30·00	30·00	70
35	12	3d. black and red	15·00	26·00	60
		a. Perf 14×13½ (1930)	60·00	65·00	80
35*b*	12a	4d. brown (23.3.28)	26·00	50·00	1·00
		bw. Wmk inverted	£650	£600	35·00
		c. Perf 14×13½ (1930)	48·00	60·00	1·25
36	13	1s. brown and deep blue	30·00	55·00	1·00
		a. Perf 14×13½ (1930)	65·00	80·00	2·00
37	14	2s.6d. green and brown	£110	£350	17·00
		a. Perf 14×13½ (1930)	£325	£550	24·00
38	15	5s. black and green	£225	£650	35·00
		a. Perf 14×13½ (1930)	£400	£850	40·00
39	16	10s. bright blue and brown	£150	£130	10·00
		a. Centre inverted (*single stamp*)	£10000		
		b. Perf 14×13½ (1930)	£190	£180	12·00
34/9 *Set of 7*			£500	£1100	55·00
34s/9s H/S "Specimen" *Set of 7*			£900		

17 De Havilland D.H.60 Cirrus Moth

(Typo Govt Ptg Wks, Pretoria)

1929 (16 Aug). *Air. Inscribed bilingually.* No wmk. P 14×13½.

			Un single	*Used single*
40	17	4d. green	5·50	2·50
41		1s. orange	16·00	13·00

PRINTER. All the following issues, except *where stated otherwise*, are printed by rotogravure (the design having either plain lines or a dotted screen) by the Government Printer, Pretoria.

I

II

The two types of the 1d. differ in the spacing of the horizontal lines in the side panels:—Type I close; Type II wide. The Afrikaans had the spacing of the words POSSEEL-INKOMSTE close in Type I and more widely spaced in Type II.

"Cobweb" variety (retouch between horns) (Cyl. 1 R. 9/5)

"Dolar" variety (Cyl. 2) R. 10/9)

Window flaw (R. 20/4 on all ptgs before 1937)

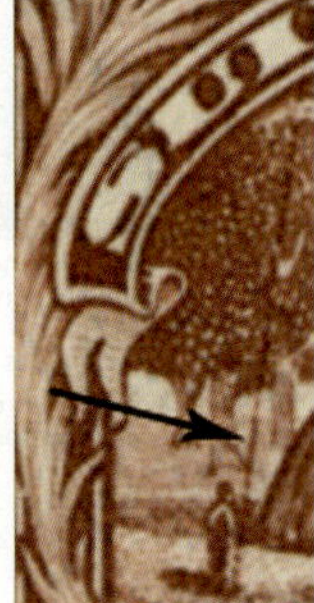

Spear flaw (R. 9/2)

"Monkey" in tree (R. 2/2)

Twisted horn (Cyl 7020 R. 1/5)

1930–45. *T* **6** *to* **8** *and* **11** *to* **14** *redrawn, "SUIDAFRIKA" (in one word) on Afrikaans stamps.* W **9**. P 15×14 (½d., 1d., and 6d.) or 14.

		Un pair	*Used pair*	*Used single*
42	½d. black and green (5.30)	3·75	3·00	10
	a. Two English or two Afrikaans stamps *se-tenant* (vert strip of 4)	40·00		
	b. *Tête-bêche*	£900		
	c. "Cobweb" variety	40·00		
	d. "Dollar" variety	40·00		
	w. Wmk inverted	3·75	2·75	10
43	1d. black and carmine (I) (4.30)	4·50	3·00	10
	a. *Tête-bêche*	£1100		
	b. Frame omitted (*single stamp*)	£450		
	cw. Wmk inverted	4·50	2·75	10
43*d*	1d. black and carmine (II) (8.32)	45·00	3·75	10
	dw. Wmk inverted	38·00	3·75	10
44	2d. slate-grey and lilac (4.31)	23·00	18·00	30
	a. *Tête-bêche*	£4250		
	b. Frame omitted (*single stamp*)	£2500		
	cw. Wmk inverted	17·00	8·50	20
44*d*	2d. blue and violet (3.38)	£325	75·00	2·50
45	3d. black and red (11.31)	60·00	80·00	2·25
	aw. Wmk inverted	32·00	60·00	1·25
	b. Window flaw	£130		
45*c*	3d. blue (10.33)	19·00	7·00	20
	cw. Wmk inverted	6·00	6·00	10
	d. Window flaw	45·00		
	e. Centre omitted	£25000		
	f. Frame omitted (*single stamp*)	£12000		
46	4d. brown (19.11.32)	£160	£120	6·00
	aw. Wmk inverted	30·00	30·00	40
	b. Spear flaw	£110		
46*c*	4d. brown (*shades*) (*again redrawn*) (1936)	3·75	2·75	10
	ca "Monkey" in tree	38·00		
	cw. Wmk inverted	13·00	8·00	10
47	6d. green and orange (*wmk inverted*) (13.5.31)	13·00	4·50	10
	w. Wmk upright (8.32)	38·00	15·00	10
48	1s. brown and deep blue (14.9.32)	75·00	45·00	40
	aw. Wmk inverted	35·00	26·00	25
	b. Twisted horn flaw	£190		
49	2s.6d. green & brown (*shades*) (24.12.32)	£110	£110	3·25
	aw. Wmk inverted	£130	£140	3·25
49*b*	2s.6d. blue and brown (1945)	26·00	12·00	20
42/9*b* *Set of 13*		£500	£275	6·50

For similar designs with "SUID-AFRIKA" hyphenated, see Nos. 54 etc. and Nos. 114 etc.

Nos. 42/3, 43*d*/4 exist in coils.

No. 42a comes from the coil printing on the cylinder for which two horizontal rows were incorrectly etched so that two Afrikaans-inscribed stamps were followed by two English. This variety is normally without a coil join, although some examples do occur showing a repair join.

The 1d. (Type I) exists without watermark from a trial printing (*Price £25 un*).

Although it appears to be printed in one colour No. 45*c* was produced from vignette and frame cylinders in the same way as the bicoloured version. The clouds in the background, which are present on No. 45e, were printed from the frame cylinder.

Nos. 45b, 45d, 46b and 48b all occur on printings with either upright or inverted watermark. The price quoted is for the cheapest version in each instance.

The Rotogravure printings may be distinguished from the preceding Typographed and Recess printed issues by the following tests:—

TYPO

ROTO

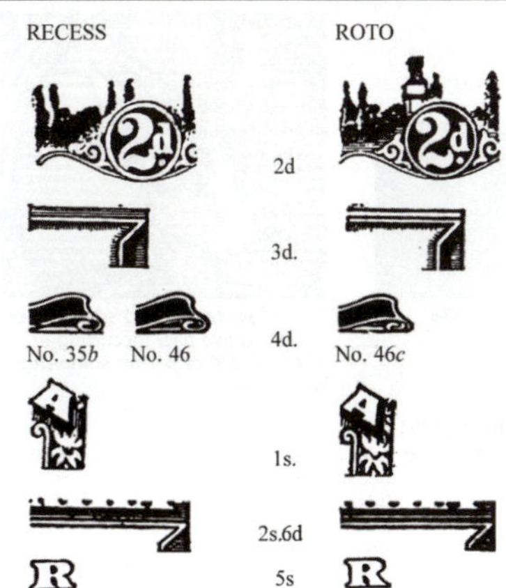

ROTOGRAVURE:

½d. 1d. and 6d. Leg of "R" in "AFR" ends squarely on the bottom line.

2d. The newly built War Memorial appears to the left of the value.

3d. Two fine lines have been removed from the top part of the frame.

4d. No. 46. The scroll is in solid colour. No. 46*c*. The scroll is white with a crooked line running through it. (No. 35*b*. The scroll is shaded by the diagonal lines.)

1s. The shading of the last "A" partly covers the flower beneath.

2s.6d. The top line of the centre frame is thick and leaves only one white line between it and the name.

5s. (Nos. 64/*b*). The leg of the "R" is straight.

Rotogravure impressions are generally coarser.

18 Church of the Vow

19 "The Great Trek" (C. Michell)

20 A Voortrekker

21 Voortrekker Woman

Blurred "SOUTH AFRICA" and red "comet" flaw (Cyls 6917/6922 R. 2/7)

(Des J. Prentice (½d., 2d., 3d.)

1933 (3 May)–**36**. *Voortrekker Memorial Fund.* W **9** (sideways). P 14.

50	**18**	½d. +½d.black and green (16.1.36)	3·50	5·00	50
51	**19**	1d. +½d.grey-black and pink	2·75	1·50	25
		a. Blurred "SOUTH AFRICA" and red "comet" flaw	45·00	48·00	
52	**20**	2d. +1d. grey-green and purple	3·50	4·00	55
53	**21**	3d. +1½d. grey-green and blue	5·50	5·00	70
50/3 *Set of 4*			14·00	14·00	1·75

22 Gold Mine

22a Groot Schuur

Dies of 6d.

I

II

III

23 Groot Constantia

"Falling ladder" flaw (R. 5/10)

1933–48. *"SUID-AFRIKA" (hyphenated) on Afrikaans stamps.* W **9**. P 15×14 (½d., 1d. and 6d.) or 14 (others).

54	**6**	½d. grey and green (*wmk inverted*) (9.35)	4·50	2·00	10
		aw. Wmk upright (1936)	8·50	7·00	10
		b. Coil stamp. Perf 13½×14 (1935)	38·00	60·00	1·00
		bw. Wmk upright	38·00	60·00	1·00
		c. Booklet pane of 6 (with adverts on margins) (*wmk upright*)	25·00		
56	**7**	1d. grey and carmine (*shades*) (19.4.34)	1·75	1·75	10
		a. Imperf (pair) (*wmk inverted*)	£160		
		b. Frame omitted (*single stamp*)	£275		
		cw. Wmk inverted	1·75	1·75	10
		d. Coil stamp. Perf 13½×14 (1935)	40·00	60·00	1·40
		dw. Wmk inverted	40·00	60·00	1·40
		e. Booklet pane of 6 (with adverts on margins) (1935)	19·00		
		f. Booklet pane of 6 (with blank margins) (1937)	19·00		
		h. Booklet pane of 6 (with postal slogans on margins) (1948)	4·00		
		i. Grey & brt rose-carm (7.48)	70	2·00	10
57	**22**	1½d. green and bright gold (12.11.36)	3·25	2·25	10
		a. Shading omitted from mine dump (in pair with normal)	£190	£140	
		bw. Wmk inverted	1·50	1·75	10
		c. Blue-green and dull gold (8.40)	6·50	3·00	10
58	**11**	2d. blue and violet (11.38)	75·00	35·00	75
58*a*		2d. grey and dull purple (5.41)	50·00	80·00	1·25
59	**22a**	3d. ultramarine (2.40)	13·00	3·25	10
61	**8**	6d. green and vermilion (I) (10.37)	70·00	30·00	70
		a. "Falling ladder" flaw	£225	£250	
61*b*		6d. green and vermilion (II) (6.38)	40·00	1·00	10
61*c*		6d. green and red-orange (III) (11.46)	20·00	75	10
62	**13**	1s. brown and chalky blue (2.39)	50·00	13·00	10
		a. Frame omitted (*single stamp*)	£4500		
64	**15**	5s. black and green (10.33)	55·00	70·00	1·75
		aw. Wmk inverted	£120	£130	3·00
		b. Black and blue-green (9.44)	38·00	16·00	35
64*c*	**23**	10s. blue and sepia (*shades*) / (8.39)	65·00	14·00	70
		ca. Blue and charcoal (1944)	42·00	5·50	30
54/9, 61*c*/64*ca* *Set of 10*			£250	£140	2·50

The ½d. and 1d. coil stamps may be found in blocks emanating from the residue of the large rolls which were cut into sheets and distributed to Post Offices.

Nos. 54 and 56 also exist in coils.

1d. Is printed from Type II. Frames of different sizes exist due to reductions made from time to time for the purpose of providing more space for the perforations.

3d. In No. 59 the frame is unscreened and composed of solid lines. Centre is diagonally screened. Scrolls above "3d." are clear lined, light in the middle and dark at sides.

6d. Die I. Green background lines faint. "SUID-AFRIKA" 16¼ mm long.

Die II. Green background lines heavy. "SUID-AFRIKA" 17 mm long. "S" near end of tablet. Scroll open.

Die III. Scroll closed up and design smaller (18×22 mm).

Single specimens of the 1933–48 issue inscribed in English may be distinguished from those of 1930–45 as follows:—

½d. and 1d. Centres in grey instead of varying intensities of black.

2d. The letters of "SOUTH AFRICA" are narrower and thinner.

3d. The trees are taller and the sky is without lines.

6d. The frame is vermilion.

1s. The frame is chalky blue.

For similar designs, but printed in screened rotogravure, see Nos. 114 to 122a.

BOOKLET PANES. Booklets issued in 1935 contained ½d. and 1d. stamps in panes with advertisements in the top and bottom margins and no margin at right (Nos. 54b and 56d). These were replaced in 1937 by editions showing blank margins on all four sides (Nos. 56e and 75ba). Following a period when the booklet panes were without margins a further 3s. booklet was issued in 1948 which had four margins on the panes and postal slogans at top and bottom (Nos. 56h, 87b and 114a).

24

JIPEX

1936
(24a)

"Cleft skull" flaw (R. 14/2)

(Des J. Booysen)

1935 (1 May). *Silver Jubilee. Inscr bilingually.* W **9**. P 15×14.

65	**24**	½d. black and blue-green.	2·75	12·00	10
		a. "Cleft skull" flaw	8·50		
66		1d. black and carmine	2·75	6·00	10
		a. "Cleft skull" flaw	8·50		
67		3d. blue	15·00	55·00	2·25
		a. "Cleft skull" flaw	48·00		
68		6d. green and orange	30·00	75·00	3·25
		a. "Cleft skull" flaw	75·00		
65/8 *Set of 4*			45·00	£130	5·00

In stamps with English at top the ½d., 3d. and 6d. have "SILWER JUBILEUM" to left of portrait, and "POSTAGE REVENUE" or "POSTAGE" (3d. and 6d.) in left value tablet. In the 1d., "SILVER JUBILEE" is to the left of portrait. In alternate stamps the positions of English and Afrikaans inscriptions are reversed.

1936 (2 Nov). *Johannesburg International Philatelic Exhibition. Optd with T* **24a**. W **9** (inverted).

		Un sheet	*Us sheet*
MS69	**6** ½d. grey and green (No. 54)	3·50	10·00
MS70	**7** 1d. grey and carmine (No. 56)	2·75	7·00

Issued each in miniature sheet of six stamps with marginal advertisements. Ten different arrangements of advertisements exist on the ½d. sheets, 21 different on the 1d.

25

"Mouse" flaw (R. 4/1)

(Des J. Prentice)

1937 (12 May). *Coronation.* W **9** (sideways*). P 14.

			Un pair	*Used pair*	*Us single*
71	**25**	½d. grey-black and blue-green	80	1·25	10
		w. Wmk horns pointing to left	80	1·25	10
72		1d. grey-black and carmine	80	1·00	10
		w. Wmk horns pointing to left	80	1·00	10
73		1½d. orange and greenish blue	80	80	10
		a. "Mouse" flaw	7·50		
		w. Wmk horns pointing to left	80	80	10
74		3d. ultramarine	1·50	3·00	10
		w. Wmk horns pointing to left	1·50	3·00	10
75		1s. red-brown and turquoise-blue	2·75	5·00	15
		a. Hyphen on Afrikaans stamp omitted (R. 2/13)	60·00		
		bw. Wmk horns pointing to left	2·75	5·00	15
71/5 *Set of 5*			6·00	10·00	40

*The normal sideways watermark shows the horns of the springbok pointing to the right, *as seen from the back of the stamp.*

No. 75a shows the hyphen completely omitted and the top of the "K" damaged. A less distinct flaw, on which part of the hyphen is still visible and with no damage to the "K", occurs on R. 4/17.

25a

"Tick" flaw on ear and spot on nose (multipositive flaw (occurring in 1947) (R. 3/4 or 3/1 on some ptgs of No. 114)

1937–40. W **9**. P 15×14.

75c	**25a**	½d. grey and green	10·00	2·00	10
		ca. Booklet pane of 6 (with blank margins) (1937)	55·00		
		cd. Grey and blue green (1940)	7·50	1·25	10
		ce. "Tick" flaw and spot on nose	55·00		

The lines of shading in T **25a** are all horizontal and thicker than in T **6**. In Nos. 75*c* and 75*cd* the design is composed of solid lines. For stamps with designs composed of dotted lines, see No. 114. Later printings of No. 75*cd* have a smaller design.

26 Voortrekker Ploughing

27 Wagon crossing Drakensberg

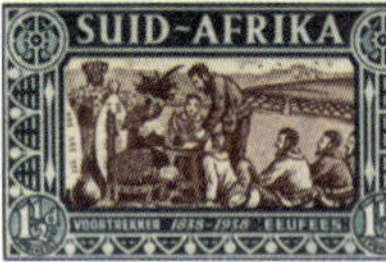

28 Signing of Dingaan–Retief Treaty

29 Voortrekker Monument

(Des W. Coetzer and J. Prentice)

1938 (14 Dec). *Voortrekker Centenary Memorial Fund.* W **9**. P 14 (Nos. 76/7) or 15×14 (others).

76	**26**	½d. +½d.blue and green	13·00	4·50	30
77	**27**	1d. +1d.blue and carmine	16·00	5·50	40
78	**28**	1½d. +1½d. chocolate and blue-green	20·00	9·00	80
79	**29**	3d. +3d.bright blue	22·00	9·00	1·00
76/9 *Set of 4*			65·00	25·00	2·25

30 Wagon Wheel

31 Voortrekker Family

Three bolts in wheel rim (R. 15/5)

(Des W. Coetzer and J. Prentice)

1938 (14 Dec). *Voortrekker Commemoration.* W **9**. P 15×14.

80	**30**	1d. blue and carmine	6·50	3·50	30
		a. Three bolts in wheel rim	38·00	27·00	
81	**31**	1½d. greenish blue and brown	8·50	3·50	30

32 Old Vicarage, Paarl, now a museum

33 Symbol of the Reformation

34 Huguenot Dwelling, Drakenstein Mountain Valley

(Des J. Prentice)

1939 (17 July). *250th Anniv of Huguenot Landing in South Africa and Huguenot Commemoration Fund.* W **9**. P 14 (Nos. 82/3) or 15×14 (No. 84).

82	**32**	½d. +½d.brown and green	5·50	6·50	30
83	**33**	1d. +1d. green and carmine	12·00	7·00	30
84	**34**	1½d. +1½d. blue-green and purple	27·00	14·00	1·00
82/4 *Set of 3*			40·00	25·00	1·40

34a Gold Mine

1941 (Aug)–**48**. W **9** (sideways). P 14×15.

87	**34a**	1½d. blue-green and yellow-buff (*shades*)	2·50	1·50	10
		a. Yellow-buff (centre) omitted	£2750	£1600	
		b. Booklet pane of 6 (with postal slogans on margins) (1948)	8·00		

35 Infantry

36 Nurse and Ambulance

37 Airman

38 Sailor, Destroyer and Lifebelts

39 Women's Auxiliary Services

40 Artillery

41 Electric Welding

42 Tank Corps

42a Signaller

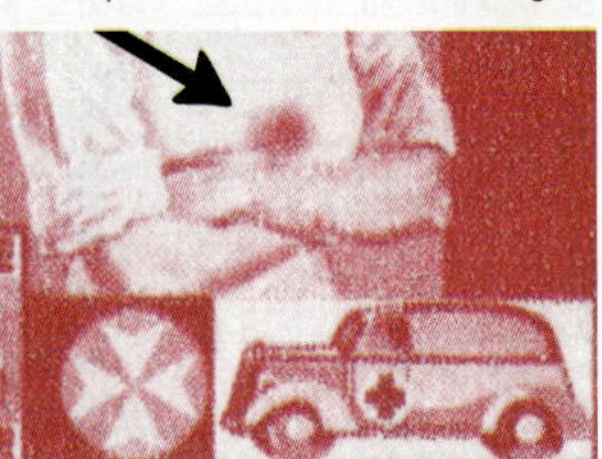
"Stain" on uniform (R. 14/11)

"Cigarette" flaw (R. 18/2)

1941–46. *War Effort.* W **9** (sideways on 2d., 4d., 6d.). P 14 (2d., 4d., 6d.) or 15×14 (others).

(a) Inscr alternately.

88	**35**	½d. green (19.11.41)	1·50	3·00	10
		a. Blue-green (7.42)	3·75	3·25	10
89	**36**	1d. carmine (3.10.41)	2·00	3·00	10
		a. "Stain" on uniform flaw	27·00		
90	**37**	1½d. myrtle-green (12.1.42)	1·50	2·75	10

91	**39**	3d. blue (1.8.41)	23·00	38·00	70
		a. "Cigarette" flaw	90·00		
92	**40**	4d. orange-brown (20.8.41)	22·00	24·00	15
		a. Red-brown (6.42)	35·00	35·00	1·25
93	**41**	6d. red-orange (3.9.41)	12·00	14·00	15
94	**42a**	1s.3d. olive-brown (2.1.43)	13·00	10·00	20
		a. Blackish brown (5.46)	4·75	8·00	20

(b) Inscr bilingually.

			Un single	*Us single*
95	**38**	2d. violet (15.9.41)	1·00	75
96	**42**	1s. brown (27.10.41)	3·75	1·00
88/96		*Set of 7 pairs and 2 singles*	65·00	85·00

43 Infantry

44 Nurse

45 Airman

46 Sailor

47 Women's Auxiliary Services

48 Electric Welding

49 Heavy Gun in Concrete Turret

50 Tank Corps

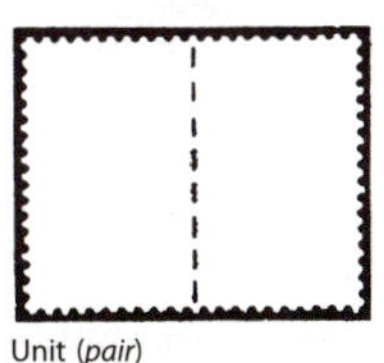
Unit (*pair*)

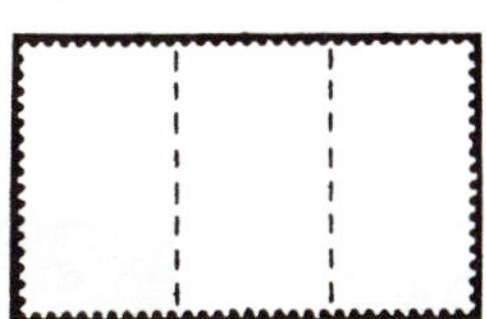
Unit (*triplet*)

Ear Flap flaw (Cyl 43 R. 13/3)

Apostrophe flaw (Cyl 6931 R. 19/1) (later corrected)

Line on Cap (Cyl 39 R. 12/11)

"Bursting Shell" (Cyl 46 R. 11/20)

Smoking "L" (Cyl 46 R. 8/2)

1942–44. *War Effort. Reduced sizes.* In pairs perf 14 (P) or strips of three, perf 15×14 (T), subdivided by roulette 6½. W **9** (sideways* on 3d., 4d. and 1s.).

(a) Inscr alternately.

			Un unit	*Us unit*	*Us single*
97	**43**	½d. blue-green (T) (10.42)	2·00	1·50	10
		a. Green (3.43)	3·00	2·00	10
		b. Greenish blue (7.44)	2·00	1·75	10
		c. Roulette omitted	£850	£600	

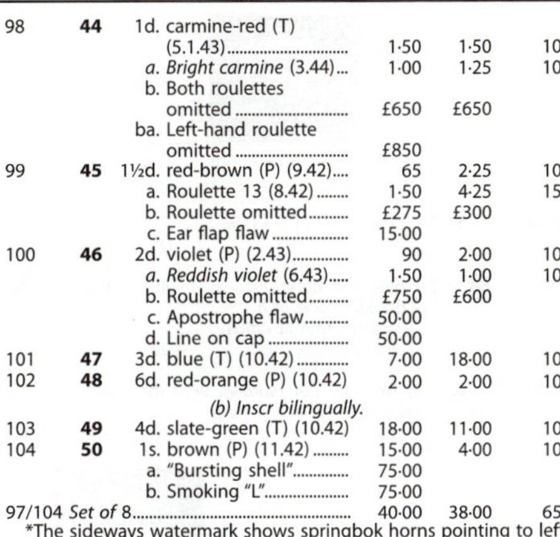

98	**44**	1d. carmine-red (T) (5.1.43)	1·50	1·50	10
		a. Bright carmine (3.44)	1·00	1·25	10
		b. Both roulettes omitted	£650	£650	
		ba. Left-hand roulette omitted	£850		
99	**45**	1½d. red-brown (P) (9.42)	65	2·25	10
		a. Roulette 13 (8.42)	1·50	4·25	15
		b. Roulette omitted	£275	£300	
		c. Ear flap flaw	15·00		
100	**46**	2d. violet (P) (2.43)	90	2·00	10
		a. Reddish violet (6.43)	1·50	1·00	10
		b. Roulette omitted	£750	£600	
		c. Apostrophe flaw	50·00		
		d. Line on cap	50·00		
101	**47**	3d. blue (T) (10.42)	7·00	18·00	10
102	**48**	6d. red-orange (P) (10.42)	2·00	2·00	10

(b) Inscr bilingually.

103	**49**	4d. slate-green (T) (10.42)	18·00	11·00	10
104	**50**	1s. brown (P) (11.42)	15·00	4·00	10
		a. "Bursting shell"	75·00		
		b. Smoking "L"	75·00		
97/104		*Set of 8*	40·00	38·00	65

*The sideways watermark shows springbok horns pointing to left on the 3d. and 1s., and to right on the 4d., *all as seen from the back of the stamp.*

52

53

1943. *Coil stamps. Redrawn. In single colours with plain background.* W **9**. P 15×14.

			Un pair	*Us pair*	*Us single*
105	**52**	½d. blue-green (18.2.43)	2·75	4·75	20
106	**53**	1d. carmine (9.43)	3·50	4·00	15

Quoted prices are for *vertical* pairs.

54 Union Buildings, Pretoria

1945–47. *Redrawn.* W **9**. P 14.

107	**54**	2d. slate and deep reddish violet (3.45)	15·00	2·50	10
		a. Slate and deep lilac (10.46)	15·00	5·00	10
		b. Slate and bright violet (1947)	3·75	10·00	15

In Nos. 107 to 107*b* the Union Buildings are shown at a different angle from Nos. 58 and 58*a*. Only the centre is screened i.e., composed of very small square dots of colour arranged in straight diagonal lines. For whole design screened and colours changed, see No. 116. No. 107*a/b* also show "2" of "2d." clear of white circle at top.

55 "Victory"

56 "Peace"

57 "Hope"

1945 (3 Dec). *Victory.* W **9**. P 14.

108	**55**	1d. brown and carmine	20	1·25	10
109	**56**	2d. slate-blue and violet	20	1·25	10
110	**57**	3d. deep blue and blue	20	1·50	10
108/10		*Set of 3*	55	3·50	25

58 King George VI

59 King George VI and Queen Elizabeth

60 Queen Elizabeth II as Princess, and Princess Margaret

"Bird" on "2" (Cyl 6912 R. 10/6)

"Black-eyed Princess" (R. 19/2)

(Des J. Prentice)

1947 (17 Feb). *Royal Visit.* W **9**. P 15×14.

111	**58**	1d. black and carmine	10	35	10
112	**59**	2d. violet	15	60	10
		a. "Bird" on "2" flaw	4·50	7·00	
113	**60**	3d. blue	15	60	10
		a. "Black-eyed Princess"	6·00	9·50	
111/13		*Set of 3*	35	1·40	20

"Flying saucer" flaw (Cyl 17 R. 17/2)

I

II

5s.

1947–54. *"SUID-AFRIKA" hyphenated on Afrikaans stamps. Printed from new cylinders with design in screened rotogravure.* W **9**. P 15×14 (½d., 1d. and 6d.) or 14 (others).

114	**25**	½d. grey and green (frame only screened) (1947)	2·00	3·75	10
		a. Booklet pane of 6 (with postal slogans on margins) (1948)	3·50		
		b. "Tick" flaw and spot on nose	38·00		
		c. Entire design screened (2.49)	2·00	3·75	10
		ca. Booklet pane of 6 (with margin at right) (1951)	3·75		
115	**7**	1d. grey and carmine (1.9.50)	2·25	4·00	10
		a. Booklet pane of 6 (with margin at right) (1951)	4·25		
116	**54**	2d. slate-blue and purple (3.50)	3·50	10·00	20
117	**22a**	3d. dull blue (4.49)	3·00	6·00	10
117*a*		3d. blue (3.51)	3·50	5·00	10
		ab. "Flying saucer" flaw	60·00	55·00	
118	**12a**	4d. brown (22.8.52)	4·50	10·00	20
119	**8**	6d. green and red-orange (III) (1.50)	3·75	1·50	10
		a. Green and brown-orange (III) (1951)	3·25	70	10
120	**13**	1s. brown and chalky blue (1.50)	10·00	10·00	10
		a. Blackish brown and ultramarine (4.52)	18·00	14·00	15
121	**14**	2s.6d. green and brown (8.49)	10·00	29·00	1·00
122	**15**	5s. black and pale blue-green (I) (9.49)	45·00	70·00	2·00
122*a*		5s. black and deep yellow-green (II) (1.54)	50·00	90·00	4·00
114/22		*Set of 9*	75·00	£130	3·25

In screened rotogravure the design is composed of very small squares of colour arranged in straight diagonal lines.

½d. Size 17¾×21¾ mm. Early printings have only the frame screened.

1d. Size 18×22 mm. For smaller, redrawn design, see No. 135.

2d. For earlier issue with centre only screened, and in different colours, see Nos. 107/*a*.

3d. No. 117. Whole stamp screened with irregular grain. Scrolls above "3d." solid and toneless. Printed from two cylinders.

No. 117*a*. Whole stamp diagonally screened. Printed from one cylinder. Clouds more pronounced. Late printings were often in deep shades.

4d. Two groups of white leaves below name tablet and a clear white line down left and right sides of stamp.

61 Gold Mine

62 King George VI and Queen Elizabeth

1948 (1 Apr). unit of four, perf 14, sub-divided by roulette 6½. W **9** (sideways).

			Un unit of 4	*Us unit*	*Used single*
124	**61**	1½d. blue-green and yellow-buff	3·25	5·00	10

(Des J. Booysen and J. Prentice)

1948 (26 Apr). *Silver Wedding.* W **9**. P 14.

			Un pair	*Used pair*	*Used single*
125	**62**	3d. blue and silver	50	1·25	10

(Typo Government Printer, Pretoria)

1948 (July). W **9**. P 14½×14.

126	**6**	½d. pale grey and blue-green	1·75	10·00	75

This was an economy printing made from the old plates of the 1926 issue for the purpose of using up a stock of cut paper. For the original printing in black and green, see No. 30.

63 *Wanderer* (emigrant ship) entering Durban

Extended rigging on mainmast (R. 14/2)

"Pennant" flaw (R. 17/5)

(Des J. Prentice)

1949 (2 May). *Centenary of Arrival of British Settlers in Natal.* W **9**. P 15×14.

127	**63**	1½d. claret	80	80	10
		a. Extended rigging	10·00	10·00	
		b. "Pennant" flaw	10·00	10·00	

64 Hermes

Serif on "C" (R. 1/1)

"Lake" in East Africa (R. 2/19)

(Des J. Booysen and J. Prentice)

1949 (1 Oct). *75th Anniv of Universal Postal Union. As T* **64** *inscr* "UNIVERSAL POSTAL UNION" *and* "WERELDPOSUNIE" *alternately.* W **9** (sideways). P 14×15.

128	**64**	½d. blue-green	50	1·00	10
129		1½d. brown-red	50	1·00	10
130		3d. bright blue	60	1·00	10
		a. Serif on "C"	38·00		
		b. "Lake" in East Africa	38·00		
128/30 *Set of 3*			1·40	2·75	25

65 Wagons approaching Bingham's Berg

67 Bible, candle and Voortrekkers

66 Voortrekker Monument, Pretoria

(Des W. Coetzer and J. Prentice)

1949 (1 Dec). *Inauguration of Voortrekker Monument, Pretoria.* W **9**. P 15×14.

			Un single	*Us single*
131	**65**	1d. magenta	10	10
132	**66**	1½d. blue-green	10	10
133	**67**	3d. blue	15	15
131/3 *Set of 3*			30	30

68 Union Buildings, Pretoria

1950 (Apr)–**51**. W **9** (sideways). P 14×15.

			Un pair	*Used pair*	*Used single*
134	**68**	2d. blue and violet	40	1·00	10
		a. Booklet pane of 6 (with margin at right) (1951)	4·00		

1951 (22 Feb). *As No. 115, but redrawn with the horizon clearly defined. Size reduced to 17¼×21¼ mm.*

135	**7**	1d. grey and carmine	1·40	2·50	10

69 Seal and monogram

70 "Maria de la Quellerie" (D. Craey)

(Des Miss R. Reeves and J. Prentice (1d., 4½d.), Mrs. T. Campbell and J. Prentice (others))

1952 (14 Mar). *Tercentenary of Landing of Van Riebeeck. T* **69/70** *and similar designs.* W **9** (sideways on 1d. and 4½d.) P 14×15 (1d. and 4½d.) or 14×15 (others).

136	½d. brown-purple and olive-grey	10	10
137	1d. deep blue-green	10	10
138	2d. deep violet	50	10
139	4½d. blue	10	10
140	1s. brown	40	10
136/40 *Set of 5*		1·10	45

Designs: *Horiz*—2d. Arrival of Van Riebeeck's ships; 1s. "Landing at the Cape" (C. Davidson Bell). *Vert*—4½d. "Jan van Riebeeck" (D. Craey).

SATISE (**74**) **SADIPU** (**75**)

76 Queen Elizabeth II

1952 (26 Mar). *South African Tercentenary International Stamp Exhibition, Cape Town. No. 137 optd with T* **74** *and No. 138 with T* **75**.

141	1d. deep blue-green	20	1·75
142	2d. deep violet	50	1·25

(Des H. Kumst)

1953 (3 June). *Coronation.* W **9** (sideways). P 14×15.

143	**76**	2d. deep violet-blue	30	10
		a. *Ultramarine*	30	10

77 1d. "Cape Triangular" Stamp

(Des H. Kumst)

1953 (1 Sept). *Centenary of First Cape of Good Hope Stamp. T* **77** *and similar horiz design.* W **9**. P 15×14.

144	1d. sepia and vermilion	10	10
145	4d. deep blue and light blue	50	20

Design:—4d. Four pence "Cape Triangular" stamp.

79 Merino Ram

80 Springbok

81 Aloes

(Des A. Hendriksz and J. Prentice (4½d.))

1953 (1 Oct). W **9**. P 14.

146	**79**	4½s. slate-purple and yellow	20	10
147	**80**	1s. 3d. chocolate	1·25	10
148	**81**	1s. 6d. vermilion and deep blue-green	60	55
146/8 *Set of 3*			1·75	65

82 Arms of Orange Free State and Scroll

(Des H. Kumst)

1954 (23 Feb). *Centenary of Orange Free State.* W **9**. P 15×14.

149	**82**	2d. sepia and pale vermilion	10	10
150		4½d. purple and slate	20	50

83 Warthog

92 Springbok

93 Gemsbok

(Des H. Kumst)

1954 (14 Oct). *T* **83**, **92/3** *and similar designs.* W **9** (sideways on large vert designs). P 15×14 (½d. to 2d.), 14 (others).

151	½d. deep blue-green	10	10
152	1d. brown-lake	10	10
153	1½d. sepia	10	10
154	2d. plum	10	10
155	3d. chocolate and turquoise-blue	1·00	10
156	4d. indigo and emerald	1·00	20
157	4½d. blue-black and grey-blue	60	1·00
158	6d. sepia and orange	50	10
159	1s. deep brown and pale chocolate	1·25	10
160	1s. 3d. brown and bluish green	2·75	10
161	1s. 6d. brown and rose	1·75	60
162	2s. 6d. brown-black and apple-green	3·50	20
163	5s. black-brown and yellow-orange	8·00	1·60
164	10s. black and cobalt	13·00	4·50
151/64 Set of 14		30·00	7·50

Designs: *Vert* (*as T* **83**)—1d. Black Wildebeest; 1½d. Leopard; 2d. Mountain Zebra. (*As T* **93**)—3d. White Rhinoceros; 4d. African Elephant; 4½d. Hippopotamus; 1s. Greater Kudu; 2s.6d. Nyala; 5s. Giraffe; 10s. Sable Antelope. *Horiz* (*as T* **92**)—6d. Lion.

No. 152 exists in coils.

See also Nos. 170/7 and 185/97.

97 President Kruger

98 President M. Pretorius

(Des H. Kumst)

1955 (21 Oct). *Centenary of Pretoria.* W **9** (sideways). P 14×15.

165	**97**	3d. slate-green	10	10
166	**98**	6d. maroon	10	30

99 A. Pretorius, Church of the Vow and Flag

100 Settlers' Block-wagon and House

(Des H. Kumst)

1955 (1 Dec). *Voortrekker Covenant Celebrations, Pietermaritzburg.* W **9**. P 14.

			Un pair	*Used pair*	*Used single*
167	**99**	2d. blue and magenta	45	3·25	10

(Des H. Kumst)

1958 (1 July). *Centenary of Arrival of German Settlers in South Africa.* W **9**. P 14.

168	**100**	2d. chocolate and pale purple	10	10

101 Arms of the Academy

(Des H. Kumst)

1959 (1 May). *50th Anniv of the South African Academy of Science and Art, Pretoria.* W **9**. P 15×14.

169	**101**	3d. deep blue and turquoise-blue	10	10
		a. Deep blue printing omitted	£2500	

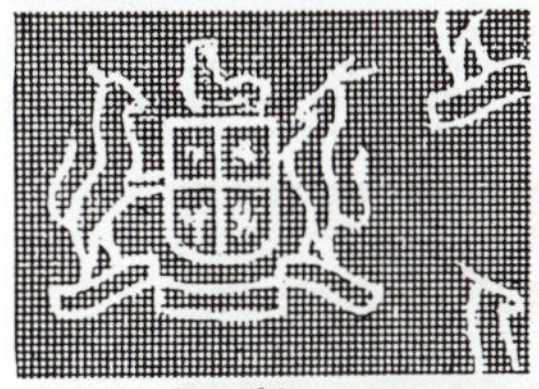

102 Union Coat of Arms

1 1
S S
I II

1959–60. *As Nos. 151/2, 155/6, 158/9 and 162/3, but* W **102** *(sideways on Nos. 172/3 and 175/7).*

170	½d. deep greenish blue (12.60)	15	4·50
171	1d. brown-lake (I) (11.59)	10	10
	a. Redrawn. Type II (10.60)	20	10
172	3d. chocolate and turquoise-blue (9.59)	15	10
173	4d. indigo and emerald (1.60)	50	20
174	6d. sepia and orange (2.60)	70	1·50
175	1s. deep brown and pale chocolate (11.59)	6·00	65
176	2s. brown-black and apple-green 6d. (12.59)	2·75	4·00
177	5s. black-brown and yellow-orange (10.60)	7·50	30·00
170/7 *Set of 8*		16·00	35·00

Nos. 171/a. In Type II "1d. Posgeld Postage" is more to the left in relation to "South Africa", with "1" almost central over "S" instead of to right as in Type I.

No. 171 exists in coils.

103 Globe and Antarctic Scene

(Des H. Kumst)

1959 (16 Nov). *South African National Antarctic Expedition.* W **102**. P 14×15.

178	**103**	3d. blue-green and orange	20	10

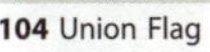

104 Union Flag **106** "Wheel of Progress"

(Des V. Ivanoff and H. Kumst (1s.), H. Kumst (others))

1960 (2 May). *50th Anniv of Union of South Africa. T* **104**, **106** *and similar designs.* W **102** (sideways on 4d. and 6d.). P 14×15 (4d., 6d.) or 15×14 (others).

179	4d. orange-red and blue	30	10
180	6d. red, brown and light green	30	10
181	1s. deep blue and light yellow	30	10
182	1s. black and light blue 6d.	70	2·25
179/82 *Set of 4*		1·40	2·25

Designs: *Vert*—6d. Union Arms. *Horiz*—1s.6d. Union Festival emblem.

See also No. 190, 192/3.

108 Steam Locomotives *Natal* (1860) and Class 25 (1950s)

(Des V. Ivanoff)

1960 (2 May). *Centenary of South African Railways.* W **102**. P 15×14.

183	**108**	1s.3d. deep blue	1·10	30

109 Prime Ministers Botha, Smuts, Hertzog, Malan, Strijdom and Verwoerd

1960 (31 May). *Union Day.* W **102**. P 15×14.

184	**109**	3d. brown and pale brown	15	10
		a. Pale brown omitted*	£3500	

*This is due to a rectangular piece of paper adhering to the background cylinder, resulting in R.2/1 missing the colour completely and six adjoining stamps having it partially omitted. The item in block of eight is probably unique.

(New Currency. 100 cents= 1 rand)

1961 (14 Feb). *As previous issues but with values in cents and rand.* W **102** (sideways on 3½ c., 7½ c., 20c., 50c., 1r.). P 15×14 (½ c., to 2½ c., 10c.), 14×15 (3½ c., 7½ c.) or 14 (others).

185	½c. deep bluish green (as 151)	10	10
186	1c. brown-lake (as 152)	10	10
187	1½c. sepia (as 153)	10	10
188	2c. plum (as 154)	10	1·00
189	2½c. brown (as 184)	20	10
190	3½c. orange-red and blue (as 179)	15	2·25
191	5c. sepia and orange (as 158)	20	10
192	7½c. red, brown and light green (as 180)	20	2·75
193	10c. deep blue and light yellow (as 181)	40	60
194	12½c. brown and bluish green (as 160)	1·00	1·25
195	20c. brown and rose (as 161)	2·25	2·75
196	50c. black-brown and orange-yellow (as 163)	4·50	10·00
197	1r. black and cobalt (as 164)	14·00	24·00
185/97 *Set of 13*		21·00	40·00

X. REPUBLIC OF SOUTH AFRICA

OUTSIDE THE COMMONWEALTH

110 African Pygmy Kingfisher **111** Kafferboom Flower **112** Afrikander Bull

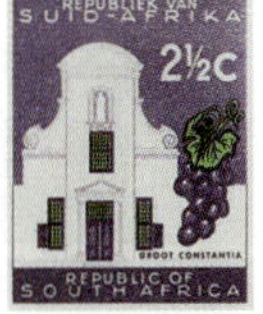

113 Pouring Gold **114** Groot Constantia

115 Burchell's Gonolek **116** Baobab Tree

117 Maize **118** Cape Town Castle Entrance **119** Protea

120 Secretary Bird **121** Cape Town Harbour

122 Strelitzia

Two types of ½c.:

I

II

Type I from sheets. Spurs of branch indistinct.
Type II from coils. Spurs strengthened.
Three types of 1c.:

I

II

III

Type I. Lowest point of flower between "OS" of "POSTAGE". Right-hand petal over "E".

Type II. Flower has moved fractionally to the right so that lowest point is over "S" of "POSTAGE". Right-hand petal over "E".

Type III. Lowest point directly over "O". Right-hand petal over "G".

Two types of 2½ c.

In Type I the lines of the building are quite faint. In Type II all lines of the building have been strengthened by re-engraving.

5c. White flaw left of tree resembling a comet (Cyl. 31-S1, R. 5/16).

(Des Mrs. T. Campbell (½ c., 3c., 1r.); Miss N. Desmond (1c.); De La Rue (2½ c., 5c., 12½ c.); H. L. Prager (50c.); Govt. Ptg Dept artist (others))

1961 (31 May)–**63**. *Unsurfaced paper.* W **102** (sideways* on ½ c., 1½ c., 2½ c., 5c. to 20c.). P 14×15 (½ c., 1½ c.), 15×14 (1c.). or 14 (others).

198	**110**	½c. bright blue, carmine and brown (I)	10	10
		a. Perf 14 (3.63)	10	15
		b. Type II (coils) (18.5.63)	80	1·60
199	**111**	1c. red and olive-grey (I)	10	10
		a. Type II (1.62)	10	10
		b. Type III (coils) (5.63)	1·25	2·00
200	**112**	1½c. brown-lake and light purple	10	10
201	**113**	2c. ultramarine and yellow	2·00	10
202	**114**	2½c. violet and green (I)	15	10
		aw. Wmk top of arms to right	30	10
		b. Type II. *Dp violet & green* (9.61)	20	10
203	**115**	3c. red and deep blue	80	10
204	**116**	5c. yellow and greenish blue	30	10
		a. "Comet" flaw	5·00	
205	**117**	7½c. yellow-brown and light green	60	10
206	**118**	10c. sepia and green	75	10
207	**119**	12½c. red, yellow and black-green	2·00	30
		a. Yellow omitted	£600	
		b. Red omitted	£700	
208	**120**	20c. turquoise-blue, carmine and brown orange	3·00	30
209	**121**	50c. black and bright blue	18·00	2·25
210	**122**	1r. orange, olive-green and light blue	10·00	2·25
198/210 *Set of 13*			32·00	4·50

*The normal sideways watermark shows the top of the arms to left, *as seen from the back of the stamp.*

1961–74 Definitives

Key to designs, perfs, watermarks, papers and phosphors

Value		*Type*	*Perf*	*W* **102** *Ordinary*	*No wmk Ordinary*	*W* **127** *Chalky*
½c.	**110**	(I)	14×15	198	—	—
		(I)	14	198a	—	—
		(II)	14×15	198b	—	—
1c.	**111**	(I)	15×14	199	211	—
		(II)		199a	211a	227
		(III)		199b	—	—
1½c.	**112**		14×15	200	—	228
2c.	**113**		14	201	212	229
2½c.	**114**	(I)	14	202	—	—
		(II)		202a	213/a	230/a
3c.	**115**		14	203	214	—
5c.	**116**		14	204	215	231
7½c.	**117**		14	205	216	232
10c.	**118**		14	206	217/b	233/a
12½c.	**119**		14	207	—	—
20c.	**120**		14	208	218	234/a
50c.	**121**		14	209	219	235
1r.	**122**		14	210	—	236

Redrawn Designs

Value	*Type*		*W* **127** *Upright or Tete-beche*	*W* **127** *Tete-beche. Phos frame*	*No wmk. Phosphorised Glossy*	*Chalky*
½c.	**130a**	14	238	—	—	—
		14×15	238b	—	—	—
		14	238c/d	—	—	—
1c.	**131**	15×14	239	—	—	—
		13½×14	239a	—	—	—
1½c.	**132**	14×15	240/b	284	—	—
		14×13½	240c	—	—	—
2c.	**133**	14	241/a	285/a	315a	—
		12½	—	—	315	315b
2½c.	**134**	14	242/a	286/a	—	—
3c.	**135**	14	243/a	287	—	—
		12½	—	—	316	316a
4c.	**134**	14	243b	288	—	—
5c.	**136**	14	244/a	289	318a	—
		12½	—	—	318	318b
6c.	**137**	14	—	290	—	—
		12½	—	—	—	319
7½c.	**137**	14	245	291	—	—
9c.	**139**	14	245a	292	—	—
		12½	—	—	320/a	—
10c.	**138**	14	246/a	293	321a	—
		12½	—	—	321	321b
12½c.	**139**	14	247/a	294	—	—
15c.	**140**	14	248	295	—	—
20c.	**141**	14	249/a	296/a	—	—
		12½	—	—	323	323a
50c.	**142**	14	250	—	—	—
		12½	—	—	324	324a
1r.	**143**	14	251	—	—	—
		12½	—	—	325	—

New Designs

			W **127** *Upright or Tete-beche. Plain or phosphorised*	*W* **127** *Tete-beche. Phos frame*	*No wmk. Phosphorised Glossy*	*Chalky*
½c.	**168**	14×13½	276	282	—	—
		14×14½	276a	—	313	—
		14×15	—	282a	—	—
1c.	**169**	13½×14	277	283	—	—
		14	—	—	314	—
4c.	**182**	14	310/a	—	—	—
		12½	—	—	317/b	317c
15c.	**182a**	14	311	—	—	—
		12½	—	—	—	322

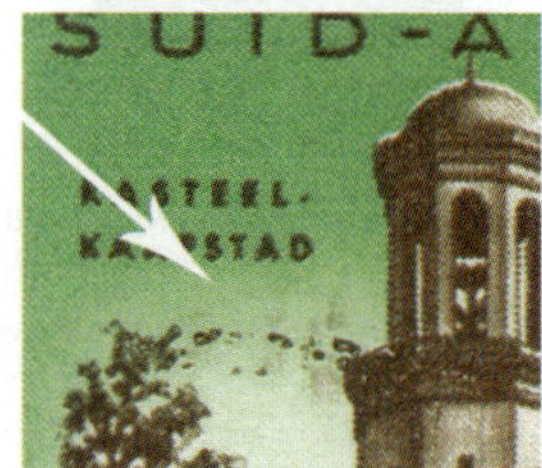

10c. Falling leaves to right of tree (Cyl. 51A-121A. R. 5/17).

1961 (1 Aug)–**63**. *As Nos. 199, 201/6 and 208/9 but without wmk.*

211	**111**	1c. red and olive-grey (I)	20	30
		a. Type II (9.62)	70	55
212	**113**	2c. ultramarine and yellow (8.63)	8·00	70
213	**114**	2½c. deep violet and green (II)	30	10
		a. *Violet and green* (12.61)	30	10
214	**115**	3c. red and deep blue (10.61)	45	10
		a. Deep blue (face value, etc) omitted	£1100	
215	**116**	5c. yellow and greenish blue (12.61)	50	10
		a. "Comet" flaw	5·00	
216	**117**	7½c. yellow-brown and light green (3.62)	80	30
217	**118**	10c. sepia and green (11.61)	1·00	40
		a. *Sepia and emerald*	40·00	17·00
		b. *Sepia-brown and light green* (7.63)	2·25	55
		c. "Falling leaves"	6·00	
218	**120**	20c. turquoise-blue carmine and brown-orange (4.63)	11·00	4·25
219	**121**	50c. black and bright blue (8.62)	11·00	4·25
211/19 *Set of 9*			30·00	9·00

123 Blériot XI Monoplane and Boeing 707 Airliner over Table Mountain

124 Folk-dancers

1961 (1 Dec). *50th Anniv of First South African Aerial Post.* W **102** (sideways). P 14×15.

220	**123**	3c. blue and red	50	10

(Des K. Esterhuysen)

1962 (1 Mar). *50th Anniv of Volkspele (folk-dancing) in South Africa.* W **102** (sideways). P 14×15.

221	**124**	2½c. orange-red and brown	15	10

125 The Chapman (emigrant ship)

1962 (20 Aug). *Unveiling of Precinct Stone, British Settlers Monument Grahamstown.* W **102**. P 15×14.

222	**125**	2½c. turquoise-green and purple	50	10
223		12½c. blue and deep chocolate	1·75	1·25

126 Red Disa (orchid), Castle Rock and Gardens

(Des M. F. Stern)

1963 (14 Mar). *50th Anniv of Kirstenbosch Botanic Gardens, Cape Town.* P 13½×14.

224	**126**	2½c. multicoloured	20	10
		a. Red (orchid, etc) omitted	£1600	£750

127 (normal version)

128 Centenary Emblem and Nurse

129 Centenary Emblem and Globe

1963 (30 Aug). *Centenary of Red Cross. Chalk-surfaced paper.* Wmk **127** (sideways on 2½ c.). P 14×13½ (2½ c.) or 15×14 (12½c.)

225	**128**	2½c. red, black and reddish purple	20	10
		w. Wmk reversed	3·00	1·40
226	**129**	12½c. red and indigo	2·25	1·00
		a. Red cross omitted	£1600	£1200

1963–67. *As 1961–3 but chalk-surfaced paper and W* **127** *(sideways on 1½ c., 2½ c., 5c., 7½ c., 10c., 20c.).* P 15×14 (1c.) 14×15 (1½ c.), or 14 (others).

227	**111**	1c. red and olive-grey (II) (9.63)	10	10
		w. Wmk reversed	65	65
228	**112**	1½c. brown-lake and light purple (1.67)	1·75	2·25
229	**113**	2c. ultramarine and yellow (11.64)	15	20
230	**114**	2½c. violet and green (I) (10.63)	10	10
		a. *Bright reddish violet and emerald (II)* (3.66)	35	20
		aw. Wmk inverted	2·50	90
231	**116**	5c. yellow and greenish blue (9.66)	1·25	30
		a. "Comet" flaw	5·00	
232	**117**	7½c. yellow-brown and bright green (23.2.66)	7·50	6·50
233	**118**	10c. sepia-brown and light emerald (9.64)	40	10
		a. *Sepia-brown and green* (1.67)	45	10
		b. "Falling leaves"	6·00	
234	**120**	20c. turquoise-blue,carmine and brown orange (7.64)	1·00	80
		a. *Deep turquoise-blue, carmine and flesh* (20.7.65)	1·75	80
235	**121**	50c. black and ultramarine (4.66)	30·00	9·50
236	**122**	1r. orange, light green and pale blue (7.64)	48·00	40·00
227/36 *Set of 10*			80·00	55·00

In the 2½ c. (No. 230a), 5c., 7½ c., 10c. (Jan 1967 printing only) and 50c. the watermark is indistinct but they can easily be distinguished from the stamps without watermark by their shades and the chalk-surfaced paper which is appreciably thicker and whiter.

130 Assembly Building, Umtata

1963 (11 Dec). *First Meeting of Transkei Legislative Assembly. Chalk-surfaced paper.* W **127**. P 15×14.

237	**130**	2½c. sepia and light green	10	10
		a. Light green omitted	£1500	

130a African Pygmy Kingfisher

131 Kafferboom Flower

132 Afrikander Bull

133 Pouring Gold

134 Groot Constantia

135 Burchell's Gonolek

136 Baobab Tree

137 Maize

138 Cape Town Castle Entrance

139 Protea

140 Industry

141 Secretary Bird

142 Cape Town Harbour

143 Strelitzia

(15c. des C. E. F. Skotnes)

Redrawn types.

½ c. "½C" larger and REPUBLIEK VAN REPUBLIC OF" smaller.

3c. and 12½ c. Inscriptions and figures of value larger.

Others. "SOUTH AFRICA" and SUID-AFRIKA larger and bolder. The differences vary in each design but are easy to see by comparing the position of the letters of the country name with "REPUBLIC OF" and "REPUBLIEK VAN".

1964–72. *As 1961–63 but designs redrawn and new values (4c., 9c. and 15c.). Chalk-surfaced paper.* W **127** (sideways on ½, 1½, 2½, 4, 5, 7½, 9, 10, 15 and 20c.). P 14×15 (1½ c.), 15×14 (1c.) or 14 (others).

238	**130a**	½c. brightt blue, carmine & brown (21.5.64)	10	10
		a. Imperf (pair)	£275	
		b. Perf 14×15. *Bright blue, carmine and yellow-brown* (6.7.67)	20	20
		c. Perf 14. *Bright blue, lake and yellow-brown* (3.68)	60	70
		d. Perf 14. *Bright blue, carmine lake and yellow-brown* (9.68)	30	10
239	**131**	1c. red and olive-grey (9.3.67)	10	10
		a. Perf 13½×14 (7.68)	30	10
240	**132**	1½c. dull red-brown and light purple (21.9.67)	15	10
		a. *Purple-brown and light purple* (1968)	15	10
		b. *Bright red-brown and light purple* (5.68)	15	10

		c. Perf 14×13½. *Red-brown and light purple* (14.8.69)	70	70
241	**133**	2c. ultramarine and yellow (8.1.68)	20	10
		a. *Blue and yellow* (10.71)	60	10
242	**134**	2½c. violet and green (19.4.67)	20	10
		a. *Reddish violet and green* (8.67)	20	10
		w. Wmk top of RSA to left	£180	65·00
243	**135**	3c. red and deep blue (11.64)	30	10
		a. *Brown-red and deep blue* (3.72)	1·50	30
243*b*	**134**	4c. violet and green (10.71)	75	30
244	**136**	5c. orange-yellow and greenish blue (14.2.68)	40	10
		a. *Lemon and deep greenish blue* (10.71)	8·00	1·00
245	**137**	7½c. yellow-brown and bright green (26.7.67)	60	10
245*a*	**139**	9c. red, yellow and slate-green (2.72)	7·50	3·75
246	**138**	10c. sepia and green (10.6.68)	1·75	10
		a. *Brown and pale green* (7.68)	4·25	3·25
247	**139**	12½c. red, yellow and black-green (3.64)	1·00	40
		a. *Red, pale yellow and blue-green* (2.2.66)	2·75	40
248	**140**	15c. black, light olive-yellow and red-orange (1.3.67)	85	25
249	**141**	20c. turquoise-blue, carmine and brown-orange (2.68)	6·00	15
		a. *Turquoise-blue, carmine and orange-buff* (12.71)	5·50	1·00
250	**142**	50c. black and bright blue (17.6.68)	1·00	40
251	**143**	1r. orange, light green & lt bl (6.65)	1·00	1·00
		w. Wmk inverted		
238/51 *Set of 16*			18·00	5·25

*The normal sideways watermark shows the top of RSA to right *as seen from the back of the stamp.*

WATERMARK. Two forms of the watermark Type **127** exist in the above issue: the normal Type **127** (sometimes indistinct), and a very faint *tête-bêche* watermark, i.e. alternately facing up and down, which was introduced in mid 1967. As it is extremely difficult to distinguish these on single stamps we do not list it. The ½ (both perfs), 1, 2, 2½, 3, 15c. and 1r. are known in both forms, the 1½, 4, 5, 7½, 9, 10, 20 and 50c. only in the *tête-bêche* form and the 12½ c. Type **127** only.

GUM. The 2, 3, 5, 20, 50c. and 1r. exist with PVA gum as well as gum arabic.

PHOSPHORISED PAPER. From October 1971 onwards phosphor bands (see Nos. 282/96) gave way to phosphorised paper which cannot be distinguished from non-phosphor stamps without the aid of a lamp. For this reason we do not distinguish these printings in the above issue, but some are slightly different shades and all have PVA gum. The 4c. and 9c. are on phosphorised paper only and differ from Nos. 288 and 292 by the lack of phosphor bands.

145 "Springbok" Badge of Rugby Board

147 Calvin

1964 (8 May). *75th Anniv of South African Rugby Board. Chalk-surfaced paper. T* **145** *and similar horiz design.* W **127** (sideways on 2½c.). P 14×15 (2½c.) or 15×14 (12½c.).

252	2½c. yellow-brown and deep green	15	10
253	12½c. black and light yellow-green	3·00	3·75

Design:—12½c. Rugby footballer.

1964 (10 July). *400th Death Anniv of Calvin (Protestant reformer). Chalk-surfaced paper.* W **127** (sideways). P 14×13½.

254	**147**	2½c. cerise, violet and brown	10	10

148 Nurse's Lamp

149 Nurse holding Lamp

I. Screened base to lamp

II. Clear base to lamp

1964 (12 Oct). *50th Anniv of South African Nursing Association. Chalk-surfaced paper.* W **127** (sideways on 2½ c.). P 14×15 (2½ c.) or 15×14 (12½c.)

255	**148**	2½c. ultramarine and dull gold (Type I)	10	10
256		2½c. bright blue and yellow-gold (Type II)	30	10
		a. *Ultramarine and dull gold*	15	10
257	**149**	12½c. bright blue and gold	2·25	1·75
		a. Gold omitted	£1400	
255/7 *Set of 3*			2·25	2·25

150 I.T.U. Emblem and Satellites

1965 (17 May). *I.T.U. Centenary. T* **150** *and similar horiz design. Chalk-surfaced paper.* W **127**. P 15×14.

258	2½c. orange and blue	25	10
259	12½c. brown-purple and green	1·25	1·00

Design:—12½ c. I.T.U. emblem and symbols.

152 Pulpit in Groote Kerk, Cape Town

153 Church Emblem

1965 (21 Oct). *Tercentenary of Nederduites Gereformeerde Kerk (Dutch Reformed Church) in South Africa. Chalk-surfaced paper.* W **127** (sideways on 2½ c., inverted on 12½ c.). P 14×15 (2½ c.) or 15×14 (12½ c.).

260	**152**	2½c. brown and light yellow	15	10
261	**153**	12½c. black, light orange and blue	70	85

154 Diamond

155 Bird in flight

(Des C.E.F. Skotnes)

1966 (31 May). *Fifth Anniv of Republic. T* **154/5** *and similar designs. Chalk-surfaced paper.* W **127** (sideways on 1c., 3c.). P 14×13½ (1c.), 13½×14 (2½c.), 14×15 (3c.) or 15×14 (7½c.).

		Un pair	Used pair	Used single
262	1c. black, bluish green and olive-yellow	45	45	10
263	2½c. blue, deep blue and yellow-green	85	1·25	10
264	3c. red, greenish yellow and red-brown	3·00	3·00	10
265	7½c. blue, ultramarine and yellow	3·75	3·75	10
262/5 *Set of 4*		7·25	7·75	35

Designs: *Vert*—3c. Maize plants. *Horiz*—7½c. Mountain landscape.

Nos. 262/5 exsist on Swiss made paper with *tête bêche* watermark from special printing made for use in presentation albums for delegates to the U.P.U. Congress in Tokyo in 1969 as supplies of the original Harrison paper were by then exhausted (*Set of 4 pairs price £140 mint*).

158 Verwoerd and Union Buildings, Pretoria

(Des from portrait by Dr. Henkel)

1966 (6 Dec). *Verwoerd Commemoration. T* **158** *and similar designs. Chalk-surfaced paper.* W **127** (sideways on 3c.). P 14×15 (3c.) or 15×14 (others).

266	2½ c. blackish brown and turquoise	10	10
267	3c. blackish brown and yellow-green	10	10
	a. Blackish brown (portrait) omitted	£3000	
268	12½ blackish brown and greenish blue c.	60	60
266/8 *Set of 3*		70	60

Designs: *Vert*—3c. "Dr. H.F. Verwoerd" (I. Henkel). *Horiz*—12½c. Verwoerd and map of South Africa.

161 "Martin Luther" (Cranach the Elder)

162 Wittenberg Church Door

1967 (31 Oct). *450th Anniv of Reformation.* W **127** ((sideways), normal on 2½ c., tête-bêche on 12½ c.). P 14×15.

269	**161**	2½c. black and rose-red	10	10
270	**162**	12½c. black and yellow-orange	1·25	2·00

163 "Profile of Pres. Fouche" (I. Henkel)

164 Portrait of Pres. Fouche

1968 (10 Apr). *Inauguration of President Fouche.* W **127** (sideways). P 14×15.

271	**163**	2½c. chocolate and pale chocolate	10	10
272	**164**	12½c. deep blue and light blue	60	1·00

No. 272 also exists with the watermark *tête-bêche* (*Price un £1; used £1.50*).

165 Hertzog in 1902

1968 (21 Sept). *Inauguration of General Hertzog Monument, Bloemfontein. T* **165** *and similar designs.* W **127** (tête-bêche on 2½ c., inverted on 3c., sideways on 12½ c.). P 14×13½ (12½ c.) or 13½×14 (others).

273	2½c. black, brown and olive-yellow	10	10
274	3c. black, red-brown, red-orange and yellow	15	10
275	12½c. red and yellow-orange	1·50	1·50
273/5 *Set of 3*		1·50	1·50

Designs: *Horiz*—3c. Hertzog in 1924. *Vert*—12½ c. Hertzog Monument.

168 African Pygmy Kingfisher

169 Kafferboom Flower

1969. W **127** (tête-bêche, sideways on ½ c.). P 14×13½ (½ c.) or 13½×14 (1c.)

276	**168**	½c. new blue, carmine-red and yellow-ochre (1.69)	10	30
		a. Coil. Perf 14×14½ (5.69)	2·25	3·00
277	**169**	1c. rose-red and olive-brown (1.69)	10	10

See also Nos. 282/3 and 313/14.

170 Springbok and Olympic Torch

171 Professor Barnard and Groote Schuur Hospital

1969 (15 Mar). *South African Games, Bloemfontein.* W **127** (tête-bêche, sideways). P 14×13½.

278	**170**	2½c. black, blue-black, red and sage-green	15	10
279		12½c. black, blue-black, red and cinnamon	70	1·50

1969 (7 July). *World's First Heart Transplant and 47th South African Medical Association Congress. T* **171** *and similar horiz design.* W **127** (tête-bêche). P 13½×14 (2½c.) or 15×14 (12½ c.).

280	2½c. plum and rose-red	15	10
281	12½c. carmine-red and royal blue	1·25	2·00

Design:—12½c. Hands holding heart.

1969–72. *As 1964–72 issue, Nos. 276/7, and new value (6c.), but with phosphor bands printed horizontally and vertically between the stamp designs, over the perforations, producing a frame effect.* W **127** arranged tête-bêche (upright on 1, 2 and 3c., sideways on others). P 14×13½ (½, 1½ c.), 13 ½×14 (1c.), or 14 (others).

282	**168**	½c. new blue, carmine-red and yellow-ochre (1.70)	15	70
		a. Coil. Perf 14×15 (2.71)	3·25	3·75

No.	Type	Description	Unused	Used
		w. Wmk reversed	65	75
283	**169**	1c. rose-red and olive-brown (12.69)	15	10
		w. Wmk reversed	55	35
284	**132**	1½c. red-brown and light purple (12.69)	20	10
285	**133**	2c. ultramarine and yellow (11.69)	70	10
		a. *Deep ultramarine and yellow* (8.70)	1·00	50
286	**134**	2½c. violet and green (1.70)	25	10
		a. *Purple and green* (24.7.70)	1·50	10
		w. Wmk reversed	20·00	17·00
287	**135**	3c. red and deep blue (30.9.69)	1·00	10
288	**134**	4c. violet and green (1.3.71)	40	70
289	**136**	5c. yellow and greenish blue (17.11.69)	85	10
290	**137**	6c. yellow-brown and bright green (3.5.71)	70	30
291		7½c. yellow-brown and bright green (17.11.69)	2·75	30
292	**139**	9c. red, yellow and black-green (17.5.71)	1·50	30
293	**138**	10c. brown and pale green (1.70)	1·50	10
294	**139**	12½c. red, yellow and black-green (2.5.70)	4·00	3·25
295	**140**	15c. black and light-yellow and red-orange (1.70)	1·50	2·00
296	**141**	20c. turquoise-blue, carmine and brown-orange 18.2.70)	8·00	2·00
		a. *Turquoise-blue, carmine and orange-buff* (9.72)	11·00	1·50
282/96		*Set of 15*	21·00	8·25

No. 286 exists on normal RSA wmk as well as RSA *tête-bêche* wmk. The 1, 2, 2½, 3, 10, 15 and 20c. exist with PVA gum as well as gum arabic, but the 4, 6 and 9c. exist with PVA gum only. For stamps without wmk, see Nos. 313, etc.

173 Mail Coach

174 Transvaal Stamp of 1869

1969 (6 Oct). *Centenary of First Stamps of South African Republic (Transvaal). Phosphor bands on all four sides (2½ c.).* W **127** (tête-bêche, sideways on 12½ c.). P 13½×14 (2½c.) or 14×13½ (12½ c.)

No.	Type	Description	Unused	Used
297	**173**	2½c. yellow, indigo and yellow-brown	15	10
298	**174**	12½c. emerald, gold and yellow-brown	2·75	3·50

PHOSPHOR FRAME. Nos. 299/306 have phosphor applied on all four sides as a frame.

175 "Water 70" Emblem

177 "The Sower"

1970 (14 Feb). *Water 70 Campaign. T* **175** *and similar design.* W **127** (tête-bêche (sideways on 2½ c.)). P 14×13½ (2½ c.) or 13½×14 (3c.)

No.	Type	Description	Unused	Used
299		2½c. green, bright blue and chocolate	30	10
300		3c. Prussian blue, royal blue and buff	30	20

Design: *Horiz*—3c. Symbolic waves.

1970 (24 Aug). *150th Anniv of Bible Society of South Africa. T* **177** *and similar horiz design (gold die-stamped on 12½ c.).* W **127** (tête-bêche, sideways on 2½ c.). P 14×13½ (2½ c.) or 13½×14 (12½c.)

No.	Type	Description	Unused	Used
301		2½c. multicoloured	15	10
302		12½c. gold, black and blue	1·50	2·00

Design:—12½ c. "Biblia" and open book.

178 J. G. Strijdom and Strijdom Tower

179 Map and Antarctic Landscape

1971 (22 May). *"Interstex" Stamp Exhibition, Cape Town.* P 14×13½.

A. W **127** (sideways tête-bêche).

No.	Type	Description	Unused	Used
303A	**178**	5c. light greenish blue, black and pale yellow	20	10

B. W **102** (sideways).

No.	Type	Description	Unused	Used
303B	**178**	5c. light greenish blue, black and pale yellow	2·00	5·00

1971 (22 May). *Tenth Anniv of Antarctic Treaty.* W **127** (tête-bêche). P 13½×14.

No.	Type	Description	Unused	Used
304	**179**	12½c. blue-black, greenish blue and orange-red	1·50	4·00

180 "Landing of British Settlers, 1820" (T. Baines)

1971 (31 May). *Tenth Anniv of the Republic of South Africa. T* **180** *and similar design.* W **127** (tête-bêche sideways on 4c.). P 13½×14 (2c.) or 14×13½ (4c.).

No.	Type	Description	Unused	Used
305		2c. pale flesh and brown-red	15	20
		w. Wmk reversed	60	60
306		4c. green and black	15	10
		w. Wmk reversed	1·40	85

Design: *Vert*—4c. Presidents Steyn and Kruger and Treaty of Vereeniging Monument.

No. 306 exists with PVA gum as well as gum arabic.

PHOSPHORISED PAPER. All issues from here are on phosphorised paper unless otherwise stated.

181 View of Dam

(Des C. Bridgeford (4c.), C. Lindsay (others))

1972 (4 Mar). *Opening of Hendrik Verwoerd Dam. T* **181** *and similar horiz designs. Multicoloured.* W **127** (tête-bêche). P 13½×14.

No.	Type	Description	Unused	Used
307		4c. Type **181**	20	10
308		5c. Aerial view of Dam	25	10
309		10c. Dam and surrounding country (58×21 mm)	1·50	2·50
307/9		*Set of 3*	1·75	2·50

182 Sheep

182a Lamb

(Des K. Esterhuysen (4c.), H. Botha (15c.))

1972 (15 May). W **127** (tête-bêche). P 14.

No.	Type	Description	Unused	Used
310	**182**	4c. olive-brown, yellow, pale blue and slate-blue	30	10
		a. yellow omitted	£425	
		b. Grey-olive, yellow, bright blue and slate-blue (10.72)	30	10
311	**182a**	15c. pale stone, deep blue and dull blue	2·25	20

Other shades exist of the 4c.

See also Nos. 317 and 322.

183 Black and Siamese Cats

184 Transport and Industry

1972 (19 Sept). *Centenary of Societies for the Prevention of Cruelty to Animals.* W **127** (sideways tête-bêche). P 14×13½.

No.	Type	Description	Unused	Used
312	**183**	5c. multicoloured	1·25	10

1972–74. *As Nos. 310/11 and 282 etc. but no wmk. Phosphorised, glossy paper.* P 14×14½ (½c.), 14 (1c.) or 12½ (others)

No.	Type	Description	Unused	Used
313	**168**	½c. bright blue, scarlet and yellow-ochre (coil) (6.73)	15·00	16·00
314	**169**	1c. rose-red and olive-brown (1.74)	40	10
315	**133**	2c. blue and orange-yellow (11.72)	15	10
		a. Perf 14. Deep ultramarine and orange-yellow (coil) (7.73)	11·00	13·00
		b. Chalk-surfaced paper (17.7.74)	40	70
316	**135**	3c. scarlet and deep blue (8.5.73)	50	20
		a. Chalk-surfaced paper (18.2.74)	1·25	1·25
317	**182**	4c. grey-blue, yellow, blue and bluish slate* (1.10.73)	30	30
		a. Olive-sepia, yellow, azure and slate-blue (18.2.74)	60	30
		b. Lavender-brown, pale yellow, blue and bluish slate* (26.7.74)	30	20
		c. Chalk-surfaed paper* (22.8.74)	60	45
318	**136**	5c. orge-yell & greenish bl (4.10.73)	2·25	1·00
		a. Perf 14. Yellow and light greenish blue (coil) (7.73)	12·00	14·00
		b. Chalk-surfaced paper (5.74)	2·25	1·50
319	**137**	6c. yellow-brown and bright green (chalky paper) (22.7.74)	2·50	3·25
320	**139**	9c. red, yellow-green and green-black (6.73)	2·00	2·25
		a. Red, deep yellowish green and green-black (4.74)	3·00	1·50
321	**138**	10c. reddish brown & brt grn (8.5.73)	85	70
		a. Perf 14 (coil) (6.73)	14·00	16·00
		b. Chalk-surfaced paper (17.7.74)	1·50	70
322	**182a**	15c. pale stone, deep blue and dull blue (chalky paper) (4.9.74)	5·50	6·00
323	**141**	20c. turquoise-blue, rose-carmine and orange-buff (8.5.73)	3·25	80
		a. Chalk-surfaced paper (5.74)	5·00	70
324	**142**	50c. black and bright blue (6.73)	4·50	2·25
		a. Chalk-surfaced paper (22.7.74)	9·50	7·50
325	**143**	1r. orange, light green and light blue (8.10.73)	9·00	2·50
		a. Orange omitted	£1800	
313/25		*Set of 13*	42·00	30·00

*On these stamps the colours are known to vary within the sheet.

No. 314 also differs in that the central design has been moved down about 1 mm.

Nos. 317/c also differ from No. 310 by measuring 26¼×21 mm instead of 27¼×21¾ mm.

No. 325a exists on the bottom row of one sheet.

(Des J. Hoekstra (4c.), M. Barnett (others))

1973 (1 Feb). *50th Anniv of ESCOM (Electricity Supply Commission). T* **184** *and similar vert designs. Multicoloured.* P 12×12½ (4c.) or 12½ (others).

No.	Type	Description	Unused	Used
326		4c. Type **184**	20	10
327		5c. Pylon (21×28 mm)	30	10
328		15c. Cooling Towers (21×28 mm)	3·00	3·50
326/8		*Set of 3*	3·25	3·50

185 University Coat of arms

187 C. J. Langenhoven

186 Rescuing Sailors

(Des P. de Wet (15c.), H. Meiring (others))

1973 (2 Apr). *Centenary of University of South Africa. T* **185** *and similar designs.* W **127** (tête-bêche) (5c.) or no wmk (others). P 12×12½ (5c.) or 12½ (others).

No.	Type	Description	Unused	Used
329		4c. multicoloured	20	10
330		5c. multicoloured	30	15
331		15c. black and gold	3·00	3·50
329/31		*Set of 3*	3·25	3·50

Designs: Horiz (37×21 mm)—5c. University Complex, Pretoria. Vert (As T **185**)—15c. Old University Building, Cape Town.

WATERMARK. All issues from this date are on unwatermarked paper, unless otherwise stated.

(Des M. Barnett)

1973 (2 June). *Bicentenary of Rescue by Wolraad Woltemade. T* **186** *and similar horiz designs.* P 11½×12½.

No.	Type	Description	Unused	Used
332		4c. light red-brown, light yellow-green and black	20	10
333		5c. yellow-olive, light yellow-green and black	40	10
334		15c. red-brown, light yellow-green and black	5·00	6·50
332/4		*Set of 3*	5·00	6·50

Designs:—5c. De Jonge Thomas foundering; 15c. De Jonge Thomas breaking up and sailors drowning.

(Des J. Mostert)

1973 (1 Aug). *Birth Centenary of C. J. Langenhoven (politician and composer of national anthem). T* **187** *and similar designs.* P 12½ (4 and 5c.) or 11½×12½ (15c.).

No.	Type	Description	Unused	Used
335	**187**	4c. multicoloured	25	10
336	–	5c. multicoloured	35	10
337	–	15c. multicoloured	3·50	5·00
335/7		*Set of 3*	5·00	5·00

Nos. 336/7 are as T **187** but with motifs rearranged. The 5c. is vert, 21×38 mm, and the 16c. is horiz, 38×21 mm.

188 Communications Map

(Des C. Webb)

1973 (1 Oct). *World Communications Day.* P 12½.

(a) No wmk. Glossy paper.

No.	Type	Description	Unused	Used
338	**188**	15c. multicoloured	50	1·40

(b) W **127** *(tête-bêche). Chalky paper.*

No.	Type	Description	Unused	Used
339	**188**	15c. multicoloured	1·50	5·00

189 Restored Buildings

190 Burgerspond (obverse and reverse)

(Des W. Jordaan)

1974 (14 Mar). *Restoration of Tulbagh. T* **189** *and similar multicoloured design.* P 12½.

340 4c. Type **189** 15 10
341 5c. Restored Church Street (58×21 mm) 40 90

(Des P. de Wet. Litho)

1974 (6 Apr). *Centenary of the Burgerspond (coin).* P 12½×12.

342 **190** 9c. brown, orange-red and pale yellow-olive .... 60 1·00

191 Dr. Malan

192 Congress Emblem

(Des I. Henkel)

1974 (22 May). *Birth Centenary of Dr. D. F. Malan (Prime Minister).* P 12½×12.

343 **191** 4c. blue and light blue 20 10

(Des Ingrid Paul)

1974 (13 June). *15th World Sugar Congress, Durban.* P 12×12½.

344 **192** 15c. deep ultramarine and silver .... 75 1·40

193 "50" and Radio Waves

(Des Ingrid Paul)

1974 (13 July). *50th Anniv of Broadcasting in South Africa.* P 12×12½.

345 **193** 4c. red and black 10 10

194 Monument Building

(Des G. Cunningham)

1974 (13 July). *Inauguration of British Settlers' Monument, Grahamstown.* P 12×12½.

346 **194** 5c. red and black 10 10

195 Stamps of the South African Provinces

(Des K. Esterhuysen)

1974 (9 Oct). *Centenary of Universal Postal Union.* P 12½.

347 **185** 15c. multicoloured 70 80

196 Iris

197 Bokmakierie Shrikes

(Des E. de Jong. Recess and photo)

1974 (20 Nov)–**76**. *Multicoloured. Glossy paper (2, 3, 4, 6, 7, 30c. and 1r.) or chalk-surfaced paper (others,).* P 12½ (1 to 25c.) or 12×12½ (others).

(a) Vert designs as T **196** *showing flowers, or horiz designs showing birds or fish.*

348 1c. Type **196** 10 10
349 2c. Wild Heath 15 10
a. Chalk-surfaced paper (2.75) 10 10
350 3c. Geranium 30 10
a. Chalk-surfaced paper (deep claret background) (6.75) 10 10

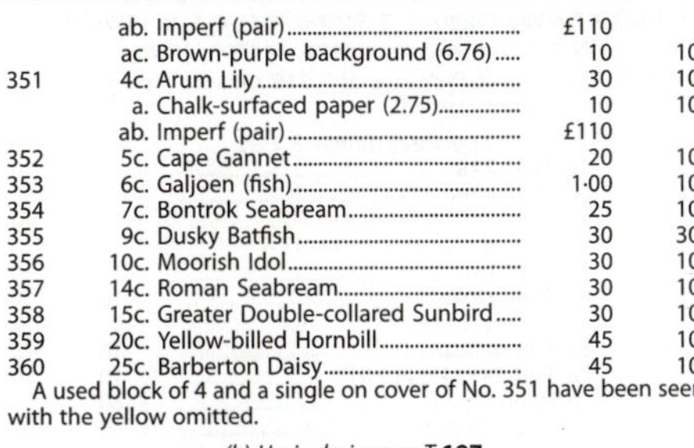
ab. Imperf (pair) £110
ac. Brown-purple background (6.76) 10 10
351 4c. Arum Lily 30 10
a. Chalk-surfaced paper (2.75) 10 10
ab. Imperf (pair) £110
352 5c. Cape Gannet 20 10
353 6c. Galjoen (fish) .... 1·00 10
354 7c. Bontrok Seabream 25 10
355 9c. Dusky Batfish 30 30
356 10c. Moorish Idol 30 10
357 14c. Roman Seabream 30 10
358 15c. Greater Double-collared Sunbird 30 10
359 20c. Yellow-billed Hornbill 45 10
360 25c. Barberton Daisy 45 10

A used block of 4 and a single on cover of No. 351 have been seen with the yellow omitted.

(b) Horiz designs as T **197**.

361 30c. Type **197** .... 7·00 70
362 50c. Stanley Cranes .... 1·00 35
363 1r. Bateleurs .... 4·00 3·00
348/63 *Set of 16* .... 14·00 4·25

1974 (20 Nov)–**76**. *Coil stamps. As Nos. 348/9, 352 and 356 but photo, colours changed. Glossy paper.* P 12½.

370 1c. reddish violet and pink 75 60
a. Perf 14. Chalk-surfaced paper (12.75) 55 60
371 2c. bronze-green and yellow-ochre 80 60
a. Chalk-surfaced paper (7.75) .... 1·40 60
b. Perf 14. Chalk-surfaced paper (11.76?) .... 1·40 50
372 5c. black and light slate-blue .... 1·75 80
373 10c. deep violet-blue and light blue .... 6·00 8·50
a. Perf 14. Chalk-surfaced paper (4.76) .... 4·00 5·25
370/3 *Set of 4* .... 6·25 6·50

198 Voortrekker Monument and Encampment

(Des J. Hoekstra)

1974 (6 Dec). *25th Anniv of Voortrekker Monument, Pretoria.* P 12½.

374 **198** 4c. multicoloured 20 30

199 SASOL Complex

200 President Diederichs

(Des C. Webb)

1975 (26 Feb). *25th Anniv of SASOL (South African Coal, Oil and Gas Corporation Ltd).* P 11½×12½.

375 **199** 15c. multicoloured .... 75 1·50

(Des J. L. Booysen. Recess (4c.) or photo (15c.))

1975 (19 Apr). *Inauguration of the State President.* P 12½×11½.

376 **200** 4c. agate and gold 10 10
377 15c. royal blue and gold .... 50 1·25

201 Jan Smuts

202 "Dutch East Indiaman, Table Bay"

(Des J. Hoekstra. Recess and photo)

1975 (24 May). *Jan Smuts Commemoration.* P 12½×11½.

378 **201** 4c. black and olive-black 10 10

(Des J. Hoekstra. Photo (Nos. 379/82) or litho (**MS**383))

1975 (18 June). *Death Centenary of Thomas Baines (painter). T* **202** *and similar horiz designs. Multicoloured.* P 11½×12½.

379 5c. Type **202** 15 10
380 9c. "Cradock, 1848" 15 15
381 15c. "Thirsty Flat, 1848" 25 25
382 30c. "Pretoria, 1874" .... 40 1·50
379/82 *Set of 4* .... 85 1·75
MS383 120×95 mm. Nos. 379/82 .... 1·00 3·75

203 Gideon Malherbe's House, Paarl

(Des P. de Wet. Recess and photo)

1975 (14 Aug). *Centenary of Genootskap van Regte Afrikaners (Afrikaner Language Movement).* P 12½.

384 **203** 4c. multicoloured 10 10

204 "Automatic Sorting"

205 Title Page of Die Afrikaanse Patriot

(Des J. Sampson)

1975 (11 Sept). *Postal Mechanisation.* P 12½×11½.

385 **204** 4c. multicoloured 10 10

(Des K. Esterhuysen. Recess and photo (4c.). Des P. de Wet. Litho (5c.))

1975 (10 Oct). *Inauguration of the Language Monument, Paarl. T* **205** *and similar vert design.* P 12½×11½.

386 4c. black, pale stone and bright orange 10 10
387 5c. multicoloured 10 10

Design:—5c. "Afrikaanse Taalmonument".

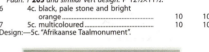

206 Table Mountain

(Des P. Bosman and J. Hoekstra. Litho)

1975 (13 Nov). *Tourism. T* **206** *and similar horiz designs. Multicoloured.* P 12½.

388 15c. Type **206** .... 2·00 3·00
a. Block of 4. Nos. 388/91 .... 7·00 11·00
ab. Yellow-orange and pale lemon ("RSA 15c") omitted £1500 £1000
389 15c. Johannesburg .... 2·00 3·00
390 15c. Cape Vineyards .... 2·00 3·00
391 15c. Lions in Kruger National Park .... 2·00 3·00
388/91 *Set of 4* .... 7·00 11·00

Nos. 388/91 were printed together, *se-tenant*, in blocks of 4 throughout the sheet.

Nos. 388/91 were printed in six colours. At least two sheets, one of which was subsequently used to prepare official first day covers at Pretoria, had the final two colours, yellow-orange and pale lemon, omitted.

207 Globe and Satellites

(Des J. Hoekstra. Litho)

1975 (3 Dec). *Satellite Communication.* P 12½.

392 **207** 15c. multicoloured 30 30

208 Bowls (**209**)

(Des J. Maskew. Litho)

1976. *Sporting Commemorations. T* **208** *and similar vert designs.* P 12½×11½.

393 15c. black and light sage-green (18.2) 20 75
394 15c. black and bright yellow-green (15.3) .... 50 1·00
395 15c. black and pale yellow-olive (16.8) 20 60
396 15c. black and apple-green (2.12) 50 60
393/6 *Set of 4* .... 1·25 1·75
MS397 161×109 mm. Nos. 393/6 (2.12) .... 1·50 4·00

Designs:—No. 393, Type **208** (World Bowls Championships, Johannesburg); 394, Batsman (Centenary of Organised Cricket in South Africa); 395, Polo player; 396, Gary Player (golfer).

1976 (6 Apr). *South Africa's Victory in World Bowls Championships. No. 393 optd with T* **209** *in gold.*

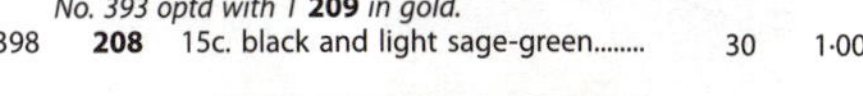
398 **208** 15c. black and light sage-green .... 30 1·00

210 "Picnic under a Baobab Tree"

(Des J. Hoekstra. Photo (4c.) or litho (others and **MS**403))

1976 (20 Apr). *Birth Centenary of Erich Mayer (painter). T* **210** *and similar horiz designs. Multicoloured.* P 11½×12½.

399	4c. Type **210**	15	10
	a. Imperf (pair)	£1100	
400	10c. "Foot of the Blaauwberg"	25	20
401	15c. "Harbeespoort Dam"	30	90
402	20c. "Street scene, Doornfontein"	40	1·25
399/402 *Set of 4*		1·00	2·25
MS403 121×95 mm. Nos. 399/402		1·50	4·00

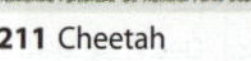

211 Cheetah

212 "Emily Hobhouse" (H. Naude)

(Des P. Bosman. Photo (3c.) or litho (others))

1976 (5 June). *World Environmental Day. T* **211** *and similar horiz designs. Multicoloured.* P 11½×12½.

404	3c. Type **211**	15	10
405	10c. Black Rhinoceros	40	30
406	15c. Blesbok	40	40
407	20c. Mountain Zebra	45	75
404/7 *Set of 4*		1·25	1·40

(Des J. Hoekstra)

1976 (8 June). *50th Death Anniv of Emily Hobhouse (welfare worker).* P 12½×11½.

408	**212**	4c. multicoloured	10	10

213 Dunrobin Castle (mail ship), 1876

214 Family with Globe

(Des K. Esterhuysen. Litho)

1976 (5 Oct). *Ocean Mail Service Centenary.* P 11½×12½.

409	**213**	10c. multicoloured	60	1·00
		a. Imperf (horiz pair)	£1100	

(Des I. Ross)

1976 (6 Nov). *Family Planning and Child Welfare.* P 12½×11½.

410	**214**	4c. chestnut and light salmon	10	10

215 Glasses of wine

oor kwa

First "die" of Afrikaans inscription at left omitted (R. 1/2) on every third sheet

216 Dr Jacob du Toit

(Des H. Botha. Litho)

1977 (14 Feb). *International Wine Symposium, Cape Town.* P 12½×11½.

411	**215**	15c. multicoloured	40	1·25
		a. "die" omitted	15·00	19·00

(Des J. Hoekstra)

1977 (21 Feb). *Birth Centenary of J. D. du Toit (theologian and poet).* P 12½×11½.

412	**216**	4c. multicoloured	10	10

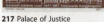

217 Palace of Justice

218 Protea repens

(Des H. Meiring)

1977 (18 May). *Centenary of Transvaal Supreme Court.* P 11½×12½.

413	**217**	4c. red-brown	10	10

(Des D. Findlay. Photo (1, 2, 3c. (No. 416), 4, 5, 8, 10 to 20c. (Nos. 425/a) and coil stamps) or litho (others))

1977 (27 May)–**82**. *Vert designs as T* **218** *showing Proteas or other Succulents. Multicoloured.*

(a) Sheet stamps. P 12½.

414	1c. Type **218**	10	10
415	2c. *P punctata*	15	50
416	3c. *P neriifolia* (photo) (p 12½)	10	10
416*a*	3c. *P neriifolia* (litho) (p 14×13½) (1.10.79)	10	60
417	4c. *P longifolia*	10	10
	a. Imperf (pair)	£100	
418	5c. *P cynaroides*	10	10
	a. Perf 14×13½ (4.3.81)	10	10
	b. Imperf (pair)	£160	
419	6c. *P canaliculata*	35	1·00
	a. Black (face value and inscr at foot) omitted	90·00	
	b. Perf 14×13½ (25.10.79*)	30	80
420	7c. *P lorea*	25	1·00
	a. Emerald ("RSA") omitted	£110	
	b. Perf 14×13½ (19.9.80)	20	80
421	8c. *P mundii*	20	30
	a. Perf 14×13½ (10.7.81)	15	10
422	9c. *P roupelliae*	20	70
	a. Perf 14×13½ (22.12.78)	3·75	2·50
423	10c. *P aristata*	30	10
	a. Perf 14×13½ (12.1.82)	20	50
424	15c. *P eximia*	25	10
425	20c. *P magnifica* (photo)	30	10
	a. Perf 14×13½ (16.2.78)	60	1·00
425*b*	20c. *P magnifica* (litho) (p 14×13½) (24.5.82)	1·25	1·25
426	25c. *P grandiceps*	60	1·00
	a. Emerald ("RSA" and leaves) omitted	£170	
	b. Black (face value and inscr) omitted	£170	
	c. Perf 14×13½ (3.6.80)	40	75
427	30c. *P amplexicaulis*	45	10
	a. Perf 14×13½ (19.10.80)	40	50
428	50c. *Leucospermum cordifolium*	65	15
	a. Perf 14×13½ (9.10.80)	45	15
429	1r. *Paranomus reflexus*	70	1·00
	a. Perf 14×13½ (30.7.80)	50	75
430	2r. *Orothamnus zeyheri*	1·25	2·50
	a. Perf 14×13½ (22.5.81)	60	1·00

(b) Coil stamps. Imperf×perf 14

431	1c. *Leucadendron argenteum*	35	1·00
432	2c. *Mimetes cucullatus*	35	1·00
433	5c. *Serruria florida*	35	1·00
434	10c. *Leucadendron sessile*	35	1·00
414/34 *Set of 21*		5·00	10·00

*Sheets dated 15 August 1979.

There were two emerald plates used for the 7c.; one for the design and background and a second, common with other values in the issue, used to apply "RSA". No. 420a shows this second emerald plate omitted.

Later printings of the coil stamps come with every fifth stamp numbered on the back.

219 Gymnast

220 Metrication Symbol on Globe

(Des D. Cowie. Litho)

1977 (15 Aug). *Eighth Congress of International Association of Physical Education and Sports for Girls and Women.* P 12½×11½.

435	**219**	15c. black, salmon-red and yellow	30	30

(Des L. Wilsenach. Litho)

1977 (15 Sept). *Metrication.* P 12×12½.

436	**220**	15c. multicoloured	30	30

221 Atomic Diagram

(Des R. Sargent. Litho)

1977 (8 Oct). *Uranium Development.* P 12×12½.

437	**221**	15c. multicoloured	40	30

222 National Flag

(Des J. Hoekstra)

1977 (11 Nov). *50th Anniv of National Flag.* P 12×12½.

438	**222**	5c. multicoloured	10	10

223 Walvis Bay, 1878

(Des A. H. Barrett. Litho)

1978 (10 Mar). *Centenary of Annexation of Walvis Bay.* P 12½.

439	**223**	15c. multicoloured	60	60

224 Dr. Andrew Murray

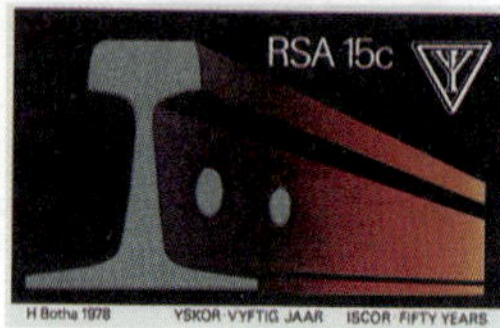

225 Steel Rail

(Des J. Hoekstra. Litho)

1978 (9 May). *150th Birth Anniv of Dr. Andrew Murray (church statesman).* P 12½×12.

440	**224**	4c. multicoloured	10	10

(Des H. Botha, Litho)

1978 (5 June). *50th Anniv of I.S.C.O.R. (South African Iron and Steel Industrial Corporation).* P 12½.

441	**225**	15c. multicoloured	30	30

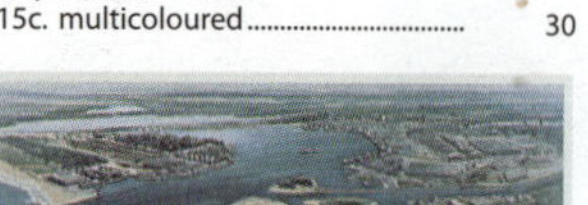

226 Richards Bay

(Des A. H. Barrett. Litho)

1978 (31 July). *Harbours. T* **226** *and similar horiz design. Multicoloured.* P 12½.

442	15c. Type **226**	50	1·00
	a. Pair. Nos. 442/3	1·00	2·00
443	15c. Saldanhabaai	50	1·00

Nos. 442/3 were printed together, *se-tenant*, in horizontal and vertical pairs throughout the sheet.

227 "Shepherd's Lonely Dwelling, Riversdale"

228 Pres. B. J. Vorster

(Des G. Mynhardt. Litho)

1978 (21 Aug). *125th Birth Anniv of J. E. A. Volschenk (painter). T* **227** *and similar horiz designs. Multicoloured.* P 12½.

444	10c. Type **227**	15	20
445	15c. "Clouds and Sunshine, Laneberg Range, Riversdale"	20	30
446	20c. "At the Foot of the Mountain"	30	75
447	25c. "Evening on the Veldt"	35	1·40
444/7 *Set of 4*		90	2·50
MS448 124×90 mm. Nos. 444/7		1·25	4·00

(Des A. H. Barrett. Litho)

1978 (10 Oct). *Inauguration of President Vorster.* P 14×13½.

449	**228**	4c. brown-purple and gold	70	20
		a. Perf 12½×12	10	10
450		15c. dull violet and gold	25	60

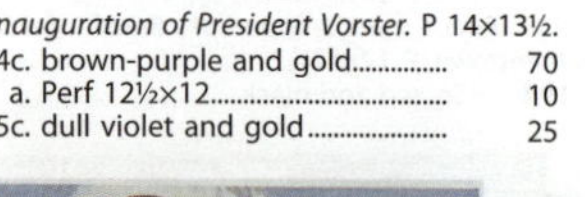

229 Golden Gate

(Des A. H. Barrett. Litho)

1978 (13 Nov). *Tourism. T* **229** *and similar horiz designs. Multicoloured.* P 12½.

451	10c. Type **229**	15	10
452	15c. Blyde River Canyon	25	35
453	20c. Amphitheatre, Drakensberg	40	1·10
454	25c. Cango Caves	55	1·50
451/4 *Set of 4*		1·25	2·75

230 Dr. Wadley (inventor) and Tellurometer

(Des A. H. Barrett. Litho)

1979 (12 Feb). *25th Anniv of Tellurometer (radio distance measurer).* P 12½.

455	**230**	15c. multicoloured	20	20

231 1929 4d. Airmail Stamp

(Des G. Mynhardt. Litho)

1979 (30 Mar). *50th Anniv of Stamp Production in South Africa.* P 14.

456 **231** 15c. green, cream and slate 30 20

232 "Save Fuel"

(Des A. H. Barrett)

1979 (2 Apr). *Fuel Conservation.* P 12×12½.

457 **232** 4c. black and vermilion 25 65
a. Pair. Nos. 457/8 .... 50 1·25
458 4c. black and vermilion 25 65

No. 458 is as T **232** but has face value and country initials in bottom left-hand corner, and Afrikaans inscription above English.

Nos. 457/8 were printed together, *se-tenant*, in horizontal and vertical pairs throughout the sheet.

233 Isandlwana **234** "Health Care"

(Des A. H. Barrett. Litho)

1979 (25 May). *Centenary of Zulu War. T* **233** *and similar horiz designs in black and rose-red, showing drawings.* P 14.

459 4c. Type **233** 20 10
460 15c. Ulundi 55 50
461 20c. Rorke's Drift .... 70 1·00
459/61 *Set of 3* .... 1·25 1·40
MS462 125×90 mm. Nos. 459/61. P 12½ .... 2·25 3·50

(Des J. Hoekstra. Litho)

1979 (19 June). *Health Year.* P 12½×12.

463 **234** 4c. multicoloured 10 10
a. Perf 14×13½ 30 30

235 Children looking at Candle

(Des G. Mynhardt. Litho)

1979 (13 Sept). *50th Anniv of Christmas Stamp Fund.* P 14.

464 **235** 4c. multicoloured 10 10
a. Gold (inscr) omitted ....

236 University of Cape Town **237** "Gary Player"

(Des G. Mynhardt. Litho)

1979 (1 Oct). *50th Anniv of University of Cape Town.* P 13½×14.

465 **236** 4c. multicoloured 20 30
a. Perf 12×12½ 15 15

(Des H. de Klerk. Litho)

1979 (4 Oct). *"Rosafari 1979" World Rose Convention, Pretoria. T* **237** *and similar vert designs. Multicoloured.* P 14×13½.

466 4c. Type **237** 15 10
467 15c. "Prof. Chris Barnard" 30 40
468 20c. "Southern Sun" 40 60
469 25c. "Soaring Wings" 40 85
466/9 *Set of 4* .... 1·10 1·75
MS470 100×125 mm. Nos. 466/9 .... 1·40 2·50

238 University of Stellenbosch **239** F.A.K. Emblem

(Des A. H. Barrett. Litho)

1979 (8 Nov). *300th Anniv of Stellenbosch (oldest town in South Africa). T* **238** *and similar horiz design. Multicoloured.* P 14.

471 4c. Type **238** 10 10
472 15c. Rhenish Church on the Braak 20 40

(Des J. Hoekstra)

1979 (18 Dec). *50th Anniv of F.A.K. (Federation of Afrikaans Cultural Societies).* P 12½×12.

473 **239** 4c. multicoloured 10 15

240 "Still-life with Sweet Peas" **241** "Cullinan II"

(Des G. Mynhardt. Litho)

1980 (6 May). *Paintings by Pieter Wenning. T* **240** *and similar multicoloured design.* P 14×13½.

474 5c. Type **240** 10 10
475 25c. "House in the Suburbs, Cape Town" (44½×37 mm) 40 60
MS476 94×121 mm. Nos. 474/5 .... 1·00 1·60

(Des A. H. Barrett. Litho)

1980 (12 May). *World Diamond Congresses, Johannesburg. T* **241** *and similar vert design. Multicoloured.* P 14.

477 15c. Type **241** 60 60
478 20c. "Cullinan I (Great Star of Africa)" 65 65

242 C. L. Leipoldt **243** University of Pretoria

(Des J. Hoekstra. Litho)

1980 (3 Sept). *Birth Centenary of C. L. Leipoldt (poet).* P 14×13½.

479 **242** 5c. multicoloured 10 10

(Des P. de Wet. Litho)

1980 (9 Oct). *50th Anniv of University of Pretoria.* P 14×13½.

480 **243** 5c. multicoloured 10 10

244 "Marine with Shipping" (Willem van de Velde)

(Des G. Mynhardt. Litho)

1980 (3 Nov). *Paintings from South African National Gallery, Cape Town. T* **244** *and similar multicoloured designs.* P 14.

481 5c. Type **244** 15 10
482 10c. "Firetail and his Trainer" (George Stubbs) 20 25
483 15c. "Lavinia" (Thomas Gainsborough) (*vert*) 25 50
484 20c. "Classical Landscape" (Pieter Post) 30 80
481/4 *Set of 4* .... 80 1·50
MS485 126×90 mm. Nos. 481/4 .... 1·00 1·75

245 Joubert, Kruger and M. Pretorius (Triumvirate Government) **246** Boers advancing up Amajuba Mountain

(Des A. H. Barrett. Litho)

1980 (15 Dec). *Centenary of Paardekraal Monument (cairn commemorating formation of Boer Triumvirate Government). T* **245** *and similar multicoloured design.* P 14×13½ (5c.) or 13½×14 (10c.)

486 5c. Type **245** 10 10
487 10c. Paardekraal Monument (*vert*) 20 65

(Des Diana Arbuthnot. Litho)

1981 (27 Feb). *Centenary of Battle of Amajuba. T* **246** *and similar multicoloured design.* P 13½×14 (5c.) or 14×13½ (15c.)

488 5c. Type **246** 20 10
489 15c. British troops defending hill (*horiz*) 40 75

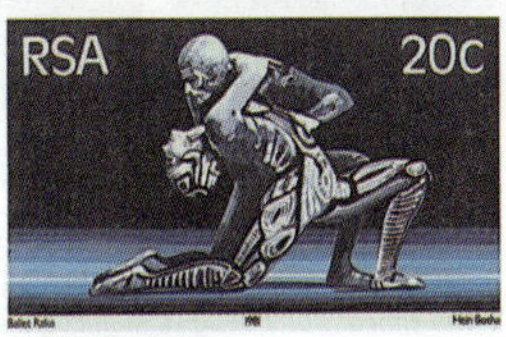

247 Ballet Raka

(Des H. Botha. Litho)

1981 (23 May). *Opening of State Theatre, Pretoria. T* **247** *and similar horiz design. Multicoloured.* P 14.

490 20c. Type **247** 25 30
491 25c. Opera Aida 40 35
MS492 110×90 mm. Nos. 490/1 .... 65 70

248 Former Presidents C. R. Swart, J. J. Fouché, N. Diederichs and B. J. Vorster

(Des A. H. Barrett. Litho)

1981 (30 May). *20th Anniv of Republic. T* **248** *and similar design.* P 14.

493 5c. black, grey-olive and bistre 15 10
494 15c. multicoloured 30 30

Design: (28×22 mm)—15c. President Marais Viljoen.

249 Girl with Hearing Aid **250** Microscope **251** *Calanthe natalensis*

(Des Mare Mouton. Litho)

1981 (12 June). *Centenary of Institutes for Deaf and Blind, Worcester. T* **249** *and similar vert design. Multicoloured.* P 13½×14.

495 5c. Type **249** 10 10
496 15c. Boy reading Braille 20 50

(Des N. Hanna. Litho)

1981 (10 July). *50th Anniv of National Cancer Association.* P 13½×14.

497 **250** 5c. multicoloured 10 10

(Des Jeanette Stead. Litho)

1981 (11 Sept). *Tenth World Orchid Conference, Durban. T* **251** *and similar vert designs. Multicoloured.* P 14.

498 5c. Type **251** 10 10
499 15c. *Eulophia speciosa* 20 35
500 20c. *Disperis fanniniae* 20 75
501 25c. *Disa uniflora* .... 25 1·10
498/501 *Set of 4* .... 65 2·00
MS502 120×91 mm. Nos. 498/501 .... 2·25 2·00

252 Voortrekkers in Uniform  **253** Lord Baden-Powell **254** Dr. Robert Koch

(Des J. Hoekstra. Litho)

1981 (30 Sept). *50th Anniv of Voortrekker Movement (Afrikaans cultural youth organization).* P 14.

503 **252** 5c. multicoloured 10 10

(Des J. Meyer. Litho)

1982 (22 Feb). *75th Anniv of Boy Scout Movement.* P 13½×14.

504 **253** 15c. multicoloured 30 30

(Des J. Meyer. Litho)

1982 (24 Mar). *Centenary of Discovery of Tubercle Bacillus by Dr. Robert Koch.* P 13½×14.

505 **254** 20c. multicoloured 20 30

255 Maria van Riebeeck (submarine)

256 Old Provost, Grahamstown

(Des A. H. Barrett. Litho)

1982 (2 Apr). *25th Anniv of Simonstown as South African Navy Base. T* **255** *and similar horiz designs. Multicoloured.* P 14.

506	8c. Type **255**	15	10
507	15c. Missile patrol vessel	20	30
508	20c. Durban (minesweeper)	25	60
509	25c. Harbour patrol boats	30	85
506/9 *Set of 4*		80	1·60
MS510 125×90 mm. Nos. 506/9		2·00	2·00

(Des A. H. Barrett. Recess (Nos. 511, 512b, 513, 514, 515a, 516a, 521, 522a, 524, 525, 526 and 527), photo (Nos. 528/31) or litho (others))

1982 (15 July)–**87**. *South African Architecture. Designs as T* **256**.

(a) *Sheet stamps.* P 14.

511	1c. reddish brown (*recess*)	15	20
511*a*	1c. reddish brown (*litho*) (2.4.84)	30	30
	ab. Imperf (horiz pair)	35·00	
512	2c. yellow-olive (*litho*)	20	30
512*a*	2c. deep green (*litho*) (9.5.83)	1·00	30
512*b*	2c. bottle green (*recess*) (28.11.83)	10	20
512*c*	2c. bottle green (*litho*) (21.11.85)	1·25	40
513	3c. violet (*recess*)	30	30
513*a*	3c. violet (*litho*) (28.11.85)	1·75	50
514	4c. brown-olive (*recess*)	20	15
514*a*	4c. brown-olive (*litho*) (25.3.85)	1·25	40
515	5c. carmine (*litho*)	30	30
515*a*	5c. brown-purple (*recess*) (11.11.83)	10	10
	ab. Imperf (pair)	£100	
516	6c. deep blue-green (*litho*)	45	40
516*a*	6c. blackish green (*recess*) (9.8.84)	80	60
517	7c. dull yellowish green (*litho*)	30	1·00
518	8c. greenish blue (*litho*)	30	30
518*a*	8c. indigo (*litho*) (3.1.83)	40	10
519	9c. deep mauve (*litho*)	40	20
520	10c. Venetian red (*litho*)	40	55
520*a*	10c. purple-brown (*litho*) (26.1.83)	35	10
520*b*	11c. cerise (*litho*) (2.4.84)	40	20
520*c*	12c. deep violet-blue (*litho*) (1.4.85)	70	10
520*d*	14c. lake-brown (*litho*) (1.4.86)	1·75	10
521	15c. deep violet-blue (*recess*)	30	15
521*a*	16c. rosine (*litho*) (1.4.87)	1·00	1·25
522	20c. vermilion (*litho*)	65	30
522*a*	20c. brownish black (*recess*) (15.6.83)	80	10
522*b*	20c. brownish black (*litho*) (14.11.85)	1·50	15
523	25c. bistre (*litho*)	50	30
523*a*	25c. ochre (*litho*) (3.6.87)	1·75	55
524	30c. agate (*recess*)	50	30
524*a*	30c. reddish brown (*litho*) (12.3.86)	1·75	30
525	50c. deep turquoise-blue (*recess*)	50	30
	a. Deep slate-blue (18.3.83)	2·00	65
525*b*	50c. turquoise-blue (*litho*) (13.10.86)	3·00	30
526	1r. deep violet (*recess*)	50	15
526*a*	1r. deep violet (*litho*) (17.12.86)	1·50	40
527	2r. deep carmine (*recess*)	65	40
527*a*	2r. deep carmine (*litho*) (5.12.85)	1·25	50

Designs: (28×20 mm)—2c. Tuynhuys, Cape Town; 3c. Appèlhof, Bloemfontein; 4c. Raadsaal, Pretoria; 5c. Cape Town Castle; 6c. Goewermentsgebou, Bloemfontein; 7c. Drostdy, Graaff-Reinet; 8c. Leeuwenhof, Cape Town; 9c. Libertas, Pretoria; 10c. City Hall, Pietermaritzburg; 11c. City Hall, Kimberley 12c. City Hall, Port Elizabeth; 14c. City Hall, Johannesburg; 15c. Matjesfontein; 16c. City Hall, Durban; 20c. Post Office, Durban; 25c. Melrose House, Pretoria. (45×28 mm)—30c. Old Legislative Assembly Building, Pietermaritzburg; 50c. Raadsaal, Bloemfontein; 1r. Houses of Parliament, Cape Town; 2r. Uniegebou, Pretoria.

For certain printings of Nos. 511/27a the design width of each stamp was reduced by a millimetre. Of the original set of 17 all showed "wide" designs with the exception of the 1r. Changes in design size occurred in subsequent printings so that Nos. 512c, 513, 521 and 524 can be found in both wide and narrow versions. Of the remainder Nos. 511a, 512b, 513a, 514a, 515a, 516a, 520b/d, 521a, 522a/b, 524a, 525a/b, 526 and 527a exist as "narrow" designs only.

(b) *Coil stamps.* P 14×imperf.

528	1c. brown	30	70
529	2c. yellow-green	30	75
530	5c. lake-brown	30	75
531	10c. light brown	30	80
528/31 *Set of 4*		1·10	2·75
511/27 *Set of 21* (one of each value)		9·00	5·50

Designs: (28×20 mm)—1c. Drostdy, Swellendam; 2c. City Hall, East London; 5c. Head Post Office, Johannesburg; 10c. Morgenster, Somerset West.

257 Bradysaurus

258 Gough Island Base

(Des Sheila Nowers. Litho)

1982 (1 Dec). *Karoo Fossils. T* **257** *and similar horiz designs. Multicoloured.* P 14.

532	8c. Type **257**	30	10
533	15c. Lystrosaurus	35	60
534	20c. Euparkeria	40	75
535	25c. Thrinaxodon	45	90
532/5 *Set of 4*		1·50	2·10
MS536 107×95 mm. Nos. 532/5		1·50	3·25

(Des D. Thorpe. Litho)

1983 (19 Jan). *Weather Stations. T* **258** *and similar horiz designs. Multicoloured.* P 13½×14.

537	8c. Type **258**	20	10
538	20c. Marion Island base	30	45
539	25c. Taking meteorological readings	30	50
540	40c. Launching weather balloon, Sanae.	40	90
537/40 *Set of 4*		1·10	1·75

259 Class S2 Krupp Locomotive, 1952

260 Rugby

(Des H. Botha. Litho)

1983 (27 Apr). *Steam Railway Locomotives. T* **259** *and similar horiz designs. Multicoloured.* P 14.

541	10c. Type **259**	30	10
542	20c. Class 16E Henschel express locomotive, 1935	50	70
543	25c. Class 6H locomotive, 1901	55	80
544	40c. Class 15F locomotive, 1939	65	1·50
541/4 *Set of 4*		1·75	2·75

(Des Sheila Nowers. Litho)

1983 (20 July). *Sport in South Africa. T* **260** *and similar multicoloured designs.* P 14.

545	10c. Type **260**	15	10
546	20c. Soccer (*horiz*)	20	30
547	25c. Yachting	25	40
548	40c. Horse-racing (*horiz*)	40	80
545/8 *Set of 4*		90	1·40

261 Plettenberg Bay

262 Thomas Pringle

(Des A. H. Barrett. Litho)

1983 (12 Oct). *Tourism. Beaches. T* **261** *and similar horiz designs. Multicoloured.* P 14.

549	10c. Type **261**	10	10
550	20c. Durban	20	30
551	25c. West coast	20	35
552	40c. Clifton	35	65
549/52 *Set of 4*		75	1·25
MS553 128×90 mm. Nos. 549/52		1·50	2·50

(Des J. van Ellinckhuijzen. Litho)

1984 (24 Feb). *South African English Authors. T* **262** *and similar vert designs.* P 14.

554	10c. olive-brown, yellow-brown and grey	10	10
555	20c. olive-brown, deep bluish green and grey	20	40
556	25c. olive-brown, deep brown-rose and grey	20	50
557	40c. olive-brown, olive-ochre and grey	35	85
554/7 *Set of 4*		75	1·75

Designs:—20c. Pauline Smith; 25c. Olive Schreiner; 40c. Sir Percy Fitzpatrick.

263 Manganese

(Des H. Botha. Litho)

1984 (8 June). *Strategic Minerals. T* **263** *and similar horiz designs. Multicoloured.* P 14.

558	11c. Type **263**	30	10
559	20c. Chromium	45	60
560	25c. Vanadium	50	80
561	30c. Titanium	60	90
558/61 *Set of 4*		1·75	2·25

264 Bloukrans River Bridge

265 Preamble to the Constitution in Afrikaans

(Des D. Bagnall. Litho)

1984 (24 Aug). *South African Bridges. T* **264** *and similar horiz designs. Multicoloured.* P 14.

562	11c. Type **264**	25	10
563	25c. Durban four level interchange	40	60
564	30c. Mfolozi Railway Bridge	45	75
565	45c. Gouritz River bridge	55	1·40
562/5 *Set of 4*		1·50	2·50

(Des G. Mynhardt. Litho)

1984 (3 Sept). *New Constitution. T* **265** *and similar vert designs.* P 14.

566	11c. stone, black and bistre	70	1·25
	a. Horiz pair. Nos. 566/7	1·40	2·50
567	11c. stone, black and bistre	70	1·25
568	25c. stone, deep claret and bistre	45	50
569	30c. multicoloured	45	50
566/9 *Set of 4*		2·00	3·25

Designs:—No. 566, Preamble to the Constitution in English; 568, Last two lines of National Anthem; 569, South African coat of arms.

Nos. 566/7 were printed together, *se-tenant*, in horizontal pairs.

266 Pres. P. W. Botha

267 Pro Patria Medal

1984 (2 Nov). *Inauguration of President Botha. Litho.* P 14.

570	**266**	11c. multicoloured	30	10
571		25c. multicoloured	55	40

(Des B. Jackson. Litho)

1984 (9 Nov). *Military Decorations. T* **267** *and similar vert designs. Multicoloured.* P 14.

572	11c. Type **267**	20	10
573	25c. De Wet Decoration	30	45
574	30c. John Chard Decoration	30	65
575	45c. Honoris Crux (Diamond) Decoration	35	1·10
572/5 *Set of 4*		1·00	2·10
MS576 71×116 mm. Nos. 572/5		1·50	3·00

268 "Reflections" (Frans Oerder)

269 Cape Parliament Building

1985 (22 Feb). *Paintings by Frans Oerder. T* **268** *and similar horiz designs. Multicoloured. Litho.* P 14.

577	11c. Type **268**	20	15
578	25c. "Ladies in a Garden"	25	35
579	30c. "Still-life with Lobster"	25	45
580	50c. "Still-life with Marigolds"	40	70
577/80 *Set of 4*		1·00	1·50
MS581 129×74 mm. Nos. 577/80		1·50	3·00

(Des A. H. Barrett. Litho)

1985 (15 May). *Centenary of Cape Parliament Building. T* **269** *and similar horiz designs. Multicoloured.* P 14.

582	12c. Type **269**	15	10
583	25c. Speaker's Chair	25	30
584	30c. "National Convention 1908–9" (Edward Roworth)	25	40
585	50c. Republic Parliamentary emblem	40	1·10
	a. Black (inscr and outline) omitted	£350	
582/5 *Set of 4*		95	2·25

270 Freesia
271 Sugar Bowl

(Des Sheila Nowers. Litho)

1985 (23 Aug). *Floral Emigrants. T* **270** *and similar vert designs. Multicoloured.* P 14.

586	12c. Type **270**	15	10
587	25c. Nerine	25	30
588	30c. Ixia	25	45
589	50c. Gladiolus	40	1·25
586/9 *Set of 4*		1·00	1·90

(Des H. Botha. Litho)

1985 (5 Nov). *Cape Silverware. T* **271** *and similar multicoloured designs.* P 14.

590	12c. Type **271**	20	10
591	25c. Teapot	30	30
592	30c. Loving cup (*vert*)	30	45
593	50c. Coffee pot (*vert*)	45	1·50
590/3 *Set of 4*		1·10	2·10

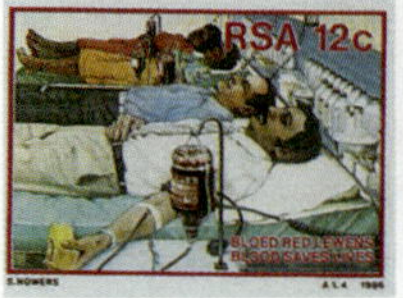

272 Blood Donor Session

273 National Flag

(Des Sheila Nowers. Litho)

1986 (20 Feb). *Blood Donor Campaign. T* **272** *and similar horiz designs. Multicoloured.* P 14.

No.	Description	Mint	Used
594	12c. Type **272**	45	10
595	20c. Baby receiving blood transfusion	75	80
596	25c. Operation in progress	80	95
597	30c. Ambulanceman and accident victim	95	1·60
594/7	*Set of 4*	2·75	3·00

(Des J. Hoekstra. Litho)

1986 (30 May). *25th Anniv of Republic of South Africa. T* **273** *and similar horiz design. Multicoloured.* P 14.

No.	Description	Mint	Used
598	14c. Type **273**	75	1·00
	a. Horiz pair. Nos. 598/9	1·50	2·00
599	14c. As Type **273**, but inscr "UNITY IS STRENGTH"	75	1·00

Nos. 598/9 were printed together, *se-tenant*, in horizontal pairs throughout the sheet.

274 Drostdyhof, Graaff-Reinet

(Des A. H. Barrett. Litho)

1986 (14 Aug). *Restoration of Historic Buildings. T* **274** *and similar horiz designs. Multicoloured.* P 14.

No.	Description	Mint	Used
600	14c. Type **274**	30	10
601	20c. Pilgrims Rest mining village	55	70
602	25c. Strapp's Store, Bethlehem	60	90
603	30c. Palmdene, Pietermaritzburg	75	1·40
600/3	*Set of 4*	2·00	2·75

PHILATELIC FOUNDATION MINIATURE SHEETS. These miniature sheets were issued by the Philatelic Foundation of Southern Africa and not the postal administration. They could be purchased by post or from a limited number of philatelic offices at a premium in aid of various national and international stamp exhibitions.

275 Von Brandis Square, Johannesburg, c. 1900

(Des J. van Niekerk. Litho)

1986 (25 Sept). *Centenary of Johannesburg. T* **275** *and similar horiz designs. Multicoloured.* P 14.

No.	Description	Mint	Used
604	14c. Type **275**	35	10
605	20c. Gold mine (26×20 mm)	1·25	1·25
606	25c. Johannesburg skyline, 1986	1·00	1·60
607	30c. Gold bars (26×20 mm)	1·75	2·50
604/7	*Set of 4*	4·00	5·00

The 30c. value exists as a Philatelic Foundation miniature sheet.

276 Gordon's Rock, Paarlberg

277 *Cicindela regalis*

(Des A. H. Barrett. Litho)

1986 (20 Nov). *Rock Formations. T* **276** *and similar vert designs. Multicoloured.* P 14.

No.	Description	Mint	Used
608	14c. Type **276**	45	10
609	20c. The Column, Drakensberg	70	80
610	25c. Maltese Cross, Sederberge	75	1·00
611	30c. Bourke's Luck Potholes, Blyde River Gorge	85	1·50
608/11	*Set of 4*	2·50	3·00

(Des E. Holm. Litho)

1987 (6 Mar). *South African Beetles. T* **277** *and similar vert designs. Multicoloured.* P 14.

No.	Description	Mint	Used
612	14c. Type **277**	40	10
613	20c. *Trichostetha fascicularis*	55	60
614	25c. *Julodis viridipes*	65	90
615	30c. *Ceroplesis militaris*	75	1·75
612/15	*Set of 4*	2·10	3·00

278 Eland, Sebaaieni Cave

(Des H. Botha. Litho)

1987 (4 June). *Rock Paintings. T* **278** *and similar horiz designs. Multicoloured.* P 14.

No.	Description	Mint	Used
616	16c. Type **278**	40	10
617	20c. Leaping lion, Clocolan	60	65
618	25c. Black Wildebeest, uMhlwazini Valley	75	90
619	30c. Bushman dance, Floukraal	80	1·60
616/19	*Set of 4*	2·25	2·75

279 Oude Pastorie, Paarl

(Des A. H. Barrett. Litho)

1987 (3 Sept). *300th Anniv of Paarl. T* **279** *and similar horiz designs. Multicoloured.* P 14.

No.	Description	Mint	Used
620	16c. Type **279**	20	10
621	20c. Grapevines	35	55
622	25c. Wagon-building	40	65
623	30c. KWV Cathedral Wine Cellar	45	1·25
620/3	*Set of 4*	1·25	2·25

The 30c. value exists as a Philatelic Foundation miniature sheet.

+10c
VLOEDRAMP
NATAL

(**280**)

281 "Belshazzar's Feast" (Rembrandt)

1987 (16 Nov). *Natal Flood Relief Fund (1st issue). No. 521a surch as T* **280** *in Afrikaans or English.*

No.	Description	Mint	Used
624	16c.+10c. rosine (surch T **280**)	30	80
	a. Pair. Nos. 624/5	60	1·60
625	16c.+10c. rosine (surch "NATAL FLOOD DISASTER")	30	80

Nos. 624/5 were surcharged together, *se-tenant*, in horizontal and vertical pairs throughout the sheet.

See also Nos. 629/30 and 635/6.

(Des Sheila Nowers. Litho)

1987 (19 Nov). *The Bible Society of South Africa. T* **281** *and similar multicoloured designs.* P 14.

No.	Description	Mint	Used
626	16c. "The Bible" in 75 languages (54×34 mm)	35	10
627	30c. Type **281**	55	70
628	50c. "St. Matthew and the Angel" (Rembrandt) (*vert*)	85	1·60
626/8	*Set of 3*	1·60	2·10

A 40c. value, showing the inscription "The Word of God" in various languages, was prepared, but due to religious objections was recalled before issue, although examples are known to have been sold to the public at some smaller post offices (*Price £450 mint, £550 used*).

1987 (1 Dec). *Natal Flood Relief Fund (2nd issue). No. 626 surch as T* **280**, *but larger (Afrikaans version 32 mm wide).*

No.	Description	Mint	Used
629	16c.+10c. multicoloured (surch "NATAL FLOOD DISASTER")	50	70
	a. Pair. Nos. 629/30	1·00	1·40
630	16c.+10c. multicoloured (surch as T **280**)	50	70

Nos. 629/30 were surcharged together, *se-tenant*, in horizontal and vertical pairs throughout the sheet. These stamps are known postmarked at Mooirivier on 25 November 1987.

282 Bartolomeu Dias and Cape of Good Hope

283 Huguenot Monument, Franschhoek

(Des Sheila Nowers. Litho)

1988 (3 Feb). *500th Anniv of Discovery of Cape of Good Hope by Bartolomeu Dias. T* **282** *and similar horiz designs. Multicoloured.* P 14.

No.	Description	Mint	Used
631	16c. Type **282**	60	10
632	30c. Kwaaihoek Monument	80	85
633	40c. Caravels	1·40	1·50
634	50c. Martellus map, c. 1489	1·75	2·25
631/4	*Set of 4*	4·00	4·25

The 50c. value exists as a Philatelic Foundation miniature sheet.

1988 (1 Mar). *Natal Flood Relief Fund (3rd issue). No. 631 surch as T* **280**, *but larger (Afrikaans version 19 mm wide).*

No.	Description	Mint	Used
635	16c.+10c. multicoloured (surch as T **280**)	50	70
	a. Pair. Nos. 635/6	1·00	1·40
636	16c.+10c. multicoloured (surch "NATAL FLOOD DISASTER")	50	70

Nos. 635/6 were surcharged together, *se-tenant*, in horizontal and vertical pairs throughout the sheet.

(Des H. Botha. Litho)

1988 (13 Apr). *300th Anniv of Arrival of First French Huguenots at the Cape. T* **283** *and similar vert designs. Multicoloured.* P 14.

No.	Description	Mint	Used
637	16c. Type **283**	30	10
638	30c. Map of France showing Huguenot areas	85	80
639	40c. Title page of French/Dutch New Testament of 1672	85	1·25
640	50c. St. Bartholomew's Day Massacre, Paris, 1572	1·10	1·50
637/40	*Set of 4*	2·75	3·25

National
Flood Disaster
+10c

(**284**)

285 Pelican Point Lighthouse, Walvis Bay

1988 (13 Apr). *National Flood Relief Fund. Nos. 637/40 surch as T* **284** *in English (E) or in Afrikaans ("Nasionale Vloedramp") (A).*

No.	Description	Mint	Used
641	16c.+10c. multicoloured (E)	40	65
	a. Pair. Nos. 641/2	80	1·25
642	16c.+10c. multicoloured (A)	40	65
643	30c.+10c. multicoloured (A)	55	75
	a. Pair. Nos. 643/4	1·10	1·50
644	30c.+10c. multicoloured (E)	55	75
645	40c.+10c. multicoloured (A)	70	90
	a. Pair. Nos. 645/6	1·40	1·75
646	40c.+10c. multicoloured (E)	70	90
647	50c.+10c. multicoloured (E)	90	1·25
	a. Pair. Nos. 647/8	1·75	2·50
648	50c.+10c. multicoloured (A)	90	1·25
641/8	*Set of 8*	4·50	6·25

The two versions of each surcharge were printed together, *se-tenant*, both horizontally and vertically, throughout the sheets.

(Des Sheila Nowers. Litho)

1988 (9 June). *Lighthouses. T* **285** *and similar horiz designs. Multicoloured.* P 14.

No.	Description	Mint	Used
649	16c. Type **285**	60	10
650	30c. Green Point, Cape Town	80	70
651	40c. Cape Agulhas	1·00	1·25
652	50c. Umhlanga Rocks, Durban	1·40	1·75
649/52	*Set of 4*	3·50	3·50
MS653	132×112 mm. Nos. 649/52	4·50	4·25

286 *Huernia zebrina*

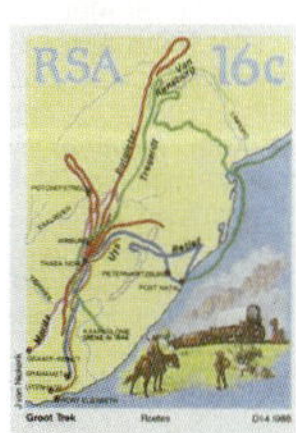

287 Map of Great Trek Routes

(Des H. Botha)

1988 (1 Sept)–**93**. *Succulents. T* **286** *and similar horiz designs. Multicoloured.*

(a) Sheet stamps. Litho. P 14.

No.	Description	Mint	Used
654	1c. Type **288**	10	10
	a. Coil strip. Nos. 654/7 and 662 (11.5.93)	50	
655	2c. *Euphorbia symmetrica*	10	10
656	5c. *Lithops dorotheae*	10	10
657	7c. *Gibbaeum nebrownii*	15	10
658	10c. *Didymaotus lapidiformis*	15	10
659	16c. *Vanheerdea divergens*	60	10
659*a*	18c. *Faucaria tigrina* (1.4.89)	50	10
660	20c. *Conophytum mundum*	80	10
660*a*	21c. *Gasteria armstrongii* (2.4.90)	40	10
661	25c. *Cheiridopsis peculiaris*	80	10
	a. Imperf (pair)	£180	
662	30c. *Tavaresia barklyi*	60	20
663	35c. *Dinteranthus witmotianus*	1·00	20
664	40c. *Frithia pulchra*	1·00	25
665	50c. *Lapidaria margaretae*	1·00	25
666	90c. *Dioscorea elephantipes*	1·25	45
667	1r. *Trichocaulon cactiforme*	1·00	50
668	2r. *Crassula columnaris*	1·25	90
668*a*	5r. *Anacampseros albissima* (1.3.90)	2·25	2·40
654/68*a*	*Set of 18*	12·00	5·25

(b) Coil stamps. Photo. P 14×imperf.

No.	Description	Mint	Used
669	1c. *Adromischus marianiae*	1·00	1·75
670	2c. *Titanopsis calcarea*	60	70
671	5c. *Dactylopsis digitata*	65	70
672	10c. *Pleiospilos bolusii*	70	85
669/72	*Set of 4*	2·75	3·50

Multi-value coil strip No. 654a was produced by the South African Post Office for use by a large direct mail marketing firm. Strips were also available from the Philatelic Service.

For similar design, but without face value and inscribed "Standardised mail" in English and Afrikaans, see No. 778.

(Des J. van Niekerk (16c.). Litho)

1988 (21 Nov). *150th Anniv of Great Trek. T* **287** *and similar multicoloured designs.* P 14.

No.	Description	Mint	Used
673	16c. Type **287**	60	10
674	30c. "Exodus" (tapestry by W. Coetzer) (56×20 mm)	90	90
675	40c. "Crossing the Drakensberg" (tapestry by W. Coetzer) (77×20 mm)	1·10	1·10
676	50c. "After the Service, Church of the Vow" (J. H. Pierneef) (*horiz*)	1·40	1·75
673/6	*Set of 4*	3·50	3·50

288 Coelacanth

289 Man-made Desert

(Des A. McBride. Litho)

1989 (9 Feb). *50th Anniv of Discovery of Coelacanth. T* **288** *and similar horiz designs. Multicoloured.* P 14.

677 16c. Type **288** ... 75 15
678 30c. Prof J. L. B. Smith and Dr. M. Courtenay-Latimer examining Coelacanth ... 1·10 1·25
679 40c. J. L. B. Smith Institute of Ichthyology, Grahamstown ... 1·40 1·60
680 50c. Coelacanth and GEO midget submarine ... 1·50 2·25
677/80 *Set of 4* ... 4·25 4·75

The 50c. value exists as a Philatelic Foundation miniature sheet and also as a corporate miniature sheet, containing two examples, sponsored by Two Oceans Environmental Trust. See note above No. 822.

(Des D. Murphy. Litho)

1989 (3 May). *National Grazing Strategy. T* **289** *and similar horiz designs. Multicoloured.* P 14.

681 18c. Type **289** ... 40 15
682 30c. Formation of erosion gully ... 65 75
683 40c. Concrete barrage in gully ... 70 1·00
684 50c. Reclaimed veldt ... 80 1·40
681/4 *Set of 4* ... 2·25 3·00

290 South Africa v France Match, 1980

291 "Composition in Blue"

(Des B. Jackson. Litho)

1989 (22 June). *Centenary of South African Rugby Board. T* **290** *and similar horiz designs. Multicoloured.* P 14.

685 15c. Type **290** ... 80 15
686 30c. South Africa v Australia, 1963 ... 1·25 90
687 40c. South Africa v New Zealand, 1937 ... 1·40 1·50
688 50c. South Africa v British Isles, 1896 ... 1·40 2·00
685/8 *Set of 4* ... 4·25 4·00

1989 (13 Aug). *Paintings by Jacob Hendrik Pierneef . T* **291** *and similar horiz designs. Multicoloured. Litho.* P 14.

689 18c. Type **291** ... 50 15
690 30c. "Zanzibar" ... 80 60
691 40c. "The Bushveld" ... 1·00 1·25
692 50c. "Cape Homestead" ... 1·10 1·75
689/92 *Set of 4* ... 3·00 3·50
MS693 114×86 mm. Nos. 689/92 ... 2·25 2·75

292 Pres. F. W. de Klerk

293 Gas-drilling Rig, Mossel Bay

1989 (20 Sept). *Inauguration of President F. W. de Klerk. T* **292** *and similar vert design. Multicoloured. Litho.* P 14.

694 18c. Type **292** ... 50 15
695 45c. F. W. de Klerk (different) ... 75 1·40

(Des H. Botha. Litho)

1989 (19 Oct). *Energy Sources. T* **293** *and similar horiz designs. Multicoloured.* P 14×14½.

696 18c. Type **293** ... 40 10
697 30c. Coal to oil conversion plant ... 70 70
698 40c. Nuclear power station ... 80 85
699 50c. Thermal electric power station ... 90 1·25
696/9 *Set of 4* ... 2·50 2·50

294 Electric Goods Train and Map of Railway Route

295 Great Britain 1840 Penny Black

(Des A. H. Barrett. Litho)

1990 (15 Feb). *Co-operation in Southern Africa. T* **294** *and similar horiz designs. Multicoloured.* P 14½×14.

700 18c. Cahora Bassa Hydro-electric Scheme, Mozambique, and map of transmission lines (68×26 mm) ... 70 25
701 30c. Type **294** ... 90 70
702 40c. Projected dam on upper Orange River, Lesotho, and map of Highlands Water Project (68×26 mm) ... 1·10 1·10
703 50c. Cow, syringe, and outline map of Africa ... 1·40 1·25
700/3 *Set of 4* ... 3·75 3·00
MS704 136×78 mm. Nos. 700/3 ... 3·25 2·75

1990 (12 May). *National Stamp Day. T* **295** *and similar vert designs showing stamps. Multicoloured. Litho.* P 14.

705 21c. Type **295** ... 40 50
a. Horiz strip of 5. Nos. 705/9 ... 1·75 2·25
706 21c. Cape of Good Hope 1853 4d.triangular pair ... 40 50
707 21c. Natal 1857 1s.40 ... 50 50
708 21c. Orange Free State 1868 1s.40 ... 50 50
709 21c. Transvaal 1869 1s.40 ... 50 50
705/9 *Set of 5* ... 1·75 2·25

Nos. 705/9 were printed together, *se-tenant*, in horizontal strips of 5 throughout the sheet.

296 Knysna Turaco

297 Karoo Landscape near Britstown

(Des C. Finch-Davies. Litho)

1990 (2 Aug). *Birds. T* **296** *and similar vert designs. Multicoloured.* P 14.

710 21c. Type **296** ... 75 20
711 35c. Red-capped Robin Chat ... 1·00 80
712 40c. Rufous-naped Bush Lark ... 1·00 1·25
713 50c. Bokmakierie Shrike ... 1·40 1·75
710/13 *Set of 4* ... 3·75 3·50

The 50c. value exists as a Philatelic Foundation miniature sheet.

1990 (1 Nov). *Tourism. T* **297** *and similar horiz designs. Multicoloured. Litho.* P 14.

714 50c. Type **297** ... 1·25 1·50
a. Block of 4. Nos. 714/17 ... 4·50 5·50
715 50c. Camps Bay, Cape of Good Hope ... 1·25 1·50
716 50c. Giraffes in Kruger National Park ... 1·25 1·50
717 50c. Boschendal Vineyard, Drakenstein Mts ... 1·25 1·50
714/17 *Set of 4* ... 4·50 5·50

Nos. 714/17 were printed together, *se-tenant*, in blocks of 4 throughout the sheet.

298 Woltemade Cross for Bravery

299 Boer Horses

(Des J. Hoekstra. Litho)

1990 (6 Dec). *National Orders. T* **298** *and similar vert designs. Multicoloured.* P 14.

718 21c. Type **298** ... 50 60
a. Horiz strip of 5. Nos. 718/22 ... 2·25 2·75
719 21c. Order of the Southern Cross ... 50 60
720 21c. Order of the Star of South Africa ... 50 60
721 21c. Order for Meritorious Service ... 50 60
722 21c. Order of Good Hope ... 50 60
718/22 *Set of 5* ... 2·25 2·75
MS723 143×70 mm. Nos. 718/22 ... 2·25 2·75

Nos. 718/22 were printed together, *se-tenant*, in horizontal strips of 5 throughout the sheet.

(Des A. Ainslie. Litho)

1991 (12 Feb). *Animal Breeding in South Africa. T* **299** *and similar horiz designs. Multicoloured.* P 14.

724 21c. Type **299** ... 80 80
a. Horiz strip of 5. Nos. 724/8 ... 3·50 3·50
725 21c. Bonsmara bull ... 80 80
726 21c. Dorper sheep ... 80 80
727 21c. Ridgeback dogs ... 80 80
728 21c. Putterie racing pigeons ... 80 80
724/8 *Set of 5* ... 3·50 3·50

Nos. 724/8 were printed together, *se-tenant*, in horizontal strips of five throughout the sheet.

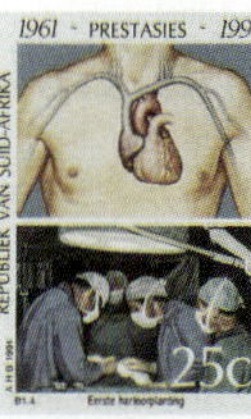

300 Diagram of Human Heart and Transplant Operation

301 State Registration of Nurses Act, 1891

(Des A. H. Barrett. Litho)

1991 (30 May). *30th Anniv of Republic. Scientific and Technological Achievements. T* **300** *and similar multicoloured designs.* P 14.

729 25c. Type **300** ... 20 10
730 40c. Marimba Power Station (*horiz*) ... 35 35
731 50c. Dolos design breakwater (*horiz*) ... 45 45
732 60c. Western Deep Levels gold mine ... 60 60
729/32 *Set of 4* ... 1·40 1·40

The 60c. value exists as a Philatelic Foundation miniature sheet.

(Des T. Marais. Litho)

1991 (15 Aug). *Centenary of State Registration for Nurses and Midwives.* P 14.

733 **301** 60c. multicoloured ... 60 60

302 South Africa Post Office Ltd Emblem

303 Sir Arnold Theiler (veterinarian)

(Des Liza van der Wal. Litho)

1991 (1 Oct). *Establishment of Post Office Ltd and Telekom Ltd. T* **302** *and similar horiz design. Multicoloured.* P 14×14½.

734 27c. Type **302** ... 50 50
a. Vert pair. Nos. 734/5 ... 1·00 1·00
735 27c. Telekom SA Ltd emblem ... 50 50

Nos. 734/5 were printed together, *se-tenant*, in vertical pairs throughout the sheet.

(Des A. H. Barrett. Litho)

1991 (9 Oct). *South African Scientists. T* **303** *and similar horiz designs. Multicoloured.* P 14.

736 27c. Type **303** ... 35 15
737 45c. Sir Basil Schonland (physicist) ... 60 60
738 65c. Dr. Robert Broom (palaeontologist) ... 1·00 1·10
739 85c. Dr. Alex du Toit (geologist) ... 1·25 2·00
736/9 *Set of 4* ... 3·00 3·50

304 Agulhas (Antarctic research ship)

305 Soil Conservation

(Des Liza van der Wal (27c.), T. Marais (65c.). Litho)

1991 (5 Dec). *30th Anniv of Antarctic Treaty. T* **304** *and similar horiz design. Multicoloured.* P 14.

740 27c. Type **304** ... 1·25 20
741 65c. Chart showing South African National Antarctic Expedition base. ... 1·50 80

(Des J. van Niekerk. Litho)

1992 (6 Feb). *Environmental Conservation. T* **305** *and similar horiz designs. Multicoloured.* P 14×14½.

742 27c. Type **305** ... 50 15
743 65c. Water pollution ... 1·25 1·10
744 85c. Air pollution ... 1·50 1·50
742/4 *Set of 3* ... 3·00 2·50

The 65c. value exists as a Philatelic Foundation miniature sheet.

306 Dutch Fleet approaching Table Bay c. 1750

307 Queen Anne Settee

(Des J. van Niekerk. Litho)

1992 (9 May). *National Stamp Day. Cape of Good Hope Postal Stones. T* **306** *and similar horiz designs. Multicoloured.* P 14.

745 35c. Type **306** ... 60 60
a. Horiz strip of 5. Nos. 745/9 ... 2·75 2·75
746 35c. Landing for water and provisions ... 60 60
747 35c. Discovering a postal stone ... 60 60
748 35c. Leaving letters under a stone ... 60 60
749 35c. Reading letters ... 60 60
745/9 *Set of 5* ... 2·75 2·75

Nos. 745/9 were printed together, *se-tenant*, in horizontal strips of 5 throughout the sheet.

1992 (9 July). *Antique Cape Furniture. T* **307** *and similar multicoloured designs. Litho.* P 14.

750 35c. Type **307** ... 50 50
a. Sheetlet. Nos. 750/9 ... 4·50
751 35c. Stinkwood settee, c. 1800 ... 50 50
752 35c. Canopy bed, c. 1800 (*vert*) ... 50 50
753 35c. 19th-century rocking cradle ... 50 50
754 35c. Waterbutt, c. 1800 (*vert*) ... 50 50
755 35c. Flemish style cabinet, c. 1700 (*vert*) ... 50 50
756 35c. Armoire, c 1780 (*vert*) ... 50 50
757 35c. Late 17th-century church chair (*vert*) ... 50 50
758 35c. Tub chair, c. 1770 (*vert*) ... 50 50
759 35c. Bible desk, c. 1750 (*vert*) ... 50 50
750/9 *Set of 10* ... 4·50 4·50

Nos. 750/9 were printed together, *se-tenant*, as a sheetlet of 10.

308 Grand Prix Motor Racing

309 "Women's Monument" (Van Wouw)

(Des Liza van der Wal (35c. (No. 761)), C. Prinsloo (55c.), B. Jackson (70, 90c., 1r.05). Litho)

1992 (24 July). *Sports. T* **308** *and similar horiz designs. Multicoloured.* P 14×14½.

760 35c. Type **308** ... 30 25

761	35c. Football	30	25
762	55c. Total Paris–Cape Motor Rally	45	35
763	70c. Athletics	55	50
764	90c. Rugby	75	65
765	1r.05 Cricket	1·25	1·00
760/5	*Set of 6*	3·25	2·75
MS766	167×69 mm. Nos. 760/5	3·50	3·00

1992 (8 Oct). *130th Birth Anniv of Anton van Wouw (sculptor). T* **309** *and similar vert designs. Multicoloured. Litho.* P 14.

767	35c. Type **309**	40	20
768	70c. "Sekupu Player"	80	60
769	90c. "The Hunter"	1·00	80
770	1r.05 "Postman Lehman"	1·10	1·00
767/70	*Set of 4*	3·00	2·40
MS771	96×149 mm. Nos. 767/70	2·75	2·40

310 Walvis Bay Harbour

311 Bristol "Boxkite", 1907

1993 (28 Jan). *South African Harbours. T* **310** *and similar horiz designs. Multicoloured. Litho.* P 14.

772	35c. Type **310**	40	20
773	55c. East London	50	35
774	70c. Port Elizabeth	75	50
775	90c. Cape Town	95	75
776	1r.05 Durban	1·00	95
772/6	*Set of 5*	3·25	2·50
MS777	147×112 mm. Nos. 777/6	2·75	2·50

(Des H. Botha. Litho)

1993 (1 1). *Succulents. Design as T* **286**, *but inscr "Standardised mail" in English and Afrikaans.* P 14.

778	(–) *Stapelia grandiflora*	60	10

No. 778 was sold at 45c.

(Des D. Stahmer. Litho)

1993 (7 May). *Aviation in South Africa. T* **311** *and similar horiz designs. Multicoloured.* P 14.

779	45c. Type **311**	65	60
	a. Sheetlet. Nos. 779/803	14·00	
780	45c. Voisin "Boxkite", 1909	65	60
781	45c. Bleriot XI, 1911	65	60
782	45c. Paterson No. 2 biplane, 1913	65	60
783	45c. Henri Farman H.F.27, 1915	65	60
784	45c. Royal Aircraft Factory B.E.2.E., 1918	65	60
785	45c. Vickers Vimy Silver Queen II, 1920	65	60
786	45c. Royal Aircraft Factory S.E.5A.,1921	65	60
787	45c. Avro 504k, 1921	65	60
788	45c. Armstrong Whitworth A.W.(15) Atalanta, 1930	35	60
789	45c. De Havilland D.H.66 Hercules, 1931	65	60
790	45c. Westland Wapiti, 1931	65	60
791	45c. Junkers F-13, 1932	65	60
792	45c. Handley Page H.P.42, 1933	65	60
793	45c. Junkers Ju 52/3m, 1934	65	60
794	45c. Junkers Ju 86, 1936	65	60
795	45c. Hawker Hartbees, 1936	65	60
796	45c. Short S.23 Empire "C" Class flying boat Canopus, 1937	65	60
797	45c. Miles Master II and Airspeed A.S.11 Oxford, (1940)	65	60
798	45c. North American AT-6 Harvard Mk IIa, (1942)	65	60
799	45c. Short S.26 Sunderland flying boat, 1945	65	60
800	45c. Avro Type **685** York, 1946	65	60
801	45c. Douglas DC-7B, 1955	65	60
802	45c. Sikorsky S-56c helicopter, 1956	65	60
803	45c. Boeing 707-344, 1959	65	60
779/803	*Set of 25*	14·00	13·00

Nos. 779/803 were printed together, *se-tenant*, in sheetlets of 25 (5×5).

Nos. 779 and 803 exist as a Philatelic Foundation miniature sheet.

312 Table Mountain Ghost Frog

313 Dragoons carrying Mail between Cape Town and False Bay, 1803

Two types of species inscr:
I. Species name in Latin.
II. Species name in English.

Two types of "Standardised mail" stamp (No. 821):
III. Small rhinoceros. Inscr "DICEROS BICORNIS".
IV. Redrawn with larger rhinoceros. Inscr "BLACK RHINOCEROS".

(Des D. Murphy. Litho)

1993 (3 Sept)–**97**. *Endangered Fauna. T* **312** *and similar horiz designs. Multicoloured.*

(a) Face values as T **312**.

804	1c. Type **312** (I)	10	50
	a. Coil strip. Nos. 804, 805×2 and 808×2 (15.4.94)	50	
	b. Coil. Imperf×p 14 (1.9.95)	20	75
	ba. Coil strip. Nos. 804b, 805b×2, 806b and 810b (50c. stamp at right)	1·00	
	bb. Coil strip. As No. 804ba, but 50c. stamp in centre (1.12.95)	1·00	
	c. Type II (coil. Imperf×p 14) (1.8.96)	20	75
	ca. Coil strip. Nos. 804c, 805c×2, 807c and 811c	1·10	
805	2c. Smith's Dwarf Chameleon (I)	10	50
	b. Coil. Imperf×p 14 (1.9.95)	20	75
	c. Type II (coil. Imperf×p 14) (1.8.96)	20	75
806	5c. Giant Girdle-tailed Lizard (I)	10	10
	a. Coil strip. Nos. 806/7, each×2, and 808 (24.8.94)	50	
	b. Coil. Imperf×p 14 (2.95)	30	30
	ba. Coil strip. Nos. 806b×2, 807b×2 and 808b	1·40	
807	10c. Geometric Tortoise (I)	10	10
	b. Coil. Imperf×p 14 (2.95)	30	30
	c. Type II (coil. Imperf×p 14) (1.8.96)	30	30
808	20c. Southern African Hedgehog (I)	10	10
	b. Coil. Imperf×p 14 (2.95)	50	50
	c. Type II (25.6.97)	30	30
809	40c. Riverine Rabbit (I)	20	10
	c. Type II (27.3.97)	20	10
810	50c. Samango Monkey (I)	25	20
	b. Coil. Imperf×p 14 (1.9.95)	30	20
	c. Type II (1.7.97)	30	30
811	55c. Aardwolf (I)	20	10
	c. Type II (coil. Imperf×p 14) (1.8.96)	30	30
812	60c. Cape Hunting Dog (I)	40	20
813	70c. Roan Antelope (I)	55	25
	c. Type II (19.5.97)	30	20
814	75c. African Striped Weasel (I)	30	20
815	80c. Kori Bustard (I)	1·00	25
815*a*	85c. Lemon-breasted Seedeater (I) (20.10.95)	1·00	25
816	90c. Jackass Penguin (I)	1·10	30
	a. Booklet pane. No. 816×10 with outer edges of pane imperf (1.12.95)	3·50	
	c. Type II (18.6.97)	1·00	30
817	1r. Wattled Crane (I)	1·10	30
	c. Type II (6.8.96)	70	30
818	2r. Blue Swallow (I)	1·25	55
	c. Type II (23.7.97)	1·25	55
819	5r. Martial Eagle (I)	2·00	1·40
	c. Type II (18.6.97)	1·75	1·40
820	10r. Bateleur (I)	3·00	2·10
804/20	*Set of 18*	10·00	5·50

(b) Inscr "Standardised mail" in English and Afrikaans (No. 821) or "Airmail postcard rate" (others).

821	(45c.) Black Rhinoceros (III)	50	25
	a. Booklet pane. No. 821×10 with outer edges of pane imperf (14.2.95)	4·50	
	b. Type IV (9.4.96)	50	35
	ba. Booklet pane. No. 821b×10 with outer edges of pane imperf	4·50	
821*c*	(1r.) White Rhinoceros (II) (8.5.96)	50	30
	c. Horiz strip of 5. Nos. 821c/g	2·25	
	cb. Pane. Nos. 821c/g plus 3 advertising and 2 airmail labels with margins all round	3·00	
	cc. Booklet pane. Nos. 821c/g plus 5 airmail labels with outer edges of pane imperf	3·00	
	cd. Booklet pane. Nos. 821c/g plus 5 Thulamela labels with outer edges of pane imperf (27.7.97)	3·00	
821*d*	(1r.) Buffalo (II) (8.5.96)	50	30
821*e*	(1r.) Lion (II) (8.5.96)	50	30
821*f*	(1r.) Leopard (II) (8.5.96)	50	30
821*g*	(1r.) African Elephant (II) (8.5.96)	50	30
821/g	*Set of 6*	2·75	1·60

Multi-value coil strips Nos. 804a, 804ba/bb, 804ca, 806a and 806ba were produced by the South African Post Office for use by Reader's Digest. Strips were also available from the Philatelic Service and philatelic counters.

Nos. 804ba/bb and 804ca each include a label showing the Reader's Digest emblem at left. In each instance the right hand stamp (50c. on No. 804ba, 5c. on No. 804bb and 55c. on No. 804ca) is imperforate on three sides.

No. 804ba originally had a black label, but was re-issued with a red label on 1 December 1995. No. 804bb had a blue label and No. 804ca a green one, but this was re-issued with an orange label on 11 November 1996.

No. 806ba occurs with both the left and right hand stamps (5c. and 20c.), or just the right hand stamp, imperforate on three sides.

No. 821 was initially sold at 45c. and No. 821b was only issued in stamp booklets, initially sold at 6r. The "Standardised mail" rate was increased to 50c. in August 1994, 60c. in April 1996, 70c. in August 1996, 1r. on 7 April 1997 and to 1r.10 on 14 April 1998.

Nos. 821c/g, which were each initially sold at 1r., were printed together, *se-tenant*, in sheets of 10 containing two horizontal strips of 5. No. 821b exists as a corporate miniature sheet sponsored by MILSET and commemorating the "ESI '97" Exhibition at Pretoria. No. 821e exists as a corporate miniature sheet sponsored by Coach House.

For stamps with elliptical perforations see Nos. 913/18 and for redrawn designs without frame and inscribed "South Africa" only see Nos. 1012a/49.

CORPORATE MINIATURE SHEETS. Such miniature sheets were introduced in 1996 and were produced for firms or other corporate bodies to use for advertising and publicity purposes. Each sponsor has to agree to purchase a minimum of 10,000 sheets with further supplies being placed on sale, at face value, by the South Africa Philatelic Bureau, philatelic counters and overseas agents.

(Des J. van Niekerk. Litho)

1993 (8 Oct). *National Stamp Day. Early 19th-century Postal Services. T* **313** *and similar horiz designs. Multicoloured.* P 14.

822	45c. Type **313**	30	25
823	65c. Ox wagon carrying Stellenbosch to Cape Town mail, 1803	45	50
824	85c. Khoi-Khoin mail runners from Stellenbosch, 1803	65	70
825	1r.05 Mounted postmen, 1804	80	90
822/5	*Set of 4*	2·00	2·10

314 Flowers from Namaqualand

1993 (12 Nov). *Tourism. T* **314** *and similar horiz designs. Multicoloured. Litho.* P 14.

826	85c. Type **314** (Afrikaans inscr)	65	75
	a. Horiz strip of 5. Nos. 826/30	3·00	3·25
827	85c. North Beach, Durban (English inscr)	65	75
828	85c. Lion (German inscr)	65	75
829	85c. "Appel Express" on Van Staden's Bridge (Dutch inscr)	65	75
830	85c. Gemsbok (antelope) (French inscr)	65	75
826/30	*Set of 5*	3·00	3·50

Nos. 826/30 were printed together, *se-tenant*, in horizontal strips of 5 thoughout the sheet.

315 Grapes and Packing Bench

(Des B. Jackson. Litho)

1994 (28 Jan). *Export Fruits. T* **315** *and similar horiz designs. Multicoloured.* P 14½×14.

831	85c. Type **315**	55	50
832	90c. Apple and picker	55	50
833	1r.05 Plum and fork-lift truck	65	60
834	1r.25 Orange and tractor with trailer	75	70
835	1r.40 Avocado and loading freighter	85	80
831/5	*Set of 5*	3·00	2·75

The 85c. value exists as a Philatelic Foundation miniature sheet.

316 "Children of Different Races"

317 Pres. Mandela

(Nicole Davies)

1994 (8 Apr). *Peace Campaign. Children's Paintings. T* **316** *and similar horiz designs. Multicoloured. Litho.* P 14½×14.

836	45c. Type **316**	25	20
837	70c. "Dove and Tree" (Robynne Lawrie)	40	40
838	95c. "Children and Dove" (Batami Nothmann)	55	55
839	1r.15 "Multi-racial Crowd" (Karen Uys)	75	80
836/9	*Set of 4*	1·75	1·75

No. 839 exists as a corporate miniature sheet sponsored by I.G.P.C. and commemorating Chernobyl's Children charities.

(Des Liza van der Wal (70c., 95c.). Litho)

1994 (10 May). *Inauguration of President Nelson Mandela. T* **317** *and similar multicoloured designs.* P 14×14½ (45c.) or 14½×14 (others).

840	45c. Type **317**	55	20
841	70c. South African national anthems	85	60
842	95c. New national flag	1·40	1·50
843	1r.15 Union Buildings, Pretoria	1·40	2·00
840/3	*Set of 4*	3·75	3·75

318 Tug T. S. McEwen towing Winchester Castle (liner), 1935

(Des Sheila Nowers. Litho)

1994 (13 May). *Tugboats. T* **318** *and similar horiz designs. Multicoloured.* P 14½×14.

844	45c. Type **318**	35	20
845	70c. Sir William Hoy with Karanja (liner), 1970	55	40
846	95c. Sir Charles Elliott and wreck of Dunedin Star (liner), 1942	70	55
847	1r.15 Eland and freighter at wharf, 1955	95	75
848	1r.36 Pioneer (paddle tug) and sailing ships, 1870	1·10	90
844/8	*Set of 5*	3·25	2·50
MS849	163×84 mm. Nos. 844/8	3·25	2·50

Commonwealth Member 1 June 1994

319 "Mother hands out Work" (Emile du Toit)

1994 (1 July). *International Year of the Family. Children's Paintings. T* **319** *and similar horiz designs. Multicoloured. Litho.* P 14.
850 45c. Type **319** 50 45
a. Vert strip of 5. Nos. 850/4 .... 2·25 2·00
851 45c. "My Friends and I at Play" (Patrick Mackenzie) 50 45
852 45c. "Family Life" (Michelle du Pisani) 50 45
853 45c. "Sunday in Church" (Elizabeth Nel) . 50 45
854 45c. "I visit my Brother in Hospital" (Zwelinzema Sam) 50 45
850/4 *Set of 5* .... 2·25 2·00
Nos. 850/4 were printed together, *se-tenant*, in vertical strips of 5 throughout the sheet.

320 Hands holding Invoice and Bulk Mail Envelope

(Des J. van Niekerk. Litho)

1994 (30 Sept). *National Stamp Day. T* **320** *and similar horiz designs. Multicoloured.* P 14.
855 50c. Type **320** 30 25
856 70c. Certified mail 40 40
857 95c. Registered mail 50 55
858 1r.15 Express Delivery mail 60 65
855/8 *Set of 4* .... 1·60 1·75

321 *Erica tenuifolia*

(Des J. van Niekerk. Litho)

1994 (18 Nov). *Heathers. T* **321** *and similar vert designs. Multicoloured.* P 14.
859 95c. Type **321** 65 70
a. Horiz strip of 5. Nos. 859/63 .... 3·00 3·25
860 95c. *Erica urna-viridis* 65 70
861 95c. *Erica decora* 65 70
862 95c. *Erica aristata* 65 70
863 95c. *Erica dichrus* 65 70
859/63 *Set of 5* .... 3·00 3·25
Nos. 859/63 were printed together, *se-tenant*, in horizontal strips of 5 throughout the sheet.

322 Warthogs (Eastern Transvaal) and Map

(Des A. Ainslie. Litho)

1995 (18 Jan). *Tourism. T* **322** *and similar horiz designs, each including map. Multicoloured.* P 14½×14.
(a) Face values as T **322**.
864 50c. Type **322** 60 40
865 50c. Lost City Resort (North-West Province) (15 Feb) 60 40
(b) Inscr "Standardised mail" in English and Afrikaans.
866 (60c.) White Rhinoceros and calf (Kwazulu/Natal) (28 April) 60 40
867 (60c.) Cape Town waterfront (Western Cape) (12 May) 60 40
868 (60c.) Baobab tree (Northern Transvaal) (30 June) 60 40
a. Vert strip of 5. Nos. 868/72 .... 2·75
869 (60c.) Highland Route (Free State) (30 June) 60 40
870 (60c.) Augrabies Falls (Northern Cape) (30 June) 60 40
871 (60c.) Herd of elephants, Addo National Park (Eastern Cape) (30 June) 60 40
872 (60c.) Union Buildings, Pretoria (Gauteng) (30 June) 60 40
864/72 *Set of 9* .... 4·75 3·00
Nos. 868/72 were printed together, *se-tenant*, in sheets of 10 containing two vertical *se-tenant* strips of 5.
No. 864 exists as a Philatelic Foundation miniature sheet.
No. 868 exists imperforate on three sides with a *se-tenant* stamp-size label as a corporate product sponsored by Coach House. The same value subsequently appeared as a corporate miniature sheet.

323 De Havilland D.H.9 Biplane and Cheetah D Jet Fighter

(Des Anne de Goede (50c.), A. H. Barrett (95c.). Litho)

1995 (1 Feb). *Aviation Anniversaries. T* **323** *and similar horiz design. Multicoloured.* P 14.
873 50c. Type **323** (75th anniv of South African Air Force) 55 30
874 95c. Vickers Vimy Silver Queen II (75th anniv of first Trans-African flight) 80 75

324 Player running with Ball and Silhouettes

325 Rural Water Purification System

1995 (25 May). *World Cup Rugby Championship, South Africa. T* **324** *and similar multicoloured designs. Litho.* P 14.
875 (60c.) Type **324** 30 25
a. Perf 14×imperf (booklets) 35 35
ab. Booklet pane. Nos. 875a/6a, each×5 .... 3·25
876 (60c.) Player running with ball and silhouettes (*vert*) 30 25
a. Imperf×perf 14 (booklets) 35 35
ab. Booklet pane. No. 876a×10 .... 3·25
877 1r.15 Player taking ball from scrum (68×26½ mm) 75 85
875/7 *Set of 3* .... 1·25 1·25
MS878 109×61 mm. No. 876 .... 75 75
Nos. 875/6 are inscribed "STANDARD POSTAGE" in English and Afrikaans.

(Des J. van Niekerk. Litho)

1995 (15 June). *50th Anniv of CSIR (technological research organization).* P 14.
879 **325** (60c.) multicoloured 45 45
No. 879 is inscribed "Standardised mail" in English and Afrikaans.

326 Player with Ball

327 Dr. John Gilchrist, South African Pilchards and *Africana* (oceanographic research ship)

1995 (28 June). *South Africa's Victory in Rugby World Cup. T* **326** *and similar multicoloured design. Litho.* P 14.
880 (60c.) Type **326** 40 40
881 (60c.) South African player holding trophy aloft (*vert*) 40 40
Nos. 880/1 are inscribed "STANDARD POSTAGE" in English and Afrikaans.

(Des D. Thorpe. Litho)

1995 (25 Aug). *Centenary of Marine Science in South Africa.* P 14.
882 **327** (60c.) multicoloured 30 30
No. 882 is inscribed "Standard Postage" in English and Afrikaans.

328 Singapore Lion

329 People building Flag Wall

(Des A. Ainslie. Litho)

1995 (1 Sept). *"Singapore '95" International Stamp Exhibition. Sheet 71×55 mm.* P 14.
MS883 **328** (60c.) multicoloured .... 75 1·00
No. **MS**883 is inscribed "STANDARD POSTAGE" in English and Afrikaans.
A second printing of No. **MS**883 included the date, "DEC 1995", on the sheet margin at bottom left.

1995 (16 Sept). *Masakhane Campaign. Litho.* P 14.
884 **329** (60c.) multicoloured (34×24 mm) 20 20
a. Booklet pane. No. 884×10 .... 2·00
884*b* (60c.) mult (26×20 mm) (1 Dec) 20 20
ba. Booklet pane. No. 884b×10 .... 2·00
Nos. 884 and 884b are inscribed "STANDARD POSTAGE" in English and Afrikaans.
No. 884b was only issued in 6r. stamp booklets.
Nos. 884a and 884ba show the three outer edges of the panes imperforate.

330 Papal Arms

331 Gandhi wearing Suit

1995 (16 Sept). *Visit of Pope John Paul II. Litho.* P 14.
885 **330** (60c.) multicoloured 65 30
No. 885 is inscribed "STANDARD POSTAGE" in English and Afrikaans.

(Des A. Ainslie. Litho)

1995 (2 Oct). *India-South Africa Co-operation. 125th Birth Anniv of Mahatma Gandhi (1994). T* **331** *and similar vert design.* P 14.
886 (60c.) deep violet 75 30
887 1r.40 bistre-brown .... 1·00 1·25
MS888 71×71 mm. No. 887 .... 1·40 1·40
Design:—1r.40, Gandhi wearing dhoti.
No. 886 is inscribed "STANDARD POSTAGE" in English and Afrikaans.
Stamps in similar designs were issued by India.
No. 886 exists as a corporate miniature sheet sponsored by Pradip Jain and commemorating the 50th anniversary of the Congress Alliance for a Democratic South Africa.

332 Traditional African Postman

333 "50" and UN Emblem

(Des C. Emslie. Litho)

1995 (9 Oct). *World Post Day.* P 14.
889 **332** (60c.) multicoloured 30 30
No. 889 is inscribed "STANDARD POSTAGE" in English and Afrikaans.
No. 889 exists as a corporate miniature sheet sponsored by the South African Stamp Colour Catalogue.

(Des C. Emslie. Litho)

1995 (19 Oct). *"Total Stampex '95" and "Ilsapex '98" Stamp Exhibitions. Sheet, 70×66 mm, containing T* **332** *and "ILSAPEX '98" logo. Imperf.*
MS890 5r. multicoloured .... 2·50 2·50

(Des C. Emslie (No. 891), A. Ainslie and F. Frescura (No. **MS**892). Litho)

1995 (24 Oct). *50th Annivs of United Nations and UNESCO T* **333** *and similar multicoloured design.* P 14.
891 (60c.) Type **333** 30 30
MS892 101×78 mm. (60c.) Traditional village (30×47 mm) 30 30
Nos. 891/2 are inscribed "STANDARD POSTAGE" in English and Afrikaans.

334 *Afrivoluta pringlei*

335 Map of Africa and Player

336 South African Player, Map and Trophy

(Des L. Kriedemann. Litho)

1995 (24 Nov). *Sea Shells. T* **334** *and similar vert designs. Multicoloured.* P 14½×14.
893 (60c.) Type **334** 40 40
a. Horiz strip of 5. Nos. 893/7 .... 1·75 1·75
894 (60c.) *Lyria Africana* 40 40
895 (60c.) *Marginella mosaica* 40 40
896 (60c.) *Conus pictus* 40 40
897 (60c.) *Gypreaea fultoni* 40 40
893/7 *Set of 5* .... 1·75 1·75
Nos. 893/7 were printed together, *se-tenant*, as horizontal strips of 5 in sheets of 10, each stamp being inscribed "STANDARD POSTAGE" in English and Afrikaans.
No. 893 is inscribed "priglei" in error.

(Des M. de Jong (Nos. 898/902), Z. Mashinini (No. **MS**903). Litho)

1996 (10 Jan). *African Nations Football Championship, South Africa. T* **335** *and similar vert designs showing map and players.* P 14½×14.
898 **335** (60c.) multicoloured ("RSA" in deep ultramarine) 55 55
a. Horiz strip of 5. Nos. 898/902 ... 2·50 2·50
899 (60c.) multicoloured ("RSA" in brown-ochre) 55 55
900 (60c.) multicoloured ("RSA" in bright scarlet) 55 55
901 (60c.) multicoloured ("RSA" in olive-grey) 55 55
902 (60c.) multicoloured ("RSA" in deep emerald) 55 55
898/902 *Set of 5* .... 2·50 2·50
MS903 75×55 mm. (60c.) mult (young player) 50 60
Nos. 898/902 were printed together, *se-tenant*, as horizontal strips of 5 in sheets of 10.
Nos. 898/903 are inscribed "STANDARD POSTAGE" in English and Afrikaans.

(Des M. de Jong. Litho)

1996 (8 Feb). *South Africa's Victory in African Nations Football Championship.* P 14.
904 **336** (60c.) multicoloured 40 30
a. Football missing above date at bottom right (R. 1/2) .... 4·50
No. 904 is inscribed "STANDARD POSTAGE" in English and Afrikaans.
It is understood that No. 904a occurs on every tenth sheet.

337 Historical Buildings, Bloemfontein **338** Rat

(Des J. van Beukering. Litho)

1996 (28 28). *150th Anniv of City of Bloemfontein.* P 14.

905 **337** (60c.) multicoloured 65 20

No. 905 is inscribed "Standard Postage" in English and Afrikaans.

(Des D. Murphy. Litho)

1996 (18 May). *"CHINA '96" 9th Asian International Stamp Exhibition, Peking. Sheet 109×85 mm.* P 14.

MS906 **338** 60c. multicoloured 70 70

339 "Man in a Donkey Cart"

(Gerard Sekoto)

1996 (1 June). *Gerard Sekoto (artist) Commemoration. T* **339** *and similar multicoloured designs. Litho.* P 14.

907 1r. Type **339** 30 30
908 2r. "Song of the Pick" 80 80
MS909 108×70 mm. 2r. "Yellow Houses, Sophiatown" (detail) (*vert*) .... 1·00 1·10

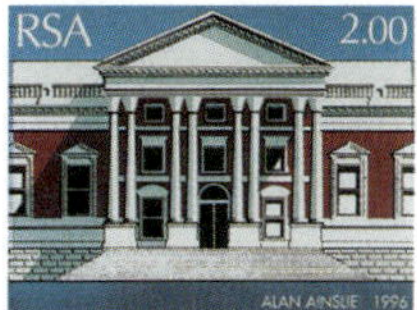

340 Parliament Building, Cape Town **341** Children playing

(Des A. Ainslie. Litho)

1996 (8 June). *"CAPEX '96" International Stamp Exhibition, Toronto. Sheet 72×49 mm.* P 14.

MS910 **340** 2r. multicoloured .... 1·00 1·10

1996 (8 June). *Youth Day. Litho.* P 14.

911 **341** (60c.) multicoloured 30 20

No. 911 is inscribed "STANDARD POSTAGE" in English and Afrikaans.

342 Marathon Runners

(Des M. de Jong. Litho)

1996 (8 June). *75th Anniv of Comrades Marathon.* P 14.

912 **342** (60c.) multicoloured 30 20

No. 912 is inscribed "Standard postage" in English and Afrikaans.

(Des D. Murphy. Litho)

1996 (1 July)–**9**. *Endangered Fauna. As Nos. 808c, 810c, 812 (but with English inscr), 817c, 821b and new value (20r.) but P 14½ (20r.) or 14 (others), each with two elliptical holes on horizontal sides.*

(a) Face values as T **312**.

913 20c. Southern African Hedgehog (II) (28.5.97) 10 10
914 50c. Samango Monkey (II) (1.7.97) 25 10
915 60c. Cape Hunting Dog (II) (12.5.97) 30 10
916 1r. Wattled Crane (II) (11.6.97) 80 25
917 20r. Fish Eagle (II) (34×24 mm) (20.3.97) .... 4·00 4·25

(b) Inscr "Standardised mail" in English and Afrikaans.

918 (60c.) Black Rhinoceros (IV) 30 30
913/18 *Set of 6* .... 5·50 4·75

The "Standardised mail" rate was increased to 70c. in August 1996, to 1r. on 7 April 1997 and to 1r.10 on 14 April 1998.

The printing of No. 918 issued on 1 July 1996 was shared between the Government Printer and Cape & Transvaal Printers.

343 Cycling **344** Constitutional Assembly Logo

(Des M. de Jong. Litho)

1996 (5 July). *Olympic Games, Atlanta. T* **343** *and similar vert designs. Multicoloured.* P 14.

919 (70c.) Type **343** 40 40
a. Horiz strip of 5. Nos. 919/23 .... 2·25 2·25
920 (70c.) Swimming 40 40
921 (70c.) Boxing 40 40
922 (70c.) Running 40 40
923 (70c.) Pole vaulting 40 40
924 (1r.40) South African Olympic emblem 40 40
919/24 *Set of 6* .... 2·25 2·25

Nos. 919/23, which are inscribed "STANDARD POSTAGE" in English and Afrikaans, were printed together in sheets of 10 containing two *se-tenant* horizontal strips of 5.

(Des M. de Jong. Litho)

1996 (1 Aug). *New Democratic Constitution.* P 14.

925 **344** (70c.) myrtle-green, orange-red and black 30 30
a. Horiz strip of 5. Nos. 925/9 .... 1·25 1·25
926 (70c.) brt turquoise-blue, dp vio, & blk 30 30
927 (70c.) deep violet, orange-yellow & black 30 30
928 (70c.) ultramarine, scarlet and black 30 30
929 (70c.) scarlet, orange-yellow and black 30 30
925/9 *Set of 5* .... 1·25 1·25

Nos. 925/9 are inscribed "Standard Postage" in English and Afrikaans and were printed together, *se-tenant*, in horizontal strips of 5 throughout the sheet.

345 Sea Pioneer (bulk carrier) **346** "Xhosa Woman" (G. Pemba)

(Des E. Wale (No. 927), P. Bilas (others). Litho)

1996 (5 Aug). *50th Anniv of South African Merchant Marine. T* **345** *and similar horiz designs. Multicoloured.* P 14.

930 (70c.) Type **345** 85 70
a. Horiz pair. Nos. 930/1 .... 1·60 1·40
931 (70c.) Winterberg (container ship) 85 70
932 1r.40 Langkloof (freighter) .... 1·25 1·40
a. Horiz pair. Nos. 932/3 .... 2·50 2·75
933 1r.40 Vaal (liner) .... 1·25 1·40
930/3 *Set of 4* .... 3·75 3·75
MS934 102×63 mm. 2r. Constantine (freighter) and tug (71×30 mm) (inscr "SOUTH AFRICAN MERCHANT MARINE 1946–1996" on top margin) .... 1·00 1·00

Nos. 930/1 are inscribed "Standard Postage" in English and Afrikaans.

Nos. 930/1 and 932/3 were printed together, *se-tenant*, in horizontal pairs throughout the sheets.

No. 931 exists as a corporate miniature sheet sponsored by Safmarine.

No. **MS**934 also comes with the top margin inscription replaced by "Safmarine" and logo.

1996 (9 Aug). *National Women's Day. Litho.* P 14.

935 **346** 70c. multicoloured 30 25

347 Postman delivering Letters **348** Candles and Holly

(Des J. van Niekerk. Litho)

1996 (9 Oct). *World Post Day.* P 14.

936 **347** 70c. multicoloured 30 25

(Des A. Ainslie. Litho)

1996 (9 Oct). *Christmas.* P 14.

937 **348** 70c. multicoloured 30 25
a. Booklet pane. No. 937×10 .... 3·00

No. 937a has the three outer edges of the pane imperforate.

No. 937 exists as a corporate miniature sheet sponsored by SANTA and sold at 2r. for charitable purposes.

349 "Liner Oranje at Cape Town" (E. Wale)

1996 (9 Oct). *"Bloemfontein 150" National Stamp Show. Sheet 86×56 mm. Litho.* P 14.

MS938 **349** 2r. multicoloured .... 1·50 1·50

350 Max Theiler (Medicine, 1951) **351** Early Motor Car

1996 (4 Nov). *South African Nobel Laureates. T* **350** *and similar vert designs. Litho.* P 14.

939 (70c.) dull violet and maroon 50 50
a. Sheetlet. Nos. 939/48 .... 4·50
940 (70c.) deep bluish green, maroon and dull violet 50 50
941 (70c.) maroon and dull violet 50 50
942 (70c.) deep bluish green, maroon and dull violet 50 50
943 (70c.) dull violet and maroon 50 50
944 (70c.) dull violet and maroon 50 50
945 (70c.) deep bluish green, maroon and dull violet 50 50
946 (70c.) maroon and dull violet 50 50
947 (70c.) deep bluish green, maroon and dull violet 50 50
948 (70c.) dull violet and maroon 50 50
939/48 *Set of 10* .... 4·50 4·50

Designs—No. 939, Type **350**; No. 940, Albert Luthuli (Peace, 1961); No. 941, Alfred Nobel; No. 942, Allan Cormack (Medicine, 1979); No. 943, Aaron Klug (Chemistry, 1982); No. 944, Desmond Tutu (Peace, 1984); No. 945, Nadine Gordimer (Literature, 1991); No. 946, Nobel Prizes symbol; No. 947, Nelson Mandela (Peace, 1993); No. 948, F. W. de Klerk (Peace, 1993).

Nos. 939/48, which are inscribed "Standard Postage" in English and Afrikaans, were printed together, *se-tenant*, in sheets of 10.

No. 941 exists as a corporate miniature sheet sponsored by AECI and celebrating the centenary of Modderfontein Industrial Complex.

(Des D. Bagnall. Litho)

1997 (4 Jan). *Centenary of Motoring in South Africa.* P 14.

949 **351** (70c.) multicoloured .... 1·00 35

No. 949 is inscribed "STANDARD POSTAGE" in English and Afrikaans.

No. 949 exists as a corporate minature sheet sponsored by Total.

352 Lion **353** Vegetables and Water Pump

(Des A. Ainslie. Litho)

1997 (12 Feb). *"Hong Kong '97" International Stamp Exhibition. Sheet 82×68 mm.* P 14 (with two elliptical holes on each vertical side).

MS950 **352** 3r. ultramarine, gold and rosine .... 1·40 1·40

(Des D. Murphy. Litho)

1997 (7 Mar). *National Water Conservation. T* **353** *and similar horiz designs. Multicoloured.* P 14 (with two elliptical holes at top or bottom).

951 (70c.) Type **353** 40 30
a. Booklet pane. Nos. 951/5, each ×2 .... 3·50
b. Perf 14 (without elliptical holes) (25 Mar) 40 40
ba. Booklet pane. Nos. 951b/5b each ×2 .... 3·50
952 (70c.) Flowers and watering can 40 30
b. Perf 14 (without elliptical holes) (25 Mar) 40 40
953 (70c.) Child in bath 40 30
b. Perf 14 (without elliptical holes) (25 Mar) 40 40
954 (70c.) Building tools 40 30
b. Perf 14 (without elliptical holes) (25 Mar) 40 40
955 (70c.) Water cart and stand pipe 40 30
b. Perf 14 (without elliptical holes) (25 Mar) 40 40
951/5 *Set of 5* .... 1·75 1·40

Nos. 951/5 and 951b/5b are inscribed "STANDARD POSTAGE" and were sold in 7r. stamp booklets containing Nos. 951a or 951ba.

Both booklet panes are imperforate on the three outer edges.

On No. 951a the elliptical holes only occur on the horizontal line of perforations separating the two rows of stamps.

Like many other modern South African booklet panes Nos. 951a and 951ba were available to collectors as uncut booklet sheets. Imperf pairs come from these sheets.

354 S.A.S. *Umkomaas* (minesweeper) **355** Election Day Poster

(Des Sheila Nowers. Litho)

1997 (1 Apr). *75th Anniv of South African Navy. T* **354** *and similar horiz designs. Multicoloured.* P 14 (with two elliptical holes on each vertical side).

956 (70c.) Type **354** 60 60
 a. Block of 4. Nos. 956/9 2·25 2·25
957 (70c.) S.A.S. *Emily Hobhouse* (submarine) and S.A.S. *President Steyn* (frigate) 60 60
958 (70c.) S.A.S. *Kobie Coetsee* (fast attack craft) 60 60
959 (70c.) S.A.S. *Protea* (hydrographic survey ship) 60 60
956/9 *Set of 4* 2·25 2·25

Nos. 956/9, which are inscribed "Standard Postage" in English and Afrikaans, were printed together, *se-tenant*, in blocks of 4 throughout the sheet.

(Des M. Maapola. Litho)

1997 (27 Apr). *Freedom Day. T* **355** *and similar vert designs. Each black and red.* P 14 (with two elliptical holes on each vertical side).

960 (1r.) Type **355** 40 40
 a. Horiz strip of 5. Nos. 960/4 1·75 1·75
961 (1r.) People queueing 40 40
962 (1r.) People registering 40 40
963 (1r.) Voting booth 40 40
964 (1r.) Woman placing vote in ballot box 40 40
960/4 *Set of 5* 1·75 1·75

Nos. 960/4, which are inscribed "STANDARD POSTAGE", were printed together, *se-tenant*, in horizontal strips of five throughout the sheet forming a composite design.

356 Brahman Bull

357 Zulu Baskets

(Des Leigh Voigt. Litho)

1997 (2 May). *Chinese New Year ("Year of the Ox"). "SAPDA '97" Stamp Exhibition, Johannesburg. Sheet 107×61 mm.* P 14.

MS965 **356** 4r.51 multicoloured 1·00 1·00

(Des D. Murphy. Litho Govt Printer (Nos. 966/75) or Questa (Nos. 966b/75b))

1997 (17 May). *Year of Cultural Experiences. T* **357** *and similar vert designs. Multicoloured.* P 14.

966 (1r.) Type **357** 40 40
 a. Sheetlet. Nos. 966/75 3·50
 b. Perf 14×15 (8 Dec) 40 40
 ba. Booklet pane. Nos. 966b/75b 3·50
967 (1r.) Southern Sotho figure 40 40
 b. Perf 14×15 (8 Dec) 40 40
968 (1r.) South Ndebele figure 40 40
 b. Perf 14×15 (8 Dec) 40 40
969 (1r.) Venda door 40 40
 b. Perf 14×15 (8 Dec) 40 40
970 (1r.) Tsonga medicine gourd 40 40
 b. Perf 14×15 (8 Dec) 40 40
971 (1r.) Wooden pot, Northern Cape 40 40
 b. Perf 14×15 (8 Dec) 40 40
972 (1r.) Khoi walking stick 40 40
 b. Perf 14×15 (8 Dec) 40 40
973 (1r.) Tswana knife handle 40 40
 b. Perf 14×15 (8 Dec) 40 40
974 (1r.) Xhosa pipe 40 40
 b. Perf 14×15 (8 Dec) 40 40
975 (1r.) Swazi vessel 40 40
966/75 *Set of 10* 3·50 3·50

Nos. 966/75 which are inscribed "Standard Postage", were printed together, *se-tenant*, in sheetlets of 10 with illustrated left-hand margin.

The stamps printed by Questa, Nos. 966b/75b, show some designs redrawn and were only issued in 20r. stamp booklets.

358 Grocott's, Muirhead and Gowie Buildings, Grahamstown

359 White breasted Cormorant

(Des A. Ainslie. Litho)

1997 (29 May). *"Pacific '97" International Stamp Exhibition, San Francisco. Sheet 94×49 mm.* P 14.

MS976 **358** 5r. multicoloured 1·25 1·25

(Des Julia Birkhead and D. Murphy. Litho Govt Printer (Nos. 977/86) or Questa (Nos. 977b/86b))

1997 (5 June). *World Environment Day. Waterbirds. T* **359** *and similar vert designs. Multicoloured.* P 14.

977 (1r.) Type **359** 40 40
 a. Sheetlet. Nos. 977/86 3·50
 b. Perf 14×15 (8 Dec) 40 40
 ba. Booklet pane. Nos. 977b/86b 3·50
978 (1r.) Hamerkop 40 40
 b. Perf 14×15 (8 Dec) 40 40
979 (1r.) Pied Kingfisher 40 40
 b. Perf 14×15 (8 Dec) 40 40
980 (1r.) Purple Heron 40 40
 b. Perf 14×15 (8 Dec) 40 40
981 (1r.) Black-headed Heron 40 40
 b. Perf 14×15 (8 Dec) 40 40
982 (1r.) Darter 40 40
 b. Perf 14×15 (8 Dec) 40 40
983 (1r.) Green-backed Heron 40 40
 b. Perf 14×15 (8 Dec) 40 40
984 (1r.) White-faced Duck 40 40
 b. Perf 14×15 (8 Dec) 40 40
985 (1r.) Saddle-billed Stork 40 40
 b. Perf 14×15 (8 Dec) 40 40
986 (1r.) Water Dikkop 40 40
 b. Perf 14×15 (8 Dec) 40 40
977/86 *Set of 10* 3·50 3·50

Nos. 977/86, are inscribed "STANDARD POSTAGE" and were printed together, *se-tenant*, in sheetlets of 10, with illustrated margin at left.

The stamps printed by Questa (Nos. 977b/86b) are in different shades and were only issued in 20r. stamp booklets.

No. 984 exists as a corporate miniature sheet sponsored by the "Junass" exhibition in aid of junior philately.

360 Double-headed Class 6E 1 Electric Locomotives

(Des A. Ainslie. Litho Govt Printer, Pretoria (Nos. 987/91) or Questa (Nos. 987b/91b))

1997 (1 Aug)–**98**. *Inauguration of Revived Blue Train Service. T* **360** *and similar horiz designs. Multicoloured.* P 14 (with four elliptical holes on each horizontal side).

987 (1r.20) Type **360** 70 70
 a. Vert strip of 5. Nos. 987/91 3·25 3·25
 b. Perf 15×14. One side phosphor band (11.98) 70 70
 ba. Booklet pane. Nos. 987b/91b, each×2 6·50
988 (1r.20) Double-headed Class 6E 1 electric locomotives (different) 70 70
 b. Perf 15×14. One side phosphor band (11.98) 70 70
989 (1r.20) Double-headed Class 25NC steam locomotives 70 70
 b. Perf 15×14. One side phosphor band (11.98) 70 70
990 (1r.20) Double-headed Class 34,900 diesel locomotives on Modder River bridge 70 70
 b. Perf 15×14. One side phosphor band (11.98) 70 70
991 (1r.20) Double-headed Class 34 diesel locomotives and Baobab tree 70 70
 b. Perf 15×14. One side phosphor band (11.98) 70 70
987/91 *Set of 5* 3·25 3·25

Nos. 987/91, which are inscribed "AIRMAIL POSTCARD RATE" were printed together, *se-tenant*, in vertical strips of 5 throughout the sheets of 10. The rate for Airmail postcards increased to 1r.30 on 14 April 1998.

Nos. 987b/91b were only available from 13r. stamp booklets with the pane folded vertically down the centre. There are no elliptical holes in the perforations of these booklet stamps. No. 989b is inscr "HUTCHINSON" instead of "HUCHINSON" (989) and No. 991b is inscr "NORTHERN PROVINCE" instead of "NORTHERN TRANSVAAL" (991).

Nos. 987 and 989 exist in separate corporate miniature sheets sponsored by Harmers of London (No. 987) or Eastgate Universal Stamps and Coins Ltd (No. 989).

361 Nguni Breed

362 Leopard Seal

(Des D. Murphy. Litho)

1997 (10 Aug). *Cattle Breeds. T* **361** *and similar horiz designs. Multicoloured.* P 14½ (with two elliptical holes on each horizontal side).

992 (1r.) Type **361** 50 50
 a. Block of 4. Nos. 992/5 1·75 1·75
993 (1r.) Bonsmara 50 50
994 (1r.) Afrikander 50 50
995 (1r.) Drakensberger 50 50
992/5 *Set of 4* 1·75 1·75

Nos. 992/5 which are inscribed "Standard Postage" in English and Afrikaans, were printed together, *se-tenant*, in blocks of four throughout the sheet.

(Des D. Murphy. Litho)

1997 (27 Aug). *Antarctic Fauna. T* **362** *and similar horiz designs. Multicoloured.* P 14.

996 (1r.) Type **362** 35 25
997 1r.20 Antarctic Skua 65 40
998 1r.70 King Penguin 1·00 70
996/8 *Set of 3* 1·75 1·25

No. 996 is inscribed "Standard Postage" in English and Afrikaans.

The Standard Postage rate increased to 1r.10 on 14 April 1998.

363 Enoch Sontonga and Verse from Nkosi Sikelel'i Afrika

(Des Thea Swanepoel and A. Ainslie. Litho)

1997 (24 Sept). *Heritage Day. Centenary of Nkosi Sikelel'i Afrika (National Anthem). T* **363** *and similar horiz design. Multicoloured.* P 14 (with two elliptical holes on each vertical side).

999 (1r.) Type **363** 50 50
 a. Horiz pair. Nos. 999/1000 1·00 1·00
1000 (1r.) As Type **363** but portrait at right 50 50

Nos. 999/1000, which are inscribed "Standard Postage", were printed together, *se-tenant*, in horizontal pairs throughout the sheet.

364 Horse-drawn Postcart delivering Mail

365 Modern Postbox

(Des D. Bagnall. Litho)

1997 (8 Oct). *"Cape Town '97" National Stamp Show. Sheet 85×64 mm.* P 14½×14.

MS1001 **364** 4r.51 multicoloured 1·50 1·50

(Des Thea Swanepoel. Litho)

1997 (9 Oct). *World Post Day. Sheet, 108×69 mm.* P 14 (with two elliptical hole on each vertical side).

MS1002 **365** (1r.) multicoloured 70 70

No. **MS**1002 is inscribed "STANDARD POSTAGE".

366 Bethlehem

367 Black Rhinoceros

1997 (3 Nov). *Christmas. 50th Anniv of S.A.N.T.A. (South African National Tuberculosis Association). T* **366** *and similar vert designs showing charity labels. Multicoloured. Litho.* P 14 (with two elliptical holes on each vertical side).

1003 (1r.) Type **366** 35 35
 a. Sheetlet. Nos. 1003/12 3·25
1004 (1r.) Cross of Lorraine and candles 35 35
1005 (1r.) Cross of Lorraine, angels and candles 35 35
1006 (1r.) Angel kneeling before Cross of Lorraine 35 35
1007 (1r.) Father Christmas carrying sack 35 35
1008 (1r.) Mary and Jesus 35 35
1009 (1r.) Christmas trees 35 35
1010 (1r.) Wise men on camels 35 35
1011 (1r.) Christmas bell 35 35
1012 (1r.) Child kneeling 35 35
1003/12 *Set of 10* 3·25 3·25

Nos. 1003/12 which are inscribed "STANDARD POSTAGE", were printed together, *se-tenant*, in sheetlets of 10, with illustrated left-hand margin.

(Des D. Murphy. Litho Cape & Transvaal Printers (No. 1029), Questa (1030p/4p, 1045/9) or Government Printer (others))

1997 (12 Dec)–**2000**. *Endangered Fauna. (3rd series). Redrawn values as 1993–97 issue and new designs (Nos. 1030/4), all without frame or imprint and inscr "South Africa" only as in T* **367**. *Multicoloured.*

(a) Designs as Nos. 806/20, and some new values, redrawn.

(i) P 14½ (10r.), P. 14 (others).

1012*a* 5c. Giant Girdle-tailed Lizard (5.6.00) 10 20
1013 10c. Geometric Tortoise (5.2.98) 10 20
1014 20c. Southern African Hedgehog (19.3.98) 10 20
1015 30c. Spotted Hyena (13.3.98) 10 20
1016 40c. Riverine Rabbit (8.1.98) 15 20
1017 50c. Samango Monkey (23.3.98) 15 10
1018 60c. Cape Hunting Dog (29.8.98) 20 15
1019 70c. Roan Antelope (18.12.97) 20 20
1020 80c. Kori Bustard (16.3.98) 1·25 20
1021 90c. Jackass Penguin (19.12.97) 1·40 25
1022 1r. Wattled Crane (12.12.97) 1·25 25
1022*a* 1r.50 Tawny Eagle (20×37 mm) (5.6.00) 1·75 30
1023 2r. Blue Swallow (9.1.99) 1·50 45
1023*a* 2r.30 Cape Vulture (20×37 mm) (5.6.00) 2·00 45
1024 3r. Giraffe (24.3.98) 2·00 65
1025 5r. Martial Eagle (17.3.98) 2·25 1·10
1026 10r. Bateleur (34×24 mm) (28.8.98) 2·75 2·25

(ii) P 14 (2r.) or 14½ (20r.), both with two elliptical holes on each horizontal side

1027 2r. Blue Swallow (18.3.98) 55 45
1028 20r. Fish Eagle (34×24 mm) (26.8.98) 4·75 4·25
1012a/28 *Set of 18* 20·00 11·00

(b) Inscr "Standard Postage" (No. 1029) or "standard postage" (others).

(i) P 14

1029 (1r.) Black Rhinoceros (12.2.98) 30 25
 a. Booklet pane. No. 1029×10 with outer edges of pane imperf 2·75
1030 (1r.10) Eland (*vert*) (18.5.98) 30 25
 a. Strip of 5. Nos. 1030/4 1·40 1·10
 p. With phosphor band (2.11.98) 20 25
 pa. Booklet pane. Nos. 1030p/4p, each ×2, with vertical edges of pane imperf 2·00
1031 (1r.10) Greater Kudu (*vert*) (18.5.98) 30 25
 p. With phosphor band (2.11.98) 20 25
1032 (1r.10) Impala (*vert*) (18.5.98) 30 25
 p. With phosphor band (2.11.98) 20 25
1033 (1r.10) Waterbuck (*vert*) (18.5.98) 30 25
 p. With phosphor band (2.11.98) 20 25
1034 (1r.10) Blue Wildebeest (*vert*) (18.5.98) 30 25
 p. With phosphor band (2.11.98) 20 25

(ii). P 14 (with two elliptical holes on each vertical side).

1035 (1r.10) Eland (*vert*) (18.5.98) 25 25

a. Booklet pane. Nos. 1035/9, each ×2 with outer edges of pane imperforate .... 2·25
1036 (1r.10) Greater Kudu (*vert*) (18.5.98) 25 25
1037 (1r.10) Impala (*vert*) (18.5.98) 25 25
1038 (1r.10) Waterbuck (*vert*) (18.5.98) 25 25
1039 (1r.10) Blue Wildebeest (*vert*) (18.5.98) 25 25

(c) Inscr "Airmail Postcard".

(i) P 14 (with two elliptical holes at top or bottom) (11.2.98).
1040 (1r.20) White Rhinoceros 50 55
a. Booklet pane. Nos. 1040/4, each ×2, with outer edges of pane imperf .... 4·50
1041 (1r.20) Buffalo 50 55
1042 (1r.20) Lion 50 55
1043 (1r.20) Leopard 50 55
1044 (1r.20) African Elephant 50 55
1040/4 *Set of 5* .... 2·25 2·50

(ii) P 14. With "L" shaped phosphor band (10.98).
1045 (1r.20) White Rhinoceros 30 35
a. Booklet pane. Nos. 1045/9, each ×2, with horiz edges of pane imperf .... 2·50
1046 (1r.20) Buffalo 30 35
1047 (1r.20) Lion 30 35
1048 (1r.20) Leopard 30 35
1049 (1r.20) African Elephant 30 35
1045/9 *Set of 5* .... 1·25 1·50

Nos. 1029, 1030p/4p and 1040/9 were only issued in booklets.

On pane No. 1040a the elliptical holes only occur on the horizontal line of perforations separating the two strips.

Nos. 1035/9 were printed together, *se-tenant* both horizontally and vertically, as strips of 5 in sheets of 100.

The Questa printings (Nos. 1030p/4p and 1045/9) are redrawn with the inscriptions smaller.

No. 1030p/4p can be easily identified by the 3 mm (instead of 1½ mm) gap between "South Africa" and "standard postage".

On Nos. 1045/9 the gap between "South Africa" and "Airmail Postcard" is 5 mm instead of 4 mm (Nos. 1040/4). Both Questa printings show the phosphor as an "L" shaped band.

For self-adhesive versions of Nos. 1030/4 see Nos. 1075/9.

The Standard Postage and Airmail Postcard rates increased to 1r.10 and 1r.30 on 14 April 1998, to 1r.20 and 1r.70 on 1 April 1999, and to 1r.30 and 1r.90 on 1 April 2000.

368 Tiger (woodcut)

369 *Rescue 8* (lifeboat)

(Des Thea Swanepoel. Litho Questa)

1998 (28 Jan). *Chinese New Year ("Year of the Tiger"). Sheet 67×85 mm.* P 14×14½.
MS1051 **368** 5r. vermilion, black and deep green. 1·50 1·50

(Des D. Bagnall. Litho)

1998 (11 Feb). *30th Anniv of National Sea Rescue Institute (1997).* P 14 (with two elliptical holes on each horizontal side).
1052 **369** (1r.) multicoloured 65 30

370 Leopard

371 Football Player

(Des J. Swanepoel. Litho)

1998 (1 May). *"SAPDA '98" National Stamp Exhibition, Johannesburg. Sheet 64×84 mm.* P 14×14½.
MS1053 **370** 5r. multicoloured .... 1·50 1·50

(Des M. de Jong. Litho)

1998 (8 June). *World Cup Football Championship, France.* P 14.
1054 **371** (1r.10) multicoloured 60 30

No. 1054 is inscribed "STANDARD POSTAGE".

372 Stone Age Hand Axe

373 Pale Chanting Goshawk

(Des Sue Wickison. Litho Questa)

1998 (28 June). *Early South African History. T* **372** *and similar vert designs. Multicoloured. Ordinary paper. Two phosphor bands.* P 14×15.
1055 (1r.10) Type **372** 45 40
a. Sheetlet. Nos. 1055/64 .... 4·00
b. Booklet pane. Nos. 1055/64 .... 4·00
1056 (1r.10) Musuku (altar) 45 40
1057 (1r.10) San rock engravings 45 40
1058 (1r.10) Early Iron Age pot 45 40
1059 (1r.10) Khoekhoe pot 45 40
1060 (1r.10) Florisbad skull 45 40
1061 (1r.10) San rock painting 45 40
1062 (1r.10) Mapungubwe gold rhinoceros and pot 45 40
1063 (1r.10) Lydenburg Head (ceremonial mask) 45 40
1064 (1r.10) Taung skull 45 40
1055/64 *Set of 10* .... 4·00 3·50

Nos. 1055/64, which are inscribed "standard postage", were printed together, *se-tenant*, in sheetlets of 10 with illustrated left-hand margin and the top, bottom and right-hand margins perforated through.

No. 1055b has these three margins imperforate.

(Des C. van Rooyen. Litho Questa)

1998 (16 Aug). *South African Raptors. T* **373** *and similar vert designs. Multicoloured. Ordinary paper. Two phosphor bands.* P 14×15.
1065 (1r.10) Type **373** 50 50
a. Sheetlet. Nos. 1065/74 .... 4·50
b. Booklet pane. Nos. 1065/74 .... 4·50
1066 (1r.10) Augur Buzzard ("Jackal Buzzard") 50 50
1067 (1r.10) Lanner Falcon 50 50
1068 (1r.10) Lammergeier ("Bearded Vulture") 50 50
1069 (1r.10) Black Harrier 50 50
1070 (1r.10) Cape Vulture 50 50
1071 (1r.10) Bateleur 50 50
1072 (1r.10) Spotted Eagle Owl 50 50
1073 (1r.10) White-headed Vulture 50 50
1074 (1r.10) African Fish Eagle 50 50
1065/74 *Set of 10* .... 4·50 4·50

Nos. 1065/74, which are inscribed "standard postage" were printed together, *se-tenant*, in sheetlets of 10 with an illustrated left-hand margin and the top, bottom and right-hand margins perforated through.

No. 1065b has these three margins imperforate.

(Litho Pemara (Nos. 1075/9) or SNP Cambec (Nos. 1075a/9a, 1075b/9b))

1998 (18 Aug)–**99**. *Endangered Fauna. Antelopes. Designs as Nos. 1030/4 but self-adhesive. Phosphor frame.* P 13×12½.
1075 (1r.10) Eland (*vert*) 50 50
a. Phosphor frame at left and foot 50 50
ab. Booklet pane. Nos. 1075a/9a, each ×2 .... 4·00
b. Perf 11 (phosphor frame at left and foot) (12.99) 50 50
ba. Booklet pane. Nos. 1075b/9b, each ×2 .... 4·00
1076 (1r.10) Greater Kudu (*vert*) 50 50
a. Phosphor frame at left and foot 50 50
b. Perf 11 (phosphor frame at left and foot) (12.99) 50 50
1077 (1r.10) Impala (*vert*) 50 50
a. Phosphor frame at left and foot 50 50
b. Perf 11 (phosphor frame at left and foot) (12.99) 50 50
1078 (1r.10) Waterbuck (*vert*) 50 50
a. Phosphor frame at left and foot 50 50
b. Perf 11 (phosphor frame at left and foot) (12.99) 50 50
1079 (1r.10) Blue Wildebeest (*vert*) 50 50
a. Phosphor frame at left and foot 50 50
b. Perf 11 (phosphor frame at left and foot) (12.99) 50 50
1075/9 *Set of 5* .... 2·25 2·25
1075a/9a *Set of 5* .... 2·25 2·25
1075b/9b *Set of 5* .... 2·25 2·25

The above are inscribed "standard postage" and were printed in rolls of 100 (Nos. 1075/9) with the surplus self-adhesive paper around each stamp removed or in booklets of 10 (Nos. 1075a/9a and 1075b/9b) with the surplus paper retained. The phosphor shows yellow under U.V. light. It forms a regular frame on Nos. 1075/9, but on Nos. 1075a/9a and 1075b/9b it is present at the left, following the outline of the antelope, and bottom only.

374 Shepherd's Tree

(Des Joan van Gogh. Litho Questa)

1998 (4 Sept). *Trees. T* **374** *and similar horiz designs. Multicoloured. Ordinary paper. One side phosphor band.* P 13½×14.
1080 (1r.10) Type **374** 70 70
a. Block of 4. Nos. 1080/3 .... 2·50 2·50
1081 (1r.10) Karee 70 70
1082 (1r.10) Baobab 70 70
1083 (1r.10) Umbrella Thorn 70 70
1080/3 *Set of 4* .... 2·50 2·50

Nos. 1080/3 are inscribed "Standard Postage" and were printed together, *se-tenant*, in sheets of 10, proving two blocks of 4 and a horizontal pair of Nos. 1080/1.

375 Sandstone Cliffs, Cape Point

376 Angel

(Des A. Ainslie. Litho Questa)

1998 (28 Sept). *"Explore South Africa" (1st series). T* **375** *and similar horiz designs. Multicoloured. Ordinary paper. Two horiz phosphor bands.* P 15×14.

(a) Western Cape.

1084 (1r.30) Type **375** 90 70
a. Booklet pane. Nos. 1084/8×2 .... 8·00
1085 (1r.30) Robben Island 90 70
1086 (1r.30) Ostrich farming, Pinehurst Homestead 90 70
1087 (1r.30) Victoria and Alfred Waterfront, Capetown 90 70
1088 (1r.30) Homestead, Boschendal Wine Estate 90 70

Nos. 1084/8 and 1089/93, which are inscribed "AIRMAIL POSTCARD", were only available from separate 13r. stamp booklets, with the panes showing an illustrated margin at top, a small blank margin at foot and the vertical sides imperforate.

See also Nos. 1138/42.

(b) KwaZulu-Natal

1089 (1r.30) Drakensberg waterfall 90 70
a. Booklet pane. Nos. 1089/93 ×2 .... 8·00
1090 (1r.30) Zulu women preparing food 90 70
1091 (1r.30) Pelicans and rhinoceros 90 70
1092 (1r.30) Rickshaw driver 90 70
1093 (1r.30) Indian dancers 90 70
1084/93 *Set of 10* .... 8·00 6·25

(Des Annamart Dednam. Litho Questa)

1998 (9 Oct). *Christmas. T* **376** *and similar vert designs. Multicoloured. Ordinary paper. One side phosphor band.* P 14×15.
1094 (1r.10) Type **376** 60 60
a. Horiz strip of 5. Nos. 1094/8 .... 2·75 2·75
1095 (1r.10) Christmas bell 60 60
1096 (1r.10) Present 60 60
1097 (1r.10) Christmas tree 60 60
1098 (1r.10) Star 60 60
1094/8 *Set of 5* .... 2·75 2·75

Nos. 1094/8 are inscribed "STANDARD POSTAGE" and were printed together, *se-tenant*, as horizontal strips of 5, in sheets of 10.

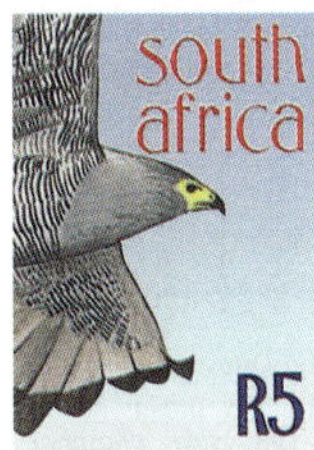

377 African Harrier Hawk

378 London Pictorial Essay, 1927

(Des C. van Rooyen. Litho Questa)

1998 (9 Oct). *World Post Day. Sheet 67×85 mm. Ordinary paper.* P 14×14½.
MS1099 **377** 5r. multicoloured .... 1·50 1·50

(Des Thea Swanepoel. Litho Questa)

1998 (20 Oct). *"ILSAPEX '98" International Stamp Exhibition, Johannesburg. Sheet, 108×80 mm, containing T* **378** *and similar vert design. Ordinary paper.* P 14½.
MS1100 5r. deep green, scarlet and cream (Type 378); 5r. black, deep green and cream (as Type **378**, but "SOUTH AFRICA" at top) .... 2·25 2·50

379 Cuvier's Beaked Whale

380 Emblem and Buildings

(Des C. Grant (Nos. 1101/4), M. Butterfield (No. **MS**1105). Litho Questa)

1998 (23 Oct). *Endangered Species. Whales of the Southern Ocean. T* **379** *and similar horiz designs. Multicoloured. Ordinary paper. One side phosphor band.* P 15×14.
1101 (1r.30) Type **379** 90 75
a. Block of 4. Nos. 1101/4 .... 3·50 2·75
1102 (1r.30) Minke Whale 90 75
1103 (1r.30) Bryde's Whale 90 75
1104 (1r.30) Pygmy Right Whale 90 75
1101/4 *Set of 4* .... 3·50 2·75
MS1105 103×68 mm. 5r. Blue Whale. No phosphor band. P 14 .... 1·75 1·75

Nos. 1101/4 are inscribed "airmail postcard" and were printed together, *se-tenant*, in sheets of 10 providing two blocks of 4 and a horizontal pair of Nos. 1101/2.

Nos. 1101/4 were also issued on 18 August 1999 in a premium booklet, No. SP1, sold at 40r.

No. **MS**1105 forms part of joint issue with Namibia and Norfolk Island.

A corporate miniature sheet, sponsored by Clover SA for their centenary, showing an ice-cream van was issued on 15 November 1998.

(Des F. Frescura. Litho Questa)

1998 (9 Dec). *50th Anniv of Universal Declaration of Human Rights. Ordinary paper. One side phosphor band.* P 14½.
1106 **380** (1r.10) multicoloured 75 35

No. 1106 is inscribed "Standard Postage".

381 Dennis Mail Van, 1913

(Des D. Bagnall. Litho Questa)

1999 (15 Feb). *125th Anniv of Universal Postal Union. T* **381** *and similar horiz designs. Multicoloured. Ordinary paper. U P U emblem and one side band in phosphor.* P 13½×14.

1107 (1r.10) Type **381** ... 70 60
a. Block of 4. Nos. 1107/10 ... 2·50 2·20
1108 (1r.10) Ford V8 post van, 1935 ... 70 60
1109 (1r.10) Mobile Post Office, 1937 ... 70 60
1110 (1r.10) Trojan Post Office van, 1927 ... 70 60
1107/10 *Set of 4* ... 2·50 2·20

Nos. 1107/10 are inscribed "Standard Postage", and were printed *se-tenant* in sheets of 10, providing two blocks of 4 and a horizontal pair of Nos. 1107/8.

382 Rabbit

(Des D. Murphy. Litho Questa)

1999 (16 Feb). *Chinese New Year ("Year of the Rabbit"). Sheet 85×67 mm. Ordinary paper.* P 14×13½.

MS1111 **382** 5r. multicoloured ... 1·50 1·50

383 Discovery (Scott)

(Des D. Bagnall. Litho Questa)

1999 (19 Mar). *Famous Ships. T* **383** *and similar horiz designs. Multicoloured. Ordinary paper. One side phosphor band.* P 13½×14.

1112 (1r.10) Type **383** ... 75 60
a. Block of 4. Nos. 1112/15 ... 2·50 2·20
1113 (1r.10) Heemskerk (Tasman) ... 75 60
1114 (1r.10) H.M.S. Endeavour (Cook) ... 75 60
1115 (1r.10) H.M.S. Beagle (Darwin) ... 75 60
1112/15 *Set of 4* ... 2·50 2·20

Nos. 1112/15 are inscribed "standard postage", and were printed *se-tenant* in sheets of 10, providing two blocks of 4 and a horizontal pair of Nos. 1112/13.

384 Lawhill (barque)

385 Traditional Nguni Love Token with AIDS Ribbon

(Des D. Bagnall. Litho Questa)

1999 (19 Mar). *"Australia '99" International Stamp Exhibition, Melbourne. Sheet 65×85 mm. Ordinary paper.* P 13½×14.

MS1116 **384** 5r. multicoloured ... 1·50 1·50

(Des Thea Swanepoel. Litho Questa)

1999 (1 Apr). *AIDS Awareness Campaign. One side phosphor band.* P 14½×14.

1117 **385** (1r.20) multicoloured (bluish violet background) ... 65 50
a. Booklet pane. Nos. 1117/18, each ×5 ... 6·00
1118 (1r.20) multicoloured (emerald background) ... 65 50

Nos. 1117/18 are inscribed "Standard Postage" and were printed *se-tenant* in 12r. stamp booklets containing No. 1117a which has the horizontal edges of the pane imperforate.

386 African Elephant

387 Class 19D Steam Locomotive, South African Railways

(Des C. van Rooyen. Litho)

1999 (27 Apr). *"iBRA '99" International Stamp Exhibition, Nuremburg. Sheet 100×68 mm. Ordinary paper.* P 14.

MS1119 **386** 5r. multicoloured ... 2·25 1·50

(Des H. Botha. Litho Questa)

1999 (30 Apr). *"SAPDA '99" Stamp Show, Johannesburg. Sheet 100×75 mm. Ordinary paper.* P 13½×14.

MS1120 **387** 5r. multicoloured ... 2·25 1·50

388 Nurse

389 President Thabo Mbeki

(Des Chenette Swart. Litho Questa)

1999 (1 May). *Workers' Day. T* **388** *and similar vert designs. One side phosphor band. Multicoloured.* P 14×15.

1121 (1r.20) Type **388** ... 60 50
a. Sheetlet. Nos. 1121/30 ... 5·50
1122 (1r.20) Cleaner with mop ... 60 50
1123 (1r.20) Forester with axe ... 60 50
1124 (1r.20) Farmer with spade ... 60 50
1125 (1r.20) Chef with sieve ... 60 50
1126 (1r.20) Fisherman with net ... 60 50
1127 (1r.20) Construction worker with scaffolding ... 60 50
1128 (1r.20) Miner with pick ... 60 50
1129 (1r.20) Postman with mail ... 60 50
1130 (1r.20) Road worker with pneumatic drill ... 60 50
1121/30 *Set of 10* ... 5·50 4·50

Nos. 1121/30 are inscribed "standard postage", and were printed together, *se-tenant*, in sheetlets of 10.

(Des Thea Swanepoel. Litho)

1999 (16 June). *Inauguration of President Thabo Mbeki.* P 14.

1131 **389** (1r.20) multicoloured ... 1·00 45

No. 1131 is inscribed "standard postage".

390 Nelson Mandela in Mantle of Order

391 Actress with Drama Masks

(Des Sue Dickinson. Litho Questa)

1999 (23 June). *900th Anniv of Order of St. John of Jerusalem. Sheet 108×68 mm. Ordinary paper.* P 14×14½.

MS1132 **390** 2r. multicoloured ... 1·25 1·00

(Des Thea Swanepoel. Litho)

1999 (29 June). *25th Anniv of Standard Bank National Arts Festival, Grahamstown. T* **391** *and similar vert designs. Multicoloured.* P 14.

1133 (1r.20) Type **391** ... 70 70
a. Horiz strip of 5. Nos. 1133/7 ... 3·25 3·25
1134 (1r.20) Woman with roll of film ... 70 70
1135 (1r.20) Woman playing guitar ... 70 70
1136 (1r.20) Woman dancing ... 70 70
1137 (1r.20) Painter ... 70 70
1133/7 *Set of 5* ... 3·25 3·25

Nos. 1133/7 are inscribed "STANDARD POSTAGE" and were printed together, *se-tenant*, as horizontal strips of 5 in sheets of 10.

(Des A. Ainslie. Litho Questa)

1999 (6 Aug). *"Explore South Africa" (2nd series). Mpumalanga and Northern Province. Horiz designs as T* **375**. *Multicoloured. One side phosphor band.* P 15×14.

1138 (1r.70) Blyde River Canyon ... 90 60
a. Booklet pane. Nos. 1138/42, each ×2 ... 8·00
1139 (1r.70) Lone Creek Falls, Sabie ... 90 60
1140 (1r.70) Ndebele women in traditional dress ... 90 60
1141 (1r.70) Pilgrim's Rest (historic town) ... 90 60
1142 (1r.70) Elephants, Kruger National Park ... 90 60
1138/42 *Set of 5* ... 4·00 2·75

Nos. 1138/42 are inscribed "AIRMAIL POSTCARD" and were only available from 17r. stamp booklets with the pane showing an illustrated margin at top, a small blank margin at foot and the vertical sides imperforate.

392 North Ndebele Wall Pattern

393 South African Rock Art Painting

(Des A. Ainslie. Litho Enschedé)

1999 (8 Aug). *Traditional Wall Art. T* **392** *and similar square designs showing sections of wall art. Multicoloured. One side phosphor band.* P 13½×14.

1143 (1r.20) Type **392** ... 60 50
a. Sheetlet. Nos. 1143/52 ... 5·50
1144 (1r.20) South Ndebele ... 60 50
1145 (1r.20) Swazi ... 60 50
1146 (1r.20) Venda ... 60 50
1147 (1r.20) South Sotho ... 60 50
1148 (1r.20) Xhosa ... 60 50
1149 (1r.20) North Sotho ... 60 50
1150 (1r.20) Tsonga ... 60 50
1151 (1r.20) Zulu ... 60 50
1152 (1r.20) Tswana ... 60 50
1143/52 *Set of 10* ... 5·50 4·50

Nos. 1143/52 are inscribed "STANDARD POSTAGE" and were printed together, *se-tenant*, in sheetlets of 10.

(Des A. Ainslie. Litho Enschedé)

1999 (21 Aug). *China '99 International Stamp Exhibition, Beijing. Sheet 154×85 mm.* P 14×13½.

MS1153 **393** 5r. multicoloured ... 1·75 1·75

394 *Strelitzia reginae* (flower) **395** Barn Swallow

(Des C. van Rooyen. Litho)

1999 (9 Sept). *"JOPEX '99" National Stamp Exhibition, Johannesburg. Sheet 65×85 mm. Ordinary paper.* P 14½.

MS1154 **394** 5r. multicoloured ... 1·75 1·75

(Des C. van Rooyen. Litho Enschedé)

1999 (4 Oct). *Migratory Species of South Africa. T* **395** *and similar vert designs. Multicoloured. One side phosphor band.* P 14×15.

1155 (1r.20) Type **395** ... 65 60
a. Sheetlet. Nos. 1155/64 ... 5·75
1156 (1r.20) Great White Shark ... 65 60
1157 (1r.20) Lesser Kestrel ... 65 60
1158 (1r.20) Common Dolphin ... 65 60
1159 (1r.20) European Bee-eater ... 65 60
1160 (1r.20) Loggerhead Turtle ... 65 60
1161 (1r.20) Curlew Sandpiper ... 65 60
1162 (1r.20) Wandering Albatross ... 65 60
1163 (1r.20) Springbok ... 65 60
1164 (1r.20) Lesser Flamingo ... 65 60
1155/64 *Set of 10* ... 5·75 5·50

Nos. 1155/64 are inscribed "Standard Postage" and were printed together, *se-tenant*, in sheetlets of 10 with an enlarged illustrated left margin.

Nos. 1155/64 were also issued in a premium booklet, No. SP2, sold at 29r.

396 Boers leaving for Commando

(Des H. Botha. Litho Questa)

1999 (11 Oct). *Centenary of Anglo-Boer War (1st issue). T* **396** *and similar horiz design. Multicoloured. One phosphor band.* P 13½×14.

1165 (1r.20) Type **396** ... 90 75
a. Horiz pair. Nos. 1165/6 ... 1·75 1·50
1166 (1r.20) British soldiers ... 90 75

Nos. 1165/6 were printed together, *se-tenant*, as horizontal pairs in sheets of 10.

Nos. 1165/6, 1203/4, 1343/4 and **MS**1384 were also issued on 1 May 2002 in a premium booklet, No SP4, sold at 45r.

See also Nos. 1203/4, 1343/4 and **MS**1384.

397 Landscape

(Des Thea Swanepoel. Litho Enschedé)

2000 (1 Jan). *New Millennium.* P 13½×14.

1167 **397** (1r.20) multicoloured ... 70 40

No. 1167 is inscribed "Standard Postage".

398 National Lottery Logo

399 Family inside Heart

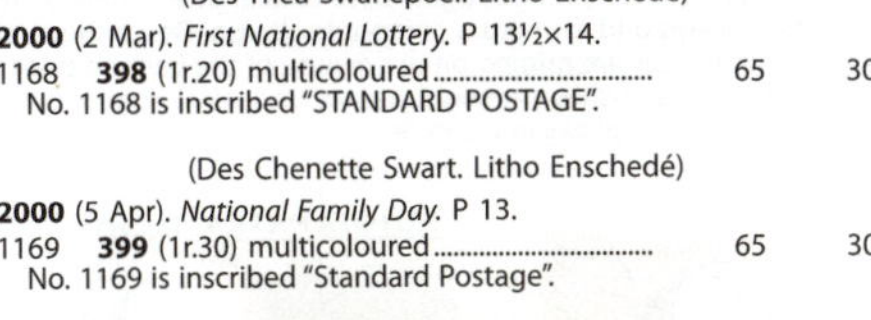

(Des Thea Swanepoel. Litho Enschedé)

2000 (2 Mar). *First National Lottery*. P 13½×14.
1168 **398** (1r.20) multicoloured 65 30
No. 1168 is inscribed "STANDARD POSTAGE".

(Des Chenette Swart. Litho Enschedé)

2000 (5 Apr). *National Family Day*. P 13.
1169 **399** (1r.30) multicoloured 65 30
No. 1169 is inscribed "Standard Postage".

400 Knysna Turaco ("Lourie")

(Des C. van Rooyen. Litho Enschedé)

2000 (22 May). *"The Stamp Show 2000" International Stamp Exhibition, London. Sheet 108×68 mm*. P 13½.
MS1170 **400** 4r.61 multicoloured .... 2·00 1·75

401 Banded Stream Frog

(Des C. van Rooyen. Litho Enschedé)

2000 (23 June). *Frogs of South Africa*. T **401** *and similar horiz designs. Multicoloured*. P 13½×14.
1171 1r.30 Type **401** 60 60
a. Sheetlet. Nos. 1171/80 .... 5·50
1172 1r.30 Yellow-striped Reed Frog 60 60
1173 1r.30 Natal Leaf-folding Frog 60 60
1174 1r.30 Paradise Toad 60 60
1175 1r.30 Table Mountain Ghost Frog 60 60
1176 1r.30 Banded Rubber Frog 60 60
1177 1r.30 Dwarf Grass Frog 60 60
1178 1r.30 Long-toed Tree Frog 60 60
1179 1r.30 Namaqua Rain Frog 60 60
1180 1r.30 Bubbling Kassina 60 60
1171/80 *Set of 10* .... 5·50 5·50
Nos. 1171/80 were printed together, *se-tenant*, in sheetlets of 10.

402 Forest Tree Frog **403** Stalked Bulbine

(Des C. van Rooyen. Litho Enschedé)

2000 (23 June). *"JUNASS 2000" National Junior Stamp Show, Boksburg. Sheet 108×68 mm*. P 13½.
MS1181 **402** 4r.60 multicoloured .... 1·75 1·75

(Des Joan van Gogh. Litho Enschedé)

2000 (1 Aug). *Medicinal Plants*. T **403** *and similar vert designs. Multicoloured*. P 14×13½.
1182 1r.30 Type **403** 45 45
a. Horiz strip of 5. Nos. 1182/6 .... 2·25 2·25
1183 1r.30 Wild Dagga 45 45
1184 1r.30 Wild Garlic 45 45
1185 1r.30 Pig's Ear 45 45
1186 1r.30 Wild Ginger 45 45
1187 2r.30 Red Paintbrush 60 60
a. Horiz strip of 5. Nos. 1187/91 .... 2·75 2·75
1188 2r.30 Cancer Bush 60 60
1189 2r.30 Yellow Star 60 60
1190 2r.30 Bitter Aloe 60 60
1191 2r.30 Sour Fig 60 60
1182/91 *Set of 10* .... 4·75 4·75
Nos. 1182/6 and 1187/91 were each printed together, *se-tenant*, as horizontal strips of 5 in sheets of 10.

404 Athlete with South African Flag **405** Globe and Peace Doves

(Des Chenette Swart. Litho Enschedé)

2000 (1 Sept). *Olympic Games, Sydney*. T **404** *and similar vert designs. Multicoloured*. P 13½×14.
1192 1r.30 Type **404** 50 25
1193 1r.51 Elana Meyer (medal winner, 1992) 50 35
1194 2r.20 Joshua Thugwane (medal winner, 1996) 70 60
1195 2r.30 Olympic Rings and South African flag 85 65
1196 6r.30 Penny Heyns (medal winner, 1996) .... 1·75 2·25
1192/6 *Set of 5* .... 3·75 3·50

(Des Alet Swarts. Litho Enschedé)

2000 (19 Sept). *United Nations International Year of Peace*. P 13.
1197 **405** 1r.30 multicoloured 65 30

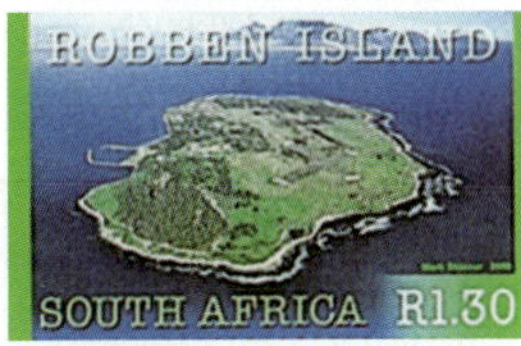

406 Robben Island

(Des Thea Swanepoel. Litho Enschedé)

2000 (22 Sept). *UNESCO World Heritage Sites*. T **406** *and similar horiz designs. Multicoloured*. P 13½×14.
1198 1r.30 Type **406** 55 35
1199 1r.30 Greater St. Lucia Wetland Park 55 35
1200 1r.30 Early skull from Sterkfontein 55 35
1198/1200 *Set of 3* .... 1·50 85

407 Dragon **408** Heart and Envelope

(Des M. Maas. Litho Enschedé)

2000 (9 Oct). *Chinese New Year ("Year of the Dragon"). Sheet 85×65 mm*. P 13.
MS1201 multicoloured .... 1·50 1·50

(Des M. Maas. Litho Enschedé)

2000 (9 Oct)–**01**. *World Post Day*. P 13.
1202 **408** 1r.30 multicoloured 70 40
a. Perf 13½×13 (22.1.01) 70 40
No. 1202 was originally printed in sheets of 10 (2×5). On 8 November 2000 it was re-issued as a sheet of 20 (4×5) with each stamp accompanied by a *se-tenant* half-size label depicting one of the cast from the Gladiators television series.
Stamps from this sheet are perforated 13½×13 (No. 1202a).
The sheets of 20 were originally sold at 35r. and stamps from them were not available at face value until 22 January 2001.

409 Sol Plaatje and Johanna Brandt

(Des H. Botha. Litho Enschedé) Centenary of Anglo-Boer War (2nd issue)

2000 (25 Oct). *Authors*. T **409** *and similar horiz design. Multicoloured*. P 13×14.
1203 1r.30 Type **409** 20 25
1204 4r.40 Arthur Conan Doyle and Winston Churchill .... 2·00 1·50

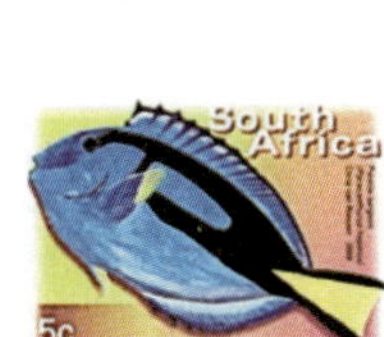

410 Palette Surgeonfish **411** The Rain Bull

(Des Joan van Gogh (1r.30), C. van Rooyen (others))

2000 (1 Nov). *Flora and Fauna*. T **410** *and similar multicoloured designs*.

(a) *Litho Questa. Phosphorised paper* P 14½×15 (*horiz*) or 15×14½ (*vert*).
1205 5c. Type **410** 10 10
1206 10c. Clown Surgeonfish ("Bluebanded Surgeon") 10 10
1207 20c. Regal Angelfish 10 10
1208 30c. Emperor Angelfish 10 10
1209 40c. Picasso Triggerfish ("Blackbar triggerfish") 10 10
1210 50c. Coral Hind ("Coral rockcod") 10 10
1211 60c. Powder-blue Surgeonfish 15 15
1212 70c. Thread-finned Butterflyfish 15 15
1213 80c. Long-horned Cowfish 15 15
1214 90c. Forceps Butterflyfish ("Longnose butterflyfish") 20 20
1215 1r. Two-spined Angelfish ("Coral Beauty") 25 20
1216 1r.30 Botterblom (*vert*) 30 25
a. Horiz strip of 5. Nos. 1216/20 .... 1·40
1217 1r.30 Blue Marguerite (*vert*) 30 25
1218 1r.30 Karoo Violet (*vert*) 30 25
1219 1r.30 Tree Pelargonium (*vert*) 30 25
1220 1r.30 Black-eyed Susy (*vert*) 30 25
1221 1r.40 Gold-banded Forester 35 25
1222 1r.51 Brenton Blue 40 30
1223 1r.90 Silver-barred Charaxes 50 35
1224 2r. Lilac-breasted Roller (*vert*) 70 35
1225 2r.30 Citrus Butterfly 70 40
1226 3r. Woodland Kingfisher (*vert*) 80 65
1227 5r. White-fronted Bee Eater (*vert*) .... 1·25 1·00
1228 6r.30 Narrow Blue-banded Swallowtail ("Green-banded swallowtail") .... 1·50 1·40
1229 10r. African Green Pigeon (*vert*) .... 2·50 1·75
1230 12r.60 False-dotted Border .... 3·00 2·50
1231 20r. Violet-crested Turaco ("Purple crested lourie") (*vert*) .... 4·50 3·75
1205/31 *Set of 27* .... 19·00 15·00

(b) *Photo Enschedé. Designs as Nos. 1216/20, but smaller (20×25 mm). Self-adhesive. Phosphor frame*. P 13×12½
1232 1r.30 As No. 1216 (inscr "Afrika Borwa") 40 40
a. Booklet pane. Nos. 1232/41 .... 3·50 3·50
b. Perf 13½ 40 40
ba. Strip of 10. Nos. 1232b/41b .... 3·50
1233 1r.30 As No. 1216 (inscr "Afrika Dzonga") 40 40
b. Perf 13½ 40 40
1234 1r.30 As No. 1217 (inscr "Ningizimu Afrika") 40 40
b. Perf 13½ 40 40
1235 1r.30 As No. 1217 (inscr "Afrika Sewula") 40 40
b. Perf 13½ 40 40
1236 1r.30 As No. 1218 (inscr "Suid Afrika") 40 40
b. Perf 13½ 40 40
1237 1r.30 As No. 1218 (inscr "Afrika Borwa") 40 40
b. Perf 13½ 40 40
1238 1r.30 As No. 1219 (inscr "Afrika Tshipembe") 40 40
b. Perf 13½ 40 40
1239 1r.30 As No. 1219 (inscr "Ningizimu Afrika") 40 40
b. Perf 13½ 40 40
1240 1r.30 As No. 1220 (inscr "Afrika Borwa") 40 40
b. Perf 13½ 40 40
1241 1r.30 As No. 1220 (inscr "Mzantsi Afrika") 40 40
b. Perf 13½ 40 40
1232/41 *Set of 10* .... 3·50 3·50
Designs from 5c. to 1r. show fish, 1r.30 flowers, 1r.40 to 1r.90, 2r.30, 6r.30 and 12r.60 butterflies and the 2, 3, 5, 10 and 20r. birds.
For stamps perforated 13½×13 or 13×13½ see Nos. 1268/94.
Nos. 1216/20 were printed together *se-tenant*, as horizontal strips of 5 throughout the sheets.
Nos. 1232/41 were only available in stamp booklets, No. SB60, in which the pane had imperforate edges so that Nos. 1232/3 are imperforate on two sides and the remainder on one side.
Nos. 1232b/41b come from coils containing all 10 designs in sequence with surplus self-adhesive paper around each stamp removed.
For similar designs inscribed "Standard Postage" see Nos. 1295/1314.
See also Nos 1268/1314 and 1389/93.

(Des Siobhian Cuff (1r.50), Sophia Mazibuko (others). Litho Questa)

2001 (24 Jan). *South African Myths and Legends*. T **411** *and similar vert designs. Multicoloured*. P 13½.
1242 1r.30 Type **411** 40 25
1243 1r.51 The Grosvenor Treasure 45 30
1244 2r.20 Seven Magic Birds 60 45
1245 2r.30 The Hole in the Wall 65 55
1246 6r.30 Van Hunks and the Devil .... 1·60 2·00
1242/46 *Set of 5* .... 3·25 3·25

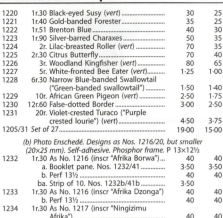

412 African Tree Snake

(Des M. Maas. Litho Questa)

2001 (1 Feb). *Chinese New Year ("Year of the Snake") and "Hong Kong (2001)" Stamp Exhibition. Sheet 65×85 mm*. P 14½×14.
MS1247 multicoloured .... 1·50 1·50

413 Ernie Els (golf)

(Des Liza van der Wal. Litho Questa)

2001 (28 Feb). *South African Sporting Heroes*. T **413** *and similar horiz designs. Multicoloured*. P 13½×14.
1248 1r.40 Type **413** 60 55
1249 1r.40 Lucas Radebe (soccer) 60 55
1250 1r.40 Francois Pienaar (rugby) 60 55
1251 1r.40 Terrence Parkin (swimming) 60 55
1252 1r.40 Rosina Magola (netball) 60 55
1253 1r.40 Hestrie Cloete (high-jumping) 60 55
1254 1r.40 Hezekiel Sepeng (athletics) 60 55
1255 1r.40 Jonty Rhodes (cricket) 60 55
a. Perf 14½×14 .... 60 55
1256 1r.40 Zanele Situ (paralympic javelin) 60 55
1257 1r.40 Vuyani Bungu (boxing) 60 55
1248/57 *Set of 10* .... 5·50 5·00
Nos. 1248/57 were each printed in sheets of 10 (2×5).
No. 1250a was printed in sheets of 15 (3×5) with each stamp accompanied by a *se-tenant* label showing a member of the South African cricket team.

414 Elephant

(Des A. Ainslie. Litho Questa)

2001 (25 Apr). *Wildlife. T* **414** *and similar horiz designs. Multicoloured. Phosphor frame.*

(a) Designs 34×26 mm. P 14½.

1258 (2r.10) Type **414** ... 80 80
a. Pane. Nos. 1258/62, each ×2 ... 7·00 7·00
1259 (2r.10) Lion ... 80 80
1260 (2r.10) Rhinoceros ... 80 80
1261 (2r.10) Leopard ... 80 80
1262 (2r.10) Buffalo ... 80 80
1258/62 *Set of 5* ... 3·50 3·50

(b) Designs 29×24 mm. Self-adhesive. P 12×11½

1263 (2r.10) Buffalo ... 60 70
a. Booklet pane. Nos. 1263/7, each ×2 ... 5·50 6·50
1264 (2r.10) Leopard ... 60 70
1265 (2r.10) Rhinoceros ... 60 70
1266 (2r.10) Lion ... 60 70
1267 (2r.10) Type **414** ... 60 70
1263/7 *Set of 5* ... 2·75 3·25

Nos. 1258/62 were printed together, *se-tenant*, in panes of 10 (5×2), either available separately or as part of a premium stamp booklet, No. SP3, sold at 49r.20.

All examples of No. 1262 are imperforate at right.

Nos. 1263/7 were only available *se-tenant*, in stamp booklets, No SB62, which have the outer edges of the pane imperforate.

Nos. 1263/66 are imperforate at left or right and No. 1267 imperforate at foot and either at left or right.

Nos. 1258/67 are inscribed "AIRMAIL POSTCARD RATE" and were initially valid for 2r.10.

(Des Joan van Gogh (Nos. 1279/83, 1284a/e and 1295/1314), C. van Rooyen (others))

2001 (25 Apr)–**03**. *Flora and Fauna (2nd series). Multicoloured designs as T* **410**.

(a) Phosphorised paper. Litho Cartor. P 13½×13 (*vert*) or 13×13½ (*horiz*)

1268 5c. Type **410** (2.10.02) ... 10 10
1269 10c. Clown surgeonfish (Bluebanded Surgeon") (22.5.03) ... 10 10
1270 20c. Regal angelfish (23.9.03) ... 10 10
1271 30c. Emperor angelfish (27.2.03) ... 10 10
1272 40c. Picasso triggerfish (23.9.03) ... 10 10
1273 50c. Coral Hind ("Coral rockcod") (7.6.02) ... 10 10
1274 60c. Powder-blue Surgeonfish (14.6.01) ... 10 15
1275 70c. Thread-finned butterflyfish (23.9.03) ... 15 15
1276 80c. Long-horned cowfish (22.9.03) ... 15 15
1277 90c. Forceps butterflyfish ("Longnose butterflyfish) (27.2.03) ... 20 20
1278 1r. Two-spined angelfish ("Coral Beauty") (23.9.03) ... 25 20
1279 1r.40 Botterblom (*vert*) ... 20 25
a. Horiz strip of 5. Nos. 1279/83 ... 1·00 1·25
1280 1r.40 Blue Marguerite (*vert*) ... 20 25
1281 1r.40 Karoo Violet (*vert*) ... 20 25
1282 1r.40 Tree Pelargonium (*vert*) ... 20 25
1283 1r.40 Black-eyed Susy (*vert*) ... 20 25
1284 1r.60 Yellow Pansy Butterfly (16.6.01) ... 25 30
1284*a* (1r.65) Botterblom (*vert*) (15.9.03) ... 25 30
ab. Horiz strip of 5. Nos. 1284a/e ... 1·25 1·50
1284*b* (1r.65) Blue Marguerite (*vert*) (15.9.03) ... 25 30
1284*c* (1r.65) Karoo Violet (*vert*) (15.9.03) ... 25 30
1284*d* (1r.65) Tree Pelegonium (*vert*) (15.9.03) ... 25 30
1284*e* (1r.65) Black-eyed Susy (*vert*) (15.9.03) ... 25 30
1285 1r.90 Large-spotted Acraea (16.6.01) ... 30 35
1286 2r. Lilac-breasted Roller (*vert*) (9.8.02) ... 35 40
1287 2r.10 Kopje Charaxes (16.6.01) ... 35 40
1288 2r.51 Common Grass-yellow (16.6.01) ... 40 45
1289 3r. Woodland Kingfisher (*vert*) (7.6.02) ... 50 55
1290 5r. White-fronted Bee-eater (*vert*) (7.6.02) ... 85 90
1291 7r. Southern Milkweed (16.6.01) ... 1·20 1·30
1292 10r. African Green Pigeon (*vert*) (1.10.01) ... 1·70 1·80
1293 14r. Lilac-tip (16.6.01) ... 2·30 2·40
1294 20r. Purple-crested Turaco ("Purplecrested lourie") (*vert*) (14.6.01) ... 3·25 3·50
1268/94 *Set of 32* ... 14·00 15·00

(b) Photo Enschedé. Designs as Nos. 1279/83, but 20×25 mm and inscr "Standard Postage" instead of face value. Self-adhesive. Phosphor frame. P 13×12½.

1295 (1r.40) As No. 1279 (inscr "Afrika Borwa") ... 20 25
a. Booklet pane. Nos. 1295/1304 ... 2·00 2·50
b. Perf 13½ ... 20 25
ba. Strip of 10. Nos. 1295b/1304b ... 2·00
1296 (1r.40) As No. 1279 (inscr "Afrika Dzonga") ... 20 25
b. Perf 13½ ... 20 25
1297 (1r.40) As No. 1280 (inscr "Ningizimu Afrika") ... 20 25
b. Perf 13½ ... 20 25
1298 (1r.40) As No. 1280 (inscr "Afrika Sewula") ... 20 25
b. Perf 13½ ... 20 25
1299 (1r.40) As No. 1281 (inscr "Suid-Afrika") ... 20 25
b. Perf 13½ ... 20 25
1300 (1r.40) As No. 1281(inscr "Afrika Borwa") ... 20 25
b. Perf 13½ ... 20 25
1301 (1r.40) As No. 1282 (inscr "Afrika Tshipembe") ... 20 25
b. Perf 13½ ... 20 25
1302 (1r.40) As No. 1282 (inscr "Ningizimu Afrika") ... 20 25
b. Perf 13½ ... 20 25
1303 (1r.40) As No. 1283 (inscr "Afrika Borwa") ... 20 25
b. Perf 13½ ... 20 25
1304 (1r.40) As No. 1283 (inscr "Mzantsi Afrika") ... 20 25
b. Perf 13½ ... 20 25
1295/1304 *Set of 10* ... 2·00 2·50

(c) Litho Southern Colour Print, New Zealand. Designs as Nos. 1279/83, but 20×25 mm and inscr "Standard Postage" instead of face value. Self-adhesive. Phosphor frame. P 13½×13.

1305 (1r.40) As No. 1279 (inscr "Afrika Borwa") (30.5.01) ... 20 25
a. Strip of 10. Nos. 1305/14 ... 2·00
b. Perf 13×12½ ... 20 25
ba. Booklet pane. Nos. 1305b/14b ... 2·00 25
1306 (1r.40) As No. 1279 (inscr "Afrika Dzonga") (30.5.01) ... 20 25
b. Perf 13×12½ ... 20 25
1307 (1r.40) As No. 1280 (inscr "Ningizimu Afrika") (30.5.01) ... 20 25
b. Perf 13×12½ ... 20 25
1308 (1r.40) As No. 1280 (inscr "Afrika Sewula") (30.5.01) ... 20 25
b. Perf 13×12½ ... 20 25
1309 (1r.40) As No. 1281 (inscr "Suid-Afrika") (30.5.01) ... 20 25
b. Perf 13×12½ ... 20 25
1310 (1r.40) As No. 1281 (inscr "Afrika Borwa") (30.5.01) ... 20 25
b. Perf 13×12½ ... 20 25
1311 (1r.40) As No. 1282 (inscr "Afrika Tshipembe") (30.5.01) ... 20 25
b. Perf 13×12½ ... 20 25
1312 (1r.40) As No. 1282 (inscr "Ningizimu Afrika") (30.5.01) ... 20 25
b. Perf 13×12½ ... 20 25
1313 (1r.40) As No. 1283 (inscr "Afrika Borwa") (30.5.01) ... 20 25
b. Perf 13×12½ ... 20 25
1314 (1r.40) As No. 1283 (inscr "Mzantsi Afrika") (30.5.01) ... 20 25
b. Perf 13×12½ ... 20 25
1305/14 *Set of 10* ... 2·00 2·50

Nos. 1279/83 and 1284/a/e were each printed together, *se-tenant*, in horizontal strips of 5 throughout the sheets.

Nos. 1284a/e, are inscribed "Standard Postage" and were initially sold for 1r.65 each.

Nos. 1284, 1285, 1287/8, 1291 and 1293 show butterflies.

Nos. 1295/1304 were only available in stamp booklets, No. SB63, in which examples of No. 1295 are imperforate at top and left, No. 1296 at bottom and left and the remainder at top or bottom. The stamps are inscribed "Standard Postage" and were initially valid for 1r.40.

Nos. 1295b/ 1304b and 1305/14 come from coils containing all 10 designs in sequence with the surplus self-adhesive paper around each stamp removed.

Nos. 1305b/14b were only available in booklets, Nos. SB64/b with the surplus paper retained.

415 Gemsbok **416** Adult holding Child's Hand

(Des Karen Odiam. Litho Cartor)

2001 (12 May). *Kgalagadi Transfrontier Wildlife Park. Joint Issue with Botswana. T* **415** *and similar multicoloured designs. Two phosphor bands.* P 13.

1315 1r.40 Type **415** ... 45 25
1316 2r.51 Cheetah ... 75 55
1317 2r.90 Sociable Weaver (bird) ... 1·00 1·00
1318 3r.60 Meercat ... 1·10 1·25
1315/1318 *Set of 4* ... 3·00 2·75
MS1319 114×78 mm. Nos. 1316/17 ... 1·50 1·50

(Des Mimi van Vuuren. Litho Questa)

2001 (16 May). *"no excuse for child abuse" Campaign.* P 13½

1320 **416** 1r.40 multicoloured ... 50 55

No. 1320 was printed in sheets of ten with the stamps arranged as two diagonal crosses.

417 Victims of Soweto Uprising **418** Cape Horsehoe Bat

(Des L. Moagi after photograph by S. Nzima. Litho Questa)

2001 (16 June). *25th Anniv of Soweto Uprising.* P 14×13½.

1321 **417** 1r.40 multicoloured ... 50 35

(Des Annemarie Wessels. Photo Questa)

2001 (22 June). *Bats of South Africa. T* **418** *and similar multicoloured designs. L-shaped phosphor band. Self-adhesive. Die-cut.* P 11½

1322 1r.40 Type **418** ... 35 35
a. Sheetlet. Nos. 1322/31 ... 3·25
1323 1r.40 Welwitsch's Hairy Bat ... 35 35
1324 1r.40 Schreiber's Long-fingered Bat ... 35 35
1325 1r.40 Wahlberg's Epauletted Fruit Bat ... 35 35
1326 1r.40 Short-eared Trident Bat ... 35 35
1327 1r.40 Common Slit-faced Bat ... 35 35
1328 1r.40 Egyptian Fruit Bat ... 35 35
1329 1r.40 Egyptian Free-tailed Bat (*vert*) ... 35 35
1330 1r.40 De Winton's Long-eared Bat ... 35 35
1331 1r.40 Large-eared Free-tailed Bat ... 35 35
1322/21 *Set of 10* ... 3·25 3·25

Nos. 1322/31 were printed together, *se-tenant*, in sheetlets of 10 with the background forming a composite design. Descriptions of the various species are printed on the reverse of the backing paper. The phosphor band shows greenish yellow under U.V. light and the sheetlet inscription glows in the dark.

419 Conference logo **420** Dominee J. D. Kestell

(Des A. Nothling. Litho Enschedé)

2001 (7 Aug). *Third U.N. World Conference Against Rascism, Durban. T* **419** *and similar vert designs. L-shaped phosphor band.* P 14×13½.

1332 **419** 1r.40 mult (inscr as in T 419) ... 30 30
a. Sheetlet. Nos. 1332/41 ... 2·75 2·75
1333 1r.40 mult (inscr "ningizimu afrika" and "kubeketelelana" at foot) ... 30 30
1334 1r.40 mult (inscr "suid-afrika") ... 30 30
1335 1r.40 mult (inscr "afrika tshipembe") ... 30 30
1336 1r.40 mult (inscr "afrika borwa" and kutlwisiso" at foot) ... 30 30
1337 1r.40 mult (inscr "afrika dzonga") ... 30 30
1338 1r.40 mult (inscr "afrika sewula") ... 30 30
1339 1r.40 mult (inscr "afrika borwa" and "kgothlelelo" at foot) ... 30 30
1340 1r.40 mult (inscr "ningizimu afrika" and "ukubekezelelana) ... 30 30
1341 1r.40 mult (inscr "mzantsi afrika") ... 30 30
1342 2r.40 mult (logo and South Africans) ... 50 50
1332/42 *Set of 11* ... 3·25 3·25

Nos. 1332/41 were printed together, *se-tenant*, in sheetlets of 10. The phosphor appears as greenish yellow under U.V. light.

(Des H. Botha. Litho Enschedé)

2001 (21 Aug). *Centenerary of Anglo-Boer War (3rd issue.) Angels of Mercy. T* **420** *and similar horiz designs. Multicoloured. Shaped phosphor band.* P 13½.

1343 1r.40 Type **420** ... 50 25
1344 3r. Captain Thomas Crean V.C., R.A.M.C ... 1·00 85

The phosphor appears as greenish yellow under U.V. light.

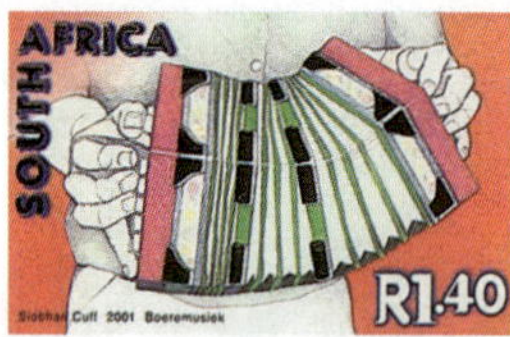

421 Boere Concertina

(Des Siobhan Cuff. Litho and die-samped Enschedé)

2001 (23 Aug). *Musical Instruments. T* **421** *and similar horiz designs. Multicoloured.* P 13½×14.

1345 1r.40 Type **421** ... 35 25
1346 1r.90 Trumpet ... 45 45
1347 2r.51 Electric guitar ... 60 55
1348 3r. African drum ... 65 65
1349 7r. Cello ... 1·60 1·75
1345/9 *Set of 5* ... 3·50 3·50

422 Field of Flowers, Namaqualand

423 Tree of Life decorated with Christmas Lights

(Des Thea Swanepoel. Litho Enschedé)

2001 (6 Sept). *Natural Wonders of South Africa. T* **422** *and similar horiz designs. Multicoloured. L-shaped phosphor band.* P 13½.

1350 (2r.10) Type **422** ... 60 60
1351 (2r.10) Cango Caves ... 60 60
1352 (2r.10) Richtersveld Desert ... 60 60
1353 (2r.10) Rocks on West Coast ... 60 60
1354 (2r.10) Snow covered mountains near Elliot ... 60 60
1355 (2r.10) Table Mountain ... 60 60
1356 (2r.10) Tsitsikamma Forest ... 60 60
1357 (2r.10) Augrabies Watefall ... 60 60
1358 (2r.10) Cape Mountain Zebra ... 60 60
1359 (2r.10) Vineyards, Stellenbosch ... 60 60
1350/59 *Set of 10* ... 5·50 5·50

Nos. 1350/9 are inscribed "Airmail Postcard Rate" and were initially valid at 2r.10 each.

(Des Siobhan Cuff. Litho Enschedé)

2001 (1 Oct). *Christmas. T* **423** *and similar square design. Multicoloured L-shaped phosphor band.* P 13½.

1360 2r. Type **423** ... 50 35
1361 3r. Angel ... 60 50

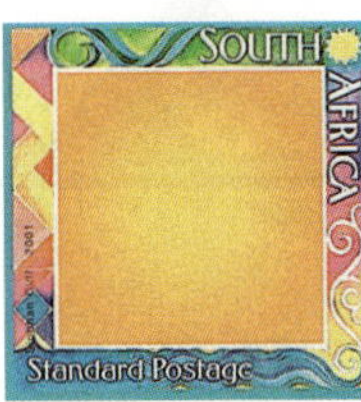

424 Frame

425 Class Volvo 60 Yacht

(Des S. Cuff. Litho Enschedé)

2001 (1 Oct). *Greeting Stamps. Self-adhesive. L-shaped phosphor band.* Die-cut. P 9.

1362 **424** (1r.40) multicoloured ... 30 20
a. Double-sided sheetlet. No. 1362 ×10 ... 2·75

No. 1362 is inscribed "Standard Postage" and was initially valid for 1r.40.

No. 1362 was printed in double-sided sheetlets of 10 (5 stamps each side) together with a selection of 20 self-adhesive labels, which were intended to be applied to the space in the centre of the frame. The surplus self-adhesive paper around the stamps and labels was retained.

(Des H. Botha. Litho Enschedé)

2001 (23 Oct). *Volvo Round the World Ocean Race. T* **425** *and similar multicoloured design. L-shaped phosphor band.* P 13.

1363 1r.40 Type **425** ... 60 35
MS1364 55×85 mm. 6r. Volvo 60 yacht (*horiz*). P 14×13½ ... 1·25 1·25

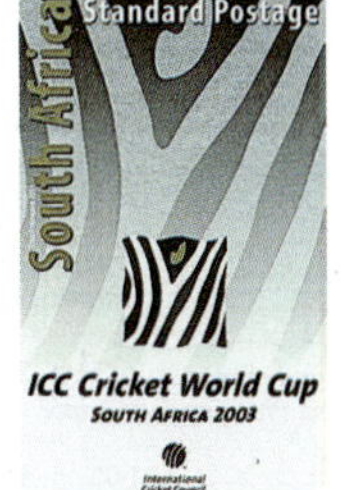

426 International Cricket Council Logo

427 Horse's Head

(Des Thea Swanepoel. Litho Questa)

2001 (1 Nov). *Cricket World Cup (2003) (1st issue). L-shaped phosphor band.* P 14×13½.

1365 **426** (1r.40) black, gold and silver ... 1·00 55

No. 1365 is inscribed "Standard Postage" and was initially valid for 1r.40.

See also Nos. 1389/94 and **MS**1418.

(Des Anna-Marié Bands. Litho Questa)

2001 (2 Nov). *Chinese New Year ("Year of the Horse"). Circular sheet 85 mm in diameter. L-shaped phosphor band.* P 14×13½.

1366 **427** 6r. multicoloured ... 1·75 1·75

428 Scalloped Hammerhead Sharks

(Des Sheila Cooper)

2001 (2 Nov). *Marine Life. T* **428** *and similar multicoloured designs. Photo. L-shaped phosphor band. Self-adhesive. Die-cut.* P 13.

1367 1r.40 Type **428** ... 45 45
a. Sheetlet. Nos. 1367/76 ... 4·00
1368 1r.40 Loggerhead Turtle (*vert*) ... 45 45
1369 1r.40 Clown Triggerfish (*vert*) ... 45 45
1370 1r.40 Cape Fur Seals (*vert*) ... 45 45
1371 1r.40 Bottlenosed Dolphins ... 45 45
1372 1r.40 Crowned Seahorses (*vert*) ... 45 45
1373 1r.40 Blue-spotted Ribbontail Ray (*vert*) ... 45 45
1374 1r.40 Moorish Idols ... 45 45
1375 1r.40 Octopus ... 45 45
1376 1r.40 Coral Rock Cod ... 45 45
1367/76 *Set of* 10 ... 4·00 4·00

Nos. 1367/76 were printed together *se-tenant* in sheetlets of 10 with the background forming a composite design. Descriptions of the various species are printed on the reverse of the backing paper.

429 Child laughing

430 Earl Kitchener

(Des P. Sibanda (No. 1380), 8 Seconds (others). Litho Enschedé)

2002 (17 Apr). *World Summit for Sustainable Development, Johannesburg (1st issue). T* **429** *and similar multicoloured designs.*

(*a*) *PVA gum.* P 14×13½ (Nos. 1377/9) or 13½×14 (1380).

1377 (1r.51) Type **429** ... 30 30
a. Sheetlet. No. 1377×4 and Nos. 1378/9 both ×3 ... 2·75
1378 (1r.51) Globe in rainforest ... 30 30
1379 (1r.51) Trees in sunset ... 30 30
1380 (1r.51) Globe and South African landmarks (48×30 mm) ... 60 60
1377/80 *Set of* 4 ... 1·50 1·50

Nos. 1381/3 were only available in stamp booklets, No. SB65, in which the pane was imperforate on one side (Nos. 1381/3) or on two adjacent sides (Nos. 1381 and 1383).

Nos. 1377/9 were printed together, *se-tenant*, in sheetlets of 10.

Nos. 1377/9 and 1381/3 were each inscribed "Standard postage" and sold for 1r.50.

See also Nos. 1386/8.

(*b*) *Designs 20×25 mm. Self-adhesive.* P 12½×13 (25 Aug).

1381 (1r.51) Type **429** ... 35 35
a. Booklet Pane. Nos. 1381×4 and 1382/3, each ×3 ... 3·50 3·50
1382 (1r.51) As No. 1378 ... 35 35
1383 (1r.51) As No. 1379 ... 35 35
1381/3 *Set of* 3 ... 1·10 1·10

(Des H. Botha. Litho Enschedé)

2002 (17 May). *Centenary of Anglo-Boer War (4th issue). Treaty of Vereeniging. Sheet, 105×65 mm, containing T* **430** *and similar square design. Multicoloured. L-shaped phosphor band.* P 13½.

MS1384 1r.50 Type **430**; 3r.30 Boer representative signing Treaty ... 1·00 1·00

No. **MS**1381was accompanied by a limited edition stamp booklet containing examples of Nos. 1165/6, 1203/4, 1343/4, in panes of two, and **MS**1381 together with two postal stationery postcards reproducing the design of No. 1344. This booklet, No. SP1, was only avalable from philatelic outlets initially at 45r., a premium of 11r.50 over the face value of the contents.

431 African Union Logo

432 Water, Sanitation and Energy

(Des A. Notling. Litho)

2002 (25 June). *First African Union Summit, Durban.* P 13½ (and around stamp).

1385 **431** 1r.51 multicoloured ... 60 40

(Des Michelle Casanova. Litho Cartor)

2002 (25 Aug). *World Summit on Sustainable Development (2nd issue). T* **432** *and similar horiz designs. Multicoloured.* P 13½×13.

1386 (1r.51) Type **432** ... 35 30
1387 (3r.) Child with hands raised to globe (Enviroment) ... 60 55
1388 (3r.30) Hands holding seedling (Food) ... 70 70
1386/8 *Set of* 3 ... 1·60 1·50

No. 1386 is inscribed "standard postage", No. 1387 "airmail postcard rate" and No. 1388 "international letter rate". The stamps were initially sold at the values quoted above.

(Des C. van Rooyen. Litho Cartor)

2002 (20 Sept). *Flora and Fauna (3rd series). Moths. Horiz designs as T* **410**. P 13.

1389 1r.80 Emperor Moth ... 40 35
1390 2r.20 Peach Moth ... 50 40
1391 2r.80 Snouted Tiger Moth ... 60 50
1392 9r. False Tiger Moth ... 1·75 1·90
1393 16r. Moon Moth ... 3·00 3·50
1389/93 *Set of* 5 ... 5·75 6·00

433 "Dazzler" Mascot Striking Ball

434 Postal Stone

(Des TBWA Gavin Reddy Litho Enschedé)

2002 (23 Sept–21 Dec). *Cricket World Cup (2003) (2nd issue). T* **433** *and similar vert designs showing "Dazzler" zebra mascot. Multicoloured. L-shaped phosphor bands.* P 12½×13.

1394 (1r.51) Type **433** ... 40 40
1395 (1r.51) Bowler (after releasing ball) ... 40 40
1396 (1r.51) Fielder (1 Nov) ... 40 40
1397 (1r.51) Batsman (on one knee) (1 Nov) ... 40 40
1398 (1r.51) Bowler (running with ball) (21 Dec) ... 40 40
1399 (1r.51) Batsman preparing to strike ball (21 Dec) ... 40 40
1394/9 *Set of* 6 ... 2·25 2·25

Nos. 1394/9×2 were each printed in sheets of six.

(Des H. Botha. Litho)

2002 (9 Oct). *World Post Day. Sheet 105×65 mm. Phosphorised paper.* P 13½.

MS1400 **434** 4r.75 multicoloured ... 1·25 1·25

435 Steve Biko

436 *Pristis microdon*

(Des Thea Swanepoel. Litho)

2002 (9 Oct). *25th Death Anniv of Steve Biko (anti-apartheid campaigner). Sheet 105×65 mm. Phosphorised paper.* P 14½.

MS1401 **435** 4r.75 black, deep rose-red and cinnamon ... 1·25 1·25

(Des H. Botha. Litho)

2002 (23 Oct). *"Algoapex" (***MS***1402) and "JUNASS" (***MS***1403) National Stamp Show. Sawfish. Two sheets containing horiz designs as T* **436**. *Multicoloured. Phosphorised Paper.* P 14×13½.

MS1402 104×65 mm. 7r. Type **436** ... 1·50 1·60
MS1403 106×65 mm. 7r. Pristis pectinata ... 1·50 1·60

437 Stylized Goat

438 "The Tree of Life"

(Des Siobhan Cuff. Litho)

2002 (1 Nov). *Chinese New Year ("Year of the Goat"). Star-shaped sheet 105×105 mm. Phosphorised paper.* P 14½.

MS1404 **437** 7r. multicoloured ... 1·50 1·60

(Des H. Nesbit. Litho)

2002 (13 Nov). *Christmas. T* **438** *and similar vert design showing stained glass. Multicoloured. Phosphorised paper.* P 14×15.

1405 1r.51 Type **438** ... 30 30
1406 3r. "The Totem" ... 70 70

Nos. 1405/6 were each printed in sheets of 10 with the top row containing two stamps and two stamp-size labels at left and right. The sheets have enlarged illustrated top margins.

439 Man wearing Sunglasses

440 Total Eclipse

(Des P. Sibanda. Litho)

2002 (29 Nov). *AIDS Prevention. Self-adhesive booklet stamps. T* **439** *and similar vert designs. Multicoloured. Phosphor frame.* P 11½×12.

1407 (1r.51) Type **439** ... 25 30
a. Booklet pane. Nos. 1407/16 ... 2·50 3·00
1408 (1r.51) Woman with AIDS ribbon on headband ... 25 30
1409 (1r.51) Woman wearing sunglasses and hat ... 25 30
1410 (1r.51) Hand holding purple candle and "STOP" ... 25 30
1411 (1r.51) Woman's face and "AIDS" ...
1412 (1r.51) Man holding purple candle and "Be safe" ... 25 30
1413 (1r.51) Hand touching AIDS ribbon and green candle ... 25 30
1414 (1r.51) Raised palm of hand and "AIDS" ... 25 30
1415 (1r.51) Woman's face in glass jar ... 25 30
1416 (1r.51) Hand catching anti-HIV drugs and AIDS ribbon in heart ... 25 30
1407/16 *Set of* 10 ... 2·50 3·00

Nos. 1407/16 are inscribed "Standard Postage" and were intially valid for 1r.50. They form a composite design and come from booklet No. SB66. Booklet pane No. 1407a was imperforate at top, bottom and left so that stamps are imperforate on one side (Nos. 1408/11 and 1413/16) or two adjacent sides (Nos. 1407, 1412).

(Des Thea Swanepoel. Litho)

2002 (4 4). *Total Solar Eclipse, 4 December 2002. Sheet 105×65 mm. Phosphorised paper.* P 14½.

MS1417 **440** 4r.75 black, yellow-orange and orange-red ... 1·25 1·25

HAVE YOU READ THE NOTES AT THE BEGINNING OF THIS CATALOGUE?

These often provide answers to the enquiries we receive

441 Traditional Thatched Huts

442 Chris Hani

(Des G. Reddy from paintings by G. Ndaba, D. Sibisi, J. Durno, B. Baqwa and V. Khumalo. Litho)

2003 (28 Feb). *Cricket World Cup (3rd issue). South Africa Scenes. T* **441** *and similar horiz designs. Multicoloured. Phosphorised paper.* P 14.

MS1418 174×90 mm. (1r.50) Type **441**; (1r.50) Man wearing brimmed hat on horse; (1r.50) Four cricketers and settlement houses; (1r.50) Passengers inside bus and on roof; (1r.50) Woman and baby; (1r.50) Double-decker bus..... 1·75 2·00

Stamps from **MS**1418 are inscribed "STANDARD POSTAGE" and were initially valid for 1r.50 each.

2003 (27 Apr). *10th Death Anniv of Chris Hani (former Secretary-General of South African Communist Party). Sheet 105×65 mm. Litho. Phosphorised paper.* P 14½×15.

MS1419 **442** (1r.65) reddish brown and vermilion 60 65

No. **MS**1419 is inscribed "Standard Postage" and was initially valid for 1r.50.

443 Women carrying Water Drums

444 Outline Map of Africa

(Des J. Lion. Litho)

2003 (16 May). *Life in Informal Settlements. T* **443** *and similar vert designs. Multicoloured. Phosphor frame.* P 14×13½.

1420 (1r.65) Type **443** ... 25 30
a. Sheetlet. Nos. 1420/9 ... 2·50 3·00
1421 (1r.65) Boy playing musical instrument ... 25 30
1422 (1r.65) Workman laying road ... 25 30
1423 (1r.65) Seamstress ... 25 30
1424 (1r.65) Two schoolchildren ... 25 30
1425 (1r.65) Shopkeeper with customer ... 25 30
1426 (1r.65) Shoemakers ... 25 30
1427 (1r.65) Woman wearing green hat ... 25 30
1428 (1r.65) Teenager leaning on tyre ... 25 30
1429 (1r.65) Mother and child ... 25 30
1420/9 *Set of 10* ... 2·50 3·00

Nos. 1420/9 were printed together, *se-tenant*, in sheetlets of 10. They are inscribed "STANDARD POSTAGE" and were initially valid for 1r.65 each.

(Des Thea Swanepoel. Litho)

2003 (25 May). *Africa Day. Sheet 105×65 mm. Phosphorised paper.* P 14½×15.

MS1430 **444** 11r.71 multicoloured ... 2·50 2·75

445 Oliver Tambo

446 Salsa Dancers

(Des Thea Swanepoel. Litho)

2003 (29 May). *10th Death Anniv of Oliver Tambo. Sheet 105×65 mm. Phosphorised paper.* P 14½×15.

MS1431 **445** (1r.65) multicoloured ... 50 60

No. **MS**1431 is inscribed "Standard Postage" and was initially valid for 1r.65.

(Des Siobhan Buff. Litho Enschedé)

2003 (23 July). *Dances. T* **446** *and similar horiz designs. Multicoloured. L-shaped phosphor bands.* P 13½×14.

1432 1r.65 Type **446** ... 45 25
1433 2r.20 Rumba ... 60 45
1434 2r.80 Waltz ... 75 75
1435 3r.30 Foxtrot ... 90 1·00
1436 3r.80 Tango ... 1·10 1·40
1432/6 *Set of 5* ... 3·50 3·50

447 African Dog

448 Robert Mangaliso Sobukwe

(Des Ellena Schmitz. Litho DLR)

2003 (1 Aug). *Dogs. Sheet 100×100 mm. containing T* **447** *and similar square designs. Multicoloured. L-shaped phosphor bands.* P 14½.

MS1437 (1r.65) Type **447**; (1r.65) Rhodesian Ridgeback; (1r.65) Boerboel; (1r.65) Basenji ... 2·00 2·00

The stamps of No. **MS**1437 were each inscribed "standard postage" and sold for 1r.65.

(Des Thea Swanepoel. Litho)

2003 (24 Sept). *25th Anniv of Robert Mangaliso Sobukwe (nationalist leader and founder of the Pan Africanist Congress). Sheet 105×65 mm.* P 14½×15.

MS1438 **448** 11r.71 multicoloured ... 3·25 3·25

449 Walter Max Ulyate Sisulu

450 Shaka

(Des Thea Swanepoel. Litho)

2003 (24 Sept). *Walter Max Ulyate Sisulu (political activist and member of the African National Congress) Commemoration. Sheet 105×65 mm.* P 14½×15.

MS1439 **449** 11r.71 muticoloured ... 3·25 3·25

(Des H. Botha. Litho Cartor)

2003 (24 Sept). *Shaka (Warrior King of the Zulu) Commemoration. Phosphorised paper.* P 13×13½.

1440 **450** (3r.) multicoloured ... 80 80

No. 1440 was printed in sheets of 10 with an enlarged, illustrated top margin. Each stamp was inscribed "Airmail Postcard" and sold for 3r.

451 Football Supporter and Globe

452 Stamp of Fortune and Post Office Logos and Cars

(Des L. Wyman. Litho)

2003 (26 Sept). *World Cup Football Bid. T* **451** *and similar horiz design. Multicoloured. Phosphorised paper.* P 15×14½.

1441 (3r.80) Type **451** ... 1·00 1·00
1442 (4r.25) Supporter and children playing football ... 1·10 1·10

Nos. 1441/2 were each printed in sheets of 10.

No. 1441 was inscribed "International Airmail Rate Small Letter" and sold for 3r.80.

No. 1442 was inscribed "B4 Domestic Large" and sold for for 4r.25.

(Des Thea Swanepoel. Litho)

2003 (29 Sept). *Television and Post Office Joint Issue.* P 14½×14.

1443 **452** (1r.65) multicoloured ... 35 35

No. 1443 was inscribed "Standard Postage" and sold for 1r.65.

453 Shongweni Dam Kwa-Zulu

(Des Rachel Joubert. Litho)

2003 (9 Oct). *Engineering and Postal Communication. Sheet 90×143 mm containing T* **453** *and similar multicoloured designs.* P 14×14½.

MS1444 (3r.30) Type **453**; (3r.30) Kimberly Microwave Tower (30×48 mm); (3r.30) Northern Cape Legislature (30×24 mm); (3r.30) Community Bridge, Limpopo (30×24 mm); (3r.30) Durban Westville Interchange (30×48 mm); (3r.30) Nelson Mandela Bridge, Gauteng (60×24 mm) .. 5·50 5·50

(Des Rachel Joubert. Litho)

2003 (19 Oct). *22nd PIARC World Road Congress. As No.* **MS**1444 *but inscr "XXIInd PIARC WORLD ROAD CONGRESS" on top margin, "CONNECTING THE WORLD" on bottom margin. Additional road agency logos are added to the left and right margins and the plate numbers, barcodes and SAICE logos are omitted. Sheet 90×143 mm containing T* **453** *and similar multicoloured designs.* P 14×14½.

MS1444*a* (3r.30) Type **453**; (3r.30) Kimberly Microwave Tower (30×48 mm); (3r.30) Northern Cape Legislature (30×24 mm); (3r.30) Community Bridge, Limpopo (30×24 mm); (3r.30) Durban Westville Interchange (30×48 mm); (3r.30) Nelson Mandela Bridge, Gauteng (60×24 mm) .. 6·00 6·00

454 Pot created by Afrikania Job Creation Project

455 "Hope"

(Des Thea Swanepoel. Litho Cartor)

2003 (16 Oct). *10th Anniv of Diplomatic Relations with India. Sheet 105×65 mm.* P 14½×15.

MS1445 **454** 3r.36 multicoloured ... 1·50 1·50

(Des Thea Swanepoel. Litho)

2003 (23 Oct). *150th Anniv of the Cape Triangular Stamp. As T* **10** *but with face value as T* **455**. *Phosphorised paper.* P 12½.

1446 **455** (1r.65) grey-blue ... 60 60
a. Tête bêche pair ... 1·20 1·20

No. 1446 was issued in sheetlets of 4 containing two tête-bêche pairs.

456 Joseph with Mary on Donkey

457 Star

(Des Thea Swanepoel and Annemarie Wessels. Litho)

2003 (3 Nov). *Christmas.*

(a) Horiz designs as T **456**. *Multicoloured. Phosphorised paper.* P 14.

1447 (1r.65) Type **456** ... 50 50
a. *se-tenant* strip of 5 ... 2·25 2·25
1448 (1r.65) Angels ... 50 50
1449 (1r.65) Three Wise Men ... 50 50
1450 (1r.65) Mary and Jesus ... 50 50
1451 (1r.65) Dove carrying holly ... 50 50
1447/51 *Set of 5* ... 2·25 2·25

(b) Vert design as T **457**. *Multicoloured. Phosphorised paper.* P 14½×15.

1452 3r.80 Type **457** ... 1·00 1·00

Nos. 1447/51 were issued in sheets of 10 comprising two strips of five stamps. Each was inscribed "Standard Postage" and sold for 1r.65.

458 African Elephant

459 Paterson Biplane

(Des A. Ainslie. Litho)

2003 (9 Dec). *10th Anniv of Diplomatic Relations with Thailand. T* **458** *and similar horiz design. Multicoloured.* P 14½×14.

1453 3r.36 Type **458** ... 1·25 1·00
a. Horiz pair. Nos. 1453/4 ... 2·50 2·00
1454 3r.36 Indian Elephant ... 1·25 1·00

Nos. 1453/4 were printed together, *se-tenant*, in horizontal pairs within sheets of 10.

(Des H. Botha. Litho)

2003 (17 Dec). *Centenery of Powered Flight. T* **459** *and similar horiz designs. Multicoloured.* P 14.

1455 (1r.65) Type **459** ... 50 50
a. Sheetlet of 10. Nos. 1455/64 ... 4·50
1456 (1r.65) Silver Queen Vickers Vimy ... 50 50
1457 (1r.65) Wapiti ... 50 50
1458 (1r.65) De Havilland DH 9 ... 50 50
1459 (1r.65) Junkers J u 52/53 ... 50 50
1460 (1r.65) Sikorsky S-55 ... 50 50
1461 (1r.65) Boeing 707 ... 50 50
1462 (1r.65) Rooivalk ... 50 50
1463 (1r.65) SUNSAT Micro satellite ... 50 50
1464 (1r.65) Mark Shuttleworth (astronaut) ... 50 50
1455/64 *Set of 10* ... 4·50 4·50

Nos. 1455/64 were printed together, *se-tenant*, in sheets of 10. The stamps were each inscribed "Standard Postage" and sold for 1r.65.

460 Monkey

(Des D. Murphy. Litho Enschedé)

2004 (27 Feb). *Chinese New Year ("Year of the Monkey"). Sheet 105×65 mm. L-shaped phosphor bands.* P 14×13½.
MS1465 **460** 11r.71 multicoloured .... 3·00 3·25

461 Patrol Sign and Pedestrian

(Des Rachel Joubert. Litho Enschedé)

2004 (24 Mar). *"Drive Alive" Road Safety Campaign. T* **461** *and similar horiz designs. Multicoloured. L-shaped phosphor bands.* P 13½×14.
1466 (1r.65) Type **461** 60 50
a. Sheetlet. Nos. 1466/70, each ×2 .... 5·50
1467 (1r.65) Slippery road sign and alcohol 60 50
1468 (1r.65) Service sign and car in disrepair 60 50
1469 (1r.65) Slow lorry Sign and steering wheel 60 50
1470 (1r.65) Danger sign and sleeping driver 60 50
1466/70 *Set of 5* .... 5·50 4·50
Nos. 1466/7 were printed together, *se-tenant*, in sheetlets of 10 (2×5) stamps. They were inscribed "Standard Postage" and initially sold for 1r.65.

462 Dove and Outline of Africa

(Des P. Sibanda. Litho Cartor)

2004 (27 Apr). *10th Anniv of Democracy. T* **462** *and similar horiz designs. Multicoloured. Phosphorised paper.* P 13½.
1471 (1r.65) Type **462** 50 50
a. Sheetlet. Nos. 1471/5, each ×2 .... 4·50
1472 (1r.65) Voters 50 50
1473 (1r.65) Accessing services (water, electricity) 50 50
1474 (1r.65) Sports supporters 50 50
1475 (1r.65) Traditional arts and crafts 50 50
1471/5 *Set of 5* .... 4·50 4·50
Nos. 1471/5 were printed together, *se-tenant*, in sheetlets of 10 (2×5) stamps. They were inscribed "Standard Postage" and initially sold for 1r.65.

463 Slave Lodge, Cape Town

464 Abstract Footballer

(Des Anne-Marie Wessels. Litho Cartor)

2004 (1 May). *The Legacy of Slaves. T* **463** *and similar horiz designs. Multicoloured. Phosphorised paper.* P 13½.
1476 (1r.70) Type **463** 50 50
a. Sheetlet. Nos. 1476/81 .... 2·75
1477 (1r.70) First book written in Arabic and Afrikaans 50 50
1478 (1r.70) Stinkwood Tulback chair and Jonkmans cupboard 50 50
1479 (1r.70) Traditional food 50 50
1480 (1r.70) Labourers on sugar cane farm 50 50
1481 (1r.70) Miners 50 50
1476/81 *Set of 6* .... 2·75 2·75
Nos. 1476/81 were printed together, *se-tenant*, in sheetlets of 6. They were inscribed "Standard Postage" and initially sold for 1r.70.

(Des Thea Swanepoel. Litho)

2004 (15 May). *Centenary of FIFA (Fédération Internationale de Football Association). Sheet 105×65 mm.* P 14½×15.
MS1482 **464** 4r.36 multicoloured .... 1·25 1·40

465 Penguins (Enviromental Helpers)

(Des J. Mocke. Litho Enschedé)

2004 (9 Aug). *Volunteers. T* **465** *and similar horiz designs. Multicoloured. L-shaped phosphor bands.* P 13½×14.
1483 (1r.70) Type **465** 55 55
a. Sheetlet. Nos. 1483/92 .... 5·00
1484 (1r.70) Volunteer assisting elderly person (Caring for the elderly) 55 55
1485 (1r.70) Child with building blocks (Education) 55 55
1486 (1r.70) Paramedics (Medical and ambulance services) 55 55
1487 (1r.70) Life guards (Surf life saving) 55 55
1488 (1r.70) Volunteer with dogs (Helping abandoned pets) 55 55
1489 (1r.70) Child in cot (Caring for orphans) 55 55
1490 (1r.70) Rescuing someone from fire (Fire fighters) 55 55
1491 (1r.70) Group gardening (Community gardens) 55 55
1492 (1r.70) Blind person and volunteer recording tape (Tape aids for the blind) 55 55
1483/92 *Set of 10* .... 5·00 5·00
Nos. 1483/92 were printed together, *se-tenant*, in sheetlets of 10. Each was inscribed "Standard Postage" and sold for 1r.70.

466 Archery **467** Cape Sugarbird

(Des Saskia van Wyk. Litho Enschedé)

2004 (13 Aug). *Sport. T* **466** *and similar vert designs. Multicoloured. L-shaped phosphor bands.* P 14×13½.
1493 (1r.70) Type **466** 55 55
a. Sheetlet. Nos. 1493/1502 .... 5·00
1494 (1r.70) Sprinting 55 55
1495 (1r.70) Show jumping 55 55
1496 (1r.70) Cycling 55 55
1497 (1r.70) Gymnastics 55 55
1498 (1r.70) Canoeing 55 55
1499 (1r.70) Football 55 55
1500 (1r.70) Swimming 55 55
1501 (1r.70) Boxing 55 55
1502 (1r.70) Tennis 55 55
1493/502 *Set of 10* .... 5·00 5·00
Nos. 1493/1502 were printed together, *se-tenant*, in sheetlets of 10. Each was inscribed "Standard Postage" and sold for 1r.70.

(Des Annamé Boshoff. Litho Southern Colour Print, New Zealand)

2004 (1 Sept). *Ecology of Table Mountain. Sheet 172×233 mm containing T* **467** *and similar multicoloured designs. Self-adhesive. L-shaped phosphor bands.* P 9×9½ (*vert*) or 9½×9.
MS1503 (4r.) Type **467**; (4r.) Dark Opal butterflies (*horiz*); (4r.); King Protea (flower) (*horiz*); (4r.) Cape Rock Hyrax (*horiz*); (4r.) Cuckoo Wasp (*horiz*); (4r.) Ghost Frog (*horiz*); (4r.) Cockroaches (*horiz*); (4r.) Staavia dodii (flower); (4r.) Spotted Skaapsteker (snake) (*horiz*); (4r.) Duvalia immaculata (*horiz*) .... 11·00 12·00
The backing paper of No. **MS**1503 is inscribed with details of all the species depicted on the stamps.
The stamps in No. **MS**1503 were each inscribed "International Airmail Rate Small Letter" and sold for 4r.

468 Children sharing Letters

(Des J. Lion. Litho Southern Colour Print, New Zealand)

2004 (23 Sept). *Universal Postal Union Congress, Romania. Phosphorised paper.* P 14.
1504 **468** 3r.45 multicoloured .... 1·00 1·00
No. 1504 was inscribed "Airmail Postcard" and sold for 3r.45.

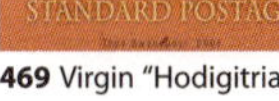

469 Virgin "Hodigitria" **470** Stylised Dove

(Des Thea Swanepoel. Litho Enschedé)

2004 (1 Oct). *Christmas. T* **469** *and similar vert design. Multicoloured. L-shaped phosphor bands.* P 14×13½.
1505 (1r.70) Type **469** 50 15
1506 (4r.) Christ Pantocrator (Almighty) .... 1·25 1·25
No. 1505 was inscribed Standard Postage" and initially sold for 1r.70.
No. 1506 was inscribed "International Airmail Letter" and initially sold for 4r.

(Des H. Botha. Litho Enschedé)

2004 (9 Oct). *World Post Day. L-shaped phosphor bands.* P 13½×14.
MS1507 **470** 12r.51 multicoloured .... 3·25 3·50

(Des Anja Denker. Litho Enschedé)

2004 (11 Oct). *First Joint Issue of Southern Africa Postal Operators Association Members. Sheet 170×95 mm containing hexagonal designs as T* **233** *of Botswana showing national birds of Association members. Multicoloured.* P 14.
MS1508 12r.51 African Fish Eagle (Namibia); 12r.51 Two African Fish Eagles perched (Zimbabwe); 12r.51 Peregrine Falcon (Angola); 12r.51 Cattle Egret (Botswana); 12r.51 Purple-crested Turaco ("Lourie") (Swaziland); 12r.51 Stanley ("Blue") Crane (South Africa); 12r.51 Bar-tailed Trogon (Malawi) (inscribed "apaloderma vittatum"); 12r.51 Two African Fish Eagles in flight (Zambia) 17·00 18·00
The stamp depicting the Bar-tailed Trogon is not inscribed with the country of which the bird is a national symbol. Minature sheets of similar designs were also issued by Namibia, Zimbabwe, Angola, Botswana, Swaziland, Malawi, and Zambia.

471 South African Large Telescope

472 South African Police Service Badge

(Des Anne-Marie Wessels. Litho Enschedé)

2004 (11 Nov). *South African Large Telescope. T* **471** *and similar vert designs. Multicoloured. L-shaped phosphor bands.* P 14×13½.
1509 4r. Type **471** 85 85
a. Sheetlet. Nos. 1509/13, each ×2 .... 7·50
1510 4r. Cross-section of observatory 85 85
1511 4r. View of the Southern Cross 85 85
1512 4r. Telescope 85 85
1513 4r. Telescope inside observatory 85 85
1509/13 *Set of 5* .... 3·75 3·75
Nos. 1509/13 were printed together, *se-tenant*, in sheetlets of 10 (2×5) stamps.

(Des SAPS Graphic Unit (1514,1522), Reáldi Marx (1515,1517/18,1521,1523), Jacqueline van Marie (1516), Rinie Voges (1519) and Joannie Ras (1520). Litho Southern Colour Print, New Zealand)

2004 (23 Nov). *South African Police Service (SAPS). T* **472** *and similar vert designs. Self-adhesive. Multicoloured. L-shaped phosphor bands.* P 13½×12½.
1514 1r.70 Type **472** 55 55
a. Sheetlet. Nos. 1514/23 .... 5·00
1515 1r.70 Handcuffed hands and drugs (Fight Against Drugs) 55 55
1516 1r.70 Police Helicopter (SAPS Air Wing) 55 55
1517 1r.70 Microscope (Fingerprint and Forensic Science Units) 55 55
1518 1r.70 Parachutists (Special Task Force) 55 55
1519 1r.70 Child and officer (Family Violence, Child Protection and Sexual Offences Unit) 55 55
1520 1r.70 Officers and map (Sector Policing) 55 55
1521 1r.70 Three police officers (The Dignified Blue) 55 55
1522 1r.70 Officer on horse (SAPS Mounted Unit) 55 55
1523 1r.70 Officer and police dog (SAPS Dog Unit) 55 55
1514/23 *Set of 10* .... 5·00 5·00
Nos. 1514/23 were printed, *se-tenant*, together in sheetlets of 10 with a brief description of the individual units inscribed on the backing paper behind the corresponding stamp. They were each inscribed **"Standard Postage"** and initially sold for 1r.70.

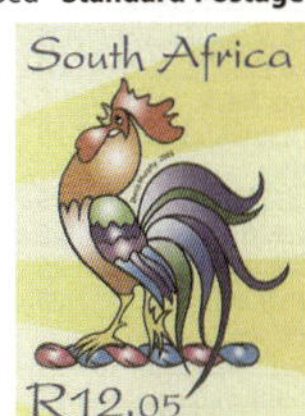

473 Rooster

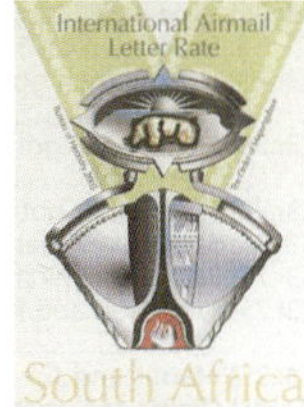

475 The Order of Mapungubwe

474 Immunising Children

(Des Denis Murphy. Litho Southern Colour Print, Dunedin)

2005 (9 Feb). *Chinese New Year ("Year of the Rooster"). Sheet 105×65 mm. Phosphorised paper.* P 14½.
MS1524 **473** 12r.50 multicoloured .... 3·50 3·50

(Des Joe Hlongwane. Litho Southern Colour Print, Dunedin)

2005 (23 Feb). *Centenary of Rotary International (humanitarian organisation). T* **474** *and similar horiz designs. L-shaped phosphor bands.* P 14.
1525 (4r.) Type **474** .... 1·25 1·25
a. Horiz pair. Nos. 1525/6 .... 2·50 2·50
1526 (4r.) Computer and metal work .... 1·25 1·25

(Des Bureau of Heraldry. Litho and embossed Southern Colour Print, Dunedin)

2005 (26 Apr). *National Orders of South Africa. T* **475** *and similar vert designs. Multicoloured. Phosphorised paper.* P 14½.

1527 (4r.25) Type **475** .... 1·40 1·40
a. Sheetlet. Nos. 1527/32 .... 7·50
1528 (4r.25) The Order of Mendi for Bravery .... 1·40 1·40
1529 (4r.25) The Order of the Baobab .... 1·40 1·40
1530 (4r.25) The Order of Luthuli .... 1·40 1·40
1531 (4r.25) The Order of Ikhamanga .... 1·40 1·40
1532 (4r.25) The Order of the Companions of O R Tambo .... 1·40 1·40
1527/32 *Set of* 6 .... 7·50 7·50

Nos. 1527/32 were printed together, *se-tenant*, in sheetlets of 6 stamps. Each was inscribed "International Airmail Letter Rate" and initially sold for 4r.25.

476 "Boland Winter" (Erik Laubscher)

477 Sunrise over the Gariep and "Freedom Charter" Reversed

(Litho Southern Colour Print, New Zealand)

2005 (6 May). *Landscape Paintings. T* **476** *and similar horiz designs. Multicoloured. Phosphorised paper.* P 14½.

1533 (3r.65) Type **476** .... 1·25 1·25
a. Sheetlet. Nos. 1533/42 .... 11·00
1534 (3r.65) "Table Mountain" (Maggie Laubser) .... 1·25 1·25
1535 (3r.65) "Fishermen Drawing Nets" (Walter Battiss) .... 1·25 1·25
1536 (3r.65) "Oh South Africa, you've turned my world completely upside down" (Lallitha Jawahirilal) .... 1·25 1·25
1537 (3r.65) "Untitled" (Lucky Sibiya) .... 1·25 1·25
1538 (3r.65) "Untitled" (Sophie Masiza) .... 1·25 1·25
1539 (3r.65) "Azibuye Emasisweni" (Trevor Makhoba) .... 1·25 1·25
1540 (3r.65) "Kontantwinkel Riebeeck-Wes" (John Kramer) .... 1·25 1·25
1541 (3r.65) "Houses in the Hills" (Gladys Mgudlandlu) .... 1·25 1·25
1542 (3r.65) "Sequence City" (Usha Seejarim) .... 1·25 1·25
1533/42 *Set of* 10 .... 11·00 11·00

Nos. 1533/42 were printed together, *se-tenant*, in sheetlets of 10 stamps. Each was inscribed "International Airmail Postcard Rate" and initially sold for 3r.65.

(Des Thea Swanepoel. Litho Southern Colour Print, Dunedin)

2005 (24 June). *50th Anniv of the Freedom Charter. Sheet, 105×65 mm, containing T* **477** *and similar horiz design. Multicoloured. L-shaped phosphor bands.* P 14½.

MS1543 (1r.77) Type **477**; (1r.77) Sunrise over the Gariep, "Freedom Charter" and "50" .... 2·50 2·50

The stamps of **MS**1543 form a panoramic design. Both were inscribed "Standard Postage" and sold for 1r.77.

478 Honeyguide's Revenge (Isi Ndebele)

479 Albert Einstein and Satellite

(Des Hein Botha. Litho Southern Colour Print, Dunedin)

2005 (1 July). *Folklore and Legends. T* **478** *and similar horiz designs. Multicoloured. L-shaped phosphor bands.* P 14½.

1544 (3r.75) Type **478** .... 1·25 1·25
a. Sheetlet. Nos. 1544/53 .... 11·00
1545 (3r.75) How Ostrich got his Long Neck (Sesotho) .... 1·25 1·25
1546 (3r.75) How Serval got his Spots (Setswana) .... 1·25 1·25
1547 (3r.75) How Zebra got his Stripes (Isi Zulu) .... 1·25 1·25
1548 (3r.75) Jackal the Tiger Eater (Cape Malay) .... 1·25 1·25
1549 (3r.75) Jackal and Wolf (Afrikaans) .... 1·25 1·25
1550 (3r.75) King Lion and King Eagle (Isi Xhosa) .... 1·25 1·25
1551 (3r.75) Mantis and the Moon (San) .... 1·25 1·25
1552 (3r.75) Words as Sweet as Honey (Tshi Venda) .... 1·25 1·25
1553 (3r.75) When Lion could Fly (Ancient Khoenkhoen languages) .... 1·25 1·25
1544/53 *Set of* 10 .... 11·00 11·00

Nos. 1544/53 were printed together, *se-tenant*, in sheetlets of ten stamps. Each was inscribed "B5" and sold initially for 3r.75.

(Des Rachel Ackermann. Litho Southern Colour Print, Dunedin)

2005 (7 July). *Year of Physics. L-shaped phosphor bands.* P 14½.

1554 **479** (3r.65) multicoloured .... 1·00 1·00

No. 1554 was inscribed "Airmail Postcard Rate" and initially sold for 3r.65.

480 Lesser Bushbaby

481 Hedgehog Spider

(Des Chris van Rooyen. Litho Southern Colour Print, Dunedin)

2005 (15 July). *JUNASS (2005). Small Indigenous Animals. Sheet, 145×90 mm, containing T* **480** *and similar multicoloured designs. L-shaped phosphor bands.* P 14.

MS1555 (1r.77) Type **480**; (1r.77) Riverine Rabbit (24×30 mm); (1r.77) African Wildcat (49×30 mm); (1r.77) Steenbok (49×30 mm); (1r.77) Cape Fox (24×30 mm);; (1r.77) Yellow Mongoose .... 4·00 4·00

The stamps of No. **MS**1555 were each inscribed "Standard Postage" and initially sold for 1r.77.

(Des Hein Botha. Litho Southern Colour Print, Dunedin)

2005 (30 July). *Spiders. Sheet, 233×172 mm, containing T* **481** *and similar multicoloured designs. L-shaped phosphor bands. Self-adhesive.* Die-cut perf 9½.

MS1556 (1r.77)×10, Type **481**; Golden orb-web spider; Lynx spider; Black button spider; Ladybird spider; Flower crab spider; Rain spider; Horn Baboon spider; Trap door spider; Spotted crab spider .... 7·00 7·50

The backing paper of No. **MS**1556 is inscribed with details of all the species depicted on the stamps. The stamps in No. **MS**1556 were each inscribed "Standard Postage" and sold for 1r.77. No. **MS**1556 was originally due to be released 30 July 2004 and the stamps show "2004" imprint date.

482 Wave

483 Christmas Tree, Candle and Heart

(Des Sulet Schulze. Litho Southern Colour Print, Dunedin)

2005 (26 Sept). *Renewable Energy Sources. T* **482** *and similar vert designs. Multicoloured. L-shaped phosphor bands.* P 14.

1557 (1r.77) Type **482** 60 60
1558 (3r.65) Wind .... 1·10 1·10
1559 (4r.25) Sun .... 1·25 1·25
1557/9 *Set of* 3 .... 2·75 2·75

Nos. 1557/9 were inscribed "Standard Postage", International Airmail Postcard" and "International Airmail Letter" and sold for 1r.77, 3r.65 and 4r.25, respectively.

(Des Peter Sibanda. Litho Southern Colour Print, New Zealand)

2005 (3 Oct). *Christmas. T* **483** *and similar vert design showing wire and bead work decorations. Multicoloured. L-shaped phosphor bands.* P 14×14½.

1560 (1r.77) Type **483** 70 25
1561 (4r.25) Angel and dove .... 1·25 1·25

No. 1560 was inscribed "Standard Postage" and sold at 1r.77.

No. 1561 was inscribed "International Airmail Letter" and sold at 4r.25.

484 "Hallo!" (Afrikaans)

(Litho Southern Colour Print, New Zealand)

2005 (7 Oct). *World Post Day. T* **484** *and similar horiz designs showing South African flag and "Hello" in South African languages. Multicoloured. L-shaped phosphor bands.* P 14½×15.

1562 (3r.65) Type **484** .... 1·10 1·10
a. Sheetlet. Nos. 1562/9 .... 8·75
1563 (3r.65) "Hi!" (English) .... 1·10 1·10
1564 (3r.65) "Sawubona" (IsiZulu and Siswati) .... 1·10 1·10
1565 (3r.65) "Ndi Masiari!" (Tshivenda) .... 1·10 1·10
1566 (3r.65) "Lotjha!" (IsiNdebele) .... 1·10 1·10
1567 (3r.65) "Avuxeni" (Xitsonga) .... 1·10 1·10
1568 (3r.65) "Dumela" (Northern Sotho) .... 1·10 1·10
1569 (3r.65) "Molo!" (IsiXhosa) .... 1·10 1·10
1562/9 *Set of* 8 .... 8·75 8·75

Nos. 1562/9 were printed together, *se-tenant*, in sheetlets of eight stamps. Each stamp was inscribed "Airmail Postcard Rate" and sold at 3r.65.

485 "Hello" embossed in Braille

(Des Saskia van Wyk. Litho and embossing Southern Colour Print)

2005 (13 Oct). *Prevention of Blindness. L-shaped phosphor bands.* P 14½×14.

1570 **485** (1r.77) multicoloured 70 50

No. 1570 was inscribed "STANDARD POSTAGE" and sold at 1r.77.

486 Labrador Guide Dog

(Des Annemarie Wessels. Litho Cartor)

2006 (27 Jan). *Chinese New Year ("Year of the Dog"). Sheet 125×65 mm. Phosphorised paper.* P 13.

MS1571 (3r.75) Type **486**; (3r.75) Customs sniffer spaniel; (3r.75) Border collie chasing birds away from airport .... 3·50 3·75

The stamps within No. **MS**1571 were inscribed "B5" and the miniature sheet was sold for 11r.25.

487 San Dancers (from Linton panel, Iziko South African Museum)

488 Lion

(Litho Cartor)

2006 (15 Feb). *Rock Art in South Africa. T* **487** *and similar horiz designs. Multicoloured. Phosphorised paper.* P 13½×13.

1572 (1r.77) Type **487** 75 75
a. Horiz strip of 5. Nos. 1572/6 .... 3·00 3·00
1573 (1r.77) Mountain reedbuck (South African Museum of Rock Art) 75 75
1574 (1r.77) San ritual specialist (South African Museum of Rock Art) 75 75
1575 (1r.77) Rhinoceros (Wildebeest Kuil) 75 75
1576 (1r.77) Eland (Game Pass) 75 75
1572/6 *Set of* 5 .... 3·00 3·00

Nos. 1572/6 were printed together, *se-tenant*, in horizontal strips of five in sheetlets of 10 (2×5) stamps. They were inscribed "Standard Postage" and sold for 1r.77 each.

(Litho Cartor)

2006 (24 Feb). *Wildlife "The Big Five". Self-adhesive booklet stamps. T* **488** *and similar vert designs. Multicoloured. L-shaped phosphor bands.* Die-cut.

1577 (3r.65) Type **488** .... 1·00 1·00
a. Booklet pane. Nos. 1577/81, each ×2 .... 10·00
1578 (3r.65) Buffalo .... 1·00 1·00
1579 (3r.65) Elephant .... 1·00 1·00
1580 (3r.65) Black rhinoceros .... 1·00 1·00
1581 (3r.65) Leopard .... 1·00 1·00
1577/81 *Set of* 5 .... 4·50 4·50

Nos. 1577/81 are inscribed "Airmail Postcard" and were initially valid for 3r.65 each. These stamps have straight edges on two adjacent sides (Type **488**) or at either top or bottom (others), with the remaining sides having wavy edges (simulating perforations).

489 Children riding Bicycles to School

490 Red Cross MBB BO105 Helicopter

(Des Jerry Lion. Litho Enschedé)

2006 (6 Mar). *Velo Mondial Conference, Cape Town. L-shaped phosphor bands.* P 13½×14.

1582 **489** (4r.25) multicoloured .... 1·40 1·10

No. 1582 is inscribed "International Airmail Letter" and was sold for 4r.25.

(Des Hein Botha. Litho Cartor)

2006 (2 May). *Medical Outreach to Rural Areas. T* **490** *and similar multicoloured designs. Phosphorised paper.* P 13½.

1583 (1r.85) Type **490** ... 90 90
a. Sheetlet. Nos. 1583/8 ... 4·75
1584 (1r.85) Clasped hands (24×30 mm) ... 90 90
1585 (1r.85) Red Cross Pilatus PC12 aircraft (48×30 mm) ... 90 90
1586 (1r.85) eRanger motorcycle ambulance (24×30 mm) ... 90 90
1587 (1r.85) Phelophepa Health Care Train (71×29 mm) ... 90 90
1588 (1r.85) St. John's ambulance (24×30 mm) .. 90 90
1583/8 *Set of 6* ... 4·75 4·75

Nos. 1583/8 were printed together, *se-tenant*, in sheetlets of six stamps. They were inscribed "STANDARD POSTAGE" and sold for 1r.85 each.

491 Bhambatha ka Mancinza Zondi and Mome Gorge

(Des Denis Murphy. Litho Enschedé)

2006 (9 June). *Centenary of the Bhambatha Rebellion. L-shaped phosphor bands.* P 14×13½.

1589 **491** (1r.85) multicoloured ... 50 40

No. 1589 is inscribed "Standard Postage" and was sold for 1r.85.

492 Nursing Sister with Child

493 African Wild Dog standing on Football

(Des Tobie Beele. Litho Enschedé)

2006 (18 June). *50th Anniv of the Red Cross War Memorial Children's Hospital. L-shaped phosphor bands.* P 14×13½ (1r.85) or 13½×14 (4r.40).

1590 (1r.85) Type **492** ... 50 25
1591 (4r.40) Hospital building (*horiz*) ... 1·25 1·40

No. 1590 has L-shaped phosphor bands at the right of the stamp, extending along the foot and halfway up the right-hand side. No. 1591 has L-shaped phosphor bands at left.

No. 1590 is inscribed "STANDARD POSTAGE" and was sold for 1r.85. No. 1591 is inscribed "INTERNATIONAL LETTER" and was sold for 4r.40.

(Des Michelle Beukes. Litho Southern Colour Print, New Zealand)

2006 (7 July). *World Cup Football, South Africa, 2010. Sheet 105×65 mm. L-shaped phosphor band.* P 14½.

MS1592 **493** (4r.40) multicoloured ... 1·25 1·40

No. **MS**1592 has L-shaped phosphor bands at right, extending along the foot and right-hand side of the stamp.

No. **MS**1592 is inscribed "International Airmail Letter" and was sold for 4r.40.

494 Sophia Williams, Rahima Moosa, Helen Joseph and Lillian Ngoyi leading March

(Des Thea Swanepoel. Litho Enschedé)

2006 (9 Aug). *50th Anniv of the Women's March to the Union Buildings, Pretoria. Sheet 105×65 mm. L-shaped phosphor bands.* P 15×14½.

MS1593 **494** (3r.75) multicoloured ... 1·10 1·10

No. **MS**1593 has inverted L-shaped phosphor bands extending along the top and left-hand side of the stamp.

No. **MS**1593 is inscribed "B5" and was sold for 3r.75.

495 *Clivia nobilis*

496 Buffalo

(Des Gillian Condy. Litho Cartor)

2006 (6 Sept). *Clivias. T* **495** *and similar vert designs. Multicoloured. Phosphorised paper.* P 13½.

1594 (1r.85) Type **495** ... 50 50
a. Sheetlet. Nos. 1594/9 ... 2·75
1595 (1r.85) *Clivia miniata* ... 50 50
1596 (1r.85) *Clivia gardenia* ... 50 50
1597 (1r.85) *Clivia caulescens* ... 50 50
1598 (1r.85) *Clivia mirabilis* ... 50 50
1599 (1r.85) *Clivia robusta* ... 50 50
1594/9 *Set of 6* ... 2·75 2·75

Nos. 1594/9 were printed together, *se-tenant*, in sheetlets of six stamps. They were inscribed "Standard Postage" and sold for 1r.85 each.

(Des Hantie Engelbrecht and Johan Schutte. Litho and die-stamped Enschedé)

2006 (15 Sept). *Animal Tracks–"Stories in the Sand". T* **496** *and similar horiz designs. Multicoloured. L-shaped phosphor bands.* P 14×13½.

1600 (1r.85) Type **496** ... 65 65
a. Sheetlet. Nos. 1600/9 ... 6·00
1601 (1r.85) Giraffe ... 65 65
1602 (1r.85) Elephant ... 65 65
1603 (1r.85) Spotted hyena ... 65 65
1604 (1r.85) Blue Wildebeest ... 65 65
1605 (1r.85) Leopard ... 65 65
1606 (1r.85) Hippopotamus ... 65 65
1607 (1r.85) Warthog ... 65 65
1608 (1r.85) Black rhinoceros ... 65 65
1609 (1r.85) Burchell's zebra ... 65 65
1600/9 *Set of 10* ... 6·00 6·00

Nos. 1600/9 were printed together, *se-tenant*, in sheetlets of ten stamps.

Nos. 1600/9 have inverted L-shaped phosphor bands extending along the top and right-hand side of the stamps.

Nos. 1600, 1602, 1604, 1606 and 1608 are inscribed "STANDARD POSTAGE", and Nos. 1601, 1603, 1605, 1607 and 1609 "standard postage". They were all sold for 1r.85.

497 Springbok

498 Climber ("Collect Stamps Start an Adventure")

(Des Dr. Jack. Litho Cartor)

2006 (2 Oct). *Christmas. "Jungle Bells". T* **497** *and similar vert designs. Multicoloured. Phosphorised paper.* P 13½×13.

1610 (1r.85) Type **497** ... 50 50
a. Horiz strip of 5. Nos. 1610/14 ... 2·50 2·50
1611 (1r.85) Warthog ... 50 50
1612 (1r.85) Zebra ... 50 50
1613 (1r.85) Hippopotamus ... 50 50
1614 (1r.85) King Lion as Father Christmas in donkey cart ... 50 50
1615 (4r.40) King Lion wearing Santa hat ... 1·25 1·25
1610/15 *Set of 6* ... 3·25 3·25

Nos. 1610/14 were printed together, *se-tenant*, in horizontal strips of five stamps throughout the sheet, each strip forming a composite design showing Springbok, Warthog, Zebra and Hippopotamus pulling Father Christmas in donkey cart.

Nos. 1610/14 are inscribed "Standard Postage" and sold for 1r.85. No. 1615 is inscribed "International Airmail Letter" and sold for 4r.40.

(Des Hein Botha. Litho Cartor)

2006 (9 Oct). *World Post Day. T* **498** *and similar horiz designs. Multicoloured. Phosphorised paper.* P 13½×13.

1616 (1r.85) Type **498** ... 55 55
a. Horiz strip of 5. Nos. 1616/20 ... 2·25 2·25
1617 (1r.85) "Be Cool Collect Stamps" ... 55 55
1618 (1r.85) Reader ("Learn More Collect Stamps") 55 55
1619 (1r.85) "Have Fun Collect Stamps" ... 55 55
1620 (1r.85) Traveller with suitcase ("Travel the World Collect Stamps") ... 55 55
1616/20 *Set of 5* ... 2·50 2·50

Nos. 1616/20 were printed together, *se-tenant*, in horizontal strips of five in sheetlets of 10 (2×5) stamps. They were inscribed "STANDARD POSTAGE" and sold for 1r.85 each.

499 *Paranthropus robustus*

(Des François Durand. Litho Enschedé)

2006 (10 Nov). *Origin of Humankind. Sheet 182×126 mm containing T* **499** *and similar vert designs. Multicoloured. L-shaped phosphor bands. Self-adhesive.* Die-cut perf 11½×12.

MS1621 (3r.80)×4, Type **499**; *Australopithecus africanus; Homo heidelbergensis; Homo ergaster*. 4·75 4·25

The stamps in **MS**1621 were each inscribed "Airmail Postcard" and sold for 3r.80 each.

They all have inverted L-shaped phosphor bands which extend along the top and left of Type **499** and *Australophithecus africanus*, and along the top and right of *Homoheidelbergensis* and *Homo ergaster*.

MACHINE LABELS

From 14 August (1986) gummed labels in the above design, ranging in value from 1c. to 99r.99, were available from an experimental machine at Sunnyside Post Office in Pretoria. The machine was moved to the "Johannesburg 100" exhibition from 6 to 11 October 1986 and was then reinstalled at Sunnyside on 17 October 1986. Further machines were introduced subsequently and each can be identified by a code number, between P.001 and P.034, at right. Commemorative labels were subsequently available at "PAARL 300" (1987), "PIETERMARITZBURG 150" (1988), "WANDERERS 101" (1989), "STAMPS 150" (1990), "CAPE TOWN 1991", "PRETORIA 92", eTHEKWINI (Durban 1993) and "BENONI '94" stamp exhibitions.

A new series of machine labels, with nine different designs showing province landscapes, was introduced on 20 October 1998 with operational values from 1r.10 upwards. Sets showing other face values from 10c. to 20r. were available against special order.

STAMP BOOKLETS

1913. *Black on red cover. With "UNION OF SOUTH AFRICA" at top and "UNIE VAN ZUID AFRIKA" at foot. Stapled.*

SB1 2s.6d. booklet containing twelve ½d. and twenty-four 1d. (Nos. 3/4) in blocks of 6 ... £5500

1913–20. *Black on red cover with "UNION OF SOUTH AFRICA" and "UNIE VAN ZUID AFRIKA" both at top. Stapled.*

SB2 2s.6d. booklet containing twelve ½d. and twenty-four 1d. (Nos. 3/4) in blocks of 6 ... £5500
a. Black on pink cover (1920) ... £5500

1921. *Black on salmon-pink cover with "UNION OF SOUTH AFRICA" and "UNIE VAN ZUID AFRIKA" either side of arms and telegraph rates beneath. Stapled.*

SB3 3s. booklet containing twelve ½d., 1d. and 1½d. (Nos. 3/5) in blocks of 6 ... £475

1922. *Black on salmon-pink cover as No. SB3 surch. Stapled.*

SB4 3s.6d. on 3s. booklet containing twelve ½d., 1d. and 2d. (Nos. 3/4, 6) in blocks of 6 ... £1000

1926. *Black on salmon-pink cover as No. SB3. Stitched.*

SB5 2s.6d. booklet containing twelve ½d. and twenty-four 1d. (Nos. 30/1) ... £2000

1927. *Black on salmon-pink cover as No. SB3, but inscr "Union of South Africa" and "Unie van Suidafrika". Stitched.*

SB6 2s.6d. booklet containing twelve ½d. and twenty-four 1d. (Nos. 30e, 31d) ... £4750

1930. *Black on pink cover as No. SB6, but with advertisement at foot instead of telegraph rates. Stitched.*

SB7 2s.6d. booklet containing twelve ½d. and twenty-four 1d. (Nos. 42/3) in blocks of 6 ... £1800

1931. *Black on pink cover. Smaller inscr and advertisement on front cover. Stitched.*

SB8 3s. booklet containing twelve 1d. (No. 43) in blocks of 6 and twelve 2d. (No. 44) in blocks of 4 ... £1900

1935. *Black on lemon cover. Advertisement on front cover. Stitched.*

SB9 2s.6d. booklet containing two panes of six ½d. (No. 54c) and four panes of six 1d. (No. 56e), all with adverts on margins ... £250

1937. *Black on lemon cover. Advertisement on front cover. Stitched.*

SB10 2s.6d. booklet containing two panes of six ½d. (No. 75ba) and four panes of six 1d. (No. 56f), all with blank margins ... £600

1937. *Machine vended booklets. Red cover. Stitched.*

SB11 6d. booklet containing four ½d. and 1d. (Nos. 75c, 56) in pairs ... 7·00

1938. *Machine vended booklets. Blue cover. Stitched.*

SB12 3d. booklet containing ½d. and 1d. (Nos. 75c, 56), each in pair ... 40·00

1938. *Black on buff cover. Union arms at top left with advertisement at foot. Stitched.*

SB13 2s.6d. booklet containing twelve ½d. and twenty-four 1d. (Nos. 75c, 56) in blocks of 6 ... £550

1939. *Black on buff cover. Union arms centred at top with advertisement at foot. Stitched.*

SB14 2s.6d. booklet containing twelve ½d. and twenty-four 1d. (Nos. 75c, 56) in blocks of 6 ... £450

1939–40. *Green on buff cover. Union arms centred at top with large advertisement at bottom left. Stitched.*

SB15 2s.6d. booklet containing twelve ½d. and twenty-four 1d. (Nos. 75c, 56) in blocks of 6 ... £2250
a. Blue on buff cover (1940) ... £120

1941. *Blue on buff cover as No. SB15. Stitched.*

SB17 2s.6d. booklet containing twelve ½d. and 1d. (Nos. 75c, 56) in blocks of 6 and 1½d. (No. 57) in block of 4 ... £150

1948. *Black on buff cover. With advertisement. Stitched.*

SB18 3s. booklet containing two panes of six ½d., 1d. and 1½d. (Nos. 114a, 56h, 87b), all with postal slogans on margins, and pane of air mail labels ... 30·00

1951. *Black on buff cover. Stitched.*

SB19 3s.6d. booklet containing two panes of six ½d., 1d. and 2d. (Nos. 114ca, 115a, 134a), each with margins at right ... 13·00

B 1 City Hall, Durban

1987 (16 Nov)–**88**. *Flood Relief Fund. Multicoloured covers as Type* B **1**. *Stamps attached by selvedge.*

SB20 2r.60 booklet (cover Type B **1**) containing 16c.+10c. (Nos. 624/5) in block of 10 ... 8·00

SB21 2r.60 booklet (cover, 139×85 mm, showing Bible) containing 16c.+10c. (Nos. 629/30) in block of 10 (1.12.87) ... 8·00

SB22 2r.60 booklet (cover showing Bartolomeu Dias) containing 16c.+10c. (Nos. 635/6) in block of 10 (1.3.88) ... 8·00

SB23 2r.60 booklet (cover, 125×90 mm, showing Huguenot Monument, Franschhoek) containing ten 16c.+10c. (Nos. 641/2) in block of 10 (13.4.88) ... 7·00

B 2 Stamp No. 787

1993 (7 May). *Aviation in South Africa. Multicoloured cover as Type* B **2**. *Stamps attached by selvedge.*

SB24 4r.50 booklet containing 45c. (Nos. 779/803) in block of 10 (back cover information in grey box) ... 14·00
a. ditto. (back cover information in red box) ... 14·00

Five versions of No. SB24/a exist showing different combinations of Nos. 779/803, *se-tenant* in panes of 10 (2×5). The Philatelic Bureau sold the booklets in sets of ten, each pane being numbered at foot.

1993 (3 Sept). *Endangered Fauna. Multicoloured cover as Type* B **2** *but showing No. 821. Stamps attached by selvedge.*

SB25 4r.50 booklet containing "Standardised mail" stamp (No. 821) in block of 10 ... 4·50

B 3 Lioness and Cubs Drinking (*Illustration further reduced. Actual size 142×64 mm*)

1993 (12 Nov). *Tourism. Multicoloured covers as Type* B **3**. *Stamps attached by selvedge. Five different cover designs: (a) Type* B **3** *(b) Luxury hotel (c) Table Mountain (d) Blue Train (e) Field of flowers.*

SB26 8r.50 booklet containing 85c. (Nos. 826/30) in block of 10 (any cover) ... 7·50

Set of 5 different cover designs ... 35·00

B 4

1995 (14 14). *Endangered Fauna. Ultramarine and bright scarlet cover as Type* B **4**. *Stamps attached by selvedge with outer edges of pane imperf.*

SB27 (4r.50) booklet containing pane of 10 "Standardised mail" stamps (No. 821a) ... 4·50
a. Containing booklet pane No. 821ba (9.4.96) ... 4·50

No. SB27 as initially sold at 4r.50 which was increased to 5r. on 30 September 1994, to 6r. on 1 April 1995 and to 7r. in August 1996.

1995 (Mar). *Tourism. Booklet No. SB26 with additional label inscr "FOR OVERSEAS POSTCARDS ONLY USE 1×85 c+1×5c = 90c".*

SB28 9r. booklet containing 85c. (Nos. 826/30 in block of 10 plus 5c. (No. 806) in strip of 10) (any cover) ... 7·00
a. With 5c. (No. 656) in block of 10 (5×2) ... 7·00
b. With 5c. (No. 806) in block of 10 (5×2) ... 7·00

1995 (Apr). *Tourism. Booklet No. SB24 with additional label inscr "FOR OVERSEAS POSTCARDS" ONLY USE 2×45c Stamps = 90 c".*

SB29 4r.50 booklet containing 45c. (Nos. 799/803) in block of 10 ... 6·00

B 5 Player running with Ball

1995 (25 May). *World Cup Rugby Championship, South Africa. Multicoloured cover as Type* B **5**. *Stamps attached by selvedge.*

SB30 (6r.) booklet containing pane of 10 "STANDARDISED POSTAGE" stamps (No. 875ab) ... 3·25

SB31 (6r.) booklet containing pane of 10 "STANDARDISED POSTAGE" stamps (No. 876ab) ... 3·25

1995 (16 Sept). *Masakhane Campaign. Bright scarlet and bright ultramarine covers as Type* B **4**. *Stamps attached by selvedge.*

SB32 (6r.) booklet containing pane of ten "STANDARD POSTAGE" stamps (No. 884a) ... 2·00

SB33 (6r.) booklet containing pane of ten "STANDARD POSTAGE" stamps (No. 884ba) (1 Dec) ... 2·00

B 6 Jackass Penguin

1995 (1 Dec). *Endangered Fauna. Multicoloured cover as Type* B **6**. *Stamps attached by selvedge.*

SB34 9r. booklet containing pane of ten 90c. (No. 816a) ... 3·50

B 7 Lion

1996 (8 May). *Tourism. Multicoloured cover as Type* B **7**. *Stamps attached by selvedge.*

SB35 (5r.) booklet containing pane of 5 "Airmail postcard rate" stamps and five labels (No. 821cc) ... 3·00
a. As No. SB35, but with additional tab and hole at right (Dec) ... 3·00

B 8 Drummer and Decorations

1996 (9 Oct). *Christmas. Multicoloured cover as Type* B **8**. *Stamps attached by selvedge.*

SB36 7r. booklet containing pane of ten 70c. (No. 937a) ... 3·00

1996 (Nov). *"Indaba '96" Tourism Exhibition, Durban. Multicoloured cover as Type* B **7**, *but 210×75 mm with inscr at right. Stamps affixed by selvedge.*

SB37 (5r.) booklet containing pane of 5 "Airmail postcard rate" stamps, 3 advertising and 2 airmail labels (No. 821cb) ... 3·00

B 9 Landscape and Sunflower (*Illustration reduced. Actual size 135×55 mm*)

1997 (7–5 March). *National Water Conservation. Multicoloured cover as Type* B **9**. *Pane attached by selvedge.*

SB38 7r. booklet containing pane of ten 70c. (No. 951a) ... 3·50
a. Containing booklet pane No. 951ba (25 Mar) ... 3·50

B 10 Black Rhinoceros (*Illustration reduced. Actual size 135×55 mm*)

1997 (1 May). *Endangered Fauna. Multicoloured cover as Type* B **10**. *"ILSAPEX 98" advertisement on the back. Stamps attached by selvedge.*

SB39 10r. booklet containing 1r. (No. 817) in block of 10 ... 8·00

1997 (June). *Endangered Fauna. Multicoloured cover as Type* B **10**. *"ILSAPEX '98" advertisement on the back. Stamps attached by selvedge.*

SB40 (10r.) booklet containing pane of 10 "Standardised mail" stamps (No. 821ba) ... 4·50
a. Human Rights Commission advertisement on back (Nov) ... 4·50

B 11 Man holding Spear (*Illustration reduced. Actual size 135×55 mm*)

1997 (27 July). *Thulamela National Heritage Site. Multicoloured cover as Type* B **11**. *Pane attached by selvedge.*

SB41 ($6) booklet containing pane of 5 and 5 commemorative labels (No. 821cd) ... 3·00

B 12 Cultural Artefacts (*Illustration reduced. Actual size 185×90 mm*)

1997 (8 Dec). *Year of Cultural Experiences. Multicoloured cover as Type* B **12**. *Booklet contains text and illustrations on left-hand margins of panes and on interleaving pages. Stitched.*

SB42 (20r.) booklet containing two panes of 10 "Standard Postage" stamps (No. 966ba) ... 6·50

B 13 Egyptian Geese (*Illustration reduced. Actual size 185×90 mm*)

1997 (8 Dec). *World Environment Day. Waterbirds. Multicoloured cover as Type* B **13**. *Booklet contains text and illustrations on left-hand margins of panes and on interleaving pages. Stitched.*

SB43 (20r.) booklet containing two panes of 10 "STANDARD POSTAGE" stamps (No. 977ba) ... 6·50

1998 (11 Feb). *Tourism. Multicoloured cover as Type* B **10** *showing lioness and inscr "10 AIRMAIL POSTCARD STAMPS". Stamps attached by selvedge.*

SB44 (12r.) booklet containing pane of 10 "Airmail Postcard" stamps (No. 1040a) ... 4·50

B 15 Technology at Work (*Illustration reduced. Actual size 135×55 mm*)

1998 (12 Feb). *Year of Science and Technology. Multicoloured cover as Type* B **15**. *Stamps attached by selvedge.*

SB45 (10r.) booklet containing pane of 10 "Standard Postage" stamps (No. 1029a) ... 2·75

B 16 Sable Antelope

1998 (18 May). *Centenary of Kruger National Park. Multicoloured cover as Type* B **16**. *Pane attached by selvedge.*

SB46 (11r.) booklet containing pane of 10 "standard postage" stamps (No. 1035a) .... 2·25

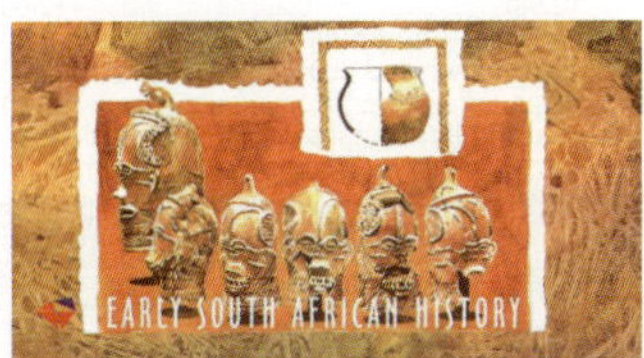

B **17** Lydenburg Heads (*Illustration reduced. Actual size* 185×92 mm)

1998 (28 June). *Early South African History. Multicoloured cover as Type* B **17**. *Booklet contains text and illustrations on left-hand margins of panes and on interleaving pages. Stitched.*

SB47 (22r.) booklet containing two panes of 10 "standard postage" stamps (No. 1055b) and two pre-paid postcards .... 7·00

B **18** Cape Vultures (*Illustration reduced. Actual size* 185×92 mm)

1998 (16 Aug). *South African Raptors. Multicoloured cover as Type* B **18**. *Booklet contains text and illustrations on left-hand margins of panes and on interleaving pages. Stitched.*

SB48 (27r.) booklet containing two panes of 10 "standard postage" stamps (No. 1065b) and two pre-paid postcards .... 8·00

B **19**

1998 (18 Aug)–**99**. *Endangered Fauna. Ultramarine and scarlet cover as Type* B **19**. *Self-adhesive.*

SB49 (11r.) booklet containing pane of 10 "standard postage" stamps (No. 1075ab) (P 13×12½)... 4·00

a. Containing pane No. 1075ba (P 11) (12.99). 4·00

B **20** Table Mountain

1998 (28 Sept). *Explore South Africa. Multicoloured covers as Type* B **20**. *Stamps attached by selvedge.*

SB50 (13r.) booklet containing pane of 10 Western Cape "AIRMAIL POSTCARD" stamps (No. 1084a) .... 8·00

SB51 (13r.) booklet containing pane of 10 KwaZulu-Natal "AIRMAIL POSTCARD" stamps (No. 1089a) (cover shows a rickshaw driver) 8·00

A limited edition booklet containing a sheet of ten of Nos. 1101/4 was only available at the "Ilsapex" Stamp Exhibition, Johannesburg, from 20 to 25 October 1998.

1998 (Oct). *Tourism. Multicoloured cover as No. SB44 (lioness), but smaller, 110×47 mm with no hole at right. Stamps attached by selvedge.*

SB52 12r. booklet containing pane of 10 "Airmail Postcard" stamps (No. 1045a) .... 2·50

B **21** Rhinoceros (from Beschryving van de Kaap de Goede Hoop, Peter Kolbe, 1727) (*Illustration reduced. Actual size* 138×55 mm)

1998 (18 Nov). *AIDS Awareness. Multicoloured cover as Type* B **21**. *Stamps attached by selvedge.*

SB53 (11r.) booklet containing "Standardised mail" (1r.10) (No. 821b) in block of 10 .... 4·50

a. Cover 110×55 mm without hang-sell hole at right. Containing No. 821 in block of 10. 4·50

The inside and back covers are printed with text and illustrations offering advice and telephone helpline numbers on AIDS. No. SB52a was adapted for use in supermarket dispensers.

B **22** The Blue Train

1998 (Nov). *Inauguration of Revived Blue Train Service. Multicoloured cover as Type* B **22**. *Stamps attached by selvedge.*

SB54 (13r.) booklet containing pane of 10 (1r.30) (No. 987ba) .... 6·50

B **23** Antelopes

1998 (2 Nov). *Centenary of Kruger National Park. Multicoloured cover as Type* B **23**. *Pane attached by selvedge.*

SB55 (11r.) booklet containing pane of 10 (standard postage) stamps (No. 1030pa) .... 2·00

B **24** Couple with AIDS Ribbon

1999 (1 Apr). *AIDS Awareness Campaign. Multicoloured cover as Type* B **24**. *Stamps attached by selvedge.*

SB56 (12r.) booklet containing pane of 10 "Standard Postage" stamps (No. 1117a) .... 6·00

1999 (6 Aug). *"Explore South Africa" (2nd series). Mpumalanga and Northern Province. Multicoloured cover as Type* B **20** *showing Pilgrim's Rest (historic town). Stamps attached by selvedge.*

SB57 17r. booklet containing pane of 10 "Airmail Postcard" stamps (No. 1138a) .... 8·00

B **27** Tree Pelargonium

2000 (1 Nov). *Flowers. Multicoloured cover as Type* B **27**. *Self-adhesive.*

SB60 13r. booklet containing pane of 10 1r.30 stamps (No. 1232a) .... 3·50

B **29** Lion

2001–2005 (25 Apr). *Wildlife. Multicoloured cover as Type* B **29** *Self-adhesive.*

SB62 (21r.) booklet containing pane of ten (2r.10) stamps (No. 1263a) .... 5·50

a. With changed telephone number, email address and website address on back cover (10.10.05) .... 4·00

No. SB62 was re-issued on 12.10.2003 dated 10.12 on inside cover.

No. SB62a is dated 2005.10.10 on the inside back cover.

2001 (25 Apr). *Flowers. Multicoloured cover as Type* B **27**, *but showing Blue Marguerite. Self-adhesive.*

SB63 (14r.) booklet containing pane of ten (1r.40) stamps (No. 1295a) .... 2·00

2001 (30 May). *Flowers. Multicoloured cover as Type* B **27** *but showing Blue Marguerite. Self-adhesive.*

SB64 (14r.) booklet containg ten (1r.40) stamps (No. 1305ba) .... 2·00

a. Institue for the Blind logo omitted from the back cover (19.8.02) .... 2·50

b. As above but with second fax number on back cover (5.5.03) .... 2·75

These booklets are dated as follows on inside back covers: SB64 2001.05.30, SB64a 2002.8.19, SB64b 2003.05.05 or 2004.02.09.

B **30** "People, planet and prosperity"

2002 (25 Aug). *World Summit on Sustainable Developemnt. Multicoloured cover as Type* B **30**. *Self-adhesive.*

SB65 (15r.) booklet containing pane of ten (1r.50) stamps (No. 1381a) .... 3·50

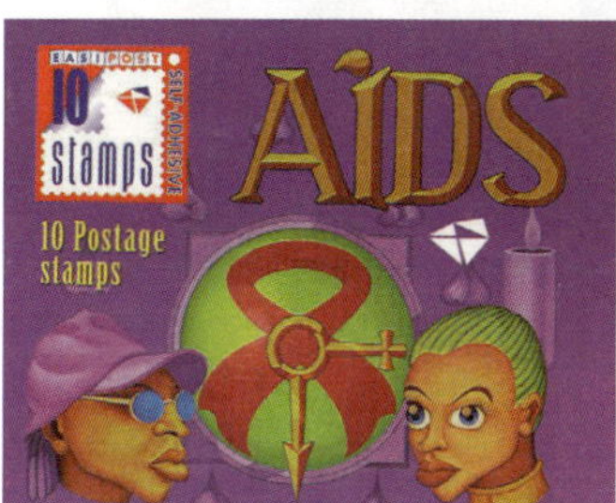

B **31** AIDS Ribbon

2002 (1 Dec). *AIDS Prevention. Multicoloured cover as Type* B **31**. *Self-adhesive.*

SB66 (15r.) booklet containing pane of ten (1r.50) stamps (No. 1407a) .... 2·50

B **32** Elephant

2006 (24 Feb). *Wildlife "The Big Five". Multicoloured cover as Type* B **32**. *Self-adhesive.*

SB67 (36r.50) booklet containing pane of ten (3r.65) stamps (No. 1577a) .... 10·00

PREMIUM BOOKLETS

The following booklets were sold at a premium over the face value of the stamps. All are stitched and have text and illustrations on interleaving pages.

A Nelson Mandela booklet issued on 26 November 2001 contained ten Airmail Postcard Rate stamps (face value 21r.), but was sold for 45r.

P 1 Tail of Blue Whale (*Illustration reduced. Actual size 190×90 mm*)

1999 (18 Aug). *Whales of the Southern Oceans. Multicoloured cover as Type* P **1**. *Stitched.*
SP1(B) 40r. booklet containing twenty "airmail postcard" (1r.70) stamps (Nos. 1101/4) in sheets of 10 plus two postal stationery postcards .... 7·00
Face value 37r.40.

P **2** Blue Marlin (*Illustration reduced. Actual size 185×92 mm*)

1999 (4 Oct). *Migratory Species of South Africa. Multicoloured cover as Type* P **2**. *Stitched.*
SP2 29r. booklet containing twenty "Standard Postage" stamps (Nos. 1155/64) in sheetlets of 10 plus two postal stationery postcards.. 10·00
Face value 26r.40.

P **3** Wildlife (*Illustration reduced. Actual size 187×92 mm*)

2001 (25 Apr). *Wildlife. Multicoloured cover as Type* P **3**. *Stitched.*
SP3 49r.20 booklet containing two panes of ten (2r.10) stamps (No. 1258a) plus two postal stationery postcards .... 8·00
Face value 46r.20.

THE ANGLO-BOER/SOUTH AFRICAN WAR • 11 OCTOBER 1899 - 31 MAY 1902

P **4** (*Illustration reduced. Actual size 185×91 mm*)

2002 (17 May). *Centenary of the Anglo-Boer War. Multicoloured cover as Type* P **4**.
SP4 45r. booklet containing three panes of 2 stamps (Nos. 1165/6, 1203/4 and 1343/4) and miniature sheet (No. **MS**1384) together with two postal stationery postcards reproducing the design of No. 1344. .... 8·00
No. SP4 was only available from philatelic outlets initially at 45r., a premium of 11r.50 over the face value of the contents.

POSTAGE DUE STAMPS

D **1**

UNION OF SOUTH AFRICA (A) UNION OF SOUTH AFRICA (B)

(Typo D.L.R.)

1914–22. *Inscribed bilingually. Lettering as A.* W **4**. P 14.

D1	D **1**	½d. black and green (19.3.15)	2·25	3·75
D2		1d. black and scarlet (19.3.15)	2·25	15
		a. Black ptd double	£1600	
		w. Wmk inverted	80·00	
D3		2d. black and reddish violet (12.12.14)	6·50	50
		a. Black and bright violet (1922)	7·00	60
		w. Wmk inverted	£130	
D4		3d. black and bright blue (2.2.15)	2·25	60
		w. Wmk inverted	45·00	
D5		5d. black and sepia (19.3.15)	4·00	28·00
D6		6d. black and slate (19.3.15)	7·00	30·00
D7		1s. red and black (19.3.15)	60·00	£150
D1/7 *Set of 7*			75·00	£190

There are interesting minor varieties in some of the above values, e.g. ½d. to 3d., thick downstroke to "d"; 1d., short serif to "1"; raised "d"; 2d., forward point of "2" blunted; 3d., raised "d"; very thick "d".

(Litho Govt Printer, Pretoria)

1922. *Lettering as A. No wmk. Rouletted.*

D8	D **1**	½d. black and bright green (6.6.22)	1·50	15·00
D9		1d. black and rose-red (3.10.22)	1·00	1·00
D10		1½d. black and yellow-brown (3.6.22)	1·25	1·75
D8/10 *Set of 3*			3·25	16·00

(Litho Govt Printer, Pretoria)

1922–26. *Type* D **1** *redrawn. Lettering as B.* P 14.

D11	½d. black and green (1.8.22)	80	1·75
D12	1d. black and rose (16.5.23)	90	15
D13	1½d. black and yellow-brown (12.1.24)	1·00	1·25
D14	2d. black and pale violet (16.5.23)	1·00	70
	a. Imperf (pair)	£275	£375
	b. Black and deep violet	12·00	1·50
D15	3d. black and blue (3.7.26)	8·00	22·00
D16	6d. black and slate (9.23)	12·00	2·00
D11/16 *Set of 6*		21·00	25·00

The locally printed stamps, perf 14, differ both in border design and in figures of value from the rouletted stamps. All values except the 3d. and 6d. are known with closed "G" in "POSTAGE" usually referred to as the "POSTADE" variety. This was corrected in later printings.

D **2**

D **3**

D **4**

2

Blunt "2" (R. 3/6, 8/6)

(Typo Pretoria)

1927–28. *Inscribed bilingually.* No wmk. P 13½×14.

D17	D **2**	½d. black and green	1·00	3·25
		a. Blunt "2"	11·00	
D18		1d. black and carmine	1·25	30
D19		2d. black and mauve	1·25	30
		a. Black and purple	19·00	80
D20		3d. black and blue	8·50	24·00
D21		6d. black and slate	21·00	3·50
D17/21 *Set of 5*			30·00	28·00

1932–42. *Type* D **2** *redrawn.* W **9**. P 15×14.

(a) Frame roto, value typo.

D22	½d. black and blue-green (1934)	2·75	1·75
	w. Wmk inverted	2·25	1·75
D23	2d. black and deep purple (10.4.33)	12·00	2·50
	w. Wmk inverted	12·00	2·50

(b) Whole stamp roto.

D25	1d. black and carmine (wmk inverted) (3.34)	2·25	10
D26	2d. black and deep purple 10.39)	28·00	10
	a. Thick (double) "2d." (R. 5/6, R. 18/2)	£325	27·00
	w. Wmk inverted	26·00	10
D27	3d. black and Prussian blue (3.8.32)	25·00	14·00
D28	3d. deep blue and blue (wmk inverted) (1935)	8·00	30
	a. Indigo and milky blue (wmk inverted) (1942)	75·00	3·25
	w. Wmk upright	50·00	2·50
D29	6d. green and brown-ochre (wmk inverted) (7.6.33)	25·00	5·00
	a. Green and bright orange (wmk inverted) (1938)	14·00	3·00
D22/9a *Set of 7*		80·00	19·00

In No. D26 the value is screened, whereas in No. D23 the black of the value is solid.

1943–44. *Inscr bilingually. Roto.* W **9**. In units of three, perf 15×14 subdivided by roulette 6½.

D30	D **3**	½d. blue-green (1944)	14·00	45·00	30
D31		1d. carmine	10·00	5·50	10
D32		2d. dull violet	6·50	11·00	15
		a. Bright violet	16·00	48·00	65
D33		3d. indigo (1943)	55·00	80·00	1·25
D30/3 *Set of 4*			75·00	£130	1·90

Split "D" (R. 7/5 on every fourth sheet)

1948–49. *New figure of value and capital "D". Whole stamp roto.* W **9**. P 15×14.

D34	D **4**	½d. black and blue-green	6·00	13·00
D35		1d. black and carmine	16·00	5·50
D36		2d. black and violet (1949)	16·00	8·50
		a. Thick (double) "2D." (R. 15/5-6, R. 16/5-6)	75·00	35·00
D37		3d. deep blue and blue	15·00	17·00
		a. Split "D"	£225	£250
D38		6d. green and bright orange (1949)	25·00	8·00
D34/8 *Set of 5*			70·00	45·00

1950–58. *As Type* D **4**, *but "SUID-AFRIKA" hyphenated. Whole stamp roto.* W **9**. P 15×14.

D39	1d. black and carmine (5.50)	70	30
D40	2d. black and violet (4.51)	50	20
	a. Thick (double) "2D." (R. 15/5-6, R. 16/5-6)	8·00	8·00
	b. Black and reddish violet (12.52)	1·00	60
	ba. Thick (double) "2D."	10·00	9·00
	bb. Black (value) omitted	£2750	
D41	3d. deep blue and blue (5.50)	4·50	2·50
	a. Split "D"	£110	60·00
D42	4d. deep myrtle-green and emerald (2.58)	12·00	15·00
D43	6d. green and bright orange (3.50)	7·00	9·00
D44	1s. black-brown and purple-brown (2.58)	12·00	15·00
D39/44 *Set of 6*		32·00	38·00

No. D40bb occurs in horizontal pair with a normal.

D **5**

D **6** Afrikaans at top

D **7** English at top

1961 (14 Feb). *Values in cents as Type* D **5**. *Whole stamp roto.* W **102**. P 15×14.

D45	1c. black and carmine	20	3·75
D46	2c. black and violet	35	3·75
D47	4c. deep myrtle-green and emerald	80	8·50
D48	5c. deep blue and blue	1·75	8·50
D49	6c. green and orange-red	6·50	8·50
D50	10c. sepia and brown-lake	7·00	10·00
D45/50 *Set of 6*		15·00	38·00

1961 (31 May)–**69**. *Roto.* W **102**. P 15×14.

D51	D **6**	1c. black and carmine	40	60
D52	D **7**	1c. black and carmine (6.62)	40	4·50
D53		2c. black and deep reddish violet	40	55
D54	D **6**	4c. deep myrtle-green and light emerald	2·25	2·25
D54*a*	D **7**	4c. deep myrtle-green and light emerald (6.69)*	12·00	22·00
D55		5c. deep blue and grey-blue	2·00	4·25
D56		5c. black and grey-blue (6.62)	1·75	7·50
D57	D **6**	6c. deep green and red-orange	8·00	5·50
D58	D **7**	10c. sepia and purple-brown	2·75	1·75
D51/8 *Set of 9*			27·00	45·00

1967 (Dec)–**71**. *Roto.* W **127** (tête-bêche). P 15×14.

D59	D **6**	1c. black and carmine	20	55
D60	D **7**	1c. black and carmine	20	30
D61	D **6**	2c. black and deep reddish violet	30	1·50
D62	D **7**	2c. black and deep reddish violet	30	1·50
D62*b*		4c. deep myrtle-green and emerald (6.69)*	29·00	29·00
D62*c*	D **6**	4c. deep myrtle-green and emerald (6.69)*	£250	£250
D63		4c. deep myrtle-green and pale green (4.71)	32·00	32·00
D64	D **7**	4c. deep myrtle-green (4.71)	32·00	32·00
D65	D **6**	5c. black and deep blue	50	50
D66	D **7**	5c. black and deep blue	50	50
D67	D **6**	6c. green and orange-red (1968)	3·50	10·00
D68	D **7**	6c. green and orange-red (1968)	3·50	10·00
D69	D **6**	10c. black and purple-brown	1·00	2·75
		a. Black and brown-lake (12.69)	1·00	2·75
D70	D **7**	10c. black and purple-brown	1·00	2·75
		a. Black and brown-lake (12.69)	1·00	2·75
D59/70a except D62b/c *Set of 12*			70·00	90·00

Nos. D59/70 were printed in two panes, one with inscriptions as Type D **6** and the other as Type D **7**.

*Nos. D54a, D62b/c and further supplies of D54 were part of a printing released in June 1969. Most sheets were printed on paper with the Arms watermark, but some were printed on RSA paper with the watermark upright and faint. Of these many were spoilt, but a few sheets were issued in Types D **7** and D **6**, the latter being very scarce.

1971. *Roto.* W **127** (tête-bêche). P 14.

D71	D **6**	2c. black and deep reddish violet	24·00	7·00
D72	D **7**	2c. black and deep reddish violet	24·00	7·00
D74		4c. deep myrtle-green and light emerald	45·00	40·00
D71/4 *Set of 3*			85·00	48·00

Nos. D71/4 were also printed in double panes as Nos. D59/70. Although the 4c. as Type D **6** must have been printed it has not been possible to confirm that any were actually issued.

D **8**

1972 (22 Mar). *English at right (1, 4 and 8c.) or at left (others).* W **127** (sideways tête-bêche). Chalk-surfaced paper (4c. to 10c.). P 14×13½.

D75	D **8**	1c. deep yellowish green	50	2·25
D76		2c. bright orange	70	3·00
D77		4c. plum	1·75	3·50
D78		6c. chrome-yellow	1·75	4·75
D79		8c. ultramarine	2·00	5·00
D80		10c. bright scarlet	6·00	7·50
D75/80 *Set of 6*			11·50	23·00

The 6c. also exists on phosphorised paper.

The printing of Postage Due stamps ceased in 1978. Isolated examples are known used as late as 1980.

OFFICIAL STAMPS

OFFICIAL. OFFISIEEL. (O 1)

OFFISIEEL OFFICIAL (O 2)

(Approximate measurements of the space between the two lines of overprint are quoted in millimetres, either in the set headings or after individual listings)

1926 (1 Dec). *Optd with Type* O **1** *(reading upwards with stops and 12½ mm between lines of opt).*

(a) On 1913 issue (No. 6).

O1 **3** 2d. purple .... 21·00 1·75

(b) On 1926 issue (Nos. 30/2).

			Un pair	Us pair	Us single
O2	**6**	½d. black and green	8·00	17·00	1·50
O3	**7**	1d. black and carmine	4·00	8·00	50
O4	**8**	6d. green and orange	£550	75·00	10·00
		w. Wmk inverted	£950	£375	30·00

The overprint occurs on both the London and Pretoria printings of Nos. 30/2. For the lower two values the overprinted London printings are scarcer than the Pretoria, but for the 6d. the ratio is reversed.

1928–30. *Nos. 32 and 34 optd as Type* O **1** *(reading upwards without stops).*

O5 **11** 2d. grey and maroon (P 14) (*17½ mm*) .... 6·00 23·00 2·00
a. Lines of opt 19 mm apart (1929) .... 7·00 18·00 1·50
ab. On No. 34a (P 14×13½) (1930) .... 35·00 42·00 5·00
O6 **8** 6d. green and orange (*11½–12 mm*) .... 21·00 42·00 2·75

1929–31. *Optd with Type* O **2**.

(a) On 1926 (Typo) issue (Nos. 30/2) (13½–15 mm between lines of opt).

O7 **6** ½d. black and green .... 2·50 4·50 35
a. Stop after "OFFISIEEL" on English inscr stamp (1930) .... 35·00 42·00 3·25
b. Ditto, but on Afrikaans inscr stamp (1930) .... 48·00 55·00 3·25
O8 **7** 1d. black and carmine .... 3·00 6·00 45
O9 **8** 6d. green and orange .... 8·00 40·00 3·25
a. Stop after "OFFISIEEL" on English inscr stamp (1930) .... 65·00 £140 10·00
b. Ditto, but on Afrikaans inscr stamp (1930) .... 75·00 £150 12·00

(b) On 1927 (Recess) issue (Nos. 36a/7) (17½–19 mm between lines of opt).

O10 **13** 1s. brown and deep blue (1931) .... 38·00 90·00 9·50
a. Stop after "OFFICIAL" on Afrikaans inscr stamp (R. 10/1, 10/7) £110 £225
b. Lines of opt 22 mm apart £325 £475
O11 **14** 2s.6d. green and brown (1931) .... 60·00 £150 19·00
a. Stop after "OFFICIAL" on Afrikaans inscr stamp (R. 10/1) £275 £500
O7/11 *Set of 5* .... £100 £250 29·00

The "stop" varieties for the ½d., and 6d. occur on R. 5/3, 5/11, 8/12, 15/3, 15/11, 18/12 with English inscriptions and R. 9/10, 9/12, 19/10, 19/12 with Afrikaans on the 1930 overprinting only.

As only the left-hand panes of the 2s.6d. were overprinted in 1931 the stop variety only occurs once. A further overprinting in 1932 was on both panes, but did not include No. O11a.

1930–47. *Nos. 42/4 and 47/9 ("SUIDAFRIKA" in one word) optd with Type* O **2**.

O12 **6** ½d. black and green (*9½–12½ mm*) (1931) .... 2·25 5·00 40
a. Stop after "OFFISIEEL" on English inscr stamp .... 38·00 55·00 4·00
b. Ditto, but on Afrikaans inscr stamp .... 27·00 48·00 3·50
c. "Cobweb" variety .... 40·00
d. "Dollar" variety .... 40·00
w. Wmk inverted (1934) .... 6·00 10·00 60
O13 **7** 1d. black and carmine (I) (*12½ mm*) .... 5·50 5·50 55
a. Stop after "OFFISIEEL" on English inscr stamp .... 50·00 65·00 4·00
b. Ditto, but on Afrikaans inscr stamp .... 35·00 48·00 3·50
cw. Wmk inverted (1931) .... 5·50 5·50 55
d. On Type II (No. 43d) (*12½–13½ mm*) (1933) .... 13·00 9·00 90
da. Opt double £275 £375
O14 **11** 2d. slate-grey and lilac (*20½–22½ mm*) (1931) .... 7·50 11·00 1·50
w. Wmk inverted (1934) .... 60·00 £110 8·00
O15 2d. blue and violet (*20½–22½ mm*) (1938) .... £140 £100 9·00
O16 **8** 6d. green and orange (*12½–13½ mm*) (*wmk inverted*) (1931) .... 8·50 8·50 85
a. Stop after "OFFISIEEL" on English inscr stamp .... 90·00 95·00 6·50
b. Ditto, but on Afrikaans inscr stamp .... 75·00 80·00 5·50
c. "OFFISIEEL" reading upwards (R. 17/12, 18/12, 19/12, 20/12) (1933) £600
w. Wmk upright (1935) .... 55·00 95·00 7·00
O17 **13** 1s. brown and deep blue (*19 mm*) (*wmk inverted*) (1932) .... 45·00 85·00 8·50
a. Twisted horn flaw £300
b. Lines of opt 21 mm apart (*wmk inverted*) (1933) .... 55·00 90·00 7·50
ba. Twisted horn flaw £300
bw. Wmk upright (1936) .... 65·00 £130 10·00
O18 **14** 2s.6d. green and brown (*17½–18½ mm*) (1933) .... 80·00 £140 15·00
a. Lines of opt 21 mm apart (1934) .... 55·00 75·00 8·50
aw. Wmk inverted (1937) £300 £350
O19 2s.6d. blue and brown (*19½–20 mm*) (11.47) .... 42·00 95·00 6·50
a. Diaeresis over second "E" of "OFFISIEEL" on Afrikaans inscr stamp (R. 6/2) £900 £1000
b. Ditto, but on English inscr stamp (R. 6/3) £900 £1000

The stop varieties for the ½d., 1d. and 6d. occur on R. 9/10, 9/12, 19/10, 19/12 with English inscriptions and R. 5/3, 5/11, 8/12, 15/3, 15/11, 18/12 with Afrikaans on the 1930 and 1931 overprintings only.

OFFICIAL OFFISIEEL (O 3) OFFISIEEL OFFICIAL (O 4)

1935–49. *Nos. 54, 56/8, 61/2 and 64a/b ("SUID-AFRIKA" hyphenated) optd.*

(a) With Type O **2** *(reading downwards with "OFFICIAL" at right).*

O20 **6** ½d. grey and green (*12½ mm*) (*wmk inverted*) (1936) .... 14·00 30·00 1·75
w. Wmk upright (1937) .... 7·00 28·00 1·75
O21 **7** 1d. grey and carmine (*11½–13 mm*) (*wmk inverted*) .... 4·75 5·50 35
aw. Wmk upright (1937) .... 4·00 3·00 20
b. Grey and bright rose-carmine (No. 56*i*) (1949) .... 4·00 5·00 30
O22 **22** 1½d. green and bright gold (*20 mm*) (*wmk inverted*) (1937) .... 50·00 32·00 1·75
aw. Wmk upright (1939) .... 28·00 24·00 1·00
b. Blue-green and dull gold (No. 57*c*) (1941) .... 50·00 11·00 1·10
O23 **11** 2d. blue and violet (*20 mm*) (1939) .... £150 35·00 2·25
O24 **8** 6d. green and vermilion (I) (*11½–13 mm*) (1937) .... 80·00 45·00 3·75
a. "Falling ladder" flaw £750 £475
b. Die II (No. 61*b*) (1938) .... 14·00 10·00 1·25
c. Die III *Green and red-orange* (No. 61c) (11.47) .... 4·00 8·50 85
O25 **13** 1s. brown and chalky blue (*20 mm*) (1939) .... 80·00 45·00 2·25
a. Diaeresis over second "E" of "OFFISIEEL" on both English and Afrikaans inscr stamps (1941) £1800 £1300
b. Ditto, but on English inscr stamp only (11.47) £1300 £900
O26 **15** 5s. black and blue-green (*20 mm*) (6.48) .... 65·00 £160 13·00
O27 **23** 10s. blue and blackish brown (No. 64*ba*) (*20 mm*) (6.48) .... £100 £275 23·00

(b) With Type O **3** *(reading downwards with "OFFICIAL" at left and 18–19 mm between lines of opt).*

O28 **15** 5s. black and blue-green (1940) .... £120 £140 12·00
O29 **23** 10s. blue and sepia (1940) .... £475 £500 38·00

(c) With Type O **4** *(reading upwards with "OFFICIAL" at right and 18½ mm between lines of opt.*

O30 **11** 2d. grey and dull purple (No. 58*a*) (1941) .... 11·00 32·00 2·25

No. O25a first appeared in the 1941 overprinting where the variety occurs on stamps 5 and 6 of an unidentified row. The variety reappears in the November 1947 overprinting where the stamps involved are R. 6/1 and 2. No. O25b occurs on R. 6/3 of the same overprinting.

Horizontal rows of 6 of the 1s. exist with "OFFICIAL" twice on the first stamp and "OFFISIEEL" twice on the last stamp. Such rows are believed to come from two half sheets which were overprinted in 1947, but not placed into normal stock (*Price for row of 6, £2500, unused*).

OFFICIAL OFFISIËEL (O 5) OFFICIAL OFFISIEEL (O 6)

1937–44. *No. 75c (redrawn design) optd.*

(a) With Type O **2** *(reading downwards with "OFFICIAL" at right and 11–12½ mm between lines of opt).*

O31 **25a** ½d. grey and green .... 23·00 19·00 1·25
a. Grey and blue-green (No. 75*cd*) (1944) .... 3·25 10·00 60

(b) With Type O **5** *(reading up and down with "OFFICIAL" at left and diaeresis over the second "E" of "OFFISIEEL". 10 mm between lines of opt).*

O32 **25a** ½d. grey and blue-green (No. 75*cd*) (1944) .... 45·00 30·00 2·00

1944–50. *Nos. 87 and 134 optd.*

(a) With Type O **2** *(reading downwards with "OFFICIAL" at right).*

O33 **34a** 1½d. blue-green and yellow-buff (*14½ mm*) .... 2·50 10·00 80
a. With diaeresis over second "E" of "OFFISIEEL" .... £550 £275 25·00
b. Lines of opt 16½ mm apart (6.48) .... 2·25 12·00 60

(b) With Type O **6** *(reading upwards with "OFFICIAL" at left and 16 mm between lines of opt).*

O34 **34a** 1½d. blue-green and yellow-buff (1949) .... 70·00 75·00 4·00
O35 **68** 2d. blue and violet (1950) £2750 £3250 £250

Two different formes were used to overprint Type **34a** between 1944 and 1946. The first, applied to the left halves of sheets only, had a diaeresis over the second "E" of "OFFISIEEL" on all positions of the setting, except for R. 1/2, 2/2 and 3/2. The second form, from which the majority of the stamps came, was applied twice to overprint complete sheets, had no diaeresis.

Examples of T**34a** overprinted with Type O2 *horizontally* exist, but their status is unclear. (*Price £750, unused pair*).

1947 (Nov)–**49.** *No. 107a optd with Type* O **2** *(reading downwards with "OFFICIAL" at right and 20 mm between lines of opt).*

O36 **54** 2d. slate and deep lilac .... 5·50 24·00 1·90
a. With diaeresis over second "E" of "OFFISIEEL" (R. 1/5-6, 11/5-6) £450 £650
b. Slate and bright violet (No. 107*b*) (1949) .... 8·00 16·00 1·60

1949–50. *Nos. 114 and 120 optd with Type* O **2** *(reading downwards with "OFFICIAL" at right).*

O37 **25a** ½d. grey and green (*11 mm*) .... 5·00 8·00 70
a. "Tick" flaw and spot on nose .... 50·00
b. Entire design screened (No. 114c) .... 5·50 10·00 90
O38 **13** 1s. brown and chalky blue (*17½–18½ mm*) (1950) .... 11·00 28·00 2·50

OFFISIEEL OFFICIAL (O 7)

1950 (June)–**54.** *Optd as Type* O **7** *using stereo blocks measuring either 10 (½d., 1d., 6d.), 14½ (1½d., 2d.) or 19 mm (others) between the lines of opt.*

O39 **25a** ½d. grey and green (No. 114c) (6.51) .... 70 1·50 15
O41 **7** 1d. grey and bright rose-carmine (No. 56*i*) .... 1·00 6·00 50
O42 1d. grey and carmine (No. 115) (3.51) .... 1·00 3·25 20
O43 1d. grey and carmine (No. 135) (6.52) .... 1·25 2·00 20
O44 **34a** 1½d. blue-green and yellow-buff (No. 87) (3.51) .... 2·00 4·50 30
O45 **68** 2d. blue and violet (No. 134) .... 1·00 2·00 20
a. Opt inverted £1000
O46 **8** 6d. green and red-orange (No. 119) .... 1·50 4·00 35
a. Green and brown-orange (No. 119*a*) (6.51) .... 1·75 3·50 35
O47 **13** 1s. brown and chalky blue (No. 120) .... 5·50 18·00 2·00
a. Blackish brown and ultram (No. 120*a*) (2.53) .... £170 £190 18·00
O48 **14** 2s.6d. green and brown (No. 121) .... 8·50 35·00 3·50
O49 **15** 5s. black and blue-green (No. 64*a*) (3.51) .... £180 £120 9·00
O50 5s. black and pale blue-green (I) (No. 122) (2.53) .... 65·00 85·00 6·50
a. Black and deep yellow-green (II) (No. 122*a*) (1.54) .... 75·00 £100 9·00
O51 **23** 10s. blue and charcoal (No. 64*ca*) .... 75·00 £250 22·00

The use of the official stamps ceased in January 1955.

XI. BOPHUTHATSWANA

The Tswana Territory Authority was established by South Africa in 1968, and was granted internal self-government in 1972 under the Bantu Homelands Constitution Act. Bophuthatswana became fully independent on 6 December 1977. This independence did not receive international political recognition, but the stamps were accepted as valid on international mail.

PRINTERS. All the following stamps were printed in lithography by the South African Government Printer, Pretoria.

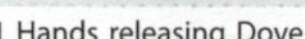

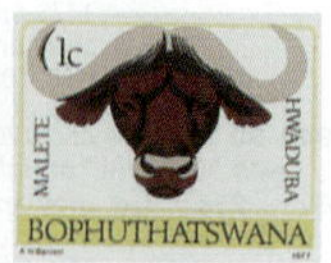

1 Hands releasing Dove　**2** African Buffalo (totem of Malete and Hwaduba tribes)

(Des A. H. Barrett)

1977 (6 Dec). *Independence. T* **1** *and similar horiz designs. Multicoloured.* P 12½.

1	4c. Type **1**	35	35
2	10c. Leopard (national emblem)	75	60
3	15c. Coat of arms	1·00	1·00
4	20c. National flag	1·25	1·40
1/4 *Set of* 4		3·00	3·00

(Des A. H. Barrett)

1977 (6 Dec)–**82**. *Tribal Totems. T* **2** *and similar horiz designs. Multicoloured.* P 12½.

5	1c. Type **2**	30	15
	a. Perf 14 (15.4.81)	20	15
6	2c. Bush Pig (Kolobeng)	30	15
	a. Perf 14 (21.6.82)	20	15
7	3c. Chacma Baboon (Hurutshe and Tlharo)	30	15
	a. Perf 14 (18.8.82)	20	15
8	4c. Leopard (national emblem)	3·00	1·25
	a. Perf 14 (6.7.79)	20	10
9	5c. Crocodile (Kwena and Fokeng)	1·00	50
	a. Perf 14 (25.1.80)	20	10
10	6c. Savanna Monkey (Kgatla)	20	10
11	7c. Lion (Taung)	1·40	60
	a. Perf 14 (18.12.79)	30	15
12	8c. Spotted Hyena (Phiring)	35	15
	a. Perf 14 (2.2.82)	20	15
13	9c. Cape Porcupine (Rokologadi)	25	15
14	10c. Aardvark (Tlokwa)	25	10
	a. Perf 14 (21.6.82)	25	10
15	15c. Tilapia (fish) (Tlhaping)	1·00	15
16	20c. Hunting Dog (Tlhalerwa)	25	20
17	25c. Common Duiker (Mfatlha)	40	30
18	30c. African Elephant (Tlhako, Tloung and Pô)	60	35
19	50c. Python (Nogeng)	70	40
20	1r. Hippopotamus (Kubung)	1·10	1·00
21	2r. Greater Kudu (Rolong)	1·10	1·75
5/21 *Set of* 17 (cheapest)		6·50	4·75

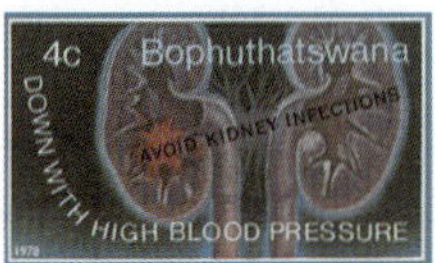

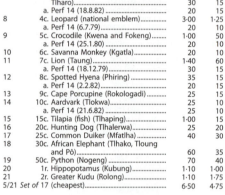

3 Infected Kidney

(Des A. H. Barrett)

1978 (4 Apr). *World Hypertension Month. T* **3** *and similar horiz designs. Multicoloured.* P 12×12½.

22	4c. Type **3**	50	25
23	10c. Heart and spoon of salt	70	70
24	15c. Spoon reflecting skull, knife and fork	1·25	1·25
22/4 *Set of* 3		2·25	2·00

4 Skull behind Wheel of Car　**5** Cutting Slabs of Travertine

1978 (12 July). *Road Safety. T* **4** *and similar horiz designs. Multicoloured.* P 12×12½.

25	4c. Type **4**	70	40
26	10c. Child knocked off tricycle	90	80
27	15c. Pedestrian stepping in front of car	1·00	1·10
28	20c. Cyclist ignoring stop sign	1·40	1·75
25/8 *Set of* 4		3·50	3·50

(Des A. H. Barrett)

1978 (3 Oct). *Semi-precious Stones. T* **5** *and similar horiz designs. Multicoloured.* P 12×12½.

29	4c. Type **5**	65	25
30	10c. Polishing travertine	1·25	85
31	15c. Sorting semi-precious stones	1·50	1·25
32	20c. Factory at Taung	2·25	1·60
29/32 *Set of* 4		5·00	3·50

6 Wright Flyer

(Des A. H. Barrett)

1978 (1 Dec). *75th Anniv of First Powered Flight by Wright Brothers. T* **6** *and similar horiz design.* P 12½.

33	10c. black, deep grey-blue and brown-red	1·00	1·00
34	15c. black, deep grey-blue and brown-red	1·40	1·50

Design:—15c. Orville and Wilbur Wright.

7 Pres. Lucas M. Mangope　**8** Drying Germinated Wheat Sorghum

(Des A. H. Barrett)

1978 (6 Dec). *First Anniv of Independence. T* **7** *and similar vert design. Multicoloured.* P 12½.

35	4c. Type **7**	25	20
36	15c. Full face portrait of President	75	60

(Des A. H. Barrett)

1979 (28 Feb). *Sorghum Beer-making. T* **8** *and similar horiz designs. Multicoloured.* P 13½×14.

37	4c. Type **8**	25	20
38	15c. Cooking the ground grain	65	70
39	20c. Sieving the liquid	70	75
40	25c. Drinking the beer	80	1·00
37/40 *Set of* 4		2·25	2·40

9 Kallie Knoetze　**10** Emblem and Drawing by Hendrick (South Africa) Sebapo of Local Fable

1979 (2 June). *Knoetze-Tate Boxing Match. T* **9** *and similar horiz design. Multicoloured.* P 13½×14.

41	15c. Type **9**	75	75
	a. Pair. Nos. 41/2	1·50	1·50
42	15c. John Tate (USA)	75	75

Nos. 41/2 were printed together, *se-tenant*, in pairs throughout the sheet.

1979 (7 June). *International Year of the Child. Children's Drawings of Local Fables. T* **10** *and similar horiz designs. Multicoloured.* P 14.

43	4c. Type **10**	20	20
44	15c. Family with animals (Daisy Morapedi)	25	25
45	20c. Man's head and landscape (Peter Tladi)	35	35
46	25c. Old man, boy and donkey (Hendrick Sebapo)	45	60
43/6 *Set of* 4		1·10	1·40

11 Miner and Molten Platinum　**12** Cattle

(Des B. Sargent)

1979 (15 Aug). *Platinum Industry. T* **11** *and similar horiz designs.* P 13½×14.

47	4c. multicoloured	25	10
48	15c. multicoloured	35	30
49	20c. multicoloured	45	45
50	25c. black, grey and deep grey	60	65
47/50 *Set of* 4		1·50	1·40

Designs:—15c. Platinum granules and industrial use; 20c. Telecommunications satellite; 25c. Jewellery.

(Des A. H. Barrett)

1979 (25 Oct). *Agriculture. T* **12** *and similar horiz designs. Multicoloured.* P 13½×14.

51	5c. Type **12**	20	20
52	15c. Picking cotton	25	25
53	20c. Scientist examining maize	30	30
54	25c. Catch of fish	35	35
51/4 *Set of* 4		1·00	1·00

13 Cigarettes forming Cross　**14** *Landolphia capensis*　**15** Pied Babbler

(Des A. H. Barrett)

1980 (5 Mar). *Anti-smoking Campaign.* P 14×13½.

55	**13**	5c. multicoloured	40	20

(Des. D. Findlay)

1980 (4 June). *Edible Wild Fruits. T* **14** *and similar vert designs. Multicoloured.* P 14×13½.

56	5c. Type **14**	15	15
57	10c. *Vangueria infausta*	30	30
58	15c. *Bequaertiodendron magalismontanum*	40	40
59	20c. *Sclerocarya caffra*	55	55
56/9 *Set of* 4		1·25	1·25

(Des D. Findlay)

1980 (10 Sept). *Birds. T* **15** *and similar vert designs. Multicoloured.* P 14×13½.

60	5c. Type **15**	30	20
61	10c. Carmine Bee Eater	40	35
62	15c. Shaft-tailed Whydah	60	60
63	20c. Meyer's Parrot	70	65
60/3 *Set of* 4		1·75	1·60

16 Sun City Hotel　**17** Deaf Child

(Des P. Roos and G. Mynhardt)

1980 (5 Dec). *Tourism. Sun City. T* **16** *and similar horiz designs. Multicoloured.* P 13½×14.

64	5c. Type **16**	10	15
65	10c. Gary Player Country Club	40	30
66	15c. Casino	45	50
67	20c. Extravaganza	50	70
64/7 *Set of* 4		1·25	1·50

(Des H. Botha)

1981 (30 Jan). *International Year of Disabled Persons. T* **17** *and similar vert designs. Multicoloured.* P 14×13½.

68	5c. Type **17**	15	10
69	15c. Blind child	30	20
70	20c. Archer in wheelchair	45	35
71	25c. Tuberculosis x-ray	60	60
68/71 *Set of* 4		1·40	1·10

18 "Behold the Lamb of God..."　**19** Siemens and Halske Wall Telephone, 1885

(Des J. Meyer)

1981 (1 Apr). *Easter. T* **18** *and similar horiz designs. Multicoloured.* P 13½×14.

72	5c. Type **18**	10	10
73	15c. Bread ("I am the bread of life")	25	25
74	20c. Shepherd ("I am the good shepherd...")	35	35
75	25c. Wheatfield ("Unless a grain of wheat falls into the earth and dies...")	45	45
72/5 *Set of* 4		1·00	1·00

(Des J. Hoekstra)

1981 (31 July). *History of the Telephone (1st series). T* **19** *and similar vert designs. Multicoloured.* P 14×13½.

76	5c. Type **19**	10	10
77	15c. Ericsson telephone, 1895	25	25
78	20c. Hasler telephone, 1900	35	35
79	25c. Mix and Genest wall telephone, 1904	45	45
76/9 *Set of* 4		1·00	1·00

See also Nos. 92/5, 108/11 and 146/9.

HAVE YOU READ THE NOTES AT THE BEGINNING OF THIS CATALOGUE?

These often provide answers to the enquiries we receive

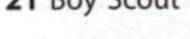

20 *Themeda triandra* **21** Boy Scout **22** Jesus arriving at Bethany (John 12:1)

(Des D. Findlay)

1981 (25 Nov). *Indigenous Grasses (1st series). T* **20** *and similar vert designs. Multicoloured.* P 14×13½.

80 5c. Type **20** ... 10 10
81 15c. *Rhynchelytrum repens* ... 20 25
82 20c. *Eragrostis capensis* ... 20 30
83 25c. *Monocymbium ceresiiforme* ... 30 45
80/3 *Set of 4* ... 70 1·00

See also Nos. 116/19.

(Des Sheila Nowers)

1982 (29 Jan). *75th Anniv of Boy Scout Movement. T* **21** *and similar vert designs. Multicoloured.* P 14×13½.

84 5c. Type **21** ... 15 10
85 15c. Mafeking siege stamps ... 35 35
86 20c. Original cadet ... 40 40
87 25c. Lord Baden-Powell ... 45 45
84/7 *Set of 4* ... 1·25 1·10

(Des J. Meyer)

1982 (1 Apr). *Easter. Palm Sunday. T* **22** *and similar vert designs. Multicoloured.* P 14×13½.

88 15c. Type **22** ... 25 25
89 20c. Jesus sending disciples for donkey (Matthew 21:1,2) ... 30 30
90 25c. Disciples taking donkey (Mark 11:5,6) ... 40 40
91 30c. Disciples with donkey and foal (Matthew 21:7) ... 45 45
88/91 *Set of 4* ... 1·25 1·25

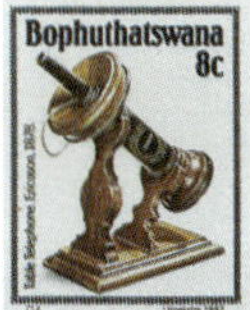

23 Ericsson Telephone **24** Old Parliament Building 1878

(Des J. Hoekstra)

1982 (3 Sept). *History of the Telephone (2nd series). T* **23** *and similar vert designs. Multicoloured.* P 14.

92 8c. Type **23** ... 15 10
93 15c. Ericsson telephone, 1885 ... 20 20
94 20c. Ericsson telephone, 1893 ... 20 20
95 25c. Siemens and Halske telephone, 1898 ... 30 30
92/5 *Set of 4* ... 75 70

(Des A. H. Barrett)

1982 (12 Dec). *Fifth Anniv of Independence. T* **24** *and similar horiz designs. Multicoloured.* P 13½×14.

96 8c. Type **24** ... 10 10
97 15c. New government offices ... 20 20
98 20c. University, Mmabatho ... 25 25
99 25c. Civic Centre, Mmabatho ... 30 30
96/9 *Set of 4* ... 75 75

25 White Rhinoceros

(Des P. Bosman)

1983 (5 Jan). *Pilanesberg Nature Reserve. T* **25** *and similar horiz designs. Multicoloured.* P 13½×14.

100 8c. Type **25** ... 30 10
101 20c. Common Zebras ... 40 30
102 25c. Sable Antelope ... 40 35
103 40c. Hartebeest ... 60 60
100/3 *Set of 4* ... 1·50 1·10

26 Disciples bringing Donkeys to Jesus (Matthew 21:7) **27** Kori Bustard

(Des Sheila Nowers)

1983 (30 Mar). *Easter. Palm Sunday. T* **26** *and similar horiz designs. Multicoloured.* P 14×13½.

104 8c. Type **26** ... 10 10
105 20c. Jesus stroking colt (Mark 11:7) ... 30 30
106 25c. Jesus enters Jerusalem on donkey (Matthew 21:8) ... 35 35
107 40c. Crowd welcoming Jesus (Mark 11:9) ... 60 60
104/7 *Set of 4* ... 1·10 1·10

(Des I. Ellithorne)

1983 (22 June). *History of the Telephone (3rd series). Vert designs as T* **19**. *Multicoloured.* P 14×13½.

108 10c. A.T.M. table telephone, c. 1920 ... 15 10
109 20c. A/S Elektrisk wall telephone, c. 1900 ... 30 30
110 25c. Ericsson wall telephone, c. 1900 ... 35 35
111 40c. Ericsson wall telephone, c. 1900 (different) ... 60 60
108/11d *Set of 4* ... 1·25 1·25

(Des D. Finlay)

1983 (14 Sept). *Birds of the Veld. T* **27** *and similar vert designs. Multicoloured.* P 14.

112 10c. Type **27** ... 30 20
113 20c. Little Black Bustard ("Black Korhaan") ... 45 45
114 25c. Crested Bustard ("Red-crested Korhaan") ... 55 55
115 40c. Barrow's Bustard ("Stanley Bustard") ... 70 80
112/15 *Set of 4* ... 1·75 1·75

(Des D. Findlay)

1984 (20 Jan). *Indigenous Grasses (2nd series). Vert designs as T* **20**. *Multicoloured.* P 14½×14.

116 10c. *Panicum maximum* ... 15 10
117 20c. *Hyparrhenia dregeana* ... 20 20
118 25c. *Cenchrus ciliaris* ... 25 35
119 40c. *Urochloa brachyura* ... 50 70
116/19 *Set of 4* ... 1·25 1·25

28 Money-lenders in the Temple (Mark 11:11)

(Des J. van Niekerk)

1984 (23 Mar). *Easter. T* **28** *and similar horiz designs. Multicoloured.* P 14½×14.

120 10c. Type **28** ... 15 10
121 20c. Jesus driving the money-lenders from the Temple (Mark 11:15) ... 25 20
122 25c. Jesus and fig tree (Matthew 21:19) ... 35 35
123 40c. The withering of the fig tree (Matthew 21:19) ... 60 70
120/3 *Set of 4* ... 1·25 1·25

29 Car Upholstery, Ga-Rankuwa

(Des A. H. Barrett)

1984 (2 Apr)–**94**. *Industries. T* **29** *and similar horiz designs. Multicoloured. Chalk-surfaced paper (except Nos. 134/5).* P 14.

124 1c. Textile mill (25.10.85) ... 10 10
a. Ordinary paper (18.7.94) ... 30 30
125 2c. Sewing sacks, Selosesha (25.10.85) ... 10 10
a. Ordinary paper (5.6.92) ... 30 30
126 3c. Ceramic tiles, Babelegi (25.10.85) ... 10 10
127 4c. Sheepskin car seat covers (25.10.85) ... 10 10
a. Ordinary paper (3.7.92) ... 30 30
128 5c. Crossbow manufacture (25.10.85) ... 15 10
a. Ordinary paper (16.11.92) ... 30 30
129 6c. Automobile parts, Babelegi (25.10.85) ... 15 10
a. Ordinary paper (26.6.92) ... 30 30
130 7c. Hosiery, Babelegi (25.10.85) ... 15 10
a. Ordinary paper (26.6.92) ... 30 30
131 8c. Specialised bicycle factory, Babelegi (25.10.85) ... 30 10
132 9c. Lawn mower assembly line (25.10.85) ... 30 15
133 10c. Dress factory, Thaba 'Nchu (25.10.85) ... 20 10
134 11c. Molten platinum (ordinary paper) ... 60 20
135 12c. Type **29** (1.4.85) (ordinary paper) ... 40 15
a. Chalk-surfaced paper (5.12.85) ... 40 15
136 14c. Maize mill, Mafeking (1.4.86) ... 50 15
137 15c. Plastic bags, Babelegi (25.10.85) ... 25 15
a. Ordinary paper (3.7.92) ... 1·25 70
137*b* 16c. Brick factory, Mmabatho (1.4.87) ... 60 15
137*c* 18c. Cutlery manufacturing, Mogwase (3.7.89) ... 60 15
138 20c. Men's clothing, Babelegi (25.10.85) ... 25 15
a. Ordinary paper (26.6.92) ... 1·40 75
138*b* 21c. Welding bus chassis (3.8.90) ... 50 50
ba. Strip of five. Nos. 138b/f ... 2·25
138*c* 21c. Fitting engine to bus chassis (3.8.90) ... 50 50
138*d* 21c. Bus body construction (3.8.90) ... 50 50
138*e* 21c. Spraying and finishing bus (3.8.90) ... 50 50
138*f* 21c. Finished buses (3.8.90) ... 50 50
139 25c. Chromium plating pram parts (25.10.85) ... 30 20
a. Ordinary paper (24.1.92) ... 60 30
140 30c. Spray painting metal beds (25.10.85) ... 40 25
a. Ordinary paper (1.2.89) ... 75 50
141 50c. Milk processing plant (25.10.85) ... 50 40
a. Ordinary paper (1.2.89) ... 85 75
142 1r. Modern printing works (25.10.85) ... 60 75
143 2r. Industrial complex, Babelegi (25.10.85) ... 1·00 2·50
124/43 *Set of 27* ... 9·00 7·50

Nos. 138*b/f* were printed together, *se-tenant*, in strips of five throughout the sheet.

(Des I. Ellithorne)

1984 (20 July). *History of the Telephone (4th series). Vert designs as T* **19**. *Multicoloured.* P 14.

146 11c. Schuchhardt table telephone, 1905 ... 15 10
147 20c. Siemens wall telephone, 1925 ... 25 20
148 25c. Ericsson table telephone, 1900 ... 30 30
149 30c. Oki table telephone, 1930 ... 40 50
146/9 *Set of 4* ... 1·00 1·00

30 Yellow-throated Plated Lizard **31** Giving Oral Vaccine against Polio

(Des Sheila Nowers)

1984 (25 Sept). *Lizards. T* **30** *and similar horiz designs. Multicoloured.* P 14×14½.

150 11c. Type **30** ... 20 10
151 25c. Transvaal Girdled Lizard ... 30 30
152 30c. Ocellated Sand Lizard ... 35 40
153 45c. Bibron's Thick-toed Gecko ... 50 60
150/3 *Set of 4* ... 1·25 1·25

(Des D. Thorpe)

1985 (25 Jan). *Health. T* **31** *and similar vert designs. Multicoloured.* P 14.

154 11c. Type **31** ... 40 10
155 25c. Vaccinating against measles ... 50 30
156 30c. Examining child for diphtheria ... 55 40
157 50c. Examining child for whooping cough ... 80 90
154/7 *Set of 4* ... 2·00 1·50

32 Chief Montshiwa Ratshidi of Barolong boo **33** The Sick flock to Jesus in the Temple (Matthew 21:14)

(Des A. H. Barrett)

1985 (11 Mar). *Centenary of Mafeking. T* **32** *and similar vert design.* P 14½×14.

158 11c. black, grey and orange ... 20 10
159 25c. black, grey and dull violet-blue ... 40 30

Design:—25c. Sir Charles Warren.

(Des J. van Niekerk)

1985 (2 Apr). *Easter. T* **33** *and similar horiz designs. Multicoloured.* P 14.

160 12c. Type **33** ... 20 10
161 25c. Jesus cures the sick (Matthew 21:14) ... 30 20
162 30c. Children praising Jesus (Matthew 21:15) ... 35 30
163 50c. Community leaders discussing Jesus's acceptance of praise (Matthew 21:15,16) ... 50 60
160/3 *Set of 4* ... 1·25 1·10

34 *Faurea saligna* and Planting Sapling **35** Jesus at the House of Mary and Martha, Bethany (John 12:2)

(Des B. Jackson)

1985 (4 July). *Tree Conservation. T* **34** *and similar vert designs. Multicoloured.* P 14.

164 12c. Type **34** ... 20 10
165 25c. *Boscia albitrunca* and Kudu ... 25 20
166 30c. *Erythrina lysistemon* and Mariqua Sunbird ... 35 30
167 50c. *Bequaertiondendron magalismontanum* and bee ... 55 50
164/7 *Set of 4* ... 1·25 1·00

(Des J. van Niekerk)

1986 (6 Mar). *Easter. T* **35** *and similar horiz designs. Multicoloured.* P 14½×14.

168 12c. Type **35** ... 25 10

169 20c. Mary anointing Jesus's feet (John 12:3) 30 20
170 25c. Mary drying Jesus's feet with her hair (John 12:3) 35 25
171 30c. Disciple condemns Mary for anointing Jesus's head with oil (Matthew 26:7) 45 50
168/71 *Set of 4* 1·25 1·00

PHILATELIC FOUNDATION MINIATURE SHEETS. These miniature sheets were issued by the Philatelic Foundation of Southern Africa and not by the postal administration. They could be purchased by post or from a limited number of philatelic offices at a premium in aid of various national and international stamp exhibitions.

36 "Wesleyan Mission Station and Residence of Moroka, Chief of the Barolong, 1834" (C. D. Bell)

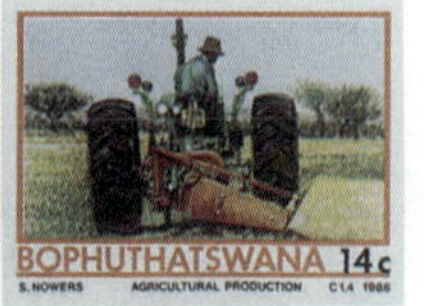

37 Farmer using Tractor (agricultural development)

1986 (15 May). *Paintings of Thaba 'Nchu. T* **36** *and similar horiz designs. Multicoloured. P* 14×14½.
172 14c. Type **36** 40 15
173 20c. "James Archbell's Congregation, 1834" (Charles Davidson Bell) 60 60
174 25c. "Mission Station at Thaba 'Nchu, 1850" (Thomas Baines) 65 80
172/4 *Set of 3* 1·50 1·40
The 25c. value exists as a Philatelic Foundation miniature sheet.

(Des Sheila Nowers)

1986 (6 Aug). *Temisano Development Project. T* **37** *and similar horiz designs. Multicoloured. P* 14.
175 14c. Type **37** 20 10
176 20c. Children at school (community development) 30 20
177 25c. Repairing engine (training) 35 30
178 30c. Grain elevator (secondary industries) 50 50
175/8 *Set of 4* 1·25 1·00

38 Stewardesses and Cessna Citation II of B.O.P. Airways

39 Netball

(Des R. Smith)

1986 (16 Oct). *B.O.P. Airways. T* **38** *and similar horiz designs. Multicoloured. P* 14.
179 14c. Type **38** 25 10
180 20c. Passengers disembarking from Boeing 707 40 20
181 25c. Mmabatho International Airport 50 35
182 30c. B.O.P. Airways Cessna Citation II 60 50
179/82 *Set of 4* 1·60 1·10

(Des B. Jackson)

1987 (22 Jan). *Sports. T* **39** *and similar vert designs. Multicoloured. P* 14×14½.
183 14c. Type **39** 20 15
184 20c. Tennis 30 30
185 25c. Football 30 30
186 30c. Athletics 45 50
183/6 *Set of 4* 1·10 1·10

40 *Berkheya zeyheri*

41 E. M. Mokgoko Farmer Training Centre

(Des Jeanette Stead)

1987 (23 Apr). *Wild Flowers. T* **40** *and similar vert designs. Multicoloured. P* 14×14½.
187 16c. Type **40** 25 15
188 20c. *Plumbago auriculata* 35 35
189 25c. *Pterodiscus speciosus* 35 35
190 30c. *Gazania krebsiana* 40 50
187/90 *Set of 4* 1·25 1·25
The 25c. value exists as a Philatelic Foundation miniature sheet.

(Des E. Dias)

1987 (6 Aug). *Tertiary Education. T* **41** *and similar horiz designs. Multicoloured. P* 14½×14.
191 16c. Type **41** 20 15
192 20c. Main lecture block, University of Bophuthatswana 30 35
193 25c. Manpower Centre 30 35
194 30c. Hotel Training School 30 50
191/4 *Set of 4* 1·00 1·25

42 Posts

43 Jesus entering Jerusalem on Donkey (John 12:12-14)

(Des J. van Niekerk)

1987 (4 Dec). *Tenth Anniv of Independence. Communications. T* **42** *and similar horiz designs. Multicoloured. P* 14½×14.
195 16c. Type **42** 25 15
196 30c. Telephone 35 35
197 40c. Radio 35 35
198 50c. Television 40 50
195/8 *Set of 4* 1·25 1·25

(Des J. van Niekerk)

1988 (31 Mar). *Easter. T* **43** *and similar horiz designs. Multicoloured. P* 14½×14.
199 16c. Type **43** 25 15
200 30c. Judas negotiating with chief priests (Mark 14:10-11) 35 35
201 40c. Jesus washing the disciples feet (John 13:5) 35 35
202 50c. Jesus handing bread to Judas (John 13:26) 40 50
199/202 *Set of 4* 1·25 1·25

44 Environment Education

(Des A. H. Barrett)

1988 (23 June). *National Parks Board. T* **44** *and similar horiz designs. Multicoloured. P* 14½×14.
203 16c. Type **44** 25 15
204 30c. Rhinoceros (Conservation) 40 40
205 40c. Catering workers 40 40
206 50c. Cheetahs (Tourism) 55 65
203/6 *Set of 4* 1·40 1·40
The 50c. value exists as a Philatelic Foundation miniature sheet.

45 Sunflowers

(Des A. H. Barrett)

1988 (15 Sept). *Crops. T* **45** *and similar horiz designs. Multicoloured. P* 14½×14.
207 16c. Type **45** 25 15
208 30c. Peanuts 35 35
209 40c. Cotton 45 45
210 50c. Cabbages 60 60
207/10 *Set of 4* 1·50 1·40

46 Ngotwane Dam

47 The Last Supper (Matthew 26:26)

(Des Estelle Marais)

1988 (17 Nov). *Dams. T* **46** *and similar horiz designs. Multicoloured. P* 14½×14.
211 16c. Type **46** 30 20
212 30c. Groothoek dam 50 50
213 40c. Sehujwane dam 50 50
214 50c. Molatedi dam 70 70
211/14 *Set of 4* 1·75 1·75

(Des J. van Niekerk)

1989 (9 Mar). *Easter. T* **47** *and similar horiz designs. Multicoloured. P* 14½×14.
215 16c. Type **47** 40 20
216 30c. Jesus praying in Garden of Gethsemane (Matthew 26.39) 60 55
217 40c. Judas kissing Jesus (Mark 14:45) 70 70
218 50c. Peter severing ear of High Priest's slave (John 18:10) 85 1·00
215/18 *Set of 4* 2·25 2·25

48 Cock (Thembi Atong)

49 Black-shouldered Kite

1989 (11 May). *Children's Art. T* **48** *and similar horiz designs depicting winning entries in National Children's Day Art Competition. Multicoloured. P* 14½×14.
219 18c. Type **48** 30 20
220 30c. Traditional thatched hut (Muhammad Mahri) 40 40
221 40c. Airplane, telephone wires and houses (Tshepo Mashokwi) 45 45
222 50c. City scene (Miles Brown) 50 60
219/22 *Set of 4* 1·50 1·50

1989 (1 Sept). *Birds of Prey. T* **49** *and similar vert designs showing paintings by Claude Finch-Davies. Multicoloured. P* 14×14½.
223 18c. Type **49** 1·25 30
224 30c. Pale Chanting Goshawk 1·40 75
225 40c. Lesser Kestrel 1·60 1·10
226 50c. Short-toed Eagle 1·75 1·50
223/6 *Set of 4* 5·50 3·25
The 50c. value exists as a Philatelic Foundation miniature sheet.

50 Bilobial House

51 Early Learning Schemes

(Des A. George)

1989 (28 Nov). *Traditional Houses. T* **50** *and similar horiz designs. Multicoloured. P* 14½×14.
227 18c. Type **50** 25 20
228 30c. House with courtyards at front and side 35 35
229 40c. House with conical roof 35 35
230 50c. House with rounded roof 40 50
227/30 *Set of 4* 1·25 1·25

(Des D. McLean)

1990 (11 Jan). *Community Services. T* **51** *and similar horiz designs. Multicoloured. P* 14.
231 18c. Type **51** 25 20
232 30c. Clinics 35 35
233 40c. Libraries 35 35
234 50c. Hospitals 40 45
231/4 *Set of 4* 1·25 1·25

52 Lesser Climbing Mouse

53 Variegated Sandgrouse

(Des A. Ainslie)

1990 (11 Apr). *Small Mammals. T* **52** *and similar horiz designs. Multicoloured. P* 14.
235 21c. Type **52** 30 20
236 30c. Zorilla 40 40
237 40c. Transvaal Elephant Shrew 60 60
238 50c. Large-toothed Rock Hyrax 80 85
235/8 *Set of 4* 1·90 1·90
The 50c. value exists as a Philatelic Foundation miniature sheet.

1990 (12 July). *Sandgrouse. T* **53** *and similar horiz designs showing paintings by Claude Finch-Davies. Multicoloured. P* 14×14½.
239 21c. Type **53** 90 30
240 35c. Double-banded Sandgrouse 1·10 75
241 40c. Namaqua Sandgrouse 1·10 90
242 50c. Yellow-throated Sandgrouse 1·40 1·40
239/42 *Set of 4* 4·00 3·00

54 Basketry

55 Sud Aviation SE 3130 Alouette III Helicopter

(Des Sheila Nowers)

1990 (4 Oct). *Traditional Crafts. T* **54** *and similar vert designs. Multicoloured. P* 14½.
243 21c. Type **54** 40 20
244 35c. Tanning 60 60
245 40c. Beer making 60 65
246 50c. Pottery 65 75
243/6 *Set of 4* 2·00 2·00

1990 (12 Dec). *Bophuthatswana Air Force. T* **55** *and similar horiz designs. Multicoloured. P* 14½×14.
247 21c. Type **55** 1·40 1·10
a. Horiz strip of 5. Nos. 247/51 6·25
248 21c. MBB-Kawasaki Bk-117 helicopter 1·40 1·10
249 21c. Pilatus PC-7 Turbo Trainer 1·40 1·10
250 21c. Pilatus PC-6 Turbo Porter 1·40 1·10
251 21c. CASA C-212 Aviocar 1·40 1·10
247/51 *Set of 5* 6·25 5·00
Nos. 247/51 were printed together, *se-tenant*, in horizontal strips of 5 throughout the sheet.

56 Wild Custard Apple **57** Arrest of Jesus (Mark 14:46)

(Des Gillian Condy)

1991 (24 Jan). *Edible Wild Fruit. T* **56** *and similar vert designs. Multicoloured.* P 14×14½.

252	21c. Type **56**	50	25
253	35c. Spine-leaved Monkey Orange	65	70
254	40c. Sycamore Fig	70	75
255	50c. Kei Apple	85	95
252/5	*Set of 4*	2·40	2·40

(Des J. van Niekerk)

1991 (21 Mar). *Easter. T* **57** *and similar horiz designs. Multicoloured.* P 14½×14.

256	21c. Type **57**	45	25
257	35c. First trial by the Sanhedrin (Mark 14:53)	60	55
258	40c. Assault and derision of Jesus after sentence (Mark 14:65)	70	70
259	50c. Servant girl recognizing Peter (Mark 14:67)	75	90
256/9	*Set of 4*	2·25	2·25

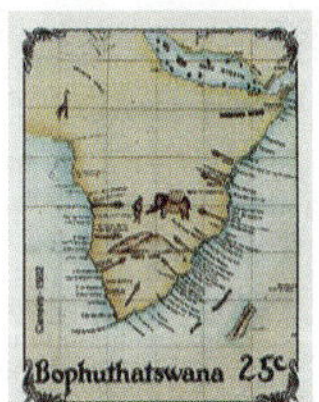

58 Class 7A Locomotive No. 350, 1897 **59** Caneiro Chart, 1502

(Des C. Becker)

1991 (4 July). *Steam Locomotives. T* **58** *and similar horiz designs. Multicoloured.* P 14.

260	25c. Class 6A locomotive No. 194 with trucks and caboose, 1897 (71×25 mm)	95	55
261	40c. Type **58**	1·25	85
262	50c. Double-boiler Class 6Z locomotives pulling Cecil Rhode's funeral train (71×25 mm)	1·40	1·25
263	60c. Class 8 locomotive at Mafeking station, 1904	1·50	1·75
260/3	*Set of 4*	4·50	4·00

The 60c. value exists as a Philatelic Foundation miniature sheet.

See also Nos. 293/6.

(Des C. Becker (25, 40c.), T. Marais (others))

1991 (12 Sept). *Old Maps (1st series). T* **59** *and similar vert designs. Multicoloured.* P 14×14½.

264	25c. Type **59**	1·10	40
265	40c. Cantino Chart, 1502	1·50	95
266	50c. Giovanni Contarini's map, 1506	1·75	1·40
267	60c. Martin Waldseemuller's map, 1507	1·75	1·90
264/7	*Set of 4*	5·50	4·25

See also Nos. 268/71 and 297/300.

60 Fracanzano Map, 1508 **61** Delivery of Jesus to Pilate (Mark 15:1)

(Des Liza van der Wal)

1992 (9 Jan). *Old Maps (2nd series). T* **60** *and similar horiz designs. Multicoloured.* P 14½×14.

268	27c. Type **60**	1·10	40
269	45c. Martin Waldseemuller's map (from edition of Ptolemy), 1513	1·50	95
270	65c. Section of Waldseemuller's woodcut Carta Marina Navigatora Portugallan Navigationes, 1516	1·75	1·50
271	85c. Map from Laurent Fries's Geographia, 1522	1·75	2·00
268/71	*Set of 4*	5·50	4·25

(Des J. van Niekerk)

1992 (1 Apr). *Easter. T* **61** *and similar horiz designs. Multicoloured.* P 14½×14.

272	27c. Type **61**	25	20
273	45c. Scourging of Jesus (Mark 15:15)	40	40
274	65c. Placing crown of thorns on Jesus's head (Mark 15:17-18)	50	70
275	85c. Soldiers mocking Jesus (Mark 15:19)	60	90
272/5	*Set of 4*	1·60	2·00

62 Sweet Thorn **63** View of Palace across Lake

(Des Gillian Coady)

1992 (18 June). *Acacia Trees. T* **62** *and similar horiz designs. Multicoloured.* P 14½×14.

276	35c. Type **62**	30	25
277	70c. Camel Thorn	50	60
278	90c. Umbrella Thorn	60	80
279	1r.05 Black Thorn	70	1·00
276/9	*Set of 4*	1·90	2·40

The 70c. value exists as a Philatelic Foundation miniature sheet.

1992 (19 Nov). *The Lost City Complex, Sun City. T* **63** *and similar horiz designs. Multicoloured.* P 14×14½.

280	35c. Type **63**	35	45
	a. Horiz strip of 5. Nos. 280/4	1·50	
281	35c. Palace façade 35	35	45
282	35c. Palace porte cochère	35	45
283	35c. Palace lobby	35	45
284	35c. Tusk Bar, Palace	35	45
280/4	*Set of 5*	1·50	2·00

Nos. 280/4 were printed together, *se-tenant*, in horizontal strips of 5 throughout the sheet.

64 Light Sussex **65** Pilate offering to release Barabbas (Luke 23:25)

(Des M. Ginn)

1993 (12 Feb). *Chickens. T* **64** *and similar horiz designs. Multicoloured.* P 14½×14.

285	35c. Type **64**	40	25
286	70c. Rhode Island Red	55	50
287	90c. Brown Leghorn	60	80
288	1r.05 White Leghorn	70	1·10
285/8	*Set of 4*	2·00	2·50

The 70c. value exists as a Philatelic Foundation miniature sheet.

(Des J. van Niekerk)

1993 (5 Mar). *Easter. T* **65** *and similar horiz designs. Multicoloured.* P 14½×14.

289	35c. Type **65**	60	30
290	70c. Jesus falling under cross (John 19:17)	95	75
291	90c. Simon of Cyrene carrying cross (Mark 15:21)	1·25	1·25
292	1r.05 Jesus being nailed to cross (Mark 15:23)	1·40	1·75
289/92	*Set of 4*	3·75	3·50

66 Mafeking Locomotive Shed, 1933

(Des C. Becker)

1993 (18 June). *Steam Locomotives (2nd series). T* **66** *and similar multicoloured designs.* P 14.

293	45c. Type **66**	65	55
294	65c. Rhodesian Railways steam locomotive No. 5, 1901 (34×25 mm)	75	65
295	85c. Class 16B locomotive pulling "White Train" during Prince George's visit, 1934	95	95
296	1r.05 Class 19D locomotive, 1938 (34×25 mm)	1·25	1·40
293/6	*Set of 4*	3·25	3·25
MS297	127×113 mm. Nos. 293/6	2·75	3·25

67 Sebastian Minister's Map (from edition of Ptolemy), 1540 **68** Crucifixion (Luke 23:33)

(Des C. Prinsloo)

1993 (20 Aug). *Old Maps (3rd series). T* **67** *and similar horiz designs. Multicoloured.* P 14½×14.

298	45c. Type **67**	50	50
299	65c. Jacopo Gastaldi's map, 1564	65	65
300	85c. Map from Mercator's Atlas, 1595	75	90
301	1r.05 Map from Ortelius's Theatrum Orbis Terrarum, 1570	90	1·25
298/301	*Set of 4*	2·50	3·50

(Des J. van Niekerk)

1994 (25 Mar). *Easter. T* **68** *and similar horiz designs. Multicoloured.* P 14½×14.

302	35c. Type **68**	65	45
303	65c. Soldiers and Jews mocking Jesus (Luke 23:35-36)	95	80
304	85c. Soldier offering Jesus vinegar (Luke 23:36)	1·10	1·25
305	1r.05 Jesus on cross and charge notice (Luke 23:38)	1·60	1·75
302/5	*Set of 4*	3·75	3·75

Bophuthatswana was reincorporated into the Republic of South Africa on 27 April 1994.

The postal service continued to operate, using South African stamps, until 1 April 1996 when it was integrated with that of the Republic.

XII. CISKEI

The Ciskei Territorial Authority was established in 1961 and autonomous government was granted in 1972 under the Bantu Homelands Constitution Act. Ciskei became fully independent on 4 December 1981. This independence did not receive international political recognition, but the stamps were accepted as valid on international mail.

PRINTERS. All the following stamps were printed in lithography by the South African Government Printer, Pretoria.

1 Dr. Lennox Sebe, Chief Minister **2** Knysna Turaco

(Des A. H. Barrett)

1981 (4 Dec). *Independence. T* **1** *and similar vert designs. Multicoloured.* P 14.

1	5c. Type **1**	10	10
2	15c. Coat of arms	20	15
3	20c. Flag	30	30
4	25c. Mace	35	25
1/4	*Set of 4*	80	75

(Des D. Findlay)

1981 (4 Dec)–**90**. *Birds. T* **2** *and similar vert designs. Multicoloured.* P 14.

5	1c. Type **2**	20	15
6	2c. Cape Wagtail	20	15
7	3c. White-browed Coucal	50	15
8	4c. Yellow-tufted Malachite Sunbird	20	15
9	5c. Stanley Crane	20	15
10	6c. African Red-winged Starling	20	15
11	7c. Giant Kingfisher	20	15
12	8c. Hadada Ibis	30	15
13	9c. Black Cuckoo	30	15
14	10c. Black-collared Barbet	30	15
14*a*	11c. African Black-headed Oriole (2.4.84)	55	30
14*b*	12c. Malachite Kingfisher (1.4.85)	1·10	30
14*c*	14c. Hoopoe (1.4.86)	1·50	30
15	15c. African Fish Eagle	30	30
15*a*	16c. Cape Puff-back Flycatcher (1.4.87)	1·00	30
15*b*	18c. Long-tailed Whydah (3.7.89)	1·50	30
16	20c. Cape Longclaw	40	30
16*a*	21c. Lemon Dove (3.7.90)	1·50	60
17	25c. Cape Dikkop	30	30
18	30c. African Green Pigeon	40	40
19	50c. Cape Parrot	60	60
20	1r. Narina Trogon	90	1·25
21	2r. Cape Eagle Owl	1·75	2·50
5/21	*Set of 23*	13·00	8·00

3 Cecilia Makiwane (first Xhosa nurse) **4** Boom Sprayer

(Des A. H. Barrett)

1982 (30 Apr). *Nursing. T* **3** *and similar multicoloured designs.* P 14×13½ (*vert*) or 13½×14 (*horiz*).

22	8c. Type **3**	15	10
23	15c. Operating theatre	30	30
24	20c. Matron lighting nurse's lamp (*horiz*)	40	40
25	25c. Nurses and patient (*horiz*)	50	50
22/5	*Set of 4*	1·25	1·10

(Des A. H. Barrett)

1982 (20 Aug). *Pineapple Industry. T* **4** *and similar horiz designs. Multicoloured.* P 13½×14.

26	8c. Type **4**	10	10
27	15c. Harvesting	20	25
28	20c. Despatch to cannery	25	30
29	30c. Packing for local market	30	35
26/9	*Set of 4*	75	85

5 Brown Hare

6 Assegai

1982 (29 Oct). *Small Mammals. T* **5** *and similar horiz designs. Multicoloured.* P 13½×14.

30	8c. Type **5**	15	15
31	15c. Cape Fox	25	25
32	20c. Cape Ground Squirrel	30	30
33	25c. Caracal	40	40
30/3	*Set of 4*	1·00	1·00

(Des D. Findlay)

1983 (2 Feb). *Trees (1st series). T* **6** *and similar vert designs. Multicoloured.* P 14×13½.

34	8c. Cabbage Tree	15	10
35	20c. Type **6**	30	30
36	25c. Cape Chestnut	35	35
37	40c. Outeniqua Yellowwood	50	55
34/7	*Set of 4*	1·10	1·10

See also Nos. 52/5.

7 Dusky Shark

8 Lovedale

(Des Sheila Nowers)

1983 (13 Apr). *Sharks. T* **7** *and similar horiz designs. Multicoloured.* P 14.

38	8c. Type **7**	15	15
39	20c. Sand Tiger ("Ragged-tooth Shark")	30	30
40	25c. Tiger Shark (57×21 mm)	35	35
41	30c. Scalloped Hammerhead (57×21 mm)	40	40
42	40c. Great White Shark (57×21 mm)	50	50
38/42	*Set of 5*	1·50	1·50

(Des A. H. Barrett)

1983 (6 July). *Educational Institutions. T* **8** *and similar horiz designs.* P 14.

43	10c. stone, light brown and black	10	10
44	20c. pale stone, olive-sepia and black	20	20
45	25c. pale cinnamon, Venetian red and black	25	25
46	40c. cinnamon, pinkish brown and black	40	45
43/6	*Set of 4*	80	85

Designs:—20c. Fort Hare; 25c. Healdtown; 40c. Lennox Sebe.

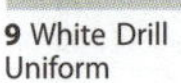

9 White Drill Uniform

10 Sandprawn

(Des A. May)

1983 (28 Sept). *British Military Uniforms (1st series). 6th (Warwickshire) Regiment of Foot, 1821–27. T* **9** *and similar vert designs. Multicoloured.* P 14.

47	20c. Type **9**	40	40
	a. Horiz strip of 5. Nos. 47/51	1·75	
48	20c. Light Company privates	40	40
49	20c. Grenadier Company sergeants	40	40
50	20c. Officers in undress blue frock-coats	40	40
51	20c. Officer and field officer in parade order	40	40
47/51	*Set of 5*	1·75	1·75

Nos. 47/51 were printed together, *se-tenant*, in horizontal strips of 5 throughout the sheet. See also Nos. 64/8 and 95/8.

(Des D. Findlay)

1984 (6 Jan). *Trees (2nd series). Vert designs as T* **6**. *Multicoloured.* P 14.

52	10c. *Rhus chirindensis*	15	15
53	20c. *Phoenix reclinata*	25	35
54	25c. *Ptaeroxylon obliquum*	30	40
	40c. *Apodytes dimidiata*	40	55
52/5	*Set of 4*	1·00	1·25

(Des D. Thorpe)

1984 (12 Apr). *Fish-bait. T* **10** *and similar horiz designs. Multicoloured.* P 14×14½.

56	11c. Type **10**	20	15
57	20c. Coral Worm	30	30
58	25c. Bloodworm	35	35
59	30c. Red-bait	40	40
56/9	*Set of 4*	1·10	1·10

11 Banded Sand Martin

(Des Sheila Nowers)

1984 (17 Aug). *Migratory Birds. T* **11** *and similar horiz designs. Multicoloured.* P 14½×14.

60	11c. Type **11**	25	20
61	25c. House Martin	50	50
62	30c. Greater Striped Swallow	60	60
63	45c. Barn Swallow ("European Swallow")	80	85
60/3	*Set of 4*	1·90	1·90

(Des A. May)

1984 (26 Oct). *British Military Uniforms (2nd series). Cape Mounted Rifles. Vert designs as T* **9**. *Multicoloured.* P 14.

64	25c. (1) Trooper in field and sergeant in undress uniforms, 1830	45	45
	a. Horiz strip of 5. Nos. 64/8	2·00	
65	25c. (2) Trooper and sergeant in full dress, 1835	45	45
66	25c. (3) Officers in undress, 1830	45	45
67	25c. (4) Officers in full dress, 1827–34	45	45
68	25c. (5) Officers in full dress, 1834	45	45
64/8	*Set of 5*	2·00	2·00

Nos. 64/8 were printed together, *se-tenant*, in horizontal strips of 5 throughout the sheet. Each stamp is inscribed at the foot with a number from "D1.5" to "D5.5". The first number is given in brackets in the listing to aid identification.

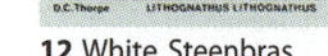

12 White Steenbras

13 Brownies holding Handmade Doll

(Des D. Thorpe)

1985 (7 Mar). *Coastal Angling. T* **12** *and similar horiz designs. Multicoloured.* P 14.

69	11c. Type **12**	20	15
70	25c. Bronze Seabream	30	30
71	30c. Kob	40	45
72	50c. Spotted Grunt	70	80
69/72	*Set of 4*	1·40	1·50

(Des Sheila Nowers)

1985 (3 May). *International Youth Year. 75th Anniv of Girl Guide Movement. T* **13** *and similar horiz designs. Multicoloured.* P 14½×14.

73	12c. Type **13**	15	15
74	25c. Rangers planting trees	25	25
75	30c. Guides with flag	30	30
76	50c. Guides building fire	60	65
73/6	*Set of 4*	1·10	1·10

14 Furniture making

15 *Antelope*

(Des B. Jackson)

1985 (8 Aug). *Small Businesses. T* **14** *and similar horiz designs. Multicoloured.* P 14.

77	12c. Type **14**	15	10
78	25c. Dressmaking	30	30
79	30c. Welding	30	30
80	50c. Basketry	60	65
77/80	*Set of 4*	1·25	1·25

(Des R. Reynolds)

1985 (15 Nov). *Sail Troopships. T* **15** *and similar horiz designs. Multicoloured.* P 14.

81	12c. Type **15**	20	15
82	25c. *Pilot*	45	45
83	30c. *Salisbury*	45	45
84	50c. *Olive Branch*	80	85
81/4	*Set of 4*	1·75	1·75

16 Earth showing Africa

17 Fifer in Winter Dress

(Des J. van Ellinckhuijzen)

1986 (20 Mar). *Appearance of Halley's Comet. T* **16** *and similar vert designs. Multicoloured.* P 14.

85	12c. (1) Earth showing South America	70	70
	a. Sheetlet. Nos. 85/94	6·50	
86	12c. (2) Type **16**	70	70
87	12c. (3) Stars and Moon	70	70
88	12c. (4) Moon and Milky Way	70	70
89	12c. (5) Milky Way and stars	70	70
90	12c. (6) Earth showing Australia	70	70
91	12c. (7) Earth and meteor	70	70
92	12c. (8) Meteor, Moon and comet tail	70	70
93	12c. (9) Comet head and Moon	70	70
94	12c. (10) Sun	70	70
85/94	*Set of 10*	6·50	6·50

Nos. 85/94 were printed together, *se-tenant*, in sheetlets of 10 forming a composite design of the southern skies in April. Each stamp is inscribed with a number from "A1-10" to "A10-10". The first number is given in brackets in the listing to aid identification.

PHILATELIC FOUNDATION MINIATURE SHEETS. These miniature sheets were issued by the Philatelic Foundation of Southern Africa and not by the postal administration. They could be purchased by post or from a limited number of philatelic offices at a premium in aid of various national and international stamp exhibitions.

(Des A. May)

1986 (12 June). *British Military Uniforms (3rd series). 98th Regiment of Foot. T* **17** *and similar vert designs. Multicoloured.* P 14.

95	14c. Type **17**	20	15
96	20c. Private in summer dress	30	30
97	25c. Grenadier in full summer dress	35	35
98	30c. Sergeant-major in full winter dress	50	50
95/8	*Set of 4*	1·25	1·10

The 30c. value exists as a Philatelic Foundation miniature sheet.

18 Welding Bicycle Frame

19 President Dr. Lennox Sebe

(Des J. van Niekerk)

1986 (18 Sept). *Bicycle Factory, Dimbaza. T* **18** *and similar horiz designs. Multicoloured.* P 14½×14.

99	14c. Type **18**	20	15
100	20c. Spray-painting frame	30	30
101	25c. Installing wheel-spokes	35	35
102	30c. Final assembly	50	50
99/102	*Set of 4*	1·25	1·10

(Des J. van Niekerk)

1986 (4 Dec). *Fifth Anniv of Independence. T* **19** *and similar horiz designs. Multicoloured.* P 14×14½.

103	14c. Type **19**	15	15
104	20c. National Shrine, Ntaba kaNdoda	20	20
105	25c. Legislative Assembly, Bisho	20	35
106	30c. Automatic telephone exchange, Bisho	25	50
103/6	*Set of 4*	70	1·10

20 *Boletus edulis*

21 Nkone Cow and Calf

(Des H. Botha)

1987 (19 Mar). *Edible Mushrooms. T* **20** *and similar vert designs. Multicoloured.* P 14×14½.

107	14c. Type **20**	25	15
108	20c. *Macrolepiota zeyheri*	40	40
109	25c. *Termitomyces sp*	50	50
110	30c. *Russula capensis*	60	60
107/10	*Set of 4*	1·60	1·50

The 20c. value exists as a Philatelic Foundation miniature sheet.

(Des D. Murphy)

1987 (18 June). *Nkone Cattle. T* **21** *and similar horiz designs. Multicoloured.* P 14½×14.

111	16c. Type **21**	20	15
112	20c. Nkone cow	25	30
113	25c. Nkone bull	30	35
114	30c. Herd of Nkone	40	55
111/14	*Set of 4*	1·00	1·25

22 Wire Windmill

23 Seven Birds

(Des A. H. Barrett)

1987 (17 Sept). *Homemade Toys. T* **22** *and similar multicoloured designs.* P 14×14½ (*vert*) or 14½×14 (*horiz*).

115	16c. Type **22**	20	15
116	20c. Rag doll	25	30
117	25c. Clay horse (*horiz*)	30	35
118	30c. Wire car (*horiz*)	40	55
115/18	*Set of 4*	1·00	1·25

(Des J. van Niekerk)

1987 (6 Nov). *Folklore (1st series). Sikulume. T* **23** *and similar horiz designs. Multicoloured.* P 14½×14.

119	16c. Type **23**	20	15
120	20c. Cannibals chasing Sikulume	25	30
121	25c. Sikulume attacking the inabulele	30	35
122	30c. Chief Mangangezulu chasing Sikulume and his bride	40	55
119/22	*Set of 4*	1·00	1·25

See also Nos. 127/36, 153/6 and 161/4.

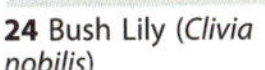

24 Bush Lily (*Clivia nobilis*)

25 Numbakatali crying and Second Wife feeding Crows

(Des A. Batten)

1988 (17 Mar). *Protected Flowers. T* **24** *and similar vert designs. Multicoloured.* P 14×14½.

123	16c. Type **24**	20	15
124	30c. Harebell (*Dierama pulcherrimum*)	35	35
125	40c. Butterfly Iris (*Moraea reticulata*)	40	40
126	50c. Vlei Lily (*Crinum campanulatum*)	60	65
123/6	*Set of 4*	1·40	1·40

The 50c. value exists as a Philatelic Foundation miniature sheet.

(Des J. van Niekerk)

1988 (27 May). *Folklore (2nd series). Mbulukazi. T* **25** *and similar horiz designs. Multicoloured.* P 14×14½.

127	16c. Type **25**	30	35
	a. Sheetlet. Nos. 127/36	2·75	
128	16c. Numbakatali telling doves of her childlessness	30	35
129	16c. Numbakatali finding children in earthenware jars	30	35
130	16c. Broad Breast sees Mbulukazi and brother at river	30	35
131	16c. Broad Breast asking to marry Mbulukazi	30	35
132	16c. Broad Breast and his two wives, Mbulukazi and her half-sister Mahlunguluza	30	35
133	16c. Mahlunguluza pushing Mbulukazi from precipice to her death	30	35
134	16c. Mbulukazi's ox tearing down Mahlunguluza's hut	30	35
135	16c. Ox licking Mbulukazi back to life	30	35
136	16c. Mahlunguluza being sent back to her father in disgrace	30	35
127/36	*Set of 10*	2·75	3·25

Nos. 127/36 were printed together, *se-tenant*, in sheetlets of 10.

26 Oranges and Grafted Rootstocks in Nursery

27 *Amanita phalloides*

(Des B. Jackson)

1988 (29 Sept). *Citrus Farming. T* **26** *and similar horiz designs. Multicoloured.* P 14×14½.

137	16c. Type **26**	20	15
138	30c. Lemons and marching rootstock onto mature tree	40	40
139	40c. Tangerines and fruit being hand picked	50	50
140	50c. Oranges and fruit being graded	60	65
137/40	*Set of 4*	1·50	1·50

(Des H. Botha)

1988 (1 Dec). *Poisonous Fungi. T* **27** *and similar vert designs. Multicoloured.* P 14×14½.

141	16c. Type **27**	75	30
142	30c. *Chlorophyllum molybdites*	1·10	75
143	40c. *Amanita muscaria*	1·40	1·10
144	50c. *Amanita pantherina*	1·60	1·25
141/4	*Set of 4*	4·25	3·00

28 Kat River Dam

29 Taking Eggs from Rainbow Trout

(Des Sheila Nowers)

1989 (2 Mar). *Dams. T* **28** *and similar horiz designs. Multicoloured.* P 14½×14.

145	16c. Type **28**	35	25
146	30c. Cata Dam	55	50
147	40c. Binfield Park Dam	65	65
148	50c. Sandile Dam	70	80
145/8	*Set of 4*	2·00	2·00

(Des B. Kent)

1989 (8 June). *Trout Hatcheries. T* **29** *and similar horiz designs. Multicoloured.* P 14½×14.

149	18c. Type **29**	25	15
150	30c. Fertilized eyed trout ova and alevins	45	45
151	40c. Five-week-old fingerlings	55	55
152	50c. Adult male	60	65
149/52	*Set of 4*	1·75	1·60

The 50c. value exists as a Philatelic Foundation miniature sheet.

30 Lion and Little Jackal killing Eland

31 Cape Horse-cart

(Des J. van Niekerk)

1989 (21 Sept). *Folklore (3rd series). Little Jackal and the Lion. T* **30** *and similar horiz designs. Multicoloured.* P 14½×14.

153	18c. Type **30**	20	15
154	30c. Little Jackal's children carrying meat to clifftop home	35	35
155	40c. Little Jackal pretending to be trapped	40	40
156	50c. Lion falling down cliff face	45	50
153/6	*Set of 4*	1·25	1·25

(Des J. Huntly)

1989 (7 Dec). *Animal-drawn Transport. T* **31** *and similar horiz designs. Multicoloured.* P 14×14½.

157	18c. Type **31**	20	15
158	30c. Jubilee spider	35	35
159	40c. Ballantine half-tent ox-drawn wagon	40	40
160	50c. Voortrekker wagon	45	50
157/60	*Set of 4*	1·25	1·25

32 Mpunzikazi offering Food to Five Heads

33 Handweaving on Loom

(Des J. van Niekerk)

1990 (15 Mar). *Folklore (4th series). The Story of Makanda Mahlanu (Five Heads). T* **32** *and similar horiz designs. Multicoloured.* P 14½×14.

161	18c. Type **32**	20	15
162	30c. Five Heads killing Mpunzikazi with his tail	35	35
163	40c. Mpunzanyana offering food to Five Heads	40	40
164	50c. Five Heads transformed into a man	45	50
161/4	*Set of 4*	1·25	1·25

(Des I. Ellithorne)

1990 (14 June). *Handmade Carpets. T* **33** *and similar vert designs. Multicoloured.* P 14×14½.

165	21c. Type **33**	30	20
166	35c. Spinning	50	50
167	40c. Dyeing yarn	70	70
168	50c. Knotting carpet	70	70
165/8	*Set of 4*	2·00	1·90

The 50c. value exists as a Philatelic Foundation miniature sheet.

34 Wooden Beam Plough, 1855

35 Prickly Pear Vendor

(Des J. Huntly)

1990 (6 Sept). *Ploughs. T* **34** *and similar horiz designs. Multicoloured.* P 14½×14.

169	21c. Type **34**	25	20
170	35c. Triple disc plough, 1895	40	40
171	40c. Reversible disc plough, 1895	50	50
172	50c. "Het Volk" double furrow plough, 1910	60	65
169/72	*Set of 4*	1·60	1·60

(Des A. H. Barrett)

1990 (29 Nov). *Prickly Pear. T* **35** *and similar horiz designs. Multicoloured.* P 14½×14.

173	21c. Type **35**	30	20
174	35c. Prickly pear bushes	50	50
175	40c. Whole and opened fruits	60	60
176	50c. Bushes in bloom	70	80
173/6	*Set of 4*	1·90	1·90

36 African Marsh Owl

37 São Bras (now Mossel Bay) on Map, 1500

(Des D. Finlay)

1991 (7 Feb). *Owls. T* **36** *and similar vert designs. Multicoloured.* P 14×14½.

177	21c. Type **36**	1·10	40
178	35c. African Scops Owl	1·40	80
179	40c. Barn Owl	1·75	1·00
180	50c. African Wood Owl	1·90	1·40
177/80	*Set of 4*	5·50	3·25

The 50c. value exists as a Philatelic Foundation miniature sheet.

(Des J. van Niekerk)

1991 (11 May). *Stamp Day. D'Ataide's Letter of 1501. T* **37** *and similar horiz designs. Multicoloured.* P 14×14½.

181	25c. Type **37**	70	70
	a. Horiz strip of 5. Nos. 181/5	3·25	
182	25c. Bartolomeo Dias's ship foundering off Cabo Tormentoso (now Cape of Good Hope) during voyage to India, 1500	70	70
183	25c. Captain Pedro d'Ataide landing at So Bras, 1501	70	70
184	25c. D'Ataide leaving letter relating death of Dias on tree	70	70
185	25c. Captain Joao da Nova finding letter, 1501	70	70
181/5	*Set of 5*	3·25	3·25

Nos. 181/5 were printed together, *se-tenant*, in horizontal strips of 5 throughout the sheet. The inscriptions at the foot of Nos. 181 and 182 are transposed.

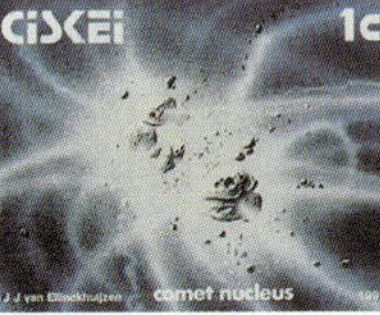

38 Comet Nucleus

39 Fort Armstrong and Xhosa Warrior

(Des J. van Ellinckhuijzen)

1991 (1 Aug). *The Solar System. T* **38** *and similar horiz designs. Multicoloured.* P 14.

186	1c. Type **38**	20	15
187	2c. Trojan asteroids	20	15
188	5c. Meteoroids	20	15
189	7c. Pluto	30	15
190	10c. Neptune	30	15
191	20c. Uranus	50	20
192	25c. Saturn	60	20
193	30c. Jupiter	65	30
194	35c. Planetoids in asteroid belt	65	40
195	40c. Mars	80	50
196	50c. The Moon	80	70
197	60c. Earth	80	80
198	1r. Venus	1·00	1·25
199	2r. Mercury	1·60	2·00
200	5r. The Sun	2·25	3·25
186/200	*Set of 15*	10·00	10·00
MS201	197×93 mm. Nos. 186/200	10·00	10·00

(Des D. Bagnall)

1991 (7 Nov). *19th-century Frontier Forts. T* **39** *and similar horiz designs. Multicoloured.* P 14×14½.

202	27c. Type **39**	30	30
203	45c. Keiskamma Hoek Post and Sir George Grey (governor of Cape Colony, 1854–58)	45	55
204	65c. Fort Hare and Xhosa Chief Sandile	55	70
205	85c. Peddie Cavalry Barracks and cavalryman	75	1·25
202/5	*Set of 4*	1·90	2·50

40 *Cumulonimbus*

41 "Intelsat VI" Communications Satellite

(Des J. Meyer)

1992 (19 Mar). *Cloud Formations. T* **40** *and similar vert designs. Multicoloured.* P 14.

206	27c. Type **40**	40	25
207	45c. *Altocumulus*	55	65
208	65c. *Cirrus*	65	80
209	85c. *Cumulus*	75	1·10
206/9	*Set of 4*	2·10	2·50

(Des J. van Ellinckhuijzen)

1992 (4 June). *International Space Year. Satellites over Southern Africa. T* **41** *and similar horiz designs. Multicoloured.* P 14.

210	35c. Type **41**	40	25
211	70c. "G P S Navstar" (navigation)	80	80

212 90c. "Meteosat" (meteorology) 1·10 1·10
213 1r.05 "Landsat VI" (Earth resources survey) 1·25 1·40
210/13 *Set of 4* 3·25 3·25

The 70c. value exists as a Philatelic Foundation miniature sheet.

42 Universal Disc-harrow, 1914

43 Mpekweni Sun Marine Resort

(Des J. Huntly)

1992 (20 Aug). *Agricultural Tools. T* **42** *and similar horiz designs. Multicoloured.* P 14.

214 35c. Type **42** 40 25
215 70c. Clod crusher and pulveriser, 1914 80 70
216 90c. Self-dump hay rake, 1910 1·10 95
217 1r.05 McCormick hay tedder, 1900 1·10 1·10
214/17 *Set of 4* 3·00 2·75

1992 (5 Nov). *Hotels. T* **43** *and similar horiz designs. Multicoloured.* P 14.

218 35c. Type **43** 40 25
219 70c. Katberg Protea Hotel 80 80
220 90c. Fish River Sun Hotel 1·10 1·10
221 1r.05 Amatola Sun Hotel, Amatole Mountains 1·10 1·25
218/21 *Set of 4* 3·00 3·00

44 Vasco da Gama, São Gabriel and Voyage round Cape of Good Hope, 1497

45 Canary

(Des J. van Niekerk)

1993 (19 May). *Navigators. T* **44** *and similar horiz designs. Multicoloured.* P 14.

222 45c. Type **44** 65 30
223 65c. James Cook, H.M.S. *Endeavour* and first voyage, 1768–71 1·10 75
224 85c. Ferdinand Magellan, *Vitoria* and circumnavigation, 1519 1·25 90
225 90c. Sir Francis Drake, *Golden Hind* and circumnavigation, 1577–80 1·25 95
226 1r.05 Abel Tasman, Heemskerk and discovery of Tasmania, 1642 1·40 1·25
222/6 *Set of 5* 5·00 3·75

The ship on No. 222 is wrongly inscribed "San Gabriel", that on No. 224 "Victoria" and that on No. 226 "Heemskerck".

(Des J. Steyn (65c.), M. Goetz (85c.))

1993 (16 July). *Cage Birds. T* **45** *and similar vert designs. Multicoloured.* P 14.

227 45c. Type **45** 45 30
228 65c. Budgerigar 70 60
229 85c. Peach-faced Lovebirds 90 80
230 90c. Cockatiel 95 85
231 1r.05 Gouldian Finch 1·00 1·10
227/31 *Set of 5* 3·50 3·25

The 85c. value exists as a Philatelic Foundation miniature sheet.

46 Goshen Church (Moravian Mission), Whittlesea

47 Jointed Cactus

(Des C. Meijer)

1993 (17 Sept). *Churches and Missions. T* **46** *and similar horiz designs.* P 14½×14.

232 45c. stone, black and scarlet 35 20
233 65c. azure, black and scarlet 60 60
234 85c. cinnamon, black and scarlet 80 80
235 1r.05 pale olive-yellow, black and scarlet 90 1·00
232/5 *Set of 4* 2·40 2·40

Designs:—65c. Kamastone Mission Church; 85c. Richie Thompson Memorial Church (Hertzog Mission), nr. Seymour; 1r.05, Bryce Ross Memorial Church (Pirie Mission), nr. Dimbaza.

(Des Auriol Batten)

1993 (5 Nov). *Invader Plants. T* **47** *and similar vert designs. Multicoloured.* P 14.

236 45c. Type **47** 40 30
237 65c. Thorn Apple 70 60
238 85c. Coffee Weed 90 80
239 1r.05 Poisonous Wild Tobacco 1·00 1·00
236/9 *Set of 4* 2·75 2·40
MS240 98×125 mm. Nos. 236/9 2·75 2·75

48 *Losna* (steamer near Fish River), 1921

49 "Herman Steyn"

(Des Sheila Nowers)

1994 (18 Feb). *Shipwrecks. T* **48** *and similar horiz designs. Multicoloured.* P 14.

241 45c. Type **48** 75 30
242 65c. *Catherine* (barque) (Waterloo Bay), 1846 1·25 60
243 85c. *Bennebroek* (East Indiaman) (near Mtana River), 1713 1·40 90
244 1r.05 *São João Baptista* (galleon) (between Fish and Kei Rivers), 1622 1·50 1·25
241/4 *Set of 4* 4·50 2·75

1994 (15 Apr). *Hybrid Roses. T* **49** *and similar horiz designs. Multicoloured.* P 14.

245 45c. Type **49** 35 30
246 70c. "Esther Geldenhuys" 60 60
247 95c. "Margaret Wasserfall" 80 80
248 1r.15 "Professor Fred Ziady" 1·00 1·00
245/8 *Set of 4* 2·50 2·75
MS249 149×114 mm. Nos. 245/8 2·50 2·75

Ciskei was reincorporated into the Republic of South Africa on 27 April 1994. Its postal service continued to operate, using South African stamps, until 1 April 1996 when it was integrated with that of the Republic.

XIII. TRANSKEI

The Natives Land Act of 1913 laid down that Transkei should be reserved entirely for Black ownership and occupation. In 1963 Transkei was granted internal self-government by the South African Parliament and subsequently the Republic of Transkei was established, on 26 October 1976, as the first of the independent "black homelands".

This independence did not receive international political recognition, but the stamps were accepted as valid on international mail.

PRINTERS. All the following stamps were printed in lithography by the South African Government Printer, Pretoria.

1 Lubisi Dam

2 K. D. Matanzima

(Des A. H. Barrett)

1976 (26 Oct)–**83**. *Transkei Scenes and Occupations. T* **1** *and similar horiz designs. Multicoloured.* P 12×12½.

1 1c. Type **1** 10 10
a. Perf 14 (28.3.83) 30 20
2 2c. Soil cultivation 10 10
a. Perf 14 (5.7.82) 15 10
3 3c. Threshing sorghum 15 10
a. Perf 14 (6.7.82) 15 10
4 4c. Transkei matron 1·75 15
a. Perf 14 (15.11.79) 15 10
5 5c. Grinding maize 1·75 15
a. Perf 14 (8.4.80) 15 10
6 6c. Cutting Phormium tenax 15 10
a. Perf 14 (8.7.82) 15 10
7 7c. Herd-boy 40 10
8 8c. Felling timber 20 10
a. Perf 14 (20.1.82) 35 15
9 9c. Agricultural schooling 15 15
a. Perf 14 (13.7.82) 25 25
10 10c. Tea picking 30 15
a. Perf 14 (11.8.80) 20 15
11 15c. Carrying wood 40 25
a. Perf 14 (16.10.81) 30 15
12 20c. Weaving industry 40 20
a. Perf 14 (15.10.80) 35 15
13 25c. Cattle 45 25
a. Perf 14 (26.10.81) 60 50
14 30c. Sledge transportation 60 50
a. Perf 14 (13.8.80) 60 45
15 50c. Coat of arms and map 85 50
a. Perf 14 (13.11.81) 60 60
16 1r. Administration building, Umtata 50 1·25
17 2r. The Bunga (Parliamentary building), Umtata 75 2·25
1/17 *Set of 17 (cheapest)* 4·50 5·25

1976 (26 Oct). *Independence. T* **2** *and similar vert designs. Multicoloured.* P 12½.

18 4c. Type **2** 20 20
19 10c. Flag and mace 45 45
20 15c. K. D. Matanzima, Paramount Chief (different) 55 75
21 20c. Coat of arms 60 80
18/21 *Set of 4* 1·60 2·00

NEW INFORMATION

The editor is always interested to correspond with people who have new information that will improve or correct the catalogue

3 Beech 100 King Air of Transkei Airways

4 *Artemisia afra*

(Des A. H. Barrett)

1977 (11 Feb). *Transkei Airways' Inaugural Flight. T* **3** *and similar horiz design. Multicoloured.* P 12×12½.

22 4c. Type **3** 25 15
23 15c. Beech 100 King Air of Transkei Airways landing at Matanzima airport and on ground 75 85

(Des D. Findlay)

1977 (16 May). *Medicinal Plants (1st series). T* **4** *and similar vert designs. Multicoloured.* P 12½×12.

24 4c. Type **4** 15 10
25 10c. *Bulbine natalensis* 45 45
26 15c. *Melianthus major* 55 65
27 20c. *Cotyledon orbiculata* 65 90
24/7 *Set of 4* 1·60 1·75

See also Nos. 88/91.

5 Disc Jockey

6 Blind Basket Weaver

(Des A. H. Barrett)

1977 (26 Oct). *First Anniv of Transkei Radio. T* **5** *and similar horiz design. Multicoloured.* P 12×12½.

28 4c. Type **5** 15 10
29 15c. Announcer 60 60

(Des A. H. Barrett)

1977 (18 Nov). *Help for the Blind. T* **6** *and similar vert designs.* P 12½×12.

30 4c. black, grey-lilac and gold 15 10
31 15c. black, drab and gold 35 35
32 20c. black, pinkish brown and gold 75 80
30/2 *Set of 3* 1·10 1·10

Designs:—15c. Hands reading braille; 20c. Blind woman spinning.

7 Men's Carved Pipes

(Des A. H. Barrett)

1978 (1 Mar). *Carved Pipes. T* **7** *and similar horiz designs. Multicoloured.* P 12×12½.

33 4c. Type **7** 10 10
34 10c. Two men's pipes 15 15
35 15c. Multi-bowled men's pipes 35 55
36 20c. Woman's pipe and witch-doctor's pipe 40 70
33/6 *Set of 4* 90 1·25

8 Angora Goat

9 *Carissa bispinosa*

(Des A. H. Barrett)

1978 (9 June). *Weaving Industry. T* **8** *and similar horiz designs. Multicoloured.* P 12×12½.

37 4c. Type **8** 10 10
38 10c. Spinning mohair 15 15
39 15c. Dyeing mohair 20 25
40 20c. Weaving mohair rug 30 40
37/40 *Set of 4* 65 80

(Des D. Findlay)

1978 (25 Sept). *Edible Wild Fruits. T* **9** *and similar vert designs. Multicoloured.* P 12½×12.

41 4c. Type **9** 15 10
42 10c. *Dovyalis caffra* 20 25
43 15c. *Harpephyllum caffrum* 35 55
44 20c. *Syzygium cordatum* 40 70
41/4 *Set of 4* 1·00 1·40

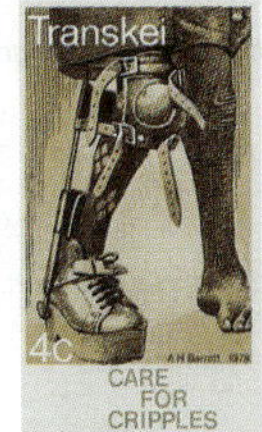

10 Calipers

11 Chi Cha Youth

(Des A. H. Barrett)

1978 (30 Nov). *Care of Cripples. T* **10** *and similar vert designs.* P 12½×12.

No.	Description	Unused	Used
45	4c. black, pale brown and gold	10	10
46	10c. black, grey and gold	25	25
47	15c. black, olive-yellow and gold	40	50
45/7	*Set of 3*	65	75

Designs:—10c. Child in wheelchair; 15c. Nurse examining child's leg.

1979 (3 Jan). *Abakwetha (coming-of-age ceremony of Xhosa males). T* **11** *and similar horiz designs. Multicoloured.* P 12½.

No.	Description	Unused	Used
48	4c. Type **11**	10	10
49	10c. Youths in three-month seclusion	20	20
50	15c. Umtshilo dance	35	35
51	20c. Burning of seclusion hut at end of final ceremony	45	45
48/51	*Set of 4*	1·00	1·00

12 President K. D. Matanzima

13 Windpump

14 Magwa Falls

1979 (20 Feb). *Inauguration of Second State President.* P 14×13½.

No.	Type	Description	Unused	Used
52	**12**	4c. brown-red and gold	15	10
53		15c. deep olive and gold	50	45

(Des K. De Beer)

1979 (13 Mar). *Water Resources. T* **13** *and similar multicoloured designs.* P 14.

No.	Description	Unused	Used
54	4c. Type **13**	15	10
55	10c. Woman ladling water into jar	20	25
56	15c. Indwe River Dam (*horiz*)	35	55
57	20c. Ncora Dam (*horiz*)	40	70
54/7	*Set of 4*	1·00	1·40

(Des A. H. Barrett)

1979 (4 Sept). *Waterfalls. T* **14** *and similar multicoloured designs.* P 14×13½ (*vert*) or 13½×14 (*horiz*).

No.	Description	Unused	Used
58	4c. Type **14**	15	10
59	10c. Bawa Falls	20	25
60	15c. Waterfall Bluff (*horiz*)	35	55
61	20c. Tsitsa Falls (*horiz*)	40	70
58/61	*Set of 4*	1·00	1·40

15 Expectant Mother pouring Milk

16 Black Gnat (dry fly)

(Des A. H. Barrett)

1979 (3 Dec). *Child Health. T* **15** *and similar vert designs. Multicoloured.* P 14×13½.

No.	Description	Unused	Used
62	5c. Type **15**	15	10
63	15c. Mother breast-feeding baby	45	45
64	20c. Immunising child	60	65
62/4	*Set of 3*	1·10	1·10

(Des A. H. Barrett)

1980 (15 Jan). *Fishing Flies (1st series). T* **16** *and similar horiz designs. Multicoloured.* P 14.

No.	Description	Unused	Used
65	5c. Type **16**	25	35
	a. Strip of 5. Nos. 65/9	1·10	1·60
66	5c. Zug Bug (nymph)	25	35
67	5c. March Brown (wet fly)	25	35
68	5c. Durham Ranger (salmon fly)	25	35
69	5c. Colonel Bates (streamer)	25	35
65/9	*Set of 5*	1·10	1·60

Nos. 65/9 were printed together, *se-tenant*, in strips of 5, both horizontally and vertically, within the sheet. See also Nos. 83/7, 99/103, 116/20 and 133/7.

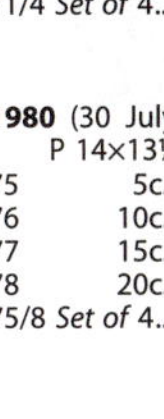

17 Rotary Emblem

18 *Encephalartos altensteinii*

19 Red-chested Cuckoo

(Des G. Mynhardt and H. De Klerk)

1980 (22 Feb). *75th Anniv of Rotary International.* P 14×13½.

No.	Type	Description	Unused	Used
70	**17**	15c. bright blue and gold	35	30

(Des D. Findlay)

1980 (30 Apr). *Cycads. T* **18** *and similar vert designs. Multicoloured.* P 14×13½.

No.	Description	Unused	Used
71	5c. Type **18**	15	10
72	10c. *Encephalartos princeps*	20	25
73	15c. *Encephalartos villosus*	25	40
74	20c. *Encephalartos friderici-guilielmi*	30	55
71/4	*Set of 4*	80	1·10

(Des D. Findlay)

1980 (30 July). *Birds. T* **19** *and similar vert designs. Multicoloured.* P 14×13½.

No.	Description	Unused	Used
75	5c. Type **19**	20	10
76	10c. Cape Puff-back Flycatcher	35	25
77	15c. South African Crowned Crane	50	60
78	20c. Spectacled Weaver	55	70
75/8	*Set of 4*	1·40	1·50

20 Hole in the Wall

(Des A. H. Barrett)

1980 (29 Oct). *Tourism. T* **20** *and similar horiz designs. Multicoloured.* P 14.

No.	Description	Unused	Used
79	5c. Type **20**	15	10
80	10c. Port St. Johns	20	25
81	15c. The Citadel (rock)	25	40
82	20c. The Archway (rock)	30	55
79/82	*Set of 4*	80	1·10

(Des A. H. Barrett)

1981 (15 Jan). *Fishing Flies (2nd series). Horiz designs as T* **16**. *Multicoloured.* P 14.

No.	Description	Unused	Used
83	10c. Kent's Lightning (streamer)	25	25
	a. Strip of 5. Nos. 83/7	1·10	1·10
84	10c. Wickham's Fancy (dry fly)	25	25
85	10c. Jock Scott (wet fly)	25	25
86	10c. Green Highlander (salmon fly)	25	25
87	10c. Tan Nymph	25	25
83/7	*Set of 5*	1·10	1·10

Nos. 83/7 were printed together, *se-tenant*, in strips of 5, both horizontally and vertically, within the sheet.

(Des D. Findlay)

1981 (15 Apr). *Medicinal Plants (2nd series). Vert designs as T* **4**. *Multicoloured.* P 14×13½.

No.	Description	Unused	Used
88	5c. *Leonotis leonurus*	15	10
89	15c. *Euphorbia bupleurifolia*	20	30
90	20c. *Pelargonium reniforme*	20	35
91	25c. *Hibiscus trionum*	20	40
88/91	*Set of 4*	70	1·00

21 Eyamakhwenkwe

(Des A. H. Barrett)

1981 (28 Aug). *Xhosa Women's Headdresses. T* **21** *and similar horiz designs. Multicoloured.* P 14.

No.	Description	Unused	Used
92	5c. Type **21**	10	10
93	15c. Eyabafana	20	35
94	20c. Umfazana	25	45
95	25c. Ixhegokazi	30	55
92/5	*Set of 4*	80	1·25
MS96	126×91 mm. Nos. 92/5	1·00	1·25

22 State House, Umtata

(Des P. Semra'd)

1981 (26 Oct). *Fifth Anniv of Independence. T* **22** *and similar horiz design.* P 14.

No.	Description	Unused	Used
97	5c. black, lake-brown and emerald	15	10
98	15c. black, lake-brown and emerald	45	30

Design:—15c. University of Transkei.

(Des A. H. Barrett)

1982 (6 Jan). *Fishing Flies (3rd series). Horiz designs as T* **16**. *Multicoloured.* P 14.

No.	Description	Unused	Used
99	10c. Blue Charm	30	30
	a. Strip of 5. Nos. 99/103	1·40	1·40
100	10c. Royal Coachman	30	30
101	10c. Light Spruce	30	30
102	10c. Montana Nymph	30	30
103	10c. Butcher	30	30
99/103	*Set of 5*	1·40	1·40

Nos. 99/103 were printed together, *se-tenant*, in strips of 5, both horizontally and vertically, within the sheet.

23 Cub Scout

24 Hippocrates

(Des H. Botha)

1982 (14 May). *75th Anniv of Boy Scout Movement. T* **23** *and similar vert designs. Multicoloured.* P 14.

No.	Description	Unused	Used
104	8c. Type **23**	15	10
105	10c. Scout planting tree	15	10
106	20c. Scout on raft	25	30
107	25c. Scout with dog	25	30
104/7	*Set of 4*	70	70

(Des J. Meyer)

1982 (5 Oct). *Celebrities of Medicine (1st series). T* **24** *and similar vert designs. Multicoloured.* P 14.

No.	Description	Unused	Used
108	15c. Type **24**	20	20
109	20c. Antonie van Leeuwenhoek	25	30
110	25c. William Harvey	30	40
111	30c. Joseph Lister	35	45
108/11	*Set of 4*	1·00	1·25

See also Nos. 125/8, 160/3, 176/9, 249/52, 273/6, 281/4 and 305/8.

25 City Hall

26 Hotel Complex, Mzamba

(Des A. H. Barrett)

1982 (10 Nov). *Centenary of Umtata. T* **25** *and similar horiz designs. Multicoloured.* P 13½×14.

No.	Description	Unused	Used
112	8c. Type **25**	10	10
113	15c. The Bunga	15	15
114	20c. Botha Sigcau Building	20	20
115	25c. Palace of Justice and K. D. Matanzima Building	25	30
112/15	*Set of 4*	65	65

(Des A. H. Barrett)

1983 (2 Mar). *Fishing Flies (4th series). Horiz designs as T* **16**. *Multicoloured.* P 14.

No.	Description	Unused	Used
116	20c. Alexandra	30	30
	a. Strip of 5. Nos. 116/20	1·40	1·40
117	20c. Kent's Marbled Sedge	30	30
118	20c. White Marabou	30	30
119	20c. Mayfly Nymph	30	30
120	20c. Silver Wilkinson	30	30
116/20	*Set of 5*	1·40	1·40

Nos. 116/20 were printed together, *se-tenant*, in strips of 5, both horizontally and vertically, within the sheet.

(Des A. H. Barrett)

1983 (25 May). *Wildcoast Holiday Complex, Mzamba. T* **26** *and similar horiz designs. Multicoloured.* P 14.

No.	Description	Unused	Used
121	10c. Type **26**	15	15
122	20c. Beach scene	25	25
123	25c. Casino	35	35
124	40c. Carousel	50	50
121/4	*Set of 4*	1·10	1·10

(Des J. Meyer)

1983 (17 Aug). *Celebrities of Medicine (2nd series). Vert designs as T* **24**. *Multicoloured.* P 14.

No.	Description	Unused	Used
125	10c. Edward Jenner	15	15
126	20c. Gregor Mendel	25	30
127	25c. Louis Pasteur	30	35
128	40c. Florence Nightingale	40	55
125/8	*Set of 4*	1·00	1·25

27 Lady Frere Post Office

(Des A. H. Barrett)

1983 (9 Nov). *Transkei Post Offices (1st series). T* **27** *and similar horiz designs. Multicoloured.* P 14.

No.	Description	Unused	Used
129	10c. Type **27**	15	15
130	20c. Idutywa	20	30
131	25c. Lusikisiki	20	35
132	40c. Cala	30	55
129/32	*Set of 4*	75	1·25

See also Nos. 156/9.

(Des A. H. Barrett)

1984 (10 Feb). *Fishing Flies (5th series). Horiz designs as T* **16**. *Multicoloured.* P 14.

133 20c. Silver Grey 45 45
a. Strip of 5. Nos. 133/7 2·00 2·00
134 20c. Ginger Quill 45 45
135 20c. Hardy's Favourite 45 45
136 20c. March Brown 45 45
137 20c. Kent's Spectrum Mohawk 45 45
133/7 *Set of 5* 2·00 2·00

Nos. 133/7 were printed together, *se-tenant*, in strips of 5, both horizontally and vertically, within the sheet.

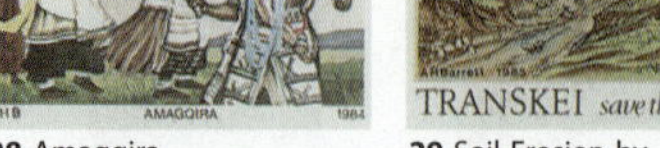

28 Amagqira **29** Soil Erosion by Overgrazing

(Des A. H. Barrett)

1984 (2 Apr)–**91**. *Xhosa Culture. T* **28** *and similar horiz designs. Multicoloured. Ordinary paper.* P 14.

138 1c. Type **28** (6.7.84) 20 10
a. Chalk-surfaced paper (7.1.91) 30 10
139 2c. Horsemen (6.7.84) 20 10
140 3c. Mat making (6.7.84) 20 10
141 4c. hosa dancers (6.7.84) 20 10
142 5c. Shopping with donkeys (6.7.84) 20 10
143 6c. Young musicians (6.7.84) 30 15
144 7c. Fingo brides (6.7.84) 30 20
145 8c. Tasting the beer (6.7.84) 30 20
146 9c. Thinning the maize (6.7.84) 30 30
147 10c. Dancing demonstration (6.7.84) 30 15
148 11c. Water from the river 30 15
148*a* 12c. Preparing a meal (1.4.85) 30 15
148*b* 14c. Weeding mealies (chalk- surfaced paper) (1.4.86) 30 20
149 15c. National sport: stick fighting (6.7.84) 20 20
149*a* 16c. Morning pasture (chalk-surfaced paper) (1.4.87) 30 20
150 20c. Abakhwetha dance (6.7.84) 30 25
150*a* 21c. Building of initiation hut (chalk surfaced paper) (3.7.90) 1·50 20
151 25c. Tribesman singing (6.7.84) 30 25
152 30c. Jovial matrons (6.7.84) 50 35
153 50c. Pipe making (6.7.84) 50 60
154 1r. Intonjane (6.7.84) 60 1·10
155 2r. Abakhwetha (6.7.84) 75 2·00
138/55 *Set of 22* 7·50 6·50

(Des A. H. Barrett)

1984 (11 May). *Transkei Post Offices (2nd series). Horiz designs as T* **27**. *Multicoloured.* P 14.

156 11c. Umzimkulu 15 15
157 20c. Mount Fletcher 20 25
158 25c. Qumbu 20 25
159 30c. Umtata 30 50
156/9 *Set of 4* 75 1·00

(Des J. Meyer)

1984 (12 Oct). *Celebrities of Medicine (3rd series). Vert designs as T* **24**. *Multicoloured.* P 14.

160 11c. Nicholas of Cusa 15 15
161 25c. William Morton 25 25
162 30c. Wilhelm Röntgen 30 40
163 45c. Karl Landsteiner 40 60
160/3 *Set of 4* 1·00 1·25

(Des A. H. Barrett)

1985 (7 Feb). *Soil Conservation. T* **29** *and similar horiz designs showing restoration of eroded landscape. Multicoloured.* P 14½×14.

164 11c. Type **29** 15 15
165 25c. Removal of stock and construction of walls as sediment collectors 25 25
166 30c. Regeneration of vegetation 30 40
167 50c. Cattle grazing in lush landscape 40 60
164/7 *Set of 4* 1·00 1·25

30 Tsitsa Bridge

(Des D. Bagnall)

1985 (18 Apr). *Bridges. T* **30** *and similar horiz designs. Multicoloured.* P 14.

168 12c. Type **30** 20 15
169 25c. White Kei Railway Bridge 25 25
170 30c. Mitchell Bridge 35 35
171 50c. Umzimvubu Bridge 55 60
168/71 *Set of 4* 1·25 1·25

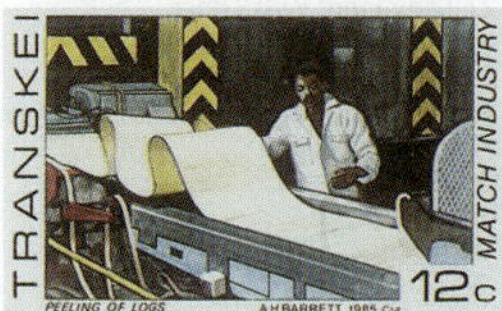

31 Veneer-peeling Machine

(Des A. H. Barrett)

1985 (25 July). *Match Industry, Butterworth. T* **31** *and similar horiz designs. Multicoloured.* P 14½×14.

172 12c. Type **31** 15 15
173 25c. Cutting wood to match-size 20 25
174 30c. Dipping splints in chemical to form match heads 25 35
175 50c. Boxing matches 40 65
172/5 *Set of 4* 90 1·25

(Des J. Meyer)

1985 (20 Sept). *Celebrities of Medicine (4th series). Vert designs as T* **24**. *Multicoloured.* P 14.

176 12c. Andreas Vesalius 20 15
177 25c. Marcello Malpighi 30 40
178 30c. Francois Magendie 35 45
179 50c. William Stewart Halsted 50 70
176/9 *Set of 4* 1·25 1·50

32 Early Street Scene **33** *Aloe ferox*

(Des A. H. Barren)

1986 (6 Feb). *Historic Port St. Johns. T* **32** *and similar horiz designs. Multicoloured.* P 14½×14.

180 12c. Type **32** 20 15
181 20c. Umzimvubu (coaster) anchored at old jetty 45 45
182 25c. Wagons off-loading maize at jetty 50 50
183 30c. View of town at end of 19th century 50 55
180/3 *Set of 4* 1·50 1·50
MS1841 30×94 mm. Nos. 180/3 1·50 1·50

PHILATELIC FOUNDATION MINIATURE SHEETS. These miniature sheets were issued by the Philatelic Foundation of Southern Africa and not the postal administration. They could be purchased by post or from a limited number of philatelic offices at a premium in aid of various national and international stamp exhibitions.

(Des D. Findlay)

1986 (1 May). *Aloes. T* **33** *and similar vert designs. Multicoloured.* P 14½×14.

185 14c. Type **33** 20 15
186 20c. *Aloe arborescens* 30 30
187 25c. *Aloe maculata* 35 35
188 30c. *Aloe ecklonis* 45 45
185/8 *Set of 4* 1·10 1·10

The 30c. value exists as a Philatelic Foundation miniature sheet.

34 First Falls Station, Umtata River **35** Prime Minister George Matanzima

(Des R. Smith)

1986 (24 July). *Hydro-electric Power Stations. T* **34** *and similar horiz designs. Multicoloured.* P 14½×14.

189 14c. Type **34** 20 15
190 20c. Second Falls, Umtata River 25 25
191 25c. Ncora, Qumanco River 40 40
192 30c. Collywobbles, Mbashe River 50 50
189/92 *Set of 4* 1·25 1·10

(Des J. van Niekerk)

1986 (26 Oct). *Tenth Anniv of Independence. T* **35** *and similar horiz designs. Multicoloured.* P 14½×14.

193 14c. Type **35** 15 15
194 20c. Technical College, Umtata 25 30
195 25c. University of Transkei, Umtata 30 40
196 30c. Palace of Justice, Umtata 40 50
193/6 *Set of 4* 1·00 1·10

36 Piper PA-23 Apache 235 *Ulundi* flying through Clouds **37** Pondo Girl

(Des H. Botha)

1987 (5 Feb). *Tenth Anniv of Transkei Airways Corporation. T* **36** *and similar horiz designs. Multicoloured.* P 14½×14.

197 14c. Type **36** 20 15
198 20c. Tail fin of *Ulundi* 30 30
199 25c. Beech 100 King Air 40 40
200 30c. Control tower, K. D. Matanzima Airport 55 60
197/200 *Set of 4* 1·25 1·25

(Des A. H. Barrett)

1987 (22 May). *Transkei Beadwork. T* **37** *and similar vert designs. Multicoloured.* P 14×14½.

201 16c. Type **37** 15 15
202 20c. Bomvana woman 25 30
203 25c. Xessibe woman 35 40
204 30c. Xhosa man 40 60
201/4 *Set of 4* 1·00 1·25

The 25c. value exists as a Philatelic Foundation miniature sheet.

38 *Latrodectus indistinctus* **39** Common Black Pigs

(Des Liza van der Wal (16, 30c.), T. Marais (others))

1987 (27 Aug). *Spiders. T* **38** *and similar vert designs. Multicoloured.* P 14×14½.

205 16c. Type **38** 20 15
206 20c. *Nephila pilipes* 30 30
207 25c. *Lycosidae sp* 40 40
208 30c. *Argiope nigrovittata* 50 55
205/8 *Set of 4* 1·25 1·25

(Des B. Jackson)

1987 (22 Oct). *Domestic Animals. T* **39** *and similar horiz designs. Multicoloured.* P 14×14½.

209 16c. Type **39** 15 15
210 30c. Goats 20 30
211 40c. Merino sheep 30 50
212 50c. Cattle 45 65
209/12 *Set of 4* 1·00 1·40

40 *Plocamium corallorhiza* **41** Spinning

(Des D. Thorpe)

1988 (18 Feb). *Seaweed. T* **40** *and similar vert designs. Multicoloured.* P 14×14½.

213 16c. Type **40** 15 15
214 30c. *Gelidium amanzii* 25 30
215 40c. *Ecklonia biruncinata* 30 40
216 50c. *Halimeda cuneata* 40 55
213/16 *Set of 4* 1·00 1·25

(Des B. Jackson)

1988 (5 May). *Blanket Factory, Butterworth. T* **41** *and similar horiz designs. Multicoloured.* P 14½×14.

217 16c. Type **41** 15 15
218 30c. Warping 25 30
219 40c. Weaving 30 40
220 50c. Raising the nap 40 55
217/20 *Set of 4* 1·00 1·25

42 Map showing Wreck Site **43** Small-spotted Cat

(Des Sheila Nowers)

1988 (4 Aug). *206th Anniv of Shipwreck of Grosvenor (East Indiaman). T* **42** *and similar horiz designs. Multicoloured.* P 14½×14.

221 16c. Type **42** 40 20
222 30c. "The Wreck of the Grosvenor" (R. Smirks) 50 50
223 40c. Dirk hilt, divider and coins from wreck 55 55
224 50c. "African Hospitality" (G. Morland) 60 70
221/4 *Set of 4* 1·90 1·75

The 50c. value exists as a Philatelic Foundation miniature sheet.

(Des D. Murphy)

1988 (20 Oct). *Endangered Animals. T* **43** *and similar horiz designs. Multicoloured.* P 14½×14.

225 16c. Type **43** 60 30
226 30c. Blue Duiker 70 60
227 40c. Oribi 85 75
228 50c. Hunting Dog 1·25 1·00
225/8 *Set of 4* 3·00 2·40

44 Class 14 CRB Steam Locomotives

45 Mat, Baskets and Jar

(Des D. Hall-Green)

1989 (19 Jan). *Trains. T* **44** *and similar multicoloured designs.* P 14×14½ (*horiz*) or 14½×14 (*vert*).

229	16c. Type **44**	20	20
230	30c. Class 14 CRB locomotive and passenger train at Toleni Halt	40	40
231	40c. Double-headed steam train on Great Kei River Bridge (*vert*)	60	70
232	50c. Double-headed steam train in Kei Valley (*vert*)	65	80
229/32 *Set of 4*		1·75	1·90

The 50c. value exists as a Philatelic Foundation miniature sheet.

(Des Sheila Nowers)

1989 (20 Apr). *Basketry. T* **45** *and similar horiz designs. Multicoloured.* P 14½×14.

233	18c. Type **45**	20	15
234	30c. Basket and jar	30	30
235	40c. Jars and bag	40	50
236	50c. Dish and jars	55	75
233/6 *Set of 4*		1·25	1·50

46 Chub Mackerel

47 Broom Cluster Fig

(Des D. Thorpe)

1989 (20 July). *Seafood. T* **46** *and similar horiz designs. Multicoloured.* P 14½×14.

237	18c. Type **46**	55	15
238	30c. Squid	70	50
239	40c. Perna or Brown Mussels	85	70
240	50c. Rock Lobster	1·00	1·00
237/40 *Set of 4*		2·75	2·10

(Des B. Jackson)

1989 (5 Oct). *Trees. T* **47** *and similar horiz designs. Multicoloured.* P 14×14½.

241	18c. Type **47**	50	20
242	30c. Natal Fig	75	55
243	40c. Broad-leaved Coral	85	85
244	50c. Cabbage Tree	1·10	1·25
241/4 *Set of 4*		2·75	2·50

48 *Ginkgo koningensis*

49 Aretaeus (discoverer of diabetes)

(Des L. Kriedemann)

1990 (18 Jan). *Plant Fossils. T* **48** *and similar horiz designs. Multicoloured.* P 14.

245	18c. Type **48**	80	25
246	30c. *Pseudoctenis spatulata*	1·10	80
247	40c. *Rissikia media*	1·25	1·10
248	50c. *Taeniopteris anavolans*	1·40	1·50
245/8 *Set of 4*		4·00	3·25

(Des A. McBride)

1990 (29 Mar). *Celebrities of Medicine (5th series). Diabetes Research. T* **49** *and similar vert designs. Multicoloured.* P 14×14½.

249	18c. Type **49**	70	20
250	30c. Claude Bernard (discovered sugar formation by liver)	1·10	70
251	40c. Oscar Minkowski (discovered pancreas removal caused diabetes)	1·25	90
252	50c. Frederick Banting (discoverer of insulin)	1·40	1·25
249/52 *Set of 4*		4·00	2·75

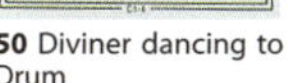

50 Diviner dancing to Drum

51 Soldier Lily

(Des A. H. Barrett)

1990 (28 June). *Diviners. T* **50** *and similar vert designs. Multicoloured.* P 14×14½.

253	21c. Type **50**	60	20
254	35c. Lecturing Imichetywa (novitiates)	90	70
255	40c. Neophyte initiation	1·00	90
256	50c. Diviner's induction ceremony	1·25	1·40
253/6 *Set of 4*		3·25	3·00

The 50c. value exists as a Philatelic Foundation miniature sheet.

(Des A. Batten)

1990 (20 Sept). *Flowers. T* **51** *and similar vert designs. Multicoloured.* P 14.

257	21c. Type **51**	65	20
258	35c. *Disa crassicornis*	90	65
259	40c. Christmas Bells	1·00	90
260	50c. Port St. John's Creeper	1·25	1·40
257/60 *Set of 4*		3·50	2·75

52 Pink Ink Plant

53 Common Dolphin

(Des A. Batten)

1991 (10 Jan). *Parasitic Plants. T* **52** *and similar vert designs. Multicoloured.* P 14×14½.

261	21c. Type **52**	60	20
262	35c. White Harveya	90	70
263	40c. *Alectra sessiliflora*	1·00	1·10
264	50c. *Hydnora africana*	1·25	1·50
261/4 *Set of 4*		3·25	3·25

(Des D. Thorpe)

1991 (4 Apr). *Dolphins. T* **53** *and similar horiz designs. Multicoloured.* P 14½×14.

265	25c. Type **53**	1·00	25
266	40c. Bottle-nosed Dolphin	1·40	85
267	50c. Humpbacked Dolphin	1·60	1·25
268	60c. Risso's Dolphin	1·60	1·60
265/8 *Set of 4*		4·75	3·50

54 South African Crowned Crane

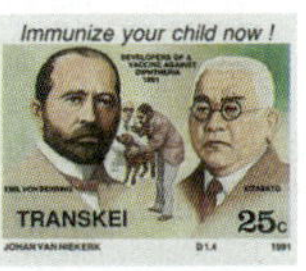

55 Emil von Behring and Shibasaburo Kitasako (diphtheria)

(Des A. Ainslie)

1991 (20 June). *Endangered Birds. T* **54** *and similar vert designs. Multicoloured.* P 14×14½.

269	25c. Type **54**	65	30
270	40c. Cape Vulture	1·00	85
271	50c. Wattled Crane	1·10	1·10
272	60c. Egyptian Vulture	1·25	1·40
269/72 *Set of 4*		3·50	3·25

The 60c. value exists as a Philatelic Foundation miniature sheet.

(Des J. van Niekerk)

1991 (26 Sept). *Celebrities of Medicine (6th series). Vaccine Development. T* **55** *and similar horiz designs. Multicoloured.* P 14×14½.

273	25c. Type **55**	90	25
274	40c. Camille Guérin and Albert Calmette (tuberculosis)	1·40	90
275	50c. Jonas Salk (poliomyelitis)	1·60	1·25
276	60c. John Enders (measles)	1·75	1·50
273/6 *Set of 4*		5·00	3·50

56 *Eulophia speciosa*

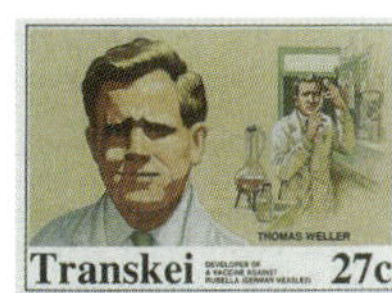

57 Thomas Weller (researcher into infectious viruses)

(Des A. Batten)

1992 (20 Feb). *Orchids. T* **56** *and similar vert designs. Multicoloured.* P 14.

277	27c. Type **56**	25	20
278	45c. *Satyrium sphaerocarpum*	40	40
279	65c. *Disa scullyi*	60	70
280	85c. *Disa tysonii*	80	1·00
277/80 *Set of 4*		1·90	2·10

(Des J. van Niekerk)

1992 (1 Apr). *Celebrities of Medicine (7th series). T* **57** *and similar horiz designs. Multicoloured.* P 14.

281	27c. Type **57**	75	25
282	45c. Ignaz Semmelweis	1·10	80
283	65c. Sir James Simpson	1·50	1·25
284	85c. René Laënnec	1·75	1·60
281/4 *Set of 4*		4·50	3·50

58 Red-billed Pintail

59 *Pseudomelania sutherlandi* (gastropod)

1992 (16 July). *Waterfowl. T* **58** *and similar horiz designs. Multicoloured.* P 14.

285	35c. Type **58**	60	60
	a. Pair. Nos. 285/6	1·10	1·10
286	35c. Hottentot Teal	60	60
287	70c. Maccoa Duck	90	90
	a. Pair. Nos. 287/8	1·75	1·75
288	70c. White-backed Duck	90	90
289	90c. African Black Duck	1·10	1·10
	a. Pair. Nos. 289/90	2·10	2·10
290	90c. Egyptian Goose	1·10	1·10
291	1r.05 Cape Shoveler	1·40	1·40
	a. Pair. Nos. 291/2	2·75	2·75
292	1r.05 Cape Teal	1·40	1·40
285/92 *Set of 8*		7·25	7·25

The two designs of each value were printed together, *se-tenant*, in pairs within the sheets.

No. 287 exists as a Philatelic Foundation miniature sheet.

(Des L. Kriedemann)

1992 (17 Sept). *Marine Fossils. T* **59** *and similar horiz designs. Multicoloured.* P 14.

293	35c. Type **59**	1·10	35
294	70c. *Gaudryceras denseplicatum* (ammonite)	1·50	1·10
295	90c. *Neithea quinquecostata* (bivalve)	1·60	1·50
296	1r.05 *Pugilina acuticarinatus* (gastropod)	1·75	1·60
293/6 *Set of 4*		5·50	4·00

60 Papillon

61 Fabrosaurus

(Des D. Murphy)

1993 (12 Feb). *Dogs. T* **60** *and similar horiz designs. Multicoloured.* P 14.

297	35c. Type **60**	60	30
298	70c. Pekinese	90	90
299	90c. Chihuahua	1·10	1·25
300	1r.05 Dachshund	1·40	1·60
297/300 *Set of 4*		3·50	3·50

The 70c. value exists as a Philatelic Foundation miniature sheet.

(Des L. Kriedemann)

1993 (18 June). *Prehistoric Animals. T* **61** *and similar horiz designs. Multicoloured.* P 14.

301	45c. Type **61**	1·10	40
302	65c. Diictodon	1·50	1·10
303	85c. Chasmatosaurus	1·75	1·60
304	1r.05 Rubidgea	1·75	1·75
301/4 *Set of 4*		5·50	4·25

62 Sir Alexander Fleming and Howard Florey

63 Laughing Doves

(Des J. van Niekerk)

1993 (20 Aug). *Celebrities of Medicine (8th series). T* **62** *and similar horiz designs. Multicoloured.* P 14.

305	45c. Type **62**	70	40
306	65c. Alexis Carrel	1·10	1·10
307	85c. James Lind	1·25	1·50
308	1r.05 Santiago Ramón y Cajal	1·40	1·60
305/8 *Set of 4*		4·00	4·25

(Des Julia Birkhead)

1993 (15 Oct). *Doves. T* **63** *and similar horiz designs. Multicoloured.* P 14.

309	45c. Type **63**	60	40
310	65c. Tambourine Doves	90	90
311	85c. Emerald-spotted Wood Doves	1·25	1·25
312	1r.05 Namaqua Doves	1·50	1·60
309/12 *Set of 4*		3·75	3·75
MS313	92×83 mm. Nos. 309/12	3·75	3·75

64 Clan Lindsay (steamer) on rocks, Mazeppa Bay, 1898

(Des J. van Niekerk)

1994 (18 Mar). *Shipwrecks. T* **64** *and similar horiz designs. Multicoloured.* P 14.

314	45c. Type **64**	1·25	60
315	65c. Horizon (freighter) on rocks near River Mngazi, 1967	1·60	1·25

316	85c. Oceanos (pleasure cruiser) sinking near Coffee Bay, 1991	1·90	1·60
317	1r.05 Forresbank (freighter) on fire near River Mtakatye, 1958	1·90	1·90
314/17	*Set of 4*	6·00	4·75

The 85c. value exists as a Philatelic Foundation miniature sheet.

Transkei was reincorporated into the Republic of South Africa on 27 April 1994. Its postal service continued to operate, using South African stamps, until 1 April 1996 when it was integrated with that of the Republic.

XIV. VENDA

The Venda Territory Authority was established in 1969 and was granted internal self-government on 1 February 1973 under the Bantu Homelands Constitution Act. Venda became fully independent on 13 September 1979. This independence did not receive international political recognition, but the stamps were accepted as valid on international mail.

PRINTERS. All the following stamps were printed in lithography by the South African Government Printer, Pretoria.

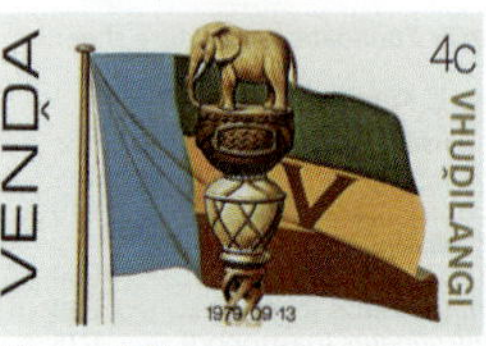

1 Flag and Mace

2 *Tecomaria capensis*

(Des A. H. Barrett)

1979 (13 Sept). *Independence. T* **1** *and similar horiz designs. Multicoloured. P* 14.

1	4c. Type **1**	25	25
2	15c. Government Buildings, Thohoyandou	30	60
3	20c. Chief Minister P. R. Mphephu	40	70
4	25c. Coat of arms	60	1·10
1/4	*Set of 4*	1·50	2·40

(Des D. Findlay)

1979 (13 Sept)–**85**. *Flowers. T* **2** *and similar vert designs. Multicoloured.* P 14 (11, 12c.) or 12½ (others).

5	1c. Type **2**	10	10
	a. Perf 14 (30.4.82)	10	10
6	2c. *Catophractes alexandri*	30	15
	a. Perf 14 (6.5.81)	20	15
7	3c. *Tricliceras lungipedunculatum*	30	10
	a. Perf 14 (18.8.82)	30	15
8	4c. *Dissotis princeps*	30	10
9	5c. *Gerbera jamesonii*	1·75	45
	a. Perf 14 (15.1.80)	30	10
10	6c. *Hibiscus mastersianus*	15	10
11	7c. *Nymphaea caerulea*	20	10
12	8c. *Crinum lagardiae*	45	25
	a. Perf 14 (27.1.82)	30	15
13	9c. *Xerophyta retinervis*	20	15
14	10c. *Hypoxis angustifolia*	40	25
	a. Perf 14 (4.3.83)	40	15
14*b*	11c. *Combretum microphyllum* (2.4.84)	55	15
14*c*	12c. *Clivia caulescens* (1.4.85)	30	15
15	15c. *Pycnostachys urticifolia*	30	15
16	20c. *Zantedeschia jucunda*	75	15
17	25c. *Leonotis mollis*	2·00	1·00
	a. Perf 14 (22.1.80)	50	40
18	30c. *Littonia modesta*	40	30
19	50c. *Protea caffra*	40	40
	a. Perf 14 (17.2.84)	1·40	1·25
20	1r. *Adenium multiflorum*	75	85
21	2r. *Strelitzia caudata*	1·25	2·00
5/21	*Set of 19* (cheapest)	7·00	5·00

3 Man drinking Beer

4 Tea Plants in Nursery

(Des A. H. Barrett)

1980 (13 Feb). *Wood Carvings. T* **3** *and similar multicoloured designs.* P 14.

22	5c. Type **3**	15	15
23	10c. Frying mealies in gourd	25	25
24	15c. King Nebuchadnezzar (*horiz*)	40	40
25	20c. Python squeezing woman to death (*horiz*)	50	60
22/5	*Set of 4*	1·10	1·25

(Des A. H. Barrett)

1980 (14 May). *Tea Cultivation. T* **4** *and similar horiz designs. Multicoloured.* P 14.

26	5c. Type **4**	15	10
27	10c. Tea pluckers	20	20
28	15c. Withering in the factory	35	35
29	20c. Cut, twist, curl unit	40	45
26/9	*Set of 4*	1·00	1·00

5 Young Banana Plants

6 *Precis tugela*

(Des A. H. Barrett)

1980 (13 Aug). *Banana Cultivation. T* **5** *and similar horiz designs. Multicoloured.* P 14.

30	5c. Type **5**	15	10
31	10c. Cutting "hands"	25	25
32	15c. Sorting and dividing into clusters	30	30
33	20c. Packing	40	45
30/3	*Set of 4*	1·00	1·00

(Des D. Findlay)

1980 (13 Nov). *Butterflies. T* **6** *and similar vert designs. Multicoloured.* P 14.

34	5c. Type **6**	20	15
35	10c. *Charaxes bohemani*	30	40
36	15c. *Catacroptera cloanthe*	40	55
37	20c. *Papilio dardanus*	50	70
34/7	*Set of 4*	1·25	1·60

7 Collared Sunbird

8 Nwanedi Dam

(Des J. Hoekstra)

1981 (16 Feb). *Sunbirds. T* **7** *and similar vert designs. Multicoloured.* P 14.

38	5c. Type **7**	20	15
39	15c. Mariqua Sunbird	30	40
40	20c. Southern White-bellied Sunbird	35	45
41	25c. Scarlet-chested Sunbird	35	55
38/41	*Set of 4*	1·10	1·40

(Des A. H. Barrett)

1981 (6 May). *Lakes and Waterfalls. T* **8** *and similar horiz designs. Multicoloured.* P 14.

42	5c. Type **8**	15	10
43	15c. Mahovhohovho Falls	30	30
44	20c. Phiphidi Falls	35	35
45	25c. Lake Fundudzi	35	40
42/5	*Set of 4*	1·00	1·00

9 *Cynorkis kassnerana*

10 Mbila

(Des Jeannette Stead)

1981 (11 Sept). *Orchids. T* **9** *and similar vert designs. Multicoloured.* P 14.

46	5c. Type **9**	15	10
47	15c. *Eulophia fridericii*	30	35
48	20c. *Bonatea densiflora*	35	45
49	25c. *Mystacidium brayboniae*	35	55
46/9	*Set of 4*	1·00	1·25
MS50	96×120 mm. Nos. 46/9	1·25	1·40

(Des J. Hoekstra)

1981 (13 Nov). *Musical Instruments. T* **10** *and similar horiz designs.* P 14.

51	5c. yellow-orange and black	10	10
52	15c. red-orange and black	25	25
53	20c. orange-brown and black	30	35
54	25c. brown-ochre and black	30	35
51/4	*Set of 4*	80	90

Designs:—15c. Phalaphala; 20c. Tshizambi; 25c. Ngoma.

11 Gathering Sisal

(Des B. Ashton)

1982 (26 Feb). *Sisal Cultivation. T* **11** *and similar horiz designs. Multicoloured.* P 13½×14.

55	5c. Type **11**	10	10
56	10c. Drying	20	20
57	20c. Grading	30	35
58	25c. Baling	30	40
55/8	*Set of 4*	80	90

12 Bison Petrograph, Altamira, Spain

(Des H. Botha)

1982 (15 June). *History of Writing (1st series). T* **12** *and similar horiz designs. Multicoloured.* P 14.

59	8c. Type **12**	15	10
60	15c. Petroglyph, Eastern California	30	30
61	20c. Pictograph script (Sumerian tablet)	40	40
62	25c. Bushman burial stone, Humansdorp	45	45
59/62	*Set of 4*	1·10	1·10

No. 59 is inscribed "AHAMIRA" in error. See also Nos. 75/8, 87/90, 107/10, 139/42, 171/4 and 203/6.

13 *Euphorbia ingens*

14 *Rana angolensis*

(Des D. Findlay)

1982 (17 Sept). *Indigenous Trees (1st series). T* **13** *and similar horiz designs. Multicoloured.* P 14.

63	8c. Type **13**	15	10
64	15c. *Pterocarpus angolensis*	25	30
65	20c. *Ficus ingens*	30	40
66	25c. *Adansonia digitata*	40	55
63/6	*Set of 4*	1·00	1·25

See also Nos. 79/82, 95/8 and 227/30.

(Des A. H. Barrett)

1982 (26 Nov). *Frogs. T* **14** *and similar horiz designs. Multicoloured.* P 14.

67	8c. Type **14**	15	10
68	15c. *Chiromantis xerampelina*	25	30
69	20c. *Leptopelis sp*	30	40
70	25c. *Ptychadena anchietae*	40	55
67/70	*Set of 4*	1·00	1·25

15 European Bee Eater

(Des Sheila Nowers)

1983 (16 Feb). *Migratory Birds (1st series). T* **15** *and similar horiz designs. Multicoloured.* P 14.

71	8c. Type **15**	25	15
72	20c. Tawny Eagle ("Steppe Eagle")	50	65
73	25c. Violet Starling ("Plum-coloured Starling")	60	75
74	40c. Abdim's Stork ("White-bellied Stork")	90	1·50
71/4	*Set of 4*	2·00	2·75

See also Nos. 91/4.

(Des H. Botha)

1983 (11 May). *History of Writing (2nd series). Multicoloured designs as T* **12**, *but vert. Multicoloured.* P 14.

75	10c. Indus Valley script	15	10
76	20c. Sumerian cuneiform	20	25
77	25c. Egyptian hieroglyphics	25	30
78	40c. Chinese handscroll	50	70
75/8	*Set of 4*	1·00	1·25

(Des D. Findlay)

1983 (3 Aug). *Indigenous Trees (2nd series). Horiz designs as T* **13**. *Multicoloured.* P 14.

79	10c. *Gardenia spatulifolia*	15	10
80	20c. *Hyphaene natalensis*	25	30
81	25c. *Albizia adianthifolia*	30	40
82	40c. *Sesamothamnus lugardii*	40	60
79/82	*Set of 4*	1·00	1·25

16 Avocado

17 African Paradise Flycatcher

(Des B. Jackson)

1983 (26 Oct). *Subtropical Fruit. T* **16** *and similar horiz designs. Multicoloured.* P 14.

83	10c. Type **16**	15	10
84	20c. Mango	25	30
85	25c. Papaya	30	40
86	40c. Litchi	40	60
83/6	*Set of 4*	1·00	1·25

(Des H. Botha)

1984 (17 Feb). *History of Writing (3rd series). Horiz designs as T* **12**. *Multicoloured.* P 14×14½.

87	10c. Evolution of cuneiform sign	15	10
88	20c. Evolution of Chinese character	25	30
89	25c. Development of Cretan hieroglyphics	30	40
90	40c. Development of Egyptian hieroglyphics	40	60
87/90	*Set of 4*	1·00	1·25

(Des Sheila Nowers)

1984 (26 Apr). *Migratory Birds (2nd series). T* **17** *and similar vert designs. Multicoloured.* P 14½×14.

91	11c. White Stork	30	20
92	20c. Type **17**	50	50
93	25c. Black Kite ("Yellow-billed Kite")	60	60
94	30c. Wood Sandpiper	70	85
91/4	*Set of 4*	1·90	1·90

(Des D. Findlay)

1984 (21 June). *Indigenous Trees (3rd series). Horiz designs as T* **13**. *Multicoloured.* P 14.

95	11c. *Afzelia quanzensis*	15	10
96	20c. *Peltophorum, africanum*	25	30
97	25c. *Gyrocarpus americanus*	30	40
98	30c. *Acacia sieberana*	40	55
95/8	*Set of 4*	1·00	1·25

18 Dzata Ruins, Nzhelele Valley

19 White-browed Robin Chat

(Des B. Jackson)

1984 (13 Sept). *Fifth Anniv of Independence. T* **18** *and similar horiz designs. Multicoloured.* P 14.

99	11c. Type **18**	15	10
100	25c. Traditional hut	25	30
101	30c. Sub-economical house	30	35
102	45c. Modern home	45	65
99/102	*Set of 4*	1·00	1·25

(Des Sheila Nowers)

1985 (10 Jan). *Songbirds. T* **19** *and similar vert designs. Multicoloured.* P 14½×14.

103	11c. Type **19** (inscr "Heuglin's Robin")	25	20
104	25c. Black-collared Barbet	35	40
105	30c. African Black-headed Oriole	40	50
106	50c. Kurrichane Thrush	60	80
103/6	*Set of 4*	1·40	1·75

(Des H. Botha)

1985 (21 Mar). *History of Writing (4th series). Horiz designs as T* **12**. *Multicoloured.* P 14.

107	11c. Southern Arabic characters	15	10
108	25c. Phoenician characters	25	30
109	30c. Aramaic characters	30	40
110	50c. Canaanite characters	50	75
107/10	*Set of 4*	1·10	1·40

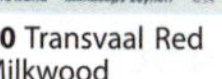

20 Transvaal Red Milkwood

21 *Pellaea dura*

(Des Sheila Nowers)

1985 (21 June). *Food from the Veld (1st series). T* **20** *and similar vert designs. Multicoloured.* P 14.

111	12c. Type **20**	15	10
112	25c. Buffalo Thorn	25	30
113	30c. Wild Water Melon	30	35
114	50c. Brown Ivory	40	60
111/14	*Set of 4*	1·00	1·25

See also Nos. 163/6.

(Des D. Findlay)

1985 (5 Sept). *Ferns. T* **21** *and similar vert designs. Multicoloured.* P 14.

115	12c. Type **21**	15	10
116	25c. Actiniopteris radiata	25	25
117	30c. Adiantum hispidulum	30	35
118	50c. Polypodium polypodioides	40	65
115/18	*Set of 4*	1·00	1·25

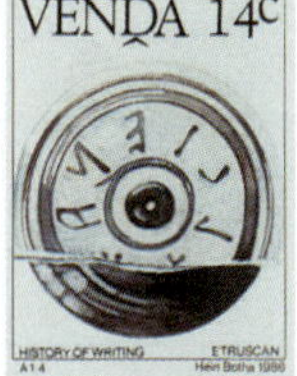

22 Three-lined Grass Snake

23 Etruscan Dish

1986 (16 Jan)–**93**. *Reptiles. T* **22** *and similar horiz designs. Multicoloured. Chalk-surfaced paper.* P 14.

119	1c. Type **22**	10	10
	a. Ordinary paper (29.5.89)	30	30
120	2c. Mole Snake	10	10
	a. Ordinary paper (29.5.89)	40	40
121	3c. Ornate Scrub Lizard	10	10
122	4c. Puff Adder	10	10
123	5c. Three-lined Skink	10	10
	a. Ordinary paper (12.7.93)	40	40
124	6c. Egyptian Cobra	15	10
125	7c. Blue-tailed Kopje Skink	15	10
126	8c. Spotted Bush Snake	20	20
	a. Ordinary paper (12.7.93)	40	40
127	9c. Yellow-throated Plated Lizard	20	20
128	10c. Northern Lined Shovelsnout	20	20
	a. Ordinary paper (20.7.93)	40	40
129	14c. Transvaal Flat Lizard (1.4.86)	1·25	20
130	15c. Soutpansberg Lizard	30	20
	a. Ordinary paper (13.9.89)	40	40
131	16c. Iguana Water Leguan (1.4.87)	60	20
132	18c. Black Mamba (ordinary paper) (3.7.89)	75	20
133	20c. Transvaal Flat Gecko	30	20
	a. Ordinary paper (17.9.90)	1·25	70
133	21c. Flap-necked Chameleon (ordinary paper) (3.8.90)	75	20
134	25c. Longtailed Garter Snake	40	30
135	30c. Tigroid Thick-toed Gecko	40	35
	a. Ordinary paper (4.9.92)	75	75
136	50c. Cape File Snake	40	50
137	1r. Soutpansberg Girdled Lizard	55	1·00
	a. Ordinary paper (9.7.90)	2·25	2·25
138	2r. African Python	70	2·00
	a. Ordinary paper (27.1.89)	3·75	3·75
119/38	*Set of 21*	7·00	6·00

(Des H. Botha)

1986 (10 Apr). *History of Writing (5th series). T* **23** *and similar vert designs. Multicoloured.* P 14×14½.

139	14c. Type **23**	15	10
140	20c. Greek inscription, AD70	30	30
141	25c. Roman inscription	40	40
142	30c. Cyrillic inscription (Byzantine mosaic)	55	60
139/42	*Set of 4*	1·25	1·25

24 Planting Pine Seedlings

(Des B. Jackson)

1986 (26 June). *Forestry. T* **24** *and similar horiz designs. Multicoloured.* P 14.

143	14c. Type **24**	20	15
144	20c. Mule hauling logs	30	30
145	25c. Off-loading logs at sawmill	40	40
146	30c. Using timber in construction	55	60
143/6	*Set of 4*	1·25	1·25

PHILATELIC FOUNDATION MINIATURE SHEETS. These miniature sheets were issued by the Philatelic Foundation of Southern Africa and not the postal administration. They could be purchased by post or from a limited number of philatelic offices at a premium in aid of various national and international stamp exhibitions.

25 Maxwell, 1910

26 Comb Duck

(Des A. H. Barrett)

1986 (4 Sept). *FIVA International Veteran Car Rally. T* **25** *and similar horiz designs. Multicoloured.* P 14½×14.

147	14c. Type **25**	20	15
148	20c. Bentley 4½ l., 1929	30	30
149	25c. Plymouth Coupé, 1933	40	40
150	30c. Mercedes Benz 220, 1958	55	60
147/50	*Set of 4*	1·25	1·25

The 30c. value exists as a Philatelic Foundation miniature sheet.

(Des A. H. Barrett)

1987 (8 Jan). *Waterfowl. T* **26** *and similar multicoloured designs.* P 14×14½ (vert) or 14½×14 (horiz).

151	14c. Type **26**	1·00	40
152	20c. White-faced Whistling Duck	1·10	70
153	25c. Spur-winged Goose (*horiz*)	1·25	90
154	30c. Egyptian Goose (*horiz*)	1·40	1·25
151/4	*Set of 4*	4·25	3·00

The 25c. value exists as a Philatelic Foundation miniature sheet.

27 "Iron Master"

28 Tigerfish

(Des L. Kriedemann)

1987 (9 Apr). *Wood Sculptures by Meshack Matamela Raphalalani. T* **27** *and similar vert designs. Multicoloured.* P 14½×14.

155	16c. Type **27**	15	15
156	20c. "Distant Drums"	25	25
157	25c. "Sunrise"	30	30
158	30c. "Obedience"	40	40
155/8	*Set of 4*	1·00	1·00

(Des D. Thorpe)

1987 (2 July). *Freshwater Fishes. T* **28** *and similar horiz designs. Multicoloured.* P 14×14½.

159	16c. Type **28**	25	20
160	20c. Barred Minnow	35	35
161	25c. Mozambique Mouthbrooder	45	45
162	30c. Sharp-toothed Catfish	55	60
159/62	*Set of 4*	1·40	1·40

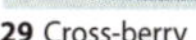

29 Cross-berry

30 Picking Berries

(Des Sheila Nowers)

1987 (2 Oct). *Food from the Veld (2nd series). T* **29** *and similar vert designs. Multicoloured.* P 14×14½.

163	16c. Type **29**	20	15
164	30c. Wild Date Palm	30	30
165	40c. Tree Fuchsia	40	40
166	50c. Wild Cucumber	50	55
163/6	*Set of 4*	1·25	1·25

(Des B. Jackson)

1988 (21 Jan). *Coffee Industry. T* **30** *and similar horiz designs. Multicoloured.* P 14½×14.

167	16c. Type **30**	20	20
168	30c. Weighing bags of berries	30	30
169	40c. Drying beans in sun	35	35
170	50c. Roasting graded beans	45	45
167/70	*Set of 4*	1·10	1·10

31 "Universal Love" in Chinese

32 College

(Des H. Botha)

1988 (28 Apr). *History of Writing (6th series). T* **31** *and similar horiz designs.* P 14½×14.

171	16c. stone, black and bright scarlet	20	20
172	30c. stone, black and bright scarlet	25	35
173	40c. stone, black and deep rose-red	35	45
174	50c. black and gold	45	60
	a. Gold omitted		
171/4	*Set of 4*	1·10	1·40

Designs:—30c. "Picture of a lion on a stone" in Devanagari (Indian script); 40c. "Information" in Russian; 50c. "Peace be upon you" in Thuluth (Arabic script).

(Des L. Kriedemann)

1988 (18 Aug). *Fifth Anniv of Shayandima Nurses' Training College. T* **32** *and similar horiz designs. Multicoloured.* P 14½×14.

175	16c. Type **32**	20	15
176	30c. Students using microscope	30	35
177	40c. Anatomy class	35	40
178	50c. Clinical training	40	50
175/8	*Set of 4*	1·10	1·25

33 "Fetching Water"

34 Ndongwana (clay bowls)

1988 (6 Oct). *Watercolours by Kenneth Thabo. T* **33** *and similar horiz designs. Multicoloured.* P 14½×14.

179	16c. Type **33**	20	15
180	30c. "Grinding Maize"	30	35
181	40c. "Offering Food"	35	40
182	50c. "Kindling the Fire"	40	50
179/82	*Set of 4*	1·10	1·25

The 50c. value exists as a Philatelic Foundation miniature sheet.

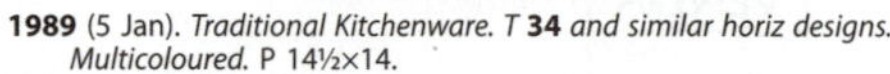

(Des L. Kriedemann)

1989 (5 Jan). *Traditional Kitchenware. T* **34** *and similar horiz designs. Multicoloured.* P 14½×14.

183 16c. Type **34** ... 15 20
184 30c. Ndilo (wooden porridge bowls) ... 25 30
185 40c. Mufaro (basket with lid) ... 30 40
186 50c. Muthatha (dish woven from ilala palm) ... 40 45
183/6 *Set of 4* ... 1·00 1·25

35 Domba

36 Southern Ground Hornbill

(Des K. Thabo)

1989 (5 Apr). *Traditional Dances. T* **35** *and similar horiz designs. Multicoloured.* P 14½×14.

187 18c. Type **35** ... 15 20
188 30c. Tshinzerere ... 25 30
189 40c. Malende ... 30 40
190 50c. Malombo ... 40 45
187/90 *Set of 4* ... 1·00 1·25

(Des M. Enslin)

1989 (27 June). *Endangered Birds. T* **36** *and similar vert designs. Multicoloured.* P 14½×14.

191 18c. Type **36** ... 80 30
192 30c. Lappet-faced Vulture ... 1·10 70
193 40c. Bateleur ... 1·40 90
194 50c. Martial Eagle ... 1·60 1·25
191/4 *Set of 4* ... 4·50 2·75

The 50c. value exists as a Philatelic Foundation miniature sheet.

37 Pres. Gota F. N. Ravele

38 Lion

(Des A. H. Barrett)

1989 (13 Sept). *Tenth Anniv of Independence. T* **37** *and similar horiz designs. Multicoloured.* P 14½×14.

195 18c. Type **37** ... 20 20
196 30c. Presidential offices ... 30 30
197 40c. President's residence ... 40 40
198 50c. Thohoyandou Sports Stadium ... 45 45
195/8 *Set of 4* ... 1·25 1·25

(Des D. Murphy)

1990 (1 Mar). *Nwanedi National Park. T* **38** *and similar vert designs. Multicoloured.* P 14×14½.

199 18c. Type **38** ... 40 25
200 30c. Common Zebra ... 70 55
201 40c. Cheetah ... 75 65
202 50c. White Rhinoceros ... 1·50 1·25
199/202 *Set of 4* ... 3·00 2·40

The 50c. value exists as a Philatelic Foundation miniature sheet.

39 Calligraphy

40 *Aloe globuligemma*

(Des H. Botha)

1990 (23 May). *History of Writing (7th series). T* **39** *and similar vert designs.* P 14½×14.

203 21c. black and grey ... 20 15
204 30c. black and reddish brown ... 40 40
205 40c. black and yellowish green ... 50 50
206 50c. blue, new blue and black ... 60 65
203/6 *Set of 4* ... 1·50 1·50

Designs:—30c. Part of score for Beethoven's Moonlight Sonata; 40c. Characters from personal computer; 50c. Television picture of message transmitted into outer space from Arecibo 1000 radio telescope.

(Des G. Marx)

1990 (23 Aug). *Aloes. T* **40** *and similar vert designs. Multicoloured.* P 14½×14.

207 21c. Type **40** ... 30 25
208 35c. *Aloe aculeata* ... 50 50
209 40c. *Aloe lutescens* ... 60 70
210 50c. *Aloe angelica* ... 70 90
207/10 *Set of 4* ... 1·90 2·10

41 *Pseudacraea boisduvalii*

42 Cape Puff-back Flycatchers

(Des E. Forbes)

1990 (15 Nov). *Butterflies. T* **41** *and similar vert designs. Multicoloured.* P 14×14½.

211 21c. Type **41** ... 70 40
212 35c. *Papilio nireus* ... 1·00 75
213 40c. *Charaxes jasius* ... 1·10 1·00
214 50c. *Aeropetes tulbaghia* ... 1·25 1·25
211/14 *Set of 4* ... 3·50 3·00

1991 (7 Mar). *Birds. T* **42** *and similar horiz designs showing paintings by Claude Finch-Davies. Multicoloured.* P 14½×14.

215 21c. Type **42** ... 50 40
216 35c. Red-capped Robin Chat ... 75 80
217 40c. Collared Seabirds ... 85 1·00
218 50c. Yellow-streaked Greenbul ... 1·10 1·40
215/18 *Set of 4* ... 2·75 3·25

43 Paper made from Pulp

44 Venda Sun Hotel Complex, Thohoyandou

(Des H. Botha)

1991 (6 June). *Inventions (1st series). T* **43** *and similar vert designs. Multicoloured.* P 14½×14.

219 25c. Type **43** ... 55 35
220 40c. Magnetic compass ... 1·00 75
221 50c. Abacus ... 1·10 1·00
222 60c. Gunpowder ... 1·75 1·25
219/22 *Set of 4* ... 4·00 3·00

The 60c. value exists as a Philatelic Foundation miniature sheet. See also Nos. 239/42 and 259/62.

1991 (29 Aug). *Tourism. T* **44** *and similar horiz designs. Multicoloured.* P 14½×14.

223 25c. Type **44** ... 55 35
224 40c. Mphephu Resort ... 85 75
225 50c. Sagole Spa ... 95 95
226 60c. Luphephe-Nwanedi Resort ... 1·00 1·25
223/6 *Set of 4* ... 3·00 3·00

(Des D. Findlay)

1991 (21 Nov). *Indigenous Trees (4th series). Horiz designs as T* **13**. *Multicoloured.* P 14½×14.

227 27c. Fever Tree ... 60 35
228 45c. Transvaal Beech ... 1·00 75
229 65c. Transvaal Wild Banana ... 1·10 1·10
230 85c. Sausage Tree ... 1·40 1·50
227/30 *Set of 4* ... 3·50 3·25

45 Setting the Web

46 *Apis mellifera*

1992 (5 Mar). *Clothing Factory. T* **45** *and similar horiz designs. Multicoloured.* P 14.

231 27c. Type **45** ... 45 25
232 45c. Knitting ... 60 55
233 65c. Making up garment ... 90 1·00
234 85c. Inspection of finished product ... 1·25 1·50
231/4 *Set of 4* ... 2·75 3·00

(Des A. Ainslie)

1992 (21 May). *Bees. T* **46** *and similar horiz designs. Multicoloured.* P 14.

235 35c. Type **46** ... 70 40
236 70c. *Anthidium cordiforme* ... 1·10 90
237 90c. *Megachile frontalis* ... 1·50 1·25
238 1r.05 *Xylocopa caffra* ... 1·60 1·40
235/8 *Set of 4* ... 4·50 3·50

The 70c. value exists as a Philatelic Foundation miniature sheet.

47 Egyptian Plough

48 Nile Crocodile

(Des H. Botha)

1992 (13 Aug). *Inventions (2nd series). T* **47** *and similar horiz designs. Multicoloured.* P 14.

239 35c. Type **47** ... 60 40
240 70c. Early wheel, Mesopotamia ... 1·00 90
241 90c. Making bricks, Egypt ... 1·40 1·25
242 1r.05 Early Egyptian sailing ship ... 1·50 1·40
239/42 *Set of 4* ... 4·00 3·50

(Des A. Ainslie)

1992 (15 Oct). *Crocodile Farming. T* **48** *and similar horiz designs. Multicoloured.* P 14½×14.

243 35c. Type **48** ... 75 40
244 70c. Egg laying ... 1·25 90
245 90c. Eggs hatching ... 1·50 1·40
246 1r.05 Mother carrying young ... 1·60 1·60
243/6 *Set of 4* ... 4·50 3·75

49 Burmese

50 Green Heron

(Des Sheila Nowers)

1993 (19 May). *Domestic Cats. T* **49** *and similar horiz designs. Multicoloured.* P 14.

247 45c. Type **49** ... 1·00 45
248 65c. Tabby ... 1·40 1·00
249 85c. Siamese ... 1·60 1·40
250 1r.05 Persian ... 1·75 1·75
247/50 *Set of 4* ... 5·25 4·25

The 65c. value exists as a Philatelic Foundation miniature sheet.

(Des Priscilla Henley)

1993 (16 July). *Herons. T* **50** *and similar horiz designs. Multicoloured.* P 14.

251 45c. Type **50** ... 80 50
252 65c. Black-crowned Night Heron ... 1·10 95
253 85c. Purple Heron ... 1·40 1·40
254 1r.05 Black-headed Heron ... 1·60 1·90
251/4 *Set of 4* ... 4·50 4·25
MS255 86×132 mm. Nos. 251/4 ... 4·50 4·75

51 Punching out Sole Lining

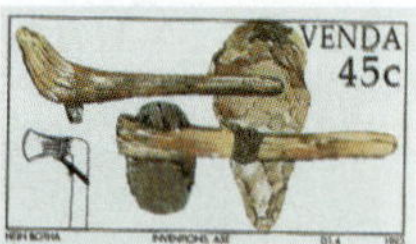

52 Axes

1993 (17 Sept). *Shoe Factory. T* **51** *and similar horiz designs. Multicoloured.* P 14×14½.

256 45c. Type **51** ... 30 25
257 65c. Shaping heel ... 55 60
258 85c. Joining the upper to inner sole ... 75 85
259 1r.05 Forming sole ... 90 1·25
256/9 *Set of 4* ... 2·25 2·75

(Des H. Botha)

1993 (5 Nov). *Inventions (3rd series). T* **52** *and similar horiz designs. Multicoloured.* P 14.

260 45c. Type **52** ... 30 35
261 65c. Armour ... 55 65
262 85c. Arches ... 75 85
263 1r.05 Pont du Gard aqueduct ... 85 1·25
260/3 *Set of 4* ... 2·25 2·75

53 Cocker Spaniel

54 Savanna Monkey

(Des D. Murphy)

1994 (14 Jan). *Dogs. T* **53** *and similar horiz designs. Multicoloured.* P 14.

264 45c. Type **53** ... 90 50
265 65c. Maltese ... 1·25 1·00
266 85c. Scottish Terrier ... 1·50 1·50
267 1r.05 Miniature Schnauzer ... 1·90 2·00
264/7 *Set of 4* ... 5·00 4·50

The 85c. value exists as a Philatelic Foundation miniature sheet.

(Des A. Ainslie)

1994 (4 Mar). *Monkeys. T* **54** *and similar horiz designs. Multicoloured.* P 14½×14.

268 45c. Type **54** ... 75 55
269 65c. Lesser Bushbaby ... 1·00 1·00
270 85c. Diademed Monkey ... 1·25 1·50
271 1r.05 Thick-tailed Bushbaby ... 1·50 2·00
268/71 *Set of 4* ... 4·00 4·50
MS272 119×70 mm. Nos. 268/71 ... 4·00 4·50

55 Red-shouldered Glossy Starlings

(Des Julia Birkhead)

1994 (29 Apr). *Starlings. T* **55** *and similar horiz designs. Multicoloured.* P 14.

273 45c. Type **55** ... 1·00 65
274 70c. Violet Starlings ... 1·50 1·50
275 95c. African Red-winged Starlings ... 1·75 1·90
276 1r.15 Wattled Starlings ... 2·00 2·25
273/6 *Set of 4* ... 5·75 5·75

Venda was reincorporated into the Republic of South Africa on 27 April 1994. Its postal service continued to operate, using South African stamps, until 1 April 1996 when it was integrated with that of the Republic.

Swaziland

PRICES FOR STAMPS ON COVER TO 1945	
Nos. 1/10	*from* × 40
Nos. 11/20	*from* × 4
Nos. 21/4	*from* × 5
Nos. 25/7	*from* × 10
Nos. 28/38	*from* × 4
Nos. 39/41	*from* × 5
Nos. D1/2	*from* × 30

TRIPARTITE GOVERNMENT

Following internal unrest and problems caused by the multitude of commercial concessions granted by the Swazi king the British and Transvaal governments intervened during 1889 to establish a tripartite administration under which the country was controlled by their representatives, acting with the agent of the Swazi king.

The Pretoria government had previously purchased the concession to run the postal service and, on the establishment of the tripartite administration, provided overprinted Transvaal stamps for use from a post office at Embekelweni and later at Bremersdorp and Darkton.

Swazieland
(**1**)

1889 (18 Oct)–**90**. *Stamps of Transvaal (South African Republic) optd with T* **1**, *in black.*

(a) P 12½×12.

No.	Type		Unused	Used
1	**18**	1d. carmine	17·00	18·00
		a. Opt inverted	£700	£650
2		2d. olive-bistre	85·00	24·00
		a. Opt inverted	—	£1200
		b. "Swazielan"	£1100	£650
		c. "Swazielan" inverted		
3		1s. green	12·00	13·00
		a. Opt inverted	£800	£475

(b) P 12½.

No.	Type		Unused	Used
4	**18**	½d. grey	9·00	18·00
		a. Opt inverted	£850	£650
		b. "Swazielan"	£1400	£800
		c. "Swazielan" inverted	—	£5000
5		2d. olive-bistre	19·00	15·00
		a. Opt inverted	£900	£450
		b. "Swazielan"	£475	£400
		c. "Swazielan" inverted	£5000	£4000
6		6d. blue	24·00	45·00
7		2s.6d. buff (20.10.90)	£250	£300
8		5s. slate-blue (20.10.90)	£150	£200
		a. Opt inverted	£1900	£2500
		b. "Swazielan"	£4500	
		c. "Swazielan" inverted		
9		10s. dull chestnut (20.10.90)	£6000	£3750

The variety without "d" occurs on R. 6/1 in each sheet of certain printings.

A printing of the ½d, 1d., 2d. and 10s. yellow-brown with stop after "Swazieland" was made in July 1894, but such stamps were not issued.

It is possible that the dates quoted above were those on which the overprinting took place in Pretoria and that the stamps were issued slightly later in Swaziland itself.

1892 (Aug). *Optd in carmine.* P 12½.

No.	Type		Unused	Used
10	**18**	½d. grey	7·50	16·00
		a. Opt inverted	£500	
		b. Opt double	£450	£450
		c. Pair, one without opt	—	£1900

No. 10 was overprinted in Pretoria during August 1892 when Swaziland was under quarantine due to smallpox. It is unlikely that it saw much postal use before all the overprints were withdrawn, although cancelled-to-order examples are plentiful.

It appears likely that no further supplies of stamps overprinted "Swazieland" were provided by Pretoria after December 1892, although stocks held at post offices were used up. The overprinted stamps were declared to be invalid from 7 November 1894. They were replaced by unoverprinted issues of the Transvaal (South African Republic).

Stamps of TRANSVAAL (SOUTH AFRICAN REPUBLIC) *used in Swaziland between* December 1892 *and* January 1900.

1885–93. *(Nos. 175/87).*

Z1	½d. grey	32·00
Z2	1d. carmine	32·00
Z3	2d. olive-bistre	16·00
Z4	2½d. mauve	32·00
Z5	3d. mauve	32·00
Z6	4d. bronze-green	32·00
Z9	2s.6d. orange-buff	

1893. *(Nos. 195/9).*

Z10	½d. on 2d. olive-bistre (Type A surch in red)	
Z11	½d. on 2d. olive-bistre (Type A surch in black)	
Z12	1d. on 6d. blue (Type A surch)	35·00
	a. Surch Type B	45·00
Z13	2½d. on 1s. green ("2½ Pence" in one line) (Type A surch)	35·00
	a. Surch Type B	45·00

1894. *(Nos. 200/4).*

Z16	1d. carmine	32·00
Z17	2d. olive-bistre	32·00

1895–96. *(Nos. 205/12a).*

Z20	½d. pearl-grey	32·00
Z21	1d. rose-red	16·00
Z22	2d. olive-bistre	16·00
Z25	6d. pale dull blue	32·00

1895. *(Nos. 213/14).*

Z27	½d. on 1s. green	

1895. *Introduction of Penny Postage (No. 215b).*

Z29	1d. red	45·00

1896–97. *(Nos. 216/24).*

Z30	½d. green	32·00
Z31	1d. rose-red and green	16·00
Z35	4d. sage-green and green	32·00
Z36	6d. lilac and green	32·00
Z37	1s. ochre and green	65·00

Prices are for clear and fairly complete postmarks. Examples dated in 1892 and 1893 are worth a premium. For list of post offices open during this period see boxed note below. Most known examples are from Bremersdorp (squared circle inscr "SWAZIEL" later replaced by "Z.A.R." or c.d.s.) or Darkton (c.d.s.).

Shortly after the outbreak of the Boer War in 1899 the Transvaal administration withdrew from Swaziland, although the post office at Darkton, which was on the border, was still operating in early 1900. There was, however, no further organised postal service in Swaziland until the country became a British Protectorate in March 1902. From that date, until the introduction of the 1933 definitives, the stamps of Transvaal and subsequently South Africa were in use.

The following post offices or postal agencies existed in Swaziland before 1933. Dates given are those on which it is generally accepted that the offices were first opened. Some were subsequently closed before the end of the period.

Bremersdorp (1890)
Darkton (1891)
Dwaleni (1918)
Embabaan (1895)
Embekelweni (1889)
Ezulweni (1910)
Forbes Reef (1906)
Goedgegun (1925)
Hlatikulu (1903)
Hluti (1912)
Ivy (1912)
Kubuta (1926)
Mahamba (1899)
Malkerns (1914)
Malomba (1928)
Mankaiana (1913)
Mbabane (*previously* Embabaan) (1905)
M'dimba (1898)
Mhlotsheni (1910)
Mooihoek (1918)
Motshane (1929)
Nomahasha (1904)
Nsoko (1927)
Piggs Peak (1899)
Sandhlan (1903)
Sicunusa (1913)
Stegi (1910)
Umkwakweni (1898)
White Umbuluzi (1925)

BRITISH PROTECTORATE

2 King George V

3 King George VI

(Des Rev. C. C. Tugman. Recess D.L.R.)

1933 (3 Jan). Wmk Mult Script CA. P 14.

No.	Type		Unused	Used
11	**2**	½d. green	30	30
12		1d. carmine	30	20
13		2d. brown	30	45
14		3d. blue	45	3·00
15		4d. orange	2·75	3·50
16		6d. bright purple	1·25	1·00
17		1s. olive	1·50	2·75
18		2s.6d. bright violet	15·00	22·00
19		5s. grey	30·00	50·00
20		10s. sepia	90·00	£110
11/20 *Set of 10*			£130	£170
11s/20s Perf "Specimen" *Set of 10*			£250	

The ½d, 1d., 2d. and 6d. values exist overprinted "OFFICIAL", but authority for their use was withdrawn before any were actually used. However, some stamps had already been issued to the Secretariat staff before instructions were received to invalidate their use (*Price £22,000 per set un*).

1935 (4 May). *Silver Jubilee. As Nos. 111/14 of Botswana.* P 11×12.

No.		Unused	Used
21	1d. deep blue and scarlet	50	1·50
	a. Extra flagstaff	£275	£325
	b. Short extra flagstaff	£400	
	c. Lightning conductor	£400	
	d. Flagstaff on right-hand turret	£100	
	e. Double flagstaff	£100	
22	2d. ultramarine and grey-black	1·00	2·00
	a. Extra flagstaff	£100	£170
	b. Short extra flagstaff	£130	
	c. Lightning conductor	£100	
23	3d. brown and deep blue	70	6·00
	a. Extra flagstaff	75·00	£200
	b. Short extra flagstaff	95·00	£170
	c. Lightning conductor	85·00	
24	6d. slate and purple	1·00	2·50
	a. Extra flagstaff	90·00	£160
	b. Short extra flagstaff	£100	
	c. Lightning conductor	£110	
21/4 *Set of 4*		2·75	11·00
21s/4s Perf "Specimen" *Set of 4*		£120	

For illustrations of plate varieties see above *No. 111 of Botswana.*

1937 (12 May). *Coronation. As Nos. 115/17 of Botswana but printed by B.W.* P 11×11½.

No.		Unused	Used
25	1d. carmine	50	2·25
26	2d. yellow-brown	50	25
27	3d. blue	50	75
25/7 *Set of 3*		1·40	3·00
25s/7s Perf "Specimen" *Set of 3*		85·00	

(Recess D.L.R.)

1938 (1 Apr)–**54**. Wmk Mult Script CA. P 13½×13.

No.	Type		Unused	Used
28	**3**	½d. green	2·50	1·25
		a. Perf 13½×14 (1.43)	30	2·75
		b. Perf 13½×14. *Bronze-green* (2.50)	2·25	7·50
29		1d. rose-red	2·75	1·25
		a. Perf 13½×14 (1.43)	1·00	1·75
30		1½d. light blue	4·25	75
		a. Perf 14 (1941)	2·75	1·00
		b. Perf 13½×14 (1.43)	30	1·00
		ba. Printed on the gummed side	£3000	
31		2d. yellow-brown	2·50	1·25
		a. Perf 13½×14 (1.43)	30	50
32		3d. ultramarine	11·00	1·75
		a. Deep blue (10.38)	16·00	1·75
		b. Perf 13½×14 *Ultramarine* (1.43)	5·00	7·00
		c. Perf 13½×14 *Light ultram* (10.46)	22·00	16·00
		d. Perf 13½×14 *Deep blue* (10.47)	12·00	12·00
33		4d. orange	6·50	2·00
		a. Perf 13½×14 (1.43)	50	1·40
34		6d. deep magenta	17·00	2·75
		a. Perf 13½×14 (1.43)	4·50	4·50
		b. Perf 13½×14. *Reddish purple (shades)* (7.44)	4·50	1·50
		c. Perf 13½×14. *Claret* (13.10.54)	7·00	6·00
35		1s. brown-olive	17·00	2·00
		a. Perf 13½×14 (1.43)	1·25	65
36		2s.6d. bright violet	25·00	4·00
		a. Perf 13½×14. *Violet* (1.43)	18·00	2·50
		b. Perf 13½×14. *Reddish violet* (10.47)	18·00	10·00
37		5s. grey	55·00	14·00
		a. Perf 13½×14. *Slate* (1.43)	55·00	50·00
		b. Perf 13½×14. *Grey* (5.44)	32·00	14·00
38		10s. sepia	60·00	6·00
		a. Perf 13½×14 (1.43)	6·50	6·00
28/38a *Set of 11*			65·00	28·00
28s/38s Perf "Specimen" *Set of 11*			£225	

The above perforations vary slightly from stamp to stamp, but the average measurements are respectively: 13.3×13.2 comb (13½×13), 14.2 line (14) and 13.3×13.8 comb (13½×14).

Swaziland
(**4**)

1945 (3 Dec). *Victory. Nos. 108/10 of South Africa optd with T* **4**.

No.		*Un pair*	*Us pair*	*Us single*
39	1d. brown and carmine	65	80	10
40	2d. slate-blue and violet	65	80	10
41	3d. deep blue and blue	65	2·50	20
39/41 *Set of 3*		1·75	3·75	35

1947 (17 Feb). *Royal Visit. As Nos. 132/5 of Botswana.*

No.		*Unused*	*Used*
42	1d. scarlet	10	10
43	2d. green	10	10
44	3d. ultramarine	10	10
45	1s. mauve	10	10
42/5 *Set of 4*		35	35
42s/5s Perf "Specimen" *Set of 4*		95·00	

1948 (1 Dec). *Royal Silver Wedding. As Nos. 136/7 of Botswana.*

No.		Unused	Used
46	1½d. ultramarine	50	70
47	10s. purple-brown	29·00	35·00

1949 (10 Oct). *75th Anniv of U.P.U. As Nos. 138/41 of Botswana.*

No.		Unused	Used
48	1½d. blue	15	20
	a. "A" of "CA" missing from wmk		
49	3d. deep blue	2·00	3·25
50	6d. magenta	30	70
51	1s. olive	30	1·50
48/51 *Set of 4*		2·25	5·00

1953 (3 June). *Coronation. As Nos. 142 of Botswana.*

No.		Unused	Used
52	2d. black and yellow-brown	20	20

5 Havelock Asbestos Mine

7 Swazi Married Woman

(Recess B.W.)

1956 (2 July). *T* **5**, **7** *and similar designs.* Wmk Mult Script CA. P 13×13½ (horiz) or 13½×13 (vert).

No.	Type		Unused	Used
53	**5**	½d. black and orange	10	10
54	–	1d. black and emerald	10	10
55	**7**	2d. black and brown	30	10
56	–	3d. black and rose-red	20	10
57	–	4½d. black and deep bright blue	60	10
58	–	6d. black and magenta	1·75	10
59	**5**	1s. black and deep olive	20	10
60	–	1s.3d. black and sepia	1·75	3·00
61	–	2s.6d. black and carmine-red	1·25	2·00
62	–	5s. deep lilac and slate-black	7·50	3·50
63	**7**	10s. black and deep lilac	17·00	16·00
64	–	£1 black and turquoise-blue	48·00	28·00
53/64 *Set of 12*			70·00	48·00

Designs: *Horiz*—1d., 2s.6d. A Highveld view; *Vert*—3d., 1s.3d. Swazi courting couple; 4½d., 5s. Swazi warrior in ceremonial dress, 6d., £1. Greater Kudu.

(New Currency. 100 cents = 1 rand)

½c (**11**) 1c (**12**) 2c (**13**) 3½c (**14**)

2½c (I) 2½c (II) 4c (I) 4c (II)

5c (I) 5c (II) 25c (I) 25c (II)

50c (I) 50c (II) 50c (III)

R1 (I) R1 (II) R1 (III) R2 (I) R2 (II)

1961 (14 Feb). *Nos. 53/64 surch as T* **11** *to* **14**.

No.	Description	Un	Used
65	½c. on ½d.	3·25	4·25
	a. Surch inverted	£900	
66	1c. on 1d.	10	1·75
	a. Surch double*	£900	
67	2c. on 2d.	10	2·00
68	2½c. on 2d.	10	1·25
69	2½c. on 3d. (Type I)	10	10
	a. Type II	10	15
70	3½c. on 2d. (May)	10	1·25
71	4c. on 4½d. (Type I)	10	10
	a. Type II	20	10
72	5c. on 6d. (Type I)	10	10
	a. Type II	10	10
73	10c. on 1s.	25·00	3·50
	a. Surch double*	£950	
74	25c. on 2s.6d. (Type I)	30	65
	a. Type II (central)	85	60
	b. Type II (bottom left)	£225	£250
75	50c. on 5s. (Type I)	30	60
	a. Type II	4·50	2·25
	b. Type III	£425	£500
76	1r. on 10s. (Type I)	1·50	60
	a. Type II	2·75	3·00
	b. Type III	45·00	50·00
77	2r. on £1 (Type I)	8·00	9·00
	a. Type II (middle left)	5·00	9·00
	b. Type II (bottom)	55·00	£100
65/77a	*Set of* 13	32·00	22·00

*On both Nos. 66a and 73a the second surcharge falls across the horizontal perforations.

No. 74b has the thin Type II surcharge at bottom left, in similar position to the thicker Type I, No. 74, with which it should not be confused.

No. 77b has the surcharge centrally placed at bottom. No. 77a has it at middle left, above "KUDU".

No. 66 with surcharge central (instead of bottom left) and No. 75a bottom left (instead of middle left) are believed to be from trial sheets released with the normal stocks. They do not represent separate printings. (No. 66 *price* £38 *un*, No. 75a *price* £120 *un*.).

(Recess B.W.)

1961. *As 1956 issue, but with values in cents and rands.* Wmk Mult Script CA. P 13×13½ (horiz) or 13½×13 (vert).

No.	Description	Un	Used
78	½c. black and orange (as ½d.) (14.2)	10	1·25
79	1c. black and emerald (as 1d.) (14.2)	10	10
80	2c. black and brown (as 2d.) (10.9)	10	2·50
81	2½c. black and rose-red (as 3d.) (14.2)	15	10
82	4c. black and deep bright blue (as 4½d.) (10.9)	15	1·50
83	5c. black and magenta (as 6d.) (10.9)	1·25	15
84	10c. black and deep olive (as 1s.) (14.2)	15	10
85	12½c. black and sepia (as 1s 3d.) (14.2)	1·25	40
86	25c. emerald and carmine-red (as 2s 6d.) (1.8)	3·00	4·25
87	50c. deep lilac and slate-black (as 5s.) (10.9)	2·50	1·40
88	1r. black and deep lilac (as 10s.) (10.9)	5·50	11·00
89	2r. black and turquoise-blue (as £1) (1.8)	12·00	11·00
78/89	*Set of* 12	23·00	30·00

15 Swazi Shields

16 Battle Axe

(Des Mrs. C. Hughes. Photo Enschedé)

1962 (24 Apr)–**66**. *Various designs as T* **15/16**. W w **12**. P 14×13 (horiz) or 13×14 (vert).

No.	Description	Un	Used
90	½c. black, brown and yellow-brown	10	10
	w. Wmk inverted	13·00	
91	1c. yellow-orange and black	10	10
	w. Wmk inverted	1·75	
92	2c. deep bluish green, black and yellow-olive	10	1·50
	w. Wmk inverted	22·00	
93	2½c. black and vermilion	10	10
	a. Black and dull red (5.66)	75	10
	w. Wmk inverted	2·25	
94	3½c. yellow-green and deep grey	10	40
	w. Wmk inverted	7·00	
95*a*	4c. black and turquoise-green	10	10
	a. Black and deep turquoise-green (5.66)	1·50	10
	w. Wmk inverted	7·00	
96	5c. black, red and orange-red	1·50	10
	w. Wmk inverted	8·00	
97	7½c. deep brown and buff	1·50	50
	a. Blackish brown and yellowish buff (5.66)	4·00	2·75
	w. Wmk inverted	9·00	
98	10c. black and light blue	4·50	20
	w. Wmk inverted	30·00	
99	12½c. carmine and grey-olive	1·50	3·25
100	15c. black and bright purple	1·50	70
101	20c. black and green	40	90
102	25c. black and bright blue	50	70
	w. Wmk inverted	28·00	
103	50c. black and rose-red	14·00	4·25
104	1r. emerald and ochre	2·50	2·25
105	2r. carmine-red and ultramarine	15·00	9·50
90/105	*Set of* 16	38·00	22·00

Designs: *Vert*—2c. Forestry; 2½c. Ceremonial headdress; 3½c. Musical instrument; 4c. Irrigation; 5c. Long-tailed Whydah; 7½ c. Rock paintings; 10c. Secretary Bird; 12½c. Pink Arum; 15c. Swazi married woman; 20c. Malaria control; 25c. Swazi warrior; 1r. Aloes. *Horiz*—50c. Southern Ground Hornbill; 2r. Msinsi in flower.

1963 (4 June). *Freedom from Hunger. As No. 182 of Botswana.*

No.	Description	Un	Used
106	15c. reddish violet	50	15

1963 (2 Sept). *Red Cross Centenary. As Nos. 183/4 of Botswana.*

No.	Description	Un	Used
107	2½c. red and black	30	10
108	15c. red and blue	70	90

31 Goods Train and Map of Swaziland Railway

(Des R. A. H. Street. Recess B.W.)

1964 (5 Nov). *Opening of Swaziland Railway.* W w **12**. P 11½.

No.	Type	Description	Un	Used
109	**31**	2½c. emerald-green and purple	55	10
110		3½c. turquoise-blue and deep yellow-olive	55	1·00
111		15c. red-orange and deep chocolate	70	70
112		25c. olive-yellow and deep ultramarine	85	80
109/12		*Set of* 4	2·40	2·25

1965 (17 May). *I.T.U. Centenary. As Nos. 190/1 of Botswana.*

No.	Description	Un	Used
113	2½c. light blue and bistre	15	10
114	15c. bright purple and rose	35	20

1965 (25 Oct). *International Co-operation Year. As Nos. 192/3 of Botswana.*

No.	Description	Un	Used
115	½c. reddish purple and turquoise-green	10	10
116	15c. deep bluish green and lavender	40	20

1966 (24 Jan). *Churchill Commemoration. As Nos. 194/7 of Botswana.*

No.	Description	Un	Used
117	½c. new blue	10	1·75
118	2½c. deep green	25	10
119	15c. brown	55	25
	w. Wmk inverted		
120	25c. bluish violet	80	70
117/20	*Set of* 4	1·50	2·50

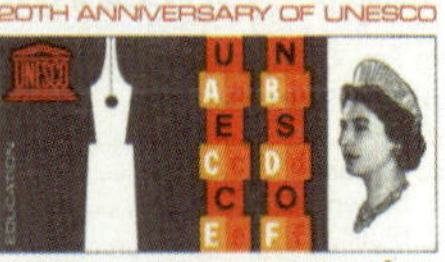

31a Education

31b Science

31c Culture

1966 (1 Dec). *20th Anniv of U.N.E.S.C.O.* W w **12** *(sideways)* P 14.

No.	Type	Description	Un	Used
121	**31a**	2½c. slate-violet, red, yellow and orange	10	10
122	**31b**	7½c. orange-yellow, violet and deep olive	40	60
123	**32c**	15c. black, bright purple and orange	65	1·25
121/3		*Set of* 3	1·00	1·75

PROTECTED STATE

32 King Sobhuza II and Map

33 King Sobhuza II

(Des and photo Harrison)

1967 (25 Apr). *Protected State.* W w **12** (sideways on horiz designs). P 14½.

No.	Type	Description	Un	Used
124	**32**	2½c. multicoloured	10	10
125	**33**	7½c. multicoloured	15	15
126	**32**	15c. multicoloured	20	30
127	**33**	25c. multicoloured	25	40
124/7		*Set of* 4	65	80

34 Students and University

(Des V. Whiteley. Photo Harrison)

1967 (7 Sept). *First Conferment of University Degrees.* P 14×14½.

No.	Type	Description	Un	Used
128	**34**	2½c. sepia, ultramarine and light yellow-orange	10	10
129		7½c. sepia, ultramarine & light greenish blue	15	15
130		15c. sepia, ultramarine and rose	25	30
131		25c. sepia, ultramarine and light violet	30	35
128/31		*Set of* 4	65	75

35 Incwala Ceremony

36 Reed Dance

(Des Mrs. G. Ellison. Photo Harrison)

1968 (5 Jan). *Traditional Customs.* P 14.

No.	Type	Description	Un	Used
132	**35**	3c. silver, vermilion and black	10	10
133	**36**	10c. silver, light brown, orange and black	10	10
134	**35**	15c. gold, vermilion and black	15	20
135	**36**	25c. gold, light brown, orange and black	15	20
132/5		*Set of* 4	40	50

(37)

38 Cattle Ploughing

1968 (1 May). *No. 96 surch with T* **37**.

No.	Description	Un	Used
136	3c. on 5c. black, red and orange-red	1·50	10
	w. Wmk inverted	5·50	1·75

INDEPENDENT

(Des Mrs. G. Ellison. Photo Enschedé)

1968 (6 Sept). *Independence. T* **38** *and similar horiz designs.* W w **12** (sideways). P 14×12½.

No.	Description	Un	Used
137	3c. multicoloured	10	10
	a. Imperf (pair)	£140	
138	4½c. multicoloured	10	45
	a. Imperf (pair)	£140	
139	17½c. yellow, green, black and gold	15	70
140	25c. slate, black and gold	45	90
137/40	*Set of* 4	65	1·75
MS141	180×162 mm. Nos. 137/40 each×5	14·00	23·00
	a. Error Imperf	£1300	

Designs:—4½c. Overhead cable carrying asbestos; 17½c. Cutting sugar cane; 25c. Iron ore mining and railway map.

Nos. 137/40 were printed in sheets of 50, but also in miniature sheets of 20 (4×5) containing *se-tenant* strips of each value.

INDEPENDENCE
1968
(42)

43 Cape Porcupine

1968 (6 Sept). *Nos. 90/105 optd as T* **42**, *and No. 93 additionally surch 3c., by Enschedé. (a) Wmk upright.*

No.	Description	Un	Used
142	½c. black, brown and yellow-brown	10	10
	a. Brown omitted	£325	
	b. Albino opt	40·00	
143	1c. yellow-orange and black	10	10
	w. Wmk inverted	40·00	
144	2c. deep bluish green, black and yellow-olive	10	10
	w. Wmk inverted	—	35·00
145	2½c. black and vermilion	60	1·40
	a. Black and dull red	2·00	10
	w. Wmk inverted	38·00	
146	3c. on 2½c. black and vermilion	10	10
	a. Black and dull red	10	10
	w. Wmk inverted	38·00	
147	3½c. yellow-green and deep grey	15	10
	w. Wmk inverted	32·00	
148	4c. black and turquoise-green	10	10
	a. Black and deep turquoise-green	25	15
	b. Black and pale turquoise-green	20	1·50

149 5c. black, red and orange-red 4·25 10
w. Wmk inverted 45·00
150 7½c. deep brown and buff 50 10
151 10c. black and light blue 4·50 10
152 12½c. carmine and grey-olive 25 1·00
w. Wmk inverted 2·00 3·00
153 15c. black and bright purple 25 1·25
154 20c. black and green 75 2·00
155 25c. black and bright blue 35 1·25
156 50c. black and rose-red 6·00 4·00
157 1r. emerald and ochre 2·00 4·50
158 2r. carmine-red and ultramarine 4·00 9·00

(b) Wmk sideways

159 50c. black and rose-red 3·50 6·50
160 2r. carmine-red and ultramarine 5·50 5·00
142/60 *Set of 19* 29·00 30·00

The 2½c., 3½c., 5c., 12½c., 50c. (No. 156) and 2r. (No. 158) exist with gum arabic only, the 1c., 2c., 3c., 4c., and 15c. with both gum arabic and PVA gum and the remainder with PVA gum only.

(Des and litho D.L.R.)

1969 (1 Aug)–**75**. *T* **43** *and similar designs showing animals. Multicoloured.* W w **12** (sideways on 3c., 3½c., 1r., 2r.). P 13×13½ (3, 3½c.), 12½×13 (1, 2r.) or 13×12½ (others).

161 ½c. Caracal 10 10
162 1c. Type **43** 10 10
163 2c. Crocodile 20 10
aw. Wmk inverted 4·00
b. Perf 12½×12 (29.9.75) 3·25 4·50
164 3c. Lion 60 10
165 3½c. African Elephant 75 10
166 5c. Bush Pig 30 10
167 7½c. Impala 35 10
168 10c. Charmer Baboon 45 10
169 12½c. Ratel 70 4·00
170 15c. Leopard 1·25 70
171 20c. Blue Wildebeest 95 60
172 25c. White Rhinoceros 1·40 1·75
w. Wmk inverted 3·25
173 50c. Common Zebra 1·50 3·25
174 1r. Waterbuck (*vert*) 3·00 6·50
175 2r. Giraffe (*vert*) 8·00 11·00
161/75 *Set of 15* 17·00 25·00

Nos. 161/73 are horizontal as Type **43** but the 3c. and 3½c. are larger, 35×24½ mm.

No. 163b was printed by the D.L.R. works in Bogota, Colombia.

Nos. 174 and 175 were reissued in new currency and no 164 with W w **12** upright in 1975.

44 King Sobhuza II and Flags

45 King Sobhuza II, U.N. Building and Emblem

(Des D.L.R. Litho P.B.)

1969 (24 Sept). *Admission of Swaziland to the United Nations.* W w **12** (sideways). P 13½.

176 **44** 3c. multicoloured 10 10
177 **45** 7½c. multicoloured 15 10
178 **44** 12½c. multicoloured 25 10
179 **45** 25c. multicoloured 40 40
176/9 *Set of 4* 75 55

46 Athlete, Shield and Spears

47 *Bauhinia galpinii*

(Des L. Curtis. Litho Format)

1970 (16 July). *Ninth Commonwealth Games, Edinburgh. T* **46** *and similar vert designs. Multicoloured.* W w **12**. P 14.

180 3c. Type **46** 10 10
181 7½c. Runner 20 10
182 12½c. Hurdler 25 10
183 25c. Procession of Swaziland competitors 35 40
180/3 *Set of 4* 75 55

(Des L. Curtis from "Wild Flowers of Natal" by Dr. W. G. Wright. Litho Questa)

1971 (1 Feb). *Flowers. T* **47** *and similar vert designs. Multicoloured.* W w **12**. P 14½.

184 3c. Type **47** 20 10
185 10c. *Crocosmia aurea* 20 10
186 15c. *Gloriosa superba* 30 25
187 25c. *Watsonia densiflora* 40 1·25
184/7 *Set of 4* 1·00 1·50

48 King Sobhuza II in Ceremonial Dress

49 UNICEF emblem

(Des L. Curtis. Litho Format)

1971 (22 Dec). *Golden Jubilee of Accession of King Sobhuza II. T* **48** *and similar vert designs. Multicoloured.* W w **12**. P 14.

188 3c. Type **48** 10 10
w. Wmk inverted 50
189 3½c. Sobhuza II in medallion 10 10
190 7½c. Sobhuza II attending Incwala ceremony 15 10
191 25c. Sobhuza II and aides at opening of Parliament 30 35
w. Wmk inverted 70
188/91 *Set of 4* 45 40

(Des Sylvia Goaman. Litho J.W.)

1972 (17 Apr). *25th Anniv of UNICEF.* W w **12** (sideways). P 13½.

192 **49** 15c. black and bright lilac 15 20
193 – 25c. black and yellow-olive 20 80

The 25c. value is as T **49**, but the inscription is rearranged.

50 Local Dancers

(Des G. Drummond. Litho Questa)

1972 (11 Sept). *Tourism. T* **50** *and similar horiz designs. Multicoloured.* W w **12**. P 13½×14.

194 3½c. Type **50** 10 10
195 7½c. Swazi beehive hut 15 15
196 15c. Ezulwini Valley 20 50
197 25c. Fishing, Usutu River 65 1·25
194/7 *Set of 4* 1·00 1·75

51 Spraying Mosquitoes

(Des PAD Studio. Litho Questa)

1973 (21 May). *25th Anniv of WHO. T* **51** *and similar horiz design. Multicoloured.* W w **12**. P 14.

198 3½c. Type **51** 20 10
199 7½c. Anti-malaria vaccination 40 80

52 Mining

(Des G. Drummond. Litho Questa)

1973 (21 June). *Natural Resources. T* **52** *and similar horiz designs. Multicoloured.* W w **12**. P 13½.

200 3½c. Type **52** 55 10
201 7½c. Cattle 25 15
202 15c. Water 30 20
203 25c. Rice 35 50
200/3 *Set of 4* 1·25 80

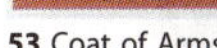
53 Coat of Arms

54 Flags and Mortarboard

(Des J.W. Litho Walsall)

1973 (7 Sept). *Fifth Anniv of Independence. T* **53** *and similar horiz designs. Multicoloured (except 3c.).* W w **12**. P 14.

204 3c. Type **53** (salmon and black) 10 10
205 10c. King Sobhuza II saluting 15 10
206 15c. Parliament Buildings 30 75
207 25c. National Somhlolo Stadium 40 1·60
204/7 *Set of 4* 80 2·25

(Des P. Powell. Litho Format)

1974 (29 Mar). *Tenth Anniv of University of Botswana, Lesotho and Swaziland. T* **54** *and similar vert designs. Multicoloured.* W w **12** (sideways). P 14.

208 7½c. Type **54** 20 10
209 12½c. University campus 25 10
210 15c. Map of Southern Africa 30 20
211 25c. University badge 40 35
208/11 *Set of 4* 1·00 60

55 King Sobhuza as College Student

56 New Post Office, Lobamba

(Des Mary Nelson; adapted PAD Studio. Litho Enschedé)

1974 (22 July). *75th Birthday of King Sobhuza II. T* **55** *and similar vert designs. Multicoloured.* W w **12**. P 13×10½.

212 3c. Type **55** 10 10
213 9c. King Sobhuza in middle-age 10 10
214 50c. King Sobhuza at 75 years of age 70 60
212/14 *Set of 3* 80 60

(Des R. Granger Barrett. Litho Questa)

1974 (9 Oct). *Centenary of Universal Postal Union. T* **56** *and similar horiz designs. Multicoloured.* W w **12** (sideways). P 14.

215 4c. Type **56** 10 10
216 10c. Mbabane Temporary Post Office, 1902 15 15
217 15c. Carrying mail by cableway 30 50
218 25c. Mule-drawn mail-coach 40 70
215/18 *Set of 4* 80 1·25

(New Currency. 100 cents = 1 lilangeni (plural emalangeni))

1975 (2 Jan). *New currency. As Nos. 174/5 but inscr in emalangeni.* W w **12** (upright). P 12½×13.

219 1e. Waterbuck 50 2·00
220 2e. Giraffe 1·10 4·00
w. Wmk inverted 75·00

57 Umcwasho Ceremony

58 Control Tower, Matsapa Airport

(Des PAD Studio. Litho Kynoch Press)

1975 (20 Mar). *Swazi Youth. T* **57** *and similar multicoloured designs.* W w **12** (sideways on 3, 10 and 25c.). P 14.

221 3c. Type **57** 10 10
222 10c. Butimba (hunting party) 15 10
223 15c. Lusekwane (sacred shrub) (*horiz*) 40 40
224 25c. Goina Regiment 60 70
221/4 *Set of 4* 1·10 1·10

(Des V. Whiteley Studio. Litho Questa)

1975 (18 Aug). *Tenth Anniv of Internal Air Service. T* **58** *and similar horiz designs. Multicoloured.* W w **14** (sideways). P 14.

225 4c. Type **58** 30 10
226 5c. Fire engine 70 20
227 15c. Douglas DC-3 1·25 1·40
228 25c. Hawker Siddeley H.S.748 2·00 2·00
225/8 Set of 4 3·75 3·25

(Litho De La Rue, Bogota, Colombia).

1975 (29 Sept). *As No. 164 but W w* **12** *upright.*

229 3c. Lion 5·00 5·50

(59)

1975 (15 Nov). *Nos. 167 and 169 surch as T* **59**.

230 3c. on 7½c. Impala 75 1·00
231 6c. on 12½c. Ratel 1·50 2·00

60 Elephant Symbol

(Des Mary-Jane Rostami. Litho Questa)

1975 (22 Dec). *International Women's Year. T* **60** *and similar designs.* W w **14** (sideways on 4 and 5c.). P 14.

232 4c. light bluish grey, black and light bright blue ... 10 10
233 5c. multicoloured ... 10 10
234 15c. multicoloured ... 30 60
235 25c. multicoloured ... 50 90
232/5 *Set of 4* ... 80 1·50

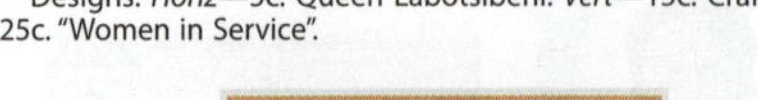
Designs: *Horiz*—5c. Queen Labotsibeni. *Vert*—15c. Craftswoman; 25c. "Women in Service".

61 African Black-headed Oriole

(Des C. Abbott. Litho Questa)

1976 (2 Jan)–**78**. *Birds. T* **61** *and similar multicoloured designs.* W w **14** (sideways on 1c., 3c., 2e.). Chalk-surfaced paper. P 14.

236 1c. Type **61** ... 75 2·50
237 2c. African Green Pigeon (*vert*) ... 80 2·50
238 3c. Green-winged Pytilia ... 1·00 1·00
239 4c. Violet Starling (*vert*) ... 80 15
aw. Wmk inverted ... † 2·00
b. Ordinary paper (31.7.78) ... 1·50 40
240 5c. Black-headed Heron (*vert*) ... 90 1·75
241 6c. Stonechat (*vert*) ... 1·50 2·50
242 7c. Chorister Robin Chat (*vert*) ... 1·40 2·75
243 10c. Four-coloured Bush-shrike (*vert*) ... 1·50 1·75
244 15c. Black-collared Barbet (*vert*) ... 2·25 55
245 20c. Grey Heron (*vert*) ... 3·25 2·00
246 25c. Giant Kingfisher (*vert*) ... 3·50 2·00
247 30c. Verreaux's Eagle (*vert*) ... 3·50 2·50
248 50c. Red Bishop (*vert*) ... 2·25 1·75
a. Ordinary paper (31.7.78) ... 90 1·00
249 1e. Pin-tailed Whydah (*vert*) ... 2·50 2·75
a. Ordinary paper (31.7.78) ... 1·40 2·50
250 2e. Lilac-breasted Roller ... 4·50 5·00
a. Ordinary paper (31.7.78) ... 1·50 5·00
236/50a *Set of 15* ... 21·00 27·00

62 Blindness from Malnutrition **63** Marathon

(Des Jennifer Toombs. Litho Questa)

1976 (15 June). *Prevention of Blindness. T* **62** *and similar horiz designs. Multicoloured.* W w **14** (sideways). P 14.

251 5c. Type **62** ... 20 10
252 10c. Infected retina ... 25 10
253 20c. Blindness from trachoma ... 45 75
254 25c. Medicines ... 50 95
251/4 *Set of 4* ... 1·60 1·75

(Des PAD Studio. Litho Walsall)

1976 (17 July). *Olympic Games, Montreal. T* **63** *and similar vert designs. Multicoloured.* W w **14** (inverted). P 14.

255 5c. Type **63** ... 15 10
256 6c. Boxing ... 20 10
257 20c. Football ... 45 45
258 25c. Olympic torch and flame ... 55 65
255/8 *Set of 4* ... 1·25 65

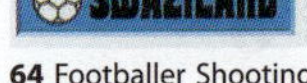

64 Footballer Shooting **65** Alexander Graham Bell and Telephone

(Des J.W. Litho Questa)

1976 (13 Sept). *FIFA Membership. T* **64** *and similar vert designs. Multicoloured.* W w **14**. P 14.

259 4c. Type **64** ... 20 10
260 6c. Heading ... 20 10
261 20c. Goalkeeping ... 50 25
262 25c. Player about to shoot ... 50 30
259/62 *Set of 4* ... 1·25 60

(Des J.W. Litho Walsall)

1976 (22 Nov). *Telephone Centenary. T* **65** *and similar horiz designs.* W w **14** (sideways). P 14.

263 4c. multicoloured ... 10 10
264 5c. multicoloured ... 10 10
265 10c. multicoloured ... 10 10
266 15c. multicoloured ... 20 20
267 20c. multicoloured ... 25 30
263/7 *Set of 5* ... 70 55

Nos. 264/7 are as T **65**, but show different telephones.

66 Queen Elizabeth II and King Sobhuza II

(Des Walsall. Litho Questa)

1977 (7 Feb). *Silver Jubilee. T* **66** *and similar horiz designs. Multicoloured.* W w **14** (sideways). P 13½.

268 20c. Type **66** ... 15 15
269 25c. Coronation Coach at Admiralty Arch ... 15 15
270 50c. Queen in coach ... 20 40
268/70 *Set of 3* ... 45 65

67 Matsapa College

(Des J. Cooter. Litho Questa)

1977 (2 May). *50th Anniv of Police Training. T* **67** *and similar multicoloured designs.* W w **14** (upright on 20c., sideways on others). P 14.

271 5c. Type **67** ... 10 10
272 10c. Uniformed police and land rover ... 50 20
273 20c. Police badge (*vert*) ... 70 95
274 25c. Dog handling ... 1·25 1·50
271/4 *Set of 4* ... 2·25 2·50

68 Animals and Hunters

(Des BG Studio. Litho Questa)

1977 (8 Aug). *Rock Paintings. T* **68** *and similar horiz designs. Multicoloured.* W w **14** (sideways*). P 14.

275 5c. Type **68** ... 25 10
276 10c. Four dancers in a procession ... 30 10
277 15c. Man with cattle ... 40 20
278 20c. Four dancers ... 45 30
275/8 *Set of 4* ... 1·25 55
MS279 103×124 mm. Nos. 275/8 ... 2·00 2·75
w. Wmk Crown to right of CA ... 6·00

*The normal sideways watermark shows Crown to left of CA, as seen from the back of the stamp.

69 Timber, Highveld Region **70** Timber, Highveld Region

(Des L. Curtis. Litho D.L.R.)

1977 (17 Oct). *Maps of the Regions. T* **69** *and similar horiz designs. Multicoloured.* W w **14** (sideways). P 13½.

280 5c. Type **69** ... 50 10
281 10c. Pineapple, Middleveld ... 60 10
282 15c. Orange and Lemon, Lowveld ... 80 65
283 20c. Cattle, Lubombo region ... 95 95
280/3 *Set of 4* ... 2·50 1·60
MS284 87×103 mm. Four 25c. designs as T **70**, together forming a composite map of Swaziland ... 1·40 1·60

71 Cabbage Tree

(Des Jennifer Toombs. Litho Walsall)

1978 (12 Jan). *Trees of Swaziland. T* **71** *and similar horiz designs. Multicoloured (except 5c.).* W w **14** (sideways). P 13½.

285 5c. Type **71** (apple-green, ochre and black) ... 15 15
286 10c. Marula ... 20 10
287 20c. Kiaat ... 45 1·25
288 25c. Lucky bean-tree ... 55 1·40
285/8 *Set of 4* ... 1·25 2·75

72 Rural Electrification at Lobamba **73** Elephant

(Des G. Drummond. Litho Questa)

1978 (6 Mar). *Hydro-electric Power. T* **72** *and similar horiz designs.* W w **14** (sideways). P 13½.

289 5c. black and buff ... 10 10
290 10c. black and light green ... 15 10
291 20c. black and pale blue ... 25 30
292 25c. black and magenta ... 30 35
289/92 *Set of 4* ... 70 65

Designs:—10c. Edwaleni Power Station; 20c. Switchgear, Magudza Power Station; 25c. Turbine Hall, Edwaleni.

(Des C. Abbott. Litho Questa)

1978 (2 June). *25th Anniv of Coronation. T* **73** *and similar vert designs.* P 15.

293 25c. chalky blue, black and sage-green ... 15 25
a. Sheetlet. Nos. 293/5×2 ... 75
294 25c. multicoloured ... 15 25
295 25c. chalky blue, black and sage-green ... 15 25
293/5 *Set of 3* ... 40 65

Designs:—No. 293, Queen's Lion; 294, Queen Elizabeth II; 295, Type **73**.

Nos. 293/5 were printed together in small sheets of 6, containing two *se-tenant* strips of 3, with horizontal gutter margin between.

74 Clay Pots

(Des C. Abbott. Litho Questa)

1978 (24 July). *Handicrafts (1st series). T* **74** *and similar horiz designs. Multicoloured.* W w **14** (sideways). P 13½×14.

296 5c. Type **74** ... 10 10
297 10c. Basketwork ... 10 10
298 20c. Wooden utensils ... 15 15
299 30c. Wooden pot ... 25 30
296/9 *Set of 4* ... 50 50

See also Nos. 310/13.

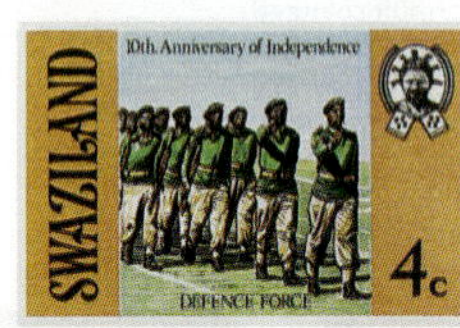

75 Defence Force

(Des BG Studio. Litho Questa)

1978 (6 Sept). *10th Anniv of Independence. T* **75** *and similar horiz designs. Multicoloured.* W w **14** (sideways). P 14.

300 4c. Type **75** ... 15 10
301 6c. The King's Regiment ... 15 10
302 10c. Tinkabi tractor (agricultural development) ... 15 10
303 15c. Water-pipe laying (self-help scheme) ... 25 10
304 25c. Sebenta adult literacy scheme ... 30 25
305 50c. Fire emergency service ... 1·25 50
300/5 *Set of 6* ... 2·00 85

76 Archangel Gabriel appearing before Shepherds **77** Prospecting at Phophonyane

(Des V. Whiteley Studio. Litho Harrison)

1978 (12 Dec). *Christmas. T* **76** *and similar horiz designs. Multicoloured.* W w **14**. P 14½×14.

306 5c. Type **76** ... 10 10
307 10c. Three Wise Men paying homage to infant Jesus ... 10 10
308 15c. Archangel Gabriel warning Joseph ... 10 10
309 25c. Flight into Egypt ... 20 20
306/9 *Set of 4* ... 30 35

(Des C. Abbott. Litho Walsall)

1979 (10 Jan). *Handicrafts (2nd series). Horiz designs as T* **74**. *Multicoloured.* W w **14** (sideways). P 13½.

310	5c. Sisal bowls	10	10
311	15c. Pottery	15	10
312	20c. Basketwork	20	15
313	30c. Hide shield	30	20
310/13	*Set of 4*	60	45

(Des L. Curtis. Litho Questa)

1979 (27 Mar). *Centenary of Discovery of Gold in Swaziland. T* **77** *and similar vert designs.* W w **14**. P 14.

314	5c. gold and deep ultramarine	25	10
315	15c. gold and deep brown	45	20
316	25c. gold and deep green	65	30
317	50c. gold and carmine-red	90	1·75
314/17	*Set of 4*	2·00	2·10

Designs:—15c. Early 3-stamp battery mill; 25c. Cyanide tanks at Piggs Peak; 50c. Pouring off molten gold.

78 "Girls at the Piano"

(Des BG Studio. Litho Questa)

1979 (8 May). *International Year of the Child. Paintings by Renoir. T* **78** *and similar horiz designs. Multicoloured.* W w **14** (sideways). P 13½.

318	5c. Type **78**	10	10
319	15c. "Madame Charpentier and her Children"	25	10
320	25c. "Girls picking Flowers"	35	15
321	50c. "Girl with Watering Can"	70	55
318/21	*Set of 4*	1·25	70
MS322	123×135 mm. Nos. 318/21	1·25	1·75

79 1933 1d. Carmine Stamp and Sir Rowland Hill

(Des J.W. Litho Walsall)

1979 (17 July). *Death Centenary of Sir Rowland Hill. T* **79** *and similar horiz designs showing stamps and portrait of Sir Rowland Hill. Multicoloured.* W w **14** (sideways*). P 14½×14.

323	10c. 1945 3d. Victory commemorative	15	10
324	20c. Type **79**	25	25
325	25c. 1968 25c. Independence commemorative	25	30
	w. Wmk Crown to right of CA	7·50	
323/5	*Set of 3*	60	60
MS326	115×90 mm. 50c. 1956 6d. Great Kudu Antelope definitive	75	85

*The normal sideways watermark shows Crown to left of CA, *as seen from the back of the stamp.*

80 Obverse and Reverse of 5 Cents

(Des G. Hutchins. Litho Walsall)

1979 (6 Sept). *Coins. T* **80** *and similar horiz designs.* W w **14** (sideways). P 13½.

327	5c. black and light brown	15	10
328	10c. black and new blue	20	10
329	20c. black and yellowish green	35	20
330	50c. black and yellow-orange	50	50
331	1e. black and cerise	75	1·00
327/31	*Set of 5*	1·75	1·60

Designs:—10c. Obverse and reverse of 10 cents; 20c. Obverse and reverse of 20 cents; 50c. Reverse of 50 cents; 1c. Reverse of 1 lilangeni.

81 Big Bend Post Office

(Des J. Cooter. Litho Questa)

1979 (22 Nov). *Post Office Anniversaries. T* **81** *and similar designs.* W w **14** (sideways on 5, 20 and 50c.). P 13½.

332	5c. multicoloured	10	10
333	15c. multicoloured	15	10
334	20c. black, sage-green and magenta	20	15
335	50c. multicoloured	40	60
332/5	*Set of 4*	70	80

Designs and commemorations: *Horiz*—5c. Type **81** (25th anniversary of Posts and Telecommunications Services); 20c. 1949 75th anniversary of UPU 1s. commemorative stamp (10th anniversary of UPU membership); 50c. 1974 centenary of UPU 25c. commemorative stamp (10th anniversary of UPU membership). *Vert*—15c. Microwave antenna, Mount Ntondozi (25th anniversary of Posts and Telecommunications Services).

82 Map of Swaziland **83** *Brunsvigia radulosa*

(Des BG Studio. Litho Walsall)

1980 (23 Feb). *75th Anniv of Rotary International. T* **82** *and similar vert designs in gold and bright blue.* W w **14**. P 13½.

336	5c. Type **82**	25	10
337	15c. Vitreous cutter and optical illuminator	45	10
338	50c. Scroll	50	55
339	1e. Rotary Headquarters, Evanston, U.S.A.	85	1·25
336/9	Set of 4	1·90	1·75

(Des BG Studio. Litho Secura, Singapore)

1980 (28 Apr)–**83**. *Flowers. Multicoloured designs as T* **83**.

A. Without imprint date below design. P 13½.

340A	1c. Type **83**	10	10
341A	2c. *Aloe suprafoliata*	10	10
342A	3c. *Haemanthus magnificus*	10	10
	c. Perf 12	3·00	2·75
343A	4c. *Aloe marlothii*	10	10
	c. Perf 12	5·00	3·25
344A	5c. *Dicoma zeyheri*	10	10
	c. Perf 12	4·00	3·25
345A	6c. *Aloe kniphofioides*	15	30
346A	7c. *Cyrtanthus bicolor*	10	10
347A	10c. *Eucomis autumnalis*	20	10
348A	15c. *Leucospermum gerrardii*	15	10
	c. Perf 12		
349A	20c. *Haemanthus multiflorus*	30	25
350A	30c. *Acridocarpus natalitius*	20	20
351A	50c. *Adenium swazicum*	20	30
352A	1e. *Protea simplex*	35	60
353A	2e. *Calodendrum capense*	80	1·25
354A	5e. *Gladiolus ecklonii*	1·10	3·00
340A/54A	*Set of 15*	3·50	5·50

B. With "1983" imprint date. P 12 (12.83).

340B	1c. Type **83**	1·00	1·00
341B	2c. *Aloe suprafoliata*	1·00	1·00
343B	4c. *Aloe marlothii*	1·50	1·00
345B	6c. *Aloe kniphofioides*	1·75	1·75
347B	10c. *Eucomis autumnalis*	2·00	1·00
349B	20c. *Haemanthus multiflorus*	2·25	2·00
340B/9B	*Set of 6*	8·50	7·00

84 Mail Runner

(Des A. Theobald. Litho Walsall)

1980 (6 May). *"London 1980" International Stamp Exhibition. T* **84** *and similar horiz designs. Multicoloured.* W w **14** (sideways*). P 14.

355	10c. Type **84**	15	10
356	20c. Post Office mail truck	25	15
	w. Wmk Crown to right of CA	6·50	
357	25c. Mail sorting office	30	20
358	50c. Ropeway conveying mail at Bulembu	70	70
355/8	*Set of 4*	1·25	1·00

*The normal sideways watermark shows Crown to left of CA, *as seen from the back of the stamp.*

85 Scaly

(Des and litho Walsall)

1980 (25 Aug). *River Fishes. T* **85** *and similar horiz designs. Multicoloured.* W w **14** (sideways). P 13½.

359	5c. Type **85**	25	10
360	10c. Silver Catfish ("Silver Barbel")	25	10
361	15c. Tiger Fish	40	15
362	30c. Brown Squeaker	50	30
363	1e. Red-breasted Tilapia ("Bream")	60	1·40
359/63	*Set of 5*	1·75	1·75

86 Oribi

(Des G. Drummond. Litho Harrison)

1980 (1 Oct). *Wildlife Conservation. T* **86** *and similar multicoloured designs.* W w **14** (sideways on 5 and 50c.). P 14.

364	5c. Type **86**	15	10
365	10c. Nile Crocodile (*vert*)	30	10
366	50c. Temminck's Ground Pangolin	50	70
367	1e. Leopard (*vert*)	1·25	1·50
364/7	*Set of 4*	2·00	2·00

87 Public Bus Service

(Des G. Hutchins. Litho Format)

1981 (5 Jan). *Transport. T* **87** *and similar horiz designs. Multicoloured. (sideways).* W w **14** P 14½.

368	5c. Type **87**	10	10
369	25c. Royal Swazi National Airways	25	15
370	30c. Swaziland United Transport	30	20
371	1e. Swaziland Railway	1·25	1·75
368/71	*Set of 4*	1·60	2·00

88 Mantenga Falls **89** Prince Charles on Hike

(Des L. Curtis. Litho Format)

1981 (16 Mar). *Tourism. T* **88** *and similar horiz designs. Multicoloured.* W w **14** (sideways). P 14.

372	5c. Type **88**	10	10
373	15c. Mananga Yacht Club	15	10
374	30c. White Rhinoceros in Mlilwane Game Sanctuary	40	30
375	1e. Roulette wheel, playing cards and dice ("casinos")	1·10	1·60
372/5	*Set of 4*	1·50	1·90

(Des J.W. Litho Walsall)

1981 (21 July). *Royal Wedding. T* **89** *and similar vert designs. Multicoloured.* W w **14**. P 14.

376	10c. Wedding bouquet from Swaziland	10	10
377	25c. Type **89**	15	10
378	1e. Prince Charles and Lady Diana Spencer	40	70
376/8	*Set of 3*	60	75

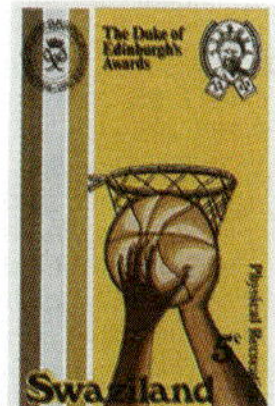
90 Installation of King Sobhuza II, 22 December 1921 **91** "Physical" Recreation

(Des J.W. Litho Harrison)

1981 (24 Aug). *Diamond Jubilee of King Sobhuza II. T* **90** *and similar horiz designs. Multicoloured.* W w **14** (sideways). P 14½.

379	5c. Type **90**	10	10
380	10c. Royal visit, 1947	10	10
381	15c. King Sobhuza II and Coronation of Queen Elizabeth II, 1953	15	15
382	25c. King Sobhuza taking Royal Salute, Independence, 1968	15	15
383	30c. King Sobuza in youth	20	20
384	1e. King Sobhuza and Parliament Buildings	50	90
379/84	*Set of 6*	1·00	1·40

(Des BG Studio. Litho Questa)

1981 (5 Nov). *25th Anniv of Duke of Edinburgh Award Scheme. T* **91** *and similar vert designs. Multicoloured.* W w **14**. P 14.

385	5c. Type **91**	10	10
386	20c. "Expeditions"	10	10
387	50c. "Skills"	25	25
388	1e. Duke of Edinburgh in ceremonial dress	50	80
385/8	*Set of 4*	80	1·00

92 Disabled Person in Wheelchair

(Des and litho Walsall)

1981 (16 Dec). *International Year of Disabled Persons. T* **92** *and similar multicoloured designs.* W w **14** (sideways on 5c. and 1c.). P 14×14½ (5c., 1c.) or 14½×14 (others).

389 5c. Type **92** ... 30 10
390 15c. Teacher with disabled child (*vert*) ... 50 15
391 25c. Disabled craftsman (*vert*) ... 75 20
392 1e. Disabled driver in invalid carriage ... 2·25 2·75
389/92 *Set of 4* ... 3·50 3·00

93 *Papilio demodocus*

94 Man holding a Flower, after discarding Cigarettes

(Des I. Loe. Litho Rosenbaum Bros, Vienna)

1982 (6 Jan). *Butterflies. T* **93** *and similar horiz designs. Multicoloured.* W w **14** (sideways*). P 14.

393 5c. Type **93** ... 50 10
w. Wmk Crown to left of CA ... 1·40
394 10c. *Charaxes candiope* ... 50 10
w. Wmk Crown to right of CA ... 2·75
395 50c. *Papilio nireus* ... 1·50 85
w. Wmk Crown to right of CA ...
396 1e. *Terias desjardinsii* ... 2·00 2·00
w. Wmk Crown to left of CA ...
393/6 *Set of 4* ... 4·00 2·75

*The normal sideways watermark shows Crown to left of CA on 10c., 50c. and to right on the other values, all *as seen from the back of the stamp.*

(Des PAD Studio. Litho Format)

1982 (27 Apr). *Pan-African Conference on Smoking and Health. T* **94** *and similar vert design. Multicoloured. W w* **14**. P 14.

397 5c. Type **94** ... 50 85
398 10c. Smoker and non-smoker climbing stairs ... 60 90

95 Male Fishing Owl

96 Swaziland Coat of Arms

(Des G. Drummond. Litho J.W.)

1982 (16 June). *Wildlife Conservation (1st series). Pel's Fishing Owl. T* **95** *and similar vert designs. Multicoloured.* W w **14**. P 13½×13.

399 35c. Type **95** ... 8·00 4·00
a. Horiz strip of 5. Nos. 399/403 ... 35·00 18·00
400 35c. Female Fishing Owl at nest ... 8·00 4·00
401 35c. Pair of Fishing Owls ... 8·00 4·00
402 35c. Fishing Owl, nest and egg ... 8·00 4·00
403 35c. Adult Fishing Owl with youngster ... 8·00 4·00
399/403 *Set of 5* ... 35·00 18·00

Nos. 399/403 were printed together, *se-tenant*, in horizontal and vertical strips of 5 throughout the sheet.

See also Nos. 425/9 and Nos. 448/52.

(Des C. Abbott. Litho W. S. Cowells Ltd)

1982 (1 July). *21st Birthday of Princess of Wales. T* **96** *and similar vert designs. Multicoloured.* W w **14**. P 14½.

404 5c. Type **96** ... 10 10
w. Wmk inverted ... 40·00
405 20c. Princess leaving Eastleigh Airport, Southampton, August 1981 ... 80 10
406 50c. Bride at Buckingham Palace ... 90 30
407 1e. Formal portrait ... 2·25 85
w. Wmk inverted ... 80·00
404/7 *Set of 4* ... 3·50 1·25

97 Irrigation

(Des G. Hutchins. Litho Walsall)

1982 (1 Sept). *Sugar Industry. T* **97** *and similar horiz designs. Multicoloured.* W w **14** (sideways). P 14×14½.

408 5c. Type **97** ... 10 10
409 20c. Harvesting ... 25 15
410 30c. Mhlume mills ... 35 25
411 1e. Sugar transportation by train ... 1·00 2·00
408/11 *Set of 4* ... 1·50 2·25

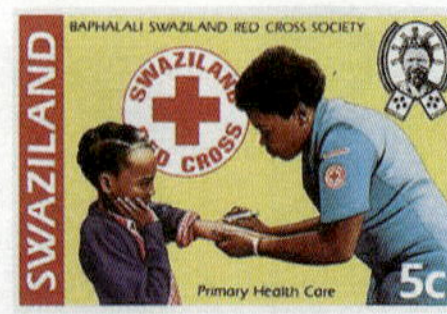

98 Nurse with Child

(Des L. Curtis. Litho Questa)

1982 (9 Nov). *Swaziland Red Cross Society (Baphaladi). T* **98** *and similar horiz designs. Multicoloured.* W w **14** (sideways). P 14.

412 5c. Type **98** ... 10 10
413 20c. Juniors carrying stretcher ... 25 15
414 50c. Disaster relief ... 55 75
415 1e. Henri Dunant (founder of Red Cross) ... 1·25 2·50
412/15 *Set of 4* ... 1·90 3·00

99 Taking the Oath

100 Satellite View of Earth

(Des B. Melton. Litho Format)

1982 (6 Dec). *75th Anniv of Boy Scout Movement. T* **99** *and similar horiz designs. Multicoloured.* W w **14** (sideways*). P 14×13½.

416 5c. Type **99** ... 10 10
417 10c. Hiking and exploration ... 15 10
418 25c. Community development ... 30 30
w. Wmk Crown to right of CA ... 9·50
419 75c. Lord Baden-Powell ... 1·00 1·25
w. Wmk Crown to right of CA ... 9·50
416/19 *Set of 4* ... 1·40 1·60
MS420 107×109 mm. 1e. World scout badge ... 1·00 1·40

*The normal sideways watermark shows Crown to left of CA, *as seen from the back of the stamp.*

(Des A. Theobald. Litho Harrison)

1983 (14 Mar). *Commonwealth Day. T* **100** *and similar multicoloured designs.* W w **14** (sideways on 50c., 1c.). P 14.

421 6c. Type **100** ... 10 10
422 10c. King Sobhuza II ... 10 10
423 50c. Swazi woman and beehive huts (*horiz*) ... 35 55
424 1e. Spraying sugar crops (*horiz*) ... 70 1·00
421/4 *Set of 4* ... 1·10 1·50

(Des G. Drummond. Litho J.W.)

1983 (16 May). *Wildlife Conservation (2nd series). Lammergeier. Vert designs as T* **95**. *Multicoloured.* W w **14**. P 13½×13.

425 35c. Adult male ... 2·50 2·50
a. Horiz strip of 5. Nos. 425/9 ... 11·00 11·00
426 35c. Pair ... 2·50 2·50
427 35c. Nest and egg ... 2·50 2·50
428 35c. Female at nest ... 2·50 2·50
429 35c. Adult bird with fledgling ... 2·50 2·50
425/9 *Set of 5* ... 11·00 11·00

Nos. 425/9 were printed together, *se-tenant*, in horizontal strips of 5 throughout the sheet.

101 Swaziland National Football Team

102 Montgolfier Balloon

(Des G. Vasarhelyi. Litho Format)

1983 (20 Aug). *Tour of Swaziland by English Football Clubs. Three sheets, 101×72 mm, each containing one 75c. stamp as T* **101**. *Multicoloured.* W w **14** (sideways). P 13½.

MS430 75c. Type **101**; 75c. Tottenham Hotspur; 75c. Manchester United *Set of 3 sheets* ... 1·50 3·00

(Des. D. Hartley-Marjoram. Litho Format)

1983 (22 Aug). *Bicentenary of Manned Flight. T* **102** *and similar multicoloured designs.* W w **14** (sideways on 10c. to 50c.). P 14.

431 5c. Type **102** ... 10 10
432 10c. Wright brothers' Flyer I (*horiz*) ... 15 10
433 25c. Fokker F.28 Fellowship (*horiz*) ... 35 35
434 50c. Bell XS-1 (*horiz*) ... 85 65
431/4 *Set of 4* ... 1·25 1·00
MS435 73×73 mm. 1e. Space shuttle *Columbia* ... 1·00 1·40

103 Dr. Albert Schweitzer (Peace Prize, 1952)

(Des G. Vasarhelyi. Litho Harrison)

1983 (21 Oct). *150th Birth Anniv of Alfred Nobel. T* **103** *and similar horiz designs. Multicoloured.* W w **14** (sideways). P 14.

436 6c. Type **103** ... 2·25 70
437 10c. Dag Hammarskjöld (Peace Prize, 1961) ... 85 15
438 50c. Albert Einstein (Physics Prize, 1921) ... 3·75 2·00
439 1e. Alfred Nobel ... 3·75 4·25
436/9 *Set of 4* ... 9·50 6·25

104 Maize

(Des Jennifer Toombs. Litho Harrison)

1983 (29 Nov). *World Food Day. T* **104** *and similar horiz designs. Multicoloured.* W w **14** (sideways). P 14.

440 6c. Type **104** ... 20 10
441 10c. Rice ... 20 10
442 50c. Cattle herding ... 90 1·00
443 1e. Ploughing ... 1·60 2·75
440/3 *Set of 4* ... 2·50 3·50

105 Women's College

106 Male Bald Ibis on Ledge

(Des C. Abbott. Litho Format)

1984 (12 Mar). *Education. T* **105** *and similar horiz designs. Multicoloured.* W w **14** (sideways). P 14.

444 5c. Type **105** ... 10 10
445 15c. Technical Training School ... 15 15
446 50c. University ... 35 60
447 1e. Primary school ... 65 1·10
444/7 *Set of 4* ... 1·10 1·75

(Des G. Drummond. Litho J.W.)

1984 (18 May). *Wildlife Conservation. (3rd series) Bald Ibis. T* **106** *and similar vert designs. Multicoloured.* W w **14**. P 13½×13.

448 35c. Type **106** ... 3·00 3·00
a. Horiz strip of 5. Nos. 448/52 ... 13·50 13·50
449 35c. Male and female ... 3·00 3·00
450 35c. Bird and egg ... 3·00 3·00
451 35c. Female on nest of eggs ... 3·00 3·00
452 35c. Adult and fledgling ... 3·00 3·00
448/52 *Set of 5* ... 13·50 13·50

Nos. 448/52 were printed together, *se-tenant*, in horizontal strips of 5 throughout the sheet.

107 Mule-drawn Passenger Coach

(Des A. Theobald. Litho Walsall)

1984 (15 June). *Universal Postal Union Congress, Hamburg. T* **107** *and similar horiz designs. Multicoloured.* W w **14** (sideways). P 14½.

453 7c. Type **107** ... 30 10
454 15c. Ox-drawn post wagon ... 45 15
455 50c. Mule-drawn mail coach ... 90 75
456 1e. Bristol to London mail coach ... 1·40 1·75
453/6 *Set of 4* ... 2·75 2·50

108 Running

(Des Harrison. Litho Walsall)

1984 (27 July). *Olympic Games, Los Angeles. T* **108** *and similar horiz designs. Multicoloured.* W w **14** (sideways). P 14.

457 7c. Type **108** ... 10 10
458 10c. Swimming ... 10 10
459 50c. Shooting ... 45 1·00
460 1e. Boxing ... 90 2·00

457/60 *Set of 4* .... 1·40 2·75
MS461 100×70 mm. Nos. 457/60 .... 3·00 5·00

109 *Suillus bovinus*

(Des J. Spencer. Litho Format)

1984 (19 Sept). *Fungi. T* **109** *and similar multicoloured designs.* W w **14** (sideways on 10c., 1c.). P 14.

462 10c. Type **109** .... 1·50 30
463 15c. *Langermannia gigantea* (*vert*) .... 2·50 55
w. Wmk inverted .... 10·00
464 50c. *Trametes versicolor* ("*Coriolus versicolor*") (*vert*) .... 2·75 2·75
465 1e. *Boletus edulis* .... 3·25 5·25
462/5 *Set of 4* .... 9·00 8·00

110 King Sobhuza opening Railway, 1964

10c
(**111**)

(Des W. Fenton. Litho Walsall)

1984 (5 Nov). *20th Anniv of Swaziland Railways. T* **110** *and similar horiz designs. Multicoloured.* W w **14** (sideways). P 14.

466 10c. Type **110** 30 15
467 25c. Type 15A locomotive at Siweni Yard 55 40
468 30c. Container loading, Matsapha Station 55 40
469 1e. Locomotive No. 268 leaving Alto Tunnel .... 1·25 2·50
466/9 *Set of 4* .... 2·40 3·00
MS470 144×74 mm. Nos. 466/9 .... 2·75 6·00

1984 (15 Dec). *Nos. 340B, 341A, 342A, 343A, 345B and 346A surch as T* **111**.

471 10c. on 4c. *Aloe marlothii* .... 50·00
a. Surch on No. 343Ac 35 10
b. Surch on No. 343B .... 4·75 4·75
472 15c. on 7c. *Cyrtanthus bicolor* 40 20
473 20c. on 3c. *Haemanthus magnificus* 35 15
a. Surch on No. 342Ac .... 4·75 4·75
474 25c. on 6c. *Aloe kniphofioides* 40 20
a. Surch triple .... † —
b. Surch double
475 30c. on 1c. Type **83** 50 20
a. Surch omitted (horiz pair with normal) £375
476 30c. on 2c. *Aloe suprafoliata* .... 2·75 3·75
a. Surch omitted (horiz pair) with normal
b. Surch on No. 341B .... 4·75 4·75
471a/6 *Set of 6* .... 4·25 4·00

112 Rotary International Logo and Map of World

113 Male Ground Hornbill

(Des G. Vasarhelyi. Litho Questa)

1985 (23 Feb). *80th Anniv of Rotary International. T* **112** *and similar horiz designs. Multicoloured.* W w **14** (sideways). P 14.

477 10c. Type **112** 75 10
478 15c. Teacher and handicapped children .... 1·00 20
479 50c. Youth exchange .... 1·25 1·40
480 1e. Nurse and children .... 3·00 4·00
477/80 *Set of 4* .... 5·50 5·25

(Des G. Drummond. Litho Harrison)

1985 (15 May). *Birth Bicentenary of John J. Audubon (ornithologist). Southern Ground Hornbills. T* **113** *and similar vert designs. Multicoloured.* W w **14**. P 14.

481 25c. Type **113** .... 2·25 3·25
a. Horiz strip of 5. Nos. 481/5 .... 10·00 14·00
482 25c. Male and female Ground Hornbills .... 2·25 3·25
483 25c. Female at nest .... 2·25 3·25
484 25c. Ground Hornbill in nest, and egg .... 2·25 3·25
485 25c. Adult and fledgling .... 2·25 3·25
481/5 *Set of 5* .... 10·00 14·00

Nos. 481/5 were printed together, *se-tenant*, in horizontal strips of 5 throughout the sheet.

114 The Queen Mother in 1975

115 Buick "Tourer"

(Des A. Theobald (2e.), C. Abbott (others). Litho Questa)

1985 (7 June). *Life and Times of Queen Elizabeth the Queen Mother. T* **114** *and similar vert designs. Multicoloured.* W w **16**. P 14½×14.

486 10c. The Queen Mother in South Africa, 1947 .... 40 10
487 15c. With the Queen and Princess Margaret, 1985 (from photo by Norman Parkinson) 40 10
488 50c. Type **114** .... 1·10 1·10
489 1e. With Prince Henry at his christening (from photo by Lord Snowdon) .... 1·40 2·50
486/9 *Set of 4* .... 3·00 3·50
MS490 91×73 mm. 2c. Greeting Prince Andrew. Wmk sideways .... 3·00 1·75

(Des D. Hartley. Litho Walsall)

1985 (16 Sept). *Century of Motoring. T* **115** *and similar horiz designs. Multicoloured. (sideways).* W w **14** P 14.

491 10c. Type **115** 50 10
492 15c. Four cylinder Rover 70 25
493 50c. De Dion Bouton .... 1·75 2·00
494 1e. "Model T" Ford .... 2·25 4·00
491/4 *Set of 4* .... 4·75 5·75

116 Youths building Bridge over Ravine

(Des Vrein Barlocher. Litho Format)

1985 (2 Dec). *International Youth Year (10, 50c.), and 75th Anniv of Girl Guide Movement (others). T* **116** *and similar horiz designs. Multicoloured.* W w **16** (sideways*). P 14.

495 10c. Type **116** 15 10
496 20c. Girl Guides in camp 20 15
w. Wmk Crown to right of CA
497 50c. Youth making model from sticks .... 45 1·00
498 1e. Guides collecting brushwood .... 80 2·00
495/8 *Set of 4* .... 1·40 3·00

*The normal sideways watermark shows Crown to left of CA, *as seen from the back of the stamp.*

117 Halley's Comet over Swaziland

117a Christening of Princess Anne, 1950

(Des Jennifer Toombs. Litho B.D.T.)

1986 (27 Feb). *Appearance of Halley's Comet.* W w **14** (sideways). P 14.

499 **117** 1e.50 multicoloured .... 2·75 4·00

(Des A. Theobald. Litho Format)

1986 (21 Apr). *60th Birthday of Queen Elizabeth II. Vert designs as T* **117a**. *Multicoloured.* W w **16**. P 14×14½.

500 10c. Type **117a** 10 10
501 30c. On Palace balcony after wedding of Prince and Princess of Wales, 1981 .... 15 25
502 45c. Royal visit to Swaziland, 1947 .... 15 30
503 1e. At Windsor Polo Ground, 1984 .... 30 70
504 2e. At Crown Agents Head Office, London, 1983 .... 60 1·40
500/4 *Set of 5* .... 1·10 2·50

118 King Mswati III

119 Emblems of Round Table and Project Orbis (eye disease campaign)

(Des L. Curtis. Litho Walsall)

1986 (25 Apr). *Coronation of King Mswati III. T* **118** *and similar designs.* W w **16** (sideways on 20c. to 2c.). P 14½×14 (10c.) or 14×14½ (others).

505 10c. black and gold 35 25
506 20c. multicoloured 70 30
507 25c. multicoloured 80 35
508 30c. multicoloured 90 50
509 40c. multicoloured .... 3·25 2·00
510 2e. multicoloured .... 4·00 8·00
505/10 *Set of 6* .... 9·00 10·00

Designs: *Horiz*—20c. Prince with King Sobhuza II at Incwala ceremony; 25c. At primary school; 30c. At school in England; 40c. Inspecting guard of honour at Matsapha Airport; 2e. Dancing the Simemo.

(Des M. Kesson, adapted G. Vasarhelyi. Litho Walsall)

1986 (6 Oct). *50th Anniv of Round Table Organization. T* **119** *and similar vert designs showing branch emblems. Multicoloured.* W w **16**. P 14.

511 15c. Type **119** 30 10
512 25c. Ehlanzeni 51 .... 40 20
513 55c. Mbabane 30 .... 85 70
514 70c. Bulembu 54 .... 1·10 1·50
515 2e. Manzini 44 .... 2·00 4·00
511/15 *Set of 5* .... 4·25 5·75

120 *Precis hierta*

(Des I. Loe. Litho Questa)

1987 (17 Mar). *Butterflies (1st series). T* **120** *and similar horiz designs. Multicoloured.* P 14.

516 10c. Type **120** .... 55 1·50
517 15c. *Hamanumida daedalus* .... 65 1·25
518 20c. *Charaxes boueti* 65 90
519 25c. *Abantis paradisea* .... 65 1·75
520 30c. *Acraea anemosa* 65 70
521 35c. *Graphium leonidas* 65 75
522 45c. *Graphium antheus* .... 70 1·75
523 50c. *Precis orithya* 70 85
524 55c. *Pinacopteryx eriphia* 70 85
525 70c. *Precis octavia* .... 80 1·40
526 1e. *Mylothris chloris* .... 1·00 3·00
527 5e. *Colotis regina* 85 90
528 10e. *Spindasis natalensis* .... 1·10 1·75
516/28 *Set of 13* .... 8·75 16·00

For these designs, and similar 5c., with different portrait of King Mswati III see Nos. 606/17.

121 Two White Rhinoceroses

122 Hybrid Tea Rose "Blue Moon"

(Des Doreen McGuinness. Litho Questa)

1987 (1 July). *White Rhinoceros. T* **121** *and similar horiz designs. Multicoloured.* W w **16** (sideways). P 14½.

529 15c. Type **121** .... 2·00 45
530 25c. Female and calf .... 2·75 1·00
531 45c. Rhinoceros charging .... 4·25 3·25
532 70c. Rhinoceros wallowing .... 6·50 7·50
529/32 *Set of 4* .... 14·00 11·00

(Des Josephine Martin. Litho Questa)

1987 (19 Oct). *Garden Flowers. T* **122** *and similar vert designs. Multicoloured.* W w **16**. P 14½.

533 15c. Type **122** .... 1·00 20
534 35c. Rambler Rose "Dense du fen" .... 2·00 80
535 55c. Pompon Dahlia "Odin" .... 2·25 1·50
536 2e. *Lilium davidii var. willmottiae* .... 6·50 11·00
533/6 *Set of 4* .... 10·50 12·00

40TH WEDDING ANNIVERSARY
122a

1987 (9 Dec). *Royal Ruby Wedding. Nos. 501/4 optd with T* **122a** *in silver.*

537 30c. On Palace balcony after wedding of Prince and Princess of Wales, 1981 .... 40 20
538 45c. Royal visit to Swaziland, 1947 .... 50 30
539 1e. At Windsor Polo Ground, 1984 .... 85 1·60
540 2e. At Crown Agents Head Office, London, 1983 .... 1·25 3·00
537/40 *Set of 4* .... 2·75 4·50

123 *Zabalius aridus* (grasshopper)

(Des I. Loe. Litho Questa)

1988 (14 Mar). *Insects. T* **123** *and similar horiz designs. Multicoloured.* W w **16** (sideways). P 14.

541	15c. Type **123**	1·40	15
542	55c. *Callidea bohemani* (shieldbug)	2·75	85
543	1e. *Phymateus viridipes* (grasshopper)	4·75	4·75
544	2e. *Nomadacris septemfasciata* (locust)	7·50	9·50
541/4	*Set of 4*	15·00	14·00

124 Athlete with Swazi Flag and Olympic Stadium

(Des C. Abbott. Litho Format)

1988 (22 Aug). *Olympic Games, Seoul. T* **124** *and similar horiz designs. Multicoloured.* W w **16** (sideways). P 14.

545	15c. Type **124**	1·00	10
546	35c. Taekwondo	1·40	45
547	1e. Boxing	1·75	2·25
548	2e. Tennis	3·50	5·00
545/8	*Set of 4*	7·00	7·00

125 Savanna Monkey ("Green Monkey")

126 Dr. David Hynd (founder of Swazi Red Cross)

(Des I. Lee. Litho Questa)

1989 (16 Jan). *Small Mammals. T* **125** *and similar horiz designs. Multicoloured.* W w **16** (sideways). P 14.

549	35c. Type **125**	2·00	30
550	55c. Large-toothed Rock Hyrax ("Rock Dassie")	2·50	75
551	1e. Zorilla	4·25	4·50
552	2e. African Wild Cat	7·50	10·00
549/52	*Set of 4*	14·50	14·00

(Des T. Chance. Litho Security Printers (M), Malaysia)

1989 (21 Sept). *125th Anniv of International Red Cross. T* **126** *and similar horiz designs. Multicoloured.* W w **14** (sideways*). P 12.

553	15c. Type **126**	25	15
554	60c. First aid training	60	40
555	1e. Sigombeni Clinic	1·00	1·40
556	2e. Refugee camp	1·50	2·75
	w. Wmk Crown to right of CA		
553/6	*Set of 4*	3·00	4·25

*The normal sideways watermark shows Crown to left of CA, as seen from the back of the stamp.

127 King Mswati III with Prince of Wales, 1987

128 Manzini to Mahamba Road

(Des L. Curtis. Litho Harrison)

1989 (15 Nov). *21st Birthday of King Mswati III. T* **127** *and similar horiz designs. Multicoloured.* P 14×14½.

557	15c. Type **127**	10	10
558	60c. King with Pope John Paul II, 1988	30	35
559	1e. Introduction of Crown Prince to people, 1983	50	55
560	2e. King Mswati III and Queen Mother	95	1·00
557/60	*Set of 4*	1·60	1·75

(Des A. Theobald. Litho Questa)

1989 (18 Dec). *25th Anniv of African Development Bank. T* **128** *and similar horiz designs. Multicoloured.* W w **16** (sideways). P 14×14½.

561	15c. Type **128**	10	10
562	60c. Microwave Radio Receiver, Mbabane	30	40
563	1e. Mbabane Government Hospital	50	1·10
564	2e. Ezulwini Power Station switchyard	95	2·25
561/4	*Set of 4*	1·60	3·50

129 International Priority Mail Van

(Des G. Vasarhelyi. Litho Security Printers (M), Malaysia)

1990 (3 May). *"Stamp World London 90" International Stamp Exhibition. T* **129** *and similar horiz designs. Multicoloured.* W w **14** (sideways). P 12½.

565	15c. Type **129**	15	10
566	60c. Facsimile Service operators	40	40
567	1e. Rural post office	75	1·00
568	2e. Ezulwini Earth Station switchyard	1·40	2·50
565/8	*Set of 4*	2·40	3·50

MS569 105×85 mm. 2e. Mail runner. Wmk upright ... 4·00 4·50

No. **MS**569 also commemorates the 150th anniversary of the Penny Black.

129a Queen Mother

129b King George VI and Queen Elizabeth visiting Civil Resettlement Unit, Hatfield House

(Des D. Miller. Litho Questa)

1990 (4 Aug). *90th Birthday of Queen Elizabeth the Queen Mother.* W w **16**. P 14×15 (75c.) or 14½ (4c.).

570	**129a**	75c. multicoloured	50	50
571	**129b**	4e. brownish black and deep turquoise-green	2·25	3·50

130 Pictorial Teaching

131 Rural Water Supply

(Des D. Aryeequaye. Litho Questa)

1990 (21 Sept). *International Literacy Year. T* **130** *and similar horiz designs. Multicoloured. W w* **14** *(sideways).* P 14.

572	15c. Type **130**	10	10
573	75c. Rural class	45	45
574	1e. Modern teaching methods	60	1·00
575	2e. Presentation of certificates	1·10	2·00
572/5	*Set of 4*	2·00	3·25

(Des D. Aryeequaye. Litho Cartor)

1990 (10 Dec). *40th Anniv of United Nations Development Programme. "Helping People to Help Themselves". T* **131** *and similar vert designs. Multicoloured.* W w **14**. P 13½×14.

576	60c. Type **131**	35	35
577	1e. Seed multiplication project	60	1·10
578	2e. Low-cost housing project	1·25	2·25
576/8	*Set of 3*	2·00	3·25

10c

(**132**)

133 Lobamba Hot Spring

1990 (17 Dec). *Nos. 519/20, 522 and 524 surch as T* **132**.

579	10c. on 25c. *Abantis paradisea*	30	30
580	15c. on 30c. *Acraea anemosa*	40	40
580*a*	15c. on 45c. *Graphium antheus*	17·00	17·00
581	20c. on 45c. *Graphium antheus*	40	40
582	40c. on 55c. *Pinacopteryx eriphia*	55	55

(Des D. Aryeequaye. Litho Harrison)

1991 (11 Feb). *National Heritage. T* **133** *and similar horiz designs. Multicoloured.* W **77** of Brunei (sideways). P 14½.

583	15c. Type **133**	30	10
584	60c. Sibebe Rock	1·00	45
585	1e. Jolobela Falls	1·50	1·75
586	2e. Mantjolo Sacred Pool	2·25	3·00
583/6	*Set of 4*	4·50	4·75

MS587 80×60 mm. 2e. Usushwana River. P 14 ... 3·75 4·25

134 King Mswati III making Speech

(Des D. Aryeequaye. Litho Cartor)

1991 (24 Apr). *5th Anniv of King Mswati III's Coronation. T* **134** *and similar horiz designs. Multicoloured.* W w **14** (sideways). P 14×13½.

588	15c. Type **134**	40	10
589	75c. Butimba Royal Hunt	1·25	60
590	1e. King and visiting school friends from Sherborne, 1986	1·50	1·75
591	2e. King opening Parliament	2·25	3·00
588/91	*Set of 4*	4·75	5·00

134a Prince Philip

135 *Xerophyta retinervis*

(Des D. Miller. Litho Questa)

1991 (17 June). *65th Birthday of Queen Elizabeth II and 70th Birthday of Prince Philip. Vert designs as T* **134a**. *Multicoloured.* W w **16** (sideways). P 14½×14.

592	1e. Prince Philip	1·75	2·00
	a. Horiz pair. Nos. 592/3 separated by label	3·75	4·25
593	2e. Queen Elizabeth II	2·00	2·25

Nos. 592/3 were printed together *se-tenant*, in sheetlets of 10 (2×5) with designs alternating and the vertical rows separated by inscribed labels.

(Des D. Aryeequaye. Litho Questa)

1991 (30 Sept). *Indigenous Flowers. T* **135** *and similar vert designs. Multicoloured.* W w **14** (sideways). P 14.

594	15c. Type **135**	50	10
595	75c. *Bauhinia galpinii*	1·25	80
596	1e. *Dombeya rotundifolia*	1·50	1·60
597	2e. *Kigelia africana*	2·25	3·25
594/7	*Set of 4*	5·00	5·00

136 Father Christmas arriving with Gifts

137 Lubombo Flat Lizard

(Des D. Aryeequaye. Litho Cartor)

1991 (18 Dec). *Christmas. T* **136** *and similar vert designs. Multicoloured.* W w **14**. P 13½.

598	20c. Type **136**	15	10
599	70c. Singing carols	65	50
600	1e. Priest reading from Bible	80	1·25
601	2e. The Nativity	1·50	2·50
598/601	*Set of 4*	2·75	4·00

(Des D. Aryeequaye. Litho Cartor)

1992 (25 Feb). *Reptiles (1st series). T* **137** *and similar horiz designs. Multicoloured.* W w **14** (sideways). P 13½.

602	20c. Type **137**	90	20
603	70c. Natal Hinged Tortoise	2·25	1·50
604	1e. Swazi Thick-toed Gecko	2·75	2·75
605	2e. Nile Monitor	3·75	5·50
602/5	*Set of 4*	8·75	9·00

See also Nos. 658/61.

138 *Precis hierta*

139 Missionaries visiting King Sobhuza II and Queen Lomawa

Two types of 55c. stamp (No. 615):

I. "Closed" letter c in 55c. "1991" imprint date
II. Redrawn design with "2000" imprint date

There are a number of other differences in the redrawn design.

(Des I. Loe. Litho Questa)

1992 (26 Aug). *Butterflies (2nd series). Designs as Nos. 516/26 and new value (5c.) showing different portrait of King Mswati III as in T* **138**. *Multicoloured. Without imprint date (5c.) or with "1991" imprint date below design (others).* P 14.

606	5c. *Colotis antevippe*	10	10
607	10c. Type **138**	15	10
608	15c. *Hamanumida daedalus*	15	10
609	20c. *Charaxes boueti*	20	10
610	25c. *Abantis paradisea*	20	10
611	30c. *Acraea anemosa*	20	15
612	35c. *Graphium leonidas*	20	20
613	45c. *Graphium antheus*	20	20
614	50c. *Precis orithya*	20	20
	a. Type II (2000)	20	20
615	55c. *Pinacopteryx eriphia*	20	20
616	70c. *Precis octavia*	30	30
617	1e. *Mylothris chloris*	40	40
618	5e. *Colotis regina* (2000)	1·20	1·40
619	10e. *Spindasis natalersis* (2000)	2·40	2·75
606/17	*Set of 12*	5·50	5·75

Nos. 606/17 are all on chalk-surfaced paper.

(Des D. Aryeequaye. Litho Cartor)

1992 (16 Dec). *Centenary of Evangelical Alliance Missions. T* **139** *and similar vert design. Multicoloured.* P 13½×14.

620 20c. Type **139** ... 50 10
621 1e. Pioneer missionaries ... 2·50 3·00

140 Calabashes

141 King Mswati III as Baby

(Des D. Aryeequaye. Litho Cartor)

1993 (18 Mar). *Archaeological and Contemporary Artifacts. T* **140** *and similar vert designs. Multicoloured.* P 13½×14.

622 20c. Type **140** ... 45 10
623 70c. Contemporary cooking pot ... 1·10 85
624 1e. Wooden bowl and containers ... 1·50 1·75
625 2e. Quern for grinding seeds ... 2·50 3·50
622/5 *Set of 4* ... 5·00 5·50

(Des D. Aryeequaye. Litho Cartor)

1993 (6 Sept). *25th Birthday of King Mswati III and 25th Anniv of Independence. T* **141** *and similar vert designs. Multicoloured.* P 13½×14.

626 25c. Type **141** ... 20 10
627 40c. King Mswati III addressing meeting 25 20
628 1e. King Sobhuza II receiving Instrument of Independence ... 75 1·25
629 2e. King Mswati III delivering Coronation speech ... 1·40 2·50
626/9 *Set of 4* ... 2·40 3·50

142 Male and Female Common Waxbills

143 Classroom and Practical Training

(Des D. Aryeequaye. Litho Cartor)

1993 (25 Nov). *Common Waxbill. T* **142** *and similar vert designs. Multicoloured.* P 13½.

630 25c. Type **142** ... 40 20
631 40c. Waxbill and eggs in nest ... 55 25
632 1e. Waxbill on nest ... 1·25 1·50
633 2e. Waxbill feeding chicks ... 2·00 2·75
630/3 *Set of 4* ... 3·75 4·25

(Des D. Aryeequaye. Litho Cartor)

1994 (22 Feb). *25th Anniv of U.S. Peace Corps in Swaziland. T* **143** *and similar vert designs. Multicoloured.* P 13½.

634 25c. Type **143** ... 35 10
635 40c. Rural water supply ... 45 20
636 1e. Americans and Swazis in traditional costumes ... 1·75 1·75
637 2e. Swazi-American co-operation ... 2·00 3·00
634/7 *Set of 4* ... 4·00 4·50

144 *Agaricus arvensis*

145 Emblem and Airliner on Runway

(Des D. Aryeequaye. Litho Cartor)

1994 (15 Sept). *Fungi. T* **144** *and similar vert designs. Multicoloured.* P 13½×14.

638 30c. Type **144** ... 1·25 50
639 40c. *Boletus edulis* ... 1·25 50
640 1e. *Russula virescens* ... 2·50 1·75
641 2e. *Armillaria mellea* ... 3·50 4·00
638/41 *Set of 4* ... 7·50 6·00

(Des D. Aryeequaye. Litho Walsall)

1994 (30 Nov). *50th Anniv of International Civil Aviation Organization. T* **145** *and similar horiz designs. Multicoloured.* P 14.

642 30c. Type **145** ... 40 10
643 40c. Control tower and dish aerial ... 45 20
644 1e. Crash tenders ... 1·00 1·25
645 2e. Air traffic controllers ... 1·50 2·50
642/5 *Set of 4* ... 3·00 3·50

146 Wooden Bowls

147 Harvesting Maize

(Des D. Aryeequaye. Litho Cartor)

1995 (7 Apr). *Handicrafts. T* **146** *and similar vert designs. Multicoloured.* P 13½×14.

646 35c. Type **146** ... 45 20
647 50c. Chicken nests ... 65 35
648 1e. Leather crafts ... 1·00 1·10
649 2e. Wood carvings ... 1·75 2·25
646/9 *Set of 4* ... 3·50 3·50

(Des D. Aryeequaye. Litho Cartor)

1995 (5 June). *50th Anniv of Food and Agriculture Organization. T* **147** *and similar vert designs. Multicoloured.* P 13½.

650 35c. Type **147** ... 20 20
651 50c. Planting vegetables ... 30 35
652 1e. Herd of cattle ... 50 75
653 2e. Harvesting sorghum ... 90 1·75
650/3 *Set of 4* ... 1·75 2·75

148 Knysna Turaco

149 Waterberry

(Des D. Aryeequaye. Litho Cartor)

1995 (27 Sept). *Turacos ("Louries"). T* **148** *and simlar horiz designs. Multicoloured.* P 13½×13.

654 35c. Type **148** ... 40 30
655 50c. Knysna Turaco in flight ... 55 45
656 1e. Violet-crested Turaco ... 80 1·00
657 2e. Livingstone's Turaco ... 1·25 2·00
654/7 *Set of 4* ... 2·75 3·25

(Des D. Aryeequaye. Litho Cartor)

1996 (17 Jan). *Reptiles (2nd series). Horiz designs as T* **137** *with King's portrait at right. Multicoloured.* P 13½×13.

658 35c. Chameleon ... 65 20
659 50c. Rock Monitor ... 75 35
660 1e. African Python ... 1·25 1·40
661 2e. Tree Agama ... 2·00 2·75
658/61 *Set of 4* ... 4·25 4·25

(Des D. Aryeequaye. Litho Cartor)

1996 (23 Apr). *Trees. T* **149** *and similar vert designs. Multicoloured.* P 13×13½.

662 40c. Type **149** ... 20 15
663 60c. Sycamore Fig ... 25 20
664 1e. Stem Fruit ... 45 80
665 2e. Wild Medlar ... 90 1·60
662/5 *Set of 4* ... 1·60 2·50

150 Mahamba Methodist Church

(Des D. Aryeequaye. Litho Cartor)

1996 (26 Aug). *Historic Monuments. T* **150** *and similar horiz designs. Multicoloured.* P 13½×13.

666 40c. Type **150** ... 50 15
667 60c. Colonial Secretariat, Mbabane ... 65 20
668 1e. King Sobhuza II Monument, Lobamba ... 1·10 1·40
669 2e. First High Court Building, Hlatikulu 1·75 2·50
666/9 *Set of 4* ... 3·50 3·75

151 Children in Class

152 Klipspringer

(Litho Enschedé)

1996 (31 Dec). *50th Anniv of UNICEF. T* **151** *and similar multicoloured designs.* P 13½×14 (40c.) or 14×13½ (others).

670 40c. Type **151** ... 15 15
671 60c. Child being inoculated (*vert*) ... 20 20
672 1e. Child on crutches (*vert*) ... 40 70
673 2e. Mother and children (*vert*) ... 80 1·60
670/3 *Set of 4* ... 1·40 2·40

(Litho Enschedé)

1997 (22 Sept). *Mammals. T* **152** *and similar multicoloured designs.* P 14×13½ (*vert*) or 13½×14 (*horiz*).

674 50c. Type **152** ... 30 20
675 70c. Grey Duiker ... 35 30
676 1e. Antbear (*horiz*) ... 50 70
677 2e. Cape Clawless Otter (*horiz*) ... 80 1·60
674/7 *Set of 4* ... 1·75 2·50

153 Umgaco Costume

154 Olive Toad

(Litho Cartor)

1997 (1 Dec). *Traditional Costumes. T* **153** *and similar vert designs. Multicoloured.* P 13×13½.

678 50c. Type **153** ... 25 15
679 70c. Sigeja cloak ... 35 25
680 1e. Umdada kilt ... 55 65
681 2e. Ligcebesha costume ... 90 1·40
678/81 *Set of 4* ... 1·90 2·25

(Des K. Addai-Yinkah. Litho Enschedé)

1998 (1 June). *Amphibians. T* **154** *and similar horiz designs. Multicoloured.* P 14½×14.

682 55c. Type **154** ... 25 15
683 75c. African Bullfrog ... 35 25
684 1e. Water Lily Frog ... 55 65
685 2e. Bushveld Rain Frog ... 90 1·40
682/5 *Set of 4* ... 1·90 2·25

155 Aerial View of King Sobhuza II Memorial Park

156 Grinding Stone

(Des K. Addai-Yinkah. Litho Enschedé)

1998 (3 Sept). *30th Anniv of Independence and 30th Birthday of King Mswati III. T* **155** *and similar multicoloured designs.* P 14×13½ (75c.) or 13½×14 (others).

686 55c. Type **155** ... 35 15
687 75c. King Mswati III taking oath (*vert*) ... 45 25
688 1e. King Mswati delivering speech ... 65 80
689 2e. King Sobhuza II receiving Instrument of Independence ... 1·10 1·60
686/9 *Set of 4* ... 2·25 2·50

(Des D. Aryeequaye. Litho Cartor)

1999 (17 May). *Local Culinary Utensils. T* **156** *and similar vert designs. Multicoloured. Two phosphor bands.* P 13½.

690 60c. Type **156** ... 35 15
691 75c. Stirring sticks ... 40 20
692 80c. Clay pot ... 40 25
693 95c. Swazi spoons ... 55 45
694 1e.75 Beer cups ... 1·00 1·10
695 2e.40 Mortar and pestle ... 1·40 1·60
690/5 *Set of 6* ... 3·75 3·50

157 Internet Service

158 Lion and Lioness

(Des K. Addai-Yinkah. Litho Cartor)

1999 (9 Oct). *125th Anniv of Universal Postal Union. T* **157** *and similar multicoloured designs. Two phosphor bands.* P 13½.

696 60c. Type **157** ... 35 15
697 80c. Cellular phone service ... 45 25
698 1e. Two post vans exchanging mail (*horiz*) ... 1·25 1·25
699 2e.40 Training school (*horiz*) ... 1·60 2·00
696/9 *Set of 4* ... 3·25 3·25

(Des K. Addai-Yinkah. Litho Cartor)

2000 (3 July). *Wildlife. T* **158** *and similar multicoloured designs. Two phosphor bands.* P 13½.

700 65c. Type **158** ... 35 15
701 90c. Leopard (*horiz*) ... 55 30
702 1e.50 Rhinoceros (*horiz*) ... 1·50 1·25
703 2e.50 Buffalo ... 1·40 1·90
700/3 *Set of 4* ... 3·50 3·25

159 Oribi with Young

(Des A. Robinson. Litho Questa)

2001 (1 Feb). *Endangered Species. Antelopes. T* **159** *and similar horiz designs. Multicoloured.* W w **14** (sideways). P 14.

704	65c. Type **159**	35	15
	a. Strip of 4. Nos. 704/7	3·00	3·00
705	90c. Oribi Buck	55	25
706	1e.50 Young Klipspringers	1·00	1·10
707	2e.50 Male and female Klipspringers	1·40	1·90
704/7 *Set of 4*		3·00	3·00

Nos. 704/7 were printed in separate sheets of 50 (two panes 5×5) or in sheets of 16 (4×4) containing the four designs *se-tenant*, both horizontally and vertically. The sheets of 16 have illustrated margins.

160 Fighting Foest Fires

(Des K. Addai-Yinkah. Litho Questa)

2001 (30 July). *Enviromental Protection. T* **160** *and similar horiz designs. Multicoloured.* P 14.

708	70c. Type **160**	50	20
709	95c. Tree planting	65	25
710	2e.05 Construction of Maguga Dam	1·40	1·50
711	2e.80 Building embankment	1·75	2·00
708/11 *Set of 4*		3·75	3·50

160a Princess Elizabeth, Prince Philip, and children, 1951

(Des A. Robinson. Litho Questa)

2002 (6 Feb). *Golden Jubilee.* W w **14** (sideways). P 14½.

712	70c. agate, viloet and gold	50	10
713	95c. multicoloured	70	25
714	2e.05 agate, viloet and gold	1·10	1·25
715	2e.80 multicoloured	1·40	1·50
712/15 *Set of 4*		3·25	2·75
MS716	16×95 mm. Nos. 712/15 and 22e.50, multicoloured. P 13½ (22e.50) or 14½ (others)	6·00	7·00

Designs: *Horiz*—70c. Type **160a**; 95c. Queen Elizebeth in blue and white beret; 2e.05 Queen Elizebeth in evening dress; 2e.80 Queen Elizebeth on visit to Norway, 2001. Vert (38×51 mm)—22e.50 Queen Elizebeth after Annigoni.

Designs as Nos. 712/15 in No. **MS**716 omit the gold frame around each stamp and the "Golden Jubilee 1952–2002" inscription.

161 Swazi Village **162** Sitolotolo (mouth organ)

(Des P. Dlamini. Litho Enschedé)

2002 (23 Dec). *Tourism. T* **161** *and similar multicoloured designs.* P 13½.

717	75c. Type **161**	20	10
718	1e.05 King Mswati and lions (*vert*)	30	20
719	2e.05 Crocodile	1·00	1·00
720	2e.80 Ostrich with young	1·50	1·75
717/20 *Set of 4*		2·75	2·75

(Des P. Dlamini. Litho Enschedé)

2003 (12 Aug). *Musical Instruments. T* **162** *and similar multicoloured designs.* P 14.

721	80c. Type **162**	25	20
722	1e.05 Emafahlawane (rattles) (*horiz*)	30	25
723	2e.35 Impalampala (Kudu horn trumpet) (*horiz*)	70	80
724	2e.80 Makhoyane (chordphone)	90	1·10
721/4 *Set of 4*		1·90	2·10

163 Community Health Worker with AIDS Patient **164** King Mswati III and outline of Africa

(Des P. Dlamini. Litho Enschedé)

2004 (9 Mar). *AIDS Awareness Campaign. T* **163** *and similar multicoloured designs.* P 13½×14 (*horiz*) or 14×13½ (*vert*).

725	85c. Type **163**	30	15
726	1e.10 Care and Voluntary Councelling and Testing Centre	40	25
727	2e.45 Testing Blood (*vert*)	90	95
728	3e.45 Nurse giving injection and sterilizer (*vert*)	1·10	1·25
725/8 *Set of 4*		2·40	2·40

(Des P. Dlamini. Litho Enschedé)

2004 (14 June). *Global 2003 Smart Partnership Movement. T* **164** *and similar multicoloured designs.* P 13½.

729	85c. Type **164**	30	15
730	1e.10 Outline of Africa and Logos (*horiz*).	40	25
731	2e.45 Stylized people holding globe	85	95
732	3e.35 King Mswati III and speaker	1·00	1·10
729/32 *Set of 4*		2·25	2·25

(Des Anja Denker. Litho Enschedé)

2004 (11 Oct). *First Joint Issue of Southern Africa Postal Operators Association Members. Hexagonal designs as T* **233** *of Botswana showing national birds of Association members. Multicoloured.* P 14.

733	85c. Purple-crested turaco ("Lourie") (Swaziland)	50	30
734	1e.10 Stanley ("Blue") crane (South Africa)	50	30
735	1e.35 Cattle egret (Botswana)	55	35
736	1e.90 Two African fish eagles perched (Zimbabwe)	90	60
737	2e. African fish eagle (Namibia)	90	60
738	2e.45 Bar-tailed trogon (Malawi) (inscribed "apaloderma vittatum")	1·00	1·10
739	3e. Two African fish eagles in flight (Zambia)	1·25	1·40
740	3e.35 Peregrine falcon (Angola)	1·40	1·50
733/40 *Set of 8*		6·25	5·50
MS741	170×95 mm. Nos. 733/40	6·00	6·50

The stamp depicting the bar-tailed trogon is not inscribed with the country of which the bird is a national symbol.

In **MS**741 No. 735 is inscribed '1e.90', no 738 is inscribed '2.25' and Nos. 739/40 are inscribed '2.30'.

Miniature sheets in similar designs were also issued by Namibia, Zimbabwe, Angola, Botswana, South Africa, Malawi and Zambia.

165 School Child under Car and Children by Road

(Des P. Dlamini. Litho Enschedé)

2005 (25 Jan). *Road Safety Council. T* **165** *and similar horiz designs. Multicoloured.* P 13½×14.

742	85c. Type **165**	50	30
743	1e.10 Fire rescue team pulling injured man from car	50	30
744	2e.45 Pedestrians and car approaching stop sign	80	90
745	3e.35 Bus and road safety officials	1·10	1·25
742/5 *Set of 4*		2·75	2·50

166 Black Mamba **166a** Pope John Paul II

(Litho Enschedé)

2005 (5 Apr). *Snakes. T* **166** *and similar horiz designs. Multicoloured.* P 13½×14.

746	85c. Type **166**	30	15
747	1e.10 Python	40	30
748	2e.45 Boomslang	80	90
749	3e.35 Puff adder	1·10	1·25
747/9 *Set of 4*		2·40	2·40

(Des Andrew Robinson. Litho BDT)

2005 (18 Aug). *Pope John Paul II Commemoration.* W w **14** (inverted). P 14.

750	**166a** 4e.50 multicoloured	1·25	1·40

No. 750 was printed in sheetlets of eight stamps with an enlarged, illustrated right margin.

167 *Schistocerca solitaria* **168** Ntombi Tfwala (1983–)

(Des P. Dlamini. Litho Enschedé)

2005 (11 Oct). *Locusts and Grasshoppers. T* **167** *and similar horiz designs. Multicoloured.* P 13½×14.

751	85c. Type **167**	30	15
752	1e.10 *Nomadacris septemfasciata* (red locust)	40	30
753	2e.45 *Schistocerca gregaria flaviventris* (South African desert locust)	80	90
754	3e.35 *Locusta migratoria migratoroides* (African migratory locust)	1·10	1·25
751/4 *Set of 4*		2·25	2·25

(Des P. Dlamini. Litho Enschedé)

2006 (10 Jan). *Queen Mothers of Swaziland. T* **168** *and similar vert designs. Multicoloured.* P 14×13½.

755	85c. Type **168**	30	15
756	1e.10 Dzeliwe Shongwe (1980–3)	40	30
757	2e. Lomawa Ndwandwe (1921–38)	60	50
758	2e.45 Labotsibeni Mdluli (1895–1921)	80	90
759	3e.35 Tibati Nkambule (1881–95)	1·10	1·25
755/9 *Set of 5*		3·00	3·00

169 District Office/Post Office, Manzini, 1920s **170** Mgubudla Falls, Northern Hhohho

2006 (8 May). *Postal History. T* **169** *and similar multicoloured designs. Litho.* P 14.

760	90c. Type **169**	30	20
761	1e.15 Ox-wagon transferring post, 1880s–90s	40	30
762	2e. Bremersdorp Post Office, 1893	70	55
763	2e.55 Mail runner (*vert*)	1·00	1·10
764	3e.50 Temporary post office, Mbabane, 1902	1·40	1·60
760/4 *Set of 4*		3·50	3·25

(Des P. Dlamini. Litho Austrian State Ptg Wks, Vienna)

2006 (26 Sept). *Waterfalls. T* **170** *and similar multicoloured designs.* P 14.

765	90c. Type **170**	30	20
766	1e.15 Phophonyane Falls, Phophonyane Nature Reserve	40	30
767	1e.40 Mantenga Falls, Mantenga Nature Reserve (*horiz*)	50	40
768	2e. Malolotja Falls, Malolotja Nature Reserve	70	55
769	2e.55 Mabhudlweni Falls, Mhlosheni, Shiselweni	1·00	1·10
770	3e.50 Manzamnyama Falls, Mdzimba Mountains (*horiz*)	1·40	1·60
765/70 *Set of 5*		3·75	3·75

171 *Cussonia spicata* (common cabbage tree)

(Des P. Dlamini. Litho Enschedé)

2007 (23 Jan). *Trees. T* **171** *and similar horiz designs. Multicoloured.* P 13½×14.

771	70c. Type **171**	30	20
772	85c. *Ficus sur* (broom cluster fig)	30	20
773	90c. *Acacia nilotica* (scented thorn)	35	25
774	1e.05 *Trichlia emetica* (Natal mahogany)	35	25
775	1e.15 *Sclerocarya birrea* (marula)	40	30
776	1e.40 *Bequaertiodendron megalismontanum* (stem fruit)	45	35
777	2e. *Acacia xanthophloea* (fever tree)	60	50
778	2e.40 *Erythrina latissima* (large-leaved coral tree)	65	60
779	2e.55 *Pterocarpus angolensis* (African teak)	65	65
780	3e.50 *Berchemia zeyheri* (red ivory)	85	85
781	5e. *Erythrina lysistemon* (common coral tree)	1·20	1·40
782	10e. *Pappea capensis* (jacket-plum)	2·40	2·75
783	20e. *Kigelia africana* (sausage tree)	4·75	5·00
771/83 *Set of 13*		12·50	12·50

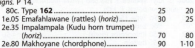

POSTAGE DUE STAMPS

D 1

Postage Due
2d
(D 2)

D 3

(Typo D.L.R.)

1933 (23 Jan)–**57**. Wmk Mult Script CA. P 14.

D1	D **1**	1d. carmine	30	11·00
		a. Chalk-surfaced paper. *Dp carmine* (24.10.51)	20	16·00
		ac. Error. St Edward's Crown, W **9b**	£275	
D2		2d. pale violet	2·25	27·00
		a. Chalk-surfaced paper (22.2.57)	4·75	40·00
		ab. Large "d"	50·00	
D1/2 Perf "Specimen" *Set of 2*			45·00	

For illustrations of No. D2ab see above No. D1 of Basutoland.

1961 (8 Feb). *No. 55 surch with Type D* **2**.

D3	**7**	2d. on 2d.	1·25	2·75

Another 2d. on 2d. Postage Due, with small surcharge as Type D **5**, was produced *after the currency change*, to meet the philatelic demand (*Price 15p unused*).

(Typo D.L.R.)

1961 (14 Feb). *Chalk-surfaced paper.* Wmk Mult Script CA. P 14.

D4	D **3**	1c. carmine	15	1·10
D5		2c. violet	15	1·10
D6		5c. green	20	1·10
D4/6 *Set of 3*			45	3·00

Postage Due
1c
(D **4**)

Postage Due
1c
(D **5**)

1961. *No. 55 surcharged. A. As Type D* **4**. *(14 Feb).*

D7	**7**	1c. on 2d.	1·25	2·50
D8		2c. on 2d.	1·25	2·50
D9		5c. on 2d.	2·25	2·50
D7/9 *Set of 3*			4·25	6·75

B. As Type D **5**. *(Date?)*

D10	**7**	1c. on 2d.	70	2·75
D11		2c. on 2d.	50	2·75
D12		5c. on 2d.	90	2·25
D10/12 *Set of 3*			1·90	7·00

D **6**

(Des and litho B.W.)

1971 (1 Feb). *Size 18×23 mm.* W w **12**. P 11½.

D13	D **6**	1c. bright rose-red	65	3·50
D14		2c. purple	75	3·50
D15		5c. dull green	1·00	4·00
D13/15 *Set of 3*			2·25	10·00

1977 (17 Jan). *Size 18×23 mm. (sideways).* W w **14**. P 11½.

D16	D **6**	1c. rose-red	85	3·50
D17		2c. purple	1·10	4·00
D18		5c. dull green	1·75	4·50
D16/18 *Set of 3*			3·25	11·00

(Litho Harrison)

1978 (20 Apr)–**85**. *Size 17½×21 mm.* W w **14**. P 15×14.

D19	D **6**	1c. carmine	30	1·75
D19*a*		1c. brown-red (13.3.85)	3·25	4·50
D20		2c. purple	30	1·50
D21		5c. blue-green	30	1·50
D19/21 *Set of 4*			3·75	8·25

(Litho Harrison)

1991 (17 July). *Size 17½×21 mm. With imprint date.* W w **14** (sideways) . P 15×14.

D23	D **6**	2c. purple	10	25
D24		5c. bright blue-green	10	25
D25		10c. pale greenish blue	10	25
D26		25c. red-brown	10	25
D23/6 *Set of 4*			25	90

www.stanleygibbons.com/mycollection

My Collection is a revolutionary tool which has been developed by the team at Stanley Gibbons to help collectors manage, view and value their collections online.

With 'My Collection' you can:

Catalogue
your stamps using the world-renowned Stanley Gibbons catalogue

Create
virtual albums to help organise your collection

Value
your entire collections at the touch of a button

Print
album pages displaying collections (and any gaps)

Produce
graphical and spreadsheet outputs quickly for insurance purposes

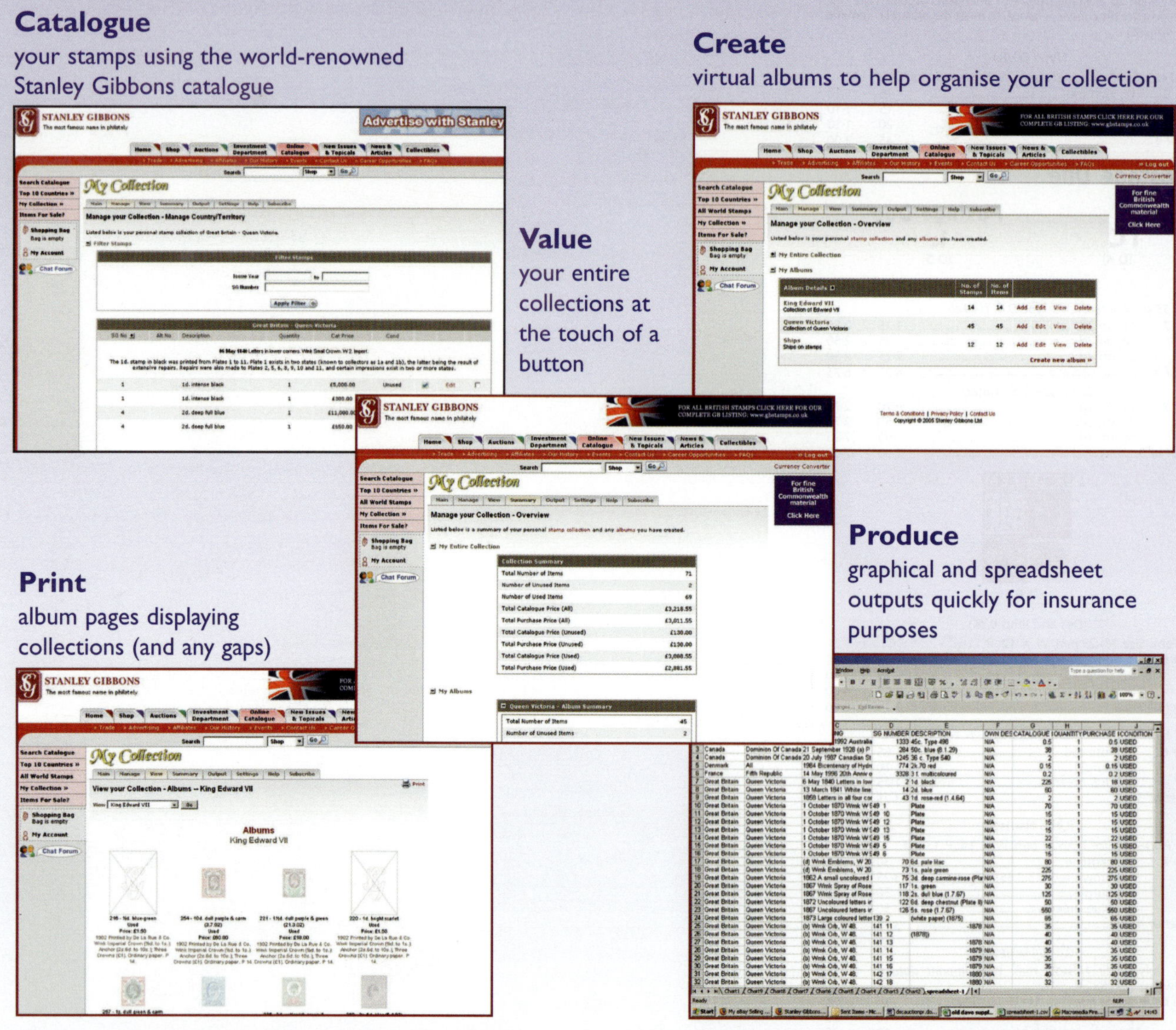

Visit www.stanleygibbons.com/mycollection now to see how 'My Collection' can help with *your collection*

Stanley Gibbons would have loved the Internet...

Stanley Gibbons built the most famous name in stamps from scratch by starting with a desk in his father's chemists and a small scale mail order business based in Plymouth.

Even in those inauspicious circumstances, Gibbons was able to build a highly successful business, which eventually grew too big for the chemist shop and even Plymouth. Just imagine if he had the Internet as a tool of his trade as well...

- over 50,000 stamps available to buy
- a philatelic reference point at your fingertips
- all Stanley Gibbons products and other leading brands available
- accessible at any time, from anywhere
- philatelic news as it breaks
- archives of images and articles
- live auctions
- catalogue your collection

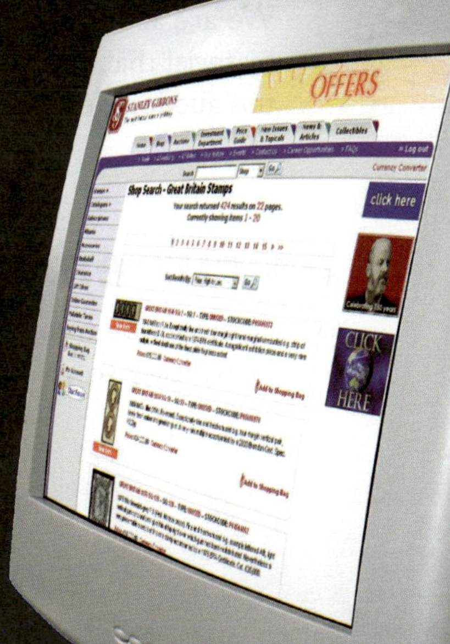

150 years of progress and invention allow us to bring you

www.stanleygibbons.com

so that you can find anything you want in the world of philately from the comfort of your own home.

www.stanleygibbons.com

COLLECT
SOUTHERN AFRICA
STAMPS

From Stanley Gibbons, THE WORLD'S LARGEST STAMP STOCK

Condition (mint/UM/used)	Country	SG No.	Description	Price	Office use only
			POSTAGE & PACKAGING	£3.60	
			GRAND TOTAL		

Minimum price. The minimum catalogue price quoted is 10p. For individual stamps, prices between 10p and 95p are provided as a guide for catalogue users. The lowest price charged for individual stamps or sets purchased from Stanley Gibbons Ltd is £1

Please complete payment, name and address details overleaf